The Sacred Actions
of Christian Worship

THE COMPLETE LIBRARY
OF
CHRISTIAN WORSHIP

THE COMPLETE LIBRARY
OF
CHRISTIAN WORSHIP

Volume 6, The Sacred Actions of Christian Worship

ROBERT E. WEBBER, EDITOR

Star Song
PUBLISHING GROUP
Nashville, Tennessee

Unless otherwise indicated, all Scripture quotations taken from the HOLY BIBLE, NEW INTERNATIONAL VERSION. Copyright © 1973, 1978, 1984 by International Bible Society. Used by permission of Zondervan Publishing House.

Scripture quotations marked (KJV) are from the HOLY BIBLE, KING JAMES VERSION.

Scripture quotations marked (NASB) are taken from the NEW AMERICAN STANDARD BIBLE. Copyright © 1960, 1962, 1963, 1968, 1971, 1972, 1973,1975, 1977, the Lockman Foundation. Used by permission.

Scripture quotations marked (RSV) are taken from the REVISED STANDARD VERSION of the Bible. Copyright © 1946, 1952, 1971, 1973, the division of the Christian Education of the National Council of Churches of Christ in the U.S.A. Used by permission.

Scripture quotations marked (NRSV) are taken from THE HOLY BIBLE: NEW REVISED STANDARD VERSION. Copyright © 1989 by Division of the Christian Education of the National Council of Churches of Christ in the United Stated of America. Used by permission.

Scripture quotations marked (TEV) are taken from TODAY's ENGLISH VERSION of the Bible, Third Edition. Copyright © 1966, 1971 American Bible Society. Used by permission.

Produced for Star Song Publishing Group by the Livingstone Corporation. Dr. James C. Galvin and J. Michael Kendrick, and Jonathan Farrar, project editors.

Star Song Publishing Group, a division of Jubilee Communications, Inc.
2325 Crestmoor, Nashville, Tennessee 37215.
Printed in the United States of America

ISBN 1-56233-016-0

1 2 3 4 5 6 7 8 9—98 97 96 95 94 93

Library of Congress Cataloging-in-Publication Data

The sacred actions of Christian worship / Robert E. Webber, editor.
        p.   cm.—(The complete library of Christian worship: vol. 6)
      Includes bibliographical references and index.
      ISBN 1-56233-016-0 $49.95
      1. Rites and ceremonies. 2. Liturgics.   3. Sacraments.
    4. Baptism. 5. Lord's Supper. I. Webber, Robert. II. Series.
    BV178.S23 1994
    264—dc20   94-21268
                                                          CIP

CONTENTS

Part 2: HISTORY AND THEOLOGY OF SACRED ACTIONS, SACRAMENTS, AND ORDINANCES

Part 3: BAPTISM

List of Illustrations

Additional Contributors

Christopher Beatty
The Upright Foundation, Lindale, Texas

Bill Rayborn
TCMR Communications, Grapevine, Texas

Board of Editorial Consultants

The Board of Editorial Consultants is made up of leaders in worship renewal from major Christian denominations. They have functioned as advisors, often through letter and telephone. Every attempt has been made to include material on worship representing the whole church. For this reason, different viewpoints are presented without any attempt to express a particular point of view or bias. A special word of thanks is due to the executive and consulting editors for their helpful input. Their ideas, suggestions and contributions have strengthened the *Complete Library of Christian Worship*. Omissions and weaknesses in all seven volumes are the sole responsibility of the compiler and editor.

Editor

Robert E. Webber, Professor of Theology, Wheaton
College, Wheaton, Illinois
Th.D., Concordia Theological Seminary

Executive Editors

Darrell A. Harris
President, Star Song Distribution Group

Stan Moser
Chief Executive Officer, Star Song Distribution Group

Matthew A. Price
Vice President, Star Song Publishing Group

David R. West, Jr.
National Sales Director, Star Song Publishing Group

Project Editors

James C. Galvin, The Livingstone Corporation
Ed.D., Northern Illinois University

J. Michael Kendrick, The Livingstone Corporation
Ph.D. (candidate) University of Wisconsin-Madison

Larry Nyberg, Liturgy and Education Consultant,
Diocese of Chicago
Ph.D. (candidate) Drew University

John D. Witvliet
Ph.D. (candidate), Notre Dame University

Substantive Editors

John Finley (Music)
M.A., University of California, SBC

David Gillaspey (Leading Worship)
M.A., University of Missouri

Richard Leonard (Scripture)
Ph.D., Boston University

Dennis Martin (Sacraments)
Ph.D., University of Waterloo

Jack Mercer (Preaching)
D.Min., Princeton Theological Seminary

Douglas Morgan
Ph.D., University of Chicago

William Mugford (Bibliography)
Ph.D. (candidate) University of Chicago

Carol Nyberg (Children's Worship)
B.A., Trinity College

Phillip Beggrov Peter
Ph.D., Northwestern University

Rebecca Slough (Arts)
Ph.D., Graduate Theological Union

Grant Sperry-White (History)
Ph.D., Notre Dame University

Consulting Editors

Douglas Adams
Pacific School of Religion, Berkeley, California

William Barker
Westminster Theological Seminary, Glenside, Pennsylvania

Paul Bassett
Nazarene Theological Seminary, Kansas City, Missouri

Harold Best
Wheaton College Conservatory of Music, Wheaton, Illinois

Donald C. Boyd
Asbury Theological Seminary, Wilmore, Kentucky

Emily Brink
Reformed Worship, Grand Rapids, Michigan

Donald Bruggink
Western Theological Seminary, Holland, Michigan

John Burkhart
McCormick Theological Seminary, Chicago, Illinois

Jeannette Scholer
American Baptist Church USA, Villa Park, Illinois

Tom Schwanda
Immanuel Reformed Church, Grand Rapids, Michigan

Dan Scott
Christ Church, Nashville, Tennessee

Mark Searle
University of Notre Dame, Notre Dame, Indiana

David L. Sebastian
Salem Church of God, Clayton, Ohio

Calvin Seerveld
Institute for Christian Studies, Toronto, Canada

Franklin M. Seglar
Broadway Baptist Church, Ft. Worth, Texas

Harold Senkbeil
Elm Grove Evangelical Lutheran Church, Elm Grove, Wisconsin

Frank C. Senn
Immanuel Lutheran Church, Evanston, Illinois

Dan Sharp
St. Andrew's Presbyterian Church, Newport Beach, California

Stephen Shoemaker
Broadway Baptist Church, Ft. Worth, Texas

George Shorney
Hope Publishing Company, Carol Stream, Illinois

Duane Sider
Eastern Mennonite Seminary, Harrisonburg, Virginia

Michael Silhary
St. Barbara Parish, Brookfield, Illinois

Rebecca J. Slough
First Mennonite Church of San Francisco, San Francisco, California

Randolph Sly
Hosanna Church of the King, Overland Park, Kansas

J. Alfred Smith, Sr.
Allen Temple Baptist Church, Oakland, California

Chuck Smith, Jr.
Calvary Chapel, Capistrano Beach, California

Gordon Smith
Canadian Bible College, Regina, Saskatchewan, Canada

Edward Sövik
Northfield, Minnesota

Bob Sorge
Zion Fellowship, Canandaigua, New York

Jack Norman Sparks
St. Athanasius Orthodox Church, Goleta, California

James Speck
Glendora, California

Jon Michael Spencer
University of North Carolina at Chapel Hill, Chapel Hill, North Carolina

Grant Sperry-White
St. Paul's School of Theology, Kansas City, Kansas

Jim Spruce
Central Nazarene Church, Flint, Michigan

Ron Sprunger
Ashland Theological Seminary, Ashland, Ohio

Gilbert W. Stafford
Anderson University School of Theology, Anderson, Indiana

Calvin Stapert
Calvin College, Grand Rapids, Michigan

Rob Staples
Nazarene Theological Seminary, Kansas City, Missouri

Alva Steffler
Wheaton College, Wheaton, Illinois

Howard Stevenson
First Evangelical Free Church, Fullerton, California

Daniel B. Stevick
Episcopal Divinity School, Cambridge, Massachusetts

Bruce Stewart
Reformed Presbyterian Theological Seminary, Pittsburgh, Pennsylvania

Sonja M. Stewart
Western Theological Seminary, Holland, Michigan

Harold Stigers
Covenant Theological Seminary, St. Louis, Missouri

Lawrence Hull Stookey
Wesley Theological Seminary, Washington, D.C.

David A. Stosur
University of Notre Dame, Notre Dame, Indiana

Raymond Sutton
Philadelphia Theological School, Philadelphia, Pennsylvania

Darius Swann
Interdenominational Theological Center, Atlanta, Georgia

Barbara Swanson
Village Presbyterian Church, Northbrook, Illinois

James Rawlings Sydnor
Presbyterian School of Christian Education, Richmond, Virginia

List of Cooperating Publishers

BOOK PUBLISHERS

Abbott-Martyn Press
2325 Crestmoor Road
Nashville, TN 37215

Abingdon Press
201 8th Avenue South
Nashville, TN 37202

Agape
Hope Publishing
Carol Stream, IL 60187

Alba House
2187 Victory Boulevard
Staten Island, NY 10314

**American Choral
Directors Association**
502 Southwest 38th
Lawton, Oklahoma 73505

**Asian Institute for
Liturgy & Music**
P.O. Box 3167
Manila 1099 Philippines

Augsburg/Fortress Press
426 S. Fifth Street
Box 1209
Minneapolis, MN 55440

Ave Maria Press
Notre Dame, IN 46556

Baker Book House
P.O. Box 6287
Grand Rapids, MI 49516-6287

Beacon Hill Press
Box 419527
Kansas City, MO 64141

Bethany House Publishers
6820 Auto Club Road
Minneapolis, MN 55438

The Brethren Press
1451 Dundee Avenue
Elgin, IL 60120

Bridge Publishing, Inc.
200 Hamilton Blvd.
South Plainfield, NJ 07080

Broadman Press
127 Ninth Avenue, North
Nashville, TN 37234

C.S.S. Publishing Company
628 South Main Street
Lima, OH 45804

Cathedral Music Press
P.O. Box 66
Pacific, MO 63069

**Catholic Book
Publishing Company**
257 W. 17th Street
New York, NY 10011

CBP Press
Box 179
St. Louis, MO 63166

Celebration
P.O. Box 309
Aliquippa, PA 15001

Channing L. Bete Company
South Deerfield, MA 01373

Choristers Guild
2834 W. Kingsley Road
Garland, TX 75041

Christian Literature Crusade
701 Pennsylvania Avenue
Box 1449
Ft. Washington, PA 19034

Christian Publications
3825 Hartzdale Drive
Camp Hill, PA 17011

**The Church
Hymnal Corporation**
800 Second Avenue
New York, NY 10017

The Columba Press
93 Merise
Mount Merrion
Blackrock, Dublin

Concordia Publishing House
3558 S. Jefferson Avenue
St. Louis, MO 63118

Covenant Publications
3200 West Foster Avenue
Chicago, IL 60625

Cowley Publications
980 Memorial Drive
Cambridge, MA 02138

CRC Publications
2850 Kalamazoo SE
Grand Rapids, MI 49560

**Creative Communications
for The Parish**
10300 Watson Road
St. Louis, MO 63127

**Crossroad Publishing
Company**
575 Lexington Avenue
New York, NY 10022

Crossroad/Continuum
370 Lexington Avenue
New York, NY 10017

Dominion Press
7112 Burns Street
Ft. Worth, TX 76118

Duke Univesity Press
Box 6697 College Station
Durham, NC 27708

Faith and Life Press
724 Main Street
Box 347
Newton, KS 67114

The Faith Press, Ltd.
7 Tufton Street
Westminster, S.W. 1
England

Fleming H. Revell Company
184 Central Avenue
Old Tappen, N.J. 07675

Folk Music Ministry
P.O. Box 3443
Annapolis, MD 21403

Franciscan Communications
1229 South Santee Street
Los Angeles, CA 90015

Georgetown University Press
111 Intercultural Center
Washington, D.C. 20057

GIA Publications
7404 S. Mason Avenue
Chicago, IL 60638

Great Commission Publications
7401 Old York Road
Philadelphia, PA 19126

Grove Books
Bramcote Notts
England

Harper & Row Publishers
Icehouse One-401
151 Union Street
San Francisco, CA 94111-1299

Harvard University Press
79 Garden Street
Cambridge, MA 02138

Harvest Publications
Baptist General Conference
2002 S. Arlington Heights Road
Arlington Heights, IL 60005

Hendrickson Publishers, Inc.
P.O. Box 3473
Peabody, MA 01961-3473

Herald Press
616 Walnut Avenue
Scottdale, PA 15683

Hinshaw Music Incorporated
P.O. Box 470
Chapel Hill, NC 27514

Holt, Rinehart & Winston
111 5th Avenue
New York, NY 10175

Hope Publishing Company
Carol Stream, IL 60188

Hymn Society of America
Texas Christian University
P.O. Box 30854
Ft. Worth, TX 76129

Indiana University Press
10th & Morton
Bloomington, IN 47405

Integrity Music
P.O. Box 16813
Mobile, AL 36616

J.S. Paluch Company, Inc.
3825 Willow Road
P.O. Box 2703
Schiller Park, IL 60176

**The Jewish Publication
Society of America**
1930 Chestnut Street
Philadelphia, PA 19103

Judson Press
P.O. Box 851
Valley Forge, PA 19482-0851

**Light and Life Publishing
Company**
P.O. Box 26421
Minneapolis, MN 55426

Liguori Publications
One Liguori Drive
Liguori, MO 63057

Lillenas Publishing Company
Box 419527
Kansas City, MO 64141

The Liturgical Conference
1017 Twelfth Street, N.W.
Washington, D.C. 20005-4091

The Liturgical Press
St. John's Abbey
Collegeville, MN 56321

Liturgy Training Publications
1800 North Heritage Avenue
Chicago, IL 60622-1101

**Macmillan Publishing
Company**
866 Third Avenue
New York, NY 10022

Maranatha! Music
25411 Cabot Road
Suite 203
Laguna Hills, CA 92653

Mel Bay Publications
Pacific, MO 63969-0066

Meriwether Publishing, Ltd.
885 Elkton Drive
Colorado Springs, CO 80907

Michael Glazier, Inc.
1723 Delaware Avenue
Wilmington, Delaware 19806

Morehouse-Barlow
78 Danbury Road
Wilton, CT 06897

Multnomah Press
10209 SE Division Street
Portland, OR 97266

**National Association
of Pastoral Musicians**
25 Sheridan Street, NW
Washington, DC 20011

NavPress
P.O. Box 6000
Colorado Springs, CO 80934

New Skete
Cambridge, NY 12816

**North American
Liturgical Resources**
1802 N. 23rd Avenue
Phoenix, AZ 85029

Oxford University Press
16-00 Pollitt Drive
Fair Lawn, NJ 07410

The Pastoral Press
225 Sheridan Street, NW
Washington, D.C. 20011

Paulist Press
997 McArthur Boulevard
Mahwah, NJ 07430

The Pilgrim Press
132 West 31st Street
New York, NY 10001

Psalmist Resources
9820 E. Watson Road
St. Louis, MO 63126

Pueblo Publishing Company
100 West 32nd Street
New York, NY 1001-3210

Regal Books
A Division of Gospel Light
    Publications
Ventura, CA 93006

Resource Publications, Inc.
160 E. Virginia Street #290
San Jose, CA 95112

The Scarecrow Press
52 Liberty Street
Box 416
Metuchen, NJ 08840

Schocken Books
62 Cooper Square
New York, NY 10003

**Schuyler Institute for
Worship & The Arts**
2757 Melandy Drive, Suite 15
San Carlos, CA 94070

SCM Press Ltd.
c/o Trinity Press International
3725 Chestnut Street
Philadelphia, PA 19104

Servant Publications
P.O. Box 8617
Petersham, MA 01366-0545

The Sharing Company
P.O. Box 2224
Austin, TX 78768-2224

Sheed & Ward
115 E. Armour Boulevard
P.O. Box 414292
Kansas City, MO 64141-0281

Shofar Publications, Inc
P.O. Box 88711
Carol Stream, IL 60188

SPCK
Holy Trinity Church
Marylebone Road
London, N.W. 4D4

St. Anthony Messenger Press
1615 Republic Street
Cincinnati, OH 45210

St. Bede's Publications
P.O. Box 545
Petersham, MA 01366-0545

St. Mary's Press
Terrace Heights
Winona, MN 55987

St. Vladimir Seminary Press
575 Scarsdale Road
Crestwood, NY 10707-1699

Thomas Nelson Publishers
P.O. Box 141000
Nashville, TN 37214

Twenty Third Publications
P.O. Box 180
Mystic, CT 06355

Tyndale House Publishers
351 Executive Drive
Carol Stream, IL 60188

United Church of Christ
Office of Church Life and
    Leadership
700 Prospect
Cleveland, OH 44115

United Church Press
132 West 31st Street
New York, NY 10001

**The United Methodist
Publishing House**
P.O. Box 801
Nashville, TN 37202

**United States
Catholic Conference**
Office of Publishing and
    Promotion Services
1312 Massachusetts Avenue, NW
Washington, DC 20005-4105

University of California Press
1010 Westward Blvd.
Los Angeles, CA 90024

**University of Notre
Dame Press**
Notre Dame, IN 46556

The Upper Room
1908 Grand Avenue
P.O. Box 189
Nashville, TN 37202

Victory House Publishers
P.O. Box 700238
Tulsa, OK 74170

Westminster John Knox Press
100 Witherspoon Street
Louisville, KY 40202-1396

**William B. Eerdmans
Publishing Company**
255 Jefferson S.E.
Grand Rapids, MI 49503

**William C. Brown
Publishing Company**
2460 Kerper Boulevard
P.O. Box 539
Dubuque, IA 52001

William H. Sadlier, Inc.
11 Park Place
New York, NY 10007

Winston Press
P.O. Box 1630
Hagerstown, MD 21741

Word Books
Tower-Williams Square
5221 N. O'Conner Blvd. Suite
    1000
Irving, TX 75039

**World Council of
Churches Publications**
P.O. Box 66
150 Route de Ferney
1211 Geneva 20, Switzerland

**World Library
Publications, Inc.**
3815 N. Willow Road
P.O. Box 2701
Schiller Park, IL 60176

**The World
Publishing Company**
Meridian Books
110 E. 59th Street
New York, NY 10022

Yale University Press
302 Temple Street
New Haven, CN 06510

Zion Fellowship
236 Gorham Street
Canadagina, NY 14424

**Zondervan Publishing
Company**
1415 Lake Drive S.E.
Grand Rapids, MI 49506

PERIODICAL PUBLISHERS

The American Center for Church Music Newsletter
3339 Burbank Drive
Ann Arbor, MI 48105

American Organist
475 Riverside Drive, Suite 1260
New York, NY 10115

ARTS: The Arts in Religious and Theological Studies
United Theological Seminary of
the Twin Cities
3000 5th Street, NW
New Brighton, MN 55112

Arts Advocate
The United Church of Christ
Fellowship in the Arts
73 S. Palvuse
Walla Walla, WA 99362

The Choral Journal
American Choral Directors
Association
P.O. Box 6310
Lawton, OK 73506

Choristers Guild Letters
2834 W. Kingsley Road
Garland, TX 75041

Christians in the Visual Arts
(newsletter)
P.O. Box 10247
Arlington, VA 22210

Church Music Quarterly
Royal School of Church Music
Addington Palace
Croyden, England CR9 5AD

The Church Musician
Southern Baptist Convention
127 9th Avenue N.
Nashville, TN 37234

Contemporary Christian Music
CCM Publications
P.O. Box 6300
Laguna Hills, CA 92654

Diapason
380 E. Northwest Highway
Des Plaines, IL 60016

Doxology
Journal of the Order of St. Luke in
the United Methodist Church

1872 Sweet Home Road
Buffalo, NY 14221

Environment and Art Letter
Liturgy Training Publications
1800 N. Hermitage Avenue
Chicago, IL 60622

GIA Quarterly
7404 S. Mason Avenue
Chicago, IL 60638

Grace Notes
Association of Lutheran Church
Musicians
4807 Idaho Circle
Ames, IA 50010

The Hymn
Hymn Society of the United States
and Canada
P.O. Box 30854
Fort Worth, TX 76129

Journal
Sacred Dance Guild
Joyce Smillie, Resource Director
10 Edge Court
Woodbury, CT 06798

Journal of Ritual Studies
Department of Religious Studies
University of Pittsburgh
Pittsburgh, PA 15260

Let the People Worship
Schuyler Institute for Worship and
the Arts
2757 Melendy Drive, Suite 15
San Carlos, CA 94070

Liturgy
The Liturgical Conference
8750 Georgia Avenue, S., Suite
123
Silver Spring, MD 20910

Liturgy 90
Liturgy Training Publications
1800 N. Hermitage Avenue
Chicago, IL 60622

Modern Liturgy
Resource Publications
160 E. Virginia Street, Suite 290
San Jose, CA 95112

Music in Worship
Selah Publishing Company
P.O. Box 103
Accord, NY 12404

Newsnotes
The Fellowship of United
Methodists in Worship, Music,
and Other Arts
P.O. Box 54367
Atlanta, GA 30308

Pastoral Music
225 Sheridian Street, NW
Washington, D.C. 20011

PRISM
Yale Institute of Sacred Music
409 Prospect Street
New Haven, CT 06510

The Psalmist
9820 E. Watson Road
St. Louis, MO 63124

Reformed Liturgy and Music
Worship and Ministry Unit
100 Witherspoon Street
Louisville, KY 40202

Reformed Music Journal
Brookside Publishing
3911 Mt. Lehman Road
Abbotsford, BC V2S 6A9

Reformed Worship
CRC Publications
2850 Kalamazoo Avenue, SE
Grand Rapids, MI 49560

Rite Reasons
Biblical Horizons
P.O. Box 1096
Niceville, FL 32588

St. Vladimirs Theological Quarterly
757 Scarsdale Road
Crestwood, NY 10707

Studia Liturgica
Department of Theology
University of Notre Dame
Notre Dame, IN 46556

Today's Liturgy
Oregon Catholic Press
5536 NE Hassalo
Portland, OR 97213

Worship
The Liturgical Press
St. John's Abbey
Collegeville, MN 56321

Worship Leader
CCM Communications, Inc.
107 Kenner Avenue
Nashville, TN 37205

Worship Today
600 Rinehard Road
Lake Mary, FL 32746

Preface to Volume 6

Communication through sign and symbol was abruptly halted by the Protestant Reformation of the sixteenth century. It was accompanied by the Gutenberg press, which effected tremendous changes in communication that altered the culture and the church, particularly its way of worshiping. At least in the Protestant world, worship ceased to be a drama enacted through the signs and symbols of the sacraments and became the exclusive domain of the Word spoken.

As many scholars have pointed out, medieval worship lacked a proper balance of Word and sign, and the renewed attention that the Reformers placed on Scripture was salutary. Yet many Protestant groups created new imbalances by denying that sacramental signs were desirable for communicating spiritual truth. Consequently, the sacred signs of worship—baptism, Eucharist, anointing, laying on of hands, marriage, funerals, and so on—were relegated to positions of inferiority. At best have played a secondary position to the Word, and at worst they were relegated to symbols without any attending supernatural power (i.e., baptism and Eucharist) or were forgotten altogether (i.e., anointing with oil). Some ceremonies, particularly weddings and funerals, become increasingly influenced and altered by secular customs.

Since the middle of the twentieth century there has been an enormous shift in communication theory that recognizes the validity of ritual expression. This shift in communication studies has been joined by a shift in biblical and theological studies that has rediscovered the power of sign and symbol, particularly in the area of worship. The imbalance of Protestant practices is being redressed, and equilibrium of Word and symbol is being sought. Today Orthodox, Catholic, and Protestant scholars have produced a growing body of material on the significance of sacramental signs and symbols in worship. More important, this scholarly material is gradually making its way out of academia and into the worship of the local church.

The Sacred Actions of Christian Worship, which is volume 6 of *The Complete Library of Christian Worship*, is a contribution to the conversation between the academy and the church. The articles, written by scholars and practitioners from every major denomination, are intended to be informative and practical to the congregation seeking worship renewal. Each of the sacred actions of the church is not only studied in terms of its origins and historical development, but also in terms of its value to the local church.

You will find this volume to be not only informative, but also inspirational and of supreme value in its application.

Robert Webber, Editor

Introduction

The *Complete Library of Christian Worship* has been designed to meet a need in the church. Christian leaders and congregations are becoming increasingly interested in the subjects of worship and worship renewal in the local church. Often, however, they lack adequate biblical and historical perspective or the necessary materials and resources to engage in the renewal process.

To fulfill the demand for worship resources, publishing houses, particularly those of specific denominations, have been producing materials for the local church. While these materials may find use within the constituency of a particular denomination, only a few break across denominational barriers and become known throughout the church at large.

The Complete Library of Christian Worship draws from more than one hundred publishing houses and the major Christian denominations of the world in order to bring those resources together in a seven-volume work, making them readily available to all.

The purpose of this introductory material is to acquaint the reader with *The Complete Library of Christian Worship* and to help him or her to use its information and resources in the local church. First, the reader needs to have some sense of the scope of worship studies and renewal that are addressed by *The Complete Library of Christian Worship* (see section 101 below). Second, it is important to learn how to use the *Library* (see section 102). Finally, there is a need to understand the precise content of Volume 6, *The Sacred Actions of Christian Worship.*

These three introductory entries are a key to the whole concept of the *Library*, a concept that brings together instruction in worship and vital resources for use in worship. The *Library* also directs the reader to a vast array of books, audio tapes, videotapes, model services, and resources in music and the arts. It seeks to provide direction and inspiration for everything the church does in worship.

101 • INTRODUCTION TO *THE COMPLETE LIBRARY OF CHRISTIAN WORSHIP*

The word *library* implies a collection of resources, together with a system of organization that makes them accessible to the user. Specifically, *The Complete Library of Christian Worship* is a comprehensive compilation of information pertaining to the worship of the Christian church. It draws from a large pool of scholars and practitioners in the field, and from more than two thousand books and media resources in print.

The purpose of *The Complete Library of Christian Worship* is to make biblical, historical, and contemporary resources on worship available to pastors, music ministers, worship committees, and the motivated individual worshiper. The *Library* contains biblical and historical information on all aspects of worship and numerous resource materials, as well as suggested resource books, audio tapes, and video instructional material for every worship act in the local church.

The twentieth century, more than any century in the history of Christianity, has been the century for research and study in the origins, history, theology, and practice of Christian worship. Consequently there are seven broad areas in which worship studies are taking place. These are:

1. the biblical foundations of worship;
2. historical and theological development of worship;
3. resources for worship and preaching;
4. resources for music and the arts in worship;
5. resources for the services of the Christian year;
6. resources for sacraments, ordinances, and other sacred acts; and
7. resources for worship and related ministries.

The Complete Library of Christian Worship is organized around these seven areas of worship renewal. In these seven volumes one will find a wide variety of resources for every worship act in the church, and a select but broad bibliography for additional resources.

102 ✦ How to Use *The Complete Library of Christian Worship*

The Complete Library of Christian Worship differs from an encyclopedia, which is often organized alphabetically, with information about a particular subject scattered throughout the book. The *Library* does not follow this pattern because it is a work designed to educate as well as to provide resources. Consequently, all the material in the *Library* is organized under a particular theme or issue of worship.

The difference between the *Library* and an encyclopedia may be illustrated, for example, by examining the topic of environmental art in worship. Some of the themes essential to environmental art are banners, candles, stained glass windows, lighting, pulpit hangings, table coverings, and Communion ware. In a typical encyclopedia these entries would be scattered in the B, C, S, L, P, and T sections. Although this is not a problem for people who know what environmental art is and what needs to be addressed in environmental art, it is a problem for the person whose knowledge about the subject is limited. For this reason *The Complete Library of Christian Worship* has been organized—like a textbook—into chapters dealing with particular issues. Therefore, all the matters dealing with environmental art can be found in the chapter on environmental art (see Volume 4, *Music and the Arts in Christian Worship*). In this way a reader becomes educated on environmental art while at the same time having the advantage of in-depth information on the various matters pertaining to this aspect of worship.

Therefore, the first unique feature of *The Complete Library of Christian Worship* is that each volume can be read and studied like a book.

The second unique feature of the *Library* is that the materials have been organized to follow the actual *sequence in which worship happens.*

For example, Volume 1, *The Biblical Foundations of Christian Worship,* looks at the roots of Christian worship in the biblical tradition, while Volume 2, *Twenty Centuries of Christian Worship,* presents the development of various historical models of worship along with an examination of the theology of worship. Next, Volumes 3 through 7 provide re-

sources for the various acts of worship: Volume 3, *The Renewal of Sunday Worship,* provides resources for the various parts of worship; Volume 4, *Music and the Arts in Christian Worship,* presents resources from music and the arts for the different aspects of worship. Volume 5, *The Services of the Christian Year,* branches out to the services of Advent, Christmas, Epiphany, Lent, Holy Week, Easter, and Pentecost, providing resources for those special services that celebrate the saving acts of God in Jesus Christ. Volume 6, *The Sacred Actions of Christian Worship,* deals with Communion, baptism, funerals, weddings, and other special or occasional acts of worship. Finally, Volume 7, *The Ministries of Christian Worship,* deals with evangelism, spirituality, education, social action, children's worship, and other matters impacted by Christian celebration.

Each volume contains an alphabetical index to the material in the book. This index makes desired information readily available for the reader.

The resources in these volumes are intended for use in every denomination and among all groups of Christians: liturgical, traditional Protestant, those using creative styles, and those in the praise-and-worship tradition. Resources from each of these communities may be found in the various volumes.

It is difficult to find material from the free churches (those not following a historic order of worship) and from the charismatic traditions. These communities function with an oral tradition of worship and therefore do not preserve their material through written texts. Nevertheless, a considerable amount of information has been gathered from these oral traditions. Recently, leaders in these communities have been teaching their worship practices through audio tapes and videotapes. Information on the availability of these materials has been included in the appropriate volumes.

The written texts have been the easiest to obtain. Because of this, *The Complete Library of Christian Worship* may give the appearance of favoring liturgical worship. Due to the very nature of written texts, the appearance of a strong liturgical bent is unavoidable. Nevertheless, the goal of the *Library* is not to make free churches liturgical. Rather, it is to expand the perspective of Christians across a wide range of worship traditions. In this way, liturgical resources may serve as guides and sources of inspiration and creativity for free churches, while insights from free traditions may also enrich the practices and understanding of the more liturgical communities.

In sum, the way to use *The Complete Library of Christian Worship* is as follows:

1. *Read each volume as you would read a book.* Each volume is full of biblical, historical, and theological information—a veritable feast for the curious, and for all worshipers motivated to expand their horizons.
2. *Use the alphabetical index for quick and easy access to a particular aspect of worship.* The index for each volume is as thorough as the listings for an encyclopedia.
3. *For further information and resources, order books and materials listed in the bibliography of resources.* Addresses of publishers may be found in your library's copy of *Books in Print.*
4. *Adapt the liturgical materials to the setting and worship style of your congregation.* Many of the worship materials in *The Complete Library of Christian Worship* have been intentionally published without adaptation. Most pastors, worship ministers, and worship committee members are capable of adapting the material to a style suitable to their congregations with effective results.

103 ◆ INTRODUCTION TO VOLUME 6: *THE SACRED ACTIONS OF CHRISTIAN WORSHIP*

Volume 6, *The Sacred Actions of Christian Worship*, recognizes that worship, from its very beginnings in first-century Jerusalem to its present practice around the world, has always been dependent on actions as well as words. The earliest descriptions of Christian worship in the New Testament include the acts of baptism, the breaking of bread, the washing of feet, the anointing of oil, and the laying on of hands. Throughout its history, the church practiced these sacred actions widely and added new ones as well.

This volume addresses all these actions in terms of their biblical roots, their historical development, and their worldwide observance in Christian churches today. In Part 1, the reader surveys the practice of sacred actions in all major denominations—Orthodox, Catholic, and Protestant. Part 2 considers the history of the sacraments. Here the reader will learn the origins and meaning of the sacred signs and how they were practiced in various epochs of Christian history.

Baptism is the subject of Part 3. Various chapters examine its historical development, its theological interpretation in various churches, and its actual practice in the churches. This section ends with an exploration of confirmation and the current practice of the renewal of the baptismal covenant.

Part 4 addresses the Lord's Supper. It is treated historically, theologically, and from a practical point of view. Part 5 addresses various actions of Christian worship for the seasons of life—child dedication, marriage, and funerals. Each topic contains a study of the act's historical development, a theological interpretation, and a sample liturgy for study and adaptation.

Finally, Part 6 concerns the sacred actions of the Christian community—ordination and commissioning, reconciliation, anointing of the sick, footwashing, and the solemn assembly. Again, the history, theology, and practice of each of these sacred actions is given thorough attention.

PART ONE

Sacred Actions Among the Churches

❧ ONE ❧

Sacred Actions Among the Contemporary Churches

Christians have always had diverse opinions on the sacred actions that take place in worship. Sacramental churches—Orthodox, Roman Catholic, and some mainline Protestant churches—regard the Lord's Supper, baptism, and sometimes other actions as special signs that bestow grace on those who receive them. Other Protestant groups believe that the sacraments by themselves confer no special power and do not necessarily indicate the presence of God. They tend to refer to sacred actions as ordinances, actions to be observed because Christ commanded his followers to do so. Regardless of their theology, all Christians agree on the importance of keeping these sacred actions and on the tremendous benefits that come through their proper observance in worship.

104 • ADVENTIST CHURCHES

With roots in the radical Reformation, Adventists have not placed great emphasis on sacraments. Nevertheless, they traditionally have regarded Communion, baptism, and sometimes marriage as sacred acts. Footwashing, ordination, and anointing the sick are also practiced, though with less frequency.

Throughout the history of the Seventh-day Adventist Church, there has been a tension about how to honor the presence of God in worship. The denomination developed in the era of camp-meeting revivals and moved with the frontier across America. The earliest Adventist worship occasions tended to be exuberant, with much personal vocal response. God's presence was felt to be immediate and close. Once regular weekly worship began, however, the idea of being in the presence of God was reflected in quiet reverence, which was understood to mean silence except for directed activities (hymns, Amens, etc.). Members were strongly encouraged to refrain from all conversation with one another as soon as they entered the sanctuary (the meeting place for worship). Yet the urge to continue fellowship in the worship setting remained strong, and the proper attitude toward worship remained a source of confusion and tension for many Seventh-day Adventist churches.

The history of Adventist church architecture shows the direction of its ideas on worship. For much of the first half of the twentieth century, the ideal church building was patterned after Gothic lines, having a relatively long, narrow nave and a high central pulpit that was used only during the worship service. A central lectern on a lower platform was used for all other purposes. The pulpit was considered sacred, and the platform on which it stood was basically reserved for pastor and elders. As the second half of the twentieth century progressed, churches were designed to bring worshipers much closer to the front, and the platform area (occasionally called "chancel") was greatly expanded. Today, the pulpit, while almost always central as a symbol of the centrality of the Word of God, is now much more likely to be movable, and there will almost never be a separate lectern. Older church buildings have been frequently remodeled along these same lines.

These changes have occurred primarily in response to the growing understanding that worship is a participatory act rather than a series of preliminaries and preaching. Although Adventists have been relatively quiet on this subject, I believe these changes also speak much more of the immanence of God than of his transcendence.

Seventh-day Adventists, in general, observe baptism, footwashing, and Communion as a way of following the example and instructions of Christ and thereby coming closer to him. When pastors plan these times with special care and much thought, congregations are coming to view them more and more as sacred times when God is present in a way beyond that of the regular weekly worship. Historically footwashing and the Lord's Supper have been practiced at the same service, collectively called Communion, and observed once each quarter. A few Adventist churches have felt a need to increase the frequency of Communion and have done so mostly by adding a Friday evening service devoted entirely to Communion. Specially scheduled times for Communion have probably done more to further the sense of God's presence at a time of worship than anything else done or said in the Adventist Church.

The marriage ceremony is considered sacred because God ordained marriage. Most Adventists do not think of marriage sacramentally nor do they think of the marriage ceremony as worship. They are surprised when an occasional pastor includes in the service hymns, prayers, and responses in which they will be involved. I can affirm that the results of involving the wedding guests in a worship experience are well worth the effort and tangibly enhance the awareness of God's presence.

Ordination of pastors to the gospel ministry sometimes surpasses even the Communion as *the* Seventh-day Adventist service most endued with a sense of the sacred. I find this quite interesting in a church that has roots in the radical Reformation and believes very strongly in the priesthood of all believers. It is of further significance to note that ordination of lay elders, deacons, and deaconesses has nowhere near the sacral impact of clergy ordination.

In addition to ordination of lay elders, deacons, and deaconesses, dedication services are conducted for groups of church officers from time to time. These services range from basic acknowledgement of a new office to a meaningfully planned service with response, congregational confirmation, special blessings, and commissioning.

Infant baptism is not practiced, but baby dedications are held frequently. These dedications take the form of a blessing rather than a sacrament.

The Seventh-day Adventist Church practices anointing the sick with oil by the pastor and/or a group of elders. In theory this can be done any time an ill person would call for it. In practice it is most always reserved for the very seriously ill, particularly those times when it seems that only a miracle could change the progress of disease.

In summary, the typical Seventh-day Adventist is likely to refer to the Communion as "the ordinances." Occasionally the term *sacrament* will be used in reference to the Communion, and more rarely in regard to baptism and marriage. Sacramental language is not used in reference to the other sacred actions of the church.

Merle J. Whitney

105 • AMERICAN BAPTIST CHURCHES IN THE USA

American Baptists have stressed the autonomy of local churches to determine the emphasis given to sacred actions. The radical Reformers, particularly Zwingli, have greatly influenced the development of American Baptist thought; hence Communion and baptism have tended to be simple services that have been secondary to preaching. Nevertheless, American Baptists are reexamining their practices in light of recent worship reforms in other churches.

As do other English-speaking Baptists, the American Baptist Churches in the USA (ABCUSA), one of over thirty distinct Baptist denominations in North America, trace their history and heritage to the congregational Puritans and Separatists from the Church of England. ABCUSA, like other Baptist denominations, is a voluntary association of autonomous local churches organized for mutual aid and the support of common missions and ministries; thus, there are American Baptist *churches*, but no American Baptist *Church*. In discussing events, trends, and developments among American Baptists, one is always constrained to remember that Baptists work together by persuasion, not legislation. Thus this article describes customs and trends but not mandated practices.

For the most part, Baptists trace their understanding and definition of *sacrament* and *ordinance* to the radical Reformers of the Protestant Reformation, principally Ulrich Zwingli (1484–1531) of Zurich. In 1524, Zwingli helped lead the "cleansing" of the churches of Zurich, which included removing or painting over all objects in the churches (relics, statues, murals, vestments, altarware, etc.) that "appealed to the eye."

Musical instruments were also removed or closed, and congregational singing was not allowed. By 1525, the only "appeal to the ear" was the reading and exposition of the Word of God. By this time, Zwingli had also completed his reform of the Lord's Supper, rejecting all claims that physical actions in worship, in general, and the Eucharist, in particular, provided any profit whatsoever. He claimed that the benefits were spiritual only and were only reminders rather than vehicles of grace. As far as possible, any "appeal to the physical senses" was abolished in the Zurich churches.

Zwingli's reform also provided for infrequent Communion (four times a year, approximately quarterly), which, ironically, was more than the people were used to (most partook once a year at Easter) but was much less than that advocated by some other Reformers. (Both Luther and Calvin advocated weekly Communion, but neither was successful in establishing the practice.)

Removing the Eucharist from the weekly liturgy allowed Zwingli to develop the remainder into a separate service of the Word, which today remains the model of the Sunday preaching service in most Baptist (and many other Protestant) churches. The sermon became the focus and the climax of the liturgy. He placed the confession of sin after the sermon as the proper response to the message; in this position, the confession became the historical antecedent of the altar call, or invitation, a fixture of evangelical and revivalist, not just Baptist, worship.

The sermon as call and the confession as response became the sacramental center for this liturgical form. In this form, the sermon mediates the Word of God to the hearer, communicates the need for repentance, stimulates the conviction of sin, and facilitates grace—all components of the definition of a sacrament. Indeed, over time, church architects reinforced this form by placing the pulpit above the table in the front center of a lecture-hall type worship space.

With the rise of the sermon to sacramental importance, baptism, Eucharist, and other sacraments became thoroughly devalued. This development gave rise to the memoralist definition of these acts

of the church. By this definition, baptism and the Lord's Supper become memorials, or ordinances: acts established and commanded by Christ to preserve the memory of him and little, if anything, more. Ordinances mediate no grace, facilitate no access to the divine, and provide no *objective* comfort or benefit to those who partake of them. Ordinances, in the strictest sense of the term, are merely actions Christians do because Jesus commands them, only signs (memorials) of gracious events in one's past, having no operative efficacy in the present.

According to memorialists, baptism is merely the sign that redemption has already been offered and received. The recipient of baptism elects to be baptized to publicly profess that regeneration has *already* occurred, but—most emphatically—not to receive regeneration thereby. Hand in hand with this position is the insistence that the proper subjects for such baptism are persons able to believe, understand, and confess the Christian faith for themselves. Believer's baptism—more accurately, confessor's baptism—by full immersion in the triune name, for those able to confess the faith for themselves, has been and continues to be the standard practice of American Baptist churches.

In most American Baptist churches today, the Lord's Supper is usually appended to the end of the preaching service on the first Sunday of the month. Few American Baptist churches continue the practice of closed Communion in any of its traditional forms. Where an explicit invitation to the Table is given, all baptized Christians are usually included. (Many churches leave to parents' discretion whether or not to serve their unbaptized children.) The liturgies are usually as spare and simple as Zwingli's: the reading of one of the Last Supper accounts from Scripture, the words of institution, prayer for the loaf and cup, and distribution. Usually plates of the bread (broken into chunks or cut into individual pieces) and trays of grape juice (in individual glasses) are carried to worshipers seated in the pews and passed hand to hand, emphasizing a Baptist tradition of serving one another. (This practice reinforces the Reformation prohibition against private or individual Communion by a priest or minister: Even the ministers must be served and may not serve themselves. Also at least two or three must be gathered for Baptists to properly partake of the Lord's Supper.) In Zwinglian fashion, plates are usually passed in silence or with a quiet organ accompaniment.

Because there are no Baptist standard scripts for baptism, Eucharist, or other worship services, Baptist worship leaders are free to compose or adapt liturgies as they see fit. Most often, when a fully scripted liturgy is desired, Baptist pastors will select texts from the service book of another denomination, modifying the language and actions to suit their personal theology and taste. This practice is particularly evident in weddings, funerals, ordinations, and installations, though it is indeed rare for any borrowed service to be used without adaptations.

It should be noted that today's American Baptists have not gone unaffected by the post–Vatican II reforms among Protestants and Catholics. It is not unusual to find American Baptist liturgies based on Justin and Hippolytus, though the commonest pattern is still the nineteenth-century frontier-revival model, itself rooted in Zwingli's liturgy. Also, in all fairness, in a denomination as ethnically diverse as the American Baptists, the above description applies more to European-American congregations than to African-American, Hispanic, Native American, or Asian-American congregations, all of whom retain strong expressions of their respective heritages, even when somewhat interwoven with the English Baptist heritage. American Baptist theologians and liturgy scholars, like their counterparts in other denominations, are engaged in a serious reevaluation of the Reformation—particularly its excesses—and are considering seriously non-Anglo, non-Eurocentric expressions of Word and sacrament.

The trends toward open membership and open Communion also benefit from this post–Vatican II spirit and from such dialogues as *Baptism, Eucharist, and Ministry (BEM)*, sponsored by the World Council of Churches. Out of this openness to reconsider positions on doctrine and liturgy, increasing numbers of American Baptists are participating with other Christians in examining and modifying—or even setting aside—many Eurocentric and/or Reformation misunderstandings in order to recover and adopt richer, holistic, more satisfying liturgies. If this trend continues, normative American Baptist understandings of liturgy, sacrament, and ecclesiology will grow and possibly mature to the point where the terms *liturgical Baptist* and *sacramental Baptist* may no longer be oxymorons.

Bibliography

The following titles explore more deeply the American Baptist perspective on the sacraments: William H. Brackney and Ruby J. Burke, eds., *Faith, Life and Witness: The Papers of the Study and Research Division of the Baptist Word Alliance, 1986–1990* (Birmingham, Ala.: Samford University Press, 1990); Norman Maring and Winthrop Hudson, *A Baptist Manual of Polity and Practice*, rev. ed. (Valley Forge, Pa.: Judson Press, 1991); H. Leon McBeth, *The Baptist Heritage: Four Centuries of Baptist Witness* (Nashville: Broadman, 1987) and *A Sourcebook for Baptist Heritage* (Nashville: Broadman, 1990); John Skoglund, *A Manual of Worship* (Valley Forge, Pa.: Judson Press, 1968) and "Baptist Worship" and related articles in *The New Westminster Dictionary of Liturgy and Worship*, ed. J. G. Davies (Philadelphia: Westminster, 1986); Bard Thompson, ed. *Liturgies of the Western Church* (Philadelphia: Fortress, 1982); Robert Webber, *Worship Old and New* (Grand Rapids: Zondervan, 1982).

Author's note: Because of Baptist polity, we cannot speak of the American Baptist Church the way we may speak of the Protestant Episcopal Church in the USA. Though there is substantial unity on many issues among American Baptist churches and throughout our areas, associations, and regions—even in our national General Board—use of the phrase *Baptist church* in the singular always and only means *one local church* and no more. One may discuss currents, trends, and traditions that may be generally accepted or entertained by one minority or another, but complete unanimity or full consensus among Baptists of any stripe remains elusive.

Ronal K. Freyer Nicholas

106 ✦ ANGLICAN/EPISCOPAL CHURCHES

The Book of Common Prayer has traditionally defined the sacramental life of Anglicans and Episcopalians. In addition to the Eucharist and baptism, Anglicans recognize five lesser sacraments. Recently, some congregations have opted for more variety in their liturgical practices.

To ascertain what Anglicans have believed, taught, confessed, and practiced regarding the sacraments, we must look at the Thirty-Nine

Articles of Religion (1562) and at the services in the Prayer Books (1549 to the present day).

Article XXV states: "Sacraments ordained of Christ be not only badges or tokens of Christian men's profession, but rather they be certain sure witnesses, and effectual signs of grace, and God's good will towards us, by the which he doth work invisibly in us, and doth not only quicken but also strengthen and confirm our Faith in him." The article goes on to describe the two Gospel sacraments (baptism and the Supper of the Lord) and five commonly called sacraments (confirmation, penance, orders, matrimony, and extreme unction).

High Church Anglicans have tended to accept the five commonly called sacraments as authentic sacraments but not of equal standing with the two Gospel sacraments. In this, they have usually followed Roman Catholic teaching. However, in the wake of the vast changes in Roman Catholicism since Vatican II, High Church Anglicans have revised their teachings, e.g. many think that confirmation is really part of baptism and should not be a separate rite, even with those baptized in infancy.

Baptism is a "sign of regeneration or new birth, whereby, as by an instrument, they that receive Baptism rightly are grafted into the Church" (Article XXVII). The Service of Holy Baptism likewise speaks of regeneration, and the minister declares: "Seeing now that this child is regenerate and grafted into the body of Christ's Church, let us give thanks unto Almighty God." Over the centuries Anglicans have debated when regeneration occurs. Evangelicals have tried to avoid a doctrine of baptismal regeneration, which seems to make the sacrament automatically grant new birth by the Holy Spirit. However, all agree that the Spirit works before, during, and after the rite to make the baptized a true member of the body of Christ. This means membership of the visible church, the household of faith, and also membership of the invisible or mystical body. Historically confirmation has been seen as the completion of baptism for those baptized as infants and as the gateway to their first Communion.

According to the classical tradition, the Lord's Supper, now often called the Holy Eucharist, is to be celebrated each Sunday and Holy Day. For long periods in Anglican history it was only celebrated once a month or less. However, in recent times, the weekly celebration has become common and, for most American parishes, the central act of worship. Though Anglicans have (until the advent of modern Books of Service) only used one basic form of words, or liturgy, for the Lord's Supper, they remain divided on the doctrine of the Real Presence of Christ. Some have followed the doctrines of Calvin or Zwingli, while others have looked to the Roman Catholic church or to the early church fathers. There is even disagreement on what doctrine Archbishop Cranmer had in mind when he composed the liturgy. Most are agreed, however, that the rite is much more than a mere memorial or remembering of the Lord's death. The catechism in _The Book of Common Prayer_ (1662) states that "the Body and Blood are verily and indeed taken and received by the faithful in the Lord's Supper" and that the benefit to the communicants is "the strengthening and refreshing of our souls by the Body and Blood of Christ, as our bodies are by the Bread and Wine." So there is an eating of two levels, the spiritual and the physical, and they are inseparable.

Over the centuries there has also been much discussion as to what kind of sacrifice is the Eucharist. All agree that it is a sacrifice of praise and thanksgiving. But is it more? Some see the Eucharist as a joining of the church here below with the perpetual offering of Christ himself to the Father in heaven. Others see the church as being offered as the body of Christ to the Father in union with its Head, the Lord Jesus Christ. Many see the church as lifted up into heaven to feast at the Table of the Lord at his messianic banquet, a feasting now in anticipation of the kingdom of God.

Over the last twenty years, a great change has begun to occur within the Anglican Communion. Many congregations are leaving behind the Common Prayer tradition (one liturgy used by all everywhere) and are adopting a new tradition of variety—of choosing from various possibilities. How this will affect worship and sacramental practice in the long term is difficult to predict. Certainly the new rites for the Eucharist place greater emphasis upon the community (e.g., by requiring the "Peace") than did the old tradition. In doing so, it is possible that the sense of the majesty and sovereign goodness of God are being lost in favor of an excessive emphasis upon the immanence of God in and with his people.

Peter Toon

107 ♦ Baptists (Evangelical Denominations and Independent Baptist Churches)

Baptists recognize the ordinances of baptism and the Lord's Supper. Baptism is an act of public declaration, and those making this profession are immersed in a lake, river, or baptismal tank. The Lord's Supper is observed ten to fifteen times a year. Congregations exercise some latitude in their observance of these ordinances.

Most evangelical Baptist churches are careful to never use the word *sacraments.* The word is somehow equated with nonevangelical groups. Baptists believe that the sacraments confer no means of grace as is believed in the more ancient branches of Christendom. Baptists instead embrace two *ordinances:* baptism and the Lord's Supper. Both are viewed as important reminders of our faith.

Baptism is never a private experience—rather it is a public declaration. The decision to be baptized is made by the Christian adult, never by his or her parents. Most evangelical Baptists regard baptism not as a statement of covenant theology and promises made by parents and congregation to nurture the person in the faith, but as a public affirmation of a personal and private decision to follow Jesus made at a previous time. It is normally conducted in a regular church service and administered by a duly authorized representative of the church—normally one of the pastors of the church. Most Baptist churches do not recognize as baptism any "alien" forms such as sprinkling, infant baptism, or pouring. Baptism must be by total immersion in a tank of water, but sometimes a local lake, river, or swimming pool is used. It is a prerequisite for formal church membership and participation on the governing boards of the church. However, it is almost never a prerequisite for complete participation in the fellowship of the church.

The Lord's Supper or what is sometimes referred to as Communion is primarily a remembrance of Jesus' last night with his disciples. It is a time when each of us is challenged to recall the sacrifice of Jesus' life on the cross for our sins. One of the accounts of the Last Supper in the Gospels is read and a time for private confession of our known sins in provided. Following that, small glasses of grape juice and pieces of bread or crackers are distributed. As each Christian partakes, she or he is very grateful for the gift of eternal life that has been given exclusively through the plan of redemption carried out by Jesus on the cross. Often our observance of Communion is a focused response to the worship theme and preached message for that Sunday. We usually ask each person to come forward and to receive the elements individually or together as family units. Sometimes we have no music during Communion—just silence for prayer and meditation. Sometimes, the choir calls us to praise God by singing a Gloria. Sometimes we have majestic congregational hymns. Any of these forms can be particularly effective, depending upon the design of the worship service.

Neither ordinance is deemed mystical or especially a vehicle for God's presence, for he is always with us wherever we are. Both the ordinances are performed because Scripture commands us to be baptized and to remember what Jesus did on the cross.

Owing to the vast spectrum of Christians who presently belong to evangelical Baptist churches, there will be some latitude in the descriptions above. No doubt some bring with themselves their theology of the sacraments into the Baptist arena. Because of our respect for the diversity of Christians in our church and a deep reverence for anything that is dedicated to God, such as the elements used in the Lord's Supper, many churches carefully protect the unused juice and bread after the service, rather than just discard it in the garbage or feed it to the birds. It is sometimes stored for a subsequent service or even consumed by those who have prepared the elements. While such practice is by no means universal, neither is it particularly rare. It is common to enjoy Communion approximately ten to fifteen times each year.

It is not believed that either ordinance has contained within its practice any special redemptive or saving powers and that both are to be enjoyed only by those Christians who of their own volition are faithfully attempting to follow God to the best of their own ability.

Rev. Larry Ellis

108 ♦ Baptist General Conference

Like most Baptists, the Baptist General Conference (BGC) recognizes the ordinance of baptism and the Lord's Supper.

Other sacred actions, though not commanded of believers, are practiced in many churches.

Because of the nature of Baptist polity (each church is autonomous and independent from any clerical or denominational hierarchy), the following is a description of the understanding and practice of ordinances and sacred actions in the worship renewal of one church in the denomination.

The Nature of Ordinances

Theologically, Baptists do not regard the rites of baptism and Communion sacramentally. We view these rites as _ordinances_ given by our Lord to be observed and practiced on a regular basis. Therefore, God's presence in worship isn't any more or less present when these rites are observed. However, his presence in ownership _is_ manifest in a special way in the gathering of two or three believers in the name of Jesus (Matthew 18:20).

But in the past, this theological position didn't manifest itself in any mystical sense as believers gathered for morning worship. Worship was service in which one sang a few hymns, listened to special music, heard a prayer by the pastor, presented one's offerings, and listened to the sermon (which was the main point of the service). In short, worship was a service _about_ God, not an encounter _with_ God.

More recently, our congregation at Bethlehem Baptist Church has experienced renewal in worship through the teaching and influence of Dr. Bruce H. Leafblad. His definition of worship encapsulates the shift that our congregation has experienced when he says, "Worship is communion with God, in which believers, by grace, center their minds' attention and their hearts' affection on the Lord himself, humbly glorifying God in response to his greatness and his Word."

As a result of this change, worship has become the focal point of our church life in which we try to be God-centered and God-focused in every area of our lives. There is now a definite change in the spirit and tone of the service: a sense of expectancy and anticipation during the prelude that we are there to meet God and that he is there to meet us.

The Lord's Supper

The Lord's Supper in most churches of the BGC is observed at least monthly. In our church, Communion is usually held in morning worship on the first Sunday of the month. Exceptions to this practice are the evening services on New Year's Eve and Maundy Thursday.

At Bethlehem, Communion is typically a service to our people before the sermon (with opening acts of worship designed to focus people's minds and hearts on Jesus and his passion). On occasion (particularly if the sermon focuses on the Atonement), Communion will be served after the sermon.

The Lord's Supper is open to all believers who attend our church. But because of Paul's warnings in 1 Corinthians 11:27-32, visitors are always informed of the seriousness of what is about to happen and, if they aren't believers, invited to place their trust in Christ alone for the forgiveness of sin and the hope of eternal life. They are then encouraged to believe and to participate.

During the distribution of the elements, various musical elements are utilized: instrumental and vocal meditations, congregational singing, silence, etc. The purpose of these meditations is to maintain an attitude of worship in the risen Lord's presence. It is, therefore, more than a mere observance of a historical event: It is a time to examine our hearts and commune with the Lord.

Baptism

Baptismal services are held during our Sunday evening services as often as needed. For Baptists, baptism is an outward expression of their internal faith and commitment: a dying to sin and Satan (symbolized by submersion in the water) and a rising to new life in Christ (symbolized by the emergence from the water).

In our church, the baptistry is located under the floor of our platform and is large enough to include space for a married couple or family. It was designed to be out in front and open because baptism is a public proclamation of one's allegiance to Christ. During the service, we invite the congregation to stand and gather around the baptismal font, so it has a feeling of being outside near a lake or stream. Modesty issues were addressed by having special robes made of thick material in a darker color. We chose to have them be burgundy in color, representing the blood of Christ that cleanses our sin. When they come out of the water, a deacon helps them up and places a white terry cloth cape around them, symbolizing our sin being washed clean by Christ's blood (Rev. 7:14).

Since baptism is an initiatory rite into the Christian faith, a celebrative mood is instituted in our church through the use of congregational singing after the person comes out of the water. The songs used focus on themes of worship such as commitment, adoration, or an invocation of the Holy Spirit.

Other Sacred Actions

Although the following sacred actions occur in our church, they are not ordinances that every believer is commanded to observe. However, they are included in corporate times of worship because they are significant events in the life of believers. At these times we desire to gather in the Lord's presence in order to seek his blessing and power in ministry. Such events include:

Dedication of Parents and Children, including the laying on of hands by the pastor, promises made by the parents, and an affirmation by the congregation to do whatever God calls them to do to help assist the parents in their promises to train their children in the Lord;

Commissioning of Missionaries, including the kneeling of the missionaries, the laying on of hands, and prayer by several members of the congregation, family, and friends;

Ordination of Pastors, including a charge to the ordinand, ordination vows, and the laying on of hands and prayer by a few family and clergy; and

Prayer Ministry for Healing, including the laying on of hands by prayer teams after the morning worship services to pray for whatever needs people have.

On occasion, some members call on the elders of the church to come and pray for them, which includes the laying on of hands, anointing of oil, and prayer as found in James 5:14-15.

Dean Palermo

109 ◆ BRETHREN (PLYMOUTH) ASSEMBLIES

Plymouth Brethren limit the sacraments to those actions commanded in Scripture by Christ. Some differences in baptism practices exist between Open Brethren and Exclusive Brethren, while all Brethren practice Communion weekly in a service known as the Breaking of the Bread. Some congregations have introduced minor changes in recent years, but Brethren remain essentially nonsacramental.

The (Plymouth) Brethren are not a sacramental movement. They typically afford no legitimacy in their practice to such things as confirmation, ordination, or any rites of healing. Ordination, in particular, is disallowed by the brethren since it suggests a clergy/laity distinction that places the ministry in the hands of the special few rather than leaving it in the hands of the gifted many. Instead, they practice *commendation* (cf. Acts 14:23, 25, KJV), which is simply praying and giving certain individuals over to the Lord's care for itinerant, local, or foreign ministry.

Following the thinking of the Reformers, Brethren limit the sacraments to those acts directly commanded by the Lord Jesus. Further, they do not believe that these sacraments supply any means of transmitting divine grace. In fact, Brethren, like others in the free-church movement, prefer to call these practices *ordinances,* if they use a collective term at all. In this sense, they identify only two ordinances commanded by the Lord: baptism and the Lord's Supper.

Among the Brethren, the practice of baptism differs within its two main divisions. The Open Brethren (following Groves, Muller, and Craik) are more baptistic and practice believer baptism by immersion. The Exclusive Brethren (following Darby) retain the Anglican practice of household or infant baptism. In either case, baptism is practiced not in the sense of obtaining spiritual benefit, but simply as an act of obedience to the command of the Lord. It serves as an outward symbol of the union of the believer with Christ, an observable parallel of and testimony to what has already taken place by faith.

The other ordinance practiced by the Brethren is the Lord's Supper, something very near and dear to the heart of every Brethren believer. The Brethren rigorously practice the Lord's Supper on a weekly basis, and occasionally more often. This is traditionally done in a separate meeting set apart for the Breaking of the Bread, which has as its focus and culmination the remembrance of the Lord in the partaking of the elements. Most frequently they take the practice in its most literal sense: They use real (leavened) bread, since *bread* is bread, not crackers, and real (fermented) wine, since _wine_ is wine, not grape juice.

In the past, one or a few cups of wine were passed among the congregation, but more recently some assemblies have made a few changes by substituting grape juice and going to multiple disposable cups for social or hygienic reasons. But the focus of the meeting is the same, and it is a very sacred meeting indeed for the Brethren. The meeting is an open, undirected one in which any believer (traditionally only males, based on the teaching of 1 Cor. 14:34-38) may suggest a hymn, lead in reflection on a passage of Scripture, or lead the congregation in prayer. But the primary issue for Brethren is the partaking of the elements in remembrance of the Lord, and all verbal contributions during the meeting are expected to ultimately lead to the time when someone voluntarily stands up to pray for the elements, which are then distributed by another. The bread is always distributed first, and the cup last, since this is the order in which it was distributed by our Lord in the Upper Room.

The Brethren also believe that the Lord is, in a real sense, present in the midst of the congregation during this time of worship, but this presence is not connected directly with some special presence of the Lord associated with the material elements. Instead, it is based on their understanding of the promise given by the Lord, "Where two or three are gathered in my name, there am I in the midst of them" (Matt. 18:2). Brethren understand themselves to be gathered to the name of Christ to remember him and, hence, expect his presence in a special way during this meeting.

These two ordinances practiced by the Brethren are not directed by any special clergy or leadership (as mentioned, Brethren know of no clergy/laity distinction). Brethren may occasionally remember the Lord in contexts of two or three apart from the local congregation, although the normal practice is within that context. Baptism may be done by any designated believer, as may the prayer for or distribution of the elements during the Supper.

Footwashing is not practiced among the Brethren, since that is not viewed as an ordinance but simply as a dynamic example of humility given by the Lord. During cases of extreme sickness, the elders of the congregation are sometimes called for, based on James 5:14-15. They may read Scrip-

ture and pray for the sick individual, sometimes laying on hands as appropriate, but rarely, if ever, anointing with oil. This latter action is rare for one of two reasons. To some, the practice is viewed as anachronistic because oil is understood to be a medicine of the first century that is no longer used (although Brethren may, with a doctor's permission, pray over and administer other more modern medicines). Others object to the magical or mystical dimensions that the oil took on in subsequent centuries of church history, a superstition they scrupulously hope to avoid.

In the last ten years or so, some Brethren assemblies have made some changes in the practice of these ordinances, but even so, the notion of any sort of divine efficaciousness in the actions of baptism or the Lord's Supper is disallowed on scriptural grounds. But occasionally one sees elders calling up before the congregation individuals or families who are leaving, or who are involved in key ministries in the assembly, or who are being commended to North American or foreign missions. These individuals are publicly prayed for by the elders, who may place their hands on them during the event. In addition, some assemblies are celebrating the birth of new babies born to families in the congregation. Elders call the families forward, hold the baby and pray for it, and honor the mother with a flower or some such token. Some Brethren have expressed concern that it is a bit too ostentatious and overbearing to see the elders doing this too often (too active an eldership borders on clericalism in some Brethren circles).

Another observable change is the tendency to allow some sort of human direction at the start of the Lord's Supper to set a theme or focus of remembrance, rather than simply opening it for general participation at once. Changes like this have met with resistance as well, since the presence of Christ in the meeting, to the Brethren, means that he must be allowed to be Lord of the meeting as well, rather than having human leadership interpose.

The bottom line is that it is highly unlikely that the Brethren will ever move toward a more sacramental approach to their worship and ministry. It is far too alien to the very nature of the movement and far too difficult for them to support scripturally. As such, they will continually face criticism from some circles of having docetic tendencies, a charge that is often leveled at churches in the free-church tradition.

Rex Koivisto

110 ✦ CHRISTIAN CHURCHES AND CHURCHES OF CHRIST

Christian churches consciously seek to imitate the worship practices of the New Testament church, and this thinking has shaped their practice of baptism and the Lord's Supper. In recent times, churches have introduced innovations to add new meaning to traditional Communion and baptism services.

Christian churches (independent) and Churches of Christ (instrumental) consciously seek unadorned New Testament practices for their worship. Their general approach to sacred actions is more one of cool, deliberate logic than of mysterious, symbolic rite. And they carefully avoid anything that appears to be a later Catholic addition. Such an approach demonstrates itself in their use of sacraments, ordinances, and sacred actions.

For example: If believers have the gift of the Holy Spirit already, there is no need to invoke the presence of the Holy Spirit or to enter the presence of God when believers assemble. Therefore, most of the churches have "opening prayer" in the "church building" (or auditorium), rather than an "invocation" in the "sanctuary." Believers simply gather together as the body of Christ for mutual edification, instruction, encouragement, and evangelism.

Another example: The clergy has a very limited role in the life of the church. Each local eldership will ordain ministers (often called *evangelists*), elders, and deacons. Ministers marry and preside at funerals because of their training, their license, and society's expectations, but they wear no clerical robes nor are they conferred with any special authority.

The two standard ordinances recognized and practiced among Christian churches and Churches of Christ are common to most denominations: the Lord's Supper and baptism. But the churches emphasize these two acts to a much greater degree than do most evangelicals. In fact, the churches are often distinguised by their unique view of these two acts.

Historically, baptism may be the movement's greatest focus. Most sermons close with an explanation of baptism, a reference to Acts 2:38, and a call for all to be immersed for the forgiveness of sin and the gift of the Holy Spirit. Many of the members of these churches would even speculate that the "pious unimmersed" were probably not saved, based on their understanding that regeneration occurs at baptism. Coincidentally, this is a more orthodox view of baptism than is common among most evangelicals, who emphasize salvation by faith alone.

Here's how a baptism service would typically occur: Each week an evangelistic invitation is offered. Those who respond are asked to repeat the Good Confession. The most common version of the confession is "I believe that Jesus is the Christ, the Son of the Living God." For the baptism itself, the evangelist says something along the order of

On the basis of your confession and in response to your repentance, I now baptize you in the name of the Father and of the Son and of the Holy Spirit, for the forgiveness of your sins; and you shall receive the gift of the Holy Spirit.

The candidate is then lowered backwards and submersed in the water. Often during the immersion itself, the evangelist will say, "Buried with Christ in baptism; raised to walk in newness of life." In many of the churches, the refrain "Now I Belong to Jesus" is sung by the congregation as the neophyte comes out of the water. The service is simple and brief, for the churches try to avoid adding any extravagance to what they see as an otherwise simple New Testament act.

The standard practice of baptism has diversified in recent years. The basic format is similar, but the wording of the Good Confession is less uniform, the chorus of response is sometimes replaced with another song or even with applause, and private baptisms during the week are more common, perhaps with family, church staff, or elders present to celebrate with the new disciple. Anyone is considered qualified to perform a baptism, although the minister does it most often.

The Lord's Supper is the other ordinance among Christian churches. As with baptism, the Christian churches' understanding of the Supper stands out because the group's position does not fit the evangelical norm. Virtually every Christian church sees apostolic precedent in meeting on the first day of the week for the purpose of breaking bread, so they have weekly Communion.

The meal is never referred to as the Eucharist among these churches, so as to avoid any terms that developed after New Testament times. It is usually referred to as the Lord's Supper, the Lord's Table, or Communion. The meal is seen as strictly a symbolic memorial that Christ instituted, and again it is done simply, with little fanfare or dressing.

Historically, churches have participated in the Lord's Supper in this way: They sing a Communion hymn, then an elder or other male member will present a brief Communion meditation. He gleans his thoughts from a publication containing sample meditations, or he may create his own. Usually, the meditation finishes with the reading of a New Testament passage (the account in 1 Corinthians 11 is most common) and/or the words of institution. These words are followed by extemporaneous prayers for the bread and "fruit of the vine" (it is grape juice—wine is not used) offered by one or two men. Trays containing the bread (individual pieces of matzo crackers or home-baked crackers of unleavened bread) and the cups (most churches use individual cups, either glass or disposable) are then passed among the congregation. The entire service may take ten or twelve minutes altogether.

More recently, there has been an emphasis on streamlining the Communion service as churches are trying to shorten their worship service. The Communion hymn may be left out, the meditation may be shortened or merged with the prayer, and more trays used to expedite the distribution. Communion observance today often takes seven to ten minutes.

On the other hand, a growing number of churches following the example of Fellowship Christian Church in Cincinnati, Ohio. After the meditation and prayer, they have an open time lasting perhaps ten minutes or more for Communion. They may place several tables around the room that individuals can freely approach. On each table rest the elements, and members kneel or stand at the table and then serve themselves, returning to their seats whenever they wish.

Christian churches and Churches of Christ are clearly not sacramental unless the act is included and explained in the pages of the New Testament itself. They demonstrate a bias toward simplicity and the tendency toward analytical study. They have historically avoided any semblance of denominational Christianity and have a general distrust of the mystical or the supernatural. They might be described as having modern evangelical worship practices colored by primitive orthodox theology.

III ✦ Christian Church (Disciples of Christ)

Of the churches that originated in the Restoration Movement, the Christian Church (Disciples of Christ) has been most open to change in worship practices. For the most part, Disciples continue to practice baptism by immersion and weekly Communion.

In January 1832, when the Christians, led by Barton Stone in Kentucky since 1804, united with the Disciples of Christ, led by Thomas and Alexander Campbell in Pennsylvania and Virginia since 1809, a major American religious movement was established. Its distinctive idea was to combine a call for Christian unity with an appeal to restore the church along the lines of the New Testament.

The Westminster Confession influenced the founders of the Christian Church. It declared that the purpose of being alive is to enjoy God. Alexander Campbell, the most influential and prolific leader of this movement, named faith as the principle by which God is enjoyed and ordinances as the means by which people enjoy God. Worship is a way to focus our faith on God, who is revealed in Jesus Christ. God pours out grace upon those who worship.

Revivalism influenced the way Christian churches approached worship from the late nineteenth century into the twentieth century. The Lord's Supper was seen as a preliminary to the sermon, which was presumed to be the climax of worship. After 1930, liberalism affected the worship of many churches, and worship became defined in purely subjective terms such as _beautiful_ or _meaningful_.

Of the three religious bodies that emerged from the Stone-Campbell movement, the Christian Church (Disciples of Christ) has been most open to changes leading away from nineteenth-century patterns and toward beliefs and practices influenced by ecumenical dialogue. In 1968, when the _Design for the Christian Church (Disciples of Christ)_ was adopted, "churches" became "a church," allowing the group to initiate ecumenical relationships as an entity. Increased ecumenical dialogue has resulted in a renewed interest in the early church. Recent scholarship has led more congregations to place Scriptures close to the sermon, to place the sermon before the Lord's Supper, and to include the offering as part of the Communion service. The number of preachers using the Common Lectionary is growing, and there is more willingness to use the term *sacrament* to describe baptism and the Lord's Supper.

While pastors and church musicians have brought about these changes, no lasting change takes place in the Christian Church (Disciples of Christ) without the understanding and support of the laity. The shifts have been gradual as worship committees and lay elders have studied the purpose of worship.

Alexander Campbell rejected the word *sacrament* and used the word *ordinance* in its place. Although anything that imparts something of God's grace could be considered an ordinance, Campbell most often spoke of three ordinances—baptism, the Lord's Supper, and the Lord's Day.

All churches stemming from the Stone-Campbell movement baptize believers by immersion. For Disciples, baptism has no magical effect in washing away sins. Instead, it is part of the process of salvation, a process that includes believing, repenting, being baptized, letting go of guilt, and receiving the gift of the Holy Spirit. It is God's grace that saves. Baptism is a way of obediently accepting God's grace through faith in Jesus Christ. The Holy Spirit calls forth faith from the believer before baptism and continues to direct the believer after baptism.

In recent years, Disciples have placed less emphasis on repenting of sins because the majority of those receiving baptism are second-generation Christians, young people who have been raised in a Christian environment. What they need is not so much to turn around as to keep going in the same direction. Therefore, in preparation for baptism, as well as in reflection on what it means to have been baptized, pastors and teachers highlight God's initiative in loving people and in choosing a person to do God's work.

Contemporary Disciples resist rebaptizing persons previously baptized as infants and confirmed as believers. Thomas and Alexander Campbell, baptized as infants and confirmed in the Presbyterian tradition, submitted themselves to rebaptism by immersion after the birth of Alexander Campbell's daughter caused them to consider the issue. While ecumenical conversation has led to greater appreciation for baptizing believers by immersion, it also has led to greater respect for the validity of other forms of Christian initiation.

Not only is immersion the most likely method of baptism used by the earliest Christians, it also effectively represents dying and rising with Christ. It is a way of being raised up into the body of the risen Christ, a way of being incorporated into the church, the first act in a life of discipleship. Waiting until someone is old enough to think about this need not take anything away from the emphasis on God's initiative in calling persons into the covenant of love.

The Lord's Supper is central to the identity of the Christian Church (Disciples of Christ). It is the most important ingredient in worship; indeed, it is the primary purpose for gathering to worship. Therefore, from the earliest days of this movement, the Christian Church has advocated weekly observance of Holy Communion.

Christian Church congregations usually speak of the Lord's Table. Located away from the wall, it is not called an altar. One to three people will preside and offer prayers from one side of the Table. These leaders may or may not include clergy, but they almost always include lay elders chosen and ordained by the congregation. Their role at the table, however, is not a matter of authority, but of convenience.

The bread may be matzo, Communion wafers, or a loaf baked in the home of a church member. The cup will contain unfermented grape juice, a lasting effect of the Temperance movement of the 1890s. Most churches use individual cups in trays that are passed among the seated congregation; however, on certain occasions, persons walk forward to the Table and dip the bread in a chalice of grape juice.

After inviting all Christians to unite at the Lord's Table, the leaders read the words of institution from the Gospels or from 1 Corinthians 11. Then one or two prayers of thanksgiving are offered by the elders. Members of the Christian Church (Disciples of Christ) hold that the Lord's Table cannot be closed to any believer. At some point in the service, the congregation might sing a hymn, which will probably be Christ-centered in doctrine.

No supernatural change occurs during the service. The bread and wine are signs that point to the presence of the risen Christ, but at no point do they literally or physically change substance.

The Lord's Day as an ordinance may be in danger of being forgotten in an increasingly secular society. Viewing one day of the week as belonging to the Lord is not legalistic but celebrative. The purpose of the day is not to abstain from work but to abstain from sin, and thus to set a pattern for all other days. This sacramental day can transform all ordinary time.

Further information on Disciples' practices can be found in Colbert S. Cartwright, _Candles of Grace: Disciples Worship in Perspective_ (St. Louis: Chalice Press, 1992) and _People of the Chalice: Disciples of Christ in Faith and Practice_ (St. Louis: CBP Press, 1987); Ronald E. Osborn, _The Faith We Affirm: Basic Beliefs of Disciples of Christ_ (Lindsborg, Kans.: Bethany Press, 1979); Keith Watkins, ed., _Thankful Praise: A Resource for Christian Worship_ (St. Louis: CBP Press, 1987); Keith Watkins, _The Feast of Joy: The Lord's Supper in Free Churches_ (Lindsborg, Kans.: Bethany Press, 1977).

Philip V. Miller

112 ◆ THE CHRISTIAN AND MISSIONARY ALLIANCE CHURCHES

Christian and Missionary Alliance (C&MA) churches practice believer baptism and regular (usually monthly) Communion. Many congregations combine Communion with services for healing and cleansing from sin.

The Christian and Missionary Alliance observes the ordinances of baptism and the Lord's Supper. Although not called sacraments, they are generally viewed as sacramental in nature: as outward and visible signs of an inward and spiritual grace.

The C&MA practices believer baptism by immersion. Some churches hold baptismal services in a public place, using running or standing water. Other churches hold them in the church building and utilize a baptistery. In our church, we purposely make this a very public event held as often as necessary at a local lake. It is a time of celebra-tion preceded by an all-church picnic. The baptismal service itself begins with a time of worship including the ministry of the Word. Prior to the actual baptism, the candidates are led through several corporate statements concerning the renunciation of Satan and all his ways and their allegiance to the Lord Jesus Christ. In addition, each candidate makes an individual declaration that Jesus Christ is Lord and Savior immediately before immersion.

Preparation for the baptism usually includes a period of instruction concerning the meaning and significance of the ordinance. This practice is followed in our church. A required two-hour class must be taken before one may be baptized. We encourage the new believers with the need to follow the Lord in baptism early on in their relationship with him.

In some parts of the C&MA, unofficial discussion is taking place concerning the possible inclusion of participation in some type of deliverance ministry as part of the candidate's preparation. Such a decision is likely to remain in the hands of the local church and not find its way into official denominational policy. I do not know of any C&MA church in the United States that currently includes such a practice. Some do not even include statements of renunciation like those our church uses.

The C&MA does not practice infant baptism. In its place is infant dedication. The emphasis in this ministry of the church is upon the dedication of the parents before God to raise the child in the nurture and admonition of the Lord. In addition, in our fellowship, we ask the members of the congregation to indicate their commitment to support the parents and child during their years of fellowship in the body. The child is then dedicated to the Lord in prayer, during which God is asked to preserve the child and quickly bring him or her into a personal relationship with him.

The other ordinance observed in the C&MA is the Lord's Supper. The only official statement is that it should be observed regularly. Most churches practice it once a month. The bread and cup, usually grape juice, are seen as symbols of the body and blood of Jesus. However, historical practice within the denomination would indicate that many understand that, during the observance of the Lord's Supper, there is a special presence of Christ that heals and touches his people through a cleansing from sin. Our practice is to often provide the opportunity for persons to be anointed with oil and to receive prayer for healing during Communion. The denomination combines these two practices at a special service each year near the end of the General Council meetings.

Most C&MA churches observe Communion by first passing out the bread and then the cup, partaking of each separately. In our church, we have generally used the method of intinction, where the communicant comes to the ones serving, takes a piece of bread, dips it in a large cup, and partakes of both elements together. This has provided for the opportunity to speak the Word of truth to each individual such as "The body of the Lord Jesus, broken for you" and "The blood of the Lord Jesus, shed for you." This has, for many, made participation an even more personally meaningful experience.

Andrew R. Jesson

113 • CHRISTIAN REFORMED CHURCH

Following its Calvinist heritage, the Christian Reformed Church regards the sacraments of baptism and the Lord's Supper as "holy signs and seals" by which God confirms the saving promises of the gospel. Such sacraments depend on the faithful proclamation of the Word. In recent years, the fairly uniform liturgical observance of these sacraments has been eroded by the influx of ethnic groups who have contributed many of their own traditions.

The Christian Reformed Church (CRC) was traditionally an immigrant church shaped by a Dutch tradition that traces its origins back to Calvin and the Swiss Reformation of Zwingli. Like other churches in this tradition, the CRC recognizes baptism and the Lord's Supper as the two sacraments explicitly instituted by Christ and essential to the corporate life of the church. Actual sacramental practice grows out of the distinctive Calvinist conviction that in worship God is not merely present but also active by means of Word and Spirit, so that when the Bible is read and proclaimed it is in fact God who speaks, with the Holy Spirit working in the hearts of hearers to convince them of the truth and inspire them to faithful obedience. This sense of God's presence finds

expression in the prayer for illumination that constitutes a characteristic feature of many Reformed liturgies. It finds expression, too, in the arrangement of liturgical space. The pulpit invariably occupies a central and commanding place, with font and Table below it or off to the sides.

It follows that the CRC regards sacraments as neither purely human actions nor objectively valid means of grace. They are, rather, a medium through which God acts for the benefit of believers. They depend upon—and at the same time complete—the proclamation of the Word; they are the "holy signs and seals," as the Heidelberg Catechism describes them, by which God confirms and, as it were, authenticates the saving promises of the gospel. Hence the CRC has always insisted on the organic unity of Word and sacrament. Sacramental acts are normally performed only within the context of corporate worship, and the historic sacramental forms feature lengthy expositions of each rite, the purposes for which it was instituted, and the particular promises it signifies and conveys.

Baptism is a sacrament of initiation into Christ's body. It confirms the washing away of sins and so manifests God's covenant faithfulness. Because the promises of this covenant apply both to adult believers and to their children (by analogy, the Old Testament covenant of circumcision), the CRC teaches and practices infant baptism. A practical consequence, given past high birthrates, is that in many congregations baptism has typically been the more frequently celebrated of the two sacraments. The traditional baptismal rite contains an extended doctrinal introduction, after which parents are called upon to affirm their faith in Christ, their understanding of the sacrament, and their commitment to instruct their children in the faith. Baptism is administered with water in the name of the Trinity. Though no specific method is mandated, pouring or sprinkling is by far the most common mode of administration. A baptismal prayer invokes the Holy Spirit on behalf of those baptized.

The CRC regards the Lord's Supper, like baptism, as a sacrament of God's faithfulness. In it the Holy Spirit nourishes the souls of believers through the "veil of . . . earthly elements," as one historic formulary puts it, uniting them spiritually with Christ and with one another. Christ is therefore truly present in the sacrament, but in a spiritual rather than a physical sense. For adult converts, participation in the Supper follows directly from baptism. Persons baptized as infants have traditionally been admitted to the Table only upon public profession of faith, which typically occurs in one's teens or early twenties.

For generations the CRC adhered to the Zwinglian pattern of celebrating the Supper four times a year (the minimum frequency mandated by the official church order). These celebrations were typically the most solemn occasions in the life of a congregation. Liturgical forms included heavy doses of doctrinal instruction, with a strong emphasis on Christ's suffering for sin and the importance of "worthy partaking." By tradition the week prior to Communion Sunday was a period of special preparation and self-examination. The church practiced close, not closed, communion: Members of other churches were allowed to commune, but only after making their request known in advance, and the Table was "fenced" with warnings to anyone guilty of an unrepentant spirit or gross public sin about partaking. Until well into the twentieth century, many congregations preserved the Dutch custom of communing at an actual table. Over time, however, this gave way almost universally to the practice of having supervising elders serve communicants in the pews, with individual cups in place of the traditional Communion cup.

Other rites, though regarded as nonsacramental, similarly invoke the Holy Spirit and assume God's active presence in the church's life and worship. These include public profession of faith (already mentioned) as well as rites of ordination or installation for clergy and other office bearers. All of these ceremonies take place within corporate worship and involve instruction, vows by the participants, and an act of induction—the latter including, in the case of of ordination, the laying on of hands by participating clergy. Provision has also traditionally been made for the solemnization of marriage as part of corporate worship, though in practice this rarely, if ever, occurs.

Recent decades have been a time of change and ferment in the CRC as members have increasingly assimilated to mainstream American culture and attempted to embrace a broader ethnic spectrum. Once almost exclusively Dutch, the church now includes a substantial minority of African-Americans, Hispanics, Asians, and Native Americans as well as non-Dutch Anglos. This growing multiculturalism has led, perhaps inevitably, to a dramatic erosion of liturgical uniformity. As late as the 1960s, virtually all congregations still employed a common set of time-honored sacramental forms. Today they have access to a veritable cornucopia of options, both official and unofficial, ranging from eucharistic prayers and baptismal rites inspired by the postwar liturgical-renewal movement to informal models indistinguishable in many respects from typical American free-church practices.

This liturgical ferment also reflects an upsurge of interest in sacramental experience. Celebrations of the Lord's Supper, for example, are becoming more frequent and often more eucharistic in spirit. According to a recent survey, barely one congregation in ten still maintains the old pattern of quarterly celebration, and while the increase in frequency has been fairly modest in most cases, at least a few congregations have succeeded in restoring the ancient practice of the weekly Communion advocated by Calvin. The past few years have also seen a movement to open the Table to younger children; the connection between baptism and Eucharist has become a subject of lively debate. Nearly half of all congregations have experimented with some form of healing rite, from the use of prayer teams in corporate worship to the laying on of hands at sickbeds. Many congregations have also expanded the use of commissioning rites to include a variety of lay ministries such as church school teachers or mission volunteers.

Most of these trends appear likely to continue. The question now facing the church is whether the distinctive sacramental insights that shaped the CRC's Dutch Reformed heritage can continue to provide coherence in the face of increasingly divergent practice, or indeed whether they will be able to survive at all.

David J. Dipehouse

114 • CHURCH OF GOD, CLEVELAND, TENNESSEE

The Church of God, Cleveland, places foremost emphasis on the ministry of the Holy Spirit and does not regard the ordinances as special signs of God's presence. Three ordinances—baptism, the Lord's Supper, and footwash-

ing—are practiced, but other actions such as dedication, ordination, and installation are observed by many congregations.

The Pentecostal doctrine and practice of the Church of God (Cleveland) cause a constant emphasis on the presence of God through the active ministry of the Holy Spirit. Regardless of the activity in the worship service, his presence is believed to be there. It may be experienced personally and corporately. God's presence is felt within the individual believer's heart through the worship experience. However, dramatic interventions of his supernatural presence through the gifts of the Spirit are both expected and desired.

Theologically no variance of God's presence or significance is seen in either the ordinances or any other ceremonial acts. This is due to the ordinances being seen as acts of obedience to the teachings and example of Christ rather than channels or means of a special dimension of the divine presence. However, from a practical standpoint, many members view the Lord's Supper and footwashing on a different plane. It seems that the introspection and the humility required in each respectively provide an added dimension of sensitivity to God's nearness.

Three individual acts comprise the ordinances practiced by the Church of God (Cleveland)—the Lord's Supper, footwashing, and water baptism. Ministerial and congregational preference determine the time, frequency, pattern, and atmosphere of celebration. The impact of each observation varies, depending partially on the value placed upon it and the current spiritual condition of the group.

Other significant events practiced by the denomination include ordination, dedication, and installation. Ministers achieving the third and final rank of ministry are then ordained. Since there is no formally written ceremony prescribed, this time of commitment and celebration varies according to the pattern preferred by the supervising minister. Whether it takes place in a regional denominational meeting or in a local church's Sunday service, there is one common practice: Other ordained ministers and laymen from the local church lay hands on the minister and his spouse during the ordination prayer.

It should be noted that some of the large congregations have implemented an elder system. Ordination of these lay leaders then becomes a matter of local church preference, since the denomination as a whole does not ordain lay leaders.

In place of infant baptism, the Church of God (Cleveland) encourages parents to dedicate both the newborn child as well as themselves to the Lord. This usually occurs within several months after the child's birth. Some pastors also use this occasion as an opportunity for the entire congregation to dedicate itself to nurturing children and families in general.

The dedication of church sanctuaries, educational plants, and parsonages is also practiced. Some congregations dedicate other major purchases such as vehicles for ministry and the main musical instruments. It is rare to find the dedication of such items as hymnals and church pews.

Whenever the event emphasizes people, the laying on of hands regularly accompanies a wide variety of sacred actions within the Church of God (Cleveland). Besides the event of ordination, laying on of hands occurs at dedications and installations as well as at special times of sending forth individuals or groups for ministry trips. Prayer for the healing of the sick or injured who are in attendance also incorporates this action. Anointing with oil may precede the prayer. Then the pastor, along with other ministers and members of the congregation, carries out the laying on of hands. In some congregations, individuals in the pews are encouraged to lay hands on those nearby who have publicly indicated prayer needs.

Any discussion of the sacred events and actions practiced by the Church of God (Cleveland) would not be complete without including the worship gesture of the uplifted hand. This symbol of honor to God and surrender of self spontaneously occurs among the ministry and laity alike. At times, the worship leader invites and encourages this response, but it is not an orchestrated gesture for the proper celebration of any of the sacred events.

With regard to change, the ordinances of the Lord's Supper and footwashing need to be considered. It appears that many Church of God congregations have increased the number of occasions on which the Lord's Supper is celebrated. They have moved from once or twice a year to quarterly and even monthly. The practice of footwashing seems to have declined greatly among most congregations. An ever-declining number celebrate the Lord's Supper and footwashing jointly, as was the practice in earlier decades. There is, however, a renewed emphasis on this ordinance at the Church of God School of Theology due to the work of Dr. Christopher Thomas.

Due to the freestyle emphasis on all worship coupled with the lack of a written liturgy, the Church of God tends to emphasize the practice of the sacred actions. The theological significance and biblical teaching concerning each is taught but generally tends to find second place behind the expression of the ordinances and other sacred actions.

Jerald Daffe

115 ✦ CHURCHES OF CHRIST (NONINSTRUMENTAL)

Like other Restorationist churches, the Churches of Christ observe weekly Communion and baptism of believers. Many churches within this tradition are devoting more time to worship during the Lord's Supper, especially through singing.

The terms _sacrament_ and _ordinance_ rarely appear in the vocabulary of Churches of Christ. The Roman Catholic and Eastern Orthodox churches recognize seven sacraments: baptism, confirmation, Eucharist, penance (or confession), anointing of the sick, holy orders, and matrimony. Roman Catholics believe that the sacraments aid salvation, whereas most Protestants see them as visible signs of agreement between God and individuals. Churches of Christ recognize two of those seven—baptism and the Eucharist (called the Lord's Supper)—although its members would never refer to them as sacraments. Churches of Christ consider all of their acts of worship sacred in nature.

Many Churches of Christ engaged in worship renewal are placing greater emphasis on the presence of God among his people when they assemble for worship. Members of Churches of Christ have always given mental assent to Jesus' words: "For where two or three come together in my name, there am I with them" (Matt. 18:20). However, until recently, there has not been a strong emphasis upon the presence of God in worship. Over the past several decades, Churches of Christ have stressed the importance of conducting the correct form of worship, of being faithful to the biblical pattern. Critics within the church have said this emphasis on correctness of form has too often led to the view that God is present in worship, but primarily as a silent observer and not as an active participant with his people. Such a view, they contend, leads to worship services which easily become lifeless, dull, and cold.

Worship leaders in renewing churches are still concerned about a form of worship that follows biblical guidelines. They are also calling for worship services that lead worshipers to a deep awareness that God is actually among them as they worship. They want worshipers to encounter the living God and to respond to him in worship with heartfelt emotion.

Renewing churches have tried to accomplish this in a number of ways. There is a call to worship that is usually accompanied by prayers and readings from Scripture, often from the Psalms. Scripture selections are carefully chosen to help worshipers become aware that God comes among his people.

Many congregations are spending more time singing at the opening of their services. These songs tend to be praise hymns that direct worshipers' thoughts and hearts to the Lord. Hymns, prayers, and Bible readings are interspersed in an effort to create an atmosphere that aids worshipers in their desire to encounter God.

Churches of Christ observe the Lord's Supper weekly. Renewing churches work hard to make this observance meaningful. Several congregations are dedicating more time to this segment of worship. They sing songs about God's love demonstrated through Jesus' death. Carefully selected songs and Scripture readings are also used to help people focus on a number of important themes: confession of sin and the need for forgiveness, concern for the body of believers, gratitude to God and to Christ for his indescribable gift, and the anticipation that Christ is coming again in glory to take his people home to heaven.

Most congregations have at the front of the sanctuary a table from which men serve the bread and the cup to worshipers, who remain seated. Some smaller congregations place one or more tables at convenient places in the assembly hall and allow members to leave their seats, gather around a table, and break the bread and drink the cup in a more personally intimate manner.

Ken Young, president of Hallel Music, a publishing company specializing in praise music for a cappella singing, says that interest in the presence of God in worship is widespread and growing among Churches of Christ. Young introduced his company's services at the 1992 Pepperdine University Bible Lectureships in Malibu, California. With no information or promotion other than the exposure it received at this three-day event, the company in only three months sold tapes and songbooks to people representing over 500 congregations, 250 cities, 32 states, and 6 foreign countries.

Not everyone has greeted these changes with enthusiasm. Some are confused by the innovations, while others feel liberated. These new emphases are more generally accepted in urban and suburban congregations than in rural settings. They are more widely appreciated among younger generations than older ones.

Anointing and the laying on of hands for the sick is not widely practiced in Churches of Christ. Most leaders in Churches of Christ believe that apostolic miraculous powers ceased in the first century. They do believe, however, that God is very much alive, that he has all power, and that he still heals whom he will. They believe that God also uses the healing powers of medical science to accomplish his desired ends. Many elders will anoint ill Christians with oil (James 5:14) when patients request it. However, they usually comply with this desire in an effort to comfort the patient and to honor the patient's faith, not because they believe miraculous power is in the oil or in their own hands. Rather, they trust in the power of God that is unleashed through prayer (James 5:15). Preachers, elders, and members of Churches of Christ sometimes do lay their hands on the sick as a gesture of care, closeness, and the symbolic mediating touch of God.

As a symbol of endorsement and empowerment for ministry, elders in some congregations lay hands on specific individuals such as missionaries who are being commissioned for special service. There is no official ordination of ministers or elders in the Churches of Christ. Churches of Christ are nondenominational and have no centralized governing body that oversees all the congregations. Each congregation is self-governed; therefore, it is left up to each local church to determine what rites are observed in commissioning and empowering people to serve.

Dan Dozier

The Alpha and Omega. The alpha and omega, the first and last letters of the Greek alphabet, mean that Jesus Christ is the beginning and end of all things. The figure above is an example of the alpha and the omega combined with a cross.

116 ✦ EASTERN ORTHODOX CHURCHES

Worship in the Eastern Orthodox tradition has always been visibly sacramental. In this ancient tradition, the sacrament is the means by which God, through physical means, comes to his church. Baptism, chrismation, Eucharist, Holy Orders, anointing (unction), and marriage are among the sacraments celebrated by the church.

In its experience of worship, the central conviction of the Orthodox church is that God is present among us through physical means. A *mystery* or *sacrament* in Orthodox tradition is a material means by which God comes to us. God created the universe and pronounced it good. After our fall into sin, God became one with humanity in Jesus Christ, so uniting all of Creation, including materiality, to himself. Thus, one could summarize the Orthodox approach to the mystery as "incarnational." Since God himself has created and inhabited matter, he continues to meet us through material means.

When one participates in Orthodox worship, one is inundated with sensory perceptions. One sees the holy icons, or images of Christ and the saints. One hears the sacred chant and the reading and preaching of God's Word. One smells the incense and the scent of burning candle wax. One feels and tastes the Holy Eucharist and the _antidoron_ (i.e., blessed bread). For Orthodox believers, worship is a very material as well as spiritual experience.

The Orthodox derive their sacramental theology and practice from the church fathers. This patristic tradition has generally not sought to number the mysteries, but rather sees Christ and his glorified humanity as _the_ sacrament. It is in Christ's body, the church, that we continue to meet God.

In holy baptism, we are united to Christ, sharing in his life, death, and resurrection victory. The Orthodox have always affirmed with St. Paul that "as many as have been baptized into Christ have put on Christ" (Gal. 3:27). This is the work of the Holy Spirit who unites us to Christ in his glorified humanity in the baptismal waters. Although God does indeed meet us in the mysteries, we must cooperate with his grace objectively present there if we are to receive the benefit of the mystery. As St. Cyril of Jerusalem (d. A.D. 386) taught those about to be baptized, "If you abide in your evil purpose, he who speaks is blameless, but you must not look for grace: for though the water shall receive you, the Spirit will not receive you." We must cooperate with God's grace that is objectively given in the holy mysteries if we are to receive their benefits.

In Holy Chrismation, we participate personally in the charismatic gift of the Holy Spirit, given to the holy church on the day of Pentecost. Through the anointing of oil blessed by the bishop, we are all able to personally participate in the anointing of Christ as his baptism and in the anointing by the risen and ascended Christ of all his people. Chrismation is the mystery by which all believers are ordained to the order of God's people, the _laos_, who constitute in Christ one holy priesthood.

Through the mystery of Holy Orders by the laying on of the bishop's hands, those faithful who are called by the Lord to serve the church as teachers, pastors, and celebrants of the Holy Eucharist are set apart to their sacred vocation. Bishops, priests, and deacons are given the special gifts of grace (charismata) which enable them, in historic succession from the apostles, to continue to shepherd God's flock, the church.

The primary function of the bishop and his representation in the local parish, the presbyter (or ministerial priest), is to be the icon of Christ as he presides at the Holy Eucharist and in the celebration of all the mysteries. In the Holy Eucharist, Christ gives us through our gifts of bread and wine his own glorified humanity. With the saints of all the ages, the Holy Orthodox Church continues to confess Christ's actual presence with us in both his divine and human natures in the bread and wine of the Eucharist. As the people, led by their presbyter or bishop, invoke the presence of the Holy Spirit upon themselves as a worshiping community and upon the bread and wine, Christ is mysteriously and truly present in the gifts. Thus, in the Holy Eucharist, the body of Christ, the church, is constituted. In this respect, the Holy Eucharist is the preeminent mystery, the foremost means by which we offer ourselves, in union with the once-for-all sacrifice of Christ, as "living sacrifices, holy and acceptable to God" (Rom. 12:1).

Through the mystery of Holy Unction, or anointing with blessed oil, the Lord bestows upon his church the grace of divine healing of body, mind, and spirit (James 5:14-16). Closely allied with this mystery of healing is the mystery of penance or confession, in which the faithful humbly acknowledge their spiritual infirmities and receive Christ's forgiveness. In addition, the mystery of Penance is the primary means whereby the faithful are counseled and pastored in the walk of holiness, without which "no one will see the Lord" (Heb. 12:14). Fasting, a rule of prayer, almsgiving—these too are sacramental means by which we are enabled to overcome sin and grow into the likeness of God found in Christ.

Marriage is the holy mystery by which the human love of a man and a woman is taken up, or transfigured, into the kingdom of God. The bride and groom are "crowned" in the marriage service, thereby accepting martyrdom to each other, submitting themselves to each other so that each partner may thereby experience God's love and salvation.

Marriage is seen also as a living icon of the

union of Christ with his church. As Christ is the head, the source of life and sustenance for his bride, the church, so is the husband to be "martyred" to his wife in a life of service on behalf of her salvatoin. As the church willingly submits to Christ in loving service, so is the wife to love and respect her husband and aid him on the path of salvation and holiness. By mutually submitting to one another in loving service and by the combined love and care of the couple for their children, the couple provide a living icon, or image, of the union of Christ and his body, the church, in his "one flesh."

Celibacy, too, is taken up and transfigured by Christ through his body, the church. Men and women who are called to remain single and to devote themselves to prayer and spiritual warfare are set apart as monks and nuns for their high calling. Monasticism has always been viewed as a high calling by the church. The monastic is comissioned by the body of the church to pursue single mindedly the life of prayer and celibacy so that the salvation of all might be aided. The monastics often provide much-needed spiritual counsel, even for those called to remain in the world, and their vocation is highly regarded in Holy Orthodoxy.

Because the church is *the* sacrament or mystery, any action of Christ through his church is seen as sacramental. Therefore, this list of mysteries is certainly not exhaustive. Through the entire life of the worshiping community, the body of Christ, all of life is taken up and united to God through Christ. In this way the wonder of the glorious Incarnation goes on until the day of its completion in the fully realized kingdom of God at the return of Christ in glory!

Father Bill Caldaroni

117 ◆ EVANGELICAL COVENANT CHURCH

The Evangelical Covenant Church believes that God created sacraments and rituals to communicate with and express truths to the church. It allows considerable latitude in its observance of baptism: both infant and adult baptism are left to the discretion of its members. Communion is observed monthly and during key events in the Christian year.

Rituals are commonplace in life, not the exception. The ordinariness of ritual may account in part for the thought that they only occur in special places, such as churches, lodges, and military establishments, and at special times, such as weddings, funerals, initiations, and trooping of the colors.

Mealtimes have rituals: grace before eating, perhaps as hands are held; conversations that tend to center around the same questions; and observation of proper etiquette. Children are sent off to school ritualistically with gestures of affection and a wave (a form of blessing, no doubt). Bedtime has its rituals involving words and gestures.

Farewell celebrations are rituals. They provide more than a way of saying good-bye. People are thanked. Stories of the relationship are told. Gifts are presented. And perhaps most significant, relationships change and people make transitions to new patterns of life without feeling that others have been ignored and abandoned. Ritual legitimates the separation and gives "permission" for the new life to be lived and for new relationships to be formed.

Rituals belong to the life of the people of God because people require rituals in order to get on with life. The entire range of human emotion—humor and anger, hello and good-bye, tears and laughter, birth and death—are given a perspective by ritualizing them. Perspective is given because rituals not only *conserve* but *convey* a tradition. By *preserving* certain words and actions and *perpetuating* them (e.g., the actions at Holy Communion: taking bread, giving thanks, breaking and distributing it; intoning the words "Do this . . . in remembrance of me"), the church provides a context for all of the experiences and emotions of human life. The celebration of Holy Communion takes on a different meaning at a wedding than at a funeral. At the former, the union of man and woman is likened to the union of the bride of Christ (the church) with the heavenly bridegroom (Christ). At a funeral, the same words and actions call to mind the marriage supper of the Lamb when all of the people of God will be gathered together once again.

The Evangelical Covenant Church recognized early on that God uses symbols and forms to communicate with people. In a document published in 1900, the Committee on Ritual cited both the divine and human use of ritualistic and symbolic actions. From the divine side, it is seen that God did not give an abstract theoretical system for human salvation but rather "perceivable means," i.e., word and sacrament—along with words, forms, and actions having origins in both Testaments—to conserve and convey God's presence to and for persons. A human is a "spiritual-physical being" who has "continual interaction between body and soul." Thus, "even purely spiritual impressions and thoughts find their way to our inner life only through the cooperation of the senses." Hence, both impressions and expressions do not circumvent the senses, forms, rituals, and symbolic actions. Both God and persons are ritual-creating and symbol-producing beings (*Covenant Book of Worship* [Chicago: Covenant Press, 1964], xiii–xxvi).

That in mind, Covenant pastors have had a book of worship since 1900 as well. It, along with the books published subsequently, conserve and convey a growing tradition. The framers of these books, knowing humans have an "eyegate" and "eargate," have not been reluctant to let the body of ritual acts grow as ways are found to relate the creating and redeeming work of God to more and more life situations, making perceivable means of God's care available to all.

The Evangelical Covenant Church, oriented to the language of sacraments rather than ordinances, provides both infant baptism and a service of the presentation of children. Congregants, according to their interpretation of Scripture, are free to receive either rite, although by tradition the Covenant Church, given its Lutheran heritage, has tended to practice the baptism of infants. Two services of baptism are provided: one for infants and another for confessing believers. Parents whose interpretation of Scripture conflicts with the baptism of infants choose a service of the presentation of children, often called a service of dedication in other traditions. The presentations of Samuel and Jesus are cited as biblical models in the rubrics. It is also noted that this is not an alternative to baptism or a substitute for it, but rather is an anticipation of baptism.

Covenant clergy sign a statement at their ordination in which they promise to officiate the rites of both baptism and the presentation of children despite personal convictions. He or she also agrees to recognize infant baptism as a true baptism that is not a mere prelude to adult baptism; at the same time, he or she is to respect those who support adult baptism. Finally, it is the pastor's responsibility to protect the minority view of the congregation on this issue so that the freedom enjoyed by Covenanters is not compromised (see "The Position of the Evangelical Covenant Church on the Practice of Baptism," which was adopted as a policy statement in 1966). The Covenant Church understands that there is one baptism, that the minister who performs the rite does not act as an individual, and that ultimately the act of baptism is the action of Christ. Hence the pastor acts representatively and is the servant of the whole congregation, not just a segment of it.

The *Covenant Book of Worship* of 1981 includes a service of the Affirmation of the Baptismal Covenant. It is intended to serve persons in three different situations: (1) persons who have experienced spiritual renewal and desire a public witness to the same; (2) people returning to the church after a lapse in commitment; and (3) people whose discipline by the church has come to an end. Rebaptism is offered by the Covenant Church so that the one baptism may be renewed, not repeated, and so that believers have a way of demonstrating publicly by means of ritual the passages in their spiritual life.

Confirmation is also a rite in the Evangelical Covenant Church. It consists of instruction in Bible, church history, and the catechism. According to the rubrics, confirmation underscores the purposes of infant baptism. For those presented for blessing and dedication in infancy, it is intended to lead to baptism. Interestingly, the rubric also says that "when young people come to the day of confirmation without an evident profession of personal commitment, their faith is confirmed as far as it has grown." The rubric also gives the confirmand the right to silence on any of the questions eliciting a vow. The service concludes with prayers and the laying on of hands, either by the pastors, deacons, or parents.

Allowance for silence is in part related to the fact that confirmation does not lead automatically to church membership. That is a separate process whereby each person bears witness to his or her personal faith before the diaconate, and upon their recommendation, the congregation votes on each candidate. The *Covenant Book of Worship* provides a service of public reception into the congregation, including vows to each other by the new members and the receiving body.

Covenant Churches generally celebrate the sacrament of the Lord's Supper monthly. Congregations might also celebrate the sacrament on Ash Wednesday, Maundy Thursday, Good Friday, Thanksgiving, and other selected days. Two orders are provided for the sacrament. One might be called the "warrant form," since it is without narrative and makes the words of institution the heart of the service. It does include a prayer of consecration over the gifts and the confession of the Apostles' Creed.

The alternative order might be called a "narrative form" and has three sections: creation, redemption, and the work of the Holy Spirit. The words of institution take their place in the narrative in the section on redemption. No prayer of consecration is included because the narrative form is itself the prayer. Both services provide for the congregation to sing the Agnus Dei ("Lamb of God") and the Acclamation ("Christ has died, Christ has risen, Christ will come again"). This service also provides for singing the praise from Isaiah 6, "Holy, Holy, Holy . . ." (the Sanctus). This service is rich in allusions to the paschal theme of the Hebrew Bible, the presence of Jesus with his church now as he was with the Emmaus pilgrims in Luke 24, and the hope of the feast to come in the kingdom.

Both services provide prayer for the commemoration of those who have died since the last celebration of the sacrament, bringing to mind the communion of saints that transcends time and place. The narrative, while ancient in ecclesiastical tradition, is basically new to the Covenant Church and is included in the 1981 *Covenant Book of Worship*. It is also published in the hymnal so that it can be celebrated with full congregational participation.

While the *Covenant Book of Worship* contains the tradition, words, and actions for other customary rites—weddings, funerals, dedication of buildings, laying of the cornerstone, the adoption of a child, the blessing of a civil marriage, etc.—it also contains the rites for the denomination's liturgical acts. These include the ordination of pastors, the consecration of missionaries, the installation of conference superintendents, and the commissioning of educators.

With this book local congregations also have use of a service to consecrate lay workers. While this particular service may be oriented to those serving in official capacities, it could be adapted to wider use for other mission tasks undertaken by members of the congregation. Those with specific needs are provided a service of healing together with anointing with oil and the laying on of hands, both by pastors and significant laypeople.

Earlier in this article, it was said that rituals are added as the church finds new needs to address and new ways of attending to the "continued interaction between body and soul." The "cooperation of the senses" is required if the depth of human consciousness is to be reached with God's grace and promise. Perceivable means, i.e., ritual words and acts, are needed to address the needs of people hurt by abuse, those wounded by various kinds of separations, and those coping with enormous losses. Ritual allows for the public address of needs, for legitimating the need for them to be addressed by the church so that people are not denied the perceivable means by which they can both be impressed by the gospel and express praise for the gospel that makes all things new.

John Weborg

118 ✦ Evangelical Free Church of America

Traditionally, free churches have taken a stand of silence on the nature and practice of baptism and the Lord's Supper so as to avoid dividing believers. This position has resulted in a melting pot of customs and practices among member churches.

In order to understand sacraments, ordinances, and sacred actions in the Evangelical Free Church of America, one must understand what we call "the significance of silence." The Evangelical Free Church of America has chosen to remain silent on those doctrines that through the centuries have divided Christians of equal dedication, biblical knowledge, spiritual maturity, and love for Christ. We believe that in view of the imminent return of Christ, there is not time to argue about what we consider to be nonessential. The significance of this silence is important, if not essential, for understanding the way in which the Evangelical Free Church of America handles sacraments, ordinances, and sacred actions.

Our doctrinal statement is silent on such matters as the time and method of baptism and on the Lord's Supper regarding the extent and presence of Christ in the elements. It simply states, "We believe that the Lord's Supper and water baptism are ordinances to be observed by the church during this present age. They are, however, not to be regarded as a means of salvation" (Article VII of the Evangelical Free Church of America Doctrinal Statement). While some may view this as a position of weakness or compromise, it is actually a position of great strength. The early leaders of the Evangelical Free Church of America were strong and unmovable. They had convictions that had been formed through study of the Word and had been strengthened through the heat of persecution of the state churches of Sweden, Norway, and Denmark from which they fled. In drafting a simple statement to support this position of silence, the founders did not overlook certain doctrines. They simply decided to be silent. They would not introduce the historic divisive elements into the fellowship but would respect the views of all believers, even though not all could join in such a broad theological base.

The Evangelical Free Church of America is not a sacramental church in that we do not believe salvation is received through any sacrament or sacred action. We believe that Christ gave certain ordinances to the local church. The purpose of those ordinances is to bring the believer to a deeper and fuller fellowship with both the Godhead and the family of believers.

The Evangelical Free Church of America stands for the unity of all believers. Because of this, we have become something of a refugee camp for many believers who for one reason or another have chosen to leave their denomination. This has brought a very interesting mix of beliefs to the Evangelical Free Church. Our position of silence on secondary issues has allowed believers to come and enjoy the fellowship of the family of God on the basis of their confession of faith in Christ, even though they may differ on other points of doctrine. An interesting aspect of this denominational melting pot is the fact that many of our traditions and practices have roots in other denominations. For example, many of our churches offer to their young people a form of confirmation that bears a

Lutheran influence. These Bible instruction classes are for our seventh- and eighth-grade students. Upon completion of this intensive study of their faith and church history, a graduation ceremony is often held.

Our early church fathers practiced both infant baptism as well as believer's baptism, and the latter by both immersion and sprinkling. We believe, however, that the only baptism necessary for salvation is the baptism of the Holy Spirit. As a rule, the Evangelical Free Church of America has settled on the practice of believer's baptism. Believer's baptism is an outward symbol of the inward spiritual baptism of the Holy Spirit. This symbolic re-enactment of Christ's death and resurrection is an important act of obedience that allows believers to publicly testify their faith in Christ and their desire to live for him. Baptism is not a requirement for membership in the Evangelical Free Church of America. All who join an Evangelical Free church do so on the basis of their confession of faith, regardless of their views as to the time and mode of baptism.

Infant baptism is seldom practiced in our churches today; however, we do dedicate infants to the Lord. These child dedications are as much a time of dedicating the parents as they are a time of dedicating the children. In this ceremony parents are reminded of their responsibility to live pure and faithful lives and are encouraged to make their home a place where the name of Jesus is loved and is heard often. Prayer is offered for both the parents and child: The child is dedicated to the Lord, and the parents to raising their child in a Christian environment.

We believe that the observance of the Lord's Supper ought to be a time of great unity for the family of believers. The controversies, such as the extent and presence of Christ in the symbols, who may serve Communion, who may partake Communion, and how often it should be observed, have all been relegated to those areas of significant silence in the Evangelical Free Church of America.

The Lord's Table is open to all believers in our Evangelical Free churches. Customs and traditions of the local churches dictate the way in which Communion is observed. In my situation at First Evangelical Free Church in Rockford, Illinois, our Communion services are most generally a quiet, reflective time, involving personal confession, intimate worship, and quiet singing as trays of bread and trays of small cups containing grape juice are passed among the congregation. This is often followed by a sweet time of prayer, joining hands, and singing a song of commitment to Christ and to one another. We have also observed Communion as families around tables in our Fellowship Hall. At other times, we have invited people to come forward to receive individually the bread and the cup at the front of the sanctuary. Whatever the method and mode, the emphasis is placed on remembering the atoning work of Christ, the promise of his forgiveness, the certainty of his coming again, and the delight of the fellowship of believers.

Our denomination is currently discovering an awakening to worship. Historically, our denomination has excelled in discipleship and evangelism but has been weak in the area of worship. The focus of our denomination since its inception has been evangelizing the lost and discipling the new believer toward spiritual maturity. While we have done well in those areas, it has caused us to lose sight of the church's ultimate priority—worship. We are just now learning that worship is far more than gathering together to sing about God and to learn about him. We are learning to sing and speak our praise to him.

As we have discovered this vertical dimension of worship and have become aware of God's presence in worship, we have discovered acts of worship such as footwashing and the laying on of hands for the sick that have not been in great use in recent years. I have never personally participated in a footwashing service but have been intrigued by the reports of the beauty of these ceremonies and the impact they have had on the lives of those who have participated. Although we use great discretion, we also anoint with oil and lay hands on for healing. While this is usually done as a private ceremony with the pastor and elders present, it has on at least one occasion been a part of our public worship service at First Free. Through these anointing services, I have witnessed miraculous healings but have also seen God allow the disease to claim the life of the believer. The anointing and laying on of hands is viewed as a statement of faith affirming God's power to heal if he desires.

The Evangelical Free Church of America also uses the practice of laying on of hands as we ordain ministers for the gospel, dedicate men and women to Christian service, and commission missionaries for their work and ministry. Again, it would be important to note that we attach no special significance to the laying on of hands apart from the symbolic picture it gives us of the spiritual leaders of the church affirming the ministries of these people.

The significance of silence in the Evangelical Free Church of America has produced a denomination of varied traditions, with a vibrant zeal for the Lord. It has fostered a unity among our churches as well as among individual believers. The Evangelical Free Church of America remains healthy and is growing in part because of the strength of our diversity.

Douglas R. Thiesen

119 ◆ EVANGELICAL LUTHERAN CHURCH IN AMERICA

Lutheranism is sometimes seen as a paradoxical union of Catholic substance and Protestant principle. Thus, while Lutheranism has accorded an important role to the "visible words" of the sacraments and also to the postures, gestures, and symbolic actions of liturgical worship, it has also raised the concern that the set things have been a principal source of superstition among Christians. The ELCA has devoted significant attention recently to worship and the sacraments.

Christians trust the promise of Christ that "where two or three are gathered in my name, I am there among them" (Matt. 18:20). This church has held that God is present in Christ specifically through the means of grace, the Word of God, and the sacraments of Christ. The Holy Spirit works through these means, creating faith in those who hear and receive.

Martin Luther wrote, "I preach the Gospel of Christ into your heart, so that you may form him within yourself. If now you truly believe, so that your heart lays hold of the Word and holds fast within it that voice, tell me what you have in your heart? You must answer that you have the true Christ, not that he sits there, as one sits on a chair, but as he is at the right hand of the Father" (*Luther's Works*, American edition, vol. 36, p. 340). This affirmation of the real presence of Christ in the preaching of the Word is located in a treatise that deals with the real presence of Christ in the sacrament of the altar (*The Sacrament of the Body and Blood of Christ—Against the Fanatics*, 1526). Luther believed that Christ is truly present both in the preaching of the Word and in the ministration of the sacraments. He was willing to split the Protestant movement over his dogged defense of the Real Presence of Christ in the Eucharist, by which he meant the sacramental union of Christ's body and blood with the bread and the wine. A Christological concern lay behind this insistence on the sacramental union. What ultimately concerned Luther in his controversy with Zwingli was not a philosophical theory about how a body could be present in more than one place at a time, but rather the concern that "they divide the two natures of the person of Christ." In one revealing exchange at the Marburg Colloquy in 1529, the Swiss reformer Oecolampadius said: "You should not cling to the humanity and the flesh of Christ, but rather lift up your mind to His divinity." To which Luther replied: "I do not know of any God except him who was made flesh, nor do I want to have another" (quoted in Hermann Sasse, *This Is My Body*, 252).

This is the cornerstone of Lutheran sacramental theory: God in Christ enters deep into the flesh to communicate with humanity. Christ is the Word (*logos*), and this Word is not disembodied. There is no split between Word and sacrament. In Lutheran understanding the Word is sacramental and the sacraments are "visible words." Just as there is no application of water in Holy Baptism or feeding with bread and wine in Holy Communion that is not accompanied by the Word of God, so the Word concretely addresses the believer by invading the senses through water and oil, bread and wine, as well as human touch in absolution and blessings.

It is the very "visibility" of the Word that has made it difficult for Lutherans to be precise about the number of sacraments. Philip Melanchthon, in the *Apology to the Augsburg Confession*, defined sacraments as "rites which have the command of God and to which the promise of grace has been added" (*Apology*, Art. XIII; Tappert, p. 211). He had no difficulty including baptism, the Lord's Supper, and absolution among the sacraments, and saw a sacramental character to ordination and marriage because both have a divine command and promise. Both confirmation and extreme unction lacked a dominical mandate in his view, although the rite of confirmation received a new emphasis in Lutheran practice as the celebration of the completion and coalition of the study of the catechism and as an affirmation of baptism. The rites of visitation of the sick included opportunities for individual confession and absolution and the ministration of Holy Communion. But Melanchthon also wrote, "If we should list as sacraments all the things that have God's Command and promise added to them, they why not prayer, which can most truly be called a sacrament? . . . Alms could be listed here as well as afflictions, which in themselves are signs to which God has added promise" (ibid., p. 213).

How did it happen, then, that Lutherans did not retain the whole panoply of ordinances and rites that the Roman Catholic church regards as sacramental? Lutheranism has always defined itself over against two fronts: Roman Catholicism on the one side and the Reformed and Radical Reformations on the other. The major critique of Roman Catholic practice and piety has been that certain rites contribute to superstition and righteousness by works. The major critique of the Reformed position is its lack of confidence that the sacraments, as means of grace, effect what their words proclaim. Lutheranism, unlike Anglicanism, has seen itself not as a via media between Catholicism and Protestantism, but as a paradoxical union of Catholic substance and Protestant principle (Paul Tillich, Jaroslav Pelikan). Thus, while Lutheranism has accorded an important role to the visible words of the sacraments and also to the postures, gestures, and symbolic actions of liturgical worship, it has also raised the concern that the set things have been a principal source of superstition among Christians and observed that their multiplication produces a pomp that is foreign to the simplicity of the Christian cult.

Paradoxes are difficult to maintain, and at various times in its history, Lutheranism has tended more toward Catholic substance or Protestant principle, depending on what had to be theologically affirmed or denied. There is no doubt that the influence of Pietism and Rationalism in the eighteenth century pushed Lutheranism closer to the Reformed position. Proposals such as the American Lutheranism of S. S. Schmucker in the nineteenth century, which produced an altered version of the Augsburg Confession in an attempt to secure an alliance with evangelicals, caused a loss of Catholic substance in Lutheranism. The confessional revival movements, beginning in nineteenth-century Germany and spreading to North America, brought about a liturgical recovery. While this has been a slow process in terms of affecting piety in the pews, the discovery by anthropology and psychology in the twentieth century of the profound significance of ritual and symbolic actions has aided the process of retrieving certain rites and actions designed to make an impression on the physical body, such as a more ample use of water in baptism, an anointing with oil after baptism, and larger quantities of bread and a cup of wine in Holy Communion, the imposition of ashes on Ash Wednesday, the enactment of the footwashing on Maundy Thursday, the laying on of hands for individual absolution, and the anointing of the sick with oil.

If we take seriously the understanding of sacraments as visible words, then it is a miscommunication to apply little dabs of water in baptism and speak of "dying with Christ," or to dispense individual wafers and containers of wine in Holy Communion and speak of being "one body in Christ." If actions speak louder than words, our practices have regularly undermined our theology. But it is also the case that our rites must speak the gospel, and an evangelical, catholic church will constantly ask what its liturgical actions are communicating. The laying on of ashes speak to us of our mortality and our hope in the cross of Christ. The footwashing puts us in the role of servants. The laying on of hands in forgiveness demonstrates the connectedness that sin breaks. The anointing with oil proclaims God's intention for wholeness and well-being in his kingdom.

The imposition of ashes and the enactment of the footwashing are options in the special liturgies for Ash Wednesday and Maundy Thursday in the *Lutheran Book of Worship*, Ministers Edition. (Pamphlets are available for use by congregations.) Individual absolution with the laying on of hands in the orders for corporate confession and forgiveness and individual confession and forgiveness are located in the *Lutheran Book of Worship*, Pew Edition (pp. 194, 197). *Occasional Services: A Companion to Lutheran Book of Worship* provides a Service of the Word for healing (pp. 89ff.), with the laying on of hands and anointing, as well

as an order of laying on of hands and anointing the sick for use in a hospital or home with individuals who are unable to attend a corporate service for healing (pp. 99ff.). It should be noted that this rite is preceded by confession and forgiveness, psalms, lessons, and prayers (selections are provided in *Occasional Services*); and is followed by Holy Communion, for which two orders are provided: "Distribution of Holy Communion to Those in Special Circumstances" (pp. 76ff.) and "Celebration of Holy Communion with Those in Special Circumstances" (pp. 83ff.). The first may be conducted by trained and designated lay assisting ministers and the second is to be celebrated by an ordained pastor.

The recovery of liturgy as "the work of the people" has prompted a desire to empower and recognize lay ministries in the congregation with the worship service. *Occasional Services* provides orders for the installation of elected parish officers, the installation of a lay professional leader (e.g., medical worker or parish nurse, Christian education director or youth minister, church musician, administrative personnel), the recognition of ministries in the congregation (e.g., worship, education, witness, service, stewardship), as well as an affirmation of the vocation of Christians in the world. The orders for installation follow the liturgy of the Word while the orders for recognition and affirmation occur within the offertory as part of the offering of ourselves and our gifts.

Frank C. Senn

120 ✦ Independent Fundamentalist and Evangelical Churches

A decided shift has occurred in the worship of many independent fundamentalist and evangelical churches. The trend toward informal, folksy gatherings is being replaced with an emphasis on deeper encounters with the living God. Hence baptism and the Lord's Supper are taking on greater meaning in many churches.

——— God's Presence in Worship ———

Christian worship is the expression of the relationship between God and his people. What people both understand and do in practice are determined by their view of God and his relationship to them. Therefore, it behooves the worship leadership of the church to examine carefully the congregation's view of God's presence in the various acts of worship, particularly as it relates to sacraments/ordinances and sacred actions.

It is easy for worshipers to come to the service week after week with little thought or sense of expectation given to meeting with the living God. People are creatures of habit. Low expectation is an effective inoculation for authentic worship. The church has an effective inoculation for authentic worship. The church has suffered from this malady regarding worship in past years, though the condition is slowly changing. But much worship of the recent years has been casual, and a sense of the awe and transcendence of God is often difficult to find in these more informal worship settings.

Often people gather for worship much in the same manner they would congregate for any social gathering, with conversation as people meet. In the 1970s, people cultivated the familiar, folksy environment in worship. The pendulum had definitely swung to informal patterns, more in reaction to past social and religious practices than for theological reasons, though the latter was often cited. Prayers were made "to Jesus, because he seems closer than God the Father." Some people liked the casual because anything was acceptable.

In some congregations, this tendency is in the process of adjustment. It's not so much that people are in love with formality as it is their desire to worship a transcendent God. There is a growing body of people longing for a deeper spiritual encounter with God than some of the more informal experiences have so far provided. There is a growing hunger to experience and understand God in worship, particularly among those born in the 1940s and 1950s. This is expressed in various worship practices.

There is greater openness in utilizing some of the spiritually rich material of the past for ideas and worship texts. Scripture choruses and songs have contributed to a continuation of the more emotive elements, offering a simple, spiritual quality in the music of worship. Older hymns have often reappeared, sometimes with new style harmonizations or even those more in keeping with their original style. In addition, there is also a significant movement to create new hymns in the traditional metrical style with newly composed, singable tunes or settings of new texts to familiar tunes.

These trends are occurring because past worship practice has been weighed in the balance and found wanting. There is renewed genuine interest in worship. As people examine who God is and what it means to be in relationship with him, congregations want to _participate_ in worshiping with heart, soul, body, and mind. It is not uncommon to find Protestant congregations sometimes kneeling when taking Communion. Other congregations that would have been suspicious of a healing service twenty-five years ago now find this a regular part of their worship life. _As a result of these kinds of practices, there is greater interest in the meaning of baptism and the Lord's Supper._

Sacraments/Ordinances: Baptism and the Lord's Supper

This heightened sense of the presence of God has resulted in greater openness and a desire to participate in some of the sacred actions as described in the Scriptures. Often called sacraments or ordinances, these have been given a heightened view and interest as a result of the renewal in the theology of worship among the laity.

The general accepted meaning of the term _sacrament_ refers to those religious actions that "are an outward and visible sign of an inward and spiritual grace given unto us ordained by Christ himself, as a means whereby we receive the same and a pledge to assure us thereof"—according to _The Book of Common Prayer_. Though sometimes as many as thirty sacraments may be listed, with seven often being cited, baptism and the Lord's Supper are the two most generally identified and universally accepted. The Reformers attached three distinguishing marks to sacraments: (1) They were instituted by Christ; (2) Christ commanded that they be observed by his followers; and (3) they are viewed as visible symbols of divine acts. Some religious groups refer to the Lord's Supper and Baptism as "ordinances," preferring to emphasize that Christ commanded his followers to observe these practices. Such groups often deny that the sacraments by themselves confer any means of grace.

A _service of healing_ is not uncommon and generally is called in response to a specific need for healing. Typically, the elders of the congregation gather either as part of a regular service or at a special time with the person requesting the anointing with oil in a manner described in James 5:14. The actual form varies from congregation to congregation. The person is anointed, usually on the forehead, with oil marked in the sign of the cross.

Services of ordination also occur when various candidates present themselves for ministry. Generally a simple order of worship is followed with questions and responses exchanged between the ordinand and church officials.

While ordination, marriage, and healing services (including anointing with oil) are regularly a part of the worship life of the Christian community, they generally are not referred to in the Reformed tradition as sacraments or ordinances.

The Challenge to Integrate and Teach

It would be well worthwhile for worship leaders to conduct a survey of their congregation regarding the understanding and practice of sacraments/ordinances. Conversations, teaching, and preaching regarding the presence of God in worship can do nothing but improve a congregation's worship and contribute to growth in faith. Rather than going through religious acts with nebulous theological feelings or understanding, the believers will gain significantly in grasping the foundation of their own faith. The sacred actions will take on increasing significance for the individual worshipers, deepening and transforming their own view of God and his relationship to his people.

Daniel Sharp

121 ♦ LUTHERAN CHURCH–MISSOURI SYNOD

During the last fifty years, the Lutheran Church–Missouri Synod has devoted greater attention to the sacraments, particularly Communion. Lutherans have also recovered the Divine Service to express their practice and theology of worship.

"Our Lord speaks and we listen. His Word bestows what it says. Faith that is born from what is heard acknowledges the gifts received with eager thankfulness and praise." These are the opening words from the introduction of *Lutheran Worship* published by the Lutheran Church–Missouri Synod in 1982. They summarize the theological understanding of the Lutheran Church–Missouri Synod that God is the Giver, and we the receivers. We do not "make God present." We do not come into his presence. Rather he deigns to come to us through his holy Word and sacraments. We simply receive what has first been given to us.

One of the significant changes that has occurred with the introduction of a new hymnal in 1982 was the use of the term *Divine Service* for the chief Sunday service of the church. Divine Service is an old expression, but it had fallen into disuse during the past decades. It was determinately revived. The naming of the Sunday service is meant to say something about our theology and understanding of worship.

It is a service of Word and sacrament in which God comes to us. We are not the servers. We are the ones who are served by God through his Word and sacraments. We are forgiven and renewed in Word and sacrament and through that forgiving power of the Lord sent out into the world to declare the marvelous deeds of him who called us out of darkness and into light.

With the introduction of *Lutheran Worship,* another significant change occurred as the main Sunday service was structured as a celebration of both Word and sacrament. The previous hymnal, issued in a 1941, provided the first service as a Service of the Word alone. The second service was a service of Word and sacrament. The new hymnal does not provide a Sunday service of Word alone but always a full service of Word and sacrament.

During the last fifty years, there has been a growing awareness and appreciation of the sacrament of the altar, variously called Holy Communion, the Lord's Supper, and the Eucharist. During the years of World War II, most congregations of the Lutheran Church–Missouri Synod celebrated the sacrament of the altar four to six times a year. Gradually a monthly celebration has become common in many congregations of the church. That weekly celebration, common in many congregations, was reflected in the new hymnal's provision of the full service of Word and sacrament as the chief service.

Lutherans have always believed that where the Word of God is preached, there God is present through his Spirit to work faith in the hearts of believers. Lutherans also believe that when the Word of the Lord is spoken over bread and wine according to his mandate, his Word is fulfilled: "This is my body. This is my blood." Human minds cannot understand how that is possible but the heart of faith accepts what the Lord says. Christ, through the Word spoken by the pastor over bread and wine, is present in the bread and wine. We can and do say of the consecrated bread and wine that it truly is the body and the blood of the Lord.

In accordance with that understanding that Christ is there present, Lutherans believe that all who receive the consecrated elements at the Lord's altar receive his body and blood. Those who receive with penitent and believing hearts receive the fruit of Christ's work, forgiveness of sins. Where there is forgiveness of sins there is also life and salvation. Those who receive impenitently and not believing the Word of the Lord receive the Lord's body and blood as judgment (1 Cor. 11:27-29).

In the same way that God works through his Word in the sacrament of the altar, so he works in the sacrament of Holy Baptism. The Lord speaks his Word, and we listen and obey. "Baptize in the name of the Father and of the Son and of the Holy Spirit." The real baptizer is not the pastor speaking the words and pouring the water, it is the Lord who, through his Word and mandate, is doing the baptizing. The effect of that baptism is that life and salvation is imparted. Sins are forgiven, and the Holy Spirit is granted. Since Holy Baptism is the Lord's action, he can and does give what he promises with no merit or worthiness on our part.

The Lutheran Church has at various times numbered the sacraments as two. At other times it has spoken of a third sacrament, that is confession and absolution. Confession and absolution has both the mandate of the Lord and his Word of forgiveness attached. Another rite, Holy Ordination or the Office of the Ministry, has also been considered at times a sacrament, for here, too, is the Word of the Lord commands this office of preaching and administering sacraments, and through that office, forgiveness of sins is imparted. However, the actual number of sacraments is less important than the Word and mandate of the Lord to do as he has told us to do. Then we receive what he has promised in his Word.

During the second half of the twentieth century, the Lutheran Church–Missouri Synod has re-emphasized the sacramental nature of worship.

As a confessional church, the Missouri Synod has again begun to emphasize what was explicitly taught in the sixteenth-century Lutheran confessions. The liturgical movement has also been a driving force among many of the leaders of the clergy of the Missouri Synod in emphasizing sacramental worship. With the introduction of _Lutheran Worship_ in 1982, there has been a renewed emphasis on Holy Baptism and the sacrament of the altar.

However, the emphasis upon sacramental worship has not diminished an emphasis upon the preaching of the Word of God. Since preaching of the Word has a sacramental quality, it continues to be emphasized in the Sunday services of congregations of the Synod. The importance of preaching also continues to be emphasized at the seminaries of the Lutheran Church–Missouri Synod. In fact, it has been observed that in congregations that are the most sacramental in their worship, there is a heightened stress upon preaching.

God is present in his church and among his people not by human action but through his promise and by his action.

The Rev. Roger D. Pittelko

122 ✦ MENNONITE CHURCHES

The Mennonite Church is heir to a radical Reformation understanding of the Lord's Supper and baptism as ordinances, not sacraments. Mennonites, however, approach these ordinances with serious reverence because of their communal significance. Two dominant styles characterize the Mennonite approach to worship and these ordinances—charismatic and free form. The charismatic style emphasizes freedom of expression by worshipers and leaders. The free-form style emphasizes the use of a prototype of worship adapted for each week's service.

When I came to faith in Christ, I asked to be baptized into the Mennonite congregation in which I had grown up. In the preparation for church membership, we, the candidates for baptism, were told, among other things, what baptism and Communion meant. The minister made it clear that baptism does not save you; it is your act of witness to the work of grace in you. Similarly, Communion is not a corporeal eating of Christ, it is a memorial of his death and a celebration of the unity of his body, the church. Then the day came when we were baptized. As the service proceeded, I recall thinking, *There is more going on here than they told us, more than what I have words for.*

I consider my experience at this point to be typical of the Mennonite understanding of the sacred actions of the church, which Mennonites usually call ordinances. The Reformation protest against sacraments that automatically convey grace is still in the marrow of Mennonite bones. The first thing that is usually explained when the rites of the church are explained is what they are not. At the same time, these ritual moments are taken with utmost seriousness. For example, my uncle, who led a congregation that had just broken away from my family's church, bore with the strain that accompanied his return to the parent congregation in order to be at my baptism. Especially in traditional congregations, a deep quietness and a suppressed (not repressed) emotionality accompanies the celebration of the ordinances, especially the Lord's Supper.

This congregational attitude is due in part to the ecclesiological significance of these acts. In other words, when I am baptized, I enter a covenant with Christ and the church to follow Christ in all things. At the breaking of bread, Mennonites renew and restore that covenant of baptism with one another and with their Lord. For Mennonites, the individual meaning of these actions is inescapably part of a communal meaning. So, many Mennonites are taught early on that they better be serious about these ordinances or not participate in them at all.

But Mennonite participation in the ordinances has other aspects. There is a sense that something more is happening than what the participants in the ordinances are doing. It is striking that, once it is clear that salvation comes by grace through faith, some of the Anabaptists speak of the Lord's Supper as partaking of Christ or as union with Christ. (see J. Rempel, *The Lord's Supper in Anabaptism* [Scottdale, Pa.: Herald Press, 1993]). This view is also evident in the confessions of faith written before the twentieth century (see H. Loewen, *One Lord, One Church, One Hope and One God* [Elkhart: Institute of Mennonite Studies, n.d.]). Only in twentieth-century literature is the drama of the Lord's Supper reduced to an act of human memory. This reductionism is the fruit of the popular rationalism that has afflicted liberal and conservative Protestantism alike.

Beyond this historical musing, how do Mennonites today experience God in worship? Like most other denominations, the Mennonite church has become remarkably diverse in its worship and piety in the past quarter century. Almost all the impulses and influences have pushed the church to loosen or even discard traditional patterns. Mennonites found the uniformity of practice stifling and graceless. One of the first experiments in the reform of worship was a more conversational tone in worship leading, and Communion in the context of a fellowship meal. I remember one woman who had enthusiastically helped to plan their congregation's first Communion meal, being accosted by her baffled mother during the event with the question "Isn't this sin?"

Although there are reservations similar to this mother, the quest of Mennonites for worship that has immediate meaning and personal warmth has led to a revolution in worship attitudes and practices. I observe two dominant styles among Mennonites. One of them could be loosely described as *charismatic,* the other as *free form.* Sometimes both exist in the same congregation. Both styles have theologically liberal and conservative forms. By charismatic, I mean an emphasis on freedom of expression for leaders and worshipers. The leadership style is informal; the worshipers share personal experiences. By free form, I mean an emphasis on a prototype that is adapted from week to week. Two of the Mennonite conferences and the Church of the Brethren have issued the *Hymnal: A Worship Book* (Newton, Kans.: Faith and Life Press, 1992), organized according to the acts of worship. How that pattern is carried out each week varies—one week the call to worship might be verses from a psalm, the next week it might be a mime.

There is a core of sacred actions common to almost all Mennonite congregations: baptism, Communion, ordination, matrimony, and dedication of parents and children. In charismatic circles, baptism is a joyful, informal occasion, often performed by immersion, even in Mennonite conferences that have traditionally practiced sprinkling or pouring. Communion tends to be celebrated monthly with a focus on the experience of forgiveness. In free-form circles, baptism is a more solemn occasion guided by a liturgical form. Communion is celebrated less often and more quietly, with an emphasis on fellowship and memorial. Some congregations of both approaches retain a preparatory service before Communion or a penitential rite at the beginning of Communion. Some retain footwashing as part of Communion once or twice a year.

Ordination (of women as well as men) is thought of as the act of setting aside a minister for lifelong service. For the most part, deacons are commissioned (a kind of short-term ordination), and bishops, where that office is retained, are appointed. No pattern of commissioning has developed for lay ministries—strangely enough for an anticlerical denomination—although some congregations induct officers into their roles. Behind this is the assumption that baptism is the basic and universal call to ministry, but this assumption is seldom articulated at baptism or in settings where people are chosen for ministries. (For an articulation of the view which understands baptism as making the ordination of a "caste" of leaders superfluous, see J. Yoder, _The Fullness of Christ_ [Elgin: Brethren Press, 1987].)

The wedding service is widely perceived as the event in which the love two people for each other is transformed into a covenant of marriage. This transformation comes through God's blessing of the vows and the covenant that is established between the couple and the congregation. For a generation, weddings had become elaborate dramas with no role for the congregation. The older pattern of congregational singing, a sermon, and a very simple entrance rite—often only the couple coming in together—has made a comeback.

The dedication of parents and children was practiced in some Anabaptist circles, but has become the norm among mainstream North American Mennonites only since World War II. It does not have a clear theology. The general understanding is that the ceremony is an opportunity to thank God for the birth of a child and to commit the child to the care of God, the parents, and the congregation. The goal of all three "partners" is to lead the child to Christ and the Christian way.

Anointing with oil is a traditional Mennonite practice, but like infant dedication, it does not have a clear theology. People with a life-threatening illness are anointed and prayed over as a way of making God's healing power immediate and concrete and of committing them to God's care. It is often said that the purpose of anointing is as much to come to terms with a suffering person's anxieties as with their physical symptoms. The charismatic stream of Mennonite church life has breathed new meaning into this ordinance.

Excommunications and the reception of repented members is the most difficult of traditional Mennonite practices to carry out in the intended spirit. If the person identified as grievously sinning is unresponsive to the pattern set forth in Matthew 18:15-20, that person is excommunicated. If and when the sinner repents, the sinner confesses the sin and shows contrition before the congregation. Then the person is received back into the church in the presence of the congregation with assurance that the sin is forgiven and forgotten both by God and the sisters and brothers of the church. The 1992 _Hymnal_ has the congregation speak the words of reconciliation admitting its own failure to surround the person with grace and guidance (no. 800).

A public service of worship in the church prior to burial is the almost universal funeral rite among Mennonites. In earlier times, the sermon often warned people that they too would one day stand before the judgment seat of Christ. In the past generation, the emphasis had been on the grace of God rather than the achievements, or lack thereof, of the person who had died. Therefore, eulogies were held to be inappropriate. More recently, the emphasis on being personal and warm in worship has led to the introduction of personal tributes as an additional part of the service or of the funeral meal that usually follows.

The practices of the church, as described above, are deeply significant to and usually carefully prepared for by Mennonite worship leaders and congregations. Twin impulses continue to be at work in the Mennonite mind. One is that whatever God gives to us and does for us as Mennonites, we receive by faith. This understanding limits the meaning ascribed to ceremonies or to the spiritual reality behind them. The other impulse—which leads Mennonites to anticipate these sacred occasions—is the certainty that reality is condensed in these sacred gestures and that there is more going on here than we have words for!

John Rempel

123 ◆ MESSIANIC SYNAGOGUE

The Messianic synagogue enacts many of the sacred rituals of Judaism, but the meaning of these rituals is enriched by the knowledge and the belief that Yeshua b. Yosef, or Jesus, is the promised Messiah. This means that the traditional rituals of Judaism such as the Shabbat, the seder, the kiddush prayer, the bar and bat mitzvah, and other rituals are sacraments that set apart, or sanctify, time and express messianic faith—in order words, the Christian faith in Jesus.

Jewish spirituality does not ordinarily consist of self-denial or of pietism, but does entail making distinctions—between right and wrong, true and false, of course, but also between the ritually pure and the impure, the clean and the unclean. Judaism is a religion of distinctions.

The kiddush, a prayer over wine that inaugurates Shabbat (the Sabbath), marks the separation of the seventh day from the working days of the week. The kiddush prayer begins with a recitation from Genesis 1:31–2:3, followed by a benediction for the wine. Then, salvation history is briefly recalled—an acknowledgment of God's grace in the giving of the Law and the Sabbath, which is a memorial of Creation and of the Exodus from Egypt. The next sentence is translated, "Thou hast chosen us and hallowed us above all nations, and in love and forever hast given us thy holy Sabbath as a heritage" (Rabbi Hayim Halevy Donin, *To Be a Jew* [New York: Basic Books, 1972], 77–78). For those who do not drink fermented wine, a nonfermented natural kosher grape juice can be substituted.

The sanctified use of wine is not limited to the inauguration of the Sabbath. There is a festival kiddush to mark the coming of Pesach (Passover) and other holy days. At the Passover seder, a liturgical holiday meal centering around the retelling of the Exodus story, four cups of wine are consumed: the first at the Kaddesh (the recitation of the kiddush prayer), the second after the recitation of the Haggadah (the reasons for and laws concerning Passover), the third—the cup associated with the Eucharist—following after-supper prayers called *circhat Hamazon*, and the fourth after the recitation of the Hallel (psalms of praise). A fifth cup of wine is poured late in the seder. The wine is poured from the cups onto a plate as the plagues that punished Egypt are remembered.

Wine, the symbol of joy, is diminished because of suffering. (Rabbi Joseph Elias, *The Haggadah* [New York: Mesorah, 1977], 56–59, (kiddush); 129, (the ten plagues); 155, (second cup of wine); 175, (third cup of wine); 176 ff., (cup of Elijah); 199, (fourth cup of wine); cf. also Rabbi Nosson Scherman, *The Haggadah Treasure* [New York: Zeieri Agudath Israel of America, 1978].)

On the night of his arrest, Yeshua b. Yosef (Jesus) gave a new meaning to the third cup of wine (after the supper) and to the matzoh (unleavened bread) used at the seder (Michael Schiffman, *Synagogue of the Messiah* [New York: Teshuvah, 1992], 74; Marion Hatchett, *Commentary on the American Prayer Book* [New York: Harper, 1980], 349–350). In doing so, he instructed his disciples to continue his custom in remembrance of him (Luke 22:19). This injunction is obeyed by Messianic Jews, although the frequency and method of commemoration varies from one messianic synagogue to another. Some obey this injunction by remembering Christ in association with the Passover seder; others do so on holidays; still others do so more frequently in association with kiddush. Yet others have a special service for *The Lord's Seder* (cf. Phillip E. Goble, *Everything You Need to Grow a Messianic Synagogue* [Pasadena, Calif.: William Carey Library, 1974], 59–69, for an example of how such a service might be performed, although no two congregations follow exactly the same model).

After the Sabbath service, the congregations often gather for a joyous celebration, again centered on bread and wine, the *Oneg Shabbat* (translated "the joy of Sabbath," quite literally a party in celebration of the seventh day). Messianic synagogues frequently observe this custom, sometimes in association with the kiddush, the symbol of the Sabbath. The bread and wine are not the only symbols in Judaism.

One of Judaism's most powerful symbols is circumcision—the symbol of the covenant of Abraham carved in flesh—the rite of entrance into the community of Israel. The Brith Milah is the rite of entrance into the community for Messianic Jews, also. On the eighth day, as commanded in Genesis 17:10-14, each baby boy is circumcised by a *mohel*, a rabbi qualified to perform circumcision. Circumcision is so important that it is to be performed on the eighth day, even if that day is a Sabbath or holy day, even Yom Kippur.

As with so many Jewish occasions of joy, the mitzvah is usually celebrated with a feast (Donin, 274–275). Likewise, as is true of so many Jewish rites of passage, the prayers of the *brit* recall the other major events that are a part of life. After the boy's father gives thanks that God has "sanctified us with his commandments and commanded us to bring [the child] into the Covenant of our father Abraham," the guests respond by praying, "Just as he entered the covenant, so may he enter into the study of Torah, into marriage, and into the performance of good deeds" (Donin, 274–275).

A custom that dates back to the earliest days provides a living picture of the redemption obtained through the Messiah. The redemption of the firstborn—the *Pidyon ha-Ben*—has its origin in Numbers 8:18 when the tribe of Levi was set aside (sanctified), instead of the firstborn of every family. In exchange for the eldest son, the Lord required that the firstborn son be redeemed by payment of a price, which could be as little as a pair of doves or two young pigeons (Lev. 12:8) and must be paid to a *cohen* (a priest). Jesus was redeemed according to the Law (Luke 2:24). The custom still exists among traditional Jews and is still practiced among tradition-minded Messianic Jews.

A *cohen*'s role in Rabbinic Judaism is a much reduced role from that which existed when the temple still stood. In Rabbinic Judaism, rabbis have replaced priests as teachers of the Law; synagogues have replaced the temple; repentance, prayer, and good deeds have replaced sacrifice. Messianic Judaism—like Reform Judaism—takes considerable liberty in the handling of the *torah she'b'al'peh* (the oral Torah; in other words, tradition). (Schiffman explains the seriousness of the question among Messianists [76], although they view the Torah through the eyes of the apostle Paul [82–90]; Goble presents what is probably still the most common view of the subject [11]; yet Andrew P. Pilant, in his "In Defense of Talmudic Law," in David A. Rausch's *Messianic Judaism: Its History, Theology, and Polity* [Lewiston, N.Y.: Mellen, 1982], sets forth a Messianist's case for the oral Law [253–260].) Nevertheless, Jewish tradition is wrestled with by virtually every Messianic Jewish organization, rabbi, and congregation.

As universally recognized as the Brith Milah, the *Mikveh-Brit* (immersion) is the initial public profession of faith. Unlike liturgical Christianity, baptism does not serve as the act of incorporation into the community of faith (circumcision does that). Unlike the nonliturgical evangelical churches, Messianic Judaism does not view the *Mikvah-Brit* as the commencement of adult participation in the community, for that is the role of bar or bat mitzvah. Nevertheless, the initial public confession of faith, especially by means of immersion, must not be underestimated, because a Jew who makes a public confession of faith in Jesus in the context of a Messianic synagogue (thereby saying, "I am still a Jew") has done no small thing!

The bar mitzvah at age thirteen marks a boy's coming of age, his first adult participation in synagogue life. For girls, the bat mitzvah among Reform, Reconstructionist, Conservative, and Messianic synagogues has assumed a similar degree of importance (Rabbi Yechiel Eckstein, *What Christians Should Know about Jews and Judaism* [Waco, Tex.: Word, 1984], 149–150; Rabbi Morris N. Kerttzer, *What Is a Jew* [New York: Macmillan, 1953], 89). On the other hand, orthodoxy has made no provision for a bat mitzvah (Donin, 285).

The weekly experience of Shabbat, the day of rest, is in a real way an island of the holiness set in the midst of time (Rabbi Donin has called it "an island in time," chapter 5). The great Jewish religious thinker Abraham Joshua Heschel observed that the rest of the week exists for Shabbat (*The Sabbath* [New York: Farrar, Straus & Giroux, 1951], 14). The Sabbath is a beloved holy day (Donin, 61 ff.; Eckstein, 81) and messianic believers care for its holiness just as much as the community as a whole (cf. "Messianic Synagogue" in vol. III; in addition, treatment of the Sabbath in *The Messianic Times* 2:4 (spring, 1992): 23). In fact, the keeping of Shabbat is an outward and visible sign of the inward spiritual gift God has given the Jews by calling them out as the people of God (*Service of the Heart* [Union of Liberal and Progressive Synagogues (U.K.), 1967], 70, 99–100, 149–150; Joseph H. Hertz, *The Authorized Daily Prayer Book*, rev. ed. [New York: Bloch, 1948], 367, 371–373).

All of the *sacramental* elements discussed above have in common that they set apart—mark off as holy—a point in time, however long or short this time may be. The kiddush and the lighting of candles (*bentsch licht*) mark off the beginning of the Sabbath. The Sabbath reaches its conclusion with havdalah, a ceremony marking the end of the holy day. These sacraments set apart, or sanctify, time—that one day out of seven. The seder marks the beginning of an eight-day period, Pesach, set aside to commemorate the deliverance of God's people. Circumcision marks the beginning of a sanctified (set apart) life; immersion marks that point in time when the person confesses faith in Yeshua; and the bar or bat mitzvah marks the point in time when a child begins to assume adult religious responsibilities. This setting apart of time occurs because, as Heschel so aptly observed, "Judaism is a religion of time aiming at the sanctification of time" (Heschel, 8). Messianic Judaism is no different—to the extent that it is an expression of Judaism. What makes Messianic Judaism unique is that it is also an expression of the messianic faith, which it shares with other branches of the body of the Messiah of which its members are a part.

Kenneth Warren Rick

124 • THE NATIONAL BAPTIST CONVENTION OF AMERICA, INCORPORATED

Although the early history of Baptist's worship reflects an emphasis upon a public preaching service, National Baptists have recently moved from this narrow concept to a broader understanding of the worship experience. Members have expressed a deep longing to worship God rather than merely to hear the pastor preach. This broader understanding centers around the National Baptist's belief that God is truly present in their corporate worship.

Introduction. The member churches of the National Baptist Convention of America, Incorporated have always understood the significance of the worship experience in the light of their understanding of God and their understanding of the doctrine of the Trinity. They accept the fact that God has revealed himself in the Son of God, Jesus Christ, who has risen from the dead and is seated at the right hand of God the Father. The active presence of God in Jesus Christ is made real through the activity of the Holy Spirit. This means for member churches of the denomination that the worship experience is an expression of gratitude for all that God has done through Jesus Christ and that their obligation is to acknowledge God's goodness by rendering gratitude and praise.

The Presence of God in the Worship Experience

Throughout the long history of the Baptists, even though they have been soundly thrashed by critics for their seemingly unorthodox positions and so-called peculiarities in worship, a keen and intuitive sense of the presence of God in personal devotional life and in the corporate worship of the church has always existed. Even though Baptists are accused of their pie-in-the-sky faith, they have always believed that the God they worship does make himself known and present in the contemporary affairs of human beings, and that God, through the Holy Spirit, is ever present in their services of corporate worship.

Admittedly, Baptist churches, including the member churches of the National Baptist Convention of America, Incorporated, have never really focused upon the technical aspects of worship like many of the other mainline Protestant denominations. Early history reflects that Baptists assembled for the public worship of God, but the emphasis was upon a public preaching service in which the pastor/preacher was the central figure, conducting the service and proclaiming the gospel of Jesus Christ with a teaching emphasis. National Baptists have moved, however, from this narrow concept to a broader understanding of the worship experience because of their deep commitment to worship God, rather than merely to hear the pastor (preacher) preach. National Baptists know that nowhere in Scripture is it affirmed that "they who wait upon the preacher or preaching shall renew their strength." Member churches of the denomination in the twentieth century have improved their understanding of the worship experience, but more important, they have understood the spiritual reality that God is present, sensed, heard, and felt in their individual worship and each component of their corporate worship experience. Their commitment to God as Father of the risen Lord Jesus Christ acknowledges God's presence in their personal lives and in their worship services. For National Baptists, God's presence is not a physical entity nor is it limited by time. National Baptists believe that God has revealed himself through the work of the Holy Spirit. For them, this revelation is not a phantom or ghostlike presence, nor merely a symbolic presence. The congregation of the Cornerstone Baptist Church of Christ in Dallas, Texas, authenticates and expresses God's presence in a chant sung following the prayer of invocation:

> Surely the Lord is in this place. Surely the Lord is in this place.
> I can feel his presence. I can feel his presence in every place.
> Surely the Lord, surely the Lord, surely the Lord is in this place.

Recognizing their inadequacies related to worship technicalities, National Baptists have begun to examine the components of their worship in order to make God's presence more evident in every component. The result is that National Baptists have come to realize that the corporate worship of the church as the body of Christ facilitates the adoration and praise of a God worthy of praise. Furthermore, corporate worship de-emphasizes the perception that God's presence is the sole experience of the individual. The so-called pie-in-the-sky theology, or futuristic hope of God's presence reminiscent of earlier years by some member churches, has been transformed to a hope in a God perceived as living, present, and active in Jesus Christ and active in the Holy Spirit's empowering function.

The Presence of God in the Sacred Actions of the Church

The renewed acknowledgment of the presence of God in worship is incorporated into the specific sacred actions and/or consecrated acts of worship designated as baptism, Communion (Lord's Supper), confirmation, ordination, marriage, and healing.

Baptism and the Lord's Supper will be discussed at length in a subsequent section of this discussion. Suffice it here to say that baptism and the Lord's Supper are the two ordinances of the Baptist church that are practiced systematically. Every Baptist believes that God is present when performing these ordinances.

The member churches of the National Baptist Convention of America, Incorporated do not adhere to the sacred act of confirmation. When a child less than eight years (not an arbitrarily selected age) affirms that he or she wishes to commit himself or herself to the lordship of Jesus Christ through the church, he or she is counseled by the pastor and other professional religious (Christian) counselors in an attempt to ascertain the level of spiritual maturity and commitment. If the pastor and/or professional Christian counselors determine that the child's spiritual maturity and commitment are acceptable, the child is then admitted to membership and required to participate in what is described as a _new member_ class or as _orientation ministry._ Upon the completion of this experience, the child is admitted to full membership through a special act of fellowship recognition as a part of the worship service, where National Baptists believe God is present. (Contrary to much public opinion, National Baptists do not establish age twelve as the acceptable age for full church membership.)

The marriage ceremony in National Baptist churches is an act of worship by the church as the body of Christ, reaffirming the intimate relationship of the church as the bride of Christ. National Baptists believe that persons who come to the church to be married reinforce the Christian idea of the family of God and that this act of worship, praise, and thanksgiving is offered to the God revealed in Jesus Christ, who initiated Christian marriage.

There is no specific sacred act of healing in the member churches, but most member churches of the denomination conduct a period of intercessory prayer for members with all kinds of problems that accompany life. When individual members request the need for prayer for specific persons with physical, emotional, psychological, financial, and social problems, special periods are devoted to intensive prayer for these persons. Although these prayers are offered by the pastor and other members, there is never the claim that healing is a result of the pastor or other individuals, but is a demonstration of the power of God to heal through Jesus Christ. Again, the contention of member churches is that the power to heal is attributed to the powerful presence of God.

Ordinances Practiced

The National Baptist Convention of America, Incorporated practices the ordinances of baptism and the Lord's Supper; thus, it is in accord with all of the mainline churches of America with the possible exception of the Friends and the Quakers. The administrator for these two ordinances is an ordained pastor (minister) who may be assisted by ordained deacons.

The Ordinance of Baptism. Member churches of the denomination prefer the term *ordinance to sacrament* because the latter term conveys to them the negative meaning that baptism as a sacrament communicates a means of saving grace. This preference is buttressed by the conviction that salvation comes only through the redemptive act of Jesus Christ and not through the sacraments. For member churches, baptism as an ordinance has historical and spiritual roots. National Baptists believe that the ordinance was instituted and ordained by Jesus Christ himself as substantiated by his baptism in the river Jordan (Matthew 3:13-17; Mark 1:9; Luke 3:21). Additionally, they believe that baptism represents the centrality of the gospel message and that it is the initial act, following conversion, for entry into the church fellowship as the body of Christ. National Baptist churches administer the ordinance of baptism to new converts in obedience to the command of Jesus Christ. However, they also believe that baptism has a future or eschatological significance in that it is the consummation of the Christian hope for eternal life.

National Baptists, like most contemporary Baptists, consider the ordinance of baptism as a symbolic act that belongs to the church, the body of Christ, and not as an act of obedience solely for the individual convert to Christianity. The symbolism of the act removes, as indicated before, baptism from being defined as a sacramental act. National Baptists are quick to respond that this does not mean that God is not included in the act. Indeed, for Baptists, God is present in the conversion experience in addition to baptism. Thus baptism is not purely a human act nor is it a magical or mechanical distribution of salvation.

The mode of baptism for Baptists has been written about and discussed greatly. Some member churches have narrowly mandated one mode of baptism to the exclusion of modes practiced by other churches. Yet the preferred practice for most Baptists is immersion. Most Baptists encourage baptism by immersion because immersion is the root meaning of the word *baptize* and is the mode that appears in the New Testament. More important, member churches do not commit themselves to infant baptism because they believe such acceptance suggests sacramental implications, i.e., that something happens to the child that may be interpreted as God's grace. Furthermore, for member churches, baptism by immersion is rich and resplendent with symbolism related to the conversion experience—death to the old life of sin, the burial of the old life, and the rising to newness of life with Christ Jesus. This symbolic trilogy for National Baptists also symbolizes Christ's death, burial, and resurrection. The symbolism is also continued in the Trinitarian benediction formula "in the Name of the Father, the Son, and the Holy Ghost (Spirit)." While this Trinitarian formula has a meaningful history, some churches of the denomination have begun to take a hard look at the Trinitarian formula because it may not always convey that this sacred act of baptism is an initiation into Christ's church.

Nevertheless, National Baptists believe that baptism is the most distinguishing act of the church as the body of Christ with a time- and spiritual-honored place that is a preliminary for participating in the ordinance of the Lord's Supper.

The Ordinance of the Lord's Supper. Member churches believe that the observance of the Lord's Supper is predicated upon the three-pronged essential qualities that they also attribute to baptism. They believe that the Lord's Supper is observed in obedience to the command of Christ, that it represents the proclamation of the central truth of the gospel message, and that it is an act of the church as the body of Christ rather than a personal act for the individual convert. Given the many ascriptions to the ordinance (Eucharist, Communion, Holy Communion, the Last Supper, the Lord's Table), member churches prefer the Lord's Supper.

The Lord's Supper, just like baptism, is perceived by National Baptists as a symbolic experience commemorating the sacrificial act of redemption by Jesus Christ to provide humanity's salvation, but not as a means of communicating sacramental grace. The symbolism of this ordinance means that members of the churches partake of Christ's broken body and his shed blood by eating bread and drinking wine (or its substitute). The symbolism is carried further when member churches take seriously the words of the biblical injunction in John 6:53-56: "He that eateth my flesh and drinketh my blood, dwelleth in me and I in him." The biblical passage most used by National Baptists is 1 Corinthians 11:24b-26, "This do in remembrance of me." This is perceived by

National Baptists as the divine command by Christ himself. Other biblical passages such as Mark 14:22-24, Luke 22:17-20, and Luke 26:26-29 certify for them that the Lord's Supper is an act mandated for the church in the Bible. There are a few churches of the denomination that contend that the divine command of Christ is meant more for new converts (disciples), but most churches contend that the ordinance of the Lord's Supper is an act mandated for the entire church.

Varied interpretations of the meaning of the Lord's Supper can be found in the member churches of the denomination. These differing interpretations usually depend on the location of the church and the teachings of the pastor. Member churches reject the Roman Catholic view of transubstantiation (the transforming of the bread and the wine into the actual body and blood of Christ). They also reject the Lutheran view of consubstantiation, which focuses too much upon the new convert and the maturity of the new convert's faith. National Baptists straddle the fence between the Calvinistic view, which focuses upon the real presence of Christ as being spiritual rather than a bodily presence, and the Zwinglian view, which says that the Lord's Supper is a memorial meal in which Christians commemorate the sacrificial death of Christ. The Zwinglian interpretation is adopted by many member churches, but it is not the prevailing view. Some member churches adopt the Calvinistic view. Thus, contrary to the prevailing notion that Baptists have a special interpretation of the Lord's Supper, National Baptists have no special Baptist interpretation.

Within the last twenty-five years, National Baptists have moved away from a very narrow and strict interpretation of how the Supper is to be observed. As late as 1965, some member churches still contended that the Lord's Supper should be closed, i.e., only Baptists should partake the ordinance in a Baptist church. This narrow interpretation, with very few exceptions, is no longer observed in National Baptist churches. The only requisite that member churches insist upon is that the ordinance of baptism precede the Lord's Supper in logical sequence because baptism is perceived as the initial act of entry into the church as the body of Christ and the Lord's Supper is perceived as the second step, which facilitates fellowship, nurturing, teaching about the faith, and demonstrating one's commitment to Christ.

Through the observance of these two ordinances, National Baptists celebrate an affinity with most of the mainline Protestant churches in America today.

Empowering Lay Ministry

National Baptists, like most mainline churches in America, do not provide special observances for empowering lay ministry as they do for the ordained ministry of the church.

Lay ministries in member churches include many different areas of Christian service. One can participate in a teaching ministry (Christian education) or a mission ministry, which is the primary focus of the missionary society groups. On the other hand, many men are participating in the Brotherhood or Laymen's ministry, which presents the gospel to men, whose numbers are declining in the church, provides nurturing for young men, and ministers to external communities and social agencies. Furthermore, the evangelistic ministry is designed to train congregations and equip them for witnessing and soul winning.

While member churches of the denomination have no special rites empowering and/or commissioning these ministries, some local churches place a day on the calendar for special celebrations that focus upon the importance of these ministries and raise financial assistance to ensure that these ministries remain a vital force in presenting the gospel of Jesus Christ at home and abroad.

Richard A. Rollins

125 ◆ PRESBYTERIAN CHURCH (USA)

The Presbyterian Church (USA) is heir to a formal worship style based on Calvin's worship reforms and a more free worship style based on seventeenth-century Puritans. This mixed heritage has allowed the Presbyterian Church (USA) in its 1989 Directory for Worship to recover many ancient sacred acts while allowing for expressions from ethnic sources. The Presbyterian Church (USA) views these sacred acts, or sacraments, as demonstrating to the worshiper that all time, all space, and all matter are potential vehicles of God's grace. The entire worship service is filled with praise for God and with the presence of Christ.

The worship of the Presbyterian Church (USA)

traces its lineage back through John Calvin and the Genevan Reformation to the early church. The rather formal worship of Calvin, which included the singing of psalms, canticles, the creed, and the Lord's Prayer, was joined by a free worship style of the seventeenth-century Puritans and free-church Independents. These two traditions, one consisting of formal worship with high ritual and the other consisting of a free worship with minimal structure, continue in the Presbyterian church until the present.

The worship of the Presbyterian Church (USA) is guided by a Directory of Worship. The Directory gives general direction to the worship, but does not provide a mandatory prayer book or mandatory order of worship. The most recent Directory for Worship was adopted by the General Assembly of the denomination in 1989 (DW 89) and is printed in the *Book of Order,* one of the constitutional documents of the denomination. The Directory generally guides the worship of the formal segment of the denomination.

The Presbyterian church has always had a very high regard for the sacraments of baptism and the Lord's Supper, and for the concept of sacraments. DW 89 has an important section in its first chapter entitled "Time, Space, and Matter" (1.3000) that provides the theological and philosophical basis for sacramental worship. The purpose of the sacraments is not that some small portion of time, space, and matter might be "set apart from all common uses to a sacred use." Instead, the sacraments should demonstrate to Christians that all time, all space, and all matter are potentially the vehicles and instruments of God's grace.

Presbyterian worship also has a strong orientation to culture and to social righteousness. DW 89 emphasizes that worship uses cultural building blocks, and it affirms the diverse components that come from various cultural traditions, such as various ethnic expressions. At the same time, the document provides criteria for judging the appropriateness of cultural forms for expression within worship and demands that worship bear fruit as the Christian goes out to live in the world.

All Presbyterian churches practice the two sacraments of baptism and the Lord's Supper, and they also practice the laying on of hands in the ordination of pastors, elders, deacons, and the officers of the church.

Baptism

The Presbyterian church affirms both the evangelistic and the nurturing dimensions of baptism and practices the baptism of both infants and adults. The mode of baptism is predominantly sprinkling, though if it is observed, one would say that the word *dabbing* is perhaps more appropriate. DW 89 says that baptism should be "by pouring, sprinkling or immersion" (3.3605) and in that same section says that "by whatever mode, the water should be applied visibly and generously." This same phrase occurs in the Supplemental Liturgical Resource 2, *Holy Baptism and Services for the Renewal of Baptist* (31). There is a significant change in the church in the observable use of water over the last thirty to fifty years. An increasing number of pastors make the role of water much more prominent, to the extent that a significant increase in the number of churches that occasionally baptize by immersion can even be observed.

Presbyterian directories for worship, until the mid–twentieth century, frequently included a phrase that mandated that no other ceremony should be added to the water ceremony. Thus, one could interpret this phrase as meaning that there would be no laying on of the pastor's hand as a pastoral blessing, no presentation to the congregation, and so on. In fact, this minimalist form of baptism did prevail through the seventeenth to nineteenth centuries. DW 89, however, provides for the option of the laying on of hands, prayer for the anointing of the Holy Spirit, anointing with oil, presentation to the congregation, the lighting of a baptismal candle, the inscription of the name in the roll of the church, and similar acts. However, the document warns that "care shall be taken that the central act of baptizing with water is not overshadowed" (DW 89 3.3607).

The Lord's Supper

The official theology of the Presbyterian church and of the Reformed tradition very strongly affirm the dynamic and active presence of Christ in the Lord's Supper. Indeed, the Presbyterian church affirms Christ's presence in all of worship; however, this affirmation is preeminently true in the celebration of the sacraments and in the preaching of the Word. The Reformed tradition criticizes static understandings of the presence, which confines Christ to the substance of the sacrament.

Rather, Presbyterians will often state that unless Christ through his Spirit transforms the worshipers into his body, nothing very significant has happened in worship. At the same time, Presbyterians recognize that the Eternal uses and enters dynamically into the elements and actions of the Lord's Supper in order to affect that transformation.

The Presbyterian church has a performative understanding of the remembering that is mandated by Christ in both baptism and the Lord's Supper. "Do this in remembrance of me" is spoken in a covenantal context and is analogous to "remember me in your will." This is an active and life-changing remembering. This remembering implies obedience. The pastor always uses the words of institution of the Supper, either from one of the synoptic Gospels or from 1 Corinthians 11:23-26. Luke 24:30-31 is often used in conjunction with one of these passages. Pastors usually proclaim these words either before or after the eucharistic prayer, rather than within the prayer. However, both DW 89 (3.3612) and the Supplemental Liturgical Resource 1, _The Service for the Lord's Day_ (SLR 1 96–117) indicate that the institution narrative may properly be within the prayer.

The eucharistic prayer is variously used by pastors within the denomination. Some simply provide an extemporaneous prayer. Both DW 89 and SLR 1 provide a Great Thanksgiving Prayer in three parts: (1) thanksgiving for creation and providence, (2) remembrance of God's acts of salvation in Jesus Christ, and (3) an invocation of the Holy Spirit to empower both the worshipers and the whole church. The prayer is Trinitarian in form and historic in scope, moving from creation to the Day of the Lord. It concludes with the entire congregation praying together the Lord's Prayer.

Presbyterian church officers will most often serve Communion to the worshipers while the worshipers remain in the pews. This action emphasizes that Christians in the priesthood of all believers are to serve one another. DW 89 directs that the bread of Communion shall be "common to the culture of the community" (3.3605). The wine may be fermented or nonfermented, though if fermented wine is used, nonfermented should always be available "for those who prefer it" (3.3611). Churches in the denomination most often serve the bread broken or cut into small pieces and the wine in individual cups. However, DW 89 provides a great deal of latitude for the mode of serving Communion. It does not limit the servers to church officers, and it provides the options of gathering around the Table, of breaking bread from a common loaf, of using a common cup or chalice, of dipping the bread in the cup, and so on. Presbyterian churches use a variety of these options depending on the particular congregation.

A practice that formerly was dominant in the church is that of the giving of alms after receiving Communion. This practice became customary in the late sixteenth and early seventeenth centuries in order to highlight and respond to Christ's lavish gifts to believers as received in the Eucharist by giving generously to the poor. This custom of receiving a second offering after Communion is still observed in some Presbyterian churches, but the practice is disappearing, a victim of the unified budget and the unified financial pledge.

Other Rites and Actions

As the Presbyterian church entered the twentieth century, very few if any pastors practiced the laying on of hands other than in the rite of ordaining pastors, elders, and deacons. Anointing with oil was avoided entirely. Confirmation was not practiced; footwashing was considered an anachronism.

The last half of the twentieth century has seen significant change in all of these areas. DW 89 provides for all of the above practices and encourages spoken, sung, enacted, and silent prayer (DW 89 3.5302 et passim). It encourages kneeling, bowing, standing, lifting hands in prayer, dancing, clapping, anointing, and laying on of hands (DW 89 2.1005). Furthermore, it is evident that the Directory and the practices in the various churches are allowing for worship expressions from various ethnic and nontraditional sources.

The Emphasis on Praise

Presbyterian worship focuses on the inexpressible majesty and glory of God. The emphasis of Presbyterian worship, when it is truest to its tradition, is on the praise of God. It is the conscious entry of the people of God into the presence of God through Jesus Christ in the Holy Spirit. In worship, Christ is present in the midst of his people, in the midst of the congregation, not localized simply or even primarily at the Table, in the bread and cup, or in water. Christ is present in that which happens, in the time, space, and matter, including the eucharistic and baptismal words and actions.

Presbyterian worship is the lifting up of the heart by individuals and congregations as the worshipers fulfill their chief and primary goal of life—bringing glory to God in exultation and praise—with openness to a variety of means to that end.

Arlo D. Duba

126 ✦ PROGRESSIVE NATIONAL BAPTIST CONVENTION, INCORPORATED

Progressive National Baptists believe that the feeling of the spiritual presence of God in their corporate worship is assisted by intensive prayer and singing. God's presence is also felt in the ordinances of the Lord's Supper and baptism, which along with the recitation of the church covenant empower the laity to serve God.

The Progressive National Baptist Convention (PNBC) believes in the spiritual presence of God in worship and in the work of the church in the world. The Holy Spirit warms the hearts of the worshipers, convicts them of sin, cleanses and forgives them, and challenges as well as commissions them to enter the everyday world of work with the redemptive and healing message of God's love in Jesus Christ. Progressive Baptists believe that intensive involvement in prayers and deep immersion in singing assist worshipers in opening themselves to the powerful presence of God. For this reason, the length of the worship services are often predicated on how the Holy Spirit manifests the mystery and majesty of God's presence.

Sometimes the moving of the Holy Spirit will elicit verbal expressions of exclamation, tearful sounds of joy, or sad sounds of mourning. Other times, God's powerful presence broods over the service where worshipers are in an aura of pensive silence or reverential reflection.

Worship norms and styles may change as the worshipers reflect the changes within culture, but the sense of God's presence in worship permeates the cultural containers and gives vitality to the styles. The feeling of the absence of God's presence only promotes sterility and rigid formalism.

The sense of the presence of God produces life-transforming experiences. These experiences are described in the African-American spiritual:

> My feet looked new, my hands looked new. The world looked new, when I came out of the wilderness, leaning on the Lord.

God's presence is most felt in the observance of the ordinances of Progressive National Baptists. There are two ordinances: baptism and the Lord's Supper. Although many Progressive Baptist churches formally served the Lord's Supper the first Sunday evening of each month, the majority of the churches now observe the ordinance of the Lord's Supper in the morning. Of the two ordinances, the Lord's Supper has the best attendance. The beauty, majesty, and pageantry of the service may appeal to the mysticism of those who attend the service. While a few may be influenced by the magical or majestic dimensions of worship, others will remember that the Lord's Supper is a memorial. However, it is a memorial of the death of Jesus who now lives the life of the living Lord of history.

At the Communion service the members usually read the church covenant in unison. It reads:

> Having been led as we believe, by the spirit of God, to receive the Lord Jesus Christ as our Savior, and on the profession of our faith, having been baptized in the name of the Father, and of the Son, and of the Holy Ghost, we do now in the presence of God, angels, and this assembly, most solemnly and joyfully enter into covenant with one another, as one body in Christ.

This church covenant develops the way of salvation, the way of confession, the way of baptism, and the way of church organization. The church covenant is a promise to do certain things, while the articles of faith are statements of belief. Because of their belief, PNBC members in unison recite these words at Communion time:

> We engage therefore, by the aid of the Holy Spirit, to walk together in Christian love; to strive for the advancement of this church, in knowledge, holiness and comfort.

Reading the church covenant at the time of the readers' participation in the ordinance of the Lord's Supper is a means of empowering lay persons to become bold witnesses of Jesus Christ and tireless servants in the lay ministries of the church.

Although Progressive Baptist churches define

baptism and the Lord's Supper as ordinances and are committed to God and to each other by the church covenant, some of these churches resemble churches who are sacramental in that they use oil for ordinations, for rites of healing, and for footwashing. These Progressive Baptist churches do not believe in the efficacy of the oil. They simply believe that the oil is symbolic of the invisible presence of God in the midst of those participating in the worship event. God anoints; God heals; God redeems; God brings life from death; and God empowers. The use of oil is an affirmation of the theology of the sacred actions of God and the people.

J. Alfred Smith, Sr.

127 ✦ REFORMED CHURCH IN AMERICA

The Reformed Church in America understands the Lord's Supper and baptism as special means of grace, as visible signs and seals of God's promises in the Word of God. Although Reformed worship used to following a Zwinglian form and emphasize the preached Word, since the 1950s the Reformed Church has officially followed the Reformed liturgical heritage of John Calvin. This change has introduced a more ordered worship format and a renewed emphasis on the liturgy of the Lord's Supper. These changes, however, have been implemented in Reformed churches erratically.

The Reformed Church in America (RCA) understands the Lord to have instituted two sacraments: baptism and the Lord's Supper. While God is everywhere present to the Christian in prayer, the special means of grace as defined by the confessional standards of the church are the preaching of the holy gospel and the celebration of baptism and the Lord's Supper.

One goes to church to worship God. The Reformed emphasis upon the proclamation of the Word has often made worship synonymous with hearing the sermon. In the past thirty years, there has been a greater emphasis upon the totality of the worship service with a corresponding emphasis upon more active participation by the congregation and the celebration of the sacraments.

This has been the result of the worship renewal that began in the 1950s with a synodical proposal to contemporize the rather antiquated wording

of the liturgy. The committee found that the structure and the content of that liturgy failed to represent the best in the Reformed liturgical heritage. It was a service that reflected the lack of coherence of the early Reformed services of Ulrich Zwingli, rather than the studied research into the forms of worship of the early church that guided the reforms of Martin Bucer and John Calvin. The Zwinglian service lacked a coherent worship sequence, was largely a ministerial monologue, and was a service of the Word only.

In 1968, a service of worship based on Calvin's reforms was published in _The Liturgy & Psalms_ that followed more closely the pattern of worship of the early church, including prayers of confession by the congregation, words of assurance of forgiveness, and the law (in its use as a guide to Christian living, and thus placed after the words of forgiveness). Nonetheless, the liturgy for the Lord's Supper was still printed separate from the service of the Word (the church's custom was to celebrate the Lord's Supper only four times a year—a rather arbitrary number inherited from the Zwinglian Reformation).

In 1985, _Rejoice in the Lord_, a hymnbook sponsored by the RCA and edited by Erik Routley (Grand Rapids: Eerdmans) included an "Order of Worship" that, for the RCA, for the first time included the liturgy of Word and sacrament as a single unit, suggesting this service as the normal expectation for Lord's day worship. After the "Approach to God" (including Scripture verses, salutation, hymn, prayer of confession, assurance of pardon, the law, the Psalter, and the Gloria), the main body of the service, designated "The Word of God in Proclamation and Sacrament," attempts to clarify that it is Christ as the Word of God who comes to the worshiper in the sermon and the sacrament. The service concludes with "The Response to God" in a psalm of thanksgiving, prayers of intercession and the Lord's Prayer, a hymn, and benediction.

This same "Order of Worship," which also included the reintroduction of the sharing of the peace, was published in _Worship the Lord_ (eds. James R. Esther and Donald J. Brugginck [Grand Rapids: Eerdmans, 1987]). This volume also contained all the services that would be used in a congregation, as well as "The Directory for Worship." A notable liturgical advance in this volume was the attempt to allow the structure of all of the services to stand within or be guided by the classic Christian pattern of the Lord's Day worship. This is particularly helpful in "The Order of Worship for Christian Marriage" in which the approach, the Word and response, is followed by and allows for the apt inclusion of the Lord's Supper—albeit a practice found only occasionally in the RCA. Also in *Worship the Lord* are services of ordination for the offices of elder, deacon, and minister of the Word, as well as "Orders for Christian Healing."

In addition to *Worship the Lord,* alternate services are periodically produced by the Commission on Worship. Most notable is the one for baptism, which includes a heightened emphasis upon the symbolism of water. That the denomination has first emphasized the reevaluation of the water verbally and symbolically rather than moving towards pouring or immersing is reflective of the Reformed heritage. Nonetheless, in a Communion that allows all gestures from immersing to pouring to sprinkling—with the latter overwhelmingly preponderant—one must be grateful for any return to the symbolism of the sacrament. By the influence of this document, one can hope for a more generous sprinkling. Perhaps even some perceptive congregation will even build a font that permits immersion.

But how are the sacraments understood? On the contemporary scene, the RCA has affirmed the *Baptism, Eucharist and Ministry (BEM)* Statement of the World Council of Churches as a faithful convergence document. With the whole church, the denomination affirms that Christ in his incarnation and saving work gives substance both to the sacraments and to the proclamation. The Reformed tend to emphasize that both Word and sacraments point to Christ and his saving work. The sacraments are visible signs and seals of the promises of God, the "visible words of God." The sacraments are given, because of our weakness, to assure us of God's promises in Christ.

The Reformed emphasize the reality of Christ's presence in the sacrament, but that real presence is through the power of the Holy Spirit (and thus the necessity of the prayer that the Holy Spirit make Christ present to the worshipers). The Lord's Supper is essentially a meal where we as worshipers celebrate with thanksgiving Christ's death and our forgiveness and his promise of his coming again to make all things new. Past, present,

and future are bound together in this meal, so that our prayer "Come, Lord Jesus" is appropriate both for the meal and for that final manifestation of God's justice and mercy.

The RCA, while having a presbyterian form of government, is nonetheless highly congregational in its practice. Thus, in liturgical practice, churches can range from full, enthusiastic usage of the liturgy in *Worship the Lord* to totally idiosyncratic services that could at best be described as eclectic. While merely having a "Directory for Worship," the RCA nonetheless requires in its *Book of Church Order* that its ministers follow the liturgy in the celebration of the sacraments of baptism and the Lord's Supper. The synod also grants provisional use of other liturgies, such as the Lima liturgy or those liturgies proposed by the Commission on Worship of the RCA. Regretfully, even with this variety of liturgical options, the requirement is sometimes disregarded by ministers who presume that their personal understanding is to be preferred to that of the church's. The result is that some churches reduce the service of the Lord's Supper to the words of institution, with even the prayer for the power and presence of the Holy Spirit being omitted.

Like many other communions, the RCA is also heavily influenced by America's revivalistic traditions—all the more so in that one of the nation's most visible and successful evangelists, Reverend Robert Schuler, is a minister of the RCA. Unfortunately, some ministers mistake a substitution of Schuler's *Hour of Power* format for that of traditional worship as being a key to success. Lacking Schuler's perspicacious intentions, context, and charisma, the result is often only an impoverishment of worship.

Worship at a Reformed Church in America may range from the Crystal Cathedral's format to a classic Christian format with all of the traditional elements of Christian worship. For the Lord's Supper, very few congregations celebrate weekly (although this is the goal of our biblical and Calvinist heritage). Some will celebrate monthly; most will celebrate only quarterly. A few have returned to the Dutch custom of going forward to the table to partake of a loaf of bread and from a common cup of wine. However, most will be served cubes of bread and little cups of grape juice in their pews. My wife is of the opinion that as long as the churches continue to use little cups that have to be washed, they will not move toward more frequent Communion. The option of using little throwaway plastic cups seems a tawdry substitute for the solid feel of the little glass cups, let alone the feel of solemnity of pewter or the honor bestowed by a gold or silver chalice.

Musically, the organ is still the dominant instrument, closely followed by the piano. In some congregations, the organ is supplemented by brass and stringed instruments. Asian congregations are probably the most conservative musically, while Hispanic congregations most likely will use instruments traditional to their culture. The absence of a denominational hymnal in the 1930s and 1940s contributed to a diversity of hymnody that continues into the present, even while the biblical riches of _Rejoice in the Lord: A Hymn Companion to the Scriptures,_ edited by Erik Routley, is a contribution of the RCA to the entire church.

Donald J. Bruggink

128 • THE REFORMED EPISCOPAL CHURCH

The Reformed Episcopal Church identifies the Lord's Supper and baptism as sacraments, as means of grace. However, the church denies the efficacy of a sacrament unless the recipient accepts the sacrament in faith. It also understands the sacraments as God's covenantal acts in the midst of God's holy community, the church. This view encourages frequent observance of the Lord's Supper.

The Reformed Episcopal Church reflects the sacramental views of the great evangelical Anglican heritage. The church calls the special rites of baptism and the Lord's Supper _sacraments_ in accordance with what is called the Gospel sacraments in the Articles of Religion. These sacraments involve physical elements set apart for sacred purposes. They are not simply ordinances or commandments to be performed as ends in and of themselves. They are means of grace. They are outward signs of inward graces. They are signs and seals, not simply signs. As seals of God's covenant, they combine with the Word of God to convey grace.

The grace of God is applied through Christ's presence. The Reformed Episcopal Church stresses the real presence of Christ in the faithful reception of bread and wine. The church upholds the real presence of Christ with reference to Holy Communion; in no sense would it advocate a real _absence._ Yet it rejects the notion of Christ's physical presence in the elements themselves, what has been called transubstantiation (or a change of substance). It therefore defines presence in a spiritual sense. In general, it embraces what has been called a _receptionist_ view of the presence of Christ.

Receptionism denies that Christ is present apart from the reception of the elements in faith. It affirms the importance of belief for the sacrament to be effectual. In the server's actual words of administration of the elements, "Take this bread in remembrance that Christ died for thee and feed on him in the heart by faith with thanksgiving." As opposed to the medieval conviction that Christ is automatically conveyed to the recipient irrespective of true faith, what has been called _automatic grace,_ the church emphasizes the presence of Christ in relationship to faithful reception. It rejects a magical or mechanical view of the sacraments.

Generally, Reformed Episcopalians advocate one of two views of receptionism. One view be-

The Alpha and Omega—English Version. This English variation of the alpha and omega symbol features a crown.

lieves that Christ is mystically received by faith upon the actual ingestion of the sacramental elements. The other maintains that the virtue of Christ is applied when Holy Communion is received in faith. As the Reformed Episcopal Church has rediscovered its Anglican heritage in the last ten years, however, other conceptions of the presence of Christ have appeared. Some churches have been influenced by John Calvin's (Eastern Orthodox) idea of mystical ascendancy into heaven at the sursum corda, the versicle said at every Communion that means "Lift up your hearts," to which the congregation responds, "We lift them up unto the Lord." Christ is near because the people of God mystically draw near to him. This is based on Hebrews 10:19-25. In this passage, the writer exhorts the people of God to "draw near" (v. 22) into the heavenly temple (v. 19) by "not forsaking the assembling of themselves together" (v. 25). The author therefore understood that divine worship ushers the congregation into the special presence of the Christ seated at the right hand of God. The Lord of heaven and earth is at the head of the Table not because he has come down to the Table, but because the people of God have risen to his presence in heaven.

In addition to these conceptions of Christ at the Holy Supper, many in the Reformed Episcopal Church would be simply content with a mystical understanding of Christ's presence. They affirm the presence in some sense that cannot be rationally comprehended. At the same time, they reject transubstantiation, and they stress the importance of faith for the sacraments to be effectual.

The gospel sacraments of baptism and Communion are very much a part of the life of the Reformed Episcopal Church. They are understood as covenantal acts performed by God in the midst of the people of God. Under the influence of the rich reformational theology of the biblical covenant, the sacraments are understood as involved in God's initiation of a covenant union between God, the recipient, and the people of God. As such, the sacraments are normally performed in actual worship services. They are not privately administered, except in rare occasions when the recipient is ill or providentially unable to attend the divine worship service.

The dynamic covenantal role of the sacraments means they are not neglected. Baptism is performed in a worship service as soon as possible after a conversion or the birth of an infant. The family and sponsors in the case of infant baptism take a serious view of their responsibilities. The covenant child is to be raised in the nurture and admonition of the Lord. The covenantal community of God is involved. The clergy have a responsibility to catechize children and all those who are young in the Lord. The parents and sponsors share in accountability to assure that covenant children are trained in the faith. Normally in the Reformed Episcopal Church, young faith is confirmed when it comes to maturity. The bishop confirms in the midst of the congregation during a Communion service. The bishop represents the one holy, catholic, apostolic church as the bishop lays on hands to receive the confirmed into the catholic (universal and historic) faith. What has been done on a local level at baptism is applied in the universal and historical spheres by the bishop.

Confirmation is usually the occasion for first Communion. In the Reformed Episcopal Church, however, confirmation is not required before Communion. This practice is a result of an emphasis that goes back to the beginning of the Reformed Episcopal Church. Bishop David Cummins, the founding bishop, wanted to stress strongly the catholicity of the Christian faith. He strongly resisted any practice of exclusivity. Consequently, he acknowledged baptism and faith as the only requirements for Holy Communion. This resulted in the famous invitation that is required to be said at every Lord's Supper: "Our fellow Christians of other branches of Christ's Church and all who love our Divine Lord and Savior Jesus Christ in sincerity, are affectionately invited to the Lord's Table." As a result of this evangelical catholicity, the Reformed Episcopal Church has always opened its Communion to other Christians. Also, within the last decade, many Reformed Episcopal parishes have allowed young baptized children (not infants) to come the Lord's Table on the same basis.

Finally, the understanding of the sacraments as God's covenantal acts in the midst of God's holy community has encouraged frequent observance of the Lord's Supper. Holy Communion is mandated on the first Sunday of the month. It is always served at major denominational meetings. In addition, many parishes have returned to the

New Testament practice of weekly Communion.

In conclusion, the rich biblical and evangelical heritage of the Reformed Episcopal Church has enabled it to enjoy the sacred rites of the historic Christian faith that continue in history back to the Holy Scripture. The church moves forward by constantly moving back to the law, the prophets, and the Gospels.

Ray R. Sutton

129 ✦ ROMAN CATHOLIC CHURCHES

The Roman church continues to celebrate seven sacraments. However, the Second Vatican Council has implemented changes aimed at making the texts and symbolism of the sacraments more intelligible so that lay members can become more involved. To this end, the role of the faith of the assembly and the role of Scripture in sacramental worship has been emphasized. Although these changes have revitalized some members of the church, the Roman church has witnessed a decline in the number participating in the sacraments.

The Roman Catholic church continues to celebrate seven sacraments: baptism, confirmation, Eucharist, reconciliation, matrimony, holy orders, and anointing of the sick. While Catholic scholars freely admit that only baptism and the Eucharist are clearly testified in the New Testament, the official teaching of the church is that all are instituted by Jesus Christ.

The ordinary practice of the church is to baptize infants; introduce children of seven or eight years of age to the Eucharist and reconciliation; have them confirmed during an episcopal visit to the parish soon after that; anoint the sick when there is a serious, usually life-threatening condition; and celebrate marriages and ordinations to the priesthood with considerable solemnity. From the time of the first Eucharist in childhood, all Catholics are required by the official teaching of the church to participate regularly in the Sunday Eucharist, preferably in their own parish churches.

The sacramental life, practice, and theology of the Catholic church has undergone far-reaching changes through progressive stages of implementation of the document _Sacrosanctum Concilium_ (S.C.) of the Second Vatican Council (1962–65). These changes, based on a return to sources in Scripture and of the early church, have aimed at making the texts and the symbolism of the sacramental actions more intelligible and at evoking more active and intelligent participation by the whole community. The decades of change (after many centuries of no perceptible development or change) have placed stress on the unity of the denomination. Some segments have resisted the changes bitterly, occasionally going into openly declared schism. Others have taken the changes in stride without really becoming more actively involved. A considerable number have been stimulated to renewed study of Scripture, liturgy, and doctrine in order to understand what is behind the changes and to become more fully involved. Some have reacted to the changes by concluding that there is less certainty in the church's teaching than formerly supposed and by seeing this as sufficient reason to drift away. Among all these groups, except the first, Sunday Eucharist attendance has declined.

The traditional emphasis in Catholic teaching has been on the efficacy of the sacraments in bestowing grace on the participants. The reason given is that the sacraments are actions of Jesus Christ himself, done in and through the mediation of the church. Because this emphasis in isolation can lend itself to superstition, the post–Vatican II practice and theory tried to redress the balance. The importance of the Word of God in Scripture is given a more central position in all sacramental celebrations than was formerly the case. The new three-year Sunday cycle of readings covers a much larger selection of biblical texts, and preaching on the text of that day's Scripture readings is required of the presider or designated homilist. In addition to this emphasis, there is a renewed understanding of the role of the sacramental signs; namely, that these enacted signs include not only the pouring of water, or signing with oil, etc., but that they also include the whole participation of the community and the commitment these signs imply. For instance, in baptism, particularly of an infant who is not personally capable of participating, the sign that makes the difference is the gathering of a community that pledges itself to provide an ambiance of grace for the child as he or she grows up and assimilates goals and values.

Especially in the celebration and understanding of the Eucharist, these changes in emphases are noticeable. The traditional Catholic teaching has focused on the presence of Christ to the communicants in the consecration of the bread and wine. The Vatican II teaching is that Christ is present at the Eucharist in four ways: in the Word of Scripture that is read and mediated, in the faith of the assembly, in the representative actions, and in the consecration of bread and wine (*S.C.* #7). In order to express this teaching, there is more participation by lay members of the assembly, more time given to Scripture reading and preaching, and more care given to planning and preparing the celebration so that the central action as well as the festivals and seasons of the calendar will be more intelligible and more compellingly relevant to the life situations of the community. One aspect of this latter emphasis has been the linking of social justice and peace issues with the liturgical worship of the community.

As lay participation has become more diverse and active, ceremonies for the investiture of lectors and extraordinary (lay) ministers of Communion have developed. Moreover, something of a bridge between the clerical and lay division in the church has emerged in the reestablishment of the permanent diaconate, open to mature married men who can preach as well as perform other tasks in the parish. In spite of strong, worldwide pressure and theological argument to the contrary, however, women continue to be excluded from both priesthood and diaconate. Some women do function as parish administrators with the responsibilities of pastors, but with explicit exclusion from functions understood to require holy orders, such as consecrating the Eucharist or absolving in reconciliation rites. Women may, in the absence of an ordained priest, conduct a Communion service, which is like a Eucharist but in which preconsecrated Communion bread—the consecration having been performed by a priest on another occasion—is distributed.

A noteworthy feature of the post–Vatican II church is the reintroduction of the Rite of Christian Initiation of Adults, commonly known by its initials, RCIA. This rite is a return to the catechumenate of the early church and is offered to those who have not been baptized, those who have been baptized but not confirmed, and those who, though baptized and confirmed in another church, seek membership in the Roman Catholic church. Because it also involves participation by other members of the parish, this rite is in many

cases an instrument of revitalization of the parish community.

Also of interest is the more relaxed discipline on intercommunion at the Eucharist and on mixed marriages and their mode of celebration. In relation to reconciliation, which in recent centuries was celebrated only in the form of individual, secret confession of sin to an ordained priest followed by an absolution in the name of the church, there are now three approved rites. These three are: an enhanced form of the individual rite; a communal celebration in the course of which absolution is given individually to those who step aside to make an individual, secret confession to a priest who is at hand for the occasion; and a communal celebration in which no specific confession of sins is made but a general (i.e., communal) absolution is given. Although the latter reconciliation rite is officially approved in principle and is based on sound precedent in the history of the church, there has been great reluctance on the part of Roman authorities to allow its use in practice. Actual participation in the individual reconciliation rite is greatly reduced and continues to diminish.

Monika K. Hellwig

130 ♦ THE SALVATION ARMY

The Salvation Army does not observe the traditional Protestant sacraments. This practice is based upon a sacramental theology that rejects the idea that God's gracious actions can be limited by certain means of grace (such as baptism and the Lord's Supper). Instead, all of life can be a sacrament if Christ's presence is acknowledged and celebrated.

Sacramental Worship by Nonsacramentalists

The Salvation Army's nonobservance of the traditional Protestant sacraments in worship is based not upon a Gnostic theology that disparages the material creation but upon a sacramental theology that disparages any attempt to limit the work of grace to prescribed rituals. The Salvationists' sacramental worldview, combined with a strong doctrine of practical holiness, results in a view of all of life as sacramental and each experience as a potential conveyor of grace. Their nonobservance of the sacraments in worship is consequently a witness to the sacraments of ordinary life. If Christ is incarnate today in the midst of the world and if he deigns to dwell and work out his will in the life of the believer, then the sacrament belongs not as much on the high altars of sanctuaries as in the everyday life of societies where the church lives and witnesses. The sacrament is being offered daily, hourly, moment by moment. The Christian's daily life is a constant dipping into the baptism of the Spirit and a constant fellowshiping with his or her Lord and the Lord's family at the Table.

The Salvationists' nonobservance of the sacraments in worship is not based upon any criticism of observance of sacraments in the worship of other communities. It is, rather, the affirmation of the realities to which the sacraments point and the celebration of those realities as a part of, and not apart from, everyday life.

This position is strengthened by the fruits of research, first, of the Biblical texts traditionally referred to as scriptural injunctions to observe the sacraments and, second, of theological developments in the early centuries of church history. The interpretation of biblical texts as containing commands of our Lord to observe baptism and the Lord's Supper have now been called into question by responsible scholarship. Furthermore, eminent New Testament scholar C. K. Barrett has noted that whereas the scriptural evidence indicates that initiatory washings and shared fellowship meals occurred early in the New Testament church, there is no evidence that this took place with a specific theology in mind. Indeed, says Barrett, it would be wrong to read back into the early New Testament accounts of baptism and fellowship meals sacramental doctrines that developed later (_Church, Ministry and Sacraments in the New Testament_ [Grand Rapids: Eerdmans, 1985]). The tendency to read back later theologies is very understandable in light of the gradual infusion of Greek presuppositions into Christian theology, as well as the establishment and clericalization of the church, bringing the institutionalization and formalization of grace-conveying rituals. The Salvationists' nonobservance of these specific rituals is therefore not a critique of them. Rather, it is a testimony to scriptural freedom with respect to them. It is also an endorsement of the grace-filled character of life to which they give

witness and is an assertion that this grace is conveyed within a much broader spectrum of observances and experiences.

The two key points, then, in understanding the Salvationists' non-sacramentalist worship are the following. First, all of life is a sacrament. Second, the sacramental character of life calls for freedom in sacramental expression in worship.

First, to assert that all of life is a sacrament is to insist on a direct link between worship and life. In no way ought there to be a great divide between life in the church and life in the world—a divide that has been fed historically by the institutionalization of the church and the clericalization of ministry. In no way ought formal worship to be seen as a different or higher order of spiritual life, which is a view that strengthens the divide. In no way ought some mystery to be celebrated or evoked other than the same mystery that is present in life's commonest experiences. The Salvationists' nonobservance of the traditional sacraments is an affirmation of the accessibility of grace through any means God chooses and is a refusal to limit that accessibility to formal worship and its prescribed rituals. What this means for the Salvationist is that a sacrament can take place over a common meal where Christ's presiding presence is recognized and celebrated. It can take place where, in a contemporary or equivalent form, someone's feet are lovingly washed. It can take place wherever Christ reveals his redemptive presence in the midst of life.

The second key to understanding the Salvationists' nonsacramentalist worship is that this understanding of the sacramental character of life calls for freedom in sacramental expression in worship. Salvationists believe that since Christ did not institute specific sacraments to be observed as such, worship—while maintaining the essential elements of adoration and praise, Scripture teaching, and opportunities for response—is not bound by culturally conditioned and institutionally prescribed forms. In other words, the essential character of worship is not dependent upon any certain practice. It is dependent upon openness to God's self-revelation in Christ through the work of the Holy Spirit in whatever ways, consistent with scriptural teaching, that revelation comes. Every means by which this happens in worship is a sacrament.

Philip D. Needham

131 • SOUTHERN BAPTIST CONVENTION CHURCHES

Southern Baptists inherit a radical Reformation perspective on the Lord's Supper and baptism that understands these sacred actions as ordinances and memorials. However, a worship renewal movement among Southern Baptists has emphasized the presence of Christ in the faith of the recipient of the ordinance. Thus, ordinances are to be understood as vividly enacted symbols in worship that become powerful invitations for the worshiper to enter the saving sphere of God's gracious activity in the world. In the following article, the author describes the worship renewal in his local church.

From the radical left-wing Reformation in sixteenth-century Europe (e.g., Zwingli and the Anabaptists) and the separatist Baptist movement of seventeenth-century England came the emergence of an alternative way to look at the Lord's Supper and baptism: as ordinances (orders or commands) rather than sacrament. Although the word *sacrament* was used in some early British Baptist documents, ordinance very quickly became the name given these two actions. Christ commanded believers to participate in them as symbolic acts of obedience.

Believer's baptism by immersion became the distinctive Baptist way of baptism. It was seen as an act of obedience symbolizing new life in Christ, the forgiveness of sins, and the gift of eternal life. Baptism was understood to symbolize that believers are buried with Christ in baptism and raised to walk in newness of life.

The Lord's Supper is seen as a memorial meal. "This do in remembrance of me" is carved in the front of many Baptist Communion tables. Its major symbolic reference has been to the sacrificial gift of Christ's life pointed to in the words of institution. In many Southern Baptist churches the Lord's Supper has been observed only once a quarter, and furthermore, it was tacked onto the end of the song-and-preaching service with little or no integration with what preceded it.

In Baptist documents phrases like *mere* command, *mere* symbol, *mere* memorial were used. Afraid of Christians who, in their eyes, made too much of the sacraments, Baptists have often made too little of them. Afraid of sacramentalism that made the Supper magical or claimed the automatic presence of Christ in the elements, Baptists have neglected the special presence of Christ promised in the observance of baptism and the Table.

There is, however, a worship renewal movement in some Southern Baptist congregations that is giving greater importance to the practice of these ordinances and is experimenting with other sacred actions. Some churches now celebrate Communion once a month with additional observances on special days of the Christian year like Christmas Eve or Maundy Thursday. The special presence of Christ around his Table is anticipated, invoked, and experienced.

In the categories of the historical debate concerning the presence of Christ in the sacraments, these churches would say that Christ is present in the faith the person brings to the Table and the water. Moreover, the Table and water help elicit faith in the believer's life.

The Lord's Supper, now also called Communion, also has a more integral relation to the rest of the service, more in line with the ancient liturgy of the church where the service of the Word and the service of the Table were equal in importance. Also, a fuller range of biblical meanings is given to the Table, not just as a memorial meal, but also as the messianic banquet table, a Passover meal, the family meal of the people of God, the table of Christ's peace, an agape feast, and so on.

Baptism is also undergoing renewal as it becomes a more central symbol in the worshiping life of the congregation. Baptism into Christ is a central metaphor of the Christian life. Baptism is not only Christian initiation but also the ordination of all believers into the ministry of Jesus Christ. It symbolizes newness of life, cleansing, radical obedience, death, and resurrection. I will speak more about its renewal later.

Churches like Crescent Hill Baptist Church in Louisville, Kentucky, are also experimenting with a broader range of sacred actions beyond the two ordinance. In my usage, *sacred actions* are less than sacraments and more than symbols. Evelyn Underhill used the term *sacramental* to describe them. They are vividly enacted symbols in worship that become powerful invitations for the worshiper to enter the saving sphere of God's gracious activity in the world.

The laying on of hands is a sacred action used in the ordination of clergy and deacons. In an increasing number of congregations, the whole congregation is invited to participate in the laying on of hands, not merely ordained persons. At Crescent Hill Baptist Church, everyone baptized also receives the laying on of hands as a symbol that all believers are called to minister.

The imposition of ashes on Ash Wednesday is a sacred action. It is practiced by some Baptist congregations that often direct the congregation to impose the ashes on each other. Footwashing services on Maundy Thursday and healing services with laying on of hands and anointing with oil are sacred actions practiced in some Baptist congregations.

I turn now to a description of how believer's baptism is being renewed in the life of Crescent Hill Baptist Church. Ordinance and sacred action are used in mutually empowering ways.

First, although we at Crescent Hill Baptist Church baptize persons all through the year as Christians come and request baptism, we always baptize on Christmas Eve and Easter Sunday. The powerful meanings of baptism are flooded with the meanings of the two great seasons of Christmas and Easter, and worshipers are reminded of the centrality of baptism into Christ at these key worship times. People remember their baptisms, and people begin to anticipate their own baptism as they witness believer's baptism in these services. Similarly, both Advent and Lent become times of evangelical invitation and concentration.

Second, we make the Lenten season a time of baptismal renewal, a deep reflection on the meaning of being baptized into Christ. At the culmination of the season, on Easter Sunday, the whole congregation is invited to the renewal of their baptismal vows. While still in the baptismal pool following the baptism of new Christians, I as pastor take two pitchers, dip them in the baptismal waters, and pass them over the side of the pool into the choir where they are passed to the ministers, who carry them down into the congregation and pour the water into two bowls on either side of the Communion table. The bowls are on pedestals and have a shell in them, the ancient symbol of baptism. When the water is finished being poured into the bowls, we sing the doxology. Then at the time of the last hymn, I invite anyone who wishes to come touch the water as a tangible sign of the renewal of their vows and as a reminder of their baptism ("Remember your baptism and be thankful") to do so as we sing. If they prefer to do so after the service in a more private manner, they may. It is a moving experience for people to walk down the aisle and touch the baptismal waters.

Finally, as mentioned above, we join the laying on of hands and baptism. Following the early church action (see the book of Acts where the laying on of hands as a sign of the Holy Spirit often accompanied baptism), I, on behalf of the congregation, lay hands on each person who comes up from the water. I then offer a prayer that is both blessing and commissioning. I normally use the Aaronic benediction, changing the last phrase to "May the Lord lift up his countenance upon you and through you give the world peace," or the benediction of 2 Corinthians 13:14.

The sacred action of laying on of hands at baptism symbolizes these important realities and meanings: (1) the empowering presence of the Holy Spirit in the life of the believer and (2) the ordination of every believer at their baptism to be a minister of Christ. Thus, the laying on of hands at baptism states that all are called; all are ordained; everyone is a minister of Christ. If baptism is the ordination of all believers, the whole people of God, then the ordination of clergy and deacons becomes a second ordination that is a commissioning to a more specific place of service requested by the church.

One more sacred action that has become of powerful importance to us is the dedication of infants. (Some early Baptist churches in America called this the devotion of children.) This sacred action occurs soon after children come into the world—one at a time. So we have children dedicated at fifteen or more services a year. The parents bring their child down the aisle, and a liturgy of dedication is shared, with parents and congregation making their vows. Then I as the pastor take the child in my arms and carry it into the congregation and speak to the significance of this day. The congregation listens. The carrying of the child itself becomes a sacred action, a visual reminder that God blesses and takes delight in us all and that we are all beloved children of God welcomed into the world and into God's family.

H. Stephen Shoemaker

132 ✦ UNITED METHODIST CHURCH

The Methodists' views of the sacraments have traveled through three distinct phases. At the beginning of the Wesleyan movement in the nineteenth century, Wesley emphasized a strong divinely experiential sense of the sacraments as means of grace. From the late eighteenth century to the 1960s, the Enlightenment understanding of the sacraments as marginal and mostly memorial dominated Methodism. However, beginning in the 1960s, United Methodists have experienced a sacramental renewal. The emphasis in the sacraments has shifted from a human undertaking to a divine covenant by God to make believers share in Christ's royal priesthood.

Methodist attitudes towards sacraments have gone through three quite distinct periods. Each has to be understood in the light of its predecessors, so I will treat them in sequence. Elements of each era survive in subsequent periods, but the periods are largely distinct.

The first period is that of the Wesleyan movement in England during the eighteenth century. Early Methodism was characterized by a strong experiential sense of the sacraments as divinely appointed means of grace. This is all the more striking in the context of the Enlightenment when sacramental life had been pushed to the margin of Anglican piety. Yet early Methodism in England is full of the sense of a warm, personal experience of the immediacy of God's presence in the Lord's Supper. Many, including Susannah Wesley, experienced the Lord's Supper as a converting ordinance in which a dead religion became one of the heart. Early Methodism was a sacramental revival, one of the first in Protestantism.

This was manifest in an emphasis on frequent Communion, such as in John Wesley's 1732 sermon "The Day of Constant Communion" in which he endeavored to "show that it is the city of every Christian to receive the Lord's Supper as often as he can." The same thought appears half a century later when he wrote to the Americans in 1784, "I also advise the elders to administer the supper of the Lord on every Lord's day." The 166 *Hymns of the Lord's Supper* of John and Charles Wesley are the greatest treasury of eucharistic poetry in the English language and surprisingly contemporary in their emphasis on pneumatology, eschatology, and the Eucharist as a sacrifice.

Wesley's thought on baptism is more ambigu-

ous. He affirms its importance for infants: "Infants need to be washed from original sin; therefore they are proper subjects of baptism." He retains a sense of baptismal regeneration in the case of infants, but is unwilling to allow adults to presume regeneration at their baptism, a view largely dictated by his own observations. And he echoed the Puritan belief that confirmation was superfluous by deleting any reference to it in his prayer book. One cannot speak of a baptismal piety in Wesley as one might in Luther.

The American Methodist experience of the sacraments, from the late eighteenth century to about 1960 reflects a different world, both figuratively and literally. In this case, the Enlightenment mentality that Wesley had resisted so forcibly came to prevail. For the Enlightenment mind, any supernatural aspect of the sacraments was suspect, and its God appeared to be emeritus as far as any present activity in the sacraments was concerned. Sacraments were tolerated as conducive to morality, but with little or no sense of them as moments of divine intervention into the lives of humans.

In this context, sacraments became marginal events for American Methodists. The Methodist Episcopal Church, South, did decree a monthly Eucharist, but most northern Methodists by the twentieth century were content with four times a year. The 1905 and 1935 hymnals each had only seven hymns for the Lord's Supper, none of them by the Wesleys. The 1935 hymnal reflects the high tide of the Enlightenment in one of the eucharistic rites in which all references to real presence have been converted to references to a memorial meal.

Baptism underwent a rather different trajectory, but with a similar destination. Early on, American Methodists made it clear they would have none of Wesley's lingering affirmation that baptism even signified regeneration. By 1916, the northern church had discarded the Wesleyan prayer over the water, which asked God to sanctify the water in order to affect the mystical washing away of sin. The emphasis had switched from saving infants from the condemnation of original sin to welcoming them into the church. Nineteenth-century Methodists added a probationary period for those baptized as adults. This delayed adult's admission into church membership; the twentieth century turned this practice into a preparatory membership status only for those baptized as infants. Just as the Eucharist had come to focus largely on human recollection of the past work of Christ, so baptism came to concentrate on human engagement in rearing the child in the church. Enlightenment reluctance to mention God's intervention had prevailed in both cases. A good monument of this period is Robert W. Goodloe's 1953 book _The Sacrament in Methodism_.

A third era began to emerge in the 1960s and is gradually becoming more apparent. This period is engaged more deeply in sacramental life. Indeed, there is now a United Methodist periodical entitled _Sacramental Life_. Many factors have gone into forming this new era: the excitement of the Roman Catholic reforms after the Second Vatican Council; the advent of professors of worship in all United Methodist seminaries (a process that took thirty years), a growing interest in sacramental theology, and the revision of the sacramental rites between 1972 and 1989. Now Abingdon Press finds books on worship one of its best-selling fields.

The most conspicuous demonstration of this new era is the 1989 _United Methodist Hymnal_. Its first page presents "The Basic Pattern of Worship," which presumes that the normal service involves thanksgiving and Communion. An increasing number of churches celebrate the Eucharist every Sunday. What is even more striking is the move away from the late medieval penitential rite that the Reformers inherited to the new rite that proclaims God's past work and invokes God's present work through the Holy Spirit. Though the words are nothing like Wesley's, the theology is similar to his eucharistic hymns and the early church sources on which he drew.

The changes in the baptismal rites are even more striking. The emphasis has shifted from a human undertaking to a divine covenant by God to make believers "share in Christ's royal priesthood." The prayer over the water invites the Holy Spirit to bless the water and wash away sin. The new rites are controversial because they represent such a drastic break from the Enlightenment-dominated past.

Methodism is gradually moving into a new era. The eucharistic hymns in the 1989 _Hymnal_ have increased from the twenty hymns in the 1965 _Hymnal_ to thirty hymns. The sacramental nature of other rites—marriage, burial, healing, and or-

dination—is much more apparent in the 1992 _United Methodist Book of Worship_. Even the title of a 1983 Abingdon book, _Sacraments as God's Self Giving_, indicates a whole new era. Changes come slowly, but surely.

James F. White

133 • THE WESLEYAN CHURCH

Wesleyans have in the past typically emphasized the pulpit over the sacraments. Although Wesleyan theology identifies these sacraments as a means of grace and accept many different forms or modes of these sacraments as legitimate, many members have tended to view them more as an opportunity for personal testimony. However, recent worship renewal has drawn the church to more of a balance between the preaching of the Word and the administering of the sacraments.

At their ordination, ministers in the Wesleyan Church are charged to preach the Word and administer the sacraments. In the life of the church, though, preaching is obviously the dominant assignment.

Like other churches in the Holiness movement, the Wesleyan Church is a non-sacramental denomination. The pulpit, not the Table, has always been central in the service, and priority is given to the sacred Word, rather than to sacred actions.

Still, the sacraments are not neglected or ignored. In Wesleyan congregations, the two historic Protestant sacraments are celebrated: baptism and the Lord's Supper. According to the Wesleyan _Discipline_, each is considered a means of grace, but the popular perception of the sacraments seems slanted more toward the understanding of it as personal testimony. God's presence is seldom associated with the sacraments, being acknowledged instead in the promise of his presence in corporate worship (Matt. 18:20) and in the moving of his Spirit in the services. (Not surprisingly, Wesleyans often sense that divine movement during the sacraments. Perhaps it is at this point that theology meets praxis.)

Baptism may be "the water that divides" for some. (the title of a study by Donald Bridge and David Phypers, _The Water That Divides_ [Downers Grove, Ill.: InterVarsity Press, 1977]), but not for Wesleyans. On the sacramental shoals of _who_ and *how,* Wesleyans steer a course that is intentionally inclusive. Baptism, with all its attendant controversies, is no potential barrier to fellowship in the church.

Both infant and believer's baptism are provided for in the Wesleyan *Discipline,* and both are consistent with the Wesleyan spirit. Infant baptism has always been affirmed in the Methodist family of churches; in the Twenty-Five Articles of Methodism, John Wesley specifically instructed that it was to be retained. Holiness churches in the Methodist tradition have continued that practice. Believer's baptism, on the other hand, is appropriate to the evangelistic impulse of the Wesleyan movement, particularly as the gospel is offered to those for whom infant baptism was not available in their own traditions.

In practice, however, believer's baptism is much more common in the Wesleyan Church, and paedobaptism is viewed with reservation. In fact, those previously baptized as infants are often rebaptized in the church, despite the decidedly un-Wesleyan theology behind such a practice. Even the church *Discipline,* which offers church members the right to have their infants baptized, describes baptism in its Articles of Religion as a sacrament "administered to believers" by which "believers declare their faith in Jesus Christ as Savior" (*The Discipline of the Wesleyan Church* [Indianapolis: Wesley Press, 1988], 27). It follows then that far more children are dedicated than are baptized in Wesleyan circles. (The preface to the ritual of "The Dedication and Baptism of Infants" is very Zwinglian, speaking of "dedicat[ing a child] through the sacrament of baptism." For many of these observations on the Wesleyan position on infant baptism, I am indebted to Rob L. Staples, *Outward Sign and Inward Grace: The Place of Sacraments in Wesleyan Spirituality* [Kansas City: Beacon Hill Press, 1991]).

As for *how,* baptism is available in all three modes—immersion, sprinkling, and pouring. Immersion is the most frequently practiced; pouring is by far the least. Whatever the mode, Christian baptism is a requirement for church membership, although in many congregations a new convert may actually be received into membership in anticipation of future baptism.

The Lord's Table is always open in the Wesleyan Church, and that phrase involves more than a universal invitation to all Christians, regardless of denominational affiliation. It also means that Wesleyans see Communion (to use its more common designation in the church) as an opportunity for evangelism, and thus the sacrament is open to repentant sinners. The invitation in the ritual is not only to "you who are walking in fellowship with God" but also to "you who do truly and earnestly repent of your sin and intend to lead a new life" (*Discipline* 404).

Communion is offered "at least once each three months" (*Discipline* 34), a schedule which ironically is indebted to Zwingli and not Wesley, who was a very frequent communicant. In keeping with the church's stand on abstinence from alcohol, grape juice is used in place of wine. Usually, the sacrament is received kneeling at the Communion rail.

Other sacred actions beyond the two sacraments find occasional usage in Wesleyan congregations. Anointing the sick is generally done on request, although at least one sizable church in the denomination schedules services for that purpose quarterly. (Medical and professional care are always seen as appropriate extensions of prayers for divine healing, if necessary.) Footwashing is not a Wesleyan tradition, but it has been employed in special contexts. Congregations that prepare their children for membership may use their reception ritual much like confirmation.

Another sacred action familiar to the entire church is ordination. The decision to ordain is made by a district conference of ministers and laity, not by a local church, and typically the ordination occurs at that same conference. (Ordained ministers were called *elders* until the terminology was changed at the 1992 General Conference.) Lay ministers may be commissioned to a variety of assignments in the church, with prescribed courses of study and rituals tailored to their callings.

Worship renewal is not widespread in the Wesleyan Church, but it is beginning to have a noticeable impact. Some congregations have increased the frequency of the Lord's Supper (usually to a monthly schedule). Expanded observance of the Christian year in the church is accompanied by increased opportunities for the sacrament. Variation on the customary wafer and individual cup at the Communion rail is no longer news in the pews. Wesleyans are becoming comfortable with alternative approaches, particularly intinction (dipping the bread into a common cup).

Without retreating from its historic emphasis on the Word read and preached, the Wesleyan Church's growing appreciation for sacred actions is a step toward a better worship balance.

Bob Black

134 ✦ WISCONSIN EVANGELICAL LUTHERAN SYNOD

The Wisconsin Evangelical Lutheran Synod has retained a fairly uniform observance of baptism and the Lord's Supper. Preparation for sacramental actions is strongly emphasized, particularly in instructing young people for confirmation. Many practices that can be traced to the movement's pietistic origins can still be found in contemporary Lutheran worship.

A visitor to the congregations that belong to the Wisconsin Evangelical Lutheran Synod might discover some differences in the way congregations conduct their public worship. Church members may even disagree over what is the primary objective of worship. The visitor would find no difference, however, in what these congregations and their members believe about the sacraments of baptism and the Lord's Supper and very little difference in how they use the sacraments.

This We Believe, a confessional statement accepted by the synod in 1967, reveals that the church body holds to the traditional Lutheran understanding of the sacraments:

We believe that God bestows all spiritual blessings upon sinners by special means, ordained by him. These are the means of grace, the gospel in Word and sacrament.

We believe that through the gospel of Christ's atoning sacrifice for sinners the Holy Spirit works faith in the heart of man, whose heart by nature is enmity against God. Scripture teaches that "faith comes from hearing the message, and the message is heard through the word of Christ" (Romans 10:17). This Spirit-wrought faith, or regeneration, brings about a renewal in man and makes of him an heir of eternal salvation.

We believe that also through baptism the Holy Spirit applies the gospel to sinful man, regenerating him (Titus 3:5) and cleansing him from all iniquity (Acts 2:38). The Lord points to the bless-

ing of baptism when he promises, "Whoever believes and is baptized will be saved" (Mark 16:16). We believe that the blessing of baptism is meant for all people (Matthew 28:19), including infants, who are sinful (John 3:6) and therefore need the regeneration effected through baptism.

We believe that all who partake of the sacrament of the Lord's Supper receive the true body and blood of Christ "in, with, and under" the bread and wine. This is true because, when the Lord instituted this sacrament, he said, "This is my body given for you. . . . This cup is the new covenant in my blood, which is poured out for you" (Luke 22:19-20). As we partake of his body and blood, given and shed for us, we by faith receive the comfort and assurance that our sins are indeed forgiven and that we are truly his own.

The need and power of baptism have been firmly implanted in the minds of Wisconsin Synod Lutherans. The parish pastor invariably brings along an application for baptism when he visits a new mother in the hospital. Many parents are so concerned about the baptisms of their newborn child that they request the child be baptized in the hospital. However, most babies are baptized in the worship assembly several weeks after birth. Adults who have not been baptized and have been led to confess Christ as Savior are baptized after they have completed a course of instruction. These baptisms are also performed most often in the regular service.

Since baptism was not historically a part of corporate worship and since its traditional order was composed in such a way as to be complete in itself, the traditional rite did not fit well into the Lutheran liturgical service. Its focus on the child and the child's parents and its inclusion and use of the Apostles' Creed (in question and answer form) and the Lord's Prayer (as a blessing) made it of a different cloth from the rest of the corporate worship rite. With Luther's understanding in mind, i.e., that confession and absolution are nothing else than a reliving of baptism, the synod's 1993 hymnal, _Christian Worship: A Lutheran Hymnal_, places the baptism rite in the general confession of the public service. The rite is congregational in focus. It does not address questions to the child nor expect answers from the child's sponsors. The Apostles' Creed and the Lord's Prayer function according to their regular use in the service.

Although they do not consider it a sacrament, Wisconsin Synod Lutherans have retained a strong attachment to confirmation. Most children receive doctrinal instruction during their early teenage years and are confirmed when they are able and willing to make a public confession of faith. The rite of confirmation used by the synod for many years was closely connected to baptism. Children were asked to "confirm the covenant which at your baptism you made with the Triune God." This emphasis on baptism as a two-sided covenant, very definitely a legacy of Lutheran pietism, was an embarrassment to most of the synod's pastors. Since the questions to the child have been eliminated from the baptism rite in *Christian Worship: A Lutheran Hymnal*, the difficult question in the confirmation order has been also deleted.

The instruction that precedes confirmation also prepares young adults for their reception of the sacrament of Holy Communion. There has been a strong emphasis on sacramental preparation in the synod. Members have been taught to understand what occurs at Communion, to examine themselves lest they come to the Lord's Table unrepentant, and to commune only with those who share the confessional Lutheran faith. The congregations of the synod offer the sacrament only to those in its fellowship, thus agreeing with the historic Lutheran practice of closed Communion. In an effort to make this practice a little less harsh sounding, some pastors refer to it as close Communion with the idea that those in Communion with a similar confession "are close to each other."

Although its confessional statements follow orthodox Lutheran patterns, many congregational practices recall the synod's pietistic roots. Less than ten percent of Wisconsin Synod congregations offer the sacrament every Sunday and festival; fully half celebrate it only once each month. Into the 1970s, some congregations still retained the custom of a quarterly Communion and often included the sacrament within an independent confessional service. The laity especially have seemed to feel a need for a close connection between personal confession and Communion. Thus, the congregational observance of the sacrament has tended to be less celebratory and more somber in character. It may be that these practices have combined with the church body's strong emphasis on the value of preaching to en-courage a rather infrequent reception; the average church member receives the sacrament only about four times a year.

For a number of years the church has been, for all intents and purposes, without a synodical agenda. *The Lutheran Agenda*, prepared in 1957 with the Lutheran Church—Missouri Synod, has been laid aside by most pastors because of its antiquated language. An agenda that serves *Christian Worship: A Lutheran Hymnal* should appear before the turn of the century. When this volume is in print, the Wisconsin Synod will again have a consistent set of rites for ordination, installation, dedication, and so on.

James P. Tiefel

135 ♦ An Alternative Approach to the Sacraments Among Free Churches

The following article is an example of a church in the free-church tradition that experienced a renewed focus on worship and the sacraments. This renewal centered around Communion. This church understands Communion as an occasion in which God mysteriously uses the ordinary things of life—the bread and wine—to meet the worshiper. With this understanding and the premise that the worshiper should be actively involved in worship, this church began to transform Communion from a somber occasion to a celebration of Christ's victory over death.

Our congregation consists primarily of college-educated people who are very comfortable with rational and academic discussions. Our faith, though, is limited by our minds. We can know God up to a certain point by using our intellect and scientific thinking processes. Beyond that, God meets us and touches our lives in places and ways that we cannot explain. This is because we worship a God who is beyond comprehension, reasons, and logic. We worship a God who continually defies the neat little categories into which we try to put him. There is a mystery about God that leaves us in awe and wonder at how and why God is involved in our lives.

The whole area of the sacraments is one such mystery. Our congregation celebrates the sacraments of baptism and Communion. These have to do with water, bread, and wine—common, ordinary things of life. Yet it is in these very ordinary things that the real presence of Christ is experienced and known. We come to God in the water and at the Table, and somehow God meets us!

Baptisms are generally performed once a year on Pentecost Sunday when we receive new members into our congregation. We have become convinced that the act of baptism is not merely the isolated act of one individual because God has called each of us to walk together as part of the church of God. Therefore, the implications of our baptisms, our commitments to Christ, must be lived out in the context of a community of believers.

Our practice and view of Communion has been evolving since our formation as a congregation nine years ago. The majority of our members came from a background where Communion was observed once a quarter and the mood was very somber. This was our starting place. We stayed in our seats, heads bowed low, as the wafers and disposable cups were passed down the rows. We were deep in thought and prayer as we examined the condition of our souls. But since we wanted our members to be active participants in worship, we now ask them to leave their seats, walk to the front, tear a piece of bread from the loaf, and dip it in the cup. As they do this, those holding the bread and cup call each person by name and say to that person, "Mary, the body of Christ broken for you; the blood of Christ shed for you." Our view as to what actually happens to the elements at this point falls somewhere between two poles of thought: We do not believe that the bread and wine actually become Christ's body and blood, nor do we believe that this act is just a memorial of Christ's death or an act of obedience.

The Communion is one of those mysteries for us—we believe that Christ is somehow present in this act of Communion and is at work in our individual lives and corporate life as a congregation. Coming to the Table has become a time to celebrate God's victory over death and sin in our world. The Eucharist is a meal that foreshadows the great banquet at the end of time when God shall reign. The Lord's Supper has become a time not only to recognize our frail condition but also to celebrate Christ and to come to him who alone can sustain and enable us to remain faithful to him. It has also become a time to celebrate each other in Holy Communion, a time to celebrate how Christ's blood has called together such a diverse group of people together to be his church, and a time to celebrate the love of God in our life together. It is a joy to watch people walk forward, take of the bread and cup, and realize, "This is my church family!"

Each time the welcome to the Table is extended, it is different. Sometimes we experience all those things that Communion has become for us. Other times, one facet speaks more clearly to us. Sometimes the meal is filled with joy; other times the mood of the meal is more reflective. However, Communion is no longer somber with the emphasis on ourselves and our sin. Communion has become a celebration of Christ! Our focus is turned to Christ, who by his grace invites us to the Table and by his grace meets us in the taking of the bread and cup. Our bodies feed on the simple bread and wine, but our hearts and spirits feed on Christ himself. We are nurtured and sustained by his life. The act is simple and straightforward, and done the same way each time. But the mystery is that we experience the love and grace of God over and over again in new ways and in deeper ways. This experience is the result of the supernatural work of God in these simple, ordinary things of life.

Not only did we ask our members to walk to the front to take Communion but we also began servicing Communion more frequently—once a month, instead of once a quarter. Now we serve Communion twice a month. Sharing in this meal more frequently did not diminish its significance in our life together, which we feared would happen. Instead, the frequency only served to heighten our sense of brokenness and neediness, and deepen our longing to come to Christ at the Table and to be ministered to by him. Coming to the Table has helped to build our sense of community and identity around the truth that is proclaimed at the Table—the truth of our sinful and lost condition and the truth of God's grace manifested in Jesus Christ's death on the cross for our sin. We are all sinful and in need of God's grace and redemption.

When the meal is over, we pass the peace, which proclaims the peace and reconciliation brought about by Christ's death on the cross. We greet each other, saying, "The peace of Christ be with you." As already described in an earlier volume, our first attempts at this were very stiff, formal, and awkward. Now the peace has evolved into a free, moving expression of a community that is centered around the worship and the truth of God.

Having celebrated the peace and community God has worked in our midst, we turn our hearts back to him in gratitude. We call it "Thanksgiving after Communion," where we worship God in song. Once a month during Communion, we have two elders, one situated on each side of the sanctuary, to be available to pray with anyone after he or she has taken Communion. This has proven to be a helpful time to care for individuals in our congregation.

It is very difficult to describe or explain how Communion has affected our life together. Although the preaching and teaching of God's Word clearly play a key role in shaping how we think about ourselves and about being in his church, Communion and worship have had just as great an influence in shaping how we *feel* about ourselves and towards each other. Communion has increased our awareness of how needy and dependent we are on Christ and each other if we are to be singularly devoted to God in this ungodly world. It is a neediness that is not only affirmed in our minds but also deeply felt in our hearts. As our understanding and practice of Communion continues to grow and evolve, we realize more and more that God is present and at work in our lives and life together in ways we will never be able to fathom or comprehend. Praise be to God who is not bound by the finiteness of our hands and minds!

Susie Wong

136 ♦ An Alternative Approach to the Sacraments among Pentecostal and Charismatic Churches

Although Pentecostals typically worship in a free style, they are by nature sacramentalists. They usually view sacramental actions as channels of divine power; however, they refuse to precisely define sacraments. Recently, some Pentecostal churches have adopted liturgies for use in their services and have moved to a higher view of the sacraments.

Pentecostals are by nature sacramentalists. Anointing with oil, prayer cloths, laying on of hands, footwashing, and other symbolic acts have been standard features of the movement since its inception, and its first major conflict involved an argument over the mode of baptism. The Pentecostals have always had a difficult time in either completely identifying or contrasting themselves with evangelicals. They never seem to completely fit despite their desire to do so. Actually they are closer to the Eastern churches in many of their theological presuppositions than they are to either Roman Catholic, evangelical, fundamentalist, or liberal Protestant churches. Pentecostals are mystics. They do not like to be pinned down on the specifics of where, how, and when grace is communicated. They usually go further than the evangelical idea of symbolism and tend to see sacramental actions as channels of divine power.

Popular Assembly of God pastor and writer Tommy Reid, speaking at the Communion service of a meeting of independent Pentecostal pastors, noted that in the Old Testament, after an animal was sacrificed, the blood was then sprinkled on the worshipers with the hyssop. He went on to say that while evangelicals were right in believing that the sacrifice of Christ is once and for all offered in the heavenlies and could not be repeated, they failed to recognize the Lord's strong words "This is my body; this is my blood." "At the Lord's table," Reid said, "the blood is brought down from the sacrifice and sprinkled on the worshipers. We participate in that sacrifice by faith." These would likely be strong words for believers from many evangelical traditions, but caused barely a ripple among Pentecostals. He was safe as long as he did not insist on a formal definition of real presence. Pentecostals, like Eastern Orthodox Christians, prefer experience to analysis. That is both their strength and their weakness.

This sort of thinking is having quite an impact on Pentecostal churches, however. Even though sacramental actions are not alien to the movement, Pentecostals have only lately begun to formally develop their theology on the sacraments and how they are to be practiced within the life of the church. One independent assembly, Christ Church, in Nashville, Tennessee, is a large Pentecostal church that works in a loosely knit network of several hundred like-minded assemblies. It has formally embraced a sacramental theology. The church has labored to keep alive its Pentecostal heritage, while recognizing the significance of formal rites. The church recognizes as sacraments water baptism, Communion, marriage, ordination, confirmation, the dedication of infants, the washing of feet, and the anointing of the sick. In the actual rites themselves, the church has borrowed rather freely from _The Book of Common Prayer_ and other sources, but has also developed ceremonies they believe to be compatible with their own heritage. Communion is served in the smaller chapel once a week and in the larger service once a month. On special occasions, such as Christmas Eve and Maundy Thursday, the sacraments are performed with a good deal more formality than at other times.

A major theological influence on Christ Church and its related congregations has been the catechism _Understanding God and His Covenants_ compiled by Patricia Gruits and Bethesda Christian Church in Detroit, Michigan—a church that also has roots in Pentecostalism but which has long been an advocate of sacramental theology and practice. Other major sources have been _For the Life of the World_ by Orthodox theologian Alexander Schmemann, _The Book of Common Prayer_, and C. S. Lewis's _Mere Christianity_. Lewis may seem out of context here, but his explanation of sacramental life was a vital turning point for many Pentecostals in their understanding of what transpires during sacramental acts.

Christ Church, like most Pentecostals involved in liturgical renewal, does not feel constrained to copy the style of older churches, though it gratefully acknowledges its debt to them. The music, art, and language of the rites of the church are adapted to meet the mood and need of the assembly. They use well-known gospel music, rhythm and blues, and Southern gospel as well as more traditional music to accompany the rites and ordinances of the church. They have discovered that Pentecostals rarely complain about the use of liturgy or a shift in theology concerning the sacraments if they can worship with music styles with which they are accustomed and if they are led into worship that brings them into the presence of God.

The leaders of the church attempt to prepare the worshiper for the sacraments by discussing often their worldview. They contend that a Christian worldview is one that views this universe as a small, isolated part of a much larger one. Sin separates our human race from interacting with the broader universe, but the sacraments are "windows in the wall" that allow us by faith to see and experience that place in which we will soon live. These experiences are life changing because they encourage the development of our eternal selves. A song often sung at the church during Communion says it all:

> We come to your table Lord, praying for living word.
> We on the earth, with heavenly host, gather to praise Thee.
> Walls cannot separate in this most sacred place
> Time now suspends, world without end, let it begin.
>
> We lift up this bread to Thee, Lord of all majesty.
> Father on bended knee, we pray for our unity.
> Spirit breathe through this wine,
> pierce through the walls of time,
> heaven now waits, we take our place,
> Kingdom of grace.
>
> This is a timeless space
> a kingdom of boundless grace.
> Saints gone before bow to the Lord,
> give praise with the living.
> Join now to celebrate, death cannot separate
> Life we receive, Lord we believe,
> grant us your peace.

"Kingdom of Grace" by Dan Scott and Nathan Digesare
[Star Song Music/Forefront Communications]

The Pentecostal movement as a whole is beginning to notice that a new generation of leaders are very attracted to a higher view of the sacraments in both theology and practice. While this sometimes worries older leaders of the movement, it is becoming apparent that for the most part those who are concerned with liturgical renewal in the movement have no intention of leaving behind their Pentecostal heritage. In fact, a growing understanding of the sacramental aspects of their faith represents to them a further development of seminal ideas that have been in the movement all along.

Dan Scott

137 • ALTERNATIVE VIEWS OF THE SACRAMENTS IN SEEKERS' SERVICE/BELIEVERS' WORSHIP

Willow Creek and other seeker-driven churches purposely avoid any liturgy or other sacred actions to demonstrate *the simplicity of the gospel and to draw in nonbelievers. Like other Protestant churches, Willow Creek views baptism and Communion as ordinances. At the services dedicated to these ordinances, the church emphasizes commitment to God, to the church, and to each other.*

Resources for Sacraments, Ordinances, and Sacred Actions

Like most Protestant churches in America, Willow Creek recognizes only baptism and Communion as ordinances required of Christians by the Scriptures. While these may be and have been referred to as sacraments by leadership in the church, they are not seen to have the same grace-imparting power as other churches believe. Essentially, they are symbolic acts of spiritual realities and truths. No other sacred actions are practiced or performed since Willow Creek is a non- and inter-denominational church and wants to provide as clear an offer of salvation to seekers as possible.

Central to Willow Creek's teaching on baptism and Communion is commitment: to God, to the church, and to each other. As Bill Hybels notes, these acts separate the "tire kickers" from those truly serious about the change in their lives. The church, however, wants to be sensitive to the many Catholics and Lutherans—either current or former—who worship at Willow Creek also. Many are refreshed by the spontaneity and lack of liturgy they find in the services.

Baptism classes and services are held twice a year (winter and spring) at Willow Creek. Members or people seeking membership in the church may participate. The mode of baptism is not as important as the fact that the believer is performing a public act of commitment and confession. Both sprinkling and immersion are practiced, depending on the believer's preference and on the opportunity to use the large lake on the campus.

Believers are taught that baptism is a symbol of a resurrection into a new life, imbued with new power to combat sin and to become the new person in Christ that they are meant to be. Besides instruction in the essentials of the Christian faith, they must undergo an interview with a church leader to ascertain their commitment to Christianity. After this, the whole church is called to witness the public decision of hundreds of believers

during a scheduled New Community service where teaching pastors administer baptism to new believers.

As with baptism, Communion is described as a symbolic act of commitment to Christ and his work performed because Christ ordered the apostles to remember him through it. The church does not advocate the idea of it being a literal sacramental act for the same reasons that this position has been held since the Protestant Reformation.

Again, as with baptism, Communion plays a natural part of a particular worship service, which includes much singing and encouragement to realize the seriousness of what Christ did for his church. Listeners are warned that no one should partake who is not part of the Christian fellowship or does not understand Communion's significance. Volunteer ushers from the service ministry distribute cut squares of bread and small cups of grape juice, which represent the bread and wine of Communion. There is a period of silent prayer and reflection, as well as Scripture reading, and then all participants take Communion together. Using the accounts of the Last Supper in the Gospels and 1 Corinthians, one of the teaching pastors will lead the congregation in corporate worship and Communion. The Communion service is held every second week of the month during a Wednesday or Thursday night service and also on the following Sunday morning for those who could not attend the first service. The service normally ends in songs of worship.

While these practices are not sacramental, they are taught to be vitally important to being a biblical Christian. Submission to the Lord in these areas prepares the way for a lifetime of freedom to live as God teaches. Further workshops and programs are available at Willow Creek to educate new and old believers about the gifts that God has given to his church for its strength and purpose.

The church is very open about empowering lay ministries, drawing on the resources of hundreds of qualified volunteers. There is a screening process to determine the best place for them to serve in the church, and there are plenty of opportunities. Elders will also meet with members who are sick to pray over them and anoint them with oil as a symbol of healing.

Willow Creek has the vision to be a new kind of church for America, one that is seeker driven. Any unnecessary barriers are removed to make way for the teaching and living of the gospel. The church purposely avoids any liturgy or other sacred actions to show the simplicity of the gospel. However, Willow Creek stresses the commitment of the believer to the church through confession of faith, evangelism, financial contribution, ministry, and submission to the elders. Willow Creek wants to be a church without walls for seeker and believer alike.

Steve Burdan

PART TWO

History and Theology of Sacred Actions

Christian worship finds its meaning in the death and resurrection of Jesus Christ. These events take on significance for worshipers today through not only the proclamation of the gospel of Christ, but also through the sacred actions of worship. Called *sacraments* in some traditions and *ordinances* in others, these actions bear witness to the Lord of the church and testify to the world the Good News of Jesus Christ. The following chapters outline some varied perspectives according to which worshipers in every tradition can examine their practice of the sacred actions of worship. They challenge worshipers to realize the importance of active participation in worship, to understand the power of ritual action in shaping faith and witnessing to the world, and to claim their place in the long line of Christians throughout history who have practiced the sacred actions of worship.

◈ TWO ◈

The Significance of Sacred Actions

Rituals are part of every human culture. Judaism was no exception. Jesus chose the setting of a Jewish ritual meal to express explicitly the meaning of his impending death as a sacrifice for the "life of the world" (John 6:51). After his resurrection, his followers took over the ritual structure of that meal together with the new meaning with which Christ had filled it: Christ's sacrifice once and for all put an end to the need for bloody animal sacrifice (e.g., Heb. 9). As Christianity ceased to be a persecuted Jewish sect and moved into the center of the late Roman culture, Christian liturgy and ritual incorporated elements of Roman public ceremony. The meaning Christians attached to these ritual actions was, however, purely Christian: In his death and resurrection, Jesus Christ fulfilled God's hidden yet revealed (mysterious) plan for the salvation of the world. In Christian ritual worship, members of Christ's body participate in the life of Christ.

138 ◆ AN INTRODUCTION TO RITUAL IN WORSHIP

All Christian communions, from Orthodox churches to charismatic congregations, participate in ritual when they worship. Whether one makes the sign of the cross or raises hands in worship, a ritual action takes place. Why some rituals are important and how we can deepen our worship through them is a matter of concern among those engaged in worship renewal. In the following paragraphs, a Roman Catholic writer addresses some of these issues.

In the late twentieth century, in many different religious circles, we hear the cry, "Our religious rituals are not working." From both the right and the left the cry is the same. Yet from outside the Roman Catholic circle our Christian brothers and sisters have begun to recognize our deep ritual heritage. Why is this cry all too true? What shall we do?

Some of our present rituals (notably the Eucharist) have been robbed of their power and depth. In an attempt to clarify and purify our rituals to return them to their simplicity and integrity (a noble project), we threw away too much. We made

them understandable rather that performable. We cut out the duplication of ritual which allowed for depth response and substituted an excess of words (so that we might more clearly understand the rites). We are left with superficial cerebral rites that can't bear the weight of true worship, rites which can't communicate at the level of faith, rites which educate more than appeal for devotional response.

On the other side, our present rituals, even those which have structural depth, often lack faith commitments. We as a community don't seem to understand our role in worship, and as a result, we don't know what to do with the ritual we have. At worship, people must pray and share their faith. Ritual will not pray for people. Without human spirit, ritual is meaningless or a lie. In the past, ritual has been used to bolster weak faith or supply it (as in the later stages of the early catechumenal development). Ultimately this has not worked! It will work no better today! The renewal of ritual must be accompanied by the renewal of faith and the renewal of faith must become a strong criterion for ritual adaptation. As part of this renewal, special ministers of worship, from presider to greeter, must learn their roles well. They must learn how to communicate through the ritual and not around it.

As a result of the lack of structural depth and the lack of faith content, some people have turned to substituting their own ritual creations, but the results have generally proven no better. Historical connection is often sacrificed while faith content still remains minimal. The congregation's attention is focused on the novelty, and the congregation might seem satisfied for a time, but the new quickly grows old, the entertainment subsides, and the central point is missed: The congregation does not adequately respond with faith.

A move from the left might suggest that since our present rituals don't work, there might not be a real need for any ritual. This side sees the importance of faith content, but fails to see the value of ritual structure. What will hopefully be learned soon is that without religious ritual, worship becomes ethical behavior, interiorized but also intellectualized, which quickly ceases to be worship.

_____ Concluding Guidelines _____

The insights to be kept in mind as we approach ritual are:

(1) There is a tremendous need for good religious ritual, and this ritual must be related to an awakening of faith among the worshipers.

(2) We need to take another look at what was "thrown out" in the revision of our present rituals. Perhaps some of this might be reintroduced (e.g., ritual repetition, movement, and gesture).

(3) We need to move toward ritual adaptation that preserves the simplicity of the ritual, rather than creating a screen of secondary rituals that diffuse the central mystery. The fullness of sign, the fullness of gesture, and the fullness of faith response must be given attention.

(4) We need to study the church's ritual history to find out what has worked and what has not, to discover central Christian dimensions behind the ritual activity we do.

(5) We need to study our cultures to find the naturally symbolic structures for faith response in them and to discover the important Christian needs in today's world. At the same time, we must remember that religious ritual does not merely mean Christianized culture, but it always stands in critique of our culture.

(6) We need to understand ourselves as sym-bolic people, as ritual people, as people with a history and a destiny, and as people who march in the middle of a long procession of saints and sinners on our way home.

Good religious ritual is born, not made. Its content is renewed in Christian commitment; its structure is discovered on the level of faith. It critiques itself from the inside, reflecting on its own historical development. It adapts itself to the culture and society in which it lives. Treat it carefully: the future of the church depends on it.

Bob Creslak[1]

139 ✦ HISTORICAL ORIGINS AND DEVELOPMENT OF RITUAL IN WORSHIP

Christian ritual grew out of Jewish ritual—whether the Jewish table rites that provided the setting for Jesus' announcement of his self-sacrifice in what became the Christian Eucharist, or the Jewish ritual of proselyte baptism. Graeco-Roman ritual contributed much of the liturgical ceremony that developed as Christianity was transformed from a persecuted Jewish sect to the cultural center of medieval Europe.

Ritual in its most general sense refers to an agreed-upon pattern of action. Religious ritual is a corporate symbolic activity in which people engage when they worship. It has been a part of all human cultures.

The earliest actual evidence for religious ritual dates from the third interglacial period (180,000 to 120,000 B.C.) and was left by prehistoric hunters of cave bears, who apparently dedicated the brain and the bone marrow of their kill to the dispenser of hunting fortune. The famous Ice Age cave paintings of large animals (approximately 10,000 B.C.) are generally believed to be evidence of ritual activity in connection with hunting. There are two major types of such activity: (1) sacrifice, in which the death of the animal is encompassed within a ritual in which its life is returned to the divine dispenser of hunting fortune, and permission is given to the hunting community to eat the meat; and (2) initiation, in which prospective hunters are taught the skills and lore they will need to become actual hunters, and the bonds uniting them into a single hunting band are established and nurtured. Such rituals exist even today among so-called primitive peoples.

The Roots of Christian Ritual

Christian ritual is historically rooted in Jewish ritual. In first-century Judaism there was an established sacrificial *cultus* in the Jerusalem temple. Jewish sacrifice was similar in form to Hellenistic Greek sacrifice. In both, an animal (or other offering) was offered to the deity. The animal was killed. Portions were burned upon the altar (the god's portion) and the rest was eaten in a festive meal by the worshipers. The burning of incense was often a part of these rituals. As the smoke of the incense rose to heaven, so the prayers of the worshipers were believed to rise (Psalm 141:2). Incense also served the practical purpose of covering the smell of the burning meat. Acts of ritual sacrifice were seen by Christians as fulfilled and abolished by the once-for-all sacrifice of Christ, but the theology of sacrifice continued to influence both Christian worship and theology. In 1 Corinthians 5:7, Paul identifies Christ with the *pesach*, the paschal lamb, the sacrifice eaten by the participants as the central feature of the Passover meal.

More significant for Christian ritual was the Jewish domestic celebration of a ritual common meal at festivals and on the Sabbaths. From its roots in the Jewish religious meal, itself a descendant of the primitive sacrificial meals, the Christian Eucharist, or Lord's Supper, developed. According to the New Testament accounts (Mark 14:22-25; Matt. 26:26-29; Luke 22:15-20; 1 Cor. 11:23-26), Jesus made use of two standard elements of the Jewish ritual meal in instituting the Christian Eucharist: the blessing and breaking of bread at the beginning of the meal, and the thanksgiving over a cup of wine at its close. He identified these elements with his body and blood. Probably in the late first or early second century, these ritual actions were separated from the actual meal, which Christians continued to celebrate for centuries under the name of *agape*, and they were joined to a service of prayer and Bible reading apparently derived from the worship of the synagogue.

The Christian rite of baptism is derived from the baptism of John the Baptist and probably from the Jewish ritual of proselyte baptism. This began as a ceremonial purification for converts of both sexes, since they had previously not observed the Jewish laws of ritual cleanliness. According to the Talmud, the proselyte emerged from the water a newborn babe and began a new life within the covenant. The ritual model for Christian baptism became the Gospel accounts of the baptism of Jesus (Mark 1:9-11 and parallels). The candidate went down into the water and was immersed while responding to questions concerning his or her belief in the triune God. Since Jesus was anointed with the Holy Spirit as he emerged from the water, the new Christian was anointed with the spiritual oil called *chrism* (or *myron*), symbolizing the anointing with the Spirit and participation in the Christ, the Anointed One. Just as Jesus was proclaimed to be the Son of God by the voice of the Father, the neophyte was proclaimed to be the child of God by adoption and grace by the bishop or elder, usually accompanied by the laying of hands on the new Christian.

While the rituals of Christian initiation derive from Jewish sources, the terminology of the pagan mystery religions was often used to explain the rites to converts, as preachers sought to use ideas and terms familiar to the converts as a basis for teaching Christian faith and practice in the fourth century, the great period of conversion from paganism. The mysteries were the great personal religious rituals of the Hellenistic world. Odo Casel's classic definition is: "The mystery is a sacred ritual action in which a saving deed is made present through the rite; the congregation, by performing the rite, take part in the saving act, and thereby win salvation" (Odo Casel, *The Mystery of Christian Worship and Other Writings* [Westminster, Md.: Newman Press, 1962], 54). The one clear borrowing of Christianity from the mysteries was the tradition of the *disciplina arcani*, keeping the content of Christian rituals secret from unbelievers.

Thus, the principal Christian ritual actions of washing in water, eating bread, and drinking wine, derive from Jewish ritual practice, with which both Jesus and the apostolic church were familiar. Ultimately, these rituals go back to the primitive rituals of initiation and the common meal.

Secondary Ritual Actions

Over the centuries, Christianity has acquired a number of secondary ritual practices, many of which are dependent upon the cultural contexts in which Christianity has spread. The oldest rituals go back to the first-century church and are derived from the traditions of synagogue and family worship and personal prayer. These traditions include the reading aloud of passages from the Scripture according to a fixed lectionary, responsive prayer between the presider and congregation, and the changing of prayers. The kiss of peace was exchanged by members of the first-century church. It is mentioned four times in the Pauline corpus (Rom. 16:16; 1 Cor. 16:20; 2 Cor. 13:12; 1 Thess. 5:26). Paul assumed that the readers were accustomed to its use. By the second century, we hear of the newly baptized being greeted by the kiss of peace, and are told that they were not permitted to exchange it with anyone before their baptism. In societies such as our own in which a kiss is not our customary greeting, various attempts have been made to substitute handshakes, bows, formal embraces, or hugs.

The adoption of Christianity as the religion of the Roman Empire introduced a number of secondary ceremonies clearly grounded in Roman customs. Christian bishops were given the rank of magistrates by the emperor, and their use of purple to signify this fact is a trivial, though long-lasting trace of this heritage. As the Gospel book was brought to the *ambo* (a lectern or pulpit) for the reading of the Gospel, burning torches and incense were carried before it to symbolize the living presence of Christ in the midst of the faithful, and the people stood to honor the presence of the Word of God. These actions were the external signs associated with the movement of the Roman emperor through the streets of the city.

Later, other aspects of court ceremonial were introduced into Western Christian worship. The altar was compared to the throne of the earthly emperor, and reverences, such as genuflections and prostrations, which were expected in the presence of the imperial majesty, were adopted as appropriate to the presence of the heavenly King. Eastern churches placed the mosaics of the *Pantokrator* (Christ enthroned in glory, wearing the robes of the Byzantine emperor) high on the wall of the apse, where it dominated worship. The beauty of the buildings and of the worship itself, with its use of Byzantine court ceremonial, came to symbolize the glory of God. Later, for those living in Moslem lands, participation in worship was both a reminder of the glory that had been theirs in Constantinople and a foretaste of the glory of the heavenly realm, of which the church building was the visible symbol.

Much of this secondary ritual has been abandoned by Christians who no longer live in those cultures. The conviction that Christianity is a universal faith prompts Christians to believe that they must be able to find appropriate expression for their faith in any human culture, and attempts are frequently made to inculturate Christian worship into the many cultures in which it exists.

Leonel L. Mitchell

140 ◆ THEOLOGY OF RITUAL IN JEWISH AND EARLY CHRISTIAN WORSHIP

The preceding paragraphs describe the development of early Christian rituals. The meaning, i.e., the theological significance, of the rituals connected with the Jewish Passover/Christian Eucharist, Christian baptism, the sign of the cross, and other ceremonies is explained in the following paragraphs.

Religious rituals are corporate symbolic actions in which people engage when they worship. The theological principle underlying ritual worship is that our principal access to the spiritual is through the outward and visible. Even the most spiritual ideas must be expressed in outward words or actions, which are almost necessarily symbolic. Love, for example, is expressed by symbolic words and actions, that is, by ritual acts. For Christians the supreme example of this outward and visible expression of spiritual reality is the incarnation of Christ, the Word made visible and tangible.

One of the most ancient ritual practices which we know of is the common meal held by a family or clan, not simply to assuage hunger, but to commune with the divine powers outwardly symbolized by the food which was eaten. Primitive theological reflection on this ritual suggested either that the divine powers were guests at the meal, or that the powers were the hosts. A third theory suggested that the divine powers resided in the food itself.

In early Judaism, three types of sacrifice existed. In the first, the entire sacrificial meal was eaten by the worshipers, e.g., the Passover (*pesach*). Theologically, this meal was understood to signify the total dependence of the people on Yahweh and the divine provision of food and all their needs. In the most common type of sacrifice (*zebach*), a portion of the food was burned on

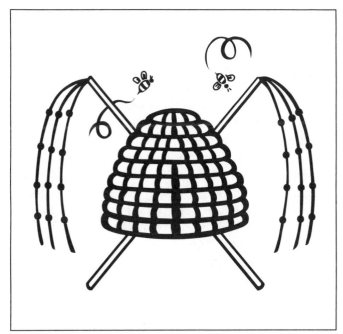

St. Ambrose. *The symbol of St. Ambrose, Bishop of Milan in the fourth century, is the beehive (a symbol of eloquence).*

the altar and a portion was eaten by the worshipers. This action was understood to be the sharing of a meal with Yahweh, theologically signifying the union and communion of God with the people. One sub-type of this sacrifice, the sacrifice of thanksgiving (*zebach todah* in Hebrew, or *thusia eucharistica* in Greek) clearly influenced early Christian understanding of the Eucharist. In the third type (*'olah*), the entire meal was burned on the altar. Theologically, this sacrifice was a gift to Yahweh, usually to give thanks for benefits received.

The purification rites of Yom Kippur involved the purification of the temple, the priesthood, and the whole people with the blood of sacrificial animals poured out before the *mercy seat* in the inner sanctuary of the temple, the Holy of Holies. The blood, symbolizing life, was seen as washing away the impurities. Hebrews interprets the sacrifice of Christ and the participation of Christians in it in terms of the rites of Yom Kippur and the *zebach todah*.

Lord's Supper

Paul, in 1 Corinthians 11:26, proclaims a connection between participation in the Lord's Supper and the death of Christ. Ritually, this is the theology of the Jewish sacrifice. To eat the flesh

of the sacrificial animal was to participate in the sacrifice and to commune with God. The bread of the Eucharist was theologically identified by Christ with his body, so for Christians to partake in the Eucharist is to be united with Christ in the power of his sacrifice.

The command, "Do this in the remembrance of me," in the synoptic Gospels reflects the Hebrew concept *zikkaron* (*anamnesis* in the Greek New Testament). It recalls the words of the Passover *haggadah* (the interpretive speech that began each Passover liturgy): "In every generation let each [person] look on himself as if he came forth from Egypt. . . . It was not only our fathers the Holy One, blessed be he, redeemed, but us as well did he redeem along with them." This idea is significant in contemporary liturgical theology. We who partake of Holy Communion are participants in the mighty acts of God in Christ by which we are saved, performed once for all in the past but made present to us in their ritual anamnesis.

Baptism

The major Christian theological understandings of baptism are Pauline (Rom. 6:3-11) and Johannine (John 3:1-16), while the ritual practice has traditionally followed the synoptic accounts of the baptism of Jesus (Mark 1:9-11 and parallels). The Pauline and Johannine theologies are usually seen as complementary.

Water in rituals is almost always purifying, destroying, and also life-giving. It symbolizes both the dissolution of what is and the renewal and rebirth of what shall be, as in the Flood and the passage through the Red Sea. To go down into the water is to die. To come up out of the water is to be born again, or to be raised from the dead. To go down into the water confessing the name of the Father, Son, and Holy Spirit, or that Jesus Christ is Lord, then, is to be buried with Christ in his death. To come up out of the water is to participate in his resurrection. An effect of this ritual death and rebirth is that the neophyte is theologically a new person. As Paul says, "It is no longer I who live, but it is Christ who lives in me" (Gal. 2:20, NRSV). This newborn person in Christ is therefore free from sin.

The other traditional ritual acts associated with baptism are the signing of the neophyte with the cross, anointing with chrism, and the laying on of hands. Theologically, the signing with the cross is a symbol of belonging to Christ. It is identified with the seal placed on the forehead of the saved in Revelation 7:3. The anointing with chrism speaks (1) of union with the anointed Messiah, (2) of participation in Jesus' anointing with the Holy Spirit at his baptism (Mark 1:10, Luke 4:18, Acts 10:38), and (3) of participation in the royal priesthood of the church (1 Pet. 2:9), following the example of the anointing of kings and priests in Israel. Although individual theologians may emphasize one meaning, all three are a part of the tradition. The laying on of hands is a multivalent ceremony, identified with ordination, healing, and blessing. Its use in baptism (or confirmation) probably combines its traditional religious use as a gesture of blessing and its use in classic Roman adoption ceremonies, where it accompanied the father's declaration that the one adopted was henceforth his child. It was identified in baptism with the voice of God the Father proclaiming, "You are my Son, the Beloved" (Mark 1:11, NRSV).

In a similar way, other ritual actions are identified as outward signs of particular spiritual benefits in which the worshipers' use of the ritual action makes them partakers.

Leonel L. Mitchell

141 ✦ WORSHIP AS A PERFORMATIVE ACT

Worship is a powerful and world-changing activity for Christian believers. When Christians worship, their view of the world is transformed and God's kingdom is made manifest. The following article examines the power of the worship event from a philosophical and social scientific point of view. These perspectives, when paired with the theological perspectives described throughout this volume, teach us about the significance of ritual action in the life of the Christian community.

The notion of the performative act is receiving the attention of those who study liturgy and worship. Essentially, the term *performance* or *performative* as applied to liturgical ritual refers to an exploration of the rite as it is enacted. Because the meaning of liturgical events is found both in the words expressed and in the actions enacted, it is useful to examine the performative from both of these perspectives. Each of these will be explored here, but only briefly.

The Performative Utterance

The English philosopher J. L. Austin first developed a theory of the *performative* as applied to language in a book entitled *How to Do Things with Words* (2d ed., Cambridge, Mass.: Harvard Univ. Press, 1975). His book laid much of the ground work for future reflection in the area of language and performance theory through a key insight into the relationship between meaning and text. He realized that words could *do* something. When a minister declares a couple married, that minister is not reporting to them that they are married or describing marriage to them. He is performing a marriage. In such instances, to speak is to do. Even statements *do* something. The simple assertion, "the temperature is seventy degrees," is more than a mere transmission of information; it is an act. In the act of uttering, a relationship is established between the speaker and hearer. Thus, the object of linguistic performative studies is not concerned with the structure of a sentence but with the emergence of an utterance in a speech situation. That is to say, the performative utterance does more than simply transmit information. Language establishes a state of affairs in the act of communicating. Theorists have coined the word *speech-act* to convey this sense of an intimate connection between speaking and doing.

Speech-act theory quickly gained the attention of those who study liturgy because it understands all speaking as *doing* something, or causing an effect. Thus, liturgical speech affects the relationships among the participants in the liturgical action, not by putting thoughts into words, but by establishing a framework for social interaction. This suggests a wider application of the word *text* to liturgy than is commonly understood. While one may examine ritual manuals in order to recognize how the liturgical books describe a celebration, it is becoming increasingly apparent that these verbal descriptions are merely summaries or idealized *scripts* of liturgical events as they are regularly celebrated. Therefore these manuals must be appreciated in relationship to the whole network of intentions that must be taken into account in order for the meaning of the rite to emerge.

The *language* of liturgy in this wider usage does not operate in the same way as ordinary human speech. It is not primarily concerned with conveying individual thoughts or intentions. Rather, it displays observable repetition in conventional structure and forms precisely because it is ritual language. By ritual, I mean the performance of more or less formal or conventional acts. Ritual by its language naturally has a social character. Ritual is a social performance and therefore its language is never individualistic or private. It carries an indelible social or communal stamp. By performing the repeated words of the liturgy, worshipers do not communicate thoughts or express private feelings. Rather, they enact something in a social context. The language of liturgy establishes conventional social forms.

For a minister or presider to say, "I baptize you in the name of the Father, and of the Son, and of the Holy Spirit," or "This is my body," is not to tell the worshiping assembly something that it did not know before; it is to enact these conventional forms for the purpose of identifying this group as a community of faith. Through the performance of these forms, an authentic affirmation of the enacted community is realized. Liturgical language is first and foremost an act; it does not describe or inform at the risk of weakening the liturgical act itself. Individuals embody these forms in order to establish their membership in the community, and through this collective embodiment the community itself is recognized and realized.

As the forms of liturgical language are conventional, so are its effects. The ritual _text_ accomplishes its end through the very performance. A couple intending to witness their love for one another in the marriage ritual knows the intended outcome in advance. The same holds true for the assembly that witnesses to their pledges of love. For the rite of marriage to be established (that is, for the change in social status to be affected), all present must conform to the forms of the rite. Everyone must play their proper part. The presider or minister must be recognized by the faith community as a duly authorized leader of that community. Someone not properly designated as the leader in that community or someone from outside of the community cannot accomplish the task. On the other hand, the couple must be free to marry, publicly declare their love for one another, and follow the forms of the marriage rite. They cannot convey their love for one another in private or create their own forms and assert that such a ceremony constitutes the proper form of marriage.

In liturgical worship, the act of acceptance on the part of all present constitutes a public act of faith. While there may be significant disparity between the public act of worship and individuals' subjective attitudes toward that act, it is the public performance of the rite that is most significant. To participate in liturgy is to conform to the religious identity expressed in the performance. By participating in a rite, individuals automatically embrace the ritual's obligations by enacting the identity expressed in the ritual performance itself. For example, an individual who is duly married may immediately engage in marital infidelity. This does not mean the rite was ineffective. On the contrary, by uttering the marriage promises and taking on the forms of the marriage rite, the married partners assume a social contract and come under its social obligations and sanctions. By entering into marriage, individuals are changed regardless of their subjective attitude toward the rite precisely because their situation in the social and public sphere is transformed by means of the performance of the rite.

The Performative Event

Many people engaged in critical liturgical reflection have come to realize that it is no longer adequate to simply examine the texts and rubrics of ritual in order to understand what a liturgy means. It is becoming increasing apparent that comparing liturgical texts and deriving one's theological interpretation of a liturgical rite based on those texts is an inadequate method for explaining what happens during a liturgical event. That is to say that the truth and effectiveness of what one claims in a theology of liturgy and sacrament can be either confused, misconstrued, or altogether obscured by concerns that have, at best, marginal claims to the deeper intentions of the liturgical act. For example, in the liturgical rite of marriage, some Christian traditions claim that the true ministers of the rite are the bride and groom themselves—that the presiding official serves only as a formal witness. Yet, multiple observations of marriage celebrations within these traditions often indicate that despite all claims to the contrary, the presiding official operatively functions as the true minister and guarantor of the transaction, with the bride and groom in a subordinate role. Attentiveness, therefore, to the liturgical event is critical because the actual _doing_ of liturgy may reveal a theology quite different from the explanation of the liturgical event. This approach to the performative takes seriously the actual experience of the liturgical celebration.

Some ritual theorists and social anthropologists have criticized the linguistic approach to the performative because of its emphasis on the primacy of ritual belief over ritual behavior. By suggesting that ritual enactment is only for the purpose of constituting a social group, these theorists contend that many of the marginalized individuals within the group often get overlooked. Women, strangers, people of color, non-ministers, the destitute—to give a few examples—may be allowed to participate in the liturgy while at the same time being excluded as proper subjects of the liturgy. Ritual establishes not only a group but a particular kind of group. Theorists concerned with the cultural performance of ritual argue that all rituals, including what we call the more traditional liturgies operate out of their own cultural context and therefore contain situational and political agendas that are often implicitly present in a ritual's performances. Because each ritual performance endorses certain intentional patterns for the group, many of these conventional forms may include patterns which suppress certain individuals within the group—patterns which are continually enacted, reinforced, and sanctioned by means of the ritual performance itself. Theorists concerned with the liturgy action, therefore, typically confront theoretical notions of the ritual with questions from the liturgy as it is enacted in order to discover the incongruities that exist between professed and observed ritual behavior.

Performance and Ritual Criticism

Liturgical theologians have been concerned with the boundaries of experience from which we look for the meaning and intention in liturgical ritual. Performative theory submits that these boundaries need to be greatly expanded beyond the areas and disciplines from which we might ordinarily inquire. The more established methods of liturgical research, such as the analysis and comparison of liturgical texts, the historical evolution of the rites, the theological and institutional pronouncements concerning these rites, and the cultural adaptations of ritual patterns, become focused in actual celebrations. Those who partici-

pate in liturgical rituals more or less unconsciously take on the patterns and intentions of the liturgical event by observing and listening, by interaction with others through responding, moving, gesturing, singing, and so forth in the collective ritual experience. Performative theory simply attempts to make more explicit this unconscious process.

To be able to discern the meaning and intention of a particular liturgical space means that one must be concerned with more than what is said about the space. It demands that critical questions be raised about how the liturgical space actually functions and affects the participants—of what things the space allows them to do and not do. Similar questions could be raised about the arrangement of the space. How do the furnishings function: To demarcate space? For what purpose? To suggest differences between *sacred* and *profane* areas? To provide a *non-intrusive space* for private worship or promote interactive space for a worshiping assembly? Does a free-standing reredos serve to bring visual focus to the sanctuary space or, because the presider's chair is placed in front of it, does it serve to highlight the role of the presider? Performative analysis trains a critical eye for such spatial relationships and a critical mind to ask the appropriate questions.

The choreography of liturgical actions, interactions, and gestures within the ritual expression are also suitable subjects of performative analysis. How is the liturgical assembly configured? Is the assembly perceived as subject of the liturgical action with ministers facilitating that action? Or is it configured as a ministerial elite with the assembly as passive observers? Is it configured to facilitate multifocused leadership that distributes roles, power, and wisdom among the members of the assembly? Performative theory focuses on the intentionality of these relationships. How are liturgical actions done? By whom? Deliberately? Casually? What is the relationship between the spoken words and the enacted gestures? What does the quality of embodiment say about the person who embraces these liturgical actions?

Furthermore, liturgical objects and art are subject to performative analysis. What do liturgical objects and art communicate about the community of which they are a part? How do they speak to this community? What do they say to others not associated with this community? How are liturgical artifacts connected to the action of the liturgical rite?

Performative questions can also be asked of music in the liturgy. Is liturgical music a matter for each individual's taste? Is music in the liturgy meant to trigger sentimentality or is its purpose to entertain? What is the function of music in the liturgy? What is the relationship between the text of music and its somatic effects—its pitch, timbre, rhythm, volume, and so on? What is the relationship between the music and the liturgical structure of the rite to which it is associated? Can liturgical music be completely variable or are there some relatively fixed elements that make it proper to the liturgy? Who sings—and who does not? Why? For whom is the music written? What needs are being met? Whose needs are being met and why?

To study liturgical performance is to realize that the actual experience of a celebration carries within itself a whole series of critical questions about the meaning and intention of a rite which are beyond the competence that descriptions of that rite provide. Furthermore, performative theory suggests that by attentiveness to the enacted liturgy, our perspective on what the ritual *means* and its intention will not only be disclosed to us, but broadened, as well as questioned, and ultimately transformed.

Paul Feela

142 ♦ RECOVERING SYMBOLISM IN WORSHIP

The concern of this article is to focus on symbolism as a medium through which the gospel of reconciliation may be communicated within the Christian community through worship.

The Place of Symbolism in Worship

It is generally recognized that a symbol both points beyond itself and participates in that which it symbolizes.

In this sense the church itself is a symbol of the kingdom. It is not the kingdom itself, but it *points* to the kingdom and *participates* in the kingdom. The church is the presence of the kingdom in the world. The church is the visible expression of the restored creation. It is not a mere ghostlike apparition but a visible, tangible society of people who have been born into the kingdom and whose new lives are taking shape in the midst of the world. This society of people, bound as they are by time, space, and history, are nevertheless the people of the "new heavens and the new earth." For this reason, the church's life and worship in this world has symbolic significance, both to itself and to the world.

The fact that the church is a symbol illustrates the significance of symbols. Therefore when we consider the function of symbols in worship as a means of communicating the Christian faith, we must not treat them as mere psychological creations but as images of an *ultimate reality*. The realm of the supernatural is as real as the natural. Thus, a symbol in the natural world corresponds to a reality of the supernatural world. The church in the world corresponds to the church in the mind of God. The worship of the church joins worship in the heavens.

The nature of faith itself demands the transformation of supernatural concepts into visible images and symbols. Because no finite language can fully and completely express supernatural truth adequately, biblical religion and the church in history has always relied on symbolism as a means of communicating that which transcends the realm of the finite. The language of faith has always, therefore, been a language of symbols (see Jean Danielow, S.J., *Primitive Christian Symbols* [Baltimore: Helicon Press, 1964]; and Gustav Aulén, *The Drama and the Symbols* [Philadelphia: Fortress, 1970]).

A glance at the history of worship suggests that it has only been recently, and especially within the Protestant Christian community, that symbolic communication has fallen into disuse. The rise of the printed page in the sixteenth century replaced the symbolic form of communication with the written word. The chief form of communication in the West, until the technological developments of the twentieth century, have been reading and writing. The invention of radio, however, signaled a shift toward the recovery of other senses in communication. Sensory communication has accelerated with the introduction of television and new advertising techniques. As people become more and more dependent on the visual means of communication, reading and writing skills will go into decline and the impact of the visual will assume greater proportions. This means it is particularly important for the church to once again recapture the use of symbolism as a means of communication. This is especially incumbent upon Protestants, whose reform was sparked and spread by the revolution introduced by the Gutenberg press.

Arguments for the Recovery of Symbolism in Worship

There is an *urgent need to recover the use of symbolism in the church.*

First, there has been a *loss of the use of symbolism in worship among most Protestants.* Protestants are accustomed to simple and straightforward language. The use of imagery, symbols, and even subtle language is relatively unknown among many Protestants who thoughtlessly have locked themselves into discursive expression as the preferable, if not the only, form of worship.

One reason why evangelicals prefer verbal communication has to do with their view of the Bible. They see the Bible as a book of words. It is God's *written* revelation. This emphasis on the written words of Scripture coupled with an attitude of neglect toward the symbolic forms of communication (which constitute a large portion of Scripture) are at the root of the neglect of the symbolic in worship. Therefore, the emphasis falls on *words* and *cognitive understanding* in communication.

While words and objective understanding play an important part in communication and should not be denied, there is nevertheless another dimension of communication that needs further exploration—symbolism. Symbolic communication is affirmed in the Scriptures. Scripture is filled with visions, dreams, imagery, and apocalyptic material.

A second reason to recover symbolism is found in the recognition that persons are *symbolic creatures.* For example, recent research in psychology, especially that branch which attempts to understand the neural organization of the human mind, has concluded that the brain functions differently in the right and left hemispheres. The left hemisphere appears to specialize in verbal functions, and right hemisphere centers on spatial functions and other nonverbal skills.

This is the concern of Stephen G. Meyer in an article entitled "Neuropsychology and Worship." He sets out to relate the findings of neural inves-tigation to the experience of worship (Stephen G. Meyer, "Neuropsychology and Worship," *Journal of Psychology and Theology* [Fall 1975], 281–89). His argument, which begins with Scripture, is that (1) while Scripture is verbal, the material it communicates is based on a variety of communication models, ranging from discursive expression to highly apocalyptic language to poetic discourse; (2) although Christianity is grounded on reason, illustrated by Paul's reasoning from the Scriptures in the synagogue (see Acts 17:2) or Peter's insisting that Christians give "an answer to everyone who asks you to give the reason for the hope that you have. . . ." (1 Pet. 3:15), there are nevertheless "definitive confrontations between God and humans where there is concurrent use of vision and word" (Meyer, 285). Meyer cites the examples of Ezekiel, Job, and John (Revelation) and concludes, "While the Bible presents the Christian faith as a rational faith, the rationale is built on symbols which outline its structure" (Meyer, 286).

Rollo May argues that the loss of symbols constitutes one of humanity's chief difficulties. When people have no symbols to identify and illustrate the meaning of life, they cannot transcend the crises of life. Hunger, war, death, unemployment, disease, and the other horrors that confront civilization on a daily basis seem to be the sum and substance of life. Without signs or symbols in *this world* to show people another world or a means of coping with the trials and strains of this world, people have nowhere to turn but to despair and absurdity.

A third reason to recover symbolism in worship is rooted in the recognition that *symbolism is at the very center of life itself.* The celebrations of birthdays, anniversaries, graduations, marriages, funerals, and the like are all ways of *acting out* the meaning of things that words alone fail to convey.

Likewise the great drama of the world as expressed in Scripture, from the Fall to the restoration of humanity in Jesus Christ, ought to be communicated not only in words but in the actions of the church. Symbolic communication in the church is a valid means of communicating truths of the Christian faith. The reenactment of the birth of Christ, the sorrow over his death, the joy of his resurrection, and the power of Pentecost cannot be completely nor adequately communicated through words alone. If the human brain is oriented toward spatial as well as verbal communication, then _Christian worship must not neglect the symbolic, nonverbal, and ritualistic means of communication._

Recovering Symbolism in Worship

In Isaiah 6 and again in Revelation 4, the creatures of God are worshiping God. Both Isaiah and John were smitten with the holiness of God and heard the creatures who surrounded the throne cry, "Holy, holy, holy, /is the Lord God Almighty, /who was, and is, and is to come" (Rev. 4:8, cf. Isa. 6:3).

A fascinating feature about this vision is the symbolism that surrounded God on the throne. Isaiah saw God "seated on a throne, high and exalted, and the train of his robe filled the temple. Above him were seraphs, each with six wings: With two wings they covered their faces, with two they covered their feet, and with two they were flying" (Isa. 6:1-2). John's description is more elaborate:

And the one who sat there had the appearance of jasper and carnelian. A rainbow, resembling an emerald, encircled the throne. Surrounding the throne were twenty-four other thrones, and seated on them were twenty-four elders. They were dressed in white and had crowns of gold on their heads. From the throne came flashes of lightning, rumblings and peals of thunder. Before the throne, seven lamps were blazing. These are the seven spirits of God. Also before the throne there was what looked like a sea of glass, clear as crystal. . . . (Rev. 4:3-6).

The important features of these visions are the visual images that speak to the greatness of God. All creatures of God, including creation itself, fall before God to ascribe power and glory.

In both the Old and New Testaments three reasons are given why God's people should be at worship. They are (1) because God created all things (see Exod. 20:11 and Rev. 4:11); (2) because God has redeemed a people (see Deut. 5:15 and Rev. 5:9); and (3) because God has entered into covenant community with his people (see Exod. 24:3-8 and Rev. 5:10).

The designation of the people of God in both the Old Testament (_Q'hal_) and the New Testament (_ecclesia_) has as its root meaning the _people who are gathered for worship._

The public worship of the church is therefore a corporate act in which the church as the covenant community rehearses both who God is and what God has done. In this way the church ascribes worth to God and gives God the glory. Consequently we must ask what principles should guide the restoration of symbolism in our worship? I will mention four.

First, it will be necessary to recognize that _earthly worship is modeled after a heavenly pattern._ The visions of Isaiah and John affirm and do not negate the use of symbolism in worship. Obviously it is impossible and not advisable to literally reproduce the elements of their visions. On the other hand, a refusal to incorporate visual symbols in worship is a resistance by the earthly church to join the heavenly hosts in ascribing worth to God. But how may the church on earth enter into visual, symbolic worship? A church building itself may represent the heavenlies while the chancel represents the throne of God. In this context the ministers, the choir, and the congregation envision themselves as the servants of God who gather around the throne to proclaim God's redemptive act. The aesthetic setting in which this takes place could range all the way from a Byzantine cathedral to a simple chapel. The thing of ultimate importance is not the gold and glitter, but the triggering of the worshipers' imaginations and spirits through the visual and symbolic setting.

Second, it is important to _recover worship as an action._ It is something we do—not something done to us. The visions given in Isaiah and Revelation indicate that worshipers are not merely passive observers. They were involved in _doing_ something. In the account of John, the creatures did not rest "day or night," the elders "[fell] down before him," and "cast their crowns before the throne" (Rev. 4:8,10, NKJV). Worship involves an active response of the worshiper.

In the history of Christian worship there has been a strong emphasis on what the worshiper does. In the Catholic and Orthodox traditions the worshiper genuflects, kneels, sings numerous responses, bows, says "amen" at the end of the prayers, walks forward for Communion, smells the incense, hears the bells, sees the Host, and passes the kiss of peace. Charismatic worship is also quite active. Charismatics raise their hands, speak in tongues, interpret, prophesy, sing in the Spirit, and sometimes dance spontaneously. In this sense the Catholics, the Orthodox, the charismatics, and others who stress the involvement of the whole person in worship are using a greater variety of symbolic actions than those who merely sit and expect to be challenged or filled.

Third, *we cannot neglect time, space, and history as elements of worship.* There is a timeless character to the worship described by Isaiah and John. Although worship takes place in time, space, and history, the church recognizes that these elements have an eternal character. For example, time has always been interpreted in relationship to the coming of Christ, to his life and ministry, to his death and resurrection, to the coming of the Holy Spirit in the life of the church, and to the second coming of Christ. These events, all of which are *historical,* are gathered up into the liturgy of the church and reenacted symbolically.

Because space also belongs to the Lord by virtue of creation and redemption, the redeemed nature of space may be demonstrated in the architectural arrangement of the building (both inside and outside). These forms of communication played an important part in the witness of the ancient church. A study of the development of the church year, of the feasts and festivals that celebrated the great drama of Christ's birth, death, and resurrection, and the coming of the Holy Spirit, as well as an examination of the redemptive understanding of art and architecture need to be revived in this age of the return to the visual.

Fourth, we must always keep in mind that *worship is a learned art.* The idea that worship is instantaneous, spontaneous, and natural betrays our lack of understanding. We are more than willing to agree that a successful musician, artist, dramatist, salesman, doctor, teacher, lawyer, carpenter, or homemaker must learn the art of doing his or her profession right! Yet when it comes to the Christian faith, to worship, and to the communication of Christian truths, we somehow feel that it should all fall into place naturally without any effort on our part. For this reason it is important to emphasize both the *learned* and *artistic* nature of worship. The process by which it has been learned is historical. The interested reader will want to examine various church liturgies for special holy days such as Christmas, Easter, and Pentecost. Symbolism can be seen also in the vestments, architecture, and music of the church.

Each of these areas will provide additional ideas for recovering symbolism in the contemporary church.

Robert Webber[2]

143 ✦ BIBLIOGRAPHY ON RITUAL IN WORSHIP

Theological and Liturgical Studies

The following are theological and liturgical studies of ritual actions. More specific studies can be found in the other bibliographies in this volume.

Bedard, Walter Maurice. *The Symbolism of the Baptismal Font in Early Christian Thought*. Washington, D.C.: Catholic University of America Press, 1951.

Collins, Mary, and David N. Power, eds. *Liturgy: A Creative Tradition*. Concilium 162. New York: Seabury Press, 1983.

Cooke, Bernard J. *The Distancing of God: The Ambiguity of Symbol in History and Theology*. Philadelphia: Fortress, 1990. Articulates a "theology of presence," a religiously effective understanding of divine providential presence and the sacramentality of Christian life and worship. In a masterful sweep through symbolic aspects of church institutions, ritual, and doctrinal formulations from New Testament times to now, Cooke traces the historical process by which that primitive sense of the immediacy of divine saving presence gave way to "religion," a sacred—and separate—realm. Cooke then identifies ways in which the modern study of symbol in anthropology, psychology, linguistic theory, and literary criticism provide means of reversing this process and reincorporating authentic human sacramentality.

Hoffman, Lawrence A.. *Beyond the Text: A Holistic Approach to Liturgy*. Bloomington, Ind.: Indiana University Press, 1987.

Kavanagh, Aidan. *Elements of Rite: A Handbook of Liturgical Style*. New York: Pueblo Publishing, 1982.

Kraybill, Donald B. "Mennonite Woman's Veiling: The Rise and Fall of a Sacred Symbol." *Mennonite Quarterly Review* 61 (1987): 298–320.

Poloma, Margaret M. *The Assemblies of God at the*

Crossroads: Charisma and Institutional Dilemmas. Knoxville, Tenn.: University of Tennessee Press, 1989. See especially chapter 11, "Maintaining a Pentecostal Worldview Through Ritual."

Power, David N. *Unsearchable Riches: The Symbolic Nature of Liturgy.* New York: Pueblo Publishing, 1984. See especially pages 5–34.

Ramshaw, Elaine. *Ritual and Pastoral Care.* Theology and Pastoral Care Series. Philadelphia: Fortress, 1987.

Rorem, Paul. *Biblical and Liturgical Symbols within the Pseudo-Dionysian Synthesis.* Studies and Texts, 71. Leiden: Brill, 1984; Toronto: Pontifical Institute of Medieval Studies, 1984.

Tripp, David. "Ambivalence in the Reception of Symbol. A Problem of Pastoral Liturgy." In *Symbolism and the Liturgy II*, ed. K. W. Stevenson, 17–23. Grove Liturgical Study, no. 26. Bramcote, U.K.: Grove Books, 1981.

———— Social Scientific Studies ————

The following works are a part of the relatively new discipline of ritual studies, which employs philosophical, sociological, and psychological insights and theories in the study of religious ritual.

Alexander, Bobby C. *Victor Turner Revisited: Ritual as Social Change.* Atlanta: Scholars Press, 1991. Victor Turner altered the way ritual is viewed by emphasizing its role as an agent of social change rather than as an agent for conserving the status quo. This book reconsiders and clarifies Turner's theory of ritual in response to its frequent misinterpretation and then demonstrates its usefulness for interpreting such phenomena as ritual possession in a politically militant African-American Pentecostal congregation and the countercultural theater experiments of Jerzy Grotowski's Polish Laboratory Theatre.

Austin, J(ohn) L(angshaw). *How to Do Things with Words.* Edited by J. O. Urmson and Marina Sbisà. 2d ed. Oxford: Oxford University Press, 1962. The classic study on the notion of the performative in language, the basis of an article in this chapter.

Bateson, Gregory, and Mary Catherine Bateson. *Angels Fear: Toward an Epistemology of the Sacred.* New York: Macmillan, 1987. This philosophical treastise is the basis for many scholarly treatments of ritual knowledge.

Bell, Catherine. *Ritual Theory, Ritual Practice.* New York: Oxford, 1992. A significant and exhaustive examination of recent critical developments in ritual studies.

Dillistone, Frederick William. *The Power of Symbols in Religion and Culture.* New York: Crossroad Publishing. 1986; *Christianity and Symbolism.* Philadelphia: Westminster, 1955. Anglican.

Douglas, Mary. *Natural Symbols: Explorations in Cosmology.* New York: Random House, 1973. One of the most influential books in shaping thinking about religious rituals.

Driver, Tom F. *The Meaning of Ritual.* San Francisco: Harper and Row, 1991. Driver asserts that bored, modern rationalist culture has lost its ability to apprehend the need for ritual and desperately needs it for cultural cohesion and transformation. Realization of three great social gifts of ritual will usher in renewal and rebirth for the community, individuals, and the church, reestablishing the vital links between earth and life. Citing that most religious rituals are moribund, the author advocates that Holy Communion ought to be, "taken more seriously, yet also more playfully, as an enactment (and embodiment) of a God-inspired freedom (socially and spiritually)." He further contends that ritual may be found in evangelical and sacramentalist camps, which provokes an important discussion for the entire church. Ecumenical.

Eliade, Mircea. *Images and Symbols.* New York: Sheed and Ward, 1962; *The Myth of the Eternal Return.* New York: Pantheon, 1954; *The Sacred and the Profane.* New York: Harper and Row, 1961; *Symbolism, the Sacred, and the Arts.* Edited by Diane Apostolos-Cappadona. New York: Crossroad, 1985. The most recent work includes sixteen essays previously published and many other works by Eliade.

Finn, Thomas M. "Ritual Process and the Survival of Early Christianity: A Study of the Apostolic Tradition of Hippolytus." *Journal of Ritual Studies* 3:1 (1989): 69–89. This article applies Victor Turner's concept of liminality and uses the work of other symbolic anthropologists. "The thesis is that the survival of Roman Christianity before Constantine depended heavily on the development of an effective catechumenate." He concludes that, "Christian survival in the face of social and legal hostility during the first three hundred years owed much to the development of a richly articulated catechumenal liturgy." He says little that Peter Brown and others haven't already said, but he works it into the language of ritual studies and anthropology.

Geertz, Clifford. "Religion as a Cultural System." In *Anthropological Approaches to Religion*, ed. Michael Banton. London: Tavistock Publications, 1966. An anthropological study of the symbolism of day-to-day rituals and routines.

Grimes, Ronald L. *Beginnings in Ritual Studies.* Lanham, Md.: University Press of America, 1982. The book is a collection of fifteen essays in an academic study of ritual. It argues for attempts that transcend textual and verbal orientation and focus on performance. Grimes states that ritual is foreign to us and wonders about the potential of studying faith from a ritological perspective, defining what it means to be Christian descriptively and gesturally, rather than confessionally. Ritual makes no sense until its meaning grasps us, the author asserts in a volume which treats worship as performance and hopes to initiate a dialogue between religious studies and the social sciences.

———. "Sources for the Study of Ritual" *Religious Studies Review* 10:2 (April 1984): 134–45. Extensive bibliography on all facets of symbolism and ritual. Grimes also prepared a full book-length bibliography published by Scarecrow Press in 1986 on this subject.

Journal of Ritual Studies. Department of Religious Studies. University of Pittsburgh, 1987–.

Miles, Margaret R. *Image as Insight: Visual Understanding in Western Christianity and Secular Culture.* Boston: Beacon, 1985.

Mitchell, Leonel L. *The Meaning of Ritual.* Wilton, Conn.: Morehouse-Barlow, 1977. This small volume is a basic introduction to the meaning and history of ritual. It examines the question, "Have ritual and symbol lost their meaning for modern culture—'the dead world of physical phenomena that points to nothing beyond itself'?" This volume defines rituals as "external actions as the necessary means of conveying and expressing interior realities." These rituals are not merely "vain repetition," but include everyone engaged in "corporate, symbolic activity." Chapters include: "The Beginnings of Ritual Worship," "Background of Christian Worship," "Origin of Christian Liturgy," "The Rituals of Christendom," and "Ritual Today." Ecumenical.

Mitchell, Nathan, ed. *Liturgy Digest* 1:1 (1993). The entire issue is devoted to ritual, with an extensive annotated bibliography on ritual and liturgy.

Philibert, Paul. "Readiness for Ritual: Psychological Aspects of Maturity in Christian Celebration." In *Alternative Futures for Worship*, vol. 1, ed. Regis Duffy. Collegeville, Minn.: Liturgical Press, 1987.

Schaller, J. "Performative Language Theory: An Exercise in the Analysis of Ritual." *Worship* 62:5 (1988): 415–25.

Shaughnessy, James, ed. *The Roots of Ritual.* Grand Rapids: Eerdmans, 1973.

Seubert, Xavier John. "Ritual Embodiment: Embellishment or Epiphany?" *Worship* 63:5 (1989): 402–16.

———. "Weaving a Pattern of Access: The Essence of Ritual." *Worship* 63:6 (1989): 490–503.

Smith, Brian K. *Reflections on Resemblance, Ritual, and Religion.* New York: Oxford University Press, 1988.

Smucker, Joseph. "Rituals, Symbols, and Relevance: Conceptual Adjustments among Mennonites." *Conrad Grebel Review* 4 (1986): 225–38.

Soskice, Janet Martin. *Metaphor and Religious Language.* New York: Oxford University Press, 1985.

Smith, Jonathan Z. *To Take Place: Toward Theory in Ritual.* Chicago: University of Chicago Press, 1987.

Turner, Victor. The Ritual Process: Structure and Anti-Structure. Chicago: Aldine, 1969.

Turner, Victor, and Edith Turner. *Image and Pilgrimage in Christian Culture: Anthropological Perspectives.* New York: Columbia Univeristy Press, 1978.

van der Leeuw, Gerardus. *Religion in Essence and Manifestation.* Rev. ed. New York: Harper and Row, 1964.

West, Edward N. *Outward Signs: The Language of Christian Symbolism.* New York: Walker and Co., 1989.

Wicker, Brian. *Culture and Liturgy.* New York: Sheed and Ward, 1963.

Wuthnow, Robert. *Rediscoverig the Sacred: Perspectives on Religion in Contemporary Society.* Grand Rapids: Eerdmans, 1992.

THREE

The History of Sacraments, Ordinances, and Sacred Actions

Christian history can be divided into two main epochs: premodern and modern. In *premodern* culture, ritual, symbol and metaphor were employed to express realities that could not be fully expressed in words. For premodern cultures, symbols were not merely notions; symbols were powerful mediators of divine activity.

Patristic Christian writers used words to discuss Christian sacred actions but they did so in a multilayered, metaphorical, evocative manner, frequently employing the symbolic language of Scripture. Patristic influence continued until the rise of university, scholastic theology in the twelfth and thirteenth centuries in Western Europe. Because Eastern Orthodox churches did not experience this scholasticism, Orthodox practices often more directly reflect the symbolic and metaphoric patristic usage.

Between the thirteenth and sixteenth centuries, scholastic theologians applied Aristotelian logic to theology and systematized all aspects of the church's life: canon law, doctrinal theology, pastoral care, and worship practice. In the sixteenth century, both Protestants and Catholics defended their views of sacramental worship by means of logical arguments. Anti-sacramental Protestants (Zwinglians, Anabaptists) argued with sacramental Protestants (Lutherans, Calvinists, Anglicans) using the same logic derived from scholastic methods. Words replaced symbolic rituals as the dominant mode of theological expression.

The *modern* political, economic, philosophical, scientific, and technological culture of the West represents a further development of the logical and systematizing thrust of scholastic theology. The rational order of modern culture leaves little room for divine reality mediated through symbolic rituals. In reaction, several Christian renewal movements emphasize experience: inward, nonsacramental Pietism (seventeenth to eighteenth centuries); Wesleyan Holiness, Pentecostal and charismatic renewals (eighteenth to twentieth centuries); and Catholic, Anglican, Lutheran, and Calvinist sacramental and liturgical renewal (nineteenth to twentieth centuries).

144 • THE MEANING OF SACRED ACTION

Sacred actions, however they may be named, have been significant in every worship tradition. This article examines the history and meaning of such actions as they have functioned in the Christian community.

The Hebrew Scriptures tell the story of God's saving action on behalf of God's people. God bound God's self to a covenant to save the people of God. With Christ a new covenant of the *kingdom of God* dawned. Christians were those who believed that the covenant promises of God were now being fulfilled in the mystery of Christ. Christ was the new oath (*sacramentum*), the new covenant. Hebrew religious rituals, in a similar manner as Hebrew theology, were transformed into Christian rituals or sacred actions.

The term *sacred action* in this article refers to the relation established between the activity of

Christ and the baptized community in its celebration of the liturgies of the sacraments.

Even during Jesus' public ministry, his disciples were becoming aware that Jesus was bringing into being a new order of things, a new breaking into human history of the *kingdom of God*. He was providing a new perspective on God, his Father, and pointing to a new way of relating to God. However, only with the Easter experience after Jesus' crucifixion, which made the disciples aware that Jesus was still humanly alive and mysteriously present to them in his Spirit, did they slowly grasp the profound transformation of life's meaning that had occurred.

Gathering together, especially for communal meals, these first Christians shared with one another their recollections of Jesus' life and death and their awareness of this enduring Christ-mystery which had changed their lives. Slowly, they developed certain rituals to celebrate the new divine-human covenant established by Jesus' death and resurrection. In particular, they gave a special form to the practice of baptizing people and used it to initiate into the community those who accepted the gospel message. They celebrated some special meals which quickly developed into *the breaking of the bread*, the Christian Eucharist. Though Jesus himself did not leave these rituals as such to his followers, it was his life and particularly his death and resurrection that "instituted these sacramental rituals" by being the mystery the rituals celebrate.

Early Christians, then, lived and prayed with the awareness of sharing in "the great mystery revealed in Christ," the mystery of God's saving presence in the lives of people. This was, in the full sense of the term, a *new life*; actually, it was the beginning of that unending life which Jesus had promised to those who would receive him as sent from his Father. Through the ritual of Christian initiation one entered into this new Spirit-life that came from Jesus' own passage into Spirit-filled risen life. As Paul explained in his letter to the Christians at Rome, in baptism one enters somehow into the death and resurrection of Christ and possesses the Spirit as the creative source of unending life.

It was this *great mystery* that was celebrated in *the breaking of the bread*. Without yet reflecting on the way in which the Eucharist *gave grace,* the early decades—indeed the early centuries—

believed that the shared bread and wine which became the body and blood of the risen Lord was a continuing *food* for the new life that had begun with baptism. At the same time, they were aware that in "proclaiming the death of the Lord until he comes in glory," they were professing together their Christian faith. They were stating their acceptance of the preached gospel, but more than that, they were pledging themselves to faithful living out of their Christianity. So, the Latin word *sacramentum* (which means "an oath, a solemn promise"), along with the earlier Greek word *mysterion*, were applied to these rituals, as well as to other Christian rituals such as *ordination* or *reconciliation* which emerged in the life of the church.

Bernard Cooke[3]

145 ◆ SACRED ACTIONS IN THE EARLY CHURCH

Understanding the sacred actions of the early church requires a short language lesson. Two words, the Greek word mysterion, *and the Latin word* sacramentum, *are important to this discussion. This article describes the history of these terms in early Christian thought and gives clues to their meaning and significance for the Christian tradition.*

As Christianity penetrated the Graeco-Roman world, it moved from the Greek East to the Latin West. Greek New Testament terms had to be translated into Latin. The *mysterion* of Christ became the *sacramentum* of Christ.

Mysterion, Mystery: Greek and Biblical Use

Christian worship initially developed out of Jewish liturgy. Jesus deliberately placed his institution of the Eucharist into the context of Jewish table ritual. Baptism, anointing, and ordination drew on Jewish precedents. Jesus' saving action was inextricably bound up with the Hebrew understanding of God's saving covenant, for Jesus himself referred to his sacrificial death as the *new covenant.*

The church took root initially in the Greek-speaking communities of the Roman Empire (even in the city of Rome, Christians were Greek-speaking during the first two hundred years). One of the

Greek terms used by New Testament writers to describe Christ's sacred action was _mysterion_. Later Latin writers translated this word as _sacramentum_. Both _mysterion_ and _sacramentum_ expressed the mystery of Christ and the church's worship of God in Christ by the power of the Spirit.

The _mysteries,_ as understood in the Greek mystery religions, were secret rites by which persons were initiated into a given religion. Initiates were expected never to reveal the details of the rite to outsiders; only those who kept the secret were said to be assured of salvation. It may be that this understanding influenced the use of the term _mysterion_ by philosophers who likened their own efforts on the path toward the understanding of truth to the steps of the religious mystics on their path to initiation. Old Testament texts, which were written in the Hellenistic period (Wisdom, Daniel, Tobit, Sirach, 2 Maccabees), used the term _mysterion_ more in its philosophical or profane sense than in its worship sense. The books of Daniel and Wisdom are especially lucid examples.

The book of Daniel refers to the _eschatological_ mysterion, that is, what is to happen in the days to come and to be revealed by God alone. Further, the book of Wisdom speaks, on the one hand, of the wicked who knew not the hidden counsels (_mysteria_) of God; on the other hand, of the mysteries of the one God revealed in the present to all who are open and seek after wisdom, who personified is seen as a mediatrix between God and humanity.

The New Testament use of the term _mysterion_ is influenced by Daniel's apocalyptic use of the term and shows a strong eschatological referent by its association with Jesus. Mark 4:11 joins mysterion with Jesus' eschatological proclamation of the _basileia_ (kingdom): "To you the mystery of the reign of God has been confided."

In the letters of Paul, especially 1 Corinthians, Ephesians, and Colossians, the uses of the term _mysterion_ taken from pre-Christian Greek worship and philosophy as well as from the Old Testament, are combined and transformed: The mysterion is essentially the Christ-event itself. Paul's entire purpose is to preach no other _wisdom_ than the apparent contradiction to wisdom, the crucified Christ. In the crucified Christ, the mystery of God is revealed and comprehended, rather than hidden. This is the mystery that is unveiled by the Spirit of God.

Paul's theology makes a clean break with any notion of elitist isolation or privatizing of the search for salvation. Rather than a secret to be preserved, the mystery of God which is Christ is proclaimed openly for all. For Paul, the crucifixion and resurrection of Jesus are the revelation and the realization of the will of God to save.

The reason why the word _mysterion_ is not used in the New Testament to refer to baptism or the Lord's Supper is to avoid any possible association of the rites of the Christian church with the secret rites of the Greek mystery religions, which were still being practiced at that time. Likewise, the desire to avoid all association with the Old Testament priesthood led to the avoidance of the word _priest_ to refer to ministers; indeed, even though Christ is referred to as a _priest,_ he is not like the Old Testament priests. However, the apologetic and missionary situation of the post-apostolic church soon led it to appropriate the Greek philosophical heritage and the Roman cultural imagery of those to whom the gospel was preached.

From the Apostles to Augustine

Justin Martyr, Irenaeus, Clement of Alexandria, and Tertullian, all of whom wrote between A.D. 150 and A.D. 220, are the most notable users of the term _mysterion_. They used the term in the first instance polemically, in apologetic defenses of the faith against the secret Hellenistic cults (e.g., Justin, _Apology_, 25, 27, 54, 66; Tertullian, _On the Prescription of Heretics_, 40), or against the secret teachings of Gnosticism (e.g., Tertullian, _On the Soul,_ 18). However, they also used the term _mysterion_ biblically to defend the unity of both the Old and the New Testaments in the divine plan of salvation. They saw events and institutions of the Old Testament as preproclamation _types_ or images, or even as an anticipation of the salvation reality which appeared in Christ. Thus they returned to Old Testament events and institutions as examples of mysterion (cf. Justin, _Dialogue with Trypho,_ 24, 40, 44, 111). Within this line of thought, the term could well be applied to certain events in the life of Jesus, especially his birth and crucifixion (Justin, _First Apology_, 113; _Dialogue_, 74, 91).

Both Justin (_First Apology_, 66) and Tertullian (_Prescription of Heretics,_ 40) referred to baptism and the Lord's Supper as mysteria. Christ is the mysterion whose reality is never limited to any created thing. Yet, because the Christ can never be separated from the members of the body, Tertullian was able to refer to both Christ and the actions of the body of Christ as mysterion. In short, the relationship between the salvation which has been worked by Christ and its ritual expression in the community of faith is such that, without denying the sinful nature of the baptized community, Christ continues to act and is therefore revealed through his action in the church.

In the translation of the Scriptures, Tertullian noted that mysterion had been translated by the Latin word *sacramentum*. As a lawyer, Tertullian recognized that sacramentum carried the connotation of an oath (in Roman legal terminology), or of personal commitment in response to the initiative of another. By combining the meaning of mysterion with that of sacramentum, Tertullian could explain baptism (and to some degree the Eucharist): From God's side, the sacramenta are the pledges of God, who wills salvation; from the faithful's side, sacramenta are the occasion for the complete response of confidence and commitment to God in Christ (*To the Martyrs*, 3.1; *On Shows*, 24.4; *On the Chaplet*, 11.1; *Scorpiace*, 4.5; *On Idolatry*, 19.2).

This attempt of Tertullian to make an account of what Christians do when they gather to worship God was one of the seeds of a fuller theological account that would be developed by Augustine and later by other theologians in the Western church over many centuries. Tertullian provided the church with yet more language by which to explain the truth that when the members of Christ's body gather with the intention of continuing to act in his name for the sake of the worship of God and the service of humanity, it is truly Christ who acts in and through the church's actions. Christ baptizes, convenes the church for the Eucharist, forgives through the ministry of the minister, consoles and heals in the sacrament of anointing, calls worship leaders to the church, and loves the church to such an extent that his love is the norm for marriage.

From this perspective, one can see why Christ is known as the mysterion/sacramentum of God, why the church in union with Christ is the *great mystery*, and why the sacraments are not merely acts of the church as though they were radically

distinct from Christ's activity. The sacraments are the events in which the members of Christ's body encounter the saving will of God in Christ and respond to that initiative. The church's worship celebration uses material things (water, oil, salt, fire, incense, etc.) or words and gestures in order to reveal and make present the saving words and deeds of Christ.

Theresa F. Koernke

146 • Sacred Actions in the Medieval and Reformation Eras

The Middle Ages witnessed some far-reaching developments in the theology and practice of the sacraments. This article traces these developments and explains the nature of the Reformation debate which arose out of them.

Medieval Christian culture was a highly ritualized culture in which all actions of social, political, and economic life (e.g., marriage negotiations, choosing and crowning kings, setting off for war, the exchange of gifts) were charged with symbolic meaning. Nearly all early medieval theologians were monks, or they were monks who became bishops. They were thus rooted in the life of daily worship. From the thirteenth century onward, theology and pastoral practice became increasingly systematized under the influence of university, scholastic theology, carried on predominantly by members of mendicant religious orders (Franciscans, Dominicans, Augustinian Friars) and other non-monastic clergy. The growing gap between ongoing popular belief in the power of sacred ritual and the increasingly complex efforts to explain logically how God acted in the sacraments eventually led to wholesale attacks on the very idea of God working through created means, beginning with the late medieval Hussite and Wycliffite movements and continuing in the more radical forms of Protestantism (Zwinglian and Anabaptist iconoclasm).

The Growing Role of the Clergy

Fairly early in the medieval era a way of receiving the sacraments different than that of the early church came into existence and slowly gained ground. This was the instrumental view, which considered the liturgical acts as means used by God, acting through the mediation of the ordained minister, to give grace to people. In this perspective Christians came to liturgy to receive sacraments, to be freed from their sins, to be blessed. This receptive approach to the role of the faithful coincided with their increasing exclusion from active participation in sacramental liturgy.

Throughout much of the first millennium, the people's sense of involvement in the Christ-mystery through sacramental ritual remained quite strong, though with diminishing understanding of the mystery. For a variety of reasons, many of them having to do with the unsettled social situation of those days, the bulk of Christians received rudimentary religious instruction at best. This, plus the fact that Latin remained the liturgical language while it was gradually becoming foreign to most people, meant that the level of theological insight into the reality of sacramental liturgy was minimal. So, by the ninth century and thereafter, we find explanations of the liturgy, very many of them allegorical, which reflect the community's loss of understanding.

As the faithful had less and less of a role in the liturgical actions, as the language became strange to them, and as the celebrant was situated at the far end of a sanctuary to perform the sacred act, the sacraments and particularly the Mass became a spectacle which people attended. Obviously, this meant that the intrinsic significance of the sacramental liturgies no longer interacted with the significance of people's lives, except for the general outlook that something was given people through sacraments that enabled them to persevere amidst conflict with "the world, the flesh, and the devil" and so to reach their heavenly destiny.

Later Theological Debates

In the twelfth century, a key development in the understanding and the practice of sacraments took place. As part of the overall intellectual struggle to understand things more clearly, there was an effort to clarify the nature of sacraments, if possible to arrive at a definition of sacrament that would permit people to say what was or was not a sacrament. This proved very difficult for an intrinsic reason: Because the Christian sacraments cannot really be fitted into a category—technically speaking, they are analogous realities—no strict definition of sacrament is possible. However,

there was one element common to all Christian sacraments: By that point in history all of them, including marriage, involved a liturgical ceremony. As a result, it was the ritual action, for example, the wedding ceremony, that by itself was identified as the sacrament, and the focus of understanding Christian sacramentality became more limited than it had been in earlier periods of the church.

Because of an increasing awareness of the decline of liturgy, the late Middle Ages witnessed movements for reform, but these were not sufficient to ward off the explosive reaction of the Protestant Reformation in the early sixteenth century. On the positive side, the Reformation drew attention to the role of personal faith and the active participation of the faithful in sacramental liturgy; on the negative side, many of the Reformation churches downgraded the role of ritual and tended to substitute reflection on the Bible for sacramental celebration.

The Roman Catholic reaction to these Protestant tenets came with the Council of Trent (1545–1563), which provided the first systematized official statement about Christian sacraments. The teaching of Trent is of special importance because it has provided the framework and basic doctrinal positions for Catholic teaching about sacraments up to the twentieth century. While the decrees of the council regarding sacraments need to be carefully studied and explained in the light of their historical context, a few of the leading notions can be mentioned here.

In the section that provides the general statements about Christian sacraments, the council insisted that Christ himself is the one who instituted the sacraments, though no explanation was given about the manner in which this took place—a later section specifically on the Mass linked the institution of Eucharist with the action of Jesus at the Supper and with his death. Countering the Protestant contention that *sacrament* could be applied in the true sense only to baptism and the Lord's Supper, Trent insisted that five other instances of liturgical celebration (confirmation, reconciliation, ordination, anointing of the sick, and marriage) were truly sacraments.

The heart of the debate between Catholics and Protestants dealt, however, with the efficacy of sacramental actions, specifically of baptism and

Eucharist. Consistent with their basic teaching about justification, namely that sinners though forgiven become *just* only in the next life, the Reformers looked on sacramental liturgies as proclaiming Christ's promise of human salvation but not yet transforming the people by grace. What liturgy did was to announce the gospel message so that people's faith might be aroused and increased; sacraments did not give grace, they only promised it.

Opposing this view, the Council of Trent insisted on the intrinsic grace-giving power of sacraments. "Sacraments contain and give grace." While its decrees took explicit account of the need for proper dispositions, including faith, in those who receive sacraments, the council viewed the sacramental liturgies as possessing in themselves a saving power that derives from the death of Christ. When properly performed by a celebrant who has the basic intention of accomplishing what the church intends in its sacramental acts, a sacrament has *ex opere operato* the power of conferring grace.

The term *ex opere operato* has been a key element in Roman Catholic sacramental teaching and in much Protestant disagreement with that teaching. If understood accurately, it refers to the belief that whenever the essential elements of the rite are carried out by a minister with a serious intention, the action, because it involves the agency of the risen Christ and his Spirit, possesses intrinsically the power of transforming people by grace. Unfortunately, the term has often been misunderstood to imply that sacramental effectiveness is automatic and independent of the care or understanding with which it is enacted or of the faith or devotion of those involved. Clearly, such was not the intention of the Council of Trent, nor do its decrees suggest such an interpretation.

Little changed in either official teaching or in popular attitudes regarding sacramental liturgies between the Council of Trent and the mid-twentieth century. However, the experience of the two great world wars and the convoking of the Second Vatican Council have opened up a new epoch in the life of Christianity and have led to a deepened interest in the role of liturgy in Christian life and to a creative development of sacramental theology.

Bernard Cooke[4]

147 ⬥ SACRED ACTIONS IN MODERN CATHOLICISM

This article traces the development of a Catholic view of the sacraments since the medieval period. This development shows a great respect for the tradition which has shaped it, but also shows new emphases offered in response to the Reformation and later theological thought.

In the later Middle Ages (from the twelfth century onward) Aristotelian philosophy provided the foundation for scholastic theology as it sought to express in logical terms how divine initiative and human response come together in the sacraments. Although both Catholic and Protestant Reformers sought in different ways to reformulate answers to this problem, their method remained, by and large, scholastic and logical. In some aspects, the reforms of the Second Vatican Council (1963) returned to the New Testament and patristic understanding of the mystery of Christ's sacred action that had characterized medieval theology up to the rise of scholasticism.

In making an account of sacramental action, that is, the relationship of the saving activity of Christ in his once-for-all death to the human response of Christians in the celebration of the sacraments, both the Roman Catholic and Reformation churches have suffered from the limitations of (1) medieval cosmology and (2) scholastic philosophy, as well as from a (3) literalist understanding of the Scriptures and (4) negative anthropology.

A Neoplatonic cosmology or worldview is characterized by the assumptions that the beings of the spiritual world are ranked on a scale of being in the shape of a pyramid, with God at the pinnacle, and that the material world is patterned on the spiritual world. With the reintroduction of Aristotelian philosophy to the European continent in the eleventh century, categories such as *cause and effect* as well as *matter and form* served to provide philosophical language for theology and, at the same time, to reinforce the hierarchical cosmology. In addition, a literalist interpretation of the Scriptures, especially of the Ascension, led to a rather physical, localized image of Christ as "seated at the right hand of the Father," distant from human history. These factors, as well as a very negative evaluation of human nature, provided the difficult task of explaining sacramental action, that is, how the divine initiative and Christian response of faith come together in the sacraments' celebration. It was asked: If God acts in sovereign freedom, and if Christ, having died once-for-all, is situated at the right hand of God, how can the graces of that saving death be related to sinful human nature in baptism, the Eucharist, and the other sacraments?

In brief, medieval scholastic theology responded: God in Christ is the primary cause of sacramental grace; the minister of the sacraments is the instrumental cause; the water, oil, bread, wine, etc., is the matter of the sacraments; and the word formula by which the meaning of the sacrament is determined is the form of the sacraments. Hence, the sacraments are the "efficacious signs of grace": they effect (bring about) the sanctifying grace (a share in the holy life of God), which they signify (mean), in the soul of the recipient _ex opere operato_ (from the work worked), that is, in virtue Christ's saving work on the cross, so long as the recipient is properly disposed to receive the gift of grace. Sacramental action was, therefore, understood to be the consequence of divine initiative in the soul of a person who responds in trust with a passive faith.

For a complex of reasons—the use of Latin; general illiteracy, even among the clergy; the extreme emphasis on the sovereign activity of God in relation to the passive faith of sinful humanity; poor catechesis and preaching; and undeniable corruption among some of the clergy—this synthesis was poorly understood and practiced. Such misunderstanding led to the sense that the grace of God was somehow automatically conferred (cheap grace), and that God could be manipulated by human actions (works righteousness), so long as the proper matter and form were used. Martin Luther and John Calvin knew this corrupt form of scholastic theology and practice, rather than the actual work of Thomas Aquinas in the _Summa Theologiae_, Part 3; it was this corrupted sacramental practice that the Reformers justifiably accused as implying the granting of "cheap grace" without personal commitment and the justifying of humans before God on the basis of "human works."

Many sixteenth-century reformers, such as Erasmus, called the church to its biblical foundations. However, the Protestant Reformers taught that only those sacraments which (they assumed to) have biblical warrant—baptism and the Lord's Supper—were to be kept; all others were said to be of merely ecclesiastical origin. Along with all other theologians of the time, the Reformers continued to assert the sovereign freedom of God and to reaffirm the importance of trusting faith in God's promises. However, in contrast to the sixteenth-century church's teaching that human nature is deeply weakened by Adam's sin, the Reformers retrieved a doctrine of human nature's total depravity from the writings of St. Augustine.

This combination of factors—a pyramidal worldview, the reaction to and entrapment in a philosophical system, a literalist interpretation of the Ascension, the (recent) limiting of the sacraments to those specifically mentioned in the New Testament, and the doctrine of the total depravity of human nature—had powerful consequences for the understanding of sacramental action and its expression in liturgical celebration among Reformation churches. Hence, even though Luther and Calvin had called for the weekly Sunday celebration of the Eucharist (Mass), the awesome sense of being depraved before God led to the reduction of Sunday worship to a preaching and word service with only an occasional celebration of the Lord's Supper, if at all, even during the Reformers' lifetimes.

In this polemical situation, the bishops at the Council of Trent reasserted the number of the principal sacraments of the church as instituted by Christ and the relation between the seven sacraments and the bestowal of sacramental grace, that is, the special participation of the grace of Christ, the head of the church, according to the purpose of each sacrament. The bishops, like the Protestant Reformers, were also laboring with some of the same assumptions: Christ's saving act on the cross is the once-for-all source of salvation; and Christ is seated at the right hand of the Father. However, Trent understood "instituted by Christ" more broadly to mean "instituted by the will of Christ in the church," and maintained that human nature is weakened rather than totally depraved.

The documents of the Council of Trent indicate that there were many abuses in pastoral practice because of poor understanding of theology. Therefore, the council mandated the correction of abuses and the reform of the clergy. Clearly, Trent had no intention of saying everything that could

The Word. Although the Word is not usually considered a sacrament, the reading and preaching of the Word embody a sacramental function—that is, the Word results in an encounter with Jesus Christ. The usual symbol of the Word is an open Bible.

be said about sacraments. Indeed, it does not represent the best of the synthesis of Thomas. Yet its tentative doctrinal synthesis became the basis for later explanations of sacramental action, especially the Eucharist, among Catholic theologians until the twentieth century. An example of the theology of the relation of Christ's saving death to Christians is present in the following: "For the Victim [Christ] is one and the same, the same [victim] now offering by the ministry of the priests, who then offered himself on the Cross, the manner alone of the offering being different. The fruits (i.e., graces) indeed of which oblation . . . are received" (Session 22, September 17, 1562).

Ironically, both the Protestant Reformers and the participants in the Council of Trent were operating from within the same worldview. On the one hand, the Protestant Reformers rejected the living tradition of the church as a source of revelation and asserted the importance of personal faith and the total depravity of human nature. On the other hand, the Council of Trent seemed simply to restate the accumulated tradition up to that point in history, but without much theological explanation.

The results of historical studies in Scripture and liturgy are moving all the churches to acknowledge the factors which led to the sixteenth-century division. The *Constitution on the Sacred Liturgy (1963),* par. 1–20, expresses in brief the retrieval of a New Testament theology of baptism into Christ's sacrifice, and hence, of the church as the primary presence of Christ, whose purpose is to proclaim the kingdom of God in history. This theology clearly asserts the sovereign initiative of God in the sacraments, but better accounts for the free human response of Christian faith: When the church gathers to celebrate the liturgy of the sacraments, it is Christ who is acting in their midst by the power of the Spirit to the glory of God. The publication *Baptism, Eucharist, and Ministry* (1982) by the Faith and Order Commission of the World Council of Churches witnesses to the growing convergence between the Western Christian churches.

Theresa F. Koernke

148 ✦ SACRED ACTIONS IN THE EASTERN CHURCHES

The Eastern Orthodox churches did not develop scholastic, logic-based systematic theologies like those of late medieval and modern Catholics and Protestants in Western Europe. Many of the differences between Eastern and Western explanations of the sacraments can be traced to this historical divergence. Moreover, the sacramental life of worship in the Eastern churches retains an important role for fasting at certain times in the church year and for the veneration of icons.

Bishops and theologians of the Orthodox church and the Roman Catholic church have been involved in the last decade in explaining how the two churches express the faith in continuity with the apostles. Both churches understand themselves as a communion of faith and sacraments, preeminently manifested in eucharistic celebrations presided over by an ordained bishop or priest. Catholics and Orthodox in the 1988 New Valamo consensus statement agreed that ". . . on all essential points concerning ordination, our churches have a common doctrine and practice, even if on certain canonical and disciplinary requirements, such as celibacy, customs can be different because of pastoral and spiritual reasons" (30).

The two churches now wish to present their sacramental beliefs in theological language that avoids the systematic categories of medieval scholastic logic (in the West) and the mystical, yet systematic categories of Gregory Palamas (d. 359) and his disciples (in the East). The new sacramental theology being formulated together draws upon scriptural, liturgical, and patristic language. Since the Eastern churches did not undergo a Renaissance, a Reformation, or an Enlightenment, they have preserved some ancient traditions forgotten in the West but have not elaborated a systematic sacramental theology. The church of Rome and the Eastern Orthodox church recognize their basic creedal affirmations on the sacraments as the same, despite the fact that the Orthodox are often puzzled and troubled by, and unwilling to imitate some practices of Rome.

To refer to the sacraments, Eastern Christians use the word derived from the Greek word *mysterion,* the holy mysteries. Eastern Christians speak of participating in the sacramental life of the church rather than *receiving* sacraments. The holy mysteries or sacraments are seen as making present and partially accessible, in sensible form, the invisible reality of God's love expressed in Trinitarian life through encounter with the incarnate Word. Christian sacramental life is a salvific union with the glorified Christ by participation in the mystery of the heavenly liturgy.

Roman Catholics note that Eastern Christians often do not use the distinction between sacraments and sacramentals. For Eastern Christians sacramental living means participating in the mystery of the Incarnation through gestures and activities which, even if practiced in the home, are linked with the church's liturgy. Numerous blessings connected with foods, water, and holy places are seen as possessing a kind of sacramental function that fosters ecclesial communion and turns the believers' minds to the heavenly liturgy where Christ intercedes without end.

Two religious practices of Eastern Christianity strongly color their sacramental life and should be noted even if, in the West, these practices are not considered directly sacramental. These practices are fasting and veneration of icons.

Through fasting Eastern Christians blend daily living with the liturgical calendar. Four major fasts are celebrated each year: Lent (seven weeks before Easter); the apostles' fast (the second Monday after Pentecost to June 28); the fast of the falling asleep of the Theotokos (August 1 to August 14), and the forty days' Christmas fast (November 15 to December 24). Fasting in the Eastern tradition is measured more by what is not eaten rather than by amount of food eaten. On most days in Great Lent and Holy Week not only is meat not allowed but neither fish nor animal products (milk, cheese, eggs, etc.), and in addition wine and oil are excluded. Eastern Christians do not use the distinction found in the West between fasting and abstinence. Observing fasting regulations in the modern living conditions of the diaspora is not always feasible. One of the preparatory commission's position papers for the forthcoming Great and Holy Synod of the Orthodox church proposes to adjust fasting requirements. Fasting is not seen as punishment of the flesh but as a gesture used to open oneself more fully to the presence of the Holy Spirit.

Secondly, through veneration of icons Eastern Christians enter into the spiritual realities signified by the sacraments. Eastern Christians venerate a spiritual presence in these religious paintings, which Westerners would never associate with statues, stained glass windows, or holy cards. In the West there is neither an equivalent of icon veneration (*proskynesis)* nor iconic incorporation into the liturgy as in the East. By the incarnation of the Word, the image of the Father, God's image (2 Cor. 4:4), is seen as being restored in every human being. The material world is viewed as sanctified and again capable of mediating divine beauty. Icons express, as far as possible, the glory of God seen in the face of Christ. And so icons are judged to be sacred words in painting or the *visible gospel.* An icon is not a random decoration but an integral part of the church's life and worship. Production and use of icons are always controlled by theological criteria. The location of the iconostasis (the screen that displays the principal icons), the location of the screen's doors, the shape of the sacred vessels, and even the shape of the church building contribute to the liturgical interplay between the visible and the invisible reality.

Michael J. Farley[5]

149 ◆ A COMPARISON OF EASTERN AND WESTERN PRACTICE OF THE SEVEN SACRAMENTS

Many of the differences between Eastern Orthodox and Roman Catholic Christians in sacramental practice stem from changes that developed in the West after the patristic period. Chrismation, originally part of baptism, became a separate rite of confirmation in the West. This led to a delay in one's first Communion, which originally took place at the time of baptism. Other differences surround the use of leavened and unleavened bread; plural and singular, first- and third-person language in baptism and reconciliation; attitudes toward remarriage after the death of a partner; and the marital status of clergy. In each case different theological assumptions underlie these variations in practice. The paragraphs that follow devote attention to Eastern practice and theology as a way of coming to understanding the differences in Roman and Eastern practice.

The doctrine of the seven sacraments, to the extent that it exists in the East, has been influenced more by the West than by Eastern theology. As is well known, the sevenfold listing of the sacraments emerged in the West during the twelfth century and became official only in the thirteenth. In the East it appears for the first time in the Profession of Faith which Pope Clement IV required of Byzantine Emperor Michael Paleologus in 1267. The East has never committed itself to any specific list of sacraments such as the Roman church did at the Council of Trent. For pedagogical reasons and to facilitate dialogue with the West, Eastern churches make use of the teaching that there are seven sacraments. At the same time, some consider other rituals as sacraments, such as monastic profession, anointing of monarchs, burial of Christians, consecration of church buildings, etc.

——————— Baptism/Chrismation ———————

Among Eastern Christians, infant baptism and chrismation are celebrated together and are seen, with the reception of eucharistic Communion (received from a golden spoon containing consecrated wine), as the sacrament or sacraments of initiation. Baptism and chrismation are deemed to belong together as the Resurrection and Pentecost. Important for the Eastern churches is the sequence of sacramental initiation: baptism, chrismation, Eucharist. Eastern Christians are puzzled, even shocked, at practices now common in Roman Catholicism: (a) of not observing the ancient sequence by allowing children to receive the Eucharist before chrismation, and (b) of depriving baptized infants of eucharistic Communion until the "age of reason." All the parts of Christian initiation in the East are administered by a priest. The liturgy begins with the blessing of the water which symbolizes the whole realm of matter. The Byzantine formula of baptism is pronounced not in the name of the minister as in the West ("I baptize you . . ."), but rather by declaration on behalf of the baptized ("The servant of God/handmaid of God is baptized . . ."). The East retains triple immersion, although the infant is not usually totally submerged. In Greece, the infant is baptized between the ages of one and two years and remains unnamed until baptism. The role of the sponsors still has strong religious and social functions.

Catechetical material explaining the Eastern liturgy of baptism does not stress a relationship between the sacramental baptism and the remission of original sin. The predominant emphasis is on entry into the body of Christ. The Orthodox do not accept baptism administered by an unbeliever who acts on behalf of the church. The minister of the sacrament must be a believer; there is even reluctance to consider a baptism as performed properly when done by a lay person.

Chrismation is seen as sign of the seal of the Holy Spirit (Acts 2:38). Unlike the normal practice in the Roman church, chrismation is not reserved to the bishop although the myron (chrism) used to anoint the person has been blessed by the bishop who thereby maintains a link with the liturgy.

The Eastern Orthodox do not use the terminology of Roman Catholic theology regarding an *indelible character* for confirmation or chrismation. They commonly confirm/reconfirm those entering the Orthodox church, even from Catholicism, as a sign that a baptism performed under irregular circumstances, outside the canonical boundaries of the church, is not regularized through this sealing. As have Roman Catholics, the Orthodox have sometimes practiced *rebaptism* of those previously baptized in another church. But by the principle of *economy* (*oikonomia*), an Orthodox bishop may declare as objectively administered something administered outside the boundaries of Orthodoxy.

Eucharist or Synaxis

This essay cannot give an account of all the eucharistic liturgies or families of eucharistic anaphoras within the Eastern churches, nor can it provide a summary of the specific theological explanations used to explain the structure and significance of eucharistic prayers.

Both Catholics and Orthodox agree on the meaning of the eucharistic celebration. The eucharistic celebration is the memorial (_anamnesis_) of Christ's work as Savior. The eucharistic sacrifice is seen as involving the active presence of Christ, the High Priest, acting through the Christian community, presided over by the bishop or persons delegated by the bishop to celebrate the eucharistic mysteries. In the eucharistic celebration, believers not only commend themselves and one another to Christ but also accept the diaconal mandate of the gospel to mediate Christ's salvation to the world. God the Father is seen as sending the Holy Spirit to consecrate the elements of bread and wine so as to become the body and blood of Jesus Christ for the sanctification of the faithful. The Holy Spirit transforms the sacred gifts into the body and blood of Christ in order to bring about the growth of the body, which is the church. In this way the entire celebration is an _epiklesis_ which at certain moments becomes more explicit. The church may be said to be continually in a state of epiklesis.

In the Byzantine liturgy and in most Eastern liturgies, the bread used in the Eucharist is leavened bread (i.e., bread made with yeast). In the Roman rite, unleavened bread (_azyme_) is used. A specially prepared loaf of bread is cut into cubes in the preparatory rites of an Eastern liturgy. Communion under the double form of bread and wine is distributed from the chalice in which the eucharistic bread soaked in eucharistic wine is administered by the priest to the communicant from a golden spoon.

Today there is a notable difference between the Eastern Orthodox and the Roman Catholics regarding the frequency of reception of the Eucharist. Orthodox believers out of reverence observe certain practices before approaching the Table of the Lord: receiving the sacrament of reconciliation, fasting for several days before reception, and neither eating nor drinking from midnight. Communicants are expected to abstain from conjugal relations prior to receiving Communion. Some pious Eastern Christians communicate only four times a year: Easter, Christmas, Dormition of the Virgin, and on their own feast day. They find the practice of weekly or daily Communion, as now practiced in the Roman church, fraught with the dangerous possibility of it becoming casual or irreverent.

Intercommunion, that is, offering eucharistic hospitality to Christians who are not Orthodox, is strictly forbidden by the Orthodox and sedulously avoided. Whereas at the Second Vatican Council and in subsequent guidelines, the Roman Catholic church expressed its willingness to permit Orthodox who approach Catholic priests to receive Communion under specific circumstances, the Orthodox did not reciprocate. Orthodoxy requires that a communicant share in the entire range of essential Orthodox beliefs before being eligible for Communion. Thus the exceptional decision by the Moscow Patriarchate (December 16, 1969) to allow some measure of intercommunion for Roman Catholics who approach the sacrament was regarded as very unusual. The Orthodox church of Greece, for example, expressed its "surprise, wonderment, and sorrow" at this decision.

Although lay participation in the Divine Liturgy is often regarded as active, even Orthodox observers are now complaining about the isolation and passivity of the laity at liturgies. The Eastern churches do not practice eucharistic devotions outside of the Divine Liturgy. Hence, Catholic devotions such as Benediction of the Blessed Sacrament are unknown.

Sacramental Reconciliation Within the Church

The Eastern churches practice private confession of postbaptismal sins to a priest. Such a confession takes place in front of the iconostasis. On a nearby stand have been placed a cross as well as an icon of the Savior or the book of the Gospels. After the penitent's confession of sins, the priest places his liturgical stole and his hands upon the penitent's head. Such a laying on of hands is seen as an important sign attesting to the power of the Holy Spirit to forgive sins.

Originally in the East and West, confession of sin or *exhomologesis* was a public act consisting of enrollment on a list of sinners and public penance over a lengthy period of time for serious sins. By the fourth century, private confession was practiced and even associated with spiritual direction from monks or other holy persons. Sacramental confession or reconciliation in the East is not practiced as frequently as it is in modern Catholicism, especially up to the 1960s. The formulas of absolution in the Byzantine *euchologia* (collections of formal prayers) and penitentials use a prayer that is declaratory and avoids the first person, as in the case of baptism. The priest was rarely ever described as judge as in Western theological writings.

Marriage

In the teaching of the East, sacramental marriage requires the mutual consent of the believing Christian partners and God's blessing imparted through a priest of the church. The discipline of the Orthodox church accepts as sacramental only those marriages sanctified through a blessing by an Orthodox priest.

The wedding service in the Byzantine tradition consists of two parts. The first part, the betrothal, takes place in the church's vestibule and includes the blessing of rings and their exchange. After a procession into the church, this is followed by the crowning, a term sometimes used for the marriage service. The bridal couple then follows the officiating priest in a circular procession to symbolize their spiritual journey to eternity.

Basing their teaching on Ephesians 5, Eastern Christians regard marriage as a *mysterion* symbolizing the union between Christ and the church. As such there can only be one, eternal bond. Unlike the view of the West which sees marriage also as a legal contract that ceases with the death of one of the partners, for the East the bond perdures. Up to the tenth century, no second marriage, not even one performed after widowhood, was ever formally blessed liturgically in Eastern churches. A distinction was drawn between first and second marriages, and a special service was introduced for the latter, dissociated from the Eucharist and penitential in character. A second marriage was not the norm and hence somewhat deficient sacramentally.

By the principle of synergy, that is humankind's cooperation with grace, marriage as a sacrament is seen as bestowing of God's grace but requiring human cooperation. The East combines a lofty ideal of indissolubility with realistic legislation that admits exceptions. Eastern teaching interprets the exception clause about divorce in Matthew 19:9 regarding *porneia* to apply to adultery. Adultery is seen as so incompatible with the nature of marriage that Jesus allowed a person to regard a matrimonial bond as non-existent after adultery. The church therefore simply testifies to a cessation when it grants a divorce. The church allows a decree of divorce and remarriage out of mercy in order to avoid greater evil and suffering.

The Roman Catholic church prefers rather to declare if possible an annulment, stating that a marriage bond in fact never existed. To the Orthodox this seems a legal fiction contrary to the intuition of those many Christians in this situation who argue that a real marriage did in fact exist but has died. Eastern churches do not have marriage tribunals or ecclesiastical courts as such.

The Orthodox are particularly concerned about the pastoral problems connected with mixed marriages in the diaspora, and how to provide religious education to the children of such marriages.

Laying on of Hands: Sacrament of Order

The sacramental life of the church also includes sharing in the ordained priesthood, which is conferred through the laying on of hands by a bishop. Ordination designates one permanently for service of the church's life and continued celebration of the Eucharistic liturgy.

The Eastern Orthodox church allows the ordination of married men but does not allow them to remarry even after the death of a spouse once they have been ordained. Since the Synod of Trullo (A.D. 691–692), only the unmarried are ordained or consecrated to the office of bishop.

The liturgy of ordination to the priesthood contains four parts: the approval of the people asserting the person's worthiness (*axios*); the invocation or epiclesis of the Holy Spirit, praying for bestowal of grace; the laying on of hands by the bishop; and the clothing in liturgical vestments.

Consecration to the episcopate is seen as entry into the fullness of priesthood. A bishop must be consecrated by at least three bishops concelebrating together.

Official Eastern Orthodox teaching corresponds to Roman Catholic teaching in affirming the traditional exclusion of women from ordination to the priesthood based on the selection of men only as apostles by Jesus Christ and on what is seen as the necessity of the priest to serve as an iconic representation of Christ.

—— Anointing with Oil for Healing ——

In its teaching on the role of anointing of the sick with holy oil, the Eastern tradition preserves a double tradition, one which associates this anointing with the forgiveness of sins, and a second which draws upon James 5:14 ff. and stresses the healing of the sick. Hence there are really two separate liturgical anointings, one of which is the anointing for the forgiveness of sin even of the healthy at the liturgy of High Thursday, and another which is anointing of the sick. These anointings are both associated with the sacrament of reconciliation.

The practice of anointing the sick, which is not frequently administered today in many Orthodox communities, has all the necessary elements of a _mysterion_: invocation of the Holy Spirit at the blessing of the oil, making it a material vehicle for the Spirit's power.

The rite of Christian burial is also sometimes listed among the sacramental liturgies belonging to the Eastern church.

Michael J. Farley[6]

150 ◆ SACRED ACTIONS IN THE REFORMATION CHURCHES

Protestant emphasis on the Word of God affected the role played by sacraments in Christian life. The more extreme Protestants (Zwinglian Reformed and Anabaptists) generally rejected the idea that God's grace was mediated to people through created things employed in sacraments. Although Lutherans, Calvinists, and Anglicans retained a place for sacraments, they insisted that sacramental practice be reformed according to the Word of God. They insisted that the New Testament authorized only two sacraments: baptism and the Lord's Supper. An emphasis on Word is also evident in the increased importance that all Protestants attached to preaching.

The Reformation understanding and practice of worship began with a sweeping critique of the sacraments and liturgical ceremonies of the medieval church. The central teaching of the Reformers, justification by faith alone (_sola fide_), was a rejection of all human works as the ground of salvation, including the actions of worship insofar as they are purely human traditions and not commanded by God in the Scriptures. For the Reformers, the Word of God rather than sacred action was the essence of Christian worship. Consequently, the actions of worship were the source of controversy with the Roman church and in turn generated disputes that seriously divided the various parties of the Reformation.

The Reformers generally agreed with Martin Luther's (1483–1546) formulation of the problem, forcefully stated in the 1520 treatise, _The Babylonian Captivity of the Church._ Luther focused his attack on the sacramental system of the Roman church. His criticism, however, comprehended the outward and visible rites and ceremonies of the liturgical order as a whole: "[W]e owe everything to faith alone and nothing to rituals" (_Luther's Works,_ ed. Jaroslav Pelikan [St. Louis: Concordia, 1968], 36:64). The inherited practice of liturgy and sacrament in Luther's view had become perverted into a human work performed by a priest for the dispensation of divine grace. The action of worship had been profoundly misconceived as a meritorious, sacrificial (with regard to the Mass), priestly action. From this fundamental misconception, all manner of practical abuses in the church's worship arose, principally those related to the sacrifice of the Mass (the offertory and canon of the Mass, Masses without communicants, private Masses, the buying and selling of Masses for various intentions).

Luther's proposals regarding the essential nature of worship were also widely received by other Reformers, at least in broad outline. Instead of the human actions of worship, Luther stressed the divine saving action in Jesus Christ proclaimed through the Word of God and received by faith. Worship is not a meritorious work but a dynamic exercise of faith in response to the Word. The sacraments (only the two instituted by Christ, baptism and Lord's Supper; not the seven of ecclesiastical tradition) are not, as the scholastic theologians taught, efficacious signs (_efficacia signa_) that operate by the performance of the ritual action (*ex opere operato*) but words of promise attached to the signs of water, bread, and wine made effective by faith. The Mass is not a sacrifice offered to God but a gift apprehended by faith and received in Communion. Finally, worship is not the action of a priest mediating the church's prayer and God's grace but an activity of the common priesthood of all believers in relation to the service of designated ministers of the Word.

Luther recognized that this critique of inherited conceptions and practices called for far-reaching liturgical reforms. Concerning the Mass, he counseled that "it would be necessary to abolish most of the books now in vogue, and to alter almost the entire external form of the churches and introduce, or rather reintroduce, a totally different kind of ceremonies" (*Luther's Works*, 36:36)—new liturgical books, space, and actions. Although the various traditions emerging from the Reformation—Lutheran, Reformed, Anabaptist, Anglican, Separatist, and Puritan—developed distinctive liturgical practices, there are a number of common characteristics and tendencies.

Preaching became an essential and, inevitably, the central action of worship. The Scriptures were read in a language that could be understood and then proclaimed in the living Word of the sermon. The restoration of the reading of Scripture and preaching as central activities in Christian worship, so critical to the reforming principle that "faith comes from hearing" (*fides ex auditu*; Rom. 10:17), has often obscured the extent to which the Reformation was equally a movement of sacramental renewal. Whether the Lord's Supper was celebrated weekly, monthly, or quarterly, people in Reformation churches generally participated in Communion much more frequently than the customary annual Communion of the medieval church. The conduct of the Lord's Supper focused on the acts of hearing Christ's words in the institution narrative and receiving Communion, including the cup previously denied to the people. For the most part, congregational participation was a hallmark of worship in the churches of the Reformation; in the singing of hymns or metrical psalms and in the use of a vernacular liturgy, the people took a more active role in the actions of worship. A tendency to reduce the amount of ceremony and to replace it with didactic prayers and exhortations accompanied this reforming concentration upon the participation of the congregation

in the essential actions of Word and sacrament.

The divisions within the Reformation over the actions of worship primarily concerned two things: (1) the relation of worship, in particular the sacraments, to God's saving action in Jesus Christ, and (2) the role of the Scriptures in determining liturgical practice. A brief survey will clarify how the Reformation generated a number of distinctive liturgical traditions.

Lutheran

The Lutheran conviction that God's Spirit creates faith through concrete means, specifically, through preaching and the sacraments, had direct implications for the actions of worship. The primacy given to the external Word (*verbum externum*) located God's saving activity precisely in the context of worship and gave significance to the outward conduct of the central liturgical actions. The gospel message of the Scriptures was heard in the living voice of a preacher; the infant was immersed (dipped) in the water of baptism; the words of institution at the heart of the Lord's Supper were publicly proclaimed by the minister, not silently prayed by a priest; and the bread and cup were received in the Communion of the people, not observed from afar. The church was, in Luther's words, a "mouth-house" (*Mundhaus*) for the act of proclaiming God's Word and the arena for the embodiment of that saving Word in the sacraments.

The other actions of worship surrounding and supporting the central, biblically mandated actions of Word and sacrament, were understood to be nonessentials (*adiaphora*), purely human traditions, and thus matters of freedom unless they contradicted the doctrine of justification by faith. As a result, the liturgical orders of the Lutheran churches in Germany and Scandinavia exhibited diversity in rite and ceremony. The practice of worship tended to be conservative in its treatment of the liturgical tradition, rich in music, especially the singing of hymns, and tolerant of artistic images. An evangelical Mass with preaching and Communion was the model for worship on Sundays and festivals, following the proposals of Luther in the *Formula missae* (1523) and *Deutsch Messe* (1526). However provision did have to be made for something less than a full celebration when there were no communicants to complete the action.

Reformed

Two divergent understandings of the external actions of worship, one from Ulrich Zwingli (1484–1531) and the other from John Calvin (1509–1564), shaped the liturgies of the Reformed churches. The Zurich Reformer held that "no external element or action can purify the soul" (_On Baptism_, in _Zwingli and Bullinger_, ed. G.W. Bromiley [Louisville, Ky.: Westminster/John Knox, 1979], 156), and consequently the sacraments and ceremonies of worship had limited theological significance. The spiritual worship of Christians was to focus on the activity of God's Word in preaching; the sacramental actions of worship did, however, stimulate the memory of Jesus Christ and provided for the witness, thanksgiving, and fellowship of the congregation. In contrast, Calvin held a view somewhat like Luther's. Calvin located God's saving action in direct relation to the external signs of worship as well as the preaching of the Word. In the sacraments, God conforms divine mercy to human capacity and there "imparts spiritual things under visible ones" (_Institutes of the Christian Religion (1559)_, 4.14.3 [Louisville, Ky.: Westminster/John Knox, 1960], 1278). Calvin developed a rich conception of the sacramental sign that embraced the whole liturgical action and presented a dynamic understanding of how the Holy Spirit uses such signs as instruments, together with the Word, to draw people into communion with God in Christ.

Reformed worship rejected most of the rites and ceremonies of the medieval church in favor of a liturgical simplicity that was thought to reflect the practice of the New Testament and the early church. Church buildings were purged of their images, and music was limited to the singing of metrical psalms. The confession of sin and acts of moral discipline attained particular prominence in Reformed worship. Despite Calvin's efforts to retain the basic structure of the Mass in a weekly service of Word and sacrament, Zwingli's preaching service, modeled after the medieval _prone_, prevailed among Reformed churches and enforced in practice his conception of spiritual worship. Zwingli's quarterly celebration of the Lord's Supper also became the Reformed standard. In contrast to Lutheran practice, where individuals communed as they desired, the Reformed practice of communion involved the entire congregation, either seated at the table(s) or in the pews.

Anabaptist

The various Anabaptist groups, located principally in Switzerland, Germany, Moravia, and the Netherlands, developed further the Zwinglian conception of spiritual worship and sought to establish patterns of worship based solely upon the instruction of the Bible without regard to human traditions. The internal testimony of the Spirit was set in opposition to the external forms of liturgy and sacrament. Anabaptists understood the actions of worship, including the sacraments, primarily as expressions of faith, bonds of communal fellowship, and ethical commitment rather than the means of God's saving activity.

Liturgical orders and fixed forms of prayer were generally rejected in favor of the freedom of the local assembly of believers to order its worship according to scriptural testimony. Worship focused on the reading and exposition of the Scriptures, prayer, and the singing of hymns. The biblically mandated actions of baptism (for adult believers only), the Lord's Supper (the norm being an occasional celebration), and even foot washing (among the Anabaptists in the Netherlands known as Mennonites) were carried out by pure assemblies of believers that practiced a rigorous church discipline, which included the use of the ban and a corresponding act of reconciliation with the laying on of hands.

Anglican

Liturgical practice in the Church of England throughout the Reformation was not governed by a single theological perspective. Thomas Cranmer (1489–1556) was a Reformer and archbishop. The liturgical rites of _The Book of Common Prayer (BCP)_, which come from him, are best understood as an attempt to comprehend the positions of various parties within the church. The result was finally more Reformed than Lutheran in its understanding of the actions of worship, including the sacraments (whether Zwinglian or Calvinist is a matter of debate). The rites of the Prayer Book and the conduct of worship were, however, distinctively Anglican in their reform of the inherited tradition.

The _BCP_, first issued in 1549, provided vernacular liturgies for the Church of England based upon the Latin rites but reformed to reflect the theology and practice of the Reformation. The revisions in the 1552 _BCP_ gave the rites a more Protestant cast in their wording and structure and eliminated much of what remained of medieval ceremony and ornament; this book was the basis of subsequent versions, although controversy continued over the outward conduct of worship. Preaching was introduced into the eucharistic liturgy, but it was not a feature of the daily services of morning and evening prayer, where the psalms, readings, canticles, and prayers were considered a sufficient act of worship. The Prayer Book provided for the celebration of the Lord's Supper on every Sunday and feast day; however, because individuals were required to receive Communion only three times a year, a truncated service with occasional celebrations of the Lord's Supper became the norm in many places. Cranmer's prayers in the English vernacular were a significant literary achievement, but, more importantly, they invigorated worship as an act of common prayer. In the English churches, metrical psalmody rather than hymnody became the staple of congregational singing.

Separatist and Puritan

The rites and ceremonies of the *BCP* were established by law as the uniform practice of the national church. A number of English Reformers influenced by the Reformed tradition on the continent opposed this arrangement. Whether Separatists, who nurtured holy congregations in opposition to any established church, or Puritans of Episcopalian, Presbyterian, or Congregationalist stripe, who sought a purified national church, they were in matters of worship united in two convictions: the reforms of the Prayer Book did not go far enough and the Scriptures were the authoritative source for all practices of worship. These Reformers were Calvinist in their regard for preaching and the sacraments as instruments of God's grace, but they went beyond Calvin and resembled the Anabaptists in their strict biblicism concerning the actions of worship.

The Puritan critique of the Prayer Book focused on ceremonial actions and prayer. Puritan Reformers regularly criticized as unbiblical the sign of the cross at baptism, kneeling at the Eucharist, and the ring given at marriage. They also argued against the use of vestments. To Puritan sensibilities, the prayers in the Prayer Book were either too limited or too complex in form and often irrelevant in content. Although there are examples of printed liturgies, the Puritan position gravitated

toward the Congregationalist practice of free prayer, something that the Separatists had always insisted upon. Consequently, when the Puritans came to power, they instituted a set of detailed instructions for worship, the *Westminster Directory* (1644), rather than a new Puritan prayer book. Puritan worship centered on preaching and the worthy reception of Communion whenever the Lord's Supper was celebrated, which was as often as every Lord's Day among some Separatists and Congregationalists. The Puritans rejected hymns of human composition and limited congregational song to metrical versions of biblical Psalms.

Thomas H. Schattauer

151 ✦ SACRED ACTIONS IN THE PROTESTANT CHURCHES AFTER THE REFORMATION

The emphasis on words and the Word of God in Reformation theologies and the adoption of a fundamentally scholastic method by Protestants developed, under the impact of the Enlightenment, into modern Protestant rationalism. But Protestant scholasticism and rationalism provoked experience-based responses: Pietism (seventeenth century), Methodism and revivalism (eighteenth to nineteenth centuries), and a variety of efforts at worship renewal (nineteenth century).

Three major historical currents have shaped the Protestant understanding and practice of worship during the modern period: Pietism, Rationalism, and Restorationism. The rationalism of the Enlightenment largely determined the way in which Protestant churches elevated preaching and teaching over the actions of liturgy and sacrament. The spoken word was the preferred means for conveying religious concepts and moral instruction in the context of worship. Pietism and recurring movements of spiritual awakening, revival, and renewal countered the dominance of rationalist religion with emphasis on religious experience and spiritual regeneration. Preaching and Bible study, free prayer and hymn singing, rather than the outward actions of worship, however, were the principal means for arousing the religious affections. The rationalist religion of the head and the pietist religion of the heart both preferred the sermonic appeal to the individual over the liturgical and sacramental actions of corporate worship, and together they promoted the religious individualism that has pervaded the modern church and its worship.

In the nineteenth century, there arose among Protestants as well as Roman Catholics a number of movements with the aim to renew the church as a community and to restore liturgical and sacramental worship according to historic patterns. These Restorationist movements were the precursors of the modern liturgical movement, which has been reshaping the worship of many Protestant traditions in the present century. As a result of these historical influences, contemporary Protestant churches are heir to competing tendencies—Pietist, Rationalist, and Restorationist—in their approach to the actions of worship.

St. John Chrysostom. John, the Bishop of Constantinople in the late fourth century, is often called "the golden mouthed" because of his great oratorical skills. His usual symbol is the Bible and chalice, which represent him as a minister of Word and sacrament.

Pietism

Pietism was a reaction in church life and theology to the sometimes stagnant orthodoxy and scholasticism of the post-Reformation period. Thus it originated prior to the modern period, but it had long-lasting effects upon worship throughout the era issuing from the eighteenth-century Enlightenment. Lutheran Pietism in Germany, under the leadership of Philipp Spener (1635–1705) and August Francke (1663–1727), was characterized by the gathering of small groups of Christians for the nurture of personal piety through devotional study of the Bible and the exercise of spiritual and moral discipline. The reform of public worship was not an immediate concern, but the increasing emphasis on conversion and personal piety led to a disregard for the formal structures of common worship. Among the Reformed, at first in the Netherlands and later in Germany, pietist practices had direct impact on the liturgy. Jean de Labadie (1610–1674) and his followers, for example, advocated free prayer and attacked the fixed prayers of standard Reformed liturgies as the pretense of the unconverted. Among Scotch Presbyterians, the dissolution of formal liturgical worship came about under the influence of English Puritanism. After the failure of the Puritans to establish permanently the principle of liturgical freedom in the Church of England itself, there developed an evangelical party in the church with convictions similar to those of the continental Pietists.

In general, Pietist religion gave impetus to a devotional style of worship emphasizing preaching, prayer, and hymn singing and showed a lack of interest in the outward actions of liturgy and sacrament. It exalted the experience of conversion over baptism, spiritual discipline and worthiness over frequent participation in Communion, and lengthy free prayer over the structured liturgical prayer. Unwittingly, Pietism prepared the way for Rationalism and its assault upon the actions of historic Christian worship.

Rationalism

The eighteenth-century Enlightenment, with its rationalist critique of religious belief and practice, ushered in the modern period. The Reformation traditions had carried out various liturgical reforms based upon a theology of the Word and the authority of the Scriptures, but the fundamental practices of historic Christian worship were nonetheless passed on to succeeding generations. The rationalism of the Enlightenment subjected worship to a far more radical critique based upon the powers of human reason. The result was a rupture in the liturgical tradition arguably deeper than that of the Reformation itself. Whereas the Reformation critique of sacred action had reformed the inherited practice of worship, the Enlightenment critique dismissed the actions of worship as largely irrelevant to the essentially rational and moral purposes of religion. Worship was no longer an assembly for acts of communion with God, but rather a stage for the communication of ideas about God and the good.

The forces of Rationalism effectively eliminated what remained of a sacramental piety that valued baptism and the Lord's Supper as communal enactments of God's relation to humankind, but sacramental practice did not completely disappear. A marked decline in the frequency of Eucharistic celebration and participation in Communion are apparent in every tradition. Although far from central to religious faith, the sacraments were retained in obedience to the literal command of God and for their value as symbolic memorials to Christ and aids to virtuous living. Rationalist religion eliminated useless ceremonial action in favor of formal acts of speech that instructed the mind, whether in sermon or in prayer. Much of the service was regularly conducted from an elevated pulpit, and the focus fell on preaching that communicated religious and moral ideas. The formality of fixed liturgical forms was preferred to the excessive enthusiasm of free prayer. Indeed, liturgical proposals and collections of rites proliferated, most of it captive to the new theology and spirit of Rationalism. See for example the proposals of Samuel Clark (1675–1729) to reform *The Book of Common Prayer,* Jean Alphonse Turretin's (1671–1737) liturgy for the Reformed church in Geneva, and the many privately produced *Agenden* among German Lutherans. At the same time, a more churchly direction appeared in the liturgical work of the Reformed pastor, Jean Frederic Ostervald (1663–1747) at Neuchatel, Switzerland, and that of the Erlangen professor and Lutheran church leader, Georg Friedrich Seiler (1733–1807).

Moravians, Methodists, and Revivalism

The Pietistic impulse in worship continued throughout the eighteenth century and into the nineteenth, manifesting itself in many contexts, including the worship of the Moravian Brethren, the Methodist movement, and the outbreaks of religious awakening and revival. The Moravian Brethren, who established themselves at Herrnhut under the leadership of the Lutheran Pietist leader, Count Nicholas von Zinzendorf (1700–1760), developed a communitarian Pietism that placed great stress on worship in small groups and in common. The gatherings of this warm fellowship were very devotional and noteworthy for their music and hymnody. Their worship often resonated with ancient actions—love feasts, foot washings, vigils, and litanies—in a new setting that nurtured a deep piety of personal communion with the crucified Savior.

The Anglican priest and Methodist leader John Wesley (1703–1791) was himself greatly influenced by the Pietism of the Moravian Brethren, and he introduced a number of Moravian practices, including love feasts, watch nights (vigils), and the informal worship of small groups to nurture religious experience. He also devised an annual act of covenant renewal. Preaching services with free prayer and an abundance of hymns were the essentials of Methodist worship, and field preaching was adopted as a means for reaching the unchurched masses. Against the prevailing tendencies of the Enlightenment, Wesley also attempted to restore the practice of sacramental worship. He held to an understanding of the Lord's Supper as a means of grace and encouraged frequent participation in Communion. Wesley's traditional concern for the fundamental actions of worship is evident in his *Sunday Service for Methodists of North America* (1784), a revision of *The Book of Common Prayer.* In America, Methodists quickly abandoned Wesley's regard for liturgy and sacrament in favor of simple services of preaching, free prayer, and hymnody in conformity with the sensibilities of the American frontier.

Rooted in the religious awakenings of the eighteenth century, Revivalism established a distinctive practice of worship on the nineteenth-century American frontier. In contrast to the historic practices of Christian worship fashioned for a community of the converted, revivalist religion aimed at the unconverted. The camp meetings of the frontier (derived from the practice of sacramental seasons among Scottish Presbyterians) were the occasion for evangelistic preaching, free prayer, and song extending over several days and concluding with the baptism of new converts and the Lord's Supper. The sacraments had an important place in revivalist religion, but they were understood from a rationalist perspective as human acts of commitment and remembrance that prompted upright behavior. New practices involving the mourner's bench or anxious seat, the altar call, and emotional behavior all served the principal aim of worship: to produce repentance and conversion. Revivalist patterns affected the worship of most Protestant churches in America (including the black churches), particularly Baptist, Methodist, Presbyterian, and the new denominations of the frontier, the Christian Church (Disciples of Christ) and the Churches of Christ. Charles G. Finney (1792–1875) effectively promoted these _new measures_ with the argument that they worked. Such liturgical pragmatism became a powerful force shaping Protestant worship in America.

Restorationism

In the nineteenth century, there arose a number of movements seeking to restore the common life of the church, including its worship, according to historic models. Under the influence of Romanticism and in the midst of the social dislocation and political ferment of the Industrial age, these Restorationist movements acted against the rationalistic ethos dominating the churches and their worship and equally against the inwardness of Pietistic religion. In England, Anglo-Catholics fostered the liturgical revival. Edward B. Pusey (1800–1882), a leader in the Oxford Movement, advocated the restoration of eucharistic worship and the use of medieval ceremonial in the parish churches that came under his influence. John Mason Neale (1818–1866) wrote hymns based on Greek and Latin texts and founded the Cambridge Camden Society to further both ritual concerns and the Gothic revival in church architecture. American Episcopalians also felt the influence of Anglo-Catholic liturgical practice. In Germany, interest in liturgical and sacramental worship accompanied the rise of Lutheran confessionalism. From his parish in Neuendettelsau, Bavaria, Wilhelm Löhe (1808–1872) promoted a recovery of the evangelical Mass and a full range of liturgical concerns based upon his study of earlier Lutheran practice and the witness of the early church. Through his one _Agende_ and the work of his missionaries among German immigrants, Löhe's liturgical ideas spread to North America. Theodor Kliefoth (1810–1895) advanced similar liturgical interests in the Lutheran Church of Mecklenburg. In Denmark, Nikolai F. S. Grundtvig (1783–1872) inspired a renewal of sacramental worship. Out of Scottish Presbyterianism came the Catholic Apostolic Church, with its elaborate ceremonial and eucharistic liturgy based upon patristic sources. Among the German Reformed in America, the Mercersburg theology of John W. Nevin (1803–1886) and Philip Schaff (1819–1893) encouraged a renewal of sacramental life and produced a liturgy that reflected both their Catholic interests and their adherence to the Reformation.

The common concern of these Restorationist movements for the communal character of the church in contrast to the religious individualism of both Rationalist and Pietist religion generated serious attention to liturgical and sacramental action. Preaching was not forsaken, but the Eucharist gained a central place in the theology and practice of worship. The sacraments in the context of worship were understood as a locus of divine action and a means of communion with God. The appreciation for ritual and ceremony corresponded to a heightened concern for the visibility of the church. Whether they appealed to the early church, to the Middle Ages, or to more conservative reforms at the time of the Reformation, the movements for ecclesial restoration shared a common conviction: The restored actions of worship constituted a relation to the historic Christian community that would revitalize the church's identity in the modern world.

Thomas H. Schattauer

152 ✦ SACRED ACTIONS IN THE PROTESTANT CHURCHES TODAY

Ever ready to adopt new methods, Protestants have been affected by new means of communication and contemporary cultural trends during the twentieth century. In addition, powerful movements of liturgical renewal, combined with the twentieth-century Pentecostal and charismatic movements have changed the face of Protestant worship.

In regard to the actions of worship, contemporary Protestant churches have inherited competing impulses from the major movements of the modern period: Pietism, Rationalism, and Restorationism. To this should be added three additional influences: the liturgical pragmatism that grew out of revivalist religion on the American frontier and has found recent expression in televangelism and the church growth movement; the modern liturgical movement in both its Roman Catholic and Protestant manifestations, which developed out of the Restorationism of the nineteenth century; and the charismatic renewal that has emerged from twentieth-century Pentecostalism. The various Protestant traditions of worship have assimilated (or resisted) these impulses and influences in different ways, but widespread ferment concerning the actions of worship continues.

The present century has been a period of unprecedented liturgical change for Roman Catholics and most Protestants. The revision of official liturgical books and the production of such books where none previously existed is the primary symptom as well as the principal agent for the renewal of liturgical practice. Among American Protestants, this is especially true of Lutherans, Episcopalians, Presbyterians, Methodists, and, to some extent, the United Church of Christ. Baptism has gained prominence as the rite of entry into the Christian community and the foundation of life in Christ. In addition to fuller rites for baptism itself, there are provisions for the affirmation and the renewal of baptism as well as proposals to elaborate baptism further as part of an extended catechumenal process. The Eucharist has increasingly become a regular part of Protestant worship, with a renewed emphasis on the act of thanksgiving and on the communion both with Christ and among the people of God. Although frequency in the celebration of the Lord's Supper varies from tradition to tradition, a unified service of Word and sacrament on every Sunday (and feast day) is the practice envisioned by the new liturgies. The liturgical context of preaching has been stressed in the use of new lectionaries. Rites that resonate with historic ritual action have been provided for the celebration of Holy Week and the ancient Easter Vigil. Concern for ritual action is likewise evident in the services provided for ordination, marriage, and burial as well as the pastoral care of the sick and those in need of confession and forgiveness. The conduct of worship, including the gestures and movement of the congregation and those leading worship, has also received fresh attention.

Some of the factors contributing to contemporary interest among Protestant churches in the actions of worship include the following.

Theological. The recovery of eschatological categories stimulated by modern biblical studies has provided new ways to understand the fundamental nature of the church and its worship. When the church is understood as an eschatological community anticipating the kingdom of God proclaimed by Jesus and inaugurated in his death and resurrection, then it is the very nature of that community to be symbolic. The church is a symbolic community that points beyond itself to the reality of God's kingdom, and consequently symbolic action, most especially liturgy and sacrament, constitutes the life of the church. Such a view is more compatible with Protestant theology than the allegorical interpretations of sacred actions in the Middle Ages or even patristic understandings based upon incarnational categories.

Anthropological. The studies of cultural anthropologists have shown that ritual behavior is foundational to human culture and have demonstrated how it functions to establish meaning and to sustain social cohesion. The church as a genuinely human community inevitably employs ritual action to constitute its way of life and system of belief.

Ecumenical. The profound changes in Roman Catholic worship have had enormous impact upon Protestant worship. Inspired by the liturgical movement, the Second Vatican Council initiated a massive effort to reform the Roman liturgical books and to renew liturgical practice. As Roman Catholics adopted the vernacular, expanded the use of hymnody, and took seriously the use of the Scriptures and the place of preaching in the liturgy, many Protestant churches discovered a new freedom to take up Catholic practices and to participate fully in the recovery of a common liturgical heritage.

Cultural. The cultural factors include the following: the dissolution of Christendom and the crisis of Christian identity in a pluralistic and secular culture; the post-modern intellectual environment, in which the Enlightenment critique of religious practice has given way to a new appreciation of ritual and symbol; and the domination of the electronic media, especially television, over other forms of communication (oral or typographical) in contemporary society. This last factor has encouraged word-centered Protestants to give more attention to the visual and kinesthetic dimensions of worship, but among the liturgical pragmatists it has become the rationale for turning Christian worship into another form of entertainment.

Thomas H. Schattauer

153 ◆ BIBLIOGRAPHY ON THE SACRAMENTS, ORDINANCES, AND SACRED ACTIONS OF CHRISTIAN WORSHIP

Baillie, Donald. *Theology of the Sacraments and Other Papers.* New York: Scribner's, 1957. A study by a leading systematic theologian in the Reformed (Calvinist) tradition.

Bausch, William J. *A New Look at the Sacraments.* Notre Dame, Ind.: Fides/Claretian, 1977.

Barrett, C(harles) K(ingsley). *Church, Ministry, and Sacraments in the New Testament.* Grand Rapids: Eerdmans, 1986.

Beachy, Alvin J. *Worship as Celebration of Covenant and Incarnation.* Scottdale, Pa.: Herald, 1968. One of the few studies of worship and sacraments from a Mennonite perspective.

Beasley-Murray, Stephen. *Towards a Metaphysics of the Sacred.* National Association of Baptist Professors of Religion, Special Studies Series, 8. Macon, Ga.: Mercer University Press, 1984. A Baptist theologian's understanding of metaphysics, with implications for sacramental theology.

Berkouwer, G. C. *Studies in Dogmatics.* Vol. 10, *The Sacraments.* Translated by Hugo Bekker. Grand Rapids: Eerdmans, 1969. A classic study in the Reformed tradition by a Dutch Reformed theologian.

Bildstein, Walter. *Spirit in the Body: A Guide to Understanding the Catholic Sacraments.* Dubuque, Ia.: Brown Roa Publishing Media, 1989. The volume is a concise summary of sacramental theology, liturgical ritual and language of the seven sacraments. The introduction defines the sacraments as signs of the covenant between God and humanity and is followed by notes on the sacraments with scriptural texts and liturgical formulae given for each. The book also contains a glossary of terms used in sacramental theology. Roman Catholic.

Borgen, Ole E., *John Wesley on the Sacraments.* Grand Rapids: Zondervan, 1986. Methodist.

The Brethren Encyclopedia. 3 vols. Ambler, Pa.: Brethren Encyclopedia, 1983. A survey of all aspects of life in the Church of the Brethren (German Baptist Brethren), a restitutionist ("New Testament alone") believers' church group that developed its own unique manner of celebrating the Lord's Supper and baptism. The Brethren also emphasize anointing with oil for healing. These three volumes contain descriptive articles, illustrations, and extensive bibliography on all aspects of sacred actions in this denomination and related groups.

Brett, Laurence. *The Message of the Sacraments.* Vol. 8, *Redeemed Creation: The Sacramentals Today.* Wilmington, Del.: Michael Glazier, 1984. Covers the Roman Catholic sacred actions outside the seven sacraments: the liturgical year, the monastic divine office (psalmody, Scripture reading), church architecture, the rosary, veneration of the Reserved Sacrament, and footwashing.

Bromiley, Geoffrey W. *Sacramental Teaching and Practice in the Reformation Churches.* Grand Rapids: Eerdmans, 1957.

Browning, Robert L., and Roy Reed. *The Sacraments in Religious Education and Liturgy: An Ecumenical Model.* Birmingham, Ala.: Religious Education Press, 1985.

Champlin, Joseph M. *Special Signs of Grace.* Collegeville, Minn.: Liturgical Press, 1986. Champlin writes a popular, updated explanation of sacramentals. Catholic tradition, current teaching, and future thought on the subject is covered in a ten-chapter exposition. Chapters one and ten deal with sacramental/ritual theology and praxis and sandwich discourse on baptism, confirmation, Eucharist, penance, anointing, matrimony, and Holy Orders. Discussion questions and bibliography is provided for each of the chapters. Roman Catholic.

Clark, Neville. *An Approach to the Theology of the Sacraments.* London: SCM, 1956. Baptist.

Cooke, Bernard J. *Christian Sacraments and Chris-*

tian Personality. New York: Holt, Rinehart, Winston, 1965; *Ministry to Word and Sacrament.* Philadelphia: Fortress, 1976; *Sacraments and Sacramentality.* Mystic, Conn.: Twenty-Third Publications, 1983. These three works are representative of Cooke's approach, a contemporary Roman Catholic sacramental theology drawing on modern social sciences.

Costen, Melva Wilson. *African American Christian Worship.* Nashville: Abingdon, 1993. See Chapter Five on the sacraments and ordinances of worship.

Davies, J(ohn) G(ordon). *The Spirit, the Church, and the Sacraments.* London: Faith Press, 1954. Anglican.

DiGidio, Sandra. *Sacraments Alive.* Mystic, Conn.: Twenty-Third Publications, 1991. The book written by a liturgist and Christian educator is especially designed as a practical/pastoral handbook for laity regarding renewed sacramental theology in the Roman Catholic tradition. Following an introduction to the sacraments, DeGidio groups the sacraments under baptism, confirmation, and the Eucharist. Theological insights and liturgical suggestions are blended with personal reflection and descriptions of the processes related to each sacrament. Discussion questions follow each chapter. Roman Catholic.

Donlan, Thomas C., O.P., et al. *Christ and His Sacraments.* Dubuque, Ia.: Priory Press, 1960. As a textbook for Catholic college students, this work gives a good survey of Roman Catholic teaching on the sacraments before the Second Vatican Council. Together with *The Documents of Vatican II* (various editions, including the paperback edition edited by Walter M. Abbott in 1966), this book offers a good overview. See also the *Catechism of the Council of Trent for Parish Priests*, the second revised edition of the translation by John A. McHugh, O.P., and Charles J. Callan, O.P. (New York: Joseph Wagner, 1923 and many other editions). This catechism was the official doctrinal textbook for Roman Catholics from 1566 to 1992, when *The Catechism of the Catholic Church* appeared. Part Two of the Roman Catechism deals with the sacraments. Taken together, these books provide the most trustworthy access to Roman Catholic teaching.

Downey, Michael. *Clothed in Christ: The Sacraments and Christian Living.* New York: Crossroad, 1987.

Duffy, Regis A., O.F.M. *Real Presence: Worship, Sacraments, and Commitment.* San Francisco: Harper and Row, 1982. A brief study of sacramental theology from a progressive rather than traditional Roman Catholic perspective, correlating sacramental theology with contemporary developmental psychology and other social sciences.

Eller, Vernard. *In Place of Sacraments: A Study of Baptism and the Lord's Supper.* Grand Rapids: Eerdmans, 1972. Articulates a basic believers' church, non-sacramental theology of ordinances. Church of the Brethren.

Fink, Peter E. *Worship: Praying the Sacraments.* Washington, D.C.: Pastoral Press, 1991. The author's goal is to weave liturgy and doctrine of the sacraments together in a cohesive pattern of prayer that he contends shapes our lives profoundly as Christians. He addresses conciliar and preconciliar sacramental understandings, the "intersection of theology, liturgy and life," the truths conveyed in celebration, sacramental "language(s)," and the relationship of private and communal prayer. Ecumenical/Roman Catholic.

Fink, Peter, S.J., ed. *The New Dictionary of Sacramental Worship.* Collegeville, Minn.: Liturgical Press, 1990. A massive reference source written primarily from a revisionist, contemporary Roman Catholic perspective.

Ganoczy, Alexandre. *An Introduction to Catholic Sacramental Theology.* Translated by William Thomas. New York: Paulist Press, 1984.

Gelpi, Donald, *Charism and Sacrament.* New York: Paulist, 1976. A charismatic Roman Catholic approach to sacraments.

Guzie, Tad. *The Book of Sacramental Basics.* New York: Paulist Press, 1981. Guzie explores the two different perspectives of the sacraments; one understands the sacrament as either the means of giving grace or the celebration of those who have received grace. Opting for the former, he advocates that the "rhythmic" integrity of reflective experience, story, and festivity should capture the significance of sacraments, focusing on the sacraments as something we do (as actions, not things). The volume is additionally valuable for its discussion of sacramental categories, process, evangelism, and children's sacraments. Ecumenical/Roman Catholic.

Hageman, Howard G. *Pulpit and Table.* Richmond: John Knox, 1962. A history of worship and sacraments in the Reformed tradition.

Harrison, Richard L., Jr. "Early Disciples of Sacramental Theology: Catholic, Reformed, and Free." In _Classic Themes of Disciples Theology: Rethinking the Traditional Affirmations of the Christian Church (Disciples of Christ)_, ed. Kenneth Lawrence, 49–100. Fort Worth, Tex.: Texas Christian University Press, 1986. Drawing on the major denominations that emerged from the uniquely American Restorationist ("New Testament alone") movement of the early nineteenth century.

Hatchett, Marion. _Sanctifying Life, Time and Space_. New York: Crossroad/Seabury, 1976. Hatchett surveys Christian liturgical tradition and contemporary praxis, concluding that the rites and sacraments of the church sanctify life, the daily office, and the liturgical year; that music sanctifies time; and that church architecture, color, and art sanctify space. His goal is liturgical theology that firmly grasps the integrity of the Bible, theology, church history and pastoralia, while critically distinguishing what is intrinsic and extraneous. Ecumenical/Anglican.

Hellwig, Monika. _The Meaning of Sacraments_. Dayton: Pflaum/Standard, 1972.

Howard, Thomas. _Evangelical Is Not Enough: Worship of God in Liturgy and Sacrament_. Nashville: Thomas Nelson, 1984; San Francisco: Ignatius Press, 1988.

Huebsch, Bill. _Rethinking Sacraments_. Mystic, Conn.: Twenty-Third Publications, 1989. If "global renewal can (only) begin . . . in the individual human heart," Heubsch believes that the hopeful, holy moments captured in the sacraments are the place to begin that renewal. His volume is a unique composition of poetry that contemporaneously captures the meaning of each sacrament familiar to Catholics and five more that are often overlooked. The work is thought-provoking and might be considered controversial. Ecumenical/Roman Catholic.

Hugh of St. Victor. _On the Sacraments of the Christian Faith_. 2.6.13. Trans. Roy J. Deferrari. Cambridge: Mediaeval Academy of America, 1951. One of several comprehensive medieval treatises on the sacraments. At the same time, Hugh of St. Victor intended it as a basic survey of theology in general because sacraments were central to medieval theology.

Jenson, Robert W. _Visible Words: The Interpretation and Practice of Christian Sacraments_. Philadelphia: Fortress, 1978. An excellent study of sacramental theology by a Lutheran theologian, yet not narrowly confessional.

Jones, Cheslyn, Geoffrey Wainwright, Edward Yarnold, and Paul Bradshaw, eds. _The Study of Liturgy_. 2d ed. Oxford: Oxford University Press, 1992. An excellent single-volume survey of liturgical and sacramental history and theology. Protestant, Orthodox, and Roman Catholic.

Lawler, Michael. _Symbol and Sacrament_. New York: Paulist Press, 1987. The sacraments are "prophetic symbols" whose theology may be studied best by drawing together streams of historic and contemporary studies of the Bible and liturgy, and the disciplines of philosophy and anthropology. However, sacramental theology can not avoid pressing issues such as infant baptism, ordination of women, and pastoral matters arising from praxis. Lawler's format is to consider thoroughly each sacrament in order to realize his vision of a contemporary sacramental theology which lives up to the ancient goal, "Sacraments are for people." Ecumenical/Roman Catholic.

Limouris, Gennadios, and Nomikos Michael Vaporis, eds. _Orthodox Perspectives on Baptism, Eucharist, and Ministry_. Faith and Order Paper, no. 128. Brookline, Mass.: Holy Cross Orthodox Press, 1985. See also _The Greek Orthodox Theological Review_ 30:2 (Summer, 1985).

Luther, Martin. _Luther's Works_. Vols. 1–4; vols. 35–38, _Word and Sacrament,_ ed. Helmut T. Lenmann. Philadelphia: Muhlenberg, 1961, 1971.

Maring, Norman H., and Winthrop S. Hudson. _Manual of Polity and Practice_. Valley Forge, Pa.: Judson Press, 1991. A Baptist treatise which includes a section on the sacraments.

Marpeck, Pilgram. "The Writings of Pilgram Marpeck." In _Classics of the Radical Reformation_, Vol. 2, translated by William Klassen and Walter Klaassen. Scottdale, Pa.: Herald, 1978. As a whole, the Anabaptists were radically anti-sacramental, but Pilgram Marpeck came the closest to a sacramental understanding of baptism when he taught that water baptism and the Lord's Table functioned as cowitness to the effective work of the Holy Spirit.

Martos, Joseph. *Doors to the Sacred: A Historical Introduction to Sacraments in the Catholic Church.* Expanded edition. Tarrytown, N.Y.: Triumph Books, 1991; *The Message of the Sacraments.* Vol. 1, *The Catholic Sacraments.* Wilmington, Del.: Michael Glazier, 1983.

Murray, Donal. *Life and Sacrament: Reflections on the Catholic Vision.* Vol. 4, *Theology and Life.* Wilmington, Del.: Michael Glazier, 1983.

Mick, Lawrence E. *Understanding the Sacraments Today.* Collegeville, Minn.: Liturgical Press, 1987. Sacramental theology has changed significantly since the Second Vatican Council, and Mick attempts to keep the reader abreast of those changes to meaning and praxis. The volume is written in a popular style, gives a brief history of the sacraments, updates the meaning of each for the modern participant, and is designed for personal and group study at many interest levels. Roman Catholic.

Neuner, Joseph, S.J., and Jacques Dupuis, S.J., eds. *The Christian Faith in the Doctrinal Documents of the Catholic Church.* Rev. ed. Staten Island, N.Y.: Alba House, 1981. This is an English version of the standard Latin collection of Roman Catholic official doctrinal statements: Heinrich Denzinger, *Enchiridion symbolorum, definitionum, et declarationum de rebus fidei et morum,* and various editions throughout the twentieth century. Later editions were revised by another scholar—hence the collection is often referred to as Denzinger-Sch'nmetzer.

Osborne, Kenan B. *Sacramental Theology: A General Introduction.* New York: Paulist Press, 1989.

O'Neill, Colman. *Theology and Life.* Vol. 2, *Sacramental Realism: A General Theory of the Sacraments.* Wilmington, Del.: Michael Glazier, 1983.

Pachence, Ronald A. *Speaking of Sacraments.* Phoenix, Ariz.: WinterSun Publications, 1988. Sacraments are the "actions of Christ (not just things or rituals of the church), which we do (not just the priest or deacon or bishop), in memory of the Lord until He comes again," asserts Pachence. "Every Christic activity we do is sacramental." Pachence contends this view transcends the notion of cultic worship and recalls the ministry relationship of disciples to the world. He designs this volume to translate the sacraments into a modern world in a fresh way which invites dialogue and provokes answers to the discussion questions at the end of each chapter. Roman Catholic.

Palmer, Paul F., S.J., ed. *Sources of Christian Theology.* Vol. 1, *Sacraments and Worship: Liturgy and Doctrinal Development of Baptism, Confirmation, and the Eucharist.* Westminster, Md.: Newman Press, 1955; Vol. 2, *Sacraments and Forgiveness: History and Doctrinal Development of Penance, Extreme Unction, and Indulgences.* Westminster, Md.: Newman Press, 1959. These two volumes contain the essential documents regarding the sacraments from a Roman Catholic perspective (which, of course, includes the general developments in the Western church up to the Protestant Reformation) in English translation and with commentary. A standard, essential sourcebook.

Pannenberg, Wolfhart. *Christian Spirituality and Sacramental Community.* London: Darton, Longman, and Todd, 1984. A widely respected European Protestant theologian outlines a Protestant spirituality that rejects penitential pietism as too individualistic and neurotic and bases his proposal on the Eucharist, not the sermon.

Richter, Klemens. *The Meaning of the Sacramental Symbols.* Collegeville, Minn.: Liturgical Press, 1990. The liturgy, sacraments, the Easter Vigil, expressive bodily actions, places for worship activities, and the elementary symbols (candles, incense, vestments, and so on) is a sample of the fifty-nine subject headings discussed as sacramental symbols in this volume which enables participants to proclaim and celebrate Christian faith. Richter traces the origins and history of symbols in order to find contemporary significance. Ecumenical/Roman Catholic.

Rahner, Karl. *The Church and the Sacraments.* London: Burns and Oates, 1963. The statement on sacramental theology by perhaps the most influential Roman Catholic theologian of this century.

Rogers, Elizabeth Frances, trans. *Peter Lombard and the Sacramental System.* Reprint. Scarsdale, N.Y.: Richwood, 1976. A translation of portions of Peter Lombard's *Book of Sentences,* the basic medieval textbook of theology.

Schillebeeckx, Edward. *Christ, the Sacrament of the Encounter with God.* New York: Sheed and Ward, 1963. An early effort in Roman Catholic revisionism regarding the sacraments rooted in theological anthropology, i.e., taking its point of departure from human experience and correlating it with dogmatic Catholic teaching.

Schanz, John P. *Introduction to the Sacraments.* New York: Pueblo Publishing, 1983. Schanz examines the anthropological, biblical, traditional, and historico-theological base for sacramental theology in a modern framework. His work involves an examination of religion and ritual worship at the root of human existence and culminates in an understanding of the sacraments as the actualization of Christ's salvation through word and rite in the church. Roman Catholic.

Schmemann, Alexander. *For the Life of the World.* Crestwood, N.Y.: St. Vladimir's Seminary Press, 1973. Originally published as *Sacraments and Orthodoxy* (1965). Discusses the sacraments from an Eastern Orthodox perspective.

Sedgwick, Timothy F. *Sacramental Ethics: Paschal Identity and the Christian Life.* Philadelphia: Fortress Press, 1987.

Segundo, Juan Luis. *The Sacraments Today.* Translated by John Drury. Maryknoll, N.Y.: Orbis Books, 1974. A Roman Catholic liberation theologian argues that sacraments must be desacralized and secularized if they are to be meaningful today (an argument that parallels sixteenth-century Radical Protestants).

Semmelroth, Otto. *Church and Sacrament.* Notre Dame, Ind.: Fides Publishers, 1965.

Staehlin, Wilhelm. *The Mystery of God: The Presence of God with Men.* Translated by R. Birch Hoyle. St. Louis: Concordia, 1937, 1964. Lutheran.

Staples, Rob L. *Outward Sign and Inward Grace: The Place of Sacraments in Wesleyan Spirituality.* Kansas City: Beacon Hill Press, 1991. The author contends that the place of sacraments in Wesleyan spirituality has been misunderstood precisely because it does not flow from the "headwaters" of Wesley's convictions but more from the merged streams of Methodism and the early nineteenth-century Holiness movement in the United States. Through a discussion of baptism, infant baptism, and the Eucharist, Staples outlines Wesley's unique sacramentalism—which may be a surprising revelation to all interested parties. The book is scholarly and readable. Ecumenical/Methodist.

Taylor, Michael J. *The Sacraments as Encasement:*

Jesus Is with Us. Collegeville, Minn.: Liturgical Press, 1985. Surrounding the sacraments with "socio-cultural humanistic scientific relevance and value" devalues their function as proclaimers of the risen Jesus' presence with his church which tells human beings "something important, significant and striking" about their lives. The sacraments are "encasements" of the presence of Christ—tangible symbols of God's love and calling which give Christ to the church. The author laments and doubts the viability of Christianity devoid of visible, audible, and tangible symbols. Roman Catholic.

Upton, Julia. *A Church for the Next Generation.* Collegeville, Minn.: Liturgical Press, 1990. Upton's short volume focuses on the evolutionary changes that are taking place in the church since the Second Vatican Council with respect to the understanding of the sacraments. Upton notes the shift of emphasis to the participating community in the dynamic organism that is the church; presents many pastoral challenges that have arisen; and optimistically considers the future of the ecclesial model envisioned by RCIA. Ecumenical/Roman Catholic.

Vaillancourt, Raymond. *Toward a Renewal of Sacramental Theology.* Collegeville, Minn.: Liturgical Press, 1979. A liturgical approach to sacraments.

White, James F. *Sacraments as God's Self-Giving.* Nashville: Abingdon, 1983. This volume is an eminent scholar's look at the sacraments in mainline Protestant churches. White's "liturgical circle" employs liturgical exegesis, theological reflection, and praxis reform to challenge sacramental reductionism and to offer thirty-five proposals to return the power of physical symbolism to the church. His functional approach creates new and recovers some old meanings lost in Protestant sacramental theology and praxis. Ultimately, he views sacraments as "sign-acts" of God's self-giving. Ecumenical.

Worgul, George S. *From Magic to Metaphor.* New York: Paulist Press, 1980. The author employs the insights of anthropology, sociology, physiology and philosophy with the reflections of theology to develop a sacramental theology which recovers the significance of relational ritual for culture and the church. He introduces sacraments as symbols—a classification of signs that are powerful and deep, and disclose a reality by actually making it present. These symbols point to realities different than themselves and make it present without being identical to it, therefore expressing the fundamental metaphors of the Christian community. Ecumenical/Roman Catholic.

Yoder, Charles F. *God's Means of Grace.* Elgin, Ill.: Brethren Publishing House, 1908. Reprint. Winona Lake, Ind.: BMH Books, 1979. The author, a member of the Progressive Brethren, a branch of the Church of the Brethren, restates believers' church ordinance theology.

See also the bibliographies on the theology of baptism and the Lord's Supper for theological perspectives on the sacraments.

PART THREE

Baptism

One of the most joy-filled and poignant of the sacred actions of the church is Christian baptism. In this act, the candidate takes on a new identity in Christ and becomes part of Christ's body, the church. Understanding baptism is thus an act of self-understanding for every worshiper. The following chapters introduce the reader to the rich imagery, symbolism, and meaning of Christian baptism. They record how this sacred action has been celebrated throughout the history of the church. And they present liturgical texts from many worship traditions, suggesting the rich diversity of actions which accompany baptism throughout the church.

Baptism is a part of initiation into the life of the church. At times this initiation has been marked with the single occasion: baptism. At other times, it has been marked by a several-stage journey: baptism, confirmation, and first Communion. Thus, throughout this section, articles discuss the relationship of these acts of initiation. Most traditions today are moving to a single act of initiation. Notice how this movement shapes the baptismal liturgies presented in chapter 6. For the traditions that maintain a separate act of confirmation, chapter 7 is devoted to the act of confirmation.

Finally, baptism is an identity-shaping action. It names us as members of Christ's body. It is important for worshipers to remember their identity in Christ. This shapes and inspires every aspect of their life in the church and in the world. In order to develop and strengthen this sense of identity, many worship traditions are currently practicing acts of renewal of baptism. This practice is described in chapter 8.

❧ FOUR ❧

The History of Baptism

Baptism remains the point of entry into the Christian church. However, the form of baptism has developed through the centuries. Catechism shifted from before baptism to after baptism in the medieval church as infant baptism became the most common path of initiation. In the Western church, anointing with oil (chrism) became detached from baptism and developed into a separate sacrament (confirmation). First Communion was also delayed until the child was old enough to understand the significance of the Eucharist. Western scholastic theologians described baptism as marking the person and explained the relationship between Christ's work and the priest's instrumentality in the sacrament. On the other hand, Eastern Orthodox churches continued to include baptism, chrismation, and first Communion in the initiation rites of even infants.

During the Reformation, Radical Reformation sects (Anabaptists, later English Baptists, and various free churches) challenged infant baptism. The main Protestant groups (Lutherans, Reformed, Anglicans) retained infant baptism and developed theologies such as covenant theology to justify it. During the twentieth century, adult-baptizing churches began to examine their practice, realizing that it could cause difficulties for children who grow into the faith without experiencing a clear conversion. Yet some Protestant theologians of the infant-baptizing denominations rejected the legitimacy of infant baptism. Roman Catholics, on the other hand, restored the prebaptismal catechumenate, the Rite of Christian Initiation for Adults, and sought ways to ensure that parents and godparents of baptized infants were committed to the child's Christian nurture after baptism.

Most of the larger Christian communions agreed, notably in the *Baptism, Eucharist, Ministry Statement of the Faith and Order Commission of the World Council of Churches* (1982), that baptism is a nonrepeatable sacred action. As a result, most churches no longer require rebaptism of converts formerly baptized with water in the name of the Trinity. Some of the adult-baptizing free churches do not recognize the validity of other churches' baptisms and thus continue to rebaptize new members.

154 ◆ BAPTISM IN THE EARLY CHURCH

From the very beginning of the Christian church, baptism was the path for entering the church, whether as adults, children, or infants. Although the precise origins of baptismal rituals are not entirely clear, the entire process involved extensive ritual action: from the catechumenate (the period of preparation) to the actual baptism with water and anointing with the oil of chrism during the great Easter Vigil service.

A proper understanding of baptism in the ancient church requires a broad perspective that encompasses the whole initiation pattern in early Christianity. The term *baptism* in this period often refers not only to the water bath, but to the whole complex of preparation and ritual actions that marked the entrance of a new member into the community of faith. Thus, the history of baptism is really the history of the whole pattern of initiation and the various components of that process.

We know little about the rites of initiation or preparation for them in the New Testament period. The Scriptures do indicate that baptism was conferred in the name of the Trinity (e.g., Matt.

28:19) and perhaps sometimes in the name of the Lord Jesus (e.g., Acts 8:16). Romans 6 suggests that baptism may have been conferred through immersion in a pool, which was seen as going down into the tomb with Christ and rising to new life. We know from archaeological evidence that this is how baptism was celebrated in the following centuries, but it is possible that this particular manner developed after Paul's symbolic description of it in the New Testament.

Christian baptism developed in the context of a culture with a variety of baptismal rituals. Baptism accompanied the circumcision of male proselytes (converts) and was the primary ritual for female converts. Although the ancient nature of this practice is questioned, its use in the first century is most probable. The Essene communities used a variety of ritual ablutions, and they seem to be part of a widespread baptist movement in Palestine and Syria. John the Baptist stands as an obvious precedent to Christian baptism, since Jesus himself was baptized by John. Yet this baptism was clearly of a different character than Christian baptism, as the Gospels often point out. The contrast is often couched in terms of a baptism of water (John's) versus a baptism in the Spirit (Jesus'), a fact that indicates the importance of the Spirit in Christian baptism.

The Gospels are unclear about whether Jesus himself ever baptized. In one place, John seems to indicate that Jesus did baptize (3:22), while in the next chapter he says, "It was not Jesus who baptized, but his disciples" (4:1-2). In either case, this baptism is still distinct from later Christian baptism, which is understood as the way to enter into the experience of Christ's death and resurrection.

Baptism and the Holy Spirit

Clearly evident in the New Testament is a link between baptism and the gift of the Holy Spirit. Reception of the Spirit is a result of joining the Christian community of believers, but the exact relation between the water bath and the reception of the Spirit is not clear. Sometimes the Spirit precedes the water ritual (Acts 10:44-48), sometimes the Spirit accompanies it (Acts 2:38), and sometimes the Spirit follows it (Acts 8:14-17; 19:1-7).

It was natural that the community would soon develop rituals that expressed the gift of the Spirit in connection with baptism. Chief among these

were the laying on of hands (Acts 8:14-17) and the anointing with oil (2 Cor. 1:21). Anointing was a common Jewish symbol of the Spirit's power (1 Sam. 16:13), and also a common accompaniment to bathing in the ancient Mediterranean world. The shifting relationship between the water bath itself and the rituals expressing the gift of the Spirit provides a helpful thread for understanding the history of initiation in succeeding centuries.

Baptism of Children and Infants

Baptism in the early centuries of the church's life was primarily baptism of adults. From the day of Pentecost on, the early Christians preached the gospel to adults and called them to a conversion which was celebrated in baptism. At the same time, significant evidence indicates that the ancient church also baptized children. Though we have no explicit New Testament reference to infant baptism, infant initiation was a practice in Jewish proselyte baptism and circumcision, both of which are cultural antecedents for Christian baptism. Since Jewish practice included infant baptism, the fact that the New Testament mentions no prohibition of it when speaking of Christian baptism is significant. It seems probable that children were baptized when whole households converted (Acts 16:15, 33; 18:8; 1 Cor. 1:16). Polycarp (*c.* 150 C.E.), Hippolytus (*c.* 215 C.E.), and various funeral epitaphs provide more explicit evidence of infant baptism in the second and third centuries. By the fifth century, infant baptism was clearly an accepted practice, since Augustine uses it as a proof for the existence of original sin in his arguments against the Pelagians. By about the sixth century, infant baptism had become the dominant pattern.

Preparation for Baptism: The Catechumenate

Early church fathers refer to various types of preparation for initiation in their writings. In the third, fourth, and fifth centuries, this preparation developed into a complete structure called the catechumenate. Designed as a support and stimulus to the process of conversion, the catechumenate was a long-term experience. The church examined the intentions and the way of life of those who sought to join. If these were in accord with the gospel, the inquirers were admitted to the order of the catechumens. The church then instructed them over a period of two or three years, while they joined in prayer, the Christian life, and noneucharistic worship with the community. Their sponsors, who had brought them to the community and vouched for them, accompanied them throughout the process of their preparation and also served as their sponsors for the celebration of the initiation sacraments.

Various liturgical rites were celebrated with the catechumens as they continued their journey toward baptism. When the candidates, their sponsors, and the community agreed that the catechumens were ready for the sacraments, their names were enrolled for baptism, and they were called the enlightened ones. This enrollment began a period, generally lasting forty days, of intensive spiritual preparation for the reception of the sacraments at Easter. As the whole community began to share with the initiates this time of preparation, it developed into the season we call Lent.

The culmination of the catechumenate came at the Easter Vigil, when the initiates were baptized, anointed by the bishop, and brought to the eucharistic table for the first time. The Easter Vigil was the night of nights, the church's annual celebration of the death and resurrection of the Lord, manifested concretely in the new Christians who died and rose in baptism. The whole community rejoiced with them as it welcomed them into the order of the faithful. Following the reception of the sacraments, the new Christians entered a period of mystagogia, a time for reflection and meditation on the mysteries, the early church's term for the sacraments. This was also a time for them to adjust to their new responsibilities as full members of the community.

Lawrence E. Mick

155 ♦ BAPTISM IN THE MEDIEVAL WEST

As infant baptism became common, the process of catechizing shifted from before to after baptism. In the Western church, the baptismal anointing with oil (chrism) slowly developed into a separate sacrament called confirmation. First Communion was often delayed for a number of years. Scholastic theologians developed theological language to describe the way baptism left its mark on the person baptized.

The patristic form of the catechumenate was in its prime in the third, fourth and fifth centuries. The history of baptism in the early medieval period is a story of its division of the patristic unified structure of initiation into three separate ritual moments of water baptism, confirmation, and first Eucharist.

There were a variety of reasons for the decline of the catechumenate. One factor was the mass conversions of the German and Slavic tribes. Since they were largely nomadic tribes, they were not in one place long enough for an extended period of formation. Another reason was the shift toward infant baptism. Since most adults had already been baptized, the majority of baptisms celebrated gradually became infant baptisms. Augustine's teaching and others on original sin prompted an even stronger emphasis on the baptism of infants as soon as possible after birth. Without many adult candidates for initiation, the need for an extended catechumenal preparation disappeared. Catechism now took place after baptism. Parents and godparents were the primary agents of catechizing, although the bishop was responsible to see that they accomplished the task. After the reforms of the Fourth Lateran Council (1215), parish priests increasingly were responsible for catechizing children.

In the Western church, the postbaptismal anointing, now called confirmation, became separated from baptism, largely because it was reserved to the bishop. The increasing size of dioceses led to multiple celebrations of the Easter Vigil in different parts of the diocese and made it impossible for the bishop to preside at all the Easter initiations. In the East, a priest administering baptism was allowed to confirm at the same ceremony; but in the West, Pope Innocent I in a letter to Bishop Decentius of Gubbio in 412, insisted that only the bishop could anoint the forehead with chrism. Where the bishop was not present for the Easter Vigil, the anointing was deferred. At first, this deferment would generally happen during Easter Week, but over the centuries, the gap between baptism and anointing widened farther and farther, reaching as much as fourteen years in recent centuries. In the process, confirmation came to be seen as a separate sacrament, its intimate link with baptism obscured by the passage of time.

When the bishop was present, however, the integrity of the initiation pattern was preserved in many places at least into the twelfth century. Even though the initiates were usually infants, they were still baptized, confirmed, and given the Eucharist. If the infants were too young to chew the bread, their Communion consisted of the cup alone.

After about the twelfth century, the practice of giving Communion to young children disappeared in the West. The reasons for this disappearance were the decreased frequency of Communion and the increased reverence of the body and blood of the Lord, which led to some scrupulous concerns about infants, who might spit up soon after receiving the sacrament.

Though exceptions still occurred, the writings of Thomas Aquinas in the thirteenth century clearly indicated that the separation of baptism and confirmation had become common. Priests baptized; while only bishops confirmed. Aquinas defended this new practice on the basis that the church, guided by the Holy Spirit, could adapt its practices as it saw the need.

The scholastic theology represented by Thomas Aquinas provided a systematic framework for understanding medieval sacramental practice. Two aspects of scholastic theology that often are misunderstood are the character of the sacraments and the meaning of the phrase *ex opere operato*. Aquinas explained the character conferred by baptism as a permanent effect of baptism, an effect which establishes a relationship between the believer, Christ, and the worshiping community of faith. Since this relationship is permanent, baptism is not repeatable. The phrase *ex opere operato* (from the act being performed) has often been understood as a quasi-magical notion of sacrament. Aquinas made it clear, however, that the phrase simply expresses the permanent availability of God's salvation in Christ. If the sacrament is celebrated, then God is present and God's grace is available, even if the minister is unworthy or the sacrament is celebrated poorly. The notion of the *ex opere operato* nature of the sacramental action is complemented by the *ex opere operantis* (from the act of the one acting), which involves the interior attitudes and intentions of those celebrating the sacraments. The spiritual effect of the sacraments depends on both dimensions.

Thomas Aquinas and other scholastics struggled to develop a theology to explain confirmation as a sacrament separate from baptism. Aquinas spoke of confirmation as a sacrament of spiritual maturity, though it is clear that this maturity is not chronological, since even a confirmed infant is spiritually mature. Aquinas saw confirmation as conferring a fullness that brought baptism to perfection. He also adopted a language of strengthening or combatting from earlier sources to explain confirmation as a conferring of the Holy Spirit's gifts in order to carry on the church's mission.

The scholastic theological perspective and the practices upon which it was based continued largely unchanged until the Reformation and the Council of Trent in the sixteenth century.

Lawrence E. Mick

156 ♦ BAPTISM IN CONTEMPORARY ROMAN CATHOLIC THOUGHT

To implement reforms decided upon at the Second Vatican Council, the Roman Catholic church has restored the adult catechumenate as a preparation period for baptism and given it a prominent role in the church, alongside infant baptism. Like most other major Christian churches, the Roman Catholic church no longer insists on rebaptizing converts who have been baptized in water in the name of the Trinity in other churches.

The theology and celebration of baptism has undergone significant development in the twentieth century, largely as a result of the liturgical movement and developments in the areas of ecclesiology, and grace and sacramental theology. At the Second Vatican Council (1963–1965), the *Constitution on the Sacred Liturgy* called for the reform of baptismal practice (par. 64–69), and the *Decree on Ecumenism* addressed baptism in an ecumenical context (par. 22). Conciliar reform resulted in two distinct rituals for baptism: for adults and children of catechetical age, the *Rite of Christian Initiation of Adults* (RCIA), and the *Rite of Baptism for Children*.

The RCIA consists of a series of formational stages of preparation for baptism with accompanying rites and prayers to admit the baptismal candidate to each stage of preparation for baptism. The stages include: (1) the period of evangelization and precatechumenate, in which the inquirer first hears the gospel message and answers the call to conversion; (2) the period of catechumenate, lasting between one and three years, in which the church instructs the catechumens in the Scriptures, doctrine, and morals of Christian life and incorporates them into the Catholic community; (3) the period of enlightenment and purification, usually during Lent, in which the elect (as the catechumens are now called) engages in a more immediate and intense spiritual preparation for baptism through reflection and prayer.

These formational periods are accompanied by and understood in light of prayers and liturgical rites. The period of the catechumenate is introduced by a rite of admission, in which the church admits the inquirer to the household of faith and calls the person to live in the pattern of the Cross. The rite of election or enrollment of names marks the entrance into the purification and enlightenment period. At this rite, the bishop, after determining whether the catechumens are properly disposed for baptism, acknowledges, in the name of the church, their election by God to be baptized. In addition to the rites for entrance into each stage, the catechists, sponsors, and catechumens meet for prayer and the study of Scripture. During Lent, the Christian community prays for and with the elect, the catechumens, in prayers of scrutiny, which ask God to purify and cleanse the elect's heart and soul so that they may be prepared for baptismal life.

Baptism itself is, as a rule, celebrated at the Easter Vigil, along with confirmation and the Eucharist. During the Easter season, the neophytes (newborn Christians) enter the fourth stage, the period of postbaptismal catechesis or mystagogy, in which they reflect on the meaning of the rites they have celebrated in light of the paschal mystery.

The rite of baptism for children consists of a welcoming into the church, a service of the Word, the liturgy of baptism, and a blessing of the parents.

Theological Understanding of Baptism

These rites have their foundation in and reflect several theological presuppositions which are the result of the renaissance of sacramental and liturgical research.

First, the rites reflect a wider understanding of baptismal theology. Baptism not only washes away original sin; it facilitates the sharing of Christ's life in the context of the Paschal mystery, incorporates one into God's family, and calls one to live the mystery of faith in one's situation. While these concepts are not absent from the older rites, they are more clearly emphasized in the new rites—not only in the prayers of the rites, but in the structure of the initiation process. The various stages of the rites assist the internalizing of faith, which is not simply intellectual assent to theological principles, but the surrender of one's whole being to God. Even in the baptism of infants, ministers are to prepare the parents and godparents in such a manner that they can form the child in the ways of faith.

Second, baptism is understood to be communal in nature. The general introductions to the rites express the concern that not only those involved in specific ministries exercise their roles, but that the entire Christian community undertake their ministry of evangelization, prayer, and support of those seeking baptism. Baptism does not initiate one into a private relationship with God but into an existential community of faith.

Third, the rites are rooted in the Scriptures. Every celebration contains a liturgy of the Word, and the prayers draw from scriptural imagery. The first concern of the church in bringing a person to baptism is that a person hears the gospel and commits oneself to Christ.

Fourth, by returning to the ancient structure of initiation, the RCIA presupposes that the church is faithful to its mission of evangelization. In the precatechumenate, the church does not wait for people to come to it, but rather it actively proclaims the gospel, inviting people to baptismal faith.

Finally, the rites reflect a deep appreciation of the ecumenical aspects of baptism. The once common practice of conditional baptism for Christians of other denominations is now reserved for only those situations in which there is serious doubt that a Trinitarian form of baptism occurred. The RCIA is intended only for those persons who have never been baptized. In some countries, however, rites of welcome that recognize baptism in a different denomination are incorporated into the context of the rites of the RCIA for pastoral reasons. The reception of baptized persons into full communion with the Roman Catholic church is seen as a continuation of their baptismal conversion.

The *Decree on Ecumenism* recognizes that baptism establishes a sacramental bond of unity; thus, acknowledging that other Christian denominations are part of the church, although they lack full unity with the Roman Catholic church. In light of this baptismal theology, the council called for dialogue with Christian churches concerning baptism. As a result of this mandate, Catholic theologians have participated in the formulation of the World Council of Churches' statement, *Baptism, Eucharist, and Ministry*, as well as bilateral discussions on baptism. In responding to *BEM*, the Vatican affirmed many areas of consensus and called for further discussion on certain theological issues including original sin, the necessity of baptism, baptism's nonrepeatable character, infant baptism, and the relationship between baptism, confirmation and Eucharist.

Jeffrey M. Kemper

157 ✦ BAPTISM AMONG THE PROTESTANT REFORMERS

Luther, Zwingli, and Calvin all believed baptism could properly be administered to infants. Yet, whereas Luther emphasized baptism as a sign of God's promise to bring about faith in conjunction with the infant's inchoate faith, Zwingli and Calvin saw it as a Christian equivalent to circumcision in the Hebrew Scriptures, the mark of inclusion in God's covenant people. Adherents of the Radical Reformation rejected the baptism of infants entirely, arguing that infants cannot have faith in Christ, since faith comes by hearing and understanding the Word of God. They repudiated their own baptisms as infants and had themselves rebaptized. Hence they became known as Anabaptists, *or rebaptizers.*

No deeper chasm separated the various Protestant Reformers than their understanding of baptism; nor have their descendants nearly half a millennium later bridged the gap. All of the Reformers reacted strongly to medieval abuses that seemed to make infant baptism an escape hatch from the consequences of a sin inherited from Adam and Eve. One group recoiled so strongly as to insist that medieval baptism was null and void

and that true baptism could be administered only to persons capable of expressing their own faith. Adherents to this view were scornfully dubbed *Anabaptists* (rebaptizers), or even *Catabaptists* (opposed to baptism), by those who accepted medieval practice while insisting it be accompanied by a new understanding of its meaning.

Luther on Baptism

In 1519, Luther wrote a treatise on baptism in which he argued for the submersion of infants as the best way of signifying that the old nature is drowned by God's grace. That understanding does not mean an end to sin within us, but rather signifies the beginning of a continuing victorious war against sin. The battle continues until death; since the drowning of sin signified in baptism lasts as long as we live. The sacrament is a dynamic process, not a momentary event; the sign and the reality signified endure to the end of our days. In 1520, Luther expanded his view of baptism in *The Babylonian Captivity of the Church*, stressing

St. Augustine. The most common symbol for St. Augustine, the celebrated church father of the fourth century, is a heart surmounted by heraldic flames. This symbol of zeal is pierced with two arrows, signifying Augustine's remorse for his youthful sins.

baptism as a sign attached to a divine promise and attacking the current understanding of penance as debilitating to baptismal theology.

Anabaptist Attacks on Infant Baptism

For some who wish to reform the church, Luther (and Zwingli also) did not go far enough in simply reinterpreting baptism. Reacting strongly against the medieval necessity to baptize immediately after birth in order to escape limbo or hell, these more radical (or left-wing) thinkers insisted on an alternative understanding: Baptism is an enacted testimony made by individual believers to their personal faith in Christ in obedience to his command, and in imitation of the adult baptism reported in the New Testament. Believers are the consciously converted who together form a religious community zealous for righteous living and radical social reform to the point of perfectionism. Hence baptism is a mark of sanctification, though not the cause of it.

Thus between 1522 and 1525, a radical movement sprang up around Zurich, led by Conrad Grebel, Felix Manz, Michael Sattler, Balthasar Hubmaier, and others. Between 1525 and 1536, similar movements arose in Germany, Austria (including areas of present-day Italy), Moravia, and the Low Countries. (From the name of one of its leaders, Menno Simons, adherents of the movement in the Netherlands became known as Mennonites.) Although Zwingli was initially attracted by the arguments of his former disciples, by the end of 1526 the city council of Zurich had condemned Anabaptism as a heresy punishable by drowning—a cruel parody of the sect's advocacy of adult baptism.

Zwingli's Defense of Infant Baptism

In the same year, Zwingli published a treatise on baptism, consisting of four parts. He rejected the notion of original guilt and instead defended infant baptism on the basis of covenant theology, with the rite being a kind of corollary to circumcision, an initiation into the new covenant. He argued that, while articulated faith is necessary for the mature Christian life, it need not precede baptism. He rightly renounced the too close an identification of sign with the thing signified that had made baptism magical in the medieval church; but in reaction, he turned the sign into a vague symbol rather than into something with effective power to proclaim the gospel truth of redemption. In this, he went well beyond Luther (as he did also in defining the Lord's Supper as an ordinance, and not a sacrament).

In response to Anabaptist objections that the New Testament nowhere explicitly warrants infant baptism, Zwingli cleverly replied that neither does it warrant the admission of women to Communion at the Lord's Table; yet the church has never rejected a narrow biblicism on the latter issue. He also corrected misconceptions among his opponents about the historical development of infant baptism.

Zwingli saw clearly the link between baptism and ecclesiology and perceived that the Anabaptist position on initiation inexorably carried with it a sectarian view of the church. Contrary to the parables found in Matthew 13, the Anabaptists insisted that the tares should be separated from the wheat in the present age and by human discernment. When his initial work did not convince his opponents, but only produced a countertreatise by Hubmaier, Zwingli in 1531 issued a work bearing a caustic title that revealed his exasperation: _Refutation of the Tricks of the Catabaptists._

The Role of Faith in Baptism

Luther was determined that baptism remain a sacrament—a sure sign with power to affect what it signifies. He understood as well as Zwingli did the medieval abuses. But Luther held firmly to the dictum, _Abusus non tollit usum_ (abuse does not abrogate use), and he set about giving sacramental baptism the clear force of gospel proclamation. Thus according to Luther, baptism is God's word to us; it can work faith within us, and not merely express the already developed faith of the individual (as in the Anabaptists) or of the church corporately (as in Zwingli). Illustrative of the power Luther saw in the sacrament, he taught Lutherans to gain confidence in the graciousness of God by reminding themselves daily—and particularly in times of great distress—"I have been baptized."

Although not resting the case for the infant baptism primarily thereon, Luther asserted that infants indeed can have faith—not the mature faith of adults, but a faith which nevertheless is a trust recognized by God. To this extent, he moved away from what often was to be a weakness in later Protestantism—the tendency to equate faith with reason. That very tendency changed confirmation, which had been a sacramental act of a bishop theologically integral to baptism, to a non-episcopal act that signaled completed catechesis and had no clear connection with baptism. A part of this change barred unconfirmed persons from the Lord's Table until the Supper could be explained to them in the catechesis process (in distinction from the Orthodox practice of communicating infants and the Roman practice of granting children first Communion before confirmation).

In 1523, Luther translated the traditional Latin baptismal rite into German with only minor adjustments; but by 1526, he produced a significantly revised rite that dropped most subsidiary ceremonies (e.g., the exorcistic application of salt, the opening of the ears, and the presentation of a candle), thereby giving the water ceremony undisputed centrality. An unknown catechetical hymn written by Luther in 1541 is "Christ unser Herr zum Jordan kam" ("Christ, our Lord, Came to Jordan").

Zwingli based the retention of infant baptism on the covenant principal, and Luther saw baptism as a great covenant for our comfort through which God continually assures us of divine grace. Among the Protestant Reformers, however, baptismal covenant theology reached its apogee in the more extended and systematic treatment of Calvin, particularly in *The Institutes of the Christian Religion* (1559 edition; IV:14–16).

With Luther and against Zwingli, Calvin defended baptism as a sacrament affecting what it signifies. But with all the Reformers, Calvin denied that baptism affects the remission of inherited sin at the moment of administration. What is affected (as also in Luther) is a continuing proclamation of God's saving love and an assurance of God's incorporation of us into the covenant of grace. Specifically, for Calvin, baptism attests to the forgiveness of sins in the future as well as from the past; assures us of being engrafted into Christ for newness of life; and teaches us that we are united with Christ and thereby are recipients of all his blessings.

As for Luther, for Calvinist baptism is a sacrament that cannot be repeated, for it is God's incontestable and utterly dependable promise to us.

To this promise we must respond in faith, if the dynamic of the covenant is to be fulfilled. But it is God who initiates and God who, through the work of Jesus Christ, saves. The lack of baptism is not, for Calvin, a barrier to salvation (as in the medieval church). Nor is baptism magical. Some may indeed receive it idly, and thus to no advantage. But to those who correctly accept the sign, the administration of baptism is an effective seal or pledge of divine promise to be relied upon with great thanksgiving to confirm and increase our faith.

Calvin made significant use of the Old Testament, not only to defend infant baptism as a corollary to circumcision, but also to connect the church's journey with Christ to Israel's crossing of the sea and following of the cloud in the wilderness. Thus Calvin explicated themes popular in the patristic and medieval literature on baptism more fully than other Reformers.

Still, in many ways, Luther's brief treatise of 1519 and his discussion in *Babylonian Captivity* are the most balanced theological considerations of baptism, primarily because they are free of the defensive polemics that necessarily invaded writings once the Anabaptist controversy emerged.

In varying proportions, the sacramental views of Luther and Calvin and the ordinantial views of Zwingli coalesced to preserve infant baptism in the Lutheran and Reformed churches and in the Anglican Church, where Cranmer embedded sacramental teaching in his prayer book liturgies and in the *Articles of Religion*. The Anabaptist view prevailed among the left-wing groups on the continent and in the seventeenth century greatly affected the Baptist movement as it emerged in and radiated from England.

Laurence Hull Stookey

158 ◆ BAPTISM IN THE MODERN ERA

In today's churches the theology and practice of baptism continues to be shaped by the debates begun during the Protestant Reformation. Theological discussions continue about the nature of baptism and appropriate candidates for baptism. Liturgical discussions continue regarding the appropriate way to celebrate baptism. This article surveys the discussion of baptism in the contemporary church.

Until the twentieth century, baptismal practices in the Western churches persisted largely unchanged since the Reformation era. In the Roman Catholic, Reformed, Lutheran, and Anglican (including Methodist) traditions, the normal point of entry into the church continued to be baptism as an infant. In the Baptist, Anabaptist (Mennonite, Amish, Hutterite), and various free church traditions, formal entry into the church normally came with baptism administered in adolescence or early adulthood.

Yet problems inherent in each approach slowly intensified. Infant baptism in an increasingly secularized society often meant that baptized children did not receive the postbaptismal Christian nurture that once had been part of growing up in a Christian culture. Churches that baptized only adolescents or adults, since they emphasized strongly committed adult membership, found it difficult to make room in their theology and practice for their own unbaptized children, who seemed to be growing into Christianity through family nurture. The age of baptism tended to creep downward toward early adolescence. Revivalism restored the clear-cut conversion experience that had once characterized these adult-baptizing believers' churches.

Theological critique in both the infant-baptizing and adult-baptizing traditions led to changes and innovations: rites of child dedication; a renewed emphasis on catechizing both baptized children and unbaptized adults; the return to the Easter Vigil as the prime setting for baptism; and the restoration of symbols and rites that had once surrounded water baptism itself, but had been eliminated during the Protestant Reformation.

The Eastern Orthodox churches constitute the main exception to the above patterns of change, since they had retained the baptismal practice of the early church largely intact. In these churches, in the twentieth century, baptism of children continues to include anointing with oil (chrism) and first Communion. The paragraphs that follow focus on the Western churches.

Churches that Baptize Infants

The infant-baptizing tradition emphasizes the continuity of the church as a community of faith. Through the church, the redemptive life is passed, as pledged by divine promise, to the children of believers; these children are surrounded and supported by a shared life of Christian teaching and commitment. Recognizing the interconnectedness of human lives and the subtlety of influence between the generations, infant baptism represents the faith of the adult church enclosing a new life and bearing a child in its own faith until the child can acquire a measure of independence and begin to make his or her adult contribution. A number of defenders of this tradition suggest that infant baptism represents God acting on behalf of a child before the child can act towards God—a sign of justification by grace through faith.

As to practice, children in Western churches were brought to baptism a few days after birth. The ritual, since medieval times (not by necessity, but by custom), became quite individualistic and private; it was performed at a font in the church, with family and sponsors present. Sponsors were friends or relatives of the child who made the promises of baptism in the child's name and represented the commitment of the adult church to support the newly baptized.

Where the faith of the adult community was genuine and intense, this baptismal practice could express a great spiritual reality. Adult faith did in fact carry a child and provide it a vital heritage into which to grow. But where the faith of the adult community was largely nominal, and yet infant baptism remained an expected social form, the redemptive meaning of baptism could be seriously qualified. The practice could seem like a device to perpetuate a folk-church—a Christian population for which baptism served as little more than a _christening_ or a public recognition of birth. Doubtless, over the centuries, most infant baptisms in the West mingled the best and the worst of these social meanings.

Because an infant being baptized is passive—being acted for or acted upon—there is (particularly in an individualistic society) a perceived inadequacy in the rite unless more is done. In the West, especially in Protestantism, a later personal avowal of faith and owning of baptism came to be expected as a person baptized in infancy approached adulthood. The objectivity of infant baptism means that the church is not shaped by human initiative, but by divine grace; yet adolescent confirmation means that the church, by intention at least, is comprised of responsible, committed members.

In the churches of the West, again particularly

in the Protestant churches, much pastoral and catechetical effort has been devoted to preparing young persons for confirmation. The rite has been variously understood—being regarded as virtually an occasion for conversion by some groups. As a rule, one was only admitted to the Holy Communion, and thus to full sacramental and legal standing in the church, after one was confirmed. Hence the regrettable popular understanding that one was "joining the church."

In the sixteenth century, some Christians broke with this prevailing initiatory practice. They were called Anabaptists, or rebaptizers, because they could not acknowledge the legitimacy of their own infant baptisms and baptized themselves again when they consciously believed. However, Anabaptists viewed this second baptism as their first. Baptism, they held, was a sign of one's faith; to baptize a person who had not given and could not give expression to this faith was to bring a Christian rite dangerously close to magic. To shape a faith community by this infancy rite lowered the level of dedication among its members. The church could neither judge nor redeem, for it and the general population had become indistinguishable. Rather than thinking of baptism as a mark of continuity in the redemptive community, the believers' baptism practices sought a *gathered church* or a *believers' church*—a church consisting of a voluntary association of persons who had believed and sought baptism. The church does not pass from generation to generation, but is always coming into being. The believers' church forms an elite group of those who stand apart from the general population by the personal summons of God.

Since the Anabaptists' view of baptism and of the character of the church meant that they could not recognize the legitimacy of past baptism, this group had to make a new beginning—accomplished by the first Anabaptists who baptized themselves. Although there is a contradiction in this act, what else could they have done?

This radical break in baptismal theology and practice is at its best a critique of a complacent use of infant baptism. When believer's baptism is the foundation of a church, it also develops weaknesses and contradictions.

The believer's baptism pattern has had difficulty accounting for the place of children in the church. Children of believing parents are loved, taught to pray, and in many respects treated as part of the church; however they are not baptized, and they do not receive the Holy Communion. Children cannot be regarded as fit candidates for baptism until they are old enough to give an account of their own faith. This intrinsic problem has led some established populations in the believer's baptism tradition to permit baptism of very young children (not without protest from other Baptists). However, since children tend to grow up uncritically into the patterns expected of them by the adults who surround them, a child will typically experience a conversion if it is expected of them. Thus the adult faith which baptism is meant to represent is qualified. Protestant revivalism during the eighteenth, nineteenth, and twentieth centuries represents one attempt to solve this problem, by encouraging crisis conversion experiences.

The defenders of believer's baptism point justifiably to the statistics in past centers of Christian population where infant baptism had prevailed for many generations. Although a large portion of the population is baptized in infancy, only a small portion gives evidence of adult Christian practice. The system of infant baptism seemed discredited by statistics.

This continuation of the initiatory customs of Christendom into the post-Christendom era in Europe and these disconcerting statistics (reported in many of the old centers of Christian population: France, Britain, Scandinavia, Holland, and others), led some theologians in the post-World War I years to question or repudiate infant baptism. Karl Barth and Emil Brunner are the best known of these questioners, but they were seconded by other concerned pastors and thinkers.

Those who question infant baptism in the name of believer's baptism seem to imply that believers' baptism by its very character solves the problem of large baptized, but very secularized, populations. This alternative system of Christian initiation creates a church of informed, convinced members—persons who are not brought by others, but who come themselves, evidencing an interior work of God. This group should be almost one hundred percent loyal to its profession. Yet any Baptist congregation, which has been in continuous existence for several generations and will examine its register of baptisms, will report the same disappointments, lapses, and pastoral tears that other churches report. The point is not that the believer's baptism system does not produce the perfect church—that is beyond human power. The point is that the system seems to say that it *will* yield results that others do not; but it cannot deliver on such a promise.

These two patterns, with their theological dignity and their practical strengths and weaknesses, continued through the modern period of the church with little change and little new arguments. Two innovations might be noted. One is the introduction in the nineteenth-century Roman Church of a first Communion in childhood, usually a few years prior to confirmation. This development is now under some question among Roman scholars. The second is that some believer's baptism churches introduced a rite of infant dedication to express the church-relatedness of children who are not regarded as proper candidates for baptism.

Modern Critique

Among the criticisms of prevailing patterns which have developed in recent generations was the awareness of the modernity of these patterns. Baptism has been a continuous practice of the Christian community, yet significant features of the modern initiatory policies have no long history. They seem to have developed on pragmatic grounds, rather than on the basis of theology or continuity.

The earliest documents (the New Testament and the sources from several centuries following) provide no information on what Christians did to bring their own children into the church. The concern of these sources is exclusively with the introduction of adult converts into the faith community. Thus the sources to which Christians turn for a model for shaping the life of the community of grace support explicitly neither the withholding of baptism from the children of Christian parents until some age of accountability, nor the baptizing of infants of Christian parents followed by confirmation at adolescence. One looks in vain in a New Testament concordance for a heading *Infants, baptism of;* one also looks in vain for *Accountability, age of.*

In addition to historical novelty, critics point to theological insecurity. Theologians have described both infant baptism and adolescent confirmation as rites in search of a theology. These rites seem to have originated more from pastoral needs of the community than from a grasp of the gospel itself. Yet baptismal policy did speak about the divine redemptive initiative expressed through the corporate life of the faith community.

Believer's baptism, for its part, seems to build an ecclesiology around the single idea that baptism is a witness to faith—an idea appropriate to the first generation of the church, the time when the Christian message takes root in a new population and believers are sharply differentiated from society. However, Christian life comes from prior Christian life. Most people who now are or who ever have been Christians, are or have been so because their parents were Christians—clearly a fact of theological significance. Continuity is characteristic of the faith-formed society. The family is a unit in the economy of redemption. The children of believing parents do not begin where the children of unbelieving parents begin, and should not be treated, pastorally or sacramentally, as outside the church.

Both systems have shortcomings which to some extent mirror one another. If infant baptism often sentimentalizes babyhood, believer's baptism centers emotion around a specific, datable crisis of conversion.

Through much of the first two-thirds of the twentieth century, various critiques were mounted of the prevailing practice, and alternatives, some of them quite radical, were proposed. The churches have been moving into a post-Christian society, yet they have continued to use initiatory rites and arguments used in the sixteenth and seventeenth centuries, when Western Christendom was still a social reality.

Public, Congregational Rites

Several features mark the baptismal rites which have been authorized in the more liturgical churches in recent years. (Ritual changes may be taking place in the freer traditions as well, but since they are largely unwritten, they are more difficult to document.)

For many centuries baptism in the West, Catholic and Protestant, had been quite individualistic and private, administered in a church (or at times in a home) with only family and friends attending. Such practice is a hold-over from a medieval development. Martin Bucer protested against it, but to little effect. However, baptism now takes place often in the midst of a large Sunday morning congregation gathered for Word and sacrament. This change in practice is witness that baptism is not just an event for the candidate, nor for the family, but for the church. Churchgoers have an opportunity not only to witness the baptism of someone else, but also to be reminded of their own baptism, to join in the promises and prayers for another, and to express the church's welcome. The Baptist churches' practice has been held ordinarily with a congregation present, although usually not in a context of a Sunday observance of the Lord's Supper.

Baptist Openings

Ecumenical discussion and the experience of religious pluralism have brought some modifications in the believer's baptism tradition also. The introduction of a service of infant dedication has been noted. Baptist church members observed that their neighbors of the infant-baptism traditions had a powerful gesture of inclusion for their children, along with at least a rudimentary theology of childhood. This ritual development among Baptists seems to open possibilities for conversation between the two traditions on the place of children in the church.

Baptist theology traditionally has described baptism as a public act of witness to one's faith. Baptism belonged to the order of obedience, not to the order of salvation. However, in recent years, some Baptist theologians are asking whether or not this sharp distinction between God's initiative and our response is sustainable. Is not our very faith in Christ at work in us? Some Baptists are willing to speak of baptism as a performative sign "for the forgiveness of sins." Baptism is a meeting point of grace and faith. The historic contention that to admit a divine gift into one's account of baptism opened the door to magic often now sounds simplistic, at least to some Baptist theologians.

With respect to adults, some Baptist churches express misgivings—not about their own rites of initiation, but instead about the necessity for the rejection of the legitimacy of other churches' baptisms that their theology requires. Although infant baptism seems mistaken, many persons who have been baptized as infants indeed mature into courageous adult believers. Given such results, some Baptist churches seek ways in which to recognize true baptized Christians among those who have been baptized as infants and who give evidence of responsible adult commitment in later life.

An Easter Setting

The infant-baptizing traditions began to question the timing of baptism because it had come to be governed by when a child was born, rather than by the Paschal events or the central moments of the Christian year.

Baptism in the early church was annual, and the Eucharist was weekly. This ancient pattern had been set aside, perhaps rashly. With the recovery of the Easter Vigil and the great Christocentric structures of the church year in many communions, it has become desirable to locate the initiation rites in ritual time so that they can interpret, and in turn be interpreted, by such occasions as Easter, Pentecost, or All Saints' Day. Many churches have commended such correlation between baptism and the kerygmatic year; however, resistance comes from persons whose attitudes and expectations were shaped by past practice.

In this matter, most Baptist churches have paid little attention to the Christian year. Yet in the patristic tradition, there is no intrinsic reason for baptism to be unrelated to the ritual observance of Jesus' death and resurrection. However, if baptism at Easter or Pentecost would mean that a person who had given evidence of belief might have to wait until then for baptism, that delay might raise objections from those Baptists who believe that a convert should be baptized as soon as that person is converted. This trust in the stir of the Spirit is considered biblical by some. However, other traditions think this theology is founded more on confidence in untested, unreflective experience than is wise.

Serious Preparation

In the modern period, some churches (especially those with a folk church background) have become quite casual about admitting persons to baptism. The church has assumed that the persons making pledges at baptism understood what they were saying. Yet often they have not. It has been assumed that baptized children would come under strong Christian influence in family and congregation. But often they have not.

Many clergy and congregations have come to insist that the parents of a child brought to baptism must themselves have a considerable amount of instruction in the faith and that they must take some responsible part in the congregation's worship and service. Unless such preconditions are met, the baptism will not proceed. The purpose is not to keep children from baptism, but to raise the intentionality of the persons and sponsors who come to it. The parents and sponsors should accept some discipline and understand and agree with the church's interpretation of baptism. Baptisms, or for that matter conversions, are of little significance if there is inadequate concern for the conservation of results.

Such pastoral diligence is never wasted. However, the clergy and Christian educators should never feel that when families and individuals do not sustain the pledges they made at baptism that this failure is their fault. People may mean what they say at a baptism and for a period following; they may drift away, and they may return. Clergy and teachers may take credit for successes, but they should not blame themselves for losses and lapses.

Rites Made Fuller

In the sixteenth century, many of the leaders of Protestantism removed from their baptismal rites all of the supporting, interpreting acts—such as anointing with oil, the sign of the cross, the giving of a lighted candle—that had developed (with varying antiquity and authority) around baptism. The reforming groups were concerned with validity, and they went to essentials. They questioned, sometimes sarcastically, actions (in the case of the Reformed churches, questioned particularly those actions that involved physical things) which lacked express New Testament warrant. Thus attention came to focus quite exclusively on water baptism. The Roman Communion retained a postbaptismal anointing. The Anglican prayer books placed immediately after the baptism a reception of the newly baptized, a signing with the cross, and a commissioning of the baptized to fight under Christ's banner (actions and terms which some liturgical historians describe as an incomplete attempt to court Presbyterian approval). However, other churches dropped such rituals, lest they obscure the biblically-mandated water action.

Clearly, water, with its complex meanings of life, death, and washing, is the central baptismal symbol, which should not be obscured. Symbolic clutter is not edifying, yet many of the revised liturgies of Christian initiation in the later half of the twentieth century are introducing (prescriptively or as choices) some postbaptismal actions into traditions which had not known them. This enrichment of the baptismal act does not come from aesthetic or antiquarian motives, nor from fussiness (a failing that liturgists do not always avoid). Rather, it demonstrates a coming to terms with the ancient ceremonial tradition and with the Catholic affirmation of images. Fullness of meaning is expressed in fullness of sign.

In the ancient church (as to this day in the East), the sequence of initiatory events led to the Holy Communion. The new baptized members, after they were given the post-baptismal anointing, entered the eucharistic room, where they took part for the first time in the kiss of peace and the prayers of the faithful, and for the first time received the bread and wine, the body and blood of Christ—all gestures of incorporation. The baptism, signifying birth, was not repeated, but it led at once to the often-repeated Lord's Supper, which spoke of the continual need to be fed.

For many generations, the churches of the West have separated these two great sacraments of the gospel. Persons who were baptized, including adults, as a rule, only received the Holy Communion later—in the case of infants, many years later. However, the revised baptismal rites of the second half of the twentieth century commend baptism in the setting of a service of Word and sacrament in which the whole ritual event will culminate in the celebration of the first Communion of the recently baptized. This sequence is observed in the Roman Catholic rite for baptizing adults, but not in the rite for baptizing infants. Some Roman liturgists are asking why.

This union of the two evangelical sacraments is easy to accomplish in the case of adults, who after their baptism at once become full members of the eucharistic community. In the case of children, this combination of the rite of initiation and the rite of nourishment, while it is especially intelligible, requires some adjusting of attitudes, understandings, practice, and spirituality. Infant Communion is unfamiliar and to some extent uncongenial in the West. Yet any argument in favor of infant baptism is an argument in favor of infant Communion; any argument for postponing Communion is an argument for believers' baptism. The churches which are changing their initiatory rites are not all moving at the same time and in the same way to join baptism and Eucharist. Each group works from its own historic experience. Locally, pastoral reasons demand patience. Yet the idea is compelling, and the practical problems have been surmounted with considerable ease in the churches that have pioneered it.

Emphasis on Adult Baptism

The most significant event in the modern history of Christian initiation is the issuing, following the Second Vatican Council, of the Roman Church's *The Rite for the Christian Initiation of Adults* (RCIA, first English edition, 1974), a substantial work which took a number of years to prepare. In the largest and oldest Christian traditions, baptism had for centuries meant infant baptism. Of course, all churches baptized adults when missionary work brought the faith to a new population. Although all Western churches had a steady but small number of adult converts, these converts were the exception. Rites essentially developed for infant baptism were adapted for these converts. The RCIA is not adapted from infant rites, but is a modern version of the initiatory process of the early church. Adults are prepared in a lengthy catechumenate, during which the catechumens attend church on Sundays, but only for the service of the Word; they receive instruction and share in the church's works of mercy. Their baptism is ordinarily at the Easter Vigil, followed at once by confirmation (by a bishop if a bishop is present, otherwise by presbyters) and by first Communion.

This rite of the RCIA is not described as an exceptional observance, but as the norm for Christian initiation. That is not to say that there will be more adult baptisms than infant baptisms. Rather, it means that what baptism signifies is more adequately stated and enacted in the case of adults than it can be in the case of children. The infant rite is derived from the adult rite, not the reverse.

If this adult rite, prepared for by careful catechesis, is to be the church's norm, it raises important issues. What are the proper expectations for membership in the Christian community? The RCIA clearly states that members should be informed about and responsible for matters of faith and practice. The rites and pastoral customs of Christian initiation should educate a person for this responsibility. In setting standards for new members, the church also asks hard questions of those already baptized.

This rite has not taken hold equally everywhere in the Roman church, but where it has, it has proved revitalizing and revolutionary. The early church developed its processes of Christian initiation because it was an evangelizing church and needed them. In the modern church, this rite is not just a throwback to early centuries. It is a call to be once again a church engaged with society in the name of the gospel. The church's life should be a cycle of evangelizing, catechizing, baptizing, nurturing in Word and sacrament, then evangelizing again. The catechumenate must not be a *program,* but instead the church doing its essential business.

The RCIA, and the understandings of initiation and community which have followed from it, have influenced other churches as well. Out of this ecumenical stir, some common ground may develop where it has not developed for four centuries. The infant baptism system and the believers' baptism system have grown up as separate configurations of understanding and practice. Representatives of one tradition could not hear what representatives of the other tradition were saying. Now, however, the RCIA seems to be opening churches in the infant-baptizing tradition to the centrality of the adult convert, and to the necessity that the church have a dedicated adult membership. Modern expositors of the RCIA are making some of the same points that were used by defenders of believer's baptism which were supposed to be uncongenial to the Catholic ethos. Even with this emphasis on adult conversion, the churches that practice infant baptism will continue to baptize the children of believers, for such children are not outside the church; their spiritual experience does not begin where a convert's spiritual experience begins, and their experience should not be expected to replicate a convert's ritual pattern. At the same time while some of the infant-baptizing churches are developing along this line, some of the believer's baptism churches are seeking ways of acknowledging that infant baptisms (at least where such baptisms have been validated by adult faith and profession) are real baptisms. It seems possible that out of new openness on both sides, there may be possibilities for the two systems to accept the strengths and tolerate the critiques of one another, and to coexist either within a single church or side by side.

Fonts and Physical Arrangements

With the renewed interest in adult baptism has come interest in baptismal space. Churches whose fonts had been small and rather out of sight are realizing that such minimal space does less than justice to the importance of the fundamental sacrament of Christian initiation. Churches which by custom had used in baptism a token amount of water are seeking ways of using more. As new churches are being designed, they often contain baptismal pools suitable for immersion and fonts in which running water is seen and heard.

This renewed emphasis must be part of a total spatial statement. In some Baptist churches, a large, conspicuous baptismal pool had simply taken over the spatial design. The centers for baptism, preaching, the Eucharist, reading, prayer, and musical direction all must be in intelligible, expressive relation to one another. None must be ignored; and none must dominate.

Daniel Stevick

159 ✦ CONVERGENCE AT THE FONT

The actions of Christian initiation seem to be growing toward an ecumenical shape as some major traditions shift their traditional baptismal customs and do so along broadly similar lines.

History. By the time of the Reformation and the Counter-Reformation, the Western church had developed a two-stage pattern of Christian initiation. Infants a few days old were baptized by the local priest; in later childhood, after at least rudimentary education in the faith, they were confirmed by a bishop. Since the late Middle Ages, admission to the Holy Communion followed confirmation. The two ritual actions corresponded with life stages—baptism with birth, and confirmation with growth.

In the sixteenth century, this two-stage rite of becoming a Christian was all that anyone knew. The Reformers accepted the first stage, infant baptism. However, they rejected, sometimes sarcastically the bishop's postbaptismal anointing.

Yet they saw value in this second initiatory action insofar as it was an opportunity for the church to instruct and for persons baptized in infancy to own their baptism. The Reformation was an educational, catechism-writing movement—as, indeed, was the Counter-Reformation.

Some radical parts of the Reformation broke with the two-stage pattern of Christian initiation. They saw baptism as a sign of one's faith, and since infants cannot have a confessing faith, infant baptism is not true baptism. The church should consist of persons who had separated themselves from the casually Christian population by an act of conscious faith. Baptism, as the Anabaptists saw it, was not meant to consecrate a Christian society, but to identify a distinct, intentional believers' church. Thus, children were not baptized until they came to an age of accountability and could enter the faith community on an adult basis when they professed their faith.

The churches of the West have continued these patterns with a few modifications. The Roman Catholics in the nineteenth century introduced a first communion prior to confirmation. And many churches in the believer's baptism tradition introduced a service of thanksgiving and dedication for the birth of a child.

Problems. These traditions were not without critics. Scholars lamented the loss of the early church's coherent way of initiating Christians. Many persons in the infant-baptizing traditions deplored the privatization of baptism, which commonly took place in an empty church or even in the family home. Moreover, baptism had become separated by several years from first Communion. Confirmation, by contrast, had become an important congregational event, culminating an educational program and marking entry into communicant life. Theologians accorded primacy to baptism, recognizing that all the meanings assigned to confirmation were meanings derived from baptism. However, popular church members saw baptism as a private, family affair, while they saw confirmation regrettably as "joining the church."

The sacramental tradition has associated confirmation with the Holy Spirit, but the Spirit was also associated with baptism. What is the role of the Spirit in these two events? Is the second event redundant? Do they differ? If so, how?

Problems arise from the extended process of

coming of age in modern society. Children begin separating themselves from parents earlier and earlier; but they are not independent adults until later and later. The act of confirmation seems to expect that one moment in this decades-long, difficult process represents the passage into Christian adulthood.

In the believer's baptism system, when it stands on its own, parents and congregations show a demonstrable tendency to baptize children at a quite early age; thus, risking making it as predictable as baptism is at infancy in other churches. As many self-critical Baptists have observed, the adult, self-determining character of baptism becomes qualified. Despite questions, most churches retained their inherited customs—customs devised for generations which took for granted a Christian society.

New Rites. In the 1960s and 1970s, Western churches undertook the most extensive reshaping of Christian initiation since the sixteenth century.

The revision of service books drew on historical study and on the ecumenical thinking that emphasized the foundational place of baptism in the church and in the Christian life and that produced the influential *Baptism, Eucharist and Ministry* statement in 1982. A few of the resultant revisionist texts are following. After the Second Vatican Council (1962–65), the Roman church developed two rites for baptism, a rite for children (1974) and the influential *Rite of Christian Initiation of Adults* (RCIA) (1974; revised ed., 1986). Liturgical work in the Episcopal church produced a revised *Book of Common Prayer* which was authorized in 1976 and 1979. A similar process led to the *Lutheran Book of Worship* (1978), *The United Methodist Book of Worship* (1992), and the Presbyterian *Book of Common Worship* (1993). All of these rites are equally prescriptive in the churches they represent, although the texts may be modified by practice. Thus, these official service books indicate the directions being taken in the major traditions.

One should note that these instances from the major traditions are only part of the story of contemporary Christian worship. Many churches and many thousands of Christians in the free church traditions stand outside the movement described here. For the entire picture, their ways of baptism should be included, but their modes of worship are usually maintained by custom rather than by printed texts. Consequently, changes are hard to trace.

Features of a Common Shape. These liturgical texts (all of them prepared and adopted within a little more than a decade) will illustrate an emerging *ecumenical shape,* marked by some identifiable features:

(1) It hardly needs to be said that in all these rites persons are baptized with water and in the name of the Trinity. Some service books identify immersion as the preferred mode of administration and seem to have in mind much water, rather than a minimal quantity.

(2) These new rites generally commend that baptism take place at a Sunday congregational service, where there will be Scripture reading, preaching, and usually the Eucharist. The congregation takes an active role in the prayers and promises, and it voices its collective welcome. No doubt there are still private baptisms, but liturgical texts and actual practice are moving decidedly away from settings that make baptism an action of the family, rather than of the ecclesia.

(3) Most of these liturgies seek to link the baptismal act with important occasions in the church's Christocentric ordering of time; therefore, they commend that baptisms (to the extent possible) take place at the Easter Vigil—some allow other times, such as Pentecost. The Episcopal church's Prayer Book prints the order of baptism as part of a continuous complex of the Easter Vigil, Holy Baptism, and Holy Eucharist—suggesting the Easter-Baptismal-Eucharist pattern in the very layout of the text.

(4) These new rites contain renunciations, which are not too cursory nor too detailed and explanatory. The promises consist of the Apostles' Creed—the church's ancient baptismal symbol—in interrogatory form. The creed is often associated with some carefully worded supporting promises of faithfulness in Christian life. The non-Roman rites contain a thanksgiving over the water—an action which is commonly done in Roman churches annually, rather than at each baptism.

(5) In the new rites generally, signs have been added to water in churches which have tradition-

ally rejected such signs. Of course, the water is central, and it should be seen (and if possible heard). Symbolic clutter is not edifying. But in many modern rites, the baptism in water is followed by a prayer of thanksgiving for forgiveness and new life, and by acts of anointing, laying on of hands, or the sign of the cross. (Some add the giving of a lighted candle and/or a white garment.) The postbaptismal actions, associated with a prayer or declaration speaking of the Holy Spirit, do not imply that the water rite alone is somehow inadequate. Rather, they are explicatory—making apparent some of the rich baptismal meanings that might otherwise go unexpressed and unappreciated. The point of such actions is not to compensate for the incomplete nature of baptism, but rather to exhibit how complete it is.

This Spirit-act, which can be traced to the early church, had been the sacramental part of confirmation. This act and the significance it carried (anointing with the Holy Spirit royalty, priestliness, athletic contestants, and others) brought about confusion when the act became separated from baptism. Some asked what it meant apart from baptism when in fact it is intelligible only in immediate association with baptism. Because it was experienced independently, some thought that it should express independent meanings. However, confirmation had no meanings other than baptismal meanings. The initiatory significances are a unity for they cohere in Christ. When some of them came to be observed a dozen years after the others, meaning was fractured. The postbaptismal location fills out the initiatory meanings without taking on separate identities. The postbaptismal sacramental sign is no longer a life-stage rite, with a separate meaning, a separate officiating minister, and a separate time subsequent to baptism. Rather, it is part of the baptismal act no matter how old the candidate is. It is within the baptismal act, and explains the presence and agency of the Spirit with an appropriate fullness of sign.

Of course, preaching and teaching will explain some of baptism. However, power is in what we see and do. Remarkably, the testy polemics of the sixteenth century suddenly seem unimportant. A mark of late twentieth-century liturgies is that churches which had condemned signs are now describing them as edifying, admissible, and even desirable.

(6) The new rites generally commend that baptism lead at once to Holy Communion. The Methodist liturgy says that when there is a celebration of Communion, "the new members, including children, may receive first." The two primary sacraments of the gospel are linked in theology and experience. Baptism reaches forward through the Eucharist, and the Eucharist reaches back and touches its origin in baptism. It is difficult to explain why if one is administered the other is not. The contemporary rites differ as to the immediate admission of the baptized to Holy Communion. Some seem to expect it, while some do not, or at least are permissive. Some rites admit baptized adults to Communion at once, but postpone admission to the Table in the case of infants. Many churches state that one is eligible for Holy Communion because one is a Christian, and one is made a Christian in baptism. The Eucharist is not reserved for an elite within the baptized community. It is one of the rights of the baptized. Other churches have not come to that conclusion, and the discussion of this matter must continue. However, until recently such discussion would not have been conceivable.

(7) Many of the newer liturgies provide for the renewing of the initiatory promises in the years following baptism. The baptismal rite in the Presbyterian _Book of Common Worship_ has a dual title: "Baptism and Reaffirmation of the Baptismal Covenant." Clearly such acts of reaffirmation are not repetitions of baptism. Baptism signifies God's acceptance, and its unrepeatability implies that it inaugurates an enduring relation. Yet even though God is faithful, we are not. At times the pledges of baptism are disregarded, and at other times the meaning of our baptism is richly rediscovered. A Christian's promises may need to be reaffirmed. This reaffirmation is not initiatory; one must be a Christian in order to have baptismal promises to renew. Rather, it is a support for the life which begins at baptism. Although baptism is done once for each person and marks the beginning of one's life in Christ and the church, it is also an act of promise, signifying all that is to follow. If Christians are to grow into what they pledge at baptism, they must recall it, claim it, and draw on it. Its vows must be confessed in new situations.

Some of the occasions of remembering can be built into the liturgical system—which may be thought of as an ordered system of prompts for weak memories. Each Eucharist is a renewal of baptism; each time we are present at someone else's baptism, we restate our own promises. (The new liturgies usually provide for the corporate renewal of baptismal promises on occasions when there is no baptism.)

However, Christian experience in contemporary society is seldom a steady passage from strength to strength, but is marked by swings of loyalty and defection, ecstasy and dullness, departure and return. Thus the possibilities in renewing the promises of baptism were not used when the church offered this act to baptized persons once in adolescence and never made it available again. The owning of one's baptism has been made a life-stage rite, associated with an uncomfortable in-between period of maturation. But at what age is it not a good thing to recall one's baptism? Renewing one's baptismal promises is not done only once, in adolescence, but is a repeatable act, in order to interpret and support one's life in faith. This reaffirmation of our fundamental relation with God should be accessible to us through occasions of reaffirming at the unpredictable times when we need it. The personal and pastoral reality that had been represented by confirmation is now available for adult Christian life at any age, any number of times, and for a wide range of circumstances.

This *reaffirmation* is a new pastoral opportunity, and it is being given definition. In 1978, the Roman Catholic Bishops' Committee on the Liturgy, in a booklet called "Christian Commitment," spoke of Christian initiation as "the entry of a Christian into the mystery of Christ and his Church." After speaking of baptism, the text identified "Ways of Renewal," naming Eucharist, Sunday, the liturgical year, penance, and "moments of personal decision." Some "nonliturgical events which call forth the renewal of baptismal faith" were mentioned. The booklet documents ways that "in preparation for and sometimes in conjunction with these . . . events it is very appropriate to renew formally the promises of baptism, those promises which accompanied our initiation into the mystery of Christ when we first said yes to his call."

Several of the liturgies have identified three occasions of renewing the promises of baptism: *confirmation*, the first time that a person who was baptized in infancy renews formally the promises of baptism; *reception*, the time when a person who was baptized and came to mature faith in another Christian communion pledges to carry out the promises of baptism in a new community of faith; and *reaffirmation*, the time when a person makes again the foundational promises of baptism on occasions of renewal or return as they occur in any Christian's life.

The Methodist liturgy at the ritual renewals of the baptismal covenant states that water may be sprinkled and that the minister may lay hands on each person saying the same words that were used after baptism: "The power of the Holy Spirit work within you, that being born through water and the Spirit you may be a faithful witness of Jesus Christ."

The emerging shape described here has been worked out largely by churches which practice infant baptism. Yet it seems to reduce, rather than heighten the differences between these churches and those which hold to believer's baptism. The new rites and theologies are emphasizing the priority of adult baptism, which should gratify Baptists. The infant form of baptism is derived from the adult form, not the reverse. The meaning of baptism is more fully stated and enacted in the case of an adult than it can be in the case of a child.

At the same time many Baptist churches are recognizing that infant baptism, when it is validated by a later life of faith, is true baptism and should not be held in disregard. Many (not all) Baptist churches now recognize and receive such persons as baptized Christians. Through such emphases on both sides of this ecumenical barrier, some mutual understanding, recognition, and liturgical growing together seems possible. (See the initiatory material on the unofficial *A Manual of Worship* [1993] by John E. Skoglund and Nancy E. Hall, prepared for "the free churches and especially for Baptists.")

Differences. Each church has worked from its own historic experience, and the resulting rites are not uniform. Differences among churches as to whether baptism admits one to the Eucharist without any further act were mentioned above. Some further differences may be noted.

With Respect to Orders and Ministries. Initiatory rites which look rather similar in printed texts may in practice seem somewhat different as the acts of baptism or of the renewal of the covenant of baptism interact with differing polities and views of the sacramental and pastoral roles of the ordained clergy. In most churches, all parts of the rites—the preparation for and the celebration of initiatory acts and the postbaptismal occasions of renewal—are in the custody of the local minister often associated with lay catechists. The Lutheran and Methodist churches which have bishops assign the bishops no specific liturgical role either in baptism or in the adult reaffirmations of the baptismal vows. In the Episcopal Church, however, the bishop's visit, which is a community-forming, community-sustaining event, is the occasion for the liturgical reaffirmation of the promises of one's baptism.

In the Roman Church, the local priest baptizes and anoints the child after baptism. The bishop oversees confirmation later. At adult baptism, however, confirmation is administered by a priest, unless a bishop is presiding. (A bishop may ask presbyters to assist.) In this rite (but why not in both?), it is more important that the initiatory actions be kept together than that the ancient Western prerogative of the bishop be retained.

With Respect to the Functions of the Reaffirmation of One's Baptismal Promises. Reaffirmation is a new pastoral action, and its uses are described differently by different churches:

The Lutheran *Book of Worship* speaks of reaffirmation principally as a restoration of a lapsed person to membership—reinstatement in active church membership. Many persons who begin life in the church and its faith leave, and later return. But is this single function too confining? May it give the event a somewhat penitential character?

The Presbyterian liturgy has provided a number of occasions for which reaffirmation would be appropriate. They include occasions when persons are making a public profession of faith, when persons are uniting with a congregation, when a congregation reaffirms the baptismal covenant, when a person experiences growth in faith, and when a pastor counsels privately with "persons who struggle to live up to the implications of their baptism." Does so full a list of occasions open possibilities? Or does it seem like an exhaustive list which closes possibilities?

The Episcopal church distributed a pastoral/liturgical resource with no indication in the Prayer Book itself of the functions reaffirmation might fill, and with almost no pastoral directives to support the clergy who are responsible for developing it effectively. Is this a wise reticence—a trust in the Spirit, the clergy and the congregations? Or is it timidity?

No doubt churches will work for decades to discover how to use reaffirmation in support of the often troubled, inconstant, but equally fulfilling experience that people find within the contemporary community of faith.

Despite the differences, this shape of initiatory rites, worked out in the second half of the twentieth century, represents an impressive, unplanned consensus. Although these initiatory rites contain some changes for all traditions and criticizes some ineffective directions taken in previous generations, they do not repudiate large tracts of past wisdom. They will not themselves solve all the theological and practical problems that have arisen in seeking functional rituals of membership for the church in a post-Christian society. Perhaps, however, the flexibility of these revitalized initiatory rites will let it meet needs, present and emerging, rather than forcing modern experience into formal patterns that are awkward today.

History has been an important guide. The early church acted to shape a community with enough interior strength of conviction to hold together in an eclectic Hellenistic society. Perhaps the modern church is closer to the early church than it is to the intervening centuries of Christendom, whose initiatory practices have, for the most part, continued from the sixteenth century through most of this century.

From patristic sources and contemporary needs, a common structure of initiatory rites and supportive acts is emerging. This ecumenical convergence may be provincially American. Perhaps this common ritual structure will continue, and the pattern will become more widespread and will work with greater economy. Perhaps it will fragment in our fragmented culture and our divided churches. However, it is important enough and hopeful enough to merit some attention now.

Daniel B. Stevick

160 ❖ Bibliography on the History of Baptism

Aland, Kurt. *Did the Early Church Baptize Infants?*

Trans. by G. R. Beasley-Murray. Philadelphia: Westminster, 1963.

Armour, Rollin S. *Anabaptist Baptism: A Representative Study.* Scottdale, Pa.: Herald, 1966. The best study to date of the sixteenth-century Radical Reformation's understanding of believer's baptism.

Barth, Karl. *The Teaching of the Church Regarding Baptism.* Translated by E. M. Payne. London: SCM Press, 1948.

Dujarier, Michel. *A History of the Catechumenate: The First Six Centuries.* New York: Sadlier, 1979.

Finn, Thomas M. *The Liturgy of Baptism in the Baptismal Instructions of St. John Chrysostom.* Studies in Christian Antiquity, no. 15. Washington, D.C.: Catholic University of America, 1967.

Fisher, J. D. C. *Christian Initiation: Baptism in the Medieval West.* Alcuin Club Collections, 47. London: SPCK, 1955.

Jaggar, Peter J. *Christian Initiation: 1552–1969.* London: SPCK, 1970.

Jeremias, Joachim. *Infant Baptism in the First Four Centuries.* Trans. D. Cairns. Philadelphia: Westminster, 1962.

Lynch, Joseph. *Godparents and Kinship in Early Modern Europe.* Princeton, N.J.: Princeton University Press, 1986. Includes a study of baptism in the medieval West.

Old, Hughes Oliphant. *The Shaping of the Reformed Baptismal Rite in the Sixteenth Century.* Grand Rapids: Eerdmans, 1992.

Riley, Hugh. *Christian Initiation: A Comparative Study of the Interpretation of the Baptismal Liturgy in the Mystagogical Writings of Cyril of Jerusalem, John Chrysostom, Theodore of Mopsuestia, and Ambrose of Milan.* Washington, D.C.: Catholic University of America Press, 1974.

Whitaker, Edward C. *Documents of the Baptismal Liturgy.* 2d ed. London: SPCK, 1970. An important collection of baptismal liturgies and documents related to the history of baptism in every period of the church's history.

Yarnold, Keith. *The Awe-Inspiring Rites of Initiation: Baptismal Homilies of the Fourth Century.* Slough, U.K.: St. Paul Publications, 1971.

See also the bibliography on the theology of baptism. Many of those sources contain information on the history of baptism.

❧ FIVE ❧

Contemporary Theologies of Water Baptism

In the Orthodox and Roman Catholic traditions, baptism itself is a saving sacrament. For Eastern Orthodox churches, baptism begins the process of salvation and growth toward participation in the divine nature. In the Western tradition, baptism washes away the guilt of original sin. For Martin Luther also, baptism remained a saving sacrament that carried the power to drive out original sin. Subsequently, all three traditions continued to baptize infants.

In the Reformed tradition, infant baptism was also retained. However, baptism does not accomplish salvation. Instead, it is a seal confirming and ratifying the saving promise found in God's Word, setting the infant on a path toward conversion to personal faith and repentance, a path that takes place within God's covenant community, the church.

During the sixteenth and seventeenth centuries, Anglicans retained the Catholic understanding of baptism as a sacramental washing away of sin although this understanding was challenged by the nineteenth-century evangelical party that emerged from the Wesleyan revivals. After much theological discussion, most Anglicans now admit baptized but unconfirmed children to Communion. While retaining infant baptism, some twentieth-century Anglican theologians have abandoned the theology of original sin that undergirded infant baptism in the West.

Mennonites, Amish, and Hutterites are divided into hundreds of individual groups. In the twentieth century, a number of Mennonite scholars and leaders have begun to draw their theology from the sixteenth-century Anabaptists, from whom these three branches descend. For Anabaptists, baptism depended on a personal, adult faith commitment made in the context of a community of believers.

Methodists take their theology of baptism from John Wesley's insistence on infant baptism as the ordinary means of salvation. Yet Methodism also emphasized, for adults, the possibility of a conscious conversion that may not necessarily be tied to the sacrament. This conversion experience contributed to the development of Holiness, Pentecostal, and charismatic movements from the later nineteenth century onward.

North American evangelicals emerged from revivalism. Most baptize only upon profession of personal, adult faith. However, some evangelical denominations are branches of infant-baptizing Reformed or Lutheran churches.

Twentieth-century Pentecostal denominations emphasize the experience of sanctification by an inward baptism of the Holy Spirit, but also retain water baptism on the basis of personal conversion. According to these denominations, baptism has no saving efficacy.

161 ◆ An Eastern Orthodox Theology of Baptism

In the Orthodox churches, baptism is understood principally by means of scriptural language: baptism marks an infant's or an adult's repentant turning away from Satan and toward Christ by the power of the Holy Spirit. It begins the process of salvation and growth toward participation in the divine nature.

The Orthodox Christian doctrine of holy baptism stems from the teachings of the Holy Scriptures. Christ instructed his apostles to "go and make disciples of all nations, baptizing them in the name of the Father and of the Son and the Holy Spirit" (Matt. 28:18). Thus the Orthodox always baptize in the name of the Holy Trinity. In his answer to those who asked how they should respond to the gospel at Pentecost, Peter told them that they must "repent and be baptized" (Acts 2:38). Consequently, the Orthodox church has always viewed baptism as a part of the repentance that begins the Christian life. Through baptism the believer dies to sin and rises again to a new life in Christ. Paul wrote, "We were therefore buried with him through baptism into death in order that, just as Christ was raised from the dead through the glory of the Father, we too may live a new life" (Rom. 6:4). Consequently, Orthodox theologians consider baptism the new birth spoken of by Christ in his conversation with Nicodemus (John 3:1-21). Those who are baptized are not only born again; they are also united to Christ. Paul wrote, "For all of you who were baptized into Christ have clothed yourselves with Christ" (Gal. 3:27). Peter used the phrase, "baptism that now saves you" (1 Pet. 3:21). Thus, the Orthodox church has always considered baptism an essential part of salvation, not simply a means of affirming faith in Christ.

The Orthodox do not separate baptism from the repentance and profession of faith that begin the Christian life. Instead, Orthodox theologians consider baptism a necessary part of turning from sin to Christ, a precondition for salvation. Candidates for baptism must first denounce Satan and confess their faith in Christ, either personally in the case of adults, or through their sponsors in the case of infants. However, repentance and confession of faith are only the beginning of the Christian life, which according to the Orthodox must be lived within the context of the body of Christ, the church. As Peter and John prayed over the newly baptized believers in Samaria that they might receive the Holy Spirit, the priest anoints the newly baptized Christian with oil, holy chrism, that they too might receive the gift of the Holy Spirit (Acts 8:14-17). A bishop, considered by Orthodox Christians a successor of the apostles, consecrates the chrism, thereby maintaining a link back to the apostles. Finally, the new Christians complete their entrance into the church by receiving Holy Communion.

Orthodox Christians regard salvation as a mystery that is neither dependent on human understanding nor a reward for human merit. Therefore, the Orthodox church has always baptized infants. Orthodox theologians find precedence for infant baptism in the baptism of whole households in the book of Acts (16:15; 18:8). They also find justification for infant baptism in the practice of all Christians until the Protestant Reformation. Finally, since Christ himself scolded his apostles when they tried to deny children access to him, the Orthodox church cannot deny children access to the grace of baptism (Matt. 19:13-15). Because baptized Christians are full members of the church, the Orthodox church also gives children the sacrament of Holy Communion. Naturally, the church expects the parents and sponsors to teach children to live like Christ so they will grow to Christian maturity and thereby realize the potential that they received at their baptism.

Orthodox theologians do not draw a sharp distinction between justification and sanctification. Instead, they consider them part of growth towards deification, the transformation of Christians through grace into the image and likeness of God, and into becoming partakers of the divine nature (2 Pet. 1:4). Baptism is the beginning of this process. Peter wrote, "Like newborn babies, crave pure spiritual milk, so that by it you may grow up in your salvation" (1 Pet. 2:2). Therefore, Orthodox theologians teach that recently baptized Christians must fulfill their baptism by cooperating with the grace of God to reach spiritual maturity through a life of discipleship, repentance, and spiritual growth.

The Orthodox church baptizes through immersion because of the scriptural image of baptism as burial and resurrection, and because of the meaning of the word *baptize*—"to immerse" —in the original Greek. However, this insistence on proper form is not legalistic. In cases of emergency, the church has always accepted baptism that does not include immersion. If no water is available, it is possible to baptize in air. The church also recognizes baptism through intention or the blood of martyrdom. However, the Orthodox church does insist that baptism must be administered "in the name of the Father and of the Son and of the Holy Spirit."

Although Orthodox theologians teach that forgiveness of sins is one of the fruits of baptism, they do not subscribe to the traditional Western view of baptism as the washing away of original sin. Orthodoxy rejects Augustine's doctrine of original sin as inherited guilt. Instead, the Orthodox church teaches that humans inherit the consequences of ancestral sin, such as mortality, corruption, and estrangement from God. However, people are only guilty of sins that they commit themselves.

Baptism is more than a symbolic act for Orthodox Christians. Orthodoxy teaches that sinful, finite humans cannot understand the mysteries of the perfect, infinite God. The Orthodox church believes that baptism is such a mystery. Orthodox theologians approach baptism with faith, rather than reason. They make no effort to explain or understand the sacrament beyond the words of the Holy Scriptures or to separate profession of faith from baptism. Thus, they believe that those who are baptized are buried with Christ and born again into a new life. Baptized persons are also united with Christ and grafted onto the vine of the church. Baptism as the new birth is the beginning of the Christian life. Baptism is a potential that must be realized by the grace of God through growth beyond spiritual infancy into spiritual maturity. The spiritually mature person becomes a new creation remade in the image and likeness of God and a partaker of the divine nature.

John W. Morris

162 ♦ A ROMAN CATHOLIC THEOLOGY OF BAPTISM

This article describes a Roman Catholic theology of baptism by examining the images and actions of the liturgy itself. Note the close connection between the theological position and the liturgical action that is always an important characteristic of liturgical worship.

The sacrament of baptism in the Roman Catholic church has changed and developed in its ritual structure and the interpretation of that structure throughout the centuries. From the advantageous position of the contemporary church, we can look back and see that, just as there is not a single way to do baptism, there is also not a single theology of baptism within the tradition. Therefore, it is more correct to speak of theologies of baptism, rather than a single interpretation, and these various meanings are summarized in one of the opening paragraphs of the general introduction to Christian initiation:

> Baptism incorporates us into Christ and forms us into God's people. This first sacrament pardons all our sins, rescues us from the power of darkness, and brings us to the dignity of adopted children, a new creation through water and the Holy Spirit. Hence we are called and are indeed children of God. (_Baptism for Children_, para. 2)

Contained within this paragraph are the primary theologies of baptism. Baptism is incorporation into the body of Christ, both into the church as the representation of the body of Christ on earth and literally into participation with Christ. Baptism is a freeing, a cleansing from the sin and evil which have held power in the world ever since the first separation from God. Baptism is rebirth, a new beginning, a leaving behind of the old, and a turning to the new, the new family of God.

Throughout the actual liturgy of baptism, the rituals reveal and augment these theologies. The baptism begins with a signing of the cross on the forehead, symbolizing the belief that the person now belongs to Christ and that the powers of evil no longer hold sway. This theology of release is also symbolized in the optional exorcistic anointing, where the baptized is given strength through the ancient symbol of oil and the gesture of blessing. The reception into the church building itself articulates the belief that baptism makes one a member of the body of Christ, the kingdom of God on earth, the church.

The preferred method of baptism, immersion, reflects the theology expressed by the apostle Paul in the letter to the Romans; namely, that baptism is a sharing in the death and resurrection of Christ (Rom. 6:3-4). One dies with Christ so that one can also rise with Christ. This very central theology of baptism also contributes to the belief that baptism is a paradigm of Christian living. Christians must be willing to die and rise with Christ throughout their life if they wish to truly live in and through Christ.

The blessing of baptismal waters which precedes the actual immersion reveals the theologies of cleansing and the idea of rebirth:

> By the power of the Holy Spirit give to this water the grace of your Son, so that in the sacrament of baptism all those whom you have created in your likeness may be cleansed from sin and rise to a new birth of innocence by water and the Holy Spirit. (*Baptism for Children,* para. 54)

The baptismal formula stresses the firm Christian belief in the Trinity; one is baptized into the name of the Father, the Son, and the Holy Spirit. God is a God who exists as a community within God's self providing a model for Christian living—specifically, to live as a community in harmony with each other.

The anointing after baptism symbolizes another facet of baptismal theology—the importance of the model of the Spirit's anointing at Jesus' own baptism, and the belief that baptism crowns the person as a *Christ* to the world: "may you remain forever a member of Christ who is Priest, Prophet, and King" (*Baptism for Children,* para. 62). Here is the ritual basis for the theology which recognizes the priesthood of all believers.

The clothing in a white garment also stresses the intimate connection that the new Christian has with Christ, for baptism is a putting on of Christ. Putting on Christ means identifying with Christ in a manner so profound that a baptized member of the church is to be Christ to others in the world. Likewise, the giving of a lighted candle symbolizes the belief that one is to be a light to the world, a representative of Christ in the world.

This preceding brief survey of the baptismal liturgy reveals that symbols within the baptismal rite itself express the primary theologies of the sacrament. Baptism is the foundation of the seven official sacraments of the Roman Catholic church, and the first of three sacraments which makes up the sequence of initiation. All sacraments are believed to be an encounter with God, an action between humans and God which fills the Christian with God and contributes to the transformation of all human existence by God. Beyond this general statement of sacramental theology, baptism means many things. It is truly a sacrament and truly a symbol because of the richness of meanings which it unfolds. Baptism means new birth, cleansing from sin, salvation from eternal death, incorporation into the church, adoption as a child of God, participation in the death and resurrection of Christ, the beginning of the Christian life, salvation to eternal life, strengthening for living, being made a priest, being made a prophet, being made royalty, being filled with the Holy Spirit, and becoming Christ for the world. These meanings are the theologies of baptism founded on the command of Christ: "Go, make disciples of all nations, and baptize them in the name of the Father, and of the Son, and of the Holy Spirit" (Matt. 28:19).

Lizette Larson-Miller

163 • A Lutheran Theology of Baptism

Lutheran theology maintains a sacramental view of baptism. It links the effectiveness of baptism not with the water itself, but with the Word of God. It also values the role of faith as a response to God's Word in making the sacrament fruitful. These themes are more fully explained in the article that follows.

In Lutheran theology, baptism is one of two chief sacraments (together with the Lord's Supper). It is the foundational sacrament of the Christian life and a means of grace. Baptism conveys the promise of salvation accomplished in the death and resurrection of Jesus Christ, and it establishes the baptized within the church, where the kingdom of God is realized through faith overflowing in love and is anticipated in its fullness through hope.

Baptism exhibits all the features of a sacrament according to the Lutheran understanding. It is commanded by God; it is constituted by God's Word of promise joined to an earthly element; and it is received by faith. First, the external act of baptism is commanded by God through Jesus' instructions to his disciples to baptize in the name of the Father and of the Son and of the Holy Spirit

(Matt. 28:19). Obedience to this divine command requires the administration of water together with the Trinitarian formula. Second, God's Word is the effective power of baptism, not the sacramental water itself. The Word, however, is inseparably linked to the water of baptism. Various expressions of Lutheran baptismal theology locate the power of the sacrament in God's Word just as they describe the unity of Word and sign: "the Word of God connected with the water," "water comprehended in God's Word," and "the Word of God in water." To use the expression of Augustine, baptism is a visible Word. Third, faith receives the activity of God's Word in baptism and makes the sacrament fruitful. Baptism is not constituted by faith, which would make it a human act rather than God's own act; however, the sacrament is properly used where faith is present. Nor, in the Lutheran conception, is faith adequately understood as a response to baptism; rather, it is the result of God's creative Word acting through the sacrament.

This distinctively Lutheran understanding of baptism was forged on two fronts during the Reformation period. On the one hand, Luther and his followers pointed to the power of God's Word and its correlate, faith, as the essence of the sacrament in opposition to the medieval scholastic theology of the sacrament, which understood baptism as an efficacious sign of grace (_efficax signum gratiae_) working through the ritual act (_ex opere operato_). On the other hand, against what they regarded as spiritual enthusiasm on the left wing of the Reformation (e.g., the Anabaptists), the Lutheran Reformers argued for the inseparability of God's Word and the external sign of water, insisted on the objective validity of the sacraments apart from faith, and defended baptism as an external Word and means of grace. Despite the importance placed upon faith in relation to the sacrament, Lutheran baptismal theology has supported the practice of infant baptism because it reflects the divine initiative in the sacrament and the unconditional character of God's promise of salvation.

The purposes and benefits of baptism are manifold because it encompasses the fullness of God's saving activity toward the human race. The Lutheran confessional writings refer to baptism as deliverance from sin, death, and the devil, and as entrance into the kingdom of God. It is a washing of regeneration (Titus 3:5) and the forgiveness of sins. It is the gift of life and eternal salvation. It confers the grace of God, the entire Christ, and the Holy Spirit with its gifts. "In short," Luther writes in the Large Catechism, "the blessings of baptism are so boundless that if a timid nature considers them, it may well doubt whether they could all be true" (_Book of Concord_, 442).

Finally, it should be noted that the Lutheran theology of baptism involved a thorough reconceptualization of the understanding of baptism and, in particular, the understanding of the relationship between baptism and postbaptismal sin that had developed in the Western church. According to medieval scholastic theology, the grace of baptism did not suffice for the forgiveness of serious sin committed after baptism. The sacrament of penance was the remedy for this. The Lutheran position, however, understood the forgiveness following repentance for such sin not as a new dispensation of grace but rather as a return to baptism.

From this perspective, baptism stands as a sign of God's Word of promise over the whole span of a person's life as a Christian. Baptism signifies death and resurrection (particularly so in the practice of immersion); not only the death and resurrection of Jesus Christ, but also that of the believer united with Christ (Rom. 6:1-11). Baptism is exercised in a daily dying to sin (repentance) and rising to new life (forgiveness), a daily baptism in faith, which characterizes the Christian life. This death to sin and new life to God is finally completed only in the mystery of a person's actual death and the resurrection on the last day. Therefore, baptism is at once the sacrament of an eschatological salvation and the sacrament of a faithful daily life in Christ.

Thomas H. Schattauer

164 ✦ A REFORMED THEOLOGY OF BAPTISM

For the second generation of Reformed theologians (Heinrich Bullinger [d. 1572], John Calvin [d. 1564], John Knox [d. 1572]), baptism is a seal confirming and ratifying God's promise in the Word to save. Infant baptism does not accomplish salvation or free the child from original sin; rather, it sets the infant on a path toward repentance, conversion, and personal faith, a path that *takes place within God's covenant community, the church.*

Baptism is recognized and celebrated by Reformed churches as one of two sacraments which, when they are rightly administered, comprise the marks of the true church. Consistently, John Calvin (in *The Institutes of the Christian Religion* [1559]), Heinrich Bullinger (in the Second Helvetic Confession [1566]), and the Heidelberg Catechism ([1563], question and answer 67) insisted that the purpose of the sacraments, like Scripture, is "to offer and set forth Christ to us" through the illuminations of the Holy Spirit. Unlike the Anabaptist position, they are more than *bare signs* that announce God's initiative taken on our behalf in Jesus Christ. They are confirmatory seals that the Holy Spirit uses to authenticate God's promises to the elect. They are symbolic instruments, accommodated to the weakness of humanity's need for sensible representation, through which humans receive the benefits of God, provided recipients receive the sacraments in faith. Thus, the sacraments are the Word of God made visible, and are attached to the prior promises of God to make them more evident and ratify them. Accordingly the Reformed tradition has insisted that the sacraments must not be detached from the preached Word that explains the promises and benefits signified in the sacraments.

Within this framework, Calvin defined baptism as "the sign of initiation by which we are received into the society of the church, in order that, engrafted in Christ, we may be reckoned among God's children" (*Institutes of the Christian Religion*).

In the Reformed tradition the infant is usually called into the church through baptism. The sacrament does not affect salvation nor does it set the baptized free from original sin (the position of the Roman Catholic and Orthodox traditions). Baptism instead announces God's forgiveness of the punishment and guilt of all sin and sets the infant on a lifetime of recalling God's promise through baptism in overcoming sin. This lifelong mortification of the flesh will take place in the context of the church through which God's benefits come to nurture the child's faith. Thus, baptism is an act of the whole church that must be accomplished in the presence of the worshiping community.

While Calvin, Zwingli (d. 1531), Bullinger, and Knox found in circumcision the Old Testament prototype and anticipation of baptism, the heart of their defense of paedo-baptism did not rest on that analogical relationship, but on the one covenant into which Jews were circumcised and the children of Christian parents are baptized. It was a familiar argument of the Reformers that there has always been one covenant since the first announcement of the gospel in Genesis 3:15 with Christ as the object of faith. This singular promise has two administrations. Thus, Calvin argued that circumcision was the Old Testament Israelites' first entry into the church, while baptism is the New Testament church's entry into Christ.

Since the promise offered to Christians in baptism does not benefit them until they embrace the promise by faith, the Reformed tradition has insisted that the child is baptized into future faith and repentance (in the same way that circumcision was a sign of repentance). Baptism is completed at confirmation, the child's personal confession of faith, which is the aim and goal of baptism. The consciousness of having been baptized into God's covenant is conducive to faith as one arrives at a responsible age; the child grows into the understanding of one's baptism. In the meantime, one of the parents must be a believer, so that a parent's faith may be conscious at the infant baptism. The Reformers did not deny that there could be faith in a child, and Bullinger argued that God imputed faith to a child who had no conscious faith. In any case in the Reformed tradition, the emphasis is not on what happens to the child at baptism, but on the child's acceptance into the covenant community and on the reaffirmation of grace by the church. An adult must profess faith in Christ at the time of baptism as she or he is received into full membership in the church. There are not two sacraments––infant and adult baptism—but one sacrament with a distinction between the candidates.

Unlike the Augsburg Confession which insists that "baptism is necessary to salvation" (1530), the Reformed tradition has never argued that a child is damned who does not receive baptism (nor that a child is necessarily saved who does). Grace is not so bound to the sacrament that it cannot be obtained by faith through the Word of God alone. Nevertheless, parents who knowingly refuse baptism to their children are considered disobedient, arrogant before God's grace, and depriving the children of their right.

Calvin and Bullinger insisted that there cannot be rebaptism (as the Anabaptists practiced) any more than there can be two circumcisions. However, they did not specify the mode of baptism, encouraging immersion as much as sprinkling and insisting only that it be performed by the ecclesiastical ministry (though its efficacy does not depend on the merits of the officiant). The Westminster Confession (1646) began to insist on sprinkling and pouring over against immersion.

Dennis Okholm

165 ◆ AN ANGLICAN THEOLOGY OF BAPTISM

During the sixteenth and seventeenth centuries, Anglicans retained the Catholic understanding of baptism as a sacramental washing away of sin. As the evangelical party emerged out of the Wesleyan revivals of the eighteenth century, some nineteenth-century Anglicans challenged the theology of baptismal regeneration. It was, in turn, defended by Edward Pusey and Frederick Denison Maurice. During the twentieth century, some Anglicans have called for the sacrament of confirmation to be reunited with baptism. This reunification has not occurred, and most Anglicans have simply admitted baptized children to Communion before they have been confirmed. Some twentieth-century Anglican theologians have abandoned the theology of original guilt. Infant baptism then becomes a demonstration of the priority of God's grace in salvation. However, Anglican baptismal liturgies retain traditional forms, including the renunciation of Satan and the interrogative recitation of the Apostles' Creed.

Sixteenth- and Seventeenth- Century History

In a sense, the Anglican tradition neither had nor claims a distinctive theology of baptism. None of the English Reformers thought through an original theological approach to baptism. The Church of England, in its liturgy and in its official doctrinal formularies, largely repeated the vocabulary for interpreting baptism from the New Testament and from the patristic and the medieval traditions. The baptismal rite of the Prayer Book of 1549 affirmed that persons who are baptized are united with Christ's death and resurrection. They receive remission of sins and are made living members of the church. They are given the Holy Spirit, new life, and the pledge of eternal life. Baptism is a sign of a divine gift and human faith. Baptized persons are committed to live in righteousness.

The Articles of Religion (1571) described baptism not only as a sign of profession, but also as an instrument whereby the promise of baptism is effected (Art. 27; see G. W. Bromiley, _Baptism and the Anglican Reformers_ [1953].) As a matter of practice, the earliest English Prayer Books adapted the medieval rites for the baptism of infants and until the revision of 1662 made no provision for adult baptism. Infant baptism was the only form that existed and had an Anglican theology.

The classic English doctrinal authorities upheld central doctrinal affirmations. John Jewel (1522–1571), replying to the contention that the Church of England had strayed from true doctrine, said that his church taught that "baptism is a sacrament of the remission of sins and of that washing which we have in the blood of Christ" (_Apologie_, Part 2). Replying to the thesis that sacraments were empty signs while only faith could accomplish redemption, the great constructive theologian, Richard Hooker (1554–1600), said that one is not baptized into one's own faith, but into a given divine redemption, in which one participates through baptism. As the incarnation was the divine participation in the human, so the church and its sacraments are means of human participation in the divine. In sacraments, outward things exhibit inner reality, and inner reality is brought to outward expression. Sacraments, Hooker said, "serve as the instruments of God, . . . moral instruments, the use whereof is in our hands, the effect in his" (_Apologie_, V. lvii.5). Baptism specifically is a heavenly work of new birth, accomplished "not with the Spirit alone, but with water thereunto adjoined" (_Ecclesiastical Polity_, V. lix.5).

Puritan Objections

Some controversies introduced peripheral issues. The Puritans objected to the Prayer Book's use of the sign of the cross at baptism on the grounds that only those things which were required by obedience to Holy Scripture should be performed at worship. Without scriptural warrant, the sign of the cross was unnecessary at best, and offensive at worst. Hooker replied that the action was not scandalous, but was profitable, even though it was of human origin. The cross on the forehead appealed to the imagination as a "silent teacher." The giving of this sign sealed to the believer the solemn vow to obey Christ and suffer reproaches for his sake (*Apologie*, V. 65).

Hooker also had to deal with the Puritan objections to baptism by lay persons, particularly women. But none of these challenges drew Anglican theologians in new directions. English controversialists of the seventeenth century debated whether baptismal discipline should be relatively restrictive or relatively inclusive. Some contended that baptism should not be administered except to children whose parents showed evident signs of faith. The leadership of the Church of England was inclined to give the benefit of the doubt to children for whom sponsors would make the pledges of baptism, for it considered baptism more an act of grace and gift from God manifested through the church than an act of faith and witness on the part of the one baptized. Once children were baptized, they were within the faith-bearing community and shaped by a godly liturgy, where they should be catechized and brought to adult faith insofar as human effort can achieve that result. The church did not baptize because one had given sufficient evidence of worthiness, but it baptized in service of a divine promise, and as an instrument of acceptance into the community of divine redemption.

Later Landmarks

After the early seventeenth century, a number of significant works appeared that addressed the Anglican theology of baptism. In the late seventeenth century, the eminent theologian Jeremy Taylor (1613–1667) described the benefits and obligations of baptism. William Wall (1647–1728), on the other hand, wrote a landmark of eighteenth-century theological literature with his lengthy (usually a two volume set), descriptive, and immensely learned *History of Infant Baptism* (1705). The theologian Daniel Waterland (1683–1740), best known for his work on eucharistic doctrine, also gave a serious account of baptism.

In the nineteenth century (as a consequence of the intense personal spiritual experience engendered in the Wesleyan movement), the evangelical party questioned a passage in the Prayer Book. After baptism, this passage stated that "this child is regenerate and grafted into the body of Christ's church." This phrase had been deleted in the Prayer Book proposed by William White for the Episcopal church in 1785; however, the text adopted by that church in 1789 reinstated the wording. The objection arose because evangelicals thought regeneration was a wonderful and identifiable inward experience, not a mysterious act of God at baptism that the Prayer Book wording implied. To devout evangelicals, this objectifying of grace seemed to bring baptism close to magic, a human effort to manipulate God. To the defenders of the Prayer Book wording, the evangelicals experiential view of grace seemed to be too individualistic and implied a baptism into one's own inward experience, not the church. Baptism has reference, not just to an individual and God, but also to the community of new life, which one is born into with baptism. In the New Testament, the imagery of regeneration primarily is developed in a cosmic and eschatological sense, rather than an individual and experiential sense.

With this controversy in mind, the learned theologian of the Oxford Movement E. B. Pusey (1800–1882) devoted several of his *Tracts for the Times* to a defense of baptismal regeneration. His tracts amounted to a developed treatise, citing largely early Christian writers in favor of baptism as an effective sign of redemption. Pusey's somewhat scholastic defense of the tradition led to an original theological development by the influential English theologian Frederick Denison Maurice (1805–1872). Maurice interpreted (perhaps not with complete fairness) Pusey's simple interpretation of baptism as an act that effects regeneration as defending a conjuring trick which makes someone into something that before the person had not been. On this point, Maurice agreed with the evangelicals, but he did not accept the evangelicals' trust in subjective experience. Maurice's theology centered around Christ's lordship, which means that he is head of the human race. All human life is under Christ and stands in relation to Christ, although most humans live without knowing that crucial truth about themselves. From this conviction, Maurice understood baptism to be an act by which the church declares on behalf of a person that which is in fact true of that person—indeed, the deepest truth about that person. If one argues that such an emphasis makes baptism declarative rather than effective, a showing rather than a doing, Maurice would reply that a declaring is a kind of doing. Some things are not effectively true until they are declared. Maurice saw the unrepeatability of baptism as a sign of divine faithfulness; the baptism once given inaugurates a lasting relation. Baptism is a sign of constant union—a union which endures, even when a baptized person, in statement or in action, denies it. The practical effect of Maurice's emphasis was to extend the inclusiveness of baptism. (see A. R. Vidler, F. D. Maurice, et al., "The Sacrament of Constant Union," 1966).

To a great extent, debates over the relation of baptism to confirmation have dominated the Anglican literature through most of the twentieth century. Some students of the early church claim that the postbaptismal anointing, which had become a separate ritual event of confirmation in the medieval West, is specifically the sacramental instrument by which the Holy Spirit is given. This viewpoint makes confirmation a necessary completion of baptism; it reduces the theological and pastoral fullness of baptism; and it raises ecumenical problems concerning the standing of Christians in churches which had no bishops and no sacramental confirmation. Other scholars have replied that baptism is complete—uniting a whole person with the triune God. Their emphasis, however, leaves confirmation somewhat problematic. It is at most a pastoral act signifying the adult's owning of one's own infant baptism. However, confirmation is not initiatory. No intrinsic reason demands that the rite be administered exclusively by bishops. One can even question whether first Communion should depend on it. Several scholarly exchanges occurred on this matter in the first half of the twentieth century. Some ecumenically significant issues were perhaps explored; however the debate was not very theologically productive (see Dale Moody, "The Anglican Tradition: Baptism and Confirmation," chap. 4 in _Baptism: Foundation for Christian Unity_ [1967]).

Starting in the late 1940s, the Church of England became concerned about what was often called indiscriminate baptism. Because of the state church inheritance, baptism for a long time had been regarded as a social recognition of birth. Persons who took no part in the life of the church still thought they had a right to have their children christened in the Church of England. Incumbents, informed by the dream of a Christian society united by a single church, felt that, as a matter of conscience, they had no right to refuse. The result was that a very high (but a diminishing) proportion of the English population is baptized in the Church of England, while only a small (but fairly steady) proportion is active in the church. This discrepancy seems scandalous. The lapsed baptized member was not the exception, but the norm. Did not such results subvert one of the sacraments of the gospel? Should not the church be shamed? Yet, who was to say no to parents? And on what grounds? Many articles and booklets debated the matter. Some clergy declared a moratorium on infant baptisms, just to indicate their distress over baptizing more members into the church who became only nominal Christians. (To be fair, other historic centers of Christianity in Europe had similar figures and similar pastoral soul searching.) Although many parts of Anglicanism were aware of this discussion, it affected principally the Church of England. Other Anglican provinces which lack the state church tradition (including some provinces in which the Christian population is growing rapidly), do not show the same statistics, and, if the provinces have the same pastoral problem, they have it to a lesser degree

Modern Liturgies

Anglicanism expresses its doctrinal emphases principally through authorized Prayer Books, rather than through confessional statements. In the nineteenth and twentieth centuries, Anglican discussion concerning baptism has centered on the Prayer Book texts. Existing texts have been criticized or supported; new texts have been proposed or adopted. Hence, to establish contemporary Anglican baptismal theology, one consults the many revised Prayer Books and the teachings they appear to express. (See D. B. Stevick, _Baptismal Moments: Baptismal Meanings_ [1987] for an explication of the 1979 Prayer Book of the Episcopal Church.)

Baptism and the Corporate Life. Modern Anglican liturgies contain an implicit critique of the individualism of Western baptism. Whereby the rite (during the Middle Ages and also through the first part of the twentieth century) was usually performed in an empty church with only family and sponsors present, baptism is now understood as an ecclesial event. It is enacted at the Easter Vigil or at the principal Eucharist of a Sunday, when a congregation is present to give witness and to engage itself freshly in the baptismal life.

Baptism brings one into a new set of relationships. One is within the forgiven and forgiveness-bearing community and is bound into the common life of believers—which shares, supports, gives, loves, and judges its members (at the same time, the common life offends and inflicts pain, but asks forgiveness and begins again). No one becomes a Christian or remains a Christian alone. Clearly, baptism is an event, not just for the individual, but for the church (see T. Eastman, *The Baptizing Community* [1982]).

When adults speak the baptismal promises on behalf of a child, the act challenges the community. Not everyone is competent to enter every contract. Clearly, adults who are not mature, carrying out to their best ability the promises of baptism, are not able to make those promises on behalf of someone else. The baptismal action must be carried by the community of faith.

Baptism and Redemptive History. The modern Anglican service books surround baptism with a rich presentation of Scripture and psalmody. They set the act within the divine redemptive purpose by placing it in the Christian year at the Great Vigil of Easter. Not all baptisms will be carried out at this time, but the Prayer Book sets the rite in this context as its normative location. All baptisms, whenever they are done, are enactments of the Easter reality. One's baptism, a passage from death to life, from darkness to light, is enacted in the context of Christ's death and resurrection—which is itself set against the interpretive background of Israel's emancipation from slavery.

This redemptive emphasis touches the theology of infant baptism particularly. For several generations, most Anglican theologians realized that the common interpretation that Romans 5:12 taught a doctrine of inherited guilt imposed a legal thesis on the Pauline text. Probably since the late patristic period, the practice of infant baptism had been defended, at least in part, by an understanding of the sin at birth. At times, the rite was dominated by anxiety, an Augustinian fear which is still popular.

Sin is a terrible, collective reality, which is present before the individual consents to take part in sin. Paul speaks in Romans 5 of human solidarity in sin (in "Adam"), but he does not say that sin is (if one may express sin this way) genetically transmitted. Guilt is not a part of Paul's argument, and in any case is not inheritable. Paul identifies the solidarity of the human race in sin, but he is not fatalistic. Speaking of God's work, he describes Christ as a greater and more inclusive figure than Adam. Speaking of human sin, he emphasizes moral responsibility "because all have sinned."

When one recognizes that one does not baptize an infant because that infant is, in some sense, a sinner, one must rethink the rationale for infant baptism. Many Anglican theologians now speak of infant baptism as a ritual demonstration of divine prevenience. God has acted for each person who is baptized before he or she is capable of knowing or responding to that act. God's love anticipates our experience of that love. Infant baptism signifies the priority of grace. This account of infant baptism (common in Anglicanism, but in other communions also) is not stated in any official formula, but neither was the former account.

The Book of Common Prayer does include renunciations of evil in the baptismal rite for children. (The medieval rite included exorcisms; however, the Anglican prayer books did not.) The renunciations are the counterpoint of the baptismal promises. In a moral world, a saying yes requires also a saying no. These words are said by parents and sponsors who do not speak about what is or what had been, but about what will be or what must be. This child, who now neither believes in God nor resists temptation, must come not only to believe, but also to discriminate and to reject evil. The child must grow to be a moral person in a flawed world. The baptism speaks by anticipation, setting the child in the grace-filled, forgiveness-bearing community under the name, not of Adam, but of Christ.

Baptism and Eucharist. The two sacraments of the gospel complement each other. One signifies birth, and the other feeding. The Eucharist sustains the life that is begun in baptism. The repeated hearing of the Word and partaking of the Supper renews the fundamental relationship begun in the unrepeated act of baptism. In the earliest Christian centuries, baptism was followed at once by Holy Communion, as it still is in the East. As the initiatory rites in the West came to be observed in two stages, admission to Communion was made dependent on the second stage, confirmation at adolescence. Thus in the Western church, the two sacraments have been divided by ten or twelve years.

Most (but not all) new Anglican liturgies state clearly that persons, including infants, are eligible for the Lord's Supper by reason of baptism. This change in sacramental economy has required some adjustment of spirituality and pastoral practice insofar as it implies infant Communion. But a church that sees no reason to postpone baptism should also question the postponement of Holy Communion (see U. T. Holmes, _Young Children and the Eucharist_ [1972]; and the collective work, _Nurturing Children at Communion_ [1985]).

Baptism and Holy Spirit. The past division of initiation between baptism and confirmation at least suggested a division of the realities signified. When some Anglican theologians took the rite of confirmation (derived from the early church's postbaptismal anointing) to speak specifically of the gift of the Holy Spirit, it left water baptism a diminished—almost a pre-Christian—rite. The modern prayer books seek to clarify that baptism is a complete Christian initiation. The Holy Spirit is not reserved for a select few; Holy Spirit fills all Christians by definition. Many Anglican liturgies or pastoral practices place postbaptismal acts (laying on of hands, or anointing, with prayer for the Holy Spirit) in the baptism rite itself. Such practices follow the early church, which understood these practices to signify the anointing of Christians into a royal priesthood. These practices complete the fullness of meaning in the act of Christian initiation (see G. W. H. Lampe, _The Seal of the Spirit_ [1967]).

Baptismal Gift and Faith. The liturgies of modern prayer books suggest that baptism is a point at which divine gift and human faith coalesce. Baptism which belongs to the initiative of God belongs also to the response of humanity. Sacraments enact the great Pauline paradox: "I, yet not I, but Christ in me" (Gal. 2:20).

The prayer over the water and baptism in the triune name set the action in the context of a divine redemptive initiative. Clearly, God acts in baptism to accept a person and to bring that person into a new relationship—to set that person within a new people, representing a new order of forgiveness and promise.

Yet at the same time, the person baptized (in the case of an adult) or the community speaking for that person (in the case of a child) is expressing gratitude and faith by making revolutionary declarations. The promises at baptism include the Apostles' Creed, the early baptismal affirmation. This basic baptismal pledge (based on apostolic preaching) is followed by further promises: to continue faithful in prayer and worship, to return when one has violated the commitments of Christian life, to witness of Christ, to serve others as one encounters need, and to work through the structures of justice to affirm the dignity of every person (_The Book of Common Prayer_ of the Episcopal Church [1979], 304–5). The baptismal covenant gives expression to divine grace and human responsibility.

Baptism sets a person in a community with a mission. It makes each baptized person a sharer in that mission, which is ultimately not programs and ideals, but the mission of God. The people of God, through joy and suffering, are participants in this mission of God.

In sum, the Anglican theological tradition retains from the biblical and early Christian sources the heart of the church's understanding of baptism as a sign and actualization of the gospel. But these sources are sufficiently flexible so that Anglican baptismal theology and practice can grow and change in response to unprecedented situations that occur in the advance of history, yet can also remain true to their Christian identity.

Daniel B. Stevick

166 • AN ANABAPTIST THEOLOGY OF BAPTISM

Anabaptists rejected infant baptism because they insisted that the purpose of baptism was personal transformation and conscious adult commitment to Christ. Although dependent on personal faith, baptism occurred in the church and set the person baptized on a trajectory of witness for Christ that, in the sixteenth century, often led to persecution and even martyrdom. In later centuries, this visible witness for Christ increasingly manifested itself in a sectarian distinctiveness from the dominant culture—hence, the plain dress and way of *life characteristic of the Amish, most Mennonites (until the mid-twentieth century), and Hutterites.*

Sixteenth-Century Anabaptists and Their Descendants

The various denominations descended from the sixteenth-century Anabaptists (Mennonites, Hutterites, Amish), each developed their own organizational patterns, doctrinal statements, and worship patterns. During the early twentieth century, Mennonite leaders in Europe and North America began to study sixteenth-century Anabaptism as a means to renew their own churches. Based on this recovery of the Anabaptist vision, some scholars and church leaders have begun to employ the adjective *Anabaptist* as a generic label for the hundreds of distinct groups descended from the two main streams of sixteenth-century Anabaptists (the Dutch/North German/Russian Anabaptists and the Swiss/South German/Moravian Anabaptists). Some leaders among the various Baptist groups descended from the seventeenth-century English Baptists also have begun to identify with the theology of the sixteenth-century continental Anabaptist movements. The following summary of sixteenth-century Anabaptist views of baptism takes the place of the impossible task of generalizing about contemporary Mennonite, Amish, and Hutterite practices. Though the Anglo-American Baptist tradition is similar, its legacy is also found among North American evangelicals.

In 1524 and 1525, scattered evangelists and preachers began calling for radical repentance and faith. They insisted that respondents be baptized. This challenged the validity of infant baptism practiced in Catholic, Lutheran, and Reformed churches. For the radical preacher's renunciation of infant baptism, these churches persecuted them severely, labeling them *Anabaptists*—literally, those who baptize again. One might suppose, then, that this movement was chiefly concerned with this particular practice. The Anabaptist understanding of baptism, however, was rooted in a far broader vision of Christian life.

Anabaptists insisted, first, that God's redemptive goal was deep personal transformation, or sanctification, not merely forgiveness of sins. Second, this could be attained only through participation in Christian community, in the church. Third, this way of life involved witness to the world, accompanied almost certainly by persecution. Baptism often referred not simply to a ceremony, but to this entire process, to these three intertwined dimensions, or phases, of Christian life.

Baptism and Personal Sanctification

The first phase, baptism of the Spirit, began with the call to faith, through the Word, and with the struggle of repentance. For Anabaptists, baptism's water imagery vividly expressed experiences of being overwhelmed, tossed to and fro, and drowned (Pss. 42:7; 69:1-2). The Spirit painfully dissolved one's ties to the flesh and world, submerging the old nature in death. Yet from the Spirit, a new, divine life also flowed, assuring one of God's presence. Anabaptists often called this first baptism, which continued in some measure through sanctification, an inner baptism. This phrase could refer to daily, inwardly experienced, mortification of the flesh. More often, it indicated the outer deprivation and persecution expected from witnessing to the world. This baptism could, quite plausibly, culminate in literal blood-shedding.

The life process of baptism, then, involved experiences and choices of which infants were incapable. This was the Anabaptists' chief reason for refusing to baptize infants. Since this rite had been practiced universally for over a millennium, they marshaled additional objections against it.

Anabaptists often insisted that infant baptism was not commanded in Scripture. They argued that it was not widely practiced in the earliest centuries. Anabaptists frequently observed that Jesus himself accepted little children; he affirmed that God's kingdom consisted of such; and he stated that children, in their humility, were examples adults should follow (Matt. 18:1-5, 10; 19:13-15). Sometimes such appeals implied that infants were guiltless. Most often, however, Anabaptists claimed that infants were free from judgment only because of Christ's atonement (John 1:29; Rom. 5:18). Yet, they still were inclined toward sin. Eventually they would choose sin. Then the Spirit's baptizing work alone could set them free.

When they spoke of baptism, Anabaptists were usually articulating a radical vision of Christian life, a process of deep purgation and transformation carried out in communion with others and in tension with the world. They insisted that significant personal and communal sanctification were possible. Yet they based this hope not on optimistic opinions about human goodness, but on trust in the power and thoroughness of God's redemptive work.

Baptism as Covenant and Witness

The second phase, baptism of water, involved the outer ceremony, probably performed by pouring or immersion. Anabaptists regarded it as a pledge, or covenant, of the individual with God and the congregation. They insisted that this outer washing was meaningless without the pledge and the inner washing to which it testified. Luther and others protested that such a baptism witnessed merely to subjective experiences, not to God's objective, saving power. In several ways, however, their understanding of baptism was more objective.

First, the baptized testified to, and in the power of, the Spirit who made the entire baptismal process possible. The Anabaptists emphasized free human response, they also stressed that God must first set the will free. The baptism of water was thus a cowitness of our spirit with God's initiating Spirit. Anabaptists could speak of it, accordingly, as conveying salvation and grace. And it was cowitness, in another sense, of inner, spiritual experience with outer, material form. To Anabaptists, infant baptism seemed one-sided, concerned only with physical form.

Second, Anabaptists pledged themselves to the congregation to walk in Christ's footsteps, sharing life and goods with their brethren and submitting to discipline should they fall short. Baptism meant open identification with a severely persecuted group committing one irreversibly to the way of the cross.

Third, most Anabaptists regarded such persecution as evidence that the end of time was near. Water baptism, then, constituted an eschatological sign—God's objective mark on those who would escape coming judgment (Rev. 7:3; 9:4). In this way, the baptism of water pointed not only back to the baptism of the Spirit which undergirded it, but also forward toward the third and ultimate phase, the baptism of blood (Mark 10:38-39).

Thomas Finger

167 ✦ A WESLEYAN THEOLOGY OF BAPTISM

Arguing from tradition, apostolic practice, and a theology of covenant, John Wesley insisted on infant baptism as the ordinary means of salvation consisting of both outer sacrament and inner regeneration. To adults, however, he also preached the possibility of a conscious conversion, an experience of inward regeneration that may not necessarily be tied to the sacrament. Wesley's understanding of baptism not only formed the basis for the Methodist movement, but also contributed to a variety of Holiness denominations, which, in turn, contributed to the early twentieth-century Pentecostal movement.

John Wesley (1703–1791) believed baptism to be the ordinary means of salvation. By baptism we enter into covenant with God, are admitted into the church, and are made children of God.

To be sure, Wesley distinguished between baptism and the new birth. Not the mere outward washing, but the inward grace added thereto makes baptism a means of saving grace (_Works of John Wesley_, vol. 6 [reprint; Kansas City: Beacon Hill Press, 1978], 73–74). This applied to infants as well as to adults, and in the case of the former, he believed that "all who are baptized in their infancy are at the same time born again" (_Works_, 9:316). However, he also insisted that in adults a conscious evangelical experience of regeneration is possible that may not necessarily be tied to the sacramental rite. Perhaps unique to Wesley was the balance he maintained between his ingrained love for corporate things and the sacramental on the one hand, and his fervent and intensely personal evangelical faith on the other. This balance has sometimes been mistaken for an inconsistency.

In his treatise on baptism (_Works_, vol. 10), he argues for infant baptism on five levels:

(1) Infants are proper subjects of baptism because of the sin of Adam in which all participate. For this disease, Christ has provided a remedy. The benefit of this remedy is to be received through baptism, which is the ordinary means he has appointed for that purpose (_Works_, 10:193).

(2) Baptism is proper for infants because of the continuity between the covenant of grace God made with Abraham and the new covenant established by Christ. Both covenants were _gospel_ covenants, with the same condition (faith), the same benefits ("I will be their God"), and the same

mediator (Gal. 3:16). As circumcision was the seal of the former, baptism is the seal of the latter. Baptism is now the "circumcision of Christ" (Col. 2:11-12). Infants under the new covenant are capable of entering into the covenant with God, just as they were under the old, and are thus entitled to baptism.

(3) On the basis of Matthew 19:13-14 and Luke 18:15, where children were brought to Christ and received by him, Wesley argues that children are therefore capable of being embraced by the church. Baptism is the divinely given sign of their inclusion in the new covenant.

(4) Wesley appeals to the practice of the apostles in baptizing entire households in the book of Acts. Although he knows the New Testament does not specifically state that these households included infants, he believes it to be a valid inference. The Jews baptized all infant proselytes, and the apostles probably did the same, since the Lord did not forbid it when he commanded baptism in the Great Commission. Wesley mentions the three thousand and five thousand, who were baptized by the apostles on separate days, and appeals to Peter's Pentecost sermon, which concludes with the words, "Be baptized . . . for the promise is for you and your children" (Acts 2:38-39). Wesley knows that the New Testament does not divide persons into three groups—believers, unbelievers, and children. There are only two groups—believers and unbelievers. Nowhere does the New Testament classify children as unbelievers.

(5) Finally, he appeals to the authority of tradition and finds support for infant baptism in the church "in all ages and in all places." Citing several church Fathers, he asserts that no instance can be found in all antiquity of any orthodox Christian, who denied baptism to children when they were brought to be baptized (*Works,* 10:198). Since infant baptism has been the uninterrupted practice of the church throughout the centuries, Wesley concludes that "it was handed down from the Apostles, who best knew the mind of Christ" (*Works,* 10:198).

Not all Wesley's followers have adhered strictly to the baptismal views of their mentor. This is the case both in mainline Methodism and in the Wesleyan/Holiness tradition which grew out of the nineteenth-century revival of Wesley's teachings on scriptural holiness. Many people from various Anabaptist backgrounds embraced Wesleyan soteriology and joined Holiness denominations; however, they brought their baptismal views with them.

Wesley had made a distinction between baptism and the new birth, but insisted they should be held together as a unity. But many of his followers turned the distinction into a separation, viewing the new birth as the important thing and allowing baptism to be seen more and more as a mere human witness to personal faith and less and less as a means of receiving present grace. Naturally, with such a development, infant baptism, in many instances, was allowed to sink into disfavor. Wesley's views on baptism were quite clear, but in Wesleyanism today the significance of this sacrament remains a bit clouded.

Rob L. Staples

168 ✦ A RESTORATIONIST UNDERSTANDING OF BAPTISM

Churches of the so-called Restoration Movement are often marked by their theological view of baptism, as well as the emphasis they place upon it. The Restoration Movement's theological position on baptism can be summarized in one sentence: adults are immersed for the forgiveness of sins and the gift of the Holy Spirit. Compared to most of the major theologies of Christendom, the combination of the Restoration Movement's emphasis on adult immersion and its view of the necessity of baptism is unique.

The Restoration Movement referred to here is the Campbell/Stone movement of the nineteenth century. The emphasis of the movement was to restore primitive New Testament Christianity and to promote unity based on the Bible without the addition of human creeds or other tests of fellowship. The movement has grown to more than four million members since that beginning. Ironically, through the course of time the movement has also divided, with three major divisions being most prominent: the liberal Disciples of Christ (Christian Church), the conservative Churches of Christ (noninstrumental), and the centrist churches, generally calling themselves Christian (independent) or Churches of Christ (instrumental). The centrists are also conservative.

Baptism and Repentance

The Scripture most centrally used by Restoration Movement thinkers on the subject of baptism is Acts 2:38. Here Peter commands the convicted crowd to "Change your hearts and each one of you must be immersed by the authority of Jesus the Messiah, so that your sins may be forgiven. Then you will receive the gift of the Holy Spirit." (All citations are from the noninstrumentalist _Simple English Bible,_ American Edition.) There are two things that Peter says for them to do to be saved: repent and be baptized. Their need for repentance seems clear in light of the fact that they are cut to the heart with remorse and indicate a desire to make things right with God. They must repent. But Peter also says they must be baptized. The only mode of baptism found in the New Testament is considered by Restorationists to be immersion. Therefore, sprinkling, pouring, or any other mode is not acceptable among most Restorationists. (The major exception to this rule is the Disciples branch, which began practicing "open membership" some years ago. Disciples churches will still immerse adult converts but will also accept those baptized in other ways who wish to join formally the local congregation.) The twofold command also holds a twofold promise: your sins will be forgiven and you will receive the gift of the Holy Spirit.

Baptism and the Forgiveness of Sin

The first promise related to repentance and baptism is the forgiveness of sin. Faith and repentance are essential, but baptism is the God-intended vehicle in which sins are forgiven. If baptism without repentance is powerless to save, so is repentance without baptism. Alexander Campbell articulated this position in his _Christian System_:

Without previous faith in the blood of Christ, and deep and unfeigned repentance before God, neither immersion in water, nor any other action, can secure to us the blessings of peace and pardon. It can merit nothing. Still to the believing penitent it is the means of receiving a formal, distinct, and specific absolution, or release from guilt. . . . To such only as are truly penitent, dare we say, "arise and be baptized, and wash away your sins, calling upon the name of the Lord," and to such only can we say with assurance, "You are washed, you are justified, you are sanctified in the name of the Lord Jesus, and by the Spirit of God." (Alexander Campbell, _The Christian System in Reference to the Union of Christians, and a Restoration of Primitive Christianity, as Plead in the Current Reformation_ [Nashville: Gospel Advocate, 1974], 16:6.)

Baptism and the Gift of the Holy Spirit

The second promise of Acts 2:38 is the gift of the Holy Spirit. The correlation of repentance, baptism, and the Holy Spirit is not unique to the book of Acts. John the Baptist performed a baptism of repentance. In Matthew 3:11 he says "Whenever you change your hearts, I immerse you in water. But there is one coming later who is more important than I am. . . . He will immerse you in the Holy Spirit and in fire!" Somehow it seems that the main difference between John's baptism of repentance and the Christian baptism would involve the Holy Spirit (compare Acts 19:1-4).

The Holy Spirit certainly has the sovereignty to come when the Spirit wants. Both on the day of Pentecost when the disciples were all together (Acts 2:1-4) and at Cornelius's house (Acts 10:44-46), the Spirit came in power prior to water baptism. The general Restoration view is that these times seem to be for a purpose other than salvation, i.e., to equip the recipients with miraculous powers having evidential value. But even if these were saving events, they are clearly exceptions to the general rule, since water baptism would not have been offered without the Holy Spirit's prior intervention. And in Cornelius' case, Peter responds to the work of the Spirit by saying, "Can we refuse to allow these people to be immersed in water? They have received the Holy Spirit the same as we did!" (Acts 10:47). So water baptism is still associated with the gift of the Spirit, even in the exceptional cases.

Furthermore, the Holy Spirit occasionally was imparted by the laying on of the apostles' hands; however, again the purpose seems to have been to convey miraculous powers. But even in such cases, as in Acts 19, water baptism is again related to the Holy Spirit. Jesus in John 3:5-8 speaks of water and Spirit. Hebrews 6:1-2 mentions baptisms in the plural; yet, Ephesians 4:4 states there is only one baptism. So to which baptism—water

IHS Symbol. The IHS symbol is an abbreviation of the Greek word ΙΗΣΟΥΣ, which means "Jesus." The particular configuration above is from a card printed years ago by the Mobray people of Oxford.

baptism or spiritual baptism—is Paul referring in Ephesians? The answer seems to be both. The one baptism which Paul refers to is the Spirit/water baptism of Acts 2:38. In conclusion, the biblical norm seems to be that the act of water baptism is also the act of Spirit baptism.

Baptism and the New Birth

Water baptism also is related to the new birth in several passages, most notably Romans 6. There, Paul says, "You know that all of us were immersed into Christ Jesus. Don't you know that we were immersed into his death? So, through immersion, we were buried with him into death. Christ was raised from death through the glory of the Father. In the same way, we will live a new life" (Rom. 6:3-4). Jesus also relates water and being born again in John 3:5. The very picture of burial in water is a symbolic enactment of the spiritual death and resurrection that takes place.

Paul underscores this relationship between baptism and the new birth in Colossians 2:12-13. Here, he writes, "You were buried with Christ through immersion [in which] you were also raised with Christ through believing in the power

of God who raised Christ from death." Does Scripture intend the gift of the Holy Spirit, and the new birth to be associated with water baptism? See Titus 3:5, where Paul writes, "He saved us by a washing of rebirth and renewal of the Holy Spirit." Again, it seems the Bible considers the initiation and the new birth to be one moment in God's intention. Water baptism is, therefore, more than merely a symbolic act representing spiritual baptism; it is the very occasion of being born again. The story is told that when Ronald Reagan was running for the presidency against Jimmy Carter, he was asked if he was born again. Since he grew up in a Christian Church (Disciples of Christ), his reply was something to the order that yes, when he was immersed in his youth, he was born again.

Baptism Is Not a Response to Salvation. The Restoration Movement's view of baptism differs from those groups who baptize adults merely as an act of obedience that follows saving faith and the reception of salvation. In other words, many groups see salvation as being by faith alone and baptism as an external work symbolizing a spiritual baptism already effected. Restorationists point to Peter's statement, "Immersion saves us through the raising of Jesus Christ from death" (1 Pet. 3:21). They do not in any way discount faith as essential, but rather point to the importance of baptism as an essential part of the *saving moment.*

Baptism Does Not Precede Salvation. The Restoration Movement's view also differs from those groups who hold a high view of the significance of baptism, but who also baptize infants. Restorationists immerse adult believers only, for Restoration Movement scholars find that any infant baptism in the New Testament must be inferred—and that inference is not very easy. In truth, the Scriptures provide no clear examples of second-generation conversions. All of the New Testament passages about baptism refer to adult conversions. Also, Restorationists find no mention of *original sin* or any such doctrine. Hence, Restorationists will not advocate infant baptism, but will allow a child to grow to the point when he or she can have his or her own faith and repentance. According to Restorationists, children are born innocent, and Jesus said the kingdom of God belonged to those who are like them. Yet the promise is that "the person who believes and is immersed will be saved, but the person who doesn't believe it will be condemned" (Mark 16:16). Infants can be sprinkled. However, since they cannot be penitent believers, saving baptism cannot occur.

In short, the Restoration Movement tends to see belief, repentance, confession, and baptism all to be essential elements of conversion, with baptism as the normal moment of the gift of the Holy Spirit. They, therefore, do not baptize infants, for that would place baptism long before the other elements of salvation. And they do not see baptism as a post-salvation act of obedience or another good work, for that would place baptism after salvation.

——— Summary and Conclusion ———

What this article describes is the basics of how churches of the Restoration Movement understand Scriptures regarding baptism. Some members of the movement, especially the Disciples branch, will not agree with the statements contained here. The Disciples tend not to emphasize baptism as much as the rest of the movement. And several churches in the centrist group are inclined to accept the Zwinglian or Anabaptist doctrine, which views baptism as an act of obedience following saving faith. Furthermore, many of the more conservative members of the movement will speculate that the "pious unimmersed" are not and cannot be saved without completing their obedience in baptism.

All in all, however, most of the churches in the Restoration Movement would agree that the biblical norm regarding baptism is adult immersion for the forgiveness of sin and the gift of the Holy Spirit.

Ken Read

169 ✦ An Evangelical Theology of Baptism

The evangelical tradition is not monolithic in its understanding of water baptism. Furthermore, the importance that the Protestant Reformers gave to baptism seems to be diminished if not absent among many evangelicals. This diminished importance is perhaps due to revivalistic theology that supplanted the significance of baptism with the individual's conversion experience, which often occurred outside the church. The following article will note the divergences and the commonalities among evangelicals.

As with other traditions, baptism in the evangelical tradition is related to the beginning of the individual's Christian life and the believer's initiation into the church (both the universal invisible church and the local visible church). It is performed and received as an act of obedience to Christ who exemplified the practice in his own life (Matt. 3:13) and commissioned his followers to baptize all people (Matt. 28:19).

Baptism must always be connected with faith and repentance (see Acts 2:38), though unlike the latter two it is not indispensable to salvation nor is it a means of regeneration. Though some Christians understand baptism to be a regenerative act, evangelicals tend to offer alternative explanations for passages such as Mark 16:16, John 3:5, Acts 2:38, Titus 3:5, and 1 Peter 3:21. What troubles evangelicals in this regard is that if baptism is regenerative, it is difficult to see how salvation is by grace through faith alone. Thus, salvation is possible without baptism, and baptism is an act that expresses one's faith. The water signifies that one has been cleansed from sin (Titus 3:5).

The biblical locus of the meaning of water baptism is Romans 6:1-11. Baptism symbolizes the believer's own death and resurrection. This union is made possible through the work of the Holy Spirit. In this way, baptism is a visible sign or representation of the objective reality of Christ's saving work that makes possible the believer's own death and resurrection, resulting in the individual's rebirth, the forgiveness of the individual's sins, and the individual's consecration to a new life of holiness and service. In this sense, the act of baptism seals or cements the relationship that God has established with the people of God.

The evangelical tradition embraces a range of opinions with regard to the candidate for baptism. Evangelicals in the Reformed tradition, for instance, who emphasize the covenant into which the baptized is placed, have argued that infants should be candidates for baptism on the basis of (1) the two different administrations of the one covenant (circumcision in the Old Testament and baptism in the New Testament), (2) the precedent of household baptisms at which infants might have been present (see Acts 11:14; 16:15, 33; 18:8; 1 Cor. 1:16), (3) and the invitation of Jesus to children (Matt. 19:13-15; Mark 10:13-16; Luke 18:15-17). Since evangelicals do not subscribe to the Roman Catholic _ex opere operato_ position, which bases the sacrament's efficacy on the working of the sacrament itself, Reformed (and Lutheran) evangelicals insist that faith must accompany the infant's baptism, either through *infant faith* or through the vicarious faith of the sponsors. But this position has not been popular with the majority of evangelicals (even including some in the Reformed tradition such as Karl Barth), particularly since the scriptural evidence is not conclusive and since the requirement of faith for baptism seems inadequate. Evangelicals have tended to insist that the proper candidates for baptism are believers who have reached an age of understanding and responsibility, and are baptized as active participants.

Evangelicals also have not been in total agreement on the mode of baptism. They have preferred immersion due to the literal meaning of baptizing ("to dip, to immerse"; also see Mark 1:10 and Acts 8:38ff), and due to the symbolism of death and resurrection in Romans 6. Immersion involves the threat of drowning, from which one is delivered and raised to life.

Baptism is to be done in, for, and by the church (though there are some Baptists who baptize privately). The act is a reminder to the church that the church itself is constituted by the Word of God as it is *proclaimed to the eyes* in baptism. The baptized person becomes an active member of the people of God. These people are characterized by their confession of loyalty to Jesus Christ, whose life, death, and resurrection is the sign under which they have been placed. For this reason, baptism is also a political act. It symbolizes the new identity of each believer who is now *in Christ,* in the church that does not arrange people in a hierarchy based on their sex, race, or socioeconomic status. Baptized individuals are expected to assume their responsibilities for Christian service on the basis of the gifts and tasks that the Holy Spirit assigns to each member of the church (Eph. 4:1-16).

Dennis Okholm

170 • A Pentecostal Theology of Baptism

Although the various Pentecostal denominations that have flourished since the beginning of the twentieth century emphasize the experience of sanctification by the inward baptism of the Holy Spirit, they have consistently retained the practice of water baptism. Water baptism, according to Pentecostals, has no saving efficacy but is enjoined on believers as a way of obeying Christ's example. Infants are not baptized. Baptism is normally, but not exclusively, by immersion and in the name of the Trinity. Rebaptism of those baptized in other Christian communions who later join Pentecostal groups is common. Repeated baptism as a mark of renewed commitment to Christ is not unknown.

"I'm saved, sanctified, filled with the Holy Spirit, and on my way to heaven." For decades, this statement has served adherents of Pentecostal churches as both a personal testimony and a short doctrinal statement. Since it never was intended as a theological summary, the lack of any reference to water baptism should not be seen as disregard for this important practice.

From the very beginning of the Pentecostal movement at the beginning of the twentieth century, the individual groups have held firmly to the belief in and the practice of water baptism. It does not receive the frequent mention in either preaching or teaching that other doctrines have. Somehow it has become hidden behind the emphasis on holiness and the Pentecostal experience.

Pentecostals believe the Scriptures teach water baptism as a prescribed rite for all believers. Jesus' baptism by John in the Jordan River provides the example which all are to follow. In the Great Commission, Christ commanded his disciples to baptize those who believe. On the day of Pentecost, Peter directed potential converts first to believe and then to follow belief with the action of baptism. Further examples of water baptism are provided by the ministries of both Philip the evangelist and the apostle Paul.

Pentecostal theology projects the symbolism of water baptism. First, the outward act of baptism reflects the inward change. Baptism as a public profession indicates death to sin and putting on of Christ. In this sense baptism is also considered a sign of discipleship. Second, baptism is seen as being symbolic of Christ's death and resurrection, which will also be experienced by all believers not living at the time of Christ's return.

This symbolic view of water baptism denies its possession of any spiritual or saving power. Baptism is not essential for salvation. However, refusal to follow the Lord's example in baptism when provided with the opportunity causes doubt that the person will be an obedient, faithful Christian.

Baptism in the Name of the Trinity by Immersion

The Trinitarian formula ("in the name of the Father, and of the Son, and of the Holy Ghost") as shared in the Great Commission has been accepted by the major Pentecostal denominations. The "Jesus only" branch as represented by the United Pentecostal Church has adamantly accepted baptism only in the "name of Jesus as directed by Peter on the Day of Pentecost." The difference between these two positions on baptism includes the question of whether Peter's injunction was a prescribed formula for baptism or a recognition of the new master as the new converts submitted to baptism.

Pentecostal theology holds to believer's baptism by immersion. There is no suggested minimum age or educational requirement. Children are allowed to be baptized upon the consent of their parents. Parents, better than anyone else, can determine the understanding and depth of the child's commitment.

The mode of baptism has not been a matter for extended discussion within Pentecostal circles. Believing immersion to be the biblical directive and example, they have adopted and practiced immersion without continuing dialogue or exhaustive study. However, it is of interest to observe that the Pentecostal Holiness Church officially sanctions sprinkling. This came about through the influence of J. H. King, their long-term general superintendent.

Rebaptism

The concept of rebaptism should not be overlooked. Individuals, who were baptized as infants or backslide after their commitment to Christ, are encouraged to become rebaptized. A few suggest that the believer should consider rebaptism as a means of renewal and deeper commitment. The scriptural precedent for rebaptism is Paul's rebaptism of those disciples who had only known John's baptism (Acts 19:5).

New converts are encouraged to be baptized as soon as possible. The immediacy of this event does not seem to be pressed as strongly as in earlier decades when stories abound of breaking ice for a baptism or holding the baptismal service in other intemperate weather. Of course, the provision of baptisteries have eradicated this problem in many other denominations as well.

The availability of a baptismal service is determined by the individual pastor as the opportunity arises. No particular occasions or time periods are generally observed. The vast majority are held as part of a Sunday evening service.

Pentecostal theology has not associated water baptism and church membership. Membership in the visible body of Christ occurs as a separate act of presenting oneself for fellowship in the local church body.

In summary, Pentecostals see water baptism as an ordinance of the church, sanctioned by Christ and practiced by the early church. Baptism should be an immersion performed with the Trinitarian formula. Believers participating in this symbolic act indicate their obedient discipleship.

Jerald Daffe

171 • A Charismatic Theology of Baptism

Charismatics tend to practice believer's baptism and to maintain the practices of the worship traditions in which they stand. They distinguish between water baptism and the baptism of the Holy Spirit.

The rite of baptism has been interpreted in various ways by the church throughout history: as a sacrament that imparts grace; an ordinance acted out in obedience; an essential element for salvation; a sign of Christian commitment; or a symbol of identification with Christ. The modes of baptism have also differed, involving total immersion, pouring, or sprinkling.

The early church found its roots for Christian baptism in the purification rites of Judaism, the baptism of Jewish proselytes, and the baptism of Jesus by John the Baptist. As the church continued to develop its practices, the issue of baptism always remained in the forefront both in terms of method and meaning. The Reformation was the beginning point for some parts of the church to change their view of baptism from _sacrament,_ where it meant a mystery that served as a channel or sign of grace, to an _ordinance,_ where it meant a practice performed as a sign of obedience. This separation of understanding has formed a long-lasting breach in dialogue between the various groups that make up the body of Christ. All major Pentecostal and charismatic groups do practice water baptism as an ingredient in the early stages of a believer's commitment to Christ.

The charismatic movement does not have an actual theology of baptism. Since this renewal movement often began within existing churches, charismatics within mainline or other smaller denominations have basically continued the normative baptismal practice of their group. Nonaligned ministries, charismatic fellowships, and independent churches have spawned a variety of positions, but normally view baptism as an ordinance, and totally immerse believers who have found a personal relationship with Jesus Christ. This emphasis on ordinance also springs from the perspective that the rite of baptism has no self-contained efficacy independent from the participant's faith.

Also, Pentecostal denominations have primarily held to believer's baptism, which was common among the revivalist movements of the nineteenth century. Certain groups will even require that a believer be rebaptized if that person was baptized as an infant or by a method other than total immersion. The practice of rebaptizing after returning from a backslidden condition has also been practiced by some. One major variation in baptismal practice exists among the so-called oneness Pentecostals, who insist that persons be baptized in the name of Jesus only.

Typically, both charismatic and Pentecostals do not see a connection between water baptism and the baptism of the Holy Spirit, which they see as a distinct process.

Randolph W. Sly

172 ◆ BIBLIOGRAPHY ON THE THEOLOGY OF BAPTISM

Baptism in New Testament Theology

Beasley-Murray, G(eoffrey) R(aymond). *Baptism in the New Testament*. Grand Rapids: Eerdmans, 1962. A scholarly approach to discovering the antecedents to Christian baptism, tracing its history through Scripture (with attention to connected rites of the "laying on of hands"), and interpreting the doctrine from a Baptist point of view. The author includes a lengthy section of "The Rise and Significance of Infant Baptism," with some interesting conclusions. Baptist/Ecumenical.

Cullman, Oscar. *Baptism in the New Testament*. Philadelphia: Westminster, 1950.

Flemington, William F. *The New Testament Doctrine of Baptism*. London: SPCK, 1948.

Schnackenburg, Rudolf. *Baptism in the Thought of St. Paul*. New York: Herder and Herder, 1964.

Systematic and Pastoral Theologies of Baptism

Adult Baptism and the Catechumenate. Concilium no. 22. New York: Paulist Press, 1967.

Baptism and Church: A Believer's Church Vision. Grand Rapids: Sagamore Books, 1986.

Beasley-Murray, G(eoffrey) R(aymond). *Baptism Today and Tomorrow*. New York: Macmillan, 1966. A Baptist theologian's approach to baptism.

Brand, Eugene. *Baptism: A Pastoral Perspective*. Minneapolis: Augsburg, 1975. Designed for group or personal study, this study by a Lutheran pastor provides a helpful introduction to Christian baptism.

Bridges, Donald, and David Phypers. *The Water That Divides: The Baptism Debate*. Downers Grove, Ill.: InterVarsity Press, 1977.

Bromiley, Geoffrey W. *Children of Promise: The Case for Baptizing Infants*. Grand Rapids: Eerdmans, 1979.

Brooks, Oscar. *The Drama of Decision*. Peabody, Mass.: Hendrickson, 1987. The author's quest is to arrive at a holistic statement about baptism that emerges authentically from baptismal texts in the Bible and ancient writings. Termed "the drama of decision," the baptismal theme is uniquely and systematically exposed through analysis of each text in its context and alternative views. Technical notes are also presented. His scholarly conclusion is that "the act of baptism is that moment when the believer publicly dramatizes that he or she has come to know God and has accepted his offer of salvation." Baptist/Ecumenical.

Burnish, Raymond. *The Meaning of Baptism*. Alcuin Club Collection. London: SPCK, 1985.

Costen, Melva Wilson. *African American Christian Worship.* Nashville: Abingdon, 1993. See chapter 5 on the sacraments and ordinances of worship.

Davis, Charles. *Sacraments of Initiation: Baptism and Confirmation.* New York: Sheed and Ward, 1964.

Dunn, James D. G. *Baptism in the Holy Spirit.* Naperville, Ill.: Allenson, 1970.

Eastman, A. Theodore. *The Baptizing Community.* 2d ed. Harrisburg, Pa.: Morehouse Publishing, 1991. A study by an Episcopal bishop of the liturgy and theology of baptism.

Empie, Paul C., and T. Austin Murphy, eds. *Lutherans and Catholics in Dialogue.* Vol. 2, *One Baptism for the Remission of Sins.* New York: Lutheran World Federation, 1966.

Every, George. *The Baptismal Sacrifice.* London: SCM Press, 1959. Eastern Orthodox.

Gilmore, Alec, ed. *Christian Baptism.* Valley Forge, Pa.: Judson Press, 1959. A classic Baptist interpretation of baptism.

Green, Michael. *Baptism: Its Purpose, Practice and Power.* Downers Grove, Ill.: InterVarsity Press, 1987. Green writes about baptism from an evangelical Anglican perspective. The volume is designed to be short and readable. It advocates a merging of Catholic, Protestant, and Pentecostal strands of meaning and praxis as respecting both biblical and traditional sources. This merger would recover symbolic and sacramental understandings in a middle way, and baptize both children and adults with appropriate meaning. Anglican/Renewal/Evangelical.

Jeschke, Marlin. *Believers Baptism for Children of the Church.* Scottdale, Pa.: Herald, 1983. This is a more recent Mennonite study of the issues regarding the baptism of children.

Jewett, Paul K. *Infant Baptism and the Covenant of Grace.* Grand Rapids: Eerdmans, 1978. An appraisal of the argument that since infants were once circumcised, so they should now be baptized.

McDonnell, Kilian, O.S.B., and George Montague, S.M. *Christian Initiation and Baptism in the Holy Spirit.* Collegeville, Minn.: Liturgical Press, 1991.

Marsh, Thomas A. *The Message of the Sacraments.* Vol. 2, *Gift of Community: Baptism and Confirmation.* Wilmington, Del.: Michael Glazier, 1984.

Marty, Martin E. *Baptism.* Minneapolis: Fortress Press, 1962.

Miller, Marlin. "Baptism in the Mennonite Tradition." *Mennonite Quarterly Review* 64:3 (1990): 230–58. Miller shows the impact of Assembly Mennonites and the Concern movement (p. 257), which states that one is able to come to faith only after age fifteen. This article is very useful for addressing Mennonite theological issues in a catholic setting and shows how fundamentally different the Neo-Anabaptists are from their predecessors.

Mitchell, Leonel L. *Initiation and the Churches.* Washington, D.C.: Pastoral Press, 1991.

———. *Baptismal Anointing.* Notre Dame, Ind.: University of Notre Dame Press, 1977.

Murphy Center for Liturgical Research. *Made, Not Born: New Perspectives on Christian Initiation and the Catechumenate.* Notre Dame, Ind.: University of Notre Dame Press, 1976.

Neunheuser, Burkhard. *Baptism and Confirmation.* Trans. John Jay Hughes. New York: Herder and Herder, 1964.

Orthodox Perspectives on Baptism, Eucharist, and Ministry. Brookline, Mass.: Holy Cross Orthodox Press, 1985.

Osborne, Kenan B. *The Christian Sacraments of Initiation: Baptism, Confirmation, Eucharist.* New York: Paulist Press, 1987.

Poloma, Margaret M. *The Assemblies of God at the Crossroads: Charisma and Institutional Dilemmas.* Knoxville, Tenn.: University of Tennessee Press, 1989. See especially chapter 3, "Glossolalia and Spirit Baptism."

Reformed Liturgy and Music 15:4 (Fall 1981). The theme issue for this volume is baptism.

Riley, Hugh M. *Christian Initiation.* Studies in Christian Antiquity, no. 17. Washington, D.C.: Catholic University of America Press, 1974.

Schmemann, Alexander. *Of Water and the Spirit: A Liturgical Study of Baptism.* Crestwood, N.Y.: St. Vladimir's Seminary Press, 1974. Written by one of the most articulate spokesmen for the sacrament-centered Eastern Orthodox tradition.

Scmeiser, James, ed. *Initiation Theology.* Toronto: Anglican Book Centre, 1978.

Searle, Mark. *Christening: The Making of Christians.* Collegeville, Minn.: Liturgical Press, 1980. A study of reforms in the Roman Catholic church since the Second Vatican Council, concentrating on the baptism of infants.

Searle, Mark, ed. *Alternative Futures for Worship.* Vol. 2, *Baptism and Confirmation.* Collegeville, Minn.: Liturgical Press, 1988.

Strege, Merle D. *Baptism and Church.* Grand Rapids: Sagamore Books, 1986. A collection of essays by church theologians who defend believer's baptism. It is a somewhat skeptical response to the essentially sacramental-oriented baptism, Eucharist, and ministry statement by the Faith and Order Commission of the World Council of Churches (various editions; found in the third edition of John H. Leith, ed., *Creeds of the Churches* [Atlanta: John Knox, 1982]).

Stevick, Daniel B. *Baptismal Moments: Baptismal Meanings.* New York: Church Hymnal Corporation, 1987. Stevick contributes an important volume on the meaning of Christian baptism and its related rites of Christian initiation—confirmation and first Communion. He addresses these subjects from a modern Anglican perspective while also providing insights into other Christian traditions. Includes an examination of the "persistent issues" (e.g., infant baptism, the inherent instability of the pattern of confirmation, and others) surrounding the rites. Extensive notes, bibliography, and running commentary on the 1979 Prayer Book are part of the text. Episcopal.

Stookey, Laurence Hull. *Baptism: Christ's Act in the Church.* Nashville: Abingdon, 1982.

Thurian, Max, and Geoffrey Wainwright, eds. *Baptism and Eucharist: Ecumenical Convergence in Celebration.* Geneva: World Council of Churches, 1983; Grand Rapids: Eerdmans, 1983. A collection of the actual texts of eucharistic and baptismal liturgies from a wide variety of Orthodox, Catholic, and Protestant churches. An excellent resource for understanding the present ecumenical situation.

Wainwright, Geoffrey. *Christian Initiation.* Richmond, Va.: John Knox, 1969.

Watkins, Keith, ed. *Baptism and Belonging.* St. Louis: Chalice Press, 1991. This volume contains instructions, prayers, and liturgical texts for Christian baptism, the reception of children, and the affirmation of baptismal vows. Descriptions and liturgical texts for the Easter Vigil and a program of preparation and nurture of baptismal candidates are also included. Believer's baptism by immersion which is both regenera-tional and sacramental is envisioned. Disciples of Christ.

Waltner, James H. *Baptism and Church Membership.* Newton, Kans.: Faith and Life Press, 1979. This pamphlet teaches believer's baptism from a Mennonite/Anabaptist perspective and contains a biblical introduction to the practice, a historical discourse on symbol and sacrament, an explanation of the distinctives of the Reformation and Mennonite/Anabaptist history and practice, and some suggestions for the practice of baptismal and membership services/liturgies. Contains a bibliography.

Willimon, William. *Remember Who You Are: Baptism, a Model for Christian Life.* Nashville: The Upper Room, 1972.

Yates, Arthur S. *Why Baptize Infants? A Study of the Biblical, Traditional and Theological Evidence.* Norwich, Norfolk: Canterbury Press, 1993.

Theological Studies of the Practice of Baptism

Davies, John G. *The Architectural Setting of Baptism.* London: Barrie and Rockliff, 1962.

Ellebracht, Mary Pierre. *The Easter Passage: The RCIA Experience.* Minneapolis: Winston, 1983.

Hatchett, Marion. *Commentary on the American Prayer Book.* New York: Seabury, 1981. A theological and liturgical commentary on the 1979 *Book of Common Prayer,* including a discussion of each sacramental liturgy.

Kavanagh, Aidan. *The Shape of Baptism: The Rite of Christian Initiation.* New York: Pueblo Publishing, 1978. The book is an attempt to acquaint the reader with the Roman rite of Christian initiation done from within the tradition, but against the background of what is going on in other traditions as well. A liturgical understanding (as act, rather than text) is the goal. New Testament foundations and early ritualization are examined, with the major section of the work being reserved for reforms of the Second Vatican Council. Theological and pastoral commentary follows with "ceremonial recipes for all conceivable situations" rendered. Contains a good bibliography. Roman Catholic.

Kennedy, David. *Methodist and United Reformed Church Worship: Baptism and Communion in Two "Free" Churches.* Nottingham, U.K.: Grove Books, 1992.

Kuehn, Regina. *A Place for Baptism* Chicago: Liturgy Training Publications, 1992. Focuses on the seven most common shapes for baptismal fonts, how to design or build baptismal fonts, and the history and symbolism of baptism.

Mitchell, Leonel L. *Praying Shapes Believing.* Minneapolis: Winston, 1985. A theological commentary on the 1979 *Book of Common Prayer,* including a discussion of each of the sacramental rites.

Pfatteicher, Philip H. *Commentary on the Lutheran Book of Worship: Lutheran Liturgy in Its Ecumenical Context.* Minneapolis: Augsburg Fortress, 1990. Includes a commentary on the baptismal liturgy.

Wilde, James A., ed. *Commentaries: Rite of Christian Initiation of Adults.* Chicago: Liturgy Training Publications, 1988. Eleven essays on various aspects of the RCIA.

See also the bibliographies on the history and practice of baptism, and the bibliography on the sacraments, ordinances, and sacred actions of the church.

❧ SIX ❧

The Practice of Baptism

The documents of this chapter are representative of baptismal liturgies within Christendom. First, a foundational document from The Apostolic Tradition of Hippolytus provides the student with a sense of baptism in the early church. The baptismal liturgies of the historic churches—Orthodox and Roman Catholic churches—show how baptismal worship has developed from the historic sources. The influence of these sources is then demonstrated by presenting a wide variety of baptismal liturgies including the Reformed, Wesleyan, free church, and ecumenical traditions. In addition, a proposed service for baptism in the charismatic tradition is presented.

173 ♦ THE APOSTOLIC TRADITION OF HIPPOLYTUS

Hippolytus was an important church leader in the Roman church in the last years of the second century and early years of the third century. In the following passage, his famous Apostolic Tradition is reconstructed and translated. According to most scholars, this text describes the baptismal practice of the Roman church around the second century. It also is the foundation for later liturgical innovations and reforms.

——————— The Text ———————

XVI

1. Those who come forward for the first time to hear the word shall first be brought to the teachers at the house before all the people [of God] come in.

2. And let them be examined as to the reason why they have come forward to the faith. And those who bring them shall bear witness for them whether they were able to hear.

3. Let their life and manner of living be enquired into, whether he is a slave or free. [Sections 4–24 consist of regulations determining the conditions under which men or women might be admitted to instruction, according to the manner of their past lives and their readiness to forsake evil ways and forbidden occupations.]

XVII

1. Let a catechumen be instructed for three years.

2. But if a man be earnest and persevere well in the matter, let him be received, because it is not the time that is judged, but the conduct.

XVIII

1. Each time the teacher finishes his instruction let the catechumens pray by themselves apart from the faithful.

2. But after the prayer is finished the catechumens shall not give the kiss of peace, for their kiss is not yet pure.

XIX.

1. After the prayer let the teacher lay hands upon them and dismiss them. Whether the teacher be an ecclesiastic or a layman let him do the same.

2. If anyone being a catechumen should be apprehended for the Name, let him not be anxious about undergoing martyrdom. For if he suffer violence and be put to death before baptism, he shall be justified having been baptized in his own blood.

XX

1. And when they are chosen who are set apart to receive baptism let their life be examined,

whether they lived piously while catechumens, whether they "honored the widows," whether they visited the sick, whether they have fulfilled every good work.

2. If those who bring them bear witness to them that they have done thus, then let them hear the gospel.

3. Moreover, from the day they are chosen, let a hand be laid on them and let them be exorcised daily. And when the day draws near on which they are to be baptized, let the bishop himself exorcise each one of them, that he may be certain that he is purified.

4. But if there is one who is not purified, let him be put on one side because he did not hear the word of instruction with faith. For the strange spirit remained with him.

5. And let those who are to be baptized be instructed to wash and cleanse themselves on the fifth day of the week [i.e., Thursday].

6. And if any woman be menstruous she shall be put aside and baptized another day.

7. Those who are to receive baptism shall fast on the Preparation [Friday] and on the Sabbath [Saturday]. And on the Sabbath the bishop shall assemble those who are to be baptized in one place, and shall bid them all to pray and bow the knee.

8. And laying his hand on them he shall exorcise every evil spirit to flee away from them and never to return to them hence forward. And when he has finished exorcising, let him breathe on their faces and seal their foreheads and ears and noses and then let him raise them up.

9. And they shall spend all the night in vigil, reading the Scriptures to them and instructing them.

10. Moreover those who are to be baptized shall not bring any other vessel, save that which each will bring with him for the Eucharist. For it is right for every one to bring his oblation then.

XXI

1. And at the hour when the cock crows they shall first [of all] pray over the water.

2. When they come to the water, let the water be pure and flowing.

3. And they shall put off their clothes.

4. And they shall baptize the little children first. And if they can answer for themselves, let them answer. But if they cannot, let their parents answer or someone from their family.

5. And next they shall baptize the grown men; and last the women, who shall have loosed their hair and laid aside their gold ornaments. Let no one go down to the water having any alien object with them.

6. And at the time determined for baptizing, the bishop shall give thanks over the oil and put it into a vessel and it is called the Oil of Thanksgiving.

7. And he shall take other oil and exorcise over it, and it is called the Oil of Exorcism.

8. And let a deacon carry the Oil of Exorcism and stand on the left hand. And another deacon shall take the Oil of Thanksgiving and stand on the right hand.

9. And when the presbyter takes hold of each one of those who are to be baptized, let him bid him renounce saying: I renounce thee, Satan, and all thy service and all thy works.

10. And when he has said this let him anoint with the Oil of Exorcism. Saying: Let all evil spirits depart far from thee.

11. Then after these things let him give over to the presbyter who stands at the water. And let them stand in the water naked. And let a deacon likewise go down with him into the water.

12. And when he goes down to the water, let him who baptizes lay his hand on him saying thus: Dost thou believe in God the Father Almighty?

13. And he who is being baptized shall say: I believe.

14. Let him forthwith baptize [*baptizet:* probably, "let him dip"; see also #16 and #18] him once, having his hand laid upon his head.

15. And after [this] let him say: Dost thou believe in Christ Jesus, the Son of God? Who was born of the Holy Spirit and the Virgin Mary. Who was crucified in the days of Pontius Pilate. And died. And rose the third day living from the dead. And ascended into the heavens, And sat down at the right hand of the Father, And will come to judge the living and the dead?

16. And when he says: I believe, let him baptize him the second time.

17. And again let him say: Dost thou believe in the Holy Spirit in the Holy Church and the resurrection of the flesh?

18. And he who is being baptized shall say: I believe. And so let him baptize him the third time.

19. And afterwards when he comes up he shall

be anointed with the Oil of Thanksgiving saying: I anoint you with holy oil in the Name of Jesus Christ.

20. And so each one drying himself they shall now put on their clothes, and after this let them be together in the assembly.

XXII

1. And the bishop shall lay his hand upon them invoking and saying: O Lord God, who didst count these worthy of deserving the forgiveness of sins by the laver of regeneration, make them worthy to be filled with thy Holy Spirit and send upon them thy grace, that they may serve thee according to thy will; to thee is the glory, to the Father and to the Son with the Holy Ghost in the holy church, both now and ever and world without end. Amen.

2. After this pouring the consecrated oil and laying his hand on his head, he shall say: I anoint thee with holy oil in God the Father Almighty and Christ Jesus and the Holy Ghost.

3. And sealing him on the forehead, he shall give him the kiss of peace and say: The Lord be with you. And he who has been sealed shall say: And with thy spirit.

4. And so shall he do to each one severally.

5. Thenceforward they shall pray together with all the people. But they shall not previously pray with the faithful before they have undergone these things.

6. And after the prayers, let them give the kiss of peace.

XXIII

[This section describes the Eucharist which followed baptism. A mixture of milk and honey, and a chalice of water were offered, as well as the bread and wine. The bread was administered first, followed by the water, the milk and honey, and the eucharistic cup, in that order. It has been suggested that the compound of milk and honey referred to here and elsewhere is a last trace of the meal in which the Eucharist originated and from which it was soon detached.]

Commentary

For modern readers, Hippolytus' liturgy is valuable not only as a source of historical information, but also as a guide to the nature and meaning of Christian baptismal practices. Most striking are the stringent requirements—requirements relating to both doctrine and life—that Hippolytus sets forth for the candidates for baptism. The length of prepatory study (three years), the separation of the catechumens (baptismal candidates) from the faithful during the time of preparation, and the repeated examination of the candidates' lives suggest the significance that many early Christians attributed to the sacrament. Baptism entailed accepting an entirely new identity as a person in Christ. The rituals associated with baptism left no doubt regarding the comprehensive nature of this change in identity.

Similarly striking are the frequent references to exorcism. During the final period of preparation for baptism, the candidates are to be "exorcised daily." Further exorcism was ordered for the beginning of the final all-night vigil prior to Easter baptism and during the baptism itself, which used the Oil of Exorcism when the candidate renounced Satan and Satan's works. These references point to a basic feature of the worldview and piety of early and medieval Christians that emphasized—and even was preoccupied with—the presence and influence of Satan. Although this emphasis may have been taken too far by some early Christians, Christians today could well benefit from a greater awareness of the presence and influence of Satan as described in Scripture.

Hippolytus' liturgy is also of interest because it reflects early manifestations of some very important Christian baptismal practices. One such practice is the administering of baptism on Easter morning. Most scholars believe that "the Preparation" and "the Sabbath" in chapter XX, number 7, refer to Good Friday and Easter Sunday morning respectively. This is corroborated by various manuscript sources of both this and other early baptismal liturgies. This practice of Easter baptism is especially helpful in emphasizing the nature of our baptism with Christ into his death and resurrection (Rom. 6:1-5). This emphasis was lost in some later baptismal services. Many church traditions have recently promoted this practice, in conjunction with recent renewed interest in the Easter Vigil service.

Another important early practice is that of the use of the Apostles' Creed in conjunction with baptism. Hippolytus' liturgy is clear in emphasizing the importance of having candidates committed to adopt changes both in doctrine and in life.

With regard to their lives, candidates were examined both as they began the process of initiation into the church (chapter XVI) and just prior to the final period of preparation (chapter XX). With regard to doctrine, candidates were educated in the tenets of the Christian faith (chapter XVII) and were required to accede to the component lines of the Apostles' Creed, which was asked of them at the moment of their baptism (chapter XXI).

The use of the Apostles' Creed also reflects an early use of a Trinitarian formula for baptism. In Matthew 28:19, Jesus challenged his disciples to baptize converts into the name of the Father, Son, and Holy Spirit. This is reflected in the threefold baptism in the liturgy of Hippolytus, with one baptism occurring after each of the three sections of the creed (XXI:12–18).

Finally, in studying Hippolytus' liturgy, a modern reader can easily be impressed with the manifold use of tangible symbols in this early baptismal service. Two oils for anointings; the water for cleansing; the hands for laying on and signing; the kiss of peace; and the bread, cup, and milk and honey of the Eucharist all add both to the complexity of the ritual and to the embodied, physical nature of the baptismal actions. Real, tangible symbols and ritual actions suggest that God's action in baptism was similarly real and tangible, and that the life of the baptized would embody tangible Christian attributes.

Commentary by John D. Witvliet

174 ✦ The Eastern Orthodox Baptismal Liturgy

The following text is one example of a twentieth-century baptismal liturgy from the Eastern Orthodox tradition. It is based on an English translation of a Greek Orthodox liturgy found in An Orthodox Prayer Book, *edited by Fr. N. M. Vaporis and translated by Fr. John von Holzhausen and Fr. Michael Gelsinger (Brookline, Mass.: 1977). The following service orginates in the Syrian liturgical tradition. Given the continuity of liturgical texts within the Orthodox tradition, this text may be taken as representative of the tradition as a whole.*

In the Orthodox churches, the sacrament of baptism is as a rule administered to infants. It is rarely that adults present themselves to be baptized, partly because the Orthodox churches only have a limited organized mission among people who are not Christians. The Office of Holy Baptism is based, however, on adult baptism and is in actual fact addressed to adults. This fact is evident in the baptismal rite, which implies that an infant to be baptized is not treated in any way other than as an adult. The same liturgy is used in both cases. Baptism is immediately followed by confirmation.

Looking at the Orthodox liturgies, we first find prayers related to childbirth and delivery which are not part of the liturgy proper. They are offered at different stages and must be considered separately. There are first the "prayers on the first day after a woman hath given birth to a child." Then, the prayers follow "at the naming of a child when he receiveth his name, on the eighth day after his birth." This time, the child is brought to the church by the midwife. The priest makes the sign of the cross upon the forehead, lips, and breast of the child and says a prayer of intercession. Later, there are the prayers "for a woman on the fortieth day after childbirth." This time, the mother brings the child to the church in order that the child may be *churched*, or introduced into the church. The priest offers again a prayer of intercession and, if the child has already been baptized, performs the *churching:* the priest carries the child to the doors of the sanctuary, saying, "The Servant of God is churched. . . ."

The Office of Holy Baptism begins with the reception of the candidate as a catechumen. The priest removes the person's clothes except for one garment. The priest places the catechumen with the person's face towards the east, breathes three times in the person's face, makes the sign of the cross upon the candidate three times, lays a hand upon the catechumen's head, and prays for the candidate. The priest says the three exorcisms, ordering the devil to leave this person: "The Lord layeth thee under ban, O Devil: He who came into the world and made his abode among men. . . . Begone, and depart from this creature, with all thy powers and thy angels." After further prayers for delivery from evil, the priest breathes upon the person's mouth, brow, and breast, saying: "Expel from him every evil and impure spirit, which hideth and maketh its lair in his heart. The spirit of error, the spirit of guile, the spirit of idolatry and of every concupiscence; the spirit of deceit and of every uncleanliness. . . . And make him a reason-endowed sheep in holy flock of thy Christ. . . ."

Then follows the renunciation of the devil. The priest turns the person to the west and asks three times, "Dost thou renounce Satan, and all his Angels, and all his works, and all his service, and all his pride?" And each time the catechumen answers, "I do." If the catechumen is an infant, the infant's godparent (sponsor) answers in the infant's place. The priest questions the catechumen three times, "Hast thou renounced Satan?" And the catechumen, or the sponsor, responds each time, "I have." The catechumen is then requested to spit upon Satan, and the priest turns the person again to the east, asking the candidate three times, "Dost thou unite thyself unto Christ?" When the catechumen has answered these questions, the catechumen recites the Nicene Creed, the holy symbol of the faith. This Creed is also said three times; whereupon the question, "Hast thou united thyself unto Christ?" is repeated three times again. When the catechumen has affirmed, for the third time, "I have," the priest orders the person to "bow down also before Him!" and the person answers, "I bow down before the Father, and the Son and the Holy Spirit, the Trinity, one in Essence and undivided." A short prayer of intercession concludes this part of the liturgy.

The priest enters the altar and dresses in white vestments. While the candles are being lit, the priest takes up the censer, goes to the font, and places the censers round about. Giving up the censer, the priest makes a reverence.

PRIEST: Blessed is the Kingdom of the Father, and of the Son, and of the Holy Spirit, both now and ever, and to the ages of ages. Amen.

In peace let us pray to the Lord. Lord have mercy.

(After each petition: **Lord have mercy.**)

For the peace from above; for the salvation of our souls; let us pray to the Lord.

For the peace for the whole world; for the stability of the holy Churches of God, and for the union of all; let us pray to the Lord.

For this holy House, and for them that with faith, reverence, and the fear of God enter therein; let us pray to the Lord.

For our Most Reverend Archbishop [Name], for the venerable Priesthood, the Diaconate in Christ; for all the Clergy, and for all the people; let us pray to the Lord.

That this water may be hallowed by the might, and operation, and descent of the Holy Spirit; let us pray to the Lord.

That there may be sent down upon it the Grace of Redemption, the blessing of the Jordan; let us pray to the Lord.

That there may come down upon this water the cleansing operation of the Supersubstantial Trinity; let us pray to the Lord.

That this water may prove effectual for the averting of every plot of visible and invisible enemies; let us pray to the Lord.

That he [she] that is about to be baptized herein may be worthy of the incorruptible Kingdom; let us pray to the Lord.

That he [she] now comes to holy Illumination, and for his [her] salvation;

That he [she] may prove to be a child of Light, and an inheritor of eternal blessings; let us pray to the Lord. That he [she] may grow in, and become a partaker of the Death and Resurrection of Christ our God; let us pray to the Lord.

That he [she] may preserve the garment of Baptism, and the earnest of the Spirit undefiled and blameless in the terrible Day of Christ our God; let us pray to the Lord.

That this water may be for him [her] a laver of Regeneration unto the remission of sins, and a garment of incorruption; let us pray to the Lord.

That the Lord may listen to the voice of our prayer; let us pray to the Lord.

That He may deliver him [her] and us from tribulation, wrath, danger, and necessity; let us pray to the Lord.

Help us; save us; have mercy on us; and keep us, O God, by Your Grace.

Calling to remembrance our all-holy, exceedingly blessed glorious Lady Theotokos and Ever-Virgin Mary, with all the Saints; let us commend ourselves and one another and all our life to Christ our God.

PRIEST (inaudibly): Let us pray to the Lord.

O compassionate and merciful God, Who tries the heart and reins, and Who alone knows the secrets of men, for no deed is secret in Your sight, but all things are exposed and naked in Your eyesight: do You Yourself, Who perceives that which concerns me, neither turn away Your face from me, but overlook my offenses in this hour, O You that overlook the sins of men that they repent. Wash away the defilement of my body and the stain of my soul. Sanctify me wholly by Your all-effectual, invisible might, and by Your spiritual right hand, lest, by preaching liberty to others, and offering this in the perfect faith of Your unspeakable love for humankind, I may be condemned as a servant of sin. Nay, Sovereign Master that alone are good and loving, let me not be turned away humbled and shamed, but sent forth to me power from on high, and strengthen me for the ministration of this Your present, great and most heavenly Mystery. Form the Image of Your Christ in him [her] who is about to be born again through my humility. Build him [her] on the foundation of Your Apostles and Prophets. Cast him [her] not down, but plant him [her] as a plant of truth in Your Holy, Catholic, and Apostolic Church. Pluck him [her] not out, that, by his [her] advancing in piety, by the same may be glorified Your Most Holy Name, of Father, and of Son, and of

Holy Spirit, both now and ever, and to the ages of ages. Amen.

THE BLESSING OF THE BAPTISMAL WATERS

PRIEST: (reads aloud)

Great are You, O Lord, and wondrous are Your works, and no word will suffice to hymn Your wonders. For by Your Will have You out of nothingness brought all things into being and by Your power sustain all creation, and by Your Providence direct the world. You from the four elements have formed creation and have crowned the cycle of the year with the four seasons; all the spiritual powers tremble before You; the sun praises You; the moon glorifies You; the stars in their courses meet with You; the Light hearkens unto You; the depths shudder at Your presence; the springs of water serve You; You have stretched out the Heavens as a curtain; You have founded the earth upon the waters; You have bounded the sea with sand; You have poured forth the air for breathing; the angelic Powers minister unto You; the Choirs of Archangels worship before You; the many-eyed Cherubim and the six-winged Seraphim, as they stand and fly around You, veil themselves with fear of Your unapproachable Glory; for You, being boundless and beginningless and unutterable, did come down on earth, taking the form of a servant, being made in the likeness of men; for you, O Master, through the tenderness of Your Mercy, could not endure the race of men tormented by the devil, but You did come and save us. We confess Your Grace; we proclaim Your beneficence; we do not hide Your Mercy; You have set at liberty the generations of our nature: You did hallow the virginal Womb by Your Birth; all creation praises You, Who did manifest Yourself, for You were seen upon the earth, and did sojourn with men. You hallowed the streams of Jordan, sending down from the Heavens Your Holy Spirit, and crushed the heads of dragons that lurked therein. DO YOU YOURSELF, O LOVING KING, BE PRESENT NOW ALSO THROUGH THE DESCENT OF YOUR HOLY SPIRIT AND HALLOW THIS WATER. And give to it the Grace of Redemption, the Blessing of Jordan. Make it a fountain of incorruption, a gift of sanctification, a loosing of sins, a healing of sickness, a destruction of demons, unapproachable by hostile powers, filled with angelic might; and let them that take counsel together against Your creature flee therefrom, for I have called upon Your Name, O Lord, which is wonderful, and glorious, and terrible unto adversaries.

And the priest signs the water thrice, dipping fingers in it; and breathing upon it, the priest says: LET ALL ADVERSE POWERS BE CRUSHED BENEATH THE SIGNING OF YOUR MOST PRECIOUS CROSS. We pray You, O Lord, let every airy and invisible specter withdraw itself from us, and let not a demon of darkness conceal himself in this water; neither let an evil spirit, bringing obscurity of purpose and rebellious thoughts, descend into it with him [her] that is about to be baptized. But do You, O Master of All, declare this water to be water of redemption, water of sanctification, a cleansing of flesh and spirit, a loosing of bonds, a forgiveness of sins, an illumination of soul, a laver of regeneration, a renewal of the spirit, a gift of sonship, a garment of incorruption, a fountain of life. For You have said, O Lord, "Wash, and be clean; put away evil from your souls." You have bestowed upon us regeneration from on high by water and the spirit. Manifest Yourself, O Lord, in this water, and grant that he [she] that is to be baptized may be transformed therein to the putting away of the old man, which is corrupt according to the deceitful lusts, and to the putting on of the new, which is renewed according to the Image of Him that created him [her]. That, being planted in the likeness of Your death through Baptism, he [she] may become a sharer of Your Resurrection; and preserving the Gift of Your Holy Spirit and increasing the deposit of Grace, he [she] may attain unto the prize of his [her] high calling and accounted among the number of the first-born whose names are written in Heaven, in You our God and Lord Jesus Christ, to Whom be all Glory and Might, together with Your Eternal Father and with Your All-Holy, Good, and Life-creating Spirit, both now and ever, and to the ages of ages.

CHOIR: Amen.
PRIEST: Peace be to all (+).
CHOIR: And to your spirit.
PRIEST: Let us bow our heads before the Lord.
CHOIR: To You, O Lord.

The priest breathes thrice upon the oil and signs it thrice, while it is held by the godparent.

PRIEST: Let us pray to the Lord. Lord have mercy.

THE BLESSING OF THE OIL

Sovereign Lord and Master, God of our Fathers, Who did send to them in the Ark of Noah a dove bearing a twig of olive in its beak as a sign of reconciliation and salvation from the Flood, and through these things prefigured the Mystery of Grace; and thereby have filled them that were under the Law with the Holy Spirit, and perfected them that are under Grace: do You Yourself bless this Oil by the power (+) and operation (+) and descent of the Holy Spirit (+) that it may become an anointing of incorruption, a shield of righteousness, a renewal of soul and body, and averting of every operation of the devil, to the removal of all evils from them that are anointed with it in faith, or that are partakers of it. To Your

Glory, and that of Your Only-Begotten Son, and of Your All-Holy, Good, and Life-creating Spirit, both now and ever, and to the ages of ages.

CHOIR: Amen.
PRIEST: Let us attend.

The priest, singing Alleluia thrice with the people, makes three crosses with the Oil upon the water.

PRIEST: Alleluia, alleluia, alleluia. Blessed is God that enlightens and sanctifies every man that comes into the world, both now and ever, and to the ages of ages.
CHOIR: Amen

The priest pours some oil into the hands of the godparent. The priest then takes oil and makes the sign of the cross on the child's forehead, breast, and between his [her] shoulders, saying:
> The servant of God [Name] is anointed with the Oil of Gladness, in the Name of the Father, and of the Son, and of the Holy Spirit, both now and ever, and to the ages of ages. Amen.

And the priest signs his [her] breast and between his [her] shoulders, saying:
> For healing of soul and body.

And on the ears, saying:
> For the hearing of Faith.

And on the feet, saying:
> That he [she] may walk in the paths of Your commandments.

And on the hands, saying:
> Your hands have made me, and fashioned me.

THE BAPTIZING

When the priest has anointed the whole body, the priest baptizes him [her] holding him [her] erect, and looking towards the east, says:
> The servant of God [Name] is baptized in the Name of the Father, Amen. And of the Son, Amen. And of the Holy Spirit, Amen.

At each invocation, the priest immerses him [her] and raises him [her] up again.

After the baptizing, the priest places the child in a linen sheet held by the godparent.

The choir sings Psalm 31:
> Blessed are they whose iniquities are forgiven, and whose sins are covered. Blessed is the man whom the Lord imputes not sin, and in whose mouth there is no guile. Because I have kept silence, my bones waxed old through my crying all the day long. For day and night Your hand was heavy on me. I was turned into lowliness while the thorn was fastened in me. My sin I have acknowledged, and my iniquity I have not hid. I said, "I will confess against myself my sin unto the Lord." And You forgave the ungodliness of my heart. For this shall everyone who is holy pray to You in a seasonable time; moreover in a flood of many waters shall the billows not come nigh to him. For You are my refuge from the tribulation which surrounds me. O my rejoicing, deliver me from them that have encircled me. The Lord says, "I will give you understanding, and will teach you in this My way which you shall go; I will fix My eyes on you. Be not as the horse, or as the mule, which have no understanding. With bit and bridle would you bind their jaws, lest they come near to you." Many are the scourges of the sinner, but with mercy shall I encircle them that hope on the Lord. Be glad in the Lord, and rejoice, you righteous; and shout for joy, all you that are upright of heart.

PRAYER OF CONFIRMATION

PRIEST: Let us pray to the Lord.
CHOIR: Lord have mercy.
PRIEST: Blessed are You, Lord God Almighty, Fountain of Blessings, Sun of Righteousness, Who made to shine forth for those in darkness a light of salvation through the manifestation of Your Only-Begotten Son and our God, granting unto us, though we are unworthy, blessed cleansing in Holy Water, and divine sanctification in the

Life-effecting Anointing; Who now also has been well-pleased to regenerate this Your servant newly illuminated through Water and Spirit, giving him [her] forgiveness of his [her] voluntary and involuntary sins: do You Yourself, Sovereign Master, Compassionate King of All, bestow upon him [her] also the Seal of Your omnipotent and adorable Holy Spirit, and the Communion of the Holy Body and Most Precious Blood of Your Christ; keep him [her] in Your sanctification; confirm him [her] in the Orthodox Faith; deliver him [her] from the Evil One and all his devices; preserve his [her] soul, through Your saving fear, in purity and righteousness, that in every work and word, being acceptable before You, he [she] may become a child and heir of Your heavenly Kingdom.

For You are our God, the God of Mercy and Salvation, and to You do we send up Glory, to the Father, and to the Son, and to the Holy Spirit, both now and ever, and to the ages of ages.

CHOIR: Amen.

And after the Prayer of Confirmation, the priest chrismates the baptized and makes on the person the sign of the cross with the holy chrism (holy myron), on the forehead, the eyes, the nostrils, the mouth, the ears, the breast, the hands, and the feet. At each anointing and sealing, he says:

SEAL OF THE GIFT OF THE HOLY SPIRIT, AMEN.

The priest invests the baptized in a new, clean robe, saying: Clothed is the servant of God [Name] with the garment of righteousness, in the Name of the Father, and of the Son, and of the Holy Spirit. Amen.

THE TROPARION (in tone 8)

A robe of divine light bestow upon me, O You that for vesture array Yourself with Light; and bestow many mercies, O Christ our God, who are plenteous in mercy.

Then the priest makes, together with the godparent and the child, a circumambulation around the font, three times; and for each of the three rounds the choir sings:

As many of you as have been baptized into Christ, have put on Christ. Alleluia.

PRIEST: Louder.

CHOIR: As many of you as have been baptized into Christ, have put on Christ, Alleluia.

PRIEST: Let us attend.

THE PROKEIMENON (in tone 3)

The Lord is my light and my salvation; of whom then shall I fear?
The Lord is the Protector of my life; of whom then shall I be afraid?

PRIEST: Wisdom!

READER: The Reading from the Epistle of the Holy Apostle Paul to the Romans (Rom. 6:3-11).

PRIEST: Let us attend.

READER: Brethren, do you not know that all of us who have been baptized into Christ Jesus were baptized into his death? We were buried therefore with him by baptism into death, so that as Christ was raised from the dead by the glory of the Father, we too might walk in newness of life. For if we have been united with him in a death like his, we shall certainly be united with him in a resurrection like his. We know that our old self was crucified with him so that the sinful body might be destroyed, and we might no longer be enslaved to sin. For he who has died is freed from sin. But if we have died with Christ, we believe that we shall also live with him. For we know that Christ being raised from the dead will never die again; death no longer has dominion over him. The death he died he died to sin, once for all, but the life he lives he lives to God. So you must also consider yourselves dead to sin and alive to God in Christ Jesus.

PRIEST: Peace be to you that read. And to your spirit.

CHOIR: Alleluia, alleluia, alleluia.

PRIEST: Wisdom! Let us attend! Let us hear the Holy Gospel.
Peace be to all (+).

CHOIR: And with your spirit.

PRIEST: The Reading from the Holy Gospel according to St. Matthew. Let us attend. (Matt. 28:16-20).

CHOIR: Glory to You, O Lord; Glory to You.

PRIEST: At that time, the eleven disciples went to Galilee, to the mountain to which Jesus had directed them. And when they saw him, they worshipped him; but some doubted. And Jesus came and said to them, "All authority in heaven and on earth has been given to me. Go therefore and make disciples of all nations, baptizing them in the name of the Father and of the Son and of the Holy Spirit, teaching them to observe all that I have commanded to you; and lo, I am with you always, to the close of the age. Amen."

CHOIR: Glory to You, O Lord; Glory to You.

THE ABLUTION

PRIEST: Peace be to all (+).

CHOIR: And with your spirit.

PRIEST: Let us bow our heads before the Lord.

CHOIR: To You, O Lord.

PRIEST: Let us pray to the Lord.

CHOIR: Lord have mercy.

PRIEST: (says the Prayer)
You that through Holy Baptism have granted forgiveness of sins to this Your servant, bestowing on him [her] a life of regeneration: do You Yourself, Sovereign Master and Lord, be pleased that the Light of Your countenance evermore shine in his [her] heart; maintain the shield of his [her] faith against the plotting of enemies; preserve in him [her] the garment of incorruption, which he [she] has put on undefiled and unstained; preserve in him [her] the Seal of Your Grace, being gracious unto us, and unto him [her] according to the multitude of Your compassions, for glorified and blessed is Your all-honorable and majestic Name: of Father, and of Son,

and of the Holy Spirit, both now and ever, and to the ages of ages.

CHOIR: Amen.

PRIEST: Let us pray to the Lord.

CHOIR: Lord have mercy.

PRIEST: Sovereign Master and Lord our God, Who through the baptismal Font bestows heavenly illumination to them that are baptized; Who has regenerated this Your servant, bestowing upon him [her] forgiveness of his [her] voluntary and involuntary sins; do You lay upon him [her] Your mighty hand, and guard him [her] in the power of Your goodness. Preserve unspotted his [her] pledge of Faith in You. Account him [her] worthy of Life everlasting and Your good favor. For You are our sanctification, and to You do we send up all Glory; to the Father, and to the Son, and to the Holy Spirit, both now and ever, and to the ages of ages. Amen.
Peace be to all (+).

CHOIR: And to your spirit.

PRIEST: Let us bow our heads before the Lord.

CHOIR: To You, O Lord.

PRIEST: Let us pray to the Lord.

CHOIR: Lord have mercy.

PRIEST: He [she] that has put on You, O Christ, with us bows his [her] head unto You; ever protect him [her] a warrior invincible against them who vainly raise up enmity against him [her], or, as might be, against us; and by Your Crown of Incorruption at the last declare us all to be the victorious ones. For Yours it is to have mercy and to save, and unto You, as to Your Eternal Father and Your All-Holy, Good, and Life-creating Spirit, do we send up all Glory, both now and ever, and to the ages of ages.

CHOIR: Amen.

The priest loosens the child's girdle and garment, and, joining the ends of these, he soaks them with clean water and sprinkles the child, saying aloud:

You are justified; you are illuminated.

And taking a new sponge dipped in water, the

priest wipes his [her] head, the breast, and the rest, saying:

> You are baptized; you are illuminated; you are anointed with the Holy Myrrh; you are hallowed; you are washed clean, in the Name of Father, and of Son, and of Holy Spirit. Amen.

THE TONSURE

PRIEST: Let us pray to the Lord.

CHOIR: Lord have mercy.

PRIEST: Sovereign Master and Lord our God, Who honored man with Your own Image, providing him with reason-endowed soul and comely body, that the body might serve the reason-endowed soul; for You did set his head on high, and therein planted the greater number of the senses, which impede not one another, covering the head that it might not be injured by the changes of the weather, and did fit all the members serviceably thereunto, that by all it might render thanks unto You, the excellent Artist; do You Yourself, O Sovereign Master, Who by the Vessel of Your Election, Paul the Apostle, to do all things unto Your Glory, bless (+) this Your servant [Name], who is come now to make offering for the firstlings of hair shorn from his [her] head; and bless his [her] Sponsor (+); granting them in all things to be diligent followers of Your Law, and to do all those things that are well pleasing unto You, for a merciful and loving God are You, and to You do we send up all Glory, to the Father, and to the Son, and to the Holy Spirit, both now and ever, and to the ages of ages.

CHOIR: Amen.

PRIEST: Peace to all (+).

CHOIR: And to your spirit.

PRIEST: Let us bow our heads before the Lord.

CHOIR: To You, O Lord.

PRIEST: Let us pray to the Lord.

CHOIR: Lord have mercy.

The priest lays a right hand upon the head of the child and prays:

> O Lord our God, Who through the fulfillment of the baptismal Font have, by your Goodness, sanctified them that believe in You: (+) do You bless this child here present, and may your blessings come down upon his [her] head; as You did bless the head of Your servant David the King through the Prophet Samuel, (+) so also bless the head of this servant [Name], through the hand of me, the unworthy Priest, visiting him [her] with Your Holy Spirit, that as he [she] goes forward to the prime of his [her] years, and the grey hairs of old age, he [she] may send up Glory to You, beholding the good things of Jerusalem all the days of his [her] life. For to You are due all glory, honor and worship, to the Father, and to the Son, and to the Holy Spirit, both now and ever, and to the ages of ages.

CHOIR: Amen.

The priest shears him [her] in the form of a cross, snipping off four locks of hair—front, back, and over each ear—cross-fashion, saying:

> The servant of God [Name] is shorn in the Name of the Father, and of the Son, and of the Holy Spirit.

CHOIR: Amen.

PRIEST: Have mercy on us, O God, according to Your great mercy. We beseech You, listen, and have mercy.

CHOIR: Lord have mercy.

PRIEST: Again let us pray for mercy, life, peace, health, and salvation for the servants of God, the newly illumined [Name], the Godparents, and all those who have come here together for this holy Sacrament. For You are a merciful and loving God, and to You do we send up all Glory, to the Father, and to the Son, and to the Holy Spirit, both now and ever, and to the ages of ages.

CHOIR: Amen.

THE APOLYSIS

PRIEST: Glory to You, O Christ our God and our hope; glory to You.

PRIEST: Glory to the Father, and to the Son, and to the Holy Spirit, both now and ever, and to the ages of ages. Amen. Lord have mercy; Lord have mercy; Lord have mercy. Master, bid the blessing. He Who deigned to be baptized in the Jordan by John for our salvation, Christ our true God— through the intercessions of His all-pure Mother, of the holy and glorious prophet, Forerunner and Baptist John, of the holy, glorious all-praiseworthy Apostles, (Name of Saint whose name the child has received), and of all the Saints; have mercy and save us as our good and loving Lord. Through the prayers of our holy Fathers.

CHOIR: Amen.

Commentary

The written liturgical text can make only a small beginning in portraying the profundity of the liturgical practices of the Eastern Orthodox church. Readers of the preceding text will need to envision not only the text itself, but also both the rich, symbol-laden gestures and the sense of solemnity that accompany the text. The careful instructions that accompany the text of the liturgy, such as "[the priest] will sign the water thrice, dipping fingers in it, and breathing upon it" or "[the priest] makes the sign of the cross on the child's forehead, breast and between his [her] shoulders" only begin to suggest the significance of every movement and symbol in the Eastern Orthodox service. Western Christians can learn from Eastern practice that the mystery of the sacrament of baptism can meaningfully be reflected not only in the text of the service, but in the very manner in which the service is led.

In attempting to understand the nature of the service, it may be helpful to derive from the liturgical text a basic outline of the service:

Entrance prayer
Blessing of the baptismal waters
Blessing of the Oil
Anointing
Baptism
Psalm 31 (Psalm 32 in Protestant Bibles)
Prayer of Confirmation
Chrismation
White Garment
Lessons: Romans 6:3-11; Matthew 28:16-20
Ablution
Tonsure
Apolysis

A few of these liturgical acts require explanation:

Chrismation. The chrismation is a sacramental anointing that is understood as the "seal of the gift of the Holy Spirit." The singular gift suggests that the act is understood not merely as sealing the various gifts or benefits of the Holy Spirit, such as those mentioned in Galatians 6, but rather the gift of the divine person of the Holy Spirit. The seal is applied several times to various parts of the body, symbolizing that the entire body with the soul is the recipient of this gift.

Ablution. The ablution is a ritual washing that at one time was observed eight days after the baptism and chrismation. The prayers which accompany this act refer to the new Christian's entry into the world as a witness and warrior for the faith, even as a child. The two ritual acts are actually an undoing of earlier ritual acts: The white garment is removed and the anointing with the chrism is washed off. This points to the fact that the external signs of the sacrament are no longer significant; only their spiritual reality is important for the Christian's life in the world.

Tonsure. The tonsure is a ritual haircutting or shaving that is understood as an act of obedience, humility, and sacrifice, where the individual Christian symbolically returns to God an offering of his or her own body. The symbolism is especially striking considering that the hair is cut from the young infants and children presented for baptism. This rite is also associated with entrance rites in monastic communities.

Apolysis. The apolysis is a final exclamation of praise. The meaning is clear. All liturgical ritual is doxological, finding meaning only in light of God's mighty acts and our offerings of praise to God.

The entire liturgy clearly evidences a high sacramental view of baptism. The complex of gestures and symbols which accompany the text are understood as participating in the reality of the union with Christ and the gift of the Holy Spirit. This reality completely enfolds the new Christian, touching the person's whole being—body and soul. Notice that anointing and chrismation are applied to various parts of the candidate's body and that the text of the prayers petitions for both spiritual strength and bodily renewal.

Finally, as the apolysis amply evidences, this liturgical text is replete with doxology. Every prayer and action is accompanied with an acclamation of praise, such as "glory to you . . ." or "blessed is God. . . ." In the baptismal liturgy, this emphasis aptly suggests the simultaneous transcendence and immanence of God. In the sacrament, God is immanent, drawing near through the gift of the Holy Spirit and changing the identity of the candidate through the work of Christ. Yet the God who does this is the holy, transcendent God of the universe. The gift of Eastern Orthodox Christians to the entire Christian church is a liturgical practice which elicits from worshipers what the Bible often describes as the "fear of the Lord," a simultaneous awe, terror, love, delight and respect of God.

Commentary by John Witvliet

175 • THE ROMAN CATHOLIC BAPTISMAL LITURGY

Since the Second Vatican Council, the Roman Catholic church has been active in promoting liturgical renewal in its parishes throughout the world. The following liturgy for baptism was written in 1969 in response to the directives of the Second Vatican Council and in light of liturgical reforms of the period.

Facing the candidate, the celebrant asks him:
[Name], what do you ask of God's Church?

CANDIDATE: Faith.
CELEBRANT: What does faith offer you?
CANDIDATE: Eternal life.
CELEBRANT: This is eternal life: to know the true God and the one he sent, Jesus Christ. God raised him from the dead to be the Lord of life and of all things, seen and unseen. In asking for baptism today you ask for this life. You would not do so unless you had come to know Christ and wanted to be his disciple. Have you completed your preparation for becoming a Christian? Have you listened to Christ's word and made up your mind to keep his commandments? Have you shared in our way of life and in our prayer?

CANDIDATE: I have.

The celebrant turns to the godparents and asks:
You are this candidate's godparent. Before God, do you consider him [her] a suitable person to be received today into full communion with the Church?

GODPARENT: I do.
CELEBRANT: You have spoken in this candidate's [or: Name's] favor. Will you continue to help him [her] to serve Christ by your words and example?
GODPARENT: I will.

With hands joined the celebrant concludes:
Let us pray.
Father of love and mercy, we thank you in the name of our brother [sister] who has experienced your guiding presence in his [her] life. Today, in the presence of your Church, he [she] is answering your call to faith: let him [her] find joy and fulfillment in his [her] new life. We ask this through Christ our Lord.

RESPONSE: **Amen.**

ENTRY INTO THE CHURCH
The celebrant invites the candidate in these or similar words:
[Name] we welcome you into the Church to share with us at the table of God's Word.

Liturgy of the Word

Readings and Homily

Prayer and Penitential Rite

CONGREGATION: Let us pray for our brother [sister] who is asking for Christ's sacraments, and for ourselves, sinners that we are: may we all draw nearer to Christ in faith and repentance and walk without tiring in the new life he gives us.

READER: That the Lord will kindle in all of us a spirit of true repentance, let us pray to the Lord:

RESPONSE: **Lord, hear our prayer.**

READER: That we, who have been saved by Christ and have died to sin through baptism, may witness to his grace by our manner of life, let us pray to the Lord:

RESPONSE: **Lord, hear our prayer.**

READER: That the Lord will give our brother [sister] sorrow for his [her] sins and trust in God's love as he [she] prepares to meet Christ, his [her] Savior, let us pray to the Lord:

RESPONSE: **Lord, hear our prayer.**

READER: That by following Christ who takes away the sin of the world our brother [sister] will be healed of the infection of sin and freed from its power, let us pray to the Lord:

RESPONSE: **Lord, hear our prayer.**

READER: That the Holy Spirit will wash him [her] clean from sin and lead him [her] in the way of holiness, let us pray to the Lord:

RESPONSE: **Lord, hear our prayer.**

READER: That through his burial with Christ in baptism he [she] will die to sin and live only for God, let us pray to the Lord:

RESPONSE: **Lord, hear our prayer.**

READER: That on the day of judgment he [she] will come before the Father bearing fruits of holiness and love, let us pray to the Lord:

RESPONSE: **Lord, hear our prayer.**

READER: That the world for which the Father gave his beloved Son may believe in his love and turn to him, let us pray to the Lord:

RESPONSE: **Lord, hear our prayer.**

Prayer of Exorcism and Anointing of the Catechumen

CELEBRANT: Almighty God, you sent your only Son to rescue us from the slavery of sin and to give to us the freedom of your children. We now pray for our brother [sister] who comes before you, acknowledging his [her] sinfulness. He [she] has faced temptation and been tested by the evil one. By the passion and resurrection of your Son, bring him [her] out of the power of darkness. With the grace of Christ, make him [her] strong and guide him [her] through life. We ask this through Christ our Lord.

RESPONSE: **Amen.**

The celebrant continues:

We anoint you with the oil of salvation in the name of Christ our Savior. May he strengthen you with his power, who lives and reigns for ever and ever.

RESPONSE: **Amen.**

The candidate is anointed with the oil of catechumens on the breast or on both hands or even on other parts of the body, if this seems desirable. This anointing may be omitted.

CELEBRATION OF BAPTISM
Celebrant's Instruction

CELEBRANT: Dear friends, Let us ask God our Father to be merciful to our brother [sister] [Name] who is asking for baptism. He has called him [her] to this hour. May he grant him [her] the riches of his light and strength to follow Christ with a courageous heart and to profess the faith of the Church. May he give him [her] the new life of the Holy Spirit, the Spirit whom we are about to ask to come down upon this water.

Then the celebrant turns to the font and blesses the water:

CELEBRANT: Father, you give us grace through sacramental signs which tells us of the wonders of your unseen power. In baptism we use your gift of water which you have made a rich symbol of the grace you give us in this sacrament. At the very dawn of creation your Spirit breathed on the waters, making them the wellspring of all holiness. The waters of the great flood you made a sign

Baptism. The universal symbol of baptism is the font. Within Christian bodies that practice immersion, a larger font or water container is used as a symbol of this practice.

of the waters of baptism that make an end of sin and a new beginning of goodness. Through the waters of the Red Sea you led Israel out of slavery to be an image of God's holy people set free from sin by baptism. In the waters of the Jordan your Son was baptized by John and anointed with the Spirit. Your Son willed that water and blood should flow from his side as he hung upon the cross. After his resurrection he told his disciples: "Go out and teach all nations, baptizing them in the name of the Father, and of the Son, and of the Holy Spirit." Father, look now with love upon your Church and unseal for

it the fountain of baptism. By the power of the Spirit give to the water of this font the grace of your Son. You created man in your own likeness: cleanse him from sin in a new birth to innocence by water and the Spirit.

The celebrant touches the water with his right hand and continues:

We ask you, Father, with your Son to send the Holy Spirit upon the water of this font. May all who are buried with Christ in the death of baptism rise also with him to newness of life. We ask this through Christ our Lord.

RESPONSE: **Amen.**

RENUNCIATION

After the font is consecrated, the celebrant questions the candidate:

Formula A:

CELEBRANT: Do you reject Satan and all his works and all his empty promises?

CANDIDATE: I do.

Formula B:

CELEBRANT: Do you reject Satan?

CANDIDATE: I do.

CELEBRANT: And all his works?

CANDIDATE: I do.

CELEBRANT: And all his empty promises?

CANDIDATE: I do.

Formula C:

CELEBRANT: Do you reject sin so as to live in the freedom of God's children?

CANDIDATE: I do.

CELEBRANT: Do you reject the glamour of evil and refuse to be mastered by sin?

CANDIDATE: I do.

CELEBRANT: Do you reject Satan, father of sin and prince of darkness?

CANDIDATE: I do.

Commentary

The most striking feature of this liturgy in light of recent liturgical reform is the fundamental unity it suggests between baptism and confirmation. The Roman Catholic church has always maintained that the sacramental acts of baptism and confirmation are distinct. Baptism is an act in which the candidate is given identity in Christ, as a partaker in Christ's death and resurrection and a recipient of Christ's benefits, including forgiveness. Confirmation is a fulfillment of baptism in which the candidate is bound to the church and given in new measure the gift of the Holy Spirit. But the practice of the church has varied significantly concerning the liturgical relationship between the two. In the Middle Ages, the two rites were separated. Confirmation was not administered until after the individual Christian, who perhaps had been baptized at a young age, declared their commitment to Christ and the church. Recent emphasis, however, has restored the fundamental unity of all the Roman rites of initiation, as was practiced in the early church. A baptized Christian need not wait to be confirmed. As one Vatican document summarizes: "An adult is not to be baptized, unless he receives confirmation immediately afterward, provided no serious obstacles exist. The connection signifies the unity of the paschal mystery, the close relationship between the mission of the Son and the pouring out of the Holy Spirit, and the joint celebration of the sacraments by which the Son and the Spirit come with the Father upon those who are baptized.

Also significant about this liturgy are the opening questions to the candidate. As a text for adult initiation, this service emphasizes the importance of a candidate's own desire for the sacrament. The candidate is asked, "What do you ask of God's church?" This emphasis resembles the medieval concern for personal responsibility prior to confirmation, with the difference that this interrogation now precedes baptism. The sacraments of initiation are not to be administered lightly by the church. Evidence of faith and commitment to Christ are necessary prerequisites for the completion of this final step of the conversion process.

These questions are also accompanied by basic instruction as to the nature of baptism. In admirably simple and straightforward prose, the meaning of baptism is suggested: "In asking for baptism today you ask for this life." Such descriptions concerning the meaning of baptism are important in reminding the entire worshiping community of the nature and meaning of baptism. All liturgical actions, gestures, and symbols can appropriately be accompanied by similarly direct descriptions of their meaning.

The role of the godparent is also significant in this and other initiation rites. The godparent is a person who verifies the readiness of the candidate, assists with the symbols of the white garment and candle, and promises to serve as a spiritual mentor to the candidate. This person becomes a direct manifestation of Christ's body, the church, in the life of the candidate. This relationship between the godparent and the church is an important symbol for a rite that marks a candidate's entrance into the church.

Suggestions for Appropriation

Appropriate New Testament readings from the liturgy of the Word include Matthew 28:18-20; Ephesians 4:4-6; Galatians 3:27-28; 1 Peter 2:9; Romans 6:3-4; Acts 2:38; and Colossians 2:12.

Appropriate Old Testament readings include those accounts of the events mentioned in the prayer at the blessing of the water, including the account of the Creation, the Flood, and the crossing of the Red Sea.

Worship planners may wish to consult *Who Calls You By Name: Music for Christian Initiation* (volumes 1 and 2) by David Haas (GIA Publications) and other similar sources for liturgical music appropriate for the baptismal service.

At the profession of faith, some parishes may wish to have the candidates speak the words of the creed. The celebrant would ask, "What do you believe concerning God, the Father." The candidate would respond, "I believe in God, the Father Almighty, Creator of heaven and earth." This pattern would continue for each of the creed's three sections.

The Rite of Christian Initiation of Adults, Par. 34.
Commentary by John D. Witvliet

176 • A METHODIST BAPTISMAL LITURGY

The baptismal rite presented here is found in The United Methodist Hymnal *as approved by the 1988 General Conference of the United Methodist Church. The 1992 General Conference approved a forthcoming* United Methodist Book of Worship *in which the essential text of the rite is unaltered though instructions and rubrics are expanded. Where these 1992 elaborations are deemed particularly significant, they will be noted in the commentary. The process of revising the rite fol-*

lowing the 1968 merger of the Methodist Church and the Evangelical United Brethren Church began in 1976. During the next dozen years, various forms of the text were issued for use and evaluation, leading to the adoption of the version that appears in the 1989 hymnal.

The baptismal covenant is God's Word to us, proclaiming our adoption by grace, and our word to God promising our response of faith and love. Those within the covenant constitute the community we call the church; therefore, the services of the baptismal covenant are conducted during the public worship of the congregation where the person's membership is to be held, except in very unusual circumstances. These services are best placed in the order of worship as a response following the reading of Scripture and its exposition in the sermon.

Persons of any age are suitable candidates. Infants and others unable to take the vows for themselves are presented by parents and/or sponsors. There may also be sponsors when candidates can speak for themselves. Parents or sponsors should be members of Christ's holy church.

In cases of emergency the essential acts in baptism are the vows and the baptism with water in the name of the Father, and of the Son, and of the Holy Spirit. A candidate baptized outside of a congregational worship service should, if possible, be presented at a later time to the congregation.

Those baptized before they are old enough to take the vows for themselves make their personal profession of faith in the service called confirmation. Those who are able to take the vows for themselves at their baptism are not confirmed, for they have made their public profession of faith at the font.

After confirmation, or after baptism when candidates take the vows for themselves, Christians are encouraged to reaffirm the baptismal covenant from time to time. Such reaffirmation is not, however, to be understood as the sacrament of baptism. Baptism is not administered to any person more than once, for while our baptismal vows are less than reliable, God's promise to us in the sacrament is steadfast.

Reaffirmation of the baptismal covenant is particularly appropriate by an entire congregation at Easter, which recalls our death and resurrection with Christ. It is also especially appropriate for persons who are transferring into a congregation.

When those being received into a congregation do not wish to reaffirm the baptismal covenant, only sections 14–16 of the service are used with those coming from another denomination and only sections 15–16 with those transferring from another United Methodist congregation.

The material marked by brackets [ ] is optional and may be omitted from the service.

The Baptismal Covenant I

Holy Baptism
Confirmation
Reaffirmation of Faith
Reception into the United Methodist Church
Reception into a local congregation

This service may be used for any of the above acts, or any combination of these that may be called for on a given occasion.

INTRODUCTION TO THE SERVICE

As persons are coming forward, an appropriate hymn of baptism or confirmation may be sung.

1. The pastor makes the following statement to the congregation:

Brothers and sisters in Christ: Through the Sacrament of Baptism we are initiated into Christ's holy church. We are incorporated into God's mighty acts of salvation and given new birth through water and the Spirit. All this is God's gift, offered to us without price.

2. If there are confirmations or reaffirmations, the pastor continues:

Through confirmation, and through the reaffirmation of our faith, we renew the covenant declared at our baptism, acknowledge what God is doing for us, and affirm our commitment to Christ's holy church.

PRESENTATION OF CANDIDATES

3. A representative of the congregation presents the candidates with the appropriate statements:
I present [Name(s)] for baptism.
I present [Name(s)] for confirmation.
I present [Name(s)] to reaffirm their faith.
I present [Name(s)] who come(s) to this congregation from the _____ Church.

RENUNCIATION OF SIN AND PROFESSION OF FAITH

4. The pastor addresses parents or other spon-

sors and those candidates who can answer for themselves:

On behalf of the whole church, I ask you:

Do you renounce the spiritual forces of wickedness, reject the evil powers of this world, and repent of your sin?

I do.

Do you accept the freedom and power God gives you to resist evil, injustice, and oppression in whatever forms they present themselves?

I do.

Do you confess Jesus Christ as your Savior, put your whole trust in his grace, and promise to serve him as your Lord, in union with the church which Christ has opened to people of all ages, nations, and races?

I do.

5. The pastor addresses parents or other sponsors of candidates not able to answer for themselves:

Will you nurture these children (persons) in Christ's holy church, that by your teaching and example they may be guided to accept God's grace for themselves, to profess their faith openly, and to lead a Christian life?

I will.

6. The pastor addresses candidates who can answer for themselves:

According to the grace given to you, will you remain faithful members of Christ's holy church and serve as Christ's representatives in the world?

I will.

7. If those who have answered for themselves have sponsors, the pastor addresses the sponsors:

Will you who sponsor these candidates support and encourage them in their Christian life?

I will.

8. The pastor addresses the congregation:

Do you, as Christ's body, the church, reaffirm both your rejection of sin and your commitment to Christ?

We do.

Will you nurture one another in the Christian faith and life and include these persons now before you in your care?

With God's help we will proclaim the good news and live according to the example of Christ. We will surround these persons with a community of love and forgiveness, that they may grow in their trust of God, and be found faithful in their service to others. We will pray for them, that they may be true disciples who walk in the way that leads to life.

9. The pastor addresses all:

Let us join together in professing the Christian faith as contained in the Scriptures of the Old and New Testaments.

Do you believe in God the Father?

**I believe in God, the Father Almighty,
    creator of heaven and earth.**

Do you believe in Jesus Christ?

**I believe in Jesus Christ, his only Son, our
    Lord,
[who was conceived by the Holy Spirit,
born of the Virgin Mary,
suffered under Pontius Pilate,
was crucified, died, and was buried;
he descended to the dead.
    On the third day he rose again;
he ascended into heaven,
is seated at the right hand of the Father,
    and will come again to judge the living
        and the dead].**

Do you believe in the Holy Spirit?

**I believe in the Holy Spirit,
[the holy catholic church,
the communion of saints,
the forgiveness of sins,
the resurrection of the body,
and the life everlasting].**

THANKSGIVING OVER THE WATER

10. If there are baptisms, or if water is to be used for reaffirmation, the water may be poured into the font at this time, and the following prayer offered:

The Lord be with you.
And also with you.

Let us pray:
Eternal Father,
When nothing existed but chaos,
you swept across the dark waters
and brought forth light.
In the days of Noah
you saved those on the ark through water.
After the flood you set in the clouds a rainbow.
When you saw your people as slaves in Egypt,
you led them to freedom through the sea.
Their children you brought through the Jordan

to the land which you promised.
Sing to the Lord, all the earth.
Tell of God's mercy each day.
In the fullness of time you sent Jesus,
nurtured in the water of a womb.
He was baptized by John and anointed by your
  Spirit.
He called his disciples
to share in the baptism of his death and resurrection
and to make disciples of all nations.
Declare his works to the nations,
his glory among all the people.
Pour out your Holy Spirit,
to bless this gift of water and those who receive
  it,
to wash away their sin
and clothe them in righteousness
throughout their lives,
that, dying and being raised with Christ,
they may share in his final victory.
All praise to you, Eternal Father,
through your Son Jesus Christ,
who with you and the Holy Spirit
lives and reigns for ever.
Amen.

BAPTISM WITH LAYING ON OF HANDS

11. As each candidate is baptized, the pastor says: [Name] I baptize you in the name of the Father, and of the Son, and of the Holy Spirit.

The people respond: **Amen.**

Immediately after the administration of the water, the pastor, and others if desired, place hands on the head of each candidate, as the pastor says to each:

The Holy Spirit work within you, that being born through water and the Spirit, you may be a faithful disciple of Jesus Christ.

The people respond: **Amen.**

When all candidates have been baptized, the pastor invites the congregation to welcome them:

Now it is our joy to welcome our new sisters
  and brothers in Christ.
Through baptism you are incorporated by the
  Holy Spirit into God's new creation
and made to share in Christ's royal priesthood.
We are all one in Christ Jesus.
With joy and thanksgiving we welcome you as
  members of the family of Christ.

CONFIRMATION OR REAFFIRMATION OF FAITH

12. Here water may be used symbolically in ways that cannot be interpreted as baptism, as the pastor says:

Remember your baptism and be thankful. Amen.

As the pastor, and others if desired, place hands on the head of each person being confirmed or reaffirming faith, the pastor says to each:

[Name], the Holy Spirit work within you, that having been born through water and the Spirit, you may live as a faithful disciple of Jesus Christ.

All respond: **Amen.**

13. When there is a congregational reaffirmation of the baptismal covenant, water may be used symbolically in ways that cannot be interpreted as baptism, as the pastor says:

Remember your baptism and be thankful. Amen.

RECEPTION INTO THE UNITED METHODIST CHURCH

14. If there are persons coming into membership in the United Methodist Church from other denominations who have not yet been presented, they may be presented at this time. The pastor addresses all those transferring their membership into the United Methodist Church, together with those who, through baptism or in confirmation, have just professed their own faith:

As members of Christ's universal church, will you be loyal to the United Methodist Church, and do all in your power to strengthen its ministries?

I will.

RECEPTION INTO THE LOCAL CONGREGATION

15. If there are persons joining this congregation from other United Methodist congregations who have not yet been presented, they may be presented at this time. The pastor addresses all those transferring membership into the congregation and those who have just professed their own faith, in baptism or in confirmation:

As members of this congregation, will you faithfully participate in its ministries by your prayers, your presence, your gifts, and your service?

I will.

COMMENDATION AND WELCOME

16. The pastor addresses the congregation:

Members of the household of God, I commend these persons to your love and care. Do all in your power to increase their faith, confirm their hope, and perfect them in love.

The congregation responds: **We give thanks for all that God has already given you and we welcome you in Christian love. As members together with you in the body of Christ and in this congregation of the United Methodist Church, we renew our covenant faithfully to participate in the ministries of the church by our prayers, our presence, our gifts, and our service, that in everything God may be glorified through Jesus Christ.**

The pastor addresses those baptized, confirmed or received:

The God of all grace, who has called us to eternal glory in Christ, establish you and strengthen you by the power of the Holy Spirit, that you may live in grace and peace.

One or more lay leaders may join with the pastor in acts of welcome and peace. Appropriate thanksgiving and intercessions for those who have participated in these acts should be included in the concerns and prayers which follow.

It is most fitting that the service continue with Holy Communion, in which the union of the new members with the body of Christ is most fully expressed. The new members may receive first.

Commentary

Concerning the Service of the Baptismal Covenant. These instructions are self-explanatory with the following elaborations. Note in paragraph 4 that in contrast to previous usage (in which all baptized persons were also to be confirmed), confirmation is now seen as appropriate only for those baptized before they can answer for themselves. Confirmation is a public affirmation that is redundant if such a personal affirmation has been made in baptism itself. Hence only those baptized before they can make their own vows are proper candidates for confirmation. Also, in all denominational traditions that have converged to form the United Methodist Church, confirmation has been a pastoral act, not an episcopal act, even though the office of bishop is firmly established both in current and predecessor polities.

Title and Subtitles. Baptism is viewed theologically as a covenant between God, the church, and individual believers within the church. The covenant announces divine promises of grace and hope, and calls for human responses of faithfulness and service. Thus, baptism is both sacrament and ordinance. From the divine side, baptism is a declaration whose reliability precludes repetition. In other words, baptism itself cannot be repeated. However from the human side, a daily reaffirmation of the covenant commitment is required. This constant call to discipleship is signaled liturgically by various forms of response, which may be made at confirmation and the other occasions indicated in the subtitles. Yet all reaffirmations flow from the covenant act and are not independent of it.

Covenant reaffirmation is central in the Wesleyan tradition. This baptismal service more explicitly tied it to baptism than previous liturgies. However, this liturgical form was the form derived from John Wesley's covenant service and adapted by various Methodist denominations in the mid-twentieth century.

General Rubric. The rubric implies that within a single rite, Form I allows for a variety of things done in predecessor denominations only by using a number of separate rites for (a) the baptism of infants and children, (b) the baptism of adults, (c) confirmation, and (d) reception into membership. Therefore if certain sections are omitted, then not all of the acts indicated in the subtitles are to be employed. For this reason, sections within the rite are individually numbered for easier reference.

Forms II and IV, derived from Form I and printed separately (but not reproduced here), are the most commonly used reductions of the full rite. Form II, including only Sections 1, 3–4, 8–11, and 16, is the reduced rite for the baptism of infants and others who do not answer for themselves. Form IV, an adaptation of Sections 1–2, 4, 9–10, 12, and 16, is the form that contains those sections needed for a congregational reaffirmation of the covenant at times such as Easter when no baptisms or confirmations are to be performed.

Form III is historically unrelated to Forms, I, II, and IV. It is a combination of the rites of the predecessor denominations (the Methodist Church and the Evangelical United Brethren Church) for use with those who can answer for themselves. It was added by the 1988 General Conference to those rites proposed to the Conference, primarily as a way of including a service of traditional language and content in contrast to the contemporary wording and theology of Forms I, II, and IV.

When none are to be baptized who do not answer for themselves, these adaptations apply: (a) When there are both baptisms and confirmations, each adult receives only one laying on of hands (using 11 and 12, respectively; 5 is omitted and 13 is optional). (b) If there are baptisms, but no confirmations or reaffirmations, omit 5, 12, and 13. (c) If there are confirmations without baptisms, omit 5 and 11; however, include 10 only if water is used. If water is not used, 13 may simply be a spoken act or may be omitted. (d) If there are neither baptisms nor confirmations but persons joining a local congregation wish to renew their baptismal covenant, 5 and 11 are omitted; 10, 12, and 13 may be omitted. If transfers are only from other United Methodist congregations, 14 is omitted. (e) If those joining a congregation do not wish to renew their baptismal covenant, only 14–16 are used if they are transferring from another denomination, and only 15–16 if they are coming from a United Methodist congregation. In all of the foregoing, section 7 is omitted unless there are sponsors. (Sponsors may be used for those who answer for themselves, although usually they have been employed only in the case of those unable to answer.)

Introduction to the Service. Sections 1 and 2 are a theological warrant. The four occurrences of the preposition _through_ are crucial to a dynamic understanding of initiation and covenant-keeping. _In, at,_ and _by_ were rejected as being too static and susceptible to magical interpretations of automatic baptismal regeneration. _Through_ implies a continuing process based on what baptism proclaims without negating the sacramental force of the action: Baptism begins and facilitates a life-long participation in the covenant through which salvation is experienced. The warrant also establishes baptism as an ecumenical rather than a denominational act.

Presentation of Candidates. By the rite's instruction that a lay person present the candidates, the rubric establishes the crucial connection between congregation and candidates. The once-popular private rites attended only by clergy and candidates (and sponsors, in the case of infants) do not adequately reflect the corporate character of the baptismal covenant.

Renunciation of Sin and Profession of Faith. While not stated in the full ancient triple form, the vows seek to recover the catholic pattern of renunciation, affirmation, and adhesion. Questions in section 4 emphasize:

(1) The ecumenical character of baptism: "On behalf of the whole church . . ."

(2) The systemic and cosmic (rather than only individualistic) nature of sin: "spiritual forces," "evil powers," "evil, injustice, oppression," and sin's seductivity and subtlety "in whatever forms."

(3) The necessity of divine assistance in conquering sin: "the freedom and power God gives you."

(4) The imperative of personal trust in Christ's saving grace: "your whole trust in his grace;" and of service within his community, "in union with the church."

(5) The inclusive character of the holy catholic church: "all ages, nations and races."

Consonant with the historical dual emphases on personal faith and social action in the Wesleyan revival, this rite deliberately attempts to highlight the societal demands of discipleship, while preserving the importance of personal piety. The rubric of section 5 has two crucial implications: (1) In the case of infants whose parents are unwilling or unable to act as sponsors, others may so function (grandparents, close friends, etc.). (2) "Not able to answer for themselves" is implicit encouragement not only for the baptism of infants but for the baptism of youth and adults who may be developmentally impaired. All such persons are to be nurtured by the church and are to be seen as capable of functioning fully as disciples within the bounds of their own abilities.

In section 6, the vow deliberately pairs _the church_ and _the world_ as complementary arenas of discipleship.

Section 7 expresses the necessity of intentional activity by sponsors, who are in no way to be regarded only as _godparents_ of an honorific sort.

Section 8 stresses the congregational role in covenant-making and the responsibilities of the whole body of believers for the nurture of those received into it.

Section 9 restores the original divided form of the baptismal creed. Two features of this version of the creed require comment:

(1) Large portions of the creed are bracketed and thus presumably optional. In this, however, there is no implied suggestion that the creed normally be reduced to three brief statements. Rather, behind these omissions lies a particular legal matter. The official law code of the United Methodist Church as set forth in its Book of Discipline specifies only that in order to unite with the church a candidate shall affirm faith in God, the Father Almighty; in Jesus Christ as God's Son; and in the Holy Spirit. Hence, any candidate has the right to refuse to affirm more than that at the time of entrance into denominational membership. Rarely is such a right exercised; but the option explains the use of brackets. The ecumenical nature of baptism and the almost universal acceptance of the Apostles' Creed argues for the full use of the creed in every possible instance.

(2) The footnote *universal* to explain *catholic* was mandated at the 1988 General Conference of the United Methodist Church for inclusion with all printings of the Apostles' Creed. This came not as a recommendation from the bodies that devised the rites and proposed them for denominational use but from the Conference delegates who feared *catholic* would be interpreted to mean *Roman Catholic*, despite the fact that since the time of Wesley, the creed has appeared in Methodist rites without such added interpretation. The footnote is intended for the eye only and does not imply any alternate wording for oral use.

Thanksgiving over the Water. After the time of Wesley, the prayer over the water disappeared from most of the rites of predecessor denominations. However, this action has been restored because of the model of many of the extant prayers of the early centuries which richly allude to the scriptural mention of water in relation to God's saving acts. This prayer is Trinitarian in design— an intentional coordinate to standard eucharistic prayer, as a means of asserting the parity of the sacraments.

In Form IV (congregational reaffirmation), the wording of the Epiklesis is altered: "Pour out your Holy Spirit and by this gift of water call to our remembrance the grace declared to us in our baptism. For you have washed away our sins and you

cloth us in righteousness throughout our lives. . . ."

When the congregation does not have access to the responsive portions of the prayer, "Sing to the Lord. . . ." and "Declare his works . . ." may be deleted. However, the final response is an integral doxology used by the minister of baptism in all circumstances.

Baptism with the Laying on of Hands. The traditional opening injunction for the baptism of infants ("Name this child") has been deleted as incongruous in an age when infants are no longer presented at the font on the day after birth, but come later already bearing well-established names. Consequently these names are announced in section 3. What is conferred at the font is not the human name given by parents, but the new name of grace given by the triune God into whose holy name we are incorporated.

No mode of baptism is specified; but both by tradition and United Methodist church law, sprinkling, pouring, or submersion are acceptable forms of administration. The first two are the more usual, particularly in the case of infants and children.

The laying on of hands is best seen not as an act by the pastor only, but by all baptized persons gathered at the font (including the lay representative who made the presentation in section 3). This laying on of hands is a repeatable act, used again in reaffirmation rites. But the change of language should be noted. At baptism, the rite states "that being born . . . you may be . . ."; while at reaffirmation (including confirmation), it states "that having being born . . . you may live. . . ." This difference shows the dynamic of the covenant in which the initiation, or baptism, is the beginning of a continuing commitment throughout life.

The expansion of rubrical instruction in the 1992 text suggests additional acts following the laying on of hands: (1) signation (with or without oil) in silence or with the formula: "You are sealed by the Holy Spirit in baptism and marked as Christ's own forever"; or (2) presentation of new clothing, a lighted candle, or a baptismal certificate.

The statement of welcome draws heavily on Scripture and again asserts the congregational implications of baptism.

Confirmation or Reaffirmation of Faith. The heading intends to suggest that confirmation is the first liturgical affirmation of faith by those baptized before they can answer for themselves, but that repeated affirmations are appropriate—indeed necessary—after any first affirmation. Such reaffirmations may be made by individuals when transferring from one congregation to another or when wishing to affirm publicly a new level of commitment to Christ or recommitment after a period of lapse. Reaffirmation as an explicit congregational act may occur at times such as Easter or the Sunday of the Baptism of the Lord if there are to be no baptisms or confirmations. However whenever a baptism or confirmation occurs, that rite should be occasion for an implicit (if unstated) reaffirmation by all baptized persons present.

The rubric at both sections 12 and 13 specify that any use of water in reaffirmation be such that it cannot be mistaken for baptism (or _rebaptism_, to use the popular, if inaccurate, designation). The expanded rubrics of 1992 suggest various forms including: (a) touching the water, and using it as a means of personal signation; (b) having water symbolically sprinkled toward the congregation (though not directly on them, which is too reminiscent of baptism by aspersion); or (c) even simply observing the action of the minister of baptism who lifts a handful of water and allows it to flow back into the font.

In sections 12 and 13, the term _remember_ is to be understood theologically, not literally. Even for those who can recall the time and place of baptism, what is to be remembered is not the circumstances of the event, but its meaning: We are thankfully to recall the saving work of Christ for us, of which our baptism is an announcement. In addition, we are to remember the gracious promises of God concerning our future, of which baptism is an earnest and trustworthy pledge.

Reception into the United Methodist Church. Having originated as a renewal society within the Church of England, United Methodism has maintained a certain society stance. Thus, while having asserted for decades that baptism makes a person a member of "Christ's holy church," the denomination nevertheless continues to regard admission into the United Methodist Church as a separate act, complete with a distinctive loyalty vow to the denomination required of all who enter, whether through baptism as adults, confirmation, or transfer of membership from another denomination.

Sections 14 and 15 seek to make the best of this theologically awkward situation by sandwiching the denominational loyalty vow between an affirmation about membership in "Christ's universal church" and participation in "this congregation." Thus the focus moves in logical fashion from the catholic church to the denominational church to the local church.

Reception into the Local Congregation. Those transferring from another United Methodist Church, having previously affirmed denominational loyalty, are not required to do so again; but together with those noted above they join in a promise to be active members of the particular congregation.

The language, "your prayers, your presence, your gifts, and your service," is a much beloved phrase by those who prior to the 1968 merger were active within the Methodist Church, which incorporated this phraseology into its membership rite following the Methodist merger of 1939.

Commendation and Welcome. In section 8, those who have made their vows of faith are welcomed with a congregational pledge of support. Subsequently, section 16 seems a bit redundant except for the fact that those transferring from other congregations may or may not have participated in the vows. (The opening instructions note that Sections 14–16 may be used alone in the cases of transfer.) In earlier drafts of the rite, however, section 8 did not exist. This section was added in response to criticism that section 16 was too remote or insufficiently strong to stress the nurturing responsibility of the congregation to those taking vows, particularly in the case of infants being baptized.

After the pastoral exhortation and congregational response, a pastoral blessing serves as the verbal conclusion to the rite. Concluding acts are suggested in the closing rubrics.

177 ✦ A REFORMED BAPTISMAL LITURGY

The following baptismal liturgy is an approved form for use in the Christian Reformed Church in North America, a denomination in the Reformed tradition with roots in the Dutch Reformed Church. This particular form is intended for the baptism of children. It was approved for use in 1976 and is printed in the 1987 Psalter Hymnal

(Grand Rapids: CRC Publications). This liturgy maintains the basic structure and content of baptismal liturgies that were used in the Reformed churches of the Netherlands and the region of Germany near Heidelberg in the mid-sixteenth century.

------------------------------ **Text** ------------------------------

INTRODUCTION

Congregation of our Lord Jesus Christ: What the Lord has revealed to us in His Word about holy baptism can be summarized in this way:

First, Scripture teaches that we and our children are sinners from birth, sinful from the time our mothers conceived us (Ps. 51:5). This means that we are all under the judgment of God and for that reason cannot be members of his kingdom unless we are born again. Baptism, whether by immersion or sprinkling, teaches that sin has made us so impure that we must undergo a cleansing which only God can accomplish. Therefore, we ought to be displeased with ourselves, humble ourselves, and turn to God for our salvation.

Second, baptism is a sign and seal that our sins are washed away through Jesus Christ. For this reason we are baptized into the name of God, the Father, the Son, and the Holy Spirit.

Our baptism into the name of God the Father is assurance to us that he makes an everlasting covenant of grace with us and adopts us as his children and heirs. Therefore, he surrounds us with his goodness and protects us from evil or turns it to our profit.

When we are baptized into the name of the Son, we are assured by Christ himself that he washes us in his blood from all our sins. Christ joins us to himself so that we share in his death and resurrection. Through this union with Christ we are liberated from our sins and regarded as righteous before God.

Baptism into the name of the Holy Spirit is the assurance that the Spirit of God will make his home within us. While living within us, the Spirit will continually work to strengthen and deepen our union with Christ. He will make real in our lives Christ's work of washing away our sins. He will also help us each day to live the new life we have in Christ. As a result of his work within us, we shall one day be presented without the stain of sin among the assembly of the elect in life eternal.

Third, because all covenants have two sides, baptism also places us under obligation to live in obedience to God. We must cling to this one God, Father, Son, and Holy Spirit. We must trust him and love him with all our heart, soul, mind, and strength. We must abandon the sinful way of life, put to death our old nature, and show by our lives that we belong to God. If we through weakness should fall into sin, we must not despair of God's grace, nor use our weakness as an excuse to keep sinning. Baptism is a seal and totally reliable witness that God is always faithful to his covenant.

Our children should not be denied the sacrament of baptism because of their inability to understand its meaning. Without their knowledge, our children not only share in Adam's condemnation but are also received into God's favor in Christ. God's gracious attitude toward us and our children is revealed in what he said to Abraham, the father of all believers: "I will establish my covenant as an everlasting covenant between me and you and your descendants after you for the generations to come, to be your God and the God of your descendants after you" (Gen. 17:7). The apostle Peter also testifies to this with these words: "The promise is for you and your children and for . . . all whom the Lord our God will call" (Acts 2:39). Therefore God formerly commanded circumcision as a seal of the covenant and as a declaration that righteousness comes by faith. Christ also recognized that children are members of the covenant people when he embraced them, laid his hands on them, and blessed them (Mark 10:16). Since baptism has replaced circumcision, our children should be baptized as heirs of God's kingdom and of his covenant. As the children mature, their parents are responsible for teaching them the meaning of baptism.

Let us turn to God, asking that in this baptism his name may be glorified, we may be comforted, and the church may be edified.

Almighty, eternal God, long ago you severely punished an unbelieving and unrepentant world by sending a flood. But you showed your great mercy when you saved and protected believing Noah and his family. Your judgment upon sin and your great mercy toward us were again shown when the obstinate pharaoh and his whole army were drowned in the Red Sea, and you brought your people Israel through the same sea on dry ground.

We pray that in this baptism you will again be

merciful. Look upon these your children with favor by bringing them into union with your Son, Jesus Christ, through your Holy Spirit. May they be buried with Christ into death and be raised with him to new life. Give them true faith, firm hope, and ardent love so that they may joyfully bear their cross as they daily follow Christ.

Give these children the full assurance of your grace so that when they leave this life and its constant struggle against the power of sin they may appear before the judgment seat of Christ without fear. We ask this in the name of our Lord Jesus Christ, who with the Father and the Holy Spirit, one only God, lives and reigns forever. Amen.

ADDRESS TO THE PARENTS

People of God, as you have now heard, baptism is given to us by God as proof that he does make a covenant with us and our children. We must, therefore, use the sacrament for the purpose that God intended and not out of custom or superstition. You are asked to give an honest answer to these questions as a testimony that you are doing what God commands.

First, do you acknowledge that our children, who are sinful from the time of conception and birth and therefore subject to the misery which sin brings, even the condemnation of God, are made holy by God in Christ and so as members of his body ought to be baptized?

Second, do you acknowledge that the teaching of the Old and New Testaments, summarized in the Apostles' Creed, and taught in this Christian church, is the true and complete doctrine of salvation?

Third, do you sincerely promise to do all you can to teach these children, and to have taught this doctrine of salvation?

Answer: _We do._

[Name], I baptize you in the name of the Father and of the Son and of the Holy Spirit.

PRAYER OF THANKSGIVING

Almighty God and merciful Father, we thank you and praise your name for having forgiven our sins through the blood of your dear Son, Jesus Christ. We thank you for uniting us with Christ through your Holy Spirit and adopting us as your children, and we thank you for sealing and confirming these blessings to us and our children in the sacrament of baptism.

We pray, O Lord, that you will always govern these children by your Holy Spirit. May they, through your guidance, be so nurtured in the Christian faith and godliness as to grow and develop in Jesus Christ. Help them see your fatherly goodness and mercy which surrounds us all. Make them champions of righteousness under the direction of Jesus Christ, our chief teacher, eternal king, and only high priest. Give them the courage to fight against and overcome sin, the devil and his whole dominion. May their lives become an eternal song of praise to you, the one only true God, Father, Son, and Holy Spirit. Amen.

Commentary

Perspectives. A noteworthy feature of this as well as other liturgies from the Reformed tradition is the careful explication of the meaning and purpose of the sacrament with which it begins. In the years following the Reformation, this explanation was thought to be an important means for clearly differentiating a Reformed understanding of baptism from the traditional Roman Catholic view on the one hand and the Anabaptist view on the other. Notice, for example, the succinct paragraph which defends the practice of baptizing children. This is a response, no doubt, to the Anabaptist practice of baptizing only believing adults. These paragraphs of explanation maintain an important function in contemporary worship as well, teaching the congregation about the meaning of baptism each time the sacrament is administered. Although too much verbal instruction regarding the meaning of individual acts of worship can make a service of worship more didactic than doxological, such brief descriptions can prevent the sacrament of baptism from becoming a mere superstitious rite in the eyes of many worshipers.

This liturgy also emphasizes the important role of the parents in the nurture of the child being baptized. As they present their children for baptism, parents are asked about their own Christian commitment, doctrinal beliefs, and intent to nurture their child in faith. This practice serves as a solemn reminder for all parents of their important responsibility for Christian nurture of children. It also serves as a necessary litmus test for determining when baptism is appropriate, reserving it for the children of parents who, along with the church community, are committed to the Christ and to the Christian nurture of their children.

A key theological point imbedded in this baptismal liturgy is aptly summarized by the term *covenant*, which is mentioned frequently even in these few, brief paragraphs. The term suggests an agreement or arrangement between God and the people of God. God made a covenant with Abraham (Gen. 17:7) and a new covenant with the church through Christ (as anticipated in Jer. 31:31-34). In the Reformed tradition, baptism is seen as a sign that the child is a part of God's new covenant with God's people, even as circumcision, in the Old Testament, signaled the child's inclusion in the old covenant. This idea suggested the importance of the communal context for baptism—that in baptism the child is being joined to God's covenant people, the church. This idea also implies that God is the initiator of what takes place at baptism, even as God is the initiator of the covenant with God's people.

Suggestions for Appropriation. To emphasize the importance of God's initiative in baptism, the third question asked of the parents may be asked after the actual baptism. The question could then be phrased, "Having witnessed this gracious act of God, will you now respond in thanksgiving by teaching and nurturing this child in the Word of God and in the way of Jesus Christ?" This practice avoids the implication that the validity of baptism is contingent on our ability to live the Christian life, suggesting rather that our lives are lived as a response to a gracious act of God.

To emphasize the importance of the congregation as a covenant community of God's people, the following question may be addressed to the congregation after the questions to the parents: "Do you, the people of the Lord, promise to receive these children in love, pray for them, help instruct them in the faith, and encourage and sustain them in the fellowship of believers?" The congregation may respond, "We do, God helping us." (This question is found in a second liturgy for the baptism of children used in the Christian Reformed Church, also approved in 1976.) In addition, the final prayer of thanksgiving may be spoken by all in unison.

The paragraphs of instruction can meaningfully be read by two worship leaders—one reads the words of instruction from the baptismal font, and the other reads the passages of Scripture mentioned from the pulpit. This serves to emphasize the importance of the Bible as the church's guide to the understanding and practice of the sacraments.

Commentary by John D. Witvliet

178 • An Ecumenical Baptismal Liturgy

Some church historians have already labeled the twentieth century as the ecumenical century, noting the wide variety of institutional and attitudinal openness toward ecumenical expression. Similarly, some liturgical scholars have described the twentieth century as a great period of liturgical convergence, noting the significant cross-fertilization of liturgical practices across denominational lines. In line with such descriptions, liturgists have attempted to write sacramental liturgies for ecumenical use. The following is one such liturgy, written by Fr. Max Thurian to illustrate the famous Lima document on baptism, Eucharist, and ministry.

The baptismal liturgy takes place between the Liturgy of the Word and the Eucharist.

THE WELCOME
[Names of the parents or of the adult seeking baptism] as a Christian community we welcome you with great joy to celebrate the baptism which you request for [Name, the child's name], a baptism of water and the Spirit, in which the covenant with God, Creator and Father, is renewed in forgiveness, in which Christ makes us pass through his death and resurrection to be born into new life, in which the Holy Spirit is given us, to bring us into the body of the church.

THE THANKSGIVING (OFFERED NEAR THE WATER OF BAPTISM)
The Lord be with you.
And also with you.
Lift up your hearts.
We lift them up to the Lord.
Let us give thanks to the Lord our God.
It is right to give him thanks and praise.
It is truly right and fitting to give you glory, to offer you our thanksgiving, loving Father, all-powerful Creator, who gives us water, water which gives life, cleanses and satisfies our thirst.
Blessed be you, O Lord.
By your invisible power, O Lord, you perform

wonders in your sacraments, and in the history of salvation you have used water, which you have created, to make known to us the grace of baptism.
Blessed be you, O Lord.
At the beginning of the world your Spirit hovered over the waters, prepared your work of creation, and planted the seed of life.
Blessed be you, O Lord.
By the waters of the Flood You declared the death of sin and the birth of a new life.
Blessed be you, O Lord.
You brought the children of Abraham through the waters of the Red Sea, and the people, freed from slavery, journeyed towards the Promised Land.
Blessed be you, O Lord.
Your beloved Son was baptized by John in the waters of Jordan, was anointed by the Spirit and appointed prophet, priest and king.
Blessed be you, O Lord.
Lifted up from the earth on the cross, your Son was immersed in the baptism of suffering; he has cast fire upon the earth to set hearts aflame and draw all people to himself.
Blessed be you, O Lord.
The risen Christ said to his disciples: "All authority in heaven and on earth has been given to me. Go therefore and make disciples of all nations, baptizing them in the name of the Father and of the Son and of the Holy Spirit, teaching them to observe all that I have commanded you; and lo, I am with you always, to the close of the age."
Blessed be you, O Lord.
And now, O Lord, look in love upon your church, and by your Holy Spirit let the spring of baptism well up among us: may your servant, made in your image, God our Father, be cleansed of all that disfigures that likeness; may he/she be buried with Christ into death and be raised with him to life; may he/she receive the Holy Spirit so as to witness to the Gospel in the Church for the world.
Blessed be you, O Lord.

THE EXHORTATION
[for the baptism of a child]
Dear parents and sponsors, the child which you present for baptism is now to be baptized; in his life, God will give him/her a new life; he/she will be born again of water and the Spirit. Be careful to help him/her grow in faith, that this life of new birth may not grow weak through sin or indifference, but that it may grow stronger in him/her day

by day. As a sign that you are prepared for this responsibility, I invite you to recall your own baptism and to declare your faith in Jesus Christ, the faith of the universal church into which every Christian is baptized.

[for the baptism of an adult]
[Name], you are now to be baptized: in his love, God will give you a new life; you will be born again of water and the Spirit. Be careful to grow in faith, that this life of new birth in you may not grow weak through sin or indifference, but that it may grow stronger in you day by day. As a sign that you are ready to commit yourself in faith to the service of Christ and his Church, I invite you to fight against the power of evil, and to declare your faith in Jesus Christ, the faith of the universal church into which every Christian is baptized.

THE RENUNCIATION
[may be used at the baptism of an adult]
So as to live in the liberty of the sons and daughters of God, to be a faithful follower of Jesus Christ and to produce the fruits of the Holy Spirit, do you renounce being ruled by the desires of this world, the snare of pride, the love of money, and the power of violence?
I renounce them.

THE DECLARATION OF FAITH
Do you believe in God, the Father almighty, creator of heaven and earth?
I do so believe.
Do you believe in Jesus Christ, his only Son, our Lord; who was conceived by the power of the Holy Spirit, and born of the Virgin Mary; who suffered under Pontius Pilate, was crucified, died and was buried, and descended to the dead; who rose again on the third day, ascended into heaven, and is seated at the right hand of the Father, and will come again to judge the living and the dead?
I do so believe.
Do you believe in the Holy Spirit, the holy catholic Church, the communion of saints, the forgiveness of sins, the resurrection of the body, and the life everlasting?
I do so believe.

[or]
THE APOSTLES' CREED
At the baptism of a child, the parents and sponsors are asked: Do you wish [Name] to be baptized in

the faith of the church which we have just declared?
We do.

At the baptism of an adult, the candidate is asked:
Do you wish to be baptized in the faith of the
church which we have just declared?
I do.

THE BAPTISM
[Name], I baptize you in the name of the Father
and of the Son and of the Holy Spirit.

THE LAYING ON OF HANDS OR CHRISMATION
Receive the seal of the gift of the Spirit: may it
make you a faithful witness to Christ to the glory
of God the Father.
[silence]

CONCLUSION
For you, there is a new act of creation. You have
put on Christ. (The person baptized may receive
a white garment.) You will be guided by the Spirit
of light. (He/she may receive a candle lit from the
paschal candle.) You are now part of the body of
the Church. You are a member of the royal priesthood, the holy fellowship. (He/she may be given
the sign of the cross in oil on the forehead.) You
belong to the people chosen to proclaim the
praise of him who has called you out of darkness
into his marvelous light. Alleluia!

Commentary

Perspectives. A striking feature of this baptismal
liturgy is the resemblance of its prayer of thanksgiving to many traditional eucharistic liturgies,
even to the point of beginning with the *sursum
corda* (the text, "lift up your hearts . . . we lift
them up to the Lord"). As in eucharistic liturgies,
this prayer traces the complete history of creation
and redemption and offers thanksgiving for the
work of the Father, Son and Holy Spirit. This powerfully suggests that the baptism which will soon
follow is rooted in these mighty acts of God.

A second striking feature of this liturgy is its
balance of historical awareness and simplicity. It
retains the essential components of even the earliest Christian liturgies, including the bold renunciation of Satan's works, the use of the Apostles'
Creed as a Trinitarian structure for the candidate's
declaration of faith, and the laying on of hands or
chrismation following the sacrament. Further,

these actions, so basic and essential to the meaning of Christian baptism throughout the history
of the church, are left unobscured by any other
complex of ritual actions or long paragraphs of
extraneous texts. Rather, the language is bold and
direct, such as the final charge to the baptized,
"For you, there is a new act of creation. You have
put on Christ. . . ."

This ecumenical liturgy certainly evidences a
full-orbed view of the nature of baptism. As the
language of the welcome summarizes, this baptism is understood as being both "of water and
the Spirit," and involving a renewal of covenant
in God's forgiveness, a mortification and vivifica-
tion (dying and rising) with Christ, the gift of the
Holy Spirit, and church membership. Whereas
various baptismal liturgies tend to emphasize one
or another of these aspects of baptism, this simple
listing of each aspect suggests that baptism appropriately involves all of them.

Suggestions for Appropriation. The act of welcome may be accompanied by a brief introduction of the candidates to the congregation. As a
response to this introduction, the congregation
may be asked, "Will you support [Name] in his/
her pilgrimage in the Christian faith with encouragement and prayer?" The congregation may respond to this question, "We promise [Name] our
encouragement and prayers." This reinforces the
communal nature of the sacrament and calls attention to the inclusion of the candidate for baptism within the membership of the church.

The opening lines or the entire text of the
thanksgiving may be sung. Many musical settings
of the eucharistic prayer of thanksgiving can be
used with little or no modification because of the
similarity of the opening lines of text. In addition,
the congregational response, "Blessed be you, O
Lord," can be sung by all the people if set to a
simple musical refrain.

Following the concluding charge to the baptized person, the service can continue with an
appropriate acclamation of praise as sung by the
entire congregation, the choir, or a soloist. In addition to baptismal hymns, appropriate hymns for
baptism are Easter hymns, which highlight the
Easter imagery found throughout the liturgy and
which are unfortunately most often not sung outside of Easter Sunday.

Commentary by John D. Witvliet

179 ❖ A BELIEVER'S BAPTISMAL LITURGY

Church traditions that practice the baptism of believers tend not to prescribe specific texts for various liturgical acts and sacraments. Thus, the following service is only one possibility from among the variety of approaches to a service of believer's baptism. This text is taken from Orders and Prayers for Church Worship: A Manual for Ministers, _compiled by Ernest A. Page and Stephen F. Winward (1960)._

Baptism should be administered in the presence of the congregation during public worship.

Since we are baptized into the church, it is desirable that baptism should, if possible, be followed by the Lord's Supper, at which the reception of the new members should take place.

After the singing of a baptismal hymn, the minister may read a selection from the following passages of Scripture.

Then Jesus came from Galilee to the Jordan to John . . . (Matt. 3:13-17, RSV). (At this point the service includes the following passages, the texts of which are given in full: Luke 3:21-22; John 3:5-8; Acts 2:38; 41-42; Acts 22:16; Romans 6:3-4; Romans 10:9-11; 1 Corinthians 12:12-13; Galatians 3:26-28; Colossians 2:12; 1 Timothy 6:12; 1 Peter 3:21-22. The following additional passages are also suitable, especially for the main New Testament lesson during the service: Mark 1:1-13; Acts 8:26-40; Acts 9:1-19; Acts 10:34-48; Acts 16:11-15; Acts 16:16-34; Acts 19:1-7; Ephesians 4:1-6; Ephesians 5:21-33; Colossians 3:1-17; Titus 3:4-7; Hebrews 10:19-25; 1 John 5:6-12.) The minister may conclude the selected readings as follows: "Jesus came and said to them. . . ." (Matt. 28:18-20, RSV).

The minister may then say: Beloved brethren: You have just heard how our Lord Jesus Christ after his glorious resurrection and before his ascension into heaven, commanded his apostles to make disciples of all nations, baptizing them in the name of the Father, and of the Son, and of the Holy Spirit.

Let us now set forth the great benefits which we are to receive from the Lord, according to his word and promise, in this holy sacrament.

In baptism we are united with Christ through faith, dying with him unto sin and rising with him unto newness of life.

The washing of our bodies with water is the outward and visible sign of the cleansing of our souls from sin through the sacrifice of our Savior.

The Holy Spirit, the Lord and giver of life, by whose unseen operation we have already been brought to repentance and faith, is given and sealed to us in this sacrament of grace.

By this same Holy Spirit, we are baptized into one body and made members of the holy catholic and apostolic church, the blessed company of all Christ's faithful people. These great benefits are promised and pledged to those who profess repentance toward God and faith in our Lord Jesus Christ. For all such believers baptism is: an act of obedience to the command of our Lord Jesus Christ; a following of the example of our Lord Jesus Christ who was baptized in the river Jordan, that he might fulfill all righteousness; a public confession of personal faith in Jesus Christ as Savior and Lord; a vow or pledge of allegiance to Jesus Christ; an engagement to be his forever.

Addressing those who are to be baptized, the minister shall say: Forasmuch as you now present yourselves for baptism, it is necessary that you sincerely give answer, before God and his church, to the questions which I now put to you. Then he says to each person to be baptized: Do you make profession of repentance toward God and of faith in our Lord Jesus Christ?

Answer: _I do._

Do you promise, in dependence on divine grace, to follow Christ and serve him forever in the fellowship of his church?

Answer: _I do._

Then shall follow the prayer: Almighty and everlasting God, we give thee humble and hearty thanks for our Savior Jesus Christ, who died for our sins, was buried, and was raised on the third day. Graciously accept, we beseech thee, these thy servants, that they, coming to thee in baptism, may by faith be united with Christ in his Church, and receive according to thy promise the forgiveness of their sins, and the gift of the Holy Spirit. Grant that they, putting on the Lord Jesus Christ, may receive out of his fullness and evermore abide in him. Keep them strong in faith, steadfast in hope, abounding in love. Bestow upon them the manifold gifts of thy grace, that they may serve thee profitably in thy Church. Defend them in all trials and temptations, and grant that, persevering to the end, they may inherit eternal life; through Jesus Christ our Lord. Amen.

As each person to be baptized stands in the

water, the minister shall pronounce his or her names, and say: On thy profession of repentance toward God and faith in our Lord Jesus Christ, I baptize thee in the name of the Father and of the Son and of the Holy Spirit. Amen.

After each baptism, the minister may say: The Lord bless thee and keep thee: the Lord make his face to shine upon thee, and be gracious unto thee. The Lord lift up his countenance upon thee and give thee peace.

Alternatively the choir and congregation may sing after each baptism, or at the conclusion of the baptisms, one of the baptismal sentences from the hymn book, or the verse of a hymn, or the doxology.

After the baptisms, one of the following prayers may be offered:

Eternal Father, keep, we beseech thee, thy servants from falling, and present them faultless before the presence of thy glory with exceeding joy, and unto thee, the only wise God our Savior, be glory and majesty, dominion and power, both now and forever. Amen.

Teach them, good Lord, to serve thee with loyal and steadfast hearts; to give and not to count the cost; to fight and not to heed the wounds; to strive and not to seek for rest; to labor and to ask for no reward, save that of knowing that they do thy will; through Jesus Christ our Lord. Amen.

Grant, O Lord, that as we are baptized into the death of thy Son our Savior Jesus Christ, so by continual mortifying our corrupt affections we may be buried with him; and that through the grave, and gate of death, we may pass to our joyful resurrection; for his merits, who died, and was buried, and rose again for us, thy Son Jesus Christ our Lord. Amen.

O God of hope, fill them with all joy and peace in believing, so that by the power of the Holy Spirit, they may abound in hope: through Jesus Christ our Lord. Amen.

O God of peace, who broughtest again from the dead our Lord Jesus, the great shepherd of the sheep, by the blood of the eternal covenant, equip them with everything good that they may do thy will, and work in them that which is pleasing in thy sight: through Jesus Christ, to whom be glory forever and ever. Amen.

If desired, a hymn may now follow, and the normal order of public worship be continued. If it be the end of the service, the minister may say:

Go forth into the world in peace; be of good courage; hold fast that which is good; render to no man evil for evil; strengthen the faint-hearted; support the weak; help the afflicted; honor all men; love and serve the Lord, rejoicing in the power of the Holy Spirit. Amen.

or

May God Almighty, the Father of our Lord Jesus Christ, grant you to be strengthened with power through his Spirit in the inward man; that Christ may dwell in your hearts through faith, and that you may be filled unto all the fullness of God. Amen.

or

The grace of the Lord Jesus Christ, and the love of God, and the fellowship of the Holy Spirit, be with you all. Amen.

Christian Initiation (1980)

Among Baptists of late there has been a growing tendency to bring closer together the act of baptism, reception into membership, and admission to Communion. In other branches of the church at the same time, there has been a tendency to see the wholeness of Christian initiation in terms of strengthening the links between baptism, confession of faith (or confirmation), and Communion.

One result of this theological discussion for Baptists is that the act of baptism as a confession of faith is increasingly seen as part of a larger act of initiation which often finds expression in one service of baptism and Communion.

The practice however is by no means universal, many ministers and churches preferring to separate baptism and reception into membership either by several hours on the same day or perhaps even by several weeks. Those who wish to do this should have no difficulty in taking what is outlined below and dividing it to suit their purposes.

In either case, however, five essential elements in the whole process of Christian initiation should find expression in the worship, whether it is in one service or in two. They are:

(1) Reading of Scripture (including the Gospel) and our reasons for engaging in Christian initiation, including the fact that baptism bears witness to what God has done and continues to do and that our act of baptism is our response to that love

(2) Profession of faith and commitment

(3) Prayers, including a prayer for God's action

in the Spirit that those who are baptized may become children of God entering into newness of life in Christ, becoming part of his body, and sharing his Spirit

(4) Baptism in the name of the Trinity, possibly with the laying on of hands

(5) Reception into membership and admission to Communion

Order of Service

THE PREPARATION
Call to worship
Hymn
Prayer of confession and assurance of forgiveness
Responsive reading

THE WORD
Reading of Scripture
Hymn
Sermon

THE RESPONSE
Statement of belief concerning Christian initiation, including Gospel reading
Baptismal hymn.
Act of baptism
Invitation to baptism
Offering
Prayers of intercession

THE COMMUNION
Hymn
Reception into membership
Presentation of gifts including bread and wine
Prayer of thanksgiving
Words of institution
Distribution of elements

Commentary

Perspectives. Of the baptismal liturgies included in this series, this particular text is the most didactic, featuring the reading of several portions of Scripture and several sentences of explanation regarding the nature of the sacrament. This explanation is helpful in making clear the nature of the sacrament and may be the basis for study and reflection prior to the service itself.

The text of this liturgy suggests an emphasis on the action of the baptismal candidates as an "act of obedience," "a following of Christ's example," a "confession of faith," and a "vow of allegiance," an emphasis expected in a service constructed for only the baptism of a declared believer. This takes some emphasis away from the understanding of baptism as being primarily God's activity, by which the candidate is united with Christ and the church. This emphasis highlights one theological difference between the traditions which practice the exclusive baptism of adult believers and other traditions represented in this series.

Suggestions for Appropriation. Prior to the text of this liturgy, the worship leader should introduce the baptismal candidate to the congregation and indicate to the candidate the joy of the congregation at the occasion. An appropriate congregational response is suggested in the commentary on the ecumenical liturgy in this series.

Several of the Scripture passages may be read by members of the family of the candidate for baptism or other appropriate members of the congregation.

The explanation of the nature of baptism may be read either by the pastor of the local congregation, or by an elder, an office-bearer, or a member of the supervisory board of the congregation, reflecting their responsibility for the supervision of the sacrament.

The prayer which immediately precedes the baptism and offers petitions on behalf of the candidate may be concluded by an anthem or hymn whose text offers similar petitions.

After the baptism, the text of the blessing may be sung by the congregation or a choir.

Following the entire baptismal service, the worship leader or pastor may offer additional personal words of encouragement to the one baptized. At this point, the one baptized may be given opportunity to express the nature of his/her journey in the faith and to ask for the continued support of the congregation. The congregation may respond by singing a hymn of encouragement to the one baptized, such as, "If You Will Trust in God to Guide You"; by joining the one baptized in singing a hymn of commitment, such as, "O Jesus, I Have Promised"; or by singing a hymn that is a prayer for God's continued presence, such as, "O Master, Let Me Walk With Thee." In any case, the specific nature and purpose of the hymn text chosen should be carefully identified for the congregation.

Commentary by John D. Witvliet

180 ◆ A CHARISMATIC BAPTISMAL SERVICE

Baptism is usually held where running water is present (such as a stream or lake), but church baptisteries or swimming pools are also used. If the baptism is held indoors, the baptism, ideally, should be part of a regular service where most of the congregation can be present as witnesses to the event.

People assemble as a group near the water (or in the front of the sanctuary). In addition to one or two ministers for the actual baptism, a worship leader is needed and additional readers, if desired.

Welcome and Prayer. The pastor or worship leader offers words of welcome and explains what is to take place. The pastor may want to explain the teaching that those being baptized received and may also want to explain in greater detail what baptism is all about. One of the pastors then leads in prayer, inviting the Holy Spirit to come and minister to those who are being baptized.

Opening Worship. This part of the service is led by a worship leader with or without an additional worship team. The music usually focuses on salvation issues and the sufficiency of Christ for all that takes place in a person's life. Opportunity is given during this worship time for the Holy Spirit to work in the lives of those present, as some who are visiting to see the baptism may make a personal decision for the Lord. Others present may need a special touch.

Those being baptized may want to take this time to search their hearts for issues they may need to resolve. Since they are not yet in front of the group, their sponsors may want to pray with them during this time to rid them of anything that would hinder their walk with Christ.

Presentation. Baptismal candidates are brought forward and presented with sponsors who will assume responsibility to encourage the spiritual growth of those baptized. For one candidate, the person should select a baptized believer from the congregation to be their sponsor. If more than one candidate is present, someone should be named to present the group of candidates and sponsors.

Something close to the following can be said: "Pastor, on behalf of the church of Jesus Christ, I present this person [these persons] to be baptized in obedience to Christ's example and teaching."

Scripture Readings. Three readings are given. These can be read uninterrupted or alternated with hymns or praise choruses. Usually the texts are:
Jeremiah 31:31-34
Romans 6:3-11
Matthew 28:16-20

Message. A baptismal message may be offered by one of the pastors.

Music. Another hymn or chorus may be sung as the candidates prepare for the actual baptism.

Baptism. The minister may then offer the following questions:
To the candidates:

MINISTER:	Is it your intention to enter into the waters of baptism as a mark of Covenant with your Lord?
CANDIDATE:	It is.
MINISTER:	Do you confess with your mouth that Jesus Christ is Lord; that He is the Son of God who died on the cross for your redemption, and rose again in victory over sin and death?
CANDIDATE	I confess Jesus as Lord and Savior.
MINISTER:	Have you repented of your sin and accepted this work on the cross for your own life?
CANDIDATE:	I have.
MINISTER:	Do you intend to live a Christian life through the power of the Holy Spirit available to you?
CANDIDATE:	I so intend.

To the sponsors (if present to support the candidate):

MINISTER:	Are you willing to give of yourself to pray for, offer counsel to, and encourage this candidate through the Spirit of God that so wonderfully works within you?
SPONSOR:	That is my desire.
MINISTER:	Will you purpose to seek the best for these candidates concerning their walk and witness for Christ?
SPONSOR:	I will with God's help.

To the congregation:

MINISTER:	Will you accept these who have come as fellow members and pil-

grims on our journey of faith?

PEOPLE: **We will.**

MINISTER: Will you, along with their sponsors, offer help and encouragement as they grow in Christ?

PEOPLE: **We will, with God's help.**

Candidates then led into the water for baptism. Prior to the actual baptism, they are given an opportunity to share what Christ means to them. They are then baptized by immersion, with the pastor saying: "[Name], I baptize you in the name of the Father, and of the Son, and of the Holy Spirit. Amen."

Anointing. After all candidates have been baptized, they are, in turn, anointed with oil on their heads by one of the ministers. (This may be done in the sign of the cross.)

Minister: "[Name], you are sealed by the Holy Spirit and marked as a child of the covenant."

Prayer is then offered by the ministers for the release of the gifts and power of the Holy Spirit in the life of the one just baptized. Additional prayers, prophetic words and words of knowledge and wisdom may be offered by those in attendance.

A closing song can be offered unless the congregation is going to celebrate Communion together, which would begin at this time.

Benediction. May the God of peace, who through the blood of the eternal covenant brought back from the dead our Lord Jesus, that great Shepherd of the sheep, equip you with everything good for doing his will, and may he work in us what is pleasing to him, through Jesus Christ, to whom be glory for ever and ever. Amen (Heb.13:20-21).

Reception. After the closing song and benediction, the candidates are then greeted by the fellowship present and welcomed into the community of faith.

Randolph W. Sly

181 • BIBLIOGRAPHY ON THE PRACTICE OF BAPTISM

The Book of Common Prayer. New York: Church Hymnal Corporation, 1979. Refer to pages 299–315 for the Episcopalian baptismal rite.

The Book of Common Worship. Louisville: Westminster/John Knox, 1993; _Holy Baptism and Services for the Renewal of Baptism: Supplemental Resources._ Philadelphia: Westminster, 1985. Both Presbyterian Church–USA and Cumberland Presbyterian Church use these worship books. See pages 403–446 in the former work for baptismal rites.

Book of Worship: United Church of Christ. New York: Office of Church Life, 1986. Refer to page 127 for the United Church of Christ's baptismal rite.

Gilmore, Alec, Edward Smalley, and Michael Walker. _Praise God: A Collection of Material for Christian Worship._ London: Baptist Union, 1980. An example of Baptist baptismal rite.

Lutheran Book of Worship. Minneapolis: Augsburg; and Philadelphia: Board of Publication, Lutheran Church in America, 1978. See pages 121–125 for Evangelical Lutheran Church in America's baptismal rite.

Lutheran Worship Agenda. St. Louis: Concordia, 1984. See pages 91–104 for the Lutheran Church–Missouri Synod baptismal rite.

MacNeil, Jesse Jai. _Minister's Service Book for Pulpit and Parish._ Grand Rapids: Eerdmans, 1993. Refer to pages 29–33 for an example of a Baptist baptismal rite.

Payne, Ernest A., and Stephen F. Winward. _Orders and Prayers for Church Worship: A Manual for Ministers._ 1960. An example of Baptist baptismal rite.

The Psalter Hymnal. Grand Rapids: CRC Publications, 1987. See pages 953–971 for the Christian Reformed Church's baptismal rite.

The Rites. Vol. 1. New York: Pueblo Publishing, 1983; and _Rite of Christian Initiation of Adults: Study Edition._ Chicago: Liturgy Training Publications, 1988. Refer to these works for the Roman Catholic rite.

Thurian, Max, and Geoffrey Wainwright, eds. _Baptism and Eucharist: Ecumenical Convergence in Celebration._ Grand Rapids: Eerdmans, 1983. A collection of liturgies from various worship traditions.

Vaporis, N. M, ed. _An Orthodox Prayer Book._ Brookline, Mass.: Holy Cross, 1977. See pages 55–73 for an Orthodox baptismal liturgy.

The United Methodist Book of Worship. Nashville:

The United Methodist Publishing House, 1992. Refer to pages 81–114 for the United Methodist's rite.

Watkins, Keith, ed., *Baptism and Belonging*. St. Louis: Chalice Press, 1991. Refer to this work for the baptismal rites of the Christian Church–Disciples of Christ.

Worship the Lord. Grand Rapids: Eerdmans, 1987. See pages 13–17 for the Reformed Church in America's baptismal rite.

☙ SEVEN ☙

Confirmation

In Western Europe during the Middle Ages, the anointing with oil that was part of baptism in the early church was detached from the baptismal rite and eventually became the distinct sacred action known as *confirmation* for largely practical reasons. The almost accidental origins of this separation have led to much controversy and reexamination. The issues raised by a separate rite of confirmation are closely related to matters of catechism and the nurture of children within the context of the church.

182 ✦ HISTORICAL ORIGINS AND DEVELOPMENT OF CONFIRMATION

Large dioceses in northern Europe during the early Middle Ages made it difficult for bishops to be present at the baptism of infants. Gradually a two-part initiation process emerged spanning the period from infancy to late childhood. With increased emphasis on catechism during the Reformation era, confirmation became a rite of passage for adolescents who had been properly instructed in the faith. Whether to admit baptized but unconfirmed children to the Eucharist became a great problem.

History

Baptism is described in the book of Acts as a simple water rite, accomplished as soon as a convert showed unmistakable signs of faith. Some New Testament literature uses imagery other than water imagery, interpreting baptism in terms such as anointing, passage from darkness to light, or reclothing. Did these images grow from ritual practices which were already in place in the first century? Or were they parts of the poetry of becoming a Christian, which helped bring non-water ritual actions into use quite early? In either case, by the late second century, baptism was associated with pre- and postbaptismal acts which brought to expression initiatory images such as priesthood, royalty, and coronation, soldiering and combat, and athletic contest. The actions of Christian initiation were not uniform throughout the church. There was a prebaptismal anointing in Syria, but no postbaptismal anointing. Elsewhere, a postbaptismal anointing was common. In Milan, the feet of the newly baptized were washed. In all parts of the early church, baptism (which was ordinarily only at Easter) led at once to the first receiving of the Holy Communion.

In the East, baptism was and still is followed by an anointing (called chrismation) by the minister of baptism, which leads immediately to the Holy Communion. In most parts of the West in the early centuries, the same pattern prevailed: Easter baptism, anointing, and Eucharist. But in Rome and its immediate vicinity, the anointing of the water by the minister of baptism was followed by an anointing of the forehead of the newly baptized, by the bishop, in the eucharistic room. This second postbaptismal anointing took on meanings associated with royalty and priestliness, and with the gifts of the Holy Spirit. (A prayer for the gifts of the Spirit, based on Isaiah 11:2, became widely used.) Such meanings were not separable from the general initiatory meanings, for the anointing with chrism and the washing in water were parts of a single ritual act.

Some early Christian writers, however, began to assign separate meanings to the two actions. They spoke of water baptism as a washing from sin, but anointing acquired a more positive connotation, for it was a divine filling of the anointed person. In the course of time, this distinction led to separation of the two acts.

In the early Middle Ages, the dioceses of Northern Europe attempted to follow the model of Rome and the sequence of two postbaptismal anointings (one by the minister of the baptism, and one by the bishop). This practice was also attempted in Gaul, where dioceses were large and bishops often inaccessible. The result was that the second part of Christian initiation (the bishop's part), when it was performed at all, was administered some years after baptism. The second anointing came to be thought of as a rite of coming of age, to be prepared for by some rudimentary education—perhaps enough to support a first confession.

Thus, the West (and only the West) developed a two-stage initiatory rite. Baptism, a rite of infancy, was followed some years later by the bishop's anointing, which came to be called confirmation, a rite of coming of age. By the discipline of the late Middle Ages, entry on the life of a practicing communicant did not follow the first stage, baptism, but followed the second stage, confirmation. This second stage came to be thought appropriate for an age around seven years.

The churches of the sixteenth century Reformation inherited this two-stage rite, unaware of how it had evolved. This incremental initiation was continued, with its educational feature (which had been little developed in medieval Catholicism) heightened. Catechisms, for children and for their teachers, were written; clergy added teaching to their expected duties; confirmation became (as it remains in these traditions) an important event for the children, their families, and the congregation. The rite of confirmation seemed a ready-made opportunity for the Reformers, who sought to raise the general level of understanding among Christian people. The Counter-Reformation was also an educational movement. Schools and educational literature multiplied profusely in the Roman communion.

The Anabaptists rejected infant baptism because they believed that baptism is properly an act of witness to an engagement with Christ through vital, articulate faith. Consequently, infants, who are incapable of such faith, could not be baptized. Anabaptists brought to baptism only persons who were competent to give an account of their experience (either adult converts or else children of Christian parents who had come to an age of accountability) and who were baptized *on profession of faith*.

The Modern Church

These patterns which developed in the sixteenth century have persisted with only minor modifications. The Catholic tradition, following early liturgical understandings, observed the bishop's anointing as a performative sacramental action which bestowed the Holy Spirit. The medieval church added the understanding that the Spirit was given at confirmation for strength for combat under Christ against the world. The Protestant traditions, by contrast, developed (under the same name) a catechetical rite of children entering on adult responsibilities and owning the promises of their baptism.

In recent generations, there has been some mingling of these traditions. The Catholic churches (possibly influenced by their parochial school system) have tended to say more about confirmands entering adulthood and making, at confirmation, a responsible self-declaration. At the same time, Protestant churches have come to say more at confirmation about the divine gift and the support and agency of the Holy Spirit.

The churches which practiced infant baptism and the confirmation of adolescents permitted full, communicant membership only after confirmation. Baptism was thus incomplete Christian initiation. Children were within the life of the church, but did not feed at the Table of the Lord.

The sort of confirmation which developed in the churches of the Reformation was not a sacramental rite, but a catechetical rite. Confirmation did not speak, except quite secondarily, of the gift of the Holy Spirit; it was an occasion of declaring for oneself the promises that had been made on one's behalf by others at baptism. Confirmation was an act made by a Christian who had baptismal vows to reaffirm. Baptism without this confirmation action was patently incomplete; both stages of initiation were required to confer full sacramental standing in the church.

The Baptist tradition has stood apart from this two-stage initiatory pattern. This tradition clearly admits one to full, not partial, standing in the church when baptism is administered. However, this tradition has showed considerable awkwardness about the place in the church of the children of believers. Some Baptist groups in recent decades have instituted a service of thanksgiving for and dedication of infants. Birth in a Christian family is significant—for the child, the parents and the congregation. Baptism, however, in the Baptist churches must wait until an age of accountability. Thus, many of the Baptist churches too have developed something like a two-stage initiatory process—perhaps more out of felt pastoral and psychological necessity than out of theological inquiry.

Generally speaking, in the Roman and Anglican churches, which have the historic episcopate, the bishop has been, by ancient prerogative, the minister of confirmation. In the Roman tradition, the bishop anoints the confirmands, while in the Anglican tradition, the authorized and sufficient action has been the laying on of hands. (Some Anglican bishops began in the nineteenth century, apart from Prayer Book authorization, to add anointing as an alternative.) The Protestant churches have given the task of confirming to the local pastors, who carry it out by the laying on of hands. Significantly, the Eastern churches know nothing of this two-stage initiatory process; the local priest administers baptism, chrismation, and first Communion to a child a few days after birth.

Recent Questions

In the second third of this century, significant questions began to be raised about this longstanding pattern. The Catholic insistence on the Holy Spirit as given in confirmation seems to qualify the Trinitarian fullness of baptism. Lack of understanding on the part of an infant was not thought to be a barrier to baptism, yet entry into communicant life was made to depend on knowing what one was doing, and, on the strength of that knowing, being confirmed. Why were the two great sacraments of the gospel treated so differently? Baptism was a sign of grace; Communion had been made a sign of achievement. Is it theologically or biblically defensible to make baptism only partial Christian initiation? Practically, adolescent confirmation placed a somewhat contrived religious crisis at an age which was too early to be truly adult in character and too late to give sacramental support to childhood. Moreover, in modern, secular society, a considerable proportion of adolescents seem to leave active Christian practice within a short time after confirmation. As Christian initiation has been rethought in connection with mid-twentieth century liturgical revisions, these questions have led to changes in understandings, intentions, rites, and practices in many churches.

183 ♦ A Theology of Confirmation

A number of relatively clear theological assumptions under gird the liturgies of confirmation used by a variety of churches.

Baptism must be regarded as complete Christian initiation; it is not the first part of a staged-out action. By it, one becomes a Christian, not a partial Christian.

Many of the modern baptismal liturgies (for example, those of the Evangelical Lutheran Church of America and the Episcopal, Presbyterian, and Methodist churches) require or commend some additional actions at the actual baptism itself, such as anointing with chrism, the laying on of hands, the sign of the cross, or the giving of a lighted candle.

Such actions were rejected by the Reformation churches of the sixteenth century, which regarded them as otiose, if not actually harmful. Reformation emphasis was on what was needed for validity. In the twentieth century, however, such actions and their accompanying verbal formulas are no longer contentious. They seem to be ways of making explicit the richness of baptismal meanings. They must not overpower the basic water rite, nor take on some separate identity, but be within a clear, economical baptismal act. When they are, they can contribute valuable images.

Many churches are persuaded that if baptism is complete Christian initiation, it should admit one to the Holy Communion. The sign of birth is closely rated to the sign of feeding. No additional rite is necessary to complete baptism or to make one eligible for participation in the Eucharist. If a congregation or a family has pastoral or practical difficulties with infant Communion, they should be resolved with understanding. However, it should be a matter of principle that children who are baptized are members of the family of God and welcome at the Table of the Lord without any further ritual act or pastoral requirement. Such a conviction about baptism changes the practice that had made entry on communicant life a part of the second stage of initiation. One feeds at the sacramental table because one is a Christian, and one is formally made a Christian by baptism. (In practice, the churches that are changing their initiatory rites along somewhat similar lines are not moving uniformly on first Communion. Some quite deep emotions and long-standing practices are involved; change requires education and modeling.)

Positively, the act of confirmation is an occasion for the renewal of one's baptismal promises. Confirmation is neither the only nor the last time for such renewal, but for most persons coming to confirmation, it will be the first public occasion on which these fundamental Christian pledges are reaffirmed. Thus it is a pastoral action especially appropriate for persons who have been baptized in infancy. It provides them an occasion for an articulate response to the baptismal gift. It is a liturgical structure whereby the church can recognize the important interior events in the growth of Christian young persons. Clearly, if confirmation is the renewal of the promises of baptism, it is not an initiatory action. One is already a baptized (and, in many case, also a communicating Christian) if one has baptismal promises to renew. Confirmation is not part of becoming a Christian, but is a responsible action which appropriately falls within the life of one who had been baptized as a child and is now, as an adult, affirming that action.

Similarly, confirmation would suit the experience of an adult who had been baptized at an early age, but whose baptism has not been followed up in any way. Such a person's adult discovery of faith is appropriately recognized by confirmation. The act would be completely inappropriate for a person who had been baptized as an adult; such a person's baptism was itself a responsible, mature declaration of faith.

The implication is that confirmation should be entirely voluntary on the part of the confirmed. It should not be part of an expectation created by an adult generation and imposed on impressionable young persons. If this counsel is followed, confirmation will no doubt fall in many cases at a considerably later age than past practice has put it. But who is effectively adult at age twelve? Or even, as twenty-four-year olds see it, at age eighteen?

Daniel B. Stevick

184 ◆ A LITURGY FOR CONFIRMATION

Many church traditions which practice infant baptism also celebrate confirmation, public profession of faith, or reception into the church—that is, a service in which those baptized at an early age publicly affirm their faith and declare their acceptance of the responsibilities entailed in baptism and church membership. The use of the term confirmation *also implies a completion or fulfillment of baptism. At confirmation, the candidate is anointed with a seal of the gift of the Holy Spirit. The following service for confirmation is based on the text found in the 1979* Book of Common Prayer *of the Episcopal Church.*

——————————— **Text** ———————————

Opening

LEADER: Blessed be God: Father, Son, and Holy Spirit.

PEOPLE: **And blessed be his kingdom, now and forever. Amen.**

LEADER: There is one Body and one Spirit.

PEOPLE: **There is one hope in God's call to us.**

LEADER: One Lord, one Faith, one Baptism.

PEOPLE: **One God and Father of all.**

LEADER: The Lord be with you,

PEOPLE: **And also with you.**

LEADER: Let us pray.
Grant, Almighty God, that we, who have been redeemed from the old life of sin by our baptism into the death and resurrection of your Son Jesus Christ, may be renewed in your Holy Spirit, and live in righteousness and true holiness; through Jesus Christ our Lord, who lives and reigns with you and the Holy Spirit, one God, now and forever. Amen.

PEOPLE: **Amen.**

PROCLAMATION

LEADER: [A reading from Ephesians 2:19-22 or 1 Peter 2:9, followed by]

LEADER: The Word of the Lord.

PEOPLE: **Thanks be to God.**

LEADER: The Holy Gospel of our Lord Jesus Christ according to Matthew.

PEOPLE: **Glory to you, Lord Christ.**

LEADER: [reading from Matthew 5:14-16]

LEADER: The Gospel of the Lord.

PEOPLE: **Praise to you, Lord Christ.**

PRESENTATION OF THE CANDIDATES

LEADER: The following are now presented for Confirmation.

The leader introduces each candidate to the congregation.

LEADER: Do you reaffirm your renunciation of evil?

CANDIDATE: I do.

LEADER: Do you renew your commitment to Jesus Christ?

CANDIDATE: I do, and with God's grace I will follow him as my Savior and Lord.

LEADER: Will you who witness these vows do all in your power to support these persons in their life in Christ?

PEOPLE: **We will.**

LEADER: Let us join with those who are committing themselves to Christ and renew our own baptismal covenant.

BAPTISMAL COVENANT

LEADER: Do you believe in God the Father?

PEOPLE: **I believe in God, the Father Almighty, creator of heaven and earth.**

LEADER: Do you believe in Jesus Christ?

PEOPLE: **I believe in Jesus Christ, his only Son, our Lord,**
who was conceived by the Holy Spirit
and born of the virgin Mary.
He suffered under Pontius Pilate,
was crucified, died and was buried;
he descended to hell.
The third day he rose again from the dead.
He ascended to heaven and is seated at the right hand of God the Father almighty.
From there he will come to judge the living and the dead.

LEADER: Do you believe in God the Holy Spirit?

PEOPLE: **I believe in the Holy Spirit,**
the holy catholic church,
the communion of the saints,
the forgiveness of sins,
the resurrection of the body,
and the life everlasting. Amen.

LEADER: Will you continue in the apostles' teaching and fellowship, in the breaking of bread, and in prayer?

PEOPLE: **I will, with God's help.**

LEADER: Will you persevere in resisting evil, and, whenever you fall into sin, repent and return to the Lord?

PEOPLE: **I will, with God's help.**

LEADER: Will you proclaim by word and example the Good News of God in Christ?

PEOPLE: **I will, with God's help.**

LEADER: Will you seek and serve Christ in all persons, loving your neighbor as yourself?

PEOPLE: **I will, with God's help.**

LEADER: Will you strive for justice and peace among all people, and respect the dignity of every human being?

PEOPLE: **I will, with God's help.**

PRAYERS FOR THE CANDIDATES

LEADER: Let us now pray for these persons who have renewed their commitment to Christ.

LEADER: Deliver, O Lord, these believers from the way of sin and death.

PEOPLE: **Lord, hear our prayer.**

LEADER: Open their hearts to your grace and truth.

PEOPLE: **Lord, hear our prayer.**

LEADER: Fill them with your Holy and life-giving Spirit.

PEOPLE: **Lord, hear our prayer.**

LEADER: Keep them in the faith and communion of your holy Church.

PEOPLE: **Lord, hear our prayer.**

LEADER: Teach them to love others in the power of the Spirit.

PEOPLE: **Lord, hear our prayer.**

LEADER: Send them into the world in witness to your love.

PEOPLE: **Lord, hear our prayer.**

LEADER: Bring them to the fullness of your peace and glory.

PEOPLE: **Lord, hear our prayer.**

[time of silence]

LEADER: Almighty God, we thank you that by the death and resurrection of your Son Jesus Christ you have overcome sin and brought us to yourself, and that by the sealing of your Holy Spirit you have bound us to your service. Renew in these your servants the covenant you made with them at their Baptism. Send them forth in the power of that Spirit to perform the service you set before them; through Jesus Christ your Son our Lord, who lives and reigns with you and the Holy Spirit, one God, now and for ever.

PEOPLE: **Amen.**

LEADER: [for each candidate]
Strengthen, O Lord, your servant [Name] with your Holy Spirit, empower him/her for your service; and sustain him/her all the days of his/her life.

PEOPLE: **Amen.**

LEADER: Almighty and everliving God, let your fatherly hand ever be over these your servants; let your Holy Spirit ever be with them; and so lead them in the knowledge and obedience of your Word, that they may serve you in this life, and dwell with you in the life to come; through Jesus Christ, our Lord.

PEOPLE: **Amen.**

LEADER: The peace of the Lord be always with you.

PEOPLE: **Amen.**

The service continues with the celebration of the Eucharist or Lord's Supper.

Commentary

In the past several decades, many church traditions have sought to downplay the dichotomy suggested by the rite of confirmation, that there are two classes of baptized Christians, both confirmed and unconfirmed. This liturgy of confirmation, while intended to stand as a separate liturgical rite from baptism, de-emphasizes any such dichotomy. Rather, it emphasizes a renewal of what happened at baptism, praying for God to "renew in these your servants the covenant you made with them at their baptism." Likewise, when appropriate reference is made to the gift of the Holy Spirit, this liturgy does not assume that the gift of the Holy Spirit was not given until confirmation. Instead, prayers ask for a renewed measure of the Spirit's presence and strengthening power.

A second notable feature of this service is the important role that the congregation plays. This role is signaled by the question to the congregation regarding their support of the candidates. Then, during the section of the baptismal covenant, the congregation joins with the candidates to declare their faith and to pledge their continued allegiance to Christ. In this way, the service functions as a renewal of baptismal vows for the entire congregation. Also, the candidates for confirmation find important solidarity in their promises with the whole people of God.

Suggestions for Planning. Lectors may be chosen from among those who have been spiritual mentors to candidates for confirmation, including godparents, church education instructors, or family members.

Two hymns for confirmation, "Lord, We Have Come at Your Own Invitation" and "Holy Spirit, Lord of Love," are included in the 1982 hymnal of the Episcopal Church; similar hymns are included in nearly every denominational hymnbook. These particular hymns are prayers that should precede the confirmation. They may be sung by the congregation or choir to conclude the collect in the opening section of the liturgy.

Following the question addressed to the congregation regarding their support of the candidates, a hymn may be sung which emphasizes the unity and fellowship of the church of Christ, such as "In Christ There Is No East or West."

The occasion of confirmation can appropriately be followed by a congregational celebration after the service, extending the theme of solidarity in Christ found in the liturgy.

Worship leaders should adapt the pronouns *him, her, their,* etc. throughout the service as would be appropriate for a given occasion.

The various brief petitions included in the prayer for the candidates may each serve as a basis for longer, extemporaneous prayers offered by various members of the congregation. All such prayers should end with a common refrain, such as "through Jesus Christ," so that the congregation may appropriately respond with their refrain, "Lord, hear our prayer."

The prayer which begins "strengthen, O Lord, your servant . . ." is the prayer for confirmation proper. This may be accompanied by the laying on of hands or the anointing with the oil of chrism, as may be appropriate in a given congregation. Each of these acts has been historically associated with the gift of the Holy Spirit at confirmation.

Commentary by John D. Witvliet

185 ✦ GUIDELINES FOR PLANNING A CONFIRMATION SERVICE

The following article presents guidelines for planning a confirmation service, based on theological, pastoral, and liturgical rationale.

The Occasion

It is desirable that the service of confirmation be planned to coincide with one of the great, evangelically significant times of the year: Easter, Pentecost, or some other festival belonging to the church's proclamation of the gospel through the stewardship of liturgical time.

As to its hour, it should clearly not be at a time outside the accustomed gathering for congregational worship. Confirmation is not merely an individual or a family event, but an ecclesial one. A congregation should be present to give its vocal support to its members.

Since the substance of the act is the renewing of the promises of baptism, if confirmation can coincide with some actual baptisms, the two ritual actions—the initial making of promises by some persons and the later reaffirming of those same promises by others—will inform one another. (Perhaps it should go without saying—except that redundancy is a perennial failing of liturgy—that a liturgical event which combines two or more actions must be worked out so as to be clear and well-shaped and to avoid duplications of acts and words.)

A Service of the Word

The specific action of confirmation—a Christian's renewal of the covenant of baptism—should take place in the midst of the reading of Scriptures, the singing of psalms (psalms such as Psalm 1 or Psalm 139:1-9, for example), and the proclaiming of the Word. The origin of the act is, in one sense, within the awareness of a particular Christian who has come to a critical moment. Yet more profoundly, the origin of the act is within the divine redemptive initiative, which should be held before the congregation and the candidate through the biblical witness.

Presentation and Sponsorship. Whoever comes to confirm the promises of his/her baptism has been supported, and will continue to be supported, in a congregation of believers. This shared support should be represented at the confirmation itself by persons who have been and who pledge themselves to continue to be close to the confirmand. Christians are members of one another. We grow towards maturity in Christ in a community of caring, giving, and forgiving people—a fact which should be exhibited at confirmation by persons who present the confirmand and promise their continued interest and faithfulness. Such persons speak for themselves and for the congregation.

Minister

In churches with episcopal order and a sacramental tradition, the minister of confirmation has been the bishop. However, this ancient sacramental prerogative is not understood as a matter of divine order, and in the Roman church, presbyters may and do confirm adults who are baptized. (Anglican churches remain more rigid on the point.) However, in most churches, the minister of confirmation will be the local pastor—the person who has known and prepared the candidates. In the rite itself, the catechist/pastor is in a position to be friendly and familiar; yet being too chatty or informal would reduce the seriousness of the occasion for the confirmand and for the congregation. The introduction of little speeches might also create a distinction between those confirmands about whom a speech is made and those others who apparently merit no speech. Such distinctions will be noted and these distinctions are undesirable.

Promises

Since the pastoral intent of the rite is the renewal of the promises of baptism, those promises should figure in the service. If confirmation is combined with baptism, the promises of an actual baptism will be joined in by the congregation, including the candidates for confirmation. Otherwise, the service of confirmation should include the promises, joined in by all the baptized.

The Apostles' Creed grew from the apostolic preaching as the affirmation Christians made at baptism. This creed represents the church's normative consent to the divine redemptive acts; its use in interrogatory form at baptism is one of the oldest traditions of the church. In the early decades, the creed formed the only explicit promise made at baptism, but in a community in which candidates came to baptism after years of catechesis, many commitments belonging to the Christian profession would be understood, without being stated. Today, many churches have set along with the creed some important pledges—pledges concerning such things as prayer and worship, engagement in witness, care for the needy, and commitment to social justice. Such promises must be carefully worded, so that, while persons make serious commitments, they are not asked to over-promise. Baptism is an occasion for hope, not for church-sponsored unreality. One wants wordings to which baptized persons can return repeatedly to orient themselves to central realities of belief and life.

The fundamental Christian promises will have been formulated for use at baptism. At confirmation, they should be used without change and in their full form, not by title.

The baptized congregation will collectively renew the baptismal covenant. What the confirmands do will minister to the community by inviting all to join in what they are doing. That being the case, the promises should be spoken at some central point in the liturgical event by everyone. The confirmands should not be asked to make these full promises individually, for that might imply that they need to restate personally what they have just said with the community or that the members of the congregation who have said the baptismal promises together, as part of the common Christian commitment, did not really mean them. The united pledge is to be seriously intended by everyone.

Confirmation. The usual symbol of confirmation is the dove, reminding the worshiper of the words often spoken during this sacred action that call for an increase in the gifts of the Holy Spirit.

However, it is surely appropriate (perhaps before the baptismal covenant is spoken by all) to ask the confirmands a question pertinent to their situation, something such as, "Do you renew your commitment to Jesus Christ?" The confirmands may answer with "I do"; the pastor might say, "Let all join in the affirmation of the promises of our baptism."

Prayer

Confirmation, like all the pastoral actions of the Christian church, is fundamentally effected, not by formula, but by prayer. Even though the liturgy of confirmation should not imply that the candidate is receiving the Holy Spirit for the first time, a prayer for the empowering of the Holy Spirit may well be part of the rite. Christians meet the Holy Spirit definitively when they become Christians; however, in the lifelong baptismal relation in which God is faithful, they will claim the Holy Spirit many times, as their experience requires. Indeed, in the New Testament, the Holy Spirit is understood eschatologically, as the sign of the age to come. Thus the Spirit represents a Christian's future, as well as a Christian's past and present. The prayer should also ask for the faithfulness of the confirmands in their fundamental commitments as baptized Christians and for their continued participation in the mission of the Christian people.

Action

The prayer should be accompanied by actions—actions which demonstrate and seal the prayer, and prayer which interprets the actions. The tradition would suggest carrying out confirmation by the laying on of hands—a gesture of bonding, blessing, healing, designating, setting-apart—a powerful, wordless gesture which may mean what its context suggests it means. Some churches would prefer anointing with chrism. Others make some subordinate sprinkling with water, to connect the confirmation action with baptism.

Ordinarily, the service of confirmation should lead directly into Holy Communion. It recalls baptism, and baptism, which is done to each Christian once, is the introduction to the often repeated action of the Holy Table. The confirmation, which recalls the first great sacrament of redemption, baptism, should culminate in the second, the Supper of the Lord. The confirmation has focused on individuals and their pilgrimage. It should be followed by the collective, uniting sign of Christian sustenance. (The confirmands should not receive Communion as a class, but with their families.)

The entire event should be full of praise. The event may capture or bring to public expression some serious life-moments—some of them having conflict, struggle and pain behind them. However by the time such experience has come to this occasion of congregational liturgical expression, these serious life-moments should have been worked through, so that they can be expressed with joy and a sense of promise.

Daniel B. Stevick

186 • BIBLIOGRAPHY ON CONFIRMATION

Austin, Gerard. _Anointing with the Spirit_. New York: Pueblo Publishing, 1985.

Dix, Gregory. _The Theology of Confirmation in Relation to Baptism_. London: Dacre Press, 1946.

Fischer, J(ohn) D(ouglas) C(lose). _Confirmation Then and Now_. Alcuin Club Collection. London: SPCK, 1978.

Kavanaugh, Aidan. _Confirmation: Origins and Reform_. New York: Pueblo Publishing, 1988.

———. "The Origin and Reform of Confirmation." _St. Vladimir's Theological Quarterly_ 33:1 (1989): 5–20. Argues that confirmation was originally the bishop's public confirmation of the immediately preceding baptism and a _dismissal_ to the Eucharist—i.e., a liturgical transition point. Confirmation did not have pneumatological character invoking the gifts of the Holy Spirit (thereby taking issue with the interpretations of Dix and Botte).

Kiesling, Christopher. _Confirmation and the Full Life of the Spirit_. Cincinnati: St. Anthony Messenger Press, 1973.

Milner, Austin P. _The Theology of Confirmation_. Hales Corner, Wis.: Clergy Book Service, 1972.

Mitchell, Leonel L. "The Place of Baptismal Anointing in Christian Initiation." _Anglican Theological Review_ 68 (1986): 202–11.

Quinn, Frank C. "Confirmation Reconsidered: Rite and Meaning." _Worship_ 59 (1985): 354–70.

Turner, Paul. _Theology and Religion_. Vol. 13, _Meaning and Practice of Confirmation: Perspectives from a Sixteenth-Century Controversy_. American University Studies, series 7. New York: Peter Lang, 1988.

EIGHT

The Renewal of the Baptismal Covenant

Christian baptism represents a commitment to Christ. In later chapters, much will be said about rites of confession of sin, reconciliation, fasting, and solemn assembly that are intended to restore such a commitment when it has been broken, both individually and corporately. Another approach, used particularly in churches that baptize infants, is formal renewal of baptismal promises. Baptismal renewal is closely connected with the increased attention given to catechism of baptized children and their (nonsacramental) confirmation, often during adolescence, in Lutheran and Reformed churches. However, annual corporate renewal of baptism is also part of the baptismal liturgy of the Easter Vigil in the Roman Catholic and Anglican communions.

187 ♦ HISTORICAL ORIGINS AND DEVELOPMENT OF THE RENEWAL OF THE BAPTISMAL COVENANT

Baptism was understood as a pledge, vow, covenant, or contract early in the history of the Christian church. The very term sacrament *meant an oath in Roman culture. When children of Christian parents were baptized, whether as part of the households mentioned in the New Testament or as children born into families that had been Christian for generations, this pledge was made by the parents and baptismal sponsors. The sacrament of confirmation became separated from baptism in the West. When Protestant Reformers denied sacramental status to confirmation but retained it as catechetical device, it gradually developed into a ceremony by which, after instruction, adolescent children of Christian parents took ownership of the vows made for them at baptism.*

Early Baptism and Promises

Baptism, which represents God's gift in grace, represents also a believer's deep commitment, an act of faith. The sixteenth century theologian Richard Hooker said, "The solemnest vow that we ever made to obey Christ and to suffer willingly all reproaches for his sake was made in baptism" (*Ecclesiastical Polity*, 5. ixv.9). This baptismal commitment stays with a Christian throughout life. It may be a guiding factor all through a lifetime, but it may also be forgotten, or forgotten and later remembered. One of the functions of liturgy is to provide prompts for weak memories, bringing to mind the promises of baptism when one's inclination would be to disregard them, or providing occasions to reaffirm these promises at times of new beginnings in Christian life.

Vows at baptism may be traced to Jewish proselyte baptism, at which heavier and lighter commandments of the law were read during the action. Among the first-century Christians, there seemed to have been germinal statements of faith to which converts should hold fast—possibly "Jesus is Lord" in the Pauline churches and "Jesus was sent from the Father" in the Johannine community. It cannot be determined from the circumstantial New Testament accounts of baptism that such affirmations figured in the actual initiatory rites of the first-century church.

As early as the second-century, the church spoke of baptism as a vow or contract, suggesting that it contained some pledge on the part of the candidate. There is at least a suggestion of baptism as pledge in 1 Peter 3:21, although the language is allusive. The term *sacrament*, introduced by Tertullian, meant "military oath." In the first extant baptismal text (Hippolytus, *c.* 215 C.E.), at the point of the actual baptism, while the candidate is in the water, he or she is asked to renounce the devil and his works—a solemn turning from all previous religious loyalties. Then the three sections of the Apostles' Creed (in an early version) are asked: "Do you believe in God, the Father almighty?" At each reply of "I believe" the candidate is baptized. The Apostles' Creed was a piece of esoteric lore, known among Christians, but kept secret from the rest of the world. It would not have been said perfunctorily, but as an existential act of commitment. At a later time, the church used the brief formula of baptism, "[Name], I baptize you in the name of the Father, and of the Son, and of the Holy Spirit," at the baptismal action itself, and the creed was delivered some weeks prior to Easter, during the catechumenal preparation. This profession of the Apostle's Creed was sometimes referred to as an act of *adherence*—one's commitment to the enduring relation with Christ.

The Apostles' Creed, the central confession of the church, growing out of the apostolic preaching, was, as far as the evidence indicates, the only promise expressly made. Doubtless one's Christian faith and life involved other pledges and understandings—commitment to a disciplined life of worship and prayer, courage when called for, uprightness in one's obligations, faithfulness in marriage, and the like. Such commitments were, however, implicit—matters covered, no doubt, in the catechumenate and taken for granted at the baptism itself.

There is early evidence that the convert's children were baptized with their parents. Adults spoke for the children who were too young to speak for themselves. However, there is simply no information about the baptism of children born to Christian parents. Presumably they were baptized, and adults made the promises on their behalf, as was done for the children of converts. (There is no evidence whatever that the admission of the children of believers into full Christian membership was withheld until some later age of personal discretion.) The early sources describe the baptism of first-generation converts and say nothing of the baptism of the church's next generation.

In the early church, there was no formal occasion for the renewing of the promises once made in baptism. Yet every time one said the Apostle's Creed, or one was present, as at each Easter, when others were baptized, or, indeed, every time one received Holy Communion, one would (if one's imagination made the requisite connections) be renewed in the baptismal gift and be made aware of one's baptismal responsibilities.

In time, the bulk of the population became Christian—first in the Mediterranean basin and the Near East, later in Slavic regions and in Northern Europe. As it did, baptismal practice came to center, not on new converts from paganism, but on the children of Christian parents. Consequently, the church's educational efforts (sometimes more, sometimes less effective) shifted from catechesis before baptism to the Christian education of the baptized.

The Western Development of a Two-Stage Initiatory Rite

The New Testament describes baptism as a brief, compact water rite which holds significance beyond its apparent simplicity. From quite an early time, however, the baptismal action became more complex. It was preceded by a ritual enrolling; it took place against the church-wide observance of Easter; it was united with the receiving of Communion; and it was followed by additional actions, such as anointing or the signing with the cross (different in different regions), which separated it from the receiving of the sacramental bread and wine. Such actions are not mentioned in the New Testament (hence, they were rejected, often acrimoniously, by the sixteenth-century Protestant groups which sought to follow the Bible prescriptively). Yet, the New Testament interprets becoming a Christian by a rich body of imagery, such as coming from darkness to light, being anointed, receiving new clothing, or eating food for nourishment and delight. Did such Christian imagery develop from Jewish poetry and prophecy, followed by the rapid development of ritual actions? Or were there already in the first-century ritual actions correlative with the imagery? One could argue either way from the hints in such New Testament sources as 1 Peter or the Apocalypse.

Throughout the church in the early centuries (and in the East until the present), the entire rite of baptism—the water rite plus the postbaptismal anointing (*chrismation* in the East) leading to the Holy Communion—was observed for children, as it was for adults. Baptisms took place in a baptistery building near the bishop's church on the eve of Easter.

The early rite of Rome, and evidently only Rome, included two postbaptismal anointings: one was administered at the water, immediately after the baptism, by the minister of the water rite; the other followed directly, in the eucharistic room, performed by the bishop. This bishop's anointing was of the forehead and was accompanied by a prayer for the gifts of the Spirit.

With the rise of the system of dioceses and parishes, baptism came to be administered, in both the East and the West, a few days after the birth of a child, with the local priest officiating. This baptism was in all respects complete.

In the early medieval efforts to bring regularity to the Western church, the Roman model was put into the service books for most of Europe. A bishop's postbaptismal anointing came to be expected in places which had not known the practice. However, conditions such as large dioceses, difficult travel, and absentee bishops, made it impossible for the bishop's anointing to be administered punctually. The local minister baptized; the baptism was followed by an anointing and led to first Communion. The bishop's anointing very often had to be abandoned. When this second anointing could be done, it was usually administered some years after one had been baptized. Thus it came to be associated with the years of growing up, the receiving of some minimal learning, and the taking of some responsibility for oneself. The result of this largely accidental process was a divided, two-stage initiatory rite: The first part (baptism) was associated with infancy, and the second part (which came to be called *confirmation*) was associated with maturation. Saint Thomas said that baptism is to birth as confirmation is to growth. By disciplinary regulations no earlier than the late Middle Ages, this second part was made the proper pre-condition for receiving communion which, by then, even adults did only infrequently.

Even though meanings associated with individual competence were becoming attached to confirmation, the bishop's rite itself said nothing about coming of age nor about renewing the promises of one's baptism. The rite was understood as a performative sacramental anointing with the Spirit.

Confirmation and the Renewing of Promises

The Reformation inherited this two-stage pattern. Luther and Calvin accepted baptism as they had received it, but they both criticized confirmation, saying that it was without clear biblical warrant. Confirmation seemed to pretend to an importance beyond that of baptism; perhaps it was invented to give bishops something to do. Yet, they turned this ritual act in a direction suited to the genius of the Protestant movement. They saw this second stage of Christian initiation as an opportunity to raise the level of understanding in the faith community.

This new direction for confirmation had several sources: (1) The Bohemian Brethren (later known as the Moravians) had developed the idea that children who had been baptized as infants should be provided an occasion to own for themselves the promises that had been made for them by others at baptism. (2) The humanistic emphases of Erasmus created concern for education, and confirmation seemed like a ready-made rite requiring catechetical preparation. (3) The Reformation understanding of faith emphasized *explicit faith*—informed, rooted faith. Preparation for confirmation provided a way in which persons baptized as infants could be led to such faith. (4) Martin Bucer identified occasions in the Old Testament in which divine covenant was entered into, and then often violated, and, when violated, renewed. Confirmation seemed an act that could be interpreted as a renewal of the baptismal covenant.

From such sources, Protestant confirmation developed as a moment, prepared for by serious catechesis, when a person on whose behalf others had spoken at baptism could now speak for her or himself. The Roman and Anglican churches sustained the more sacramental rite from the medieval church, but early in the case of the Church of England and later in the case of the Roman Church, much of the sense of confirmation as a coming of age in the community of faith was added to the sacramental understandings.

Separated from baptism though it was, confirmation was taken to be initiatory. It was unrepeated, as baptism is unrepeated. It admitted one to the Holy Communion, as baptism itself did not. One became a Christian in full standing through this two-stage rite—leading to the widespread (and unfortunate) understanding of confirmation as "joining the church." The divided parts of initiation provided for birth and for coming of age. The life into which it brought one was to be sustained by the Word and by feeding at the Table of the Lord.

Modern Questions

In this century, a number of objections have arisen concerning this inherited pattern. (1) This two-stage rite has no real history except in the modern West. (2) To associate the Holy Spirit in a distinctive way with the second stage deprives baptism of its Trinitarian fullness. (3) Lack of understanding is not made a barrier to baptism, but it keeps one from participating in Holy Communion. Why are the two great sacraments of the gospel treated so differently? (4) If confirmation is meant to signify coming of age in the life of the church, what age adequately expresses that meaning? Adolescence and youth are so protracted in modern society that any age one chooses is too early to capture some of the adult meanings or too late to give sacramental support for childhood. (5) When the renewing of the baptismal promises is made a part of a second stage of Christian initiation, it is taken to be unrepeatable, as baptism is unrepeatable. Yet life stages which affect us inwardly begin prior to adolescence and continue long after it. If the substance of confirmation is the reaffirmation of vows, why can one make a solemn restatement of one's baptismal promises at one occasion in childhood, but not do so again at later points in life, when such an act might be more significant than it was at age twelve?

Such thinking recovered a position articulated by Luther, who had stressed the totality and unrepeatability of baptism, which he saw as an act by God, carrying the pledge that God is for us, now and always. Yet, he added, baptism remains uncreative unless it is remembered, claimed or drawn on. In his society, virtually everyone was baptized, yet "there are scarce any who call to mind their baptism and still fewer who glory in it" (*The Babylonian Captivity of the Church*). If one's baptism should be a vital part of one's awareness, the renewing of its promises at one moment of adolescence seems an inadequate pro-

vision for sustaining the glory of it.

In the life of Christ, one's baptismal starting place, although it is not repeated, is always accessible to one. One does not grow beyond it, but is always growing into it. One's baptism is to be claimed, reaffirmed, remembered. The promises of baptism, whenever they were made and under whatever circumstances, are always capable of being repossessed and restated in connection with new situations. Having been said once as the human part of the baptismal covenant, they may be said again; they are indefinitely repeatable.

Daniel B. Stevick

188 • A THEOLOGY FOR THE RENEWAL OF THE BAPTISMAL COVENANT

The separation of confirmation from baptism in the West has left an enduring legacy of unease among paedobaptist Christian theologians. If baptism is indeed the full and complete rite of initiation into the church, what is the role of confirmation, whether as a sacrament (Roman Catholic) or a catechetical and social rite of passage (Anglican, Lutheran, Reformed)? Is a baptized but unconfirmed child not really a full member of the church? Adult-baptizing churches maintain baptism's full initiatory status by reserving baptism until children are old enough to make their own commitments, but this still leaves the unbaptized children somehow both inside yet outside the church (see chapter 4). In infant-baptizing traditions, one way of dealing with the problem is to treat confirmation and other occasions in later life simply as renewals of baptism. In this way, baptism itself retains its significance as full, complete entry into the church while asserting that its promises are capable of being renewed after the child reaches the age of discretion.

After some decades of exploring pastoral and theological questions and seeking to understand the ritual inheritance, several churches have developed a new, but historically rooted pattern: Pastoral occasions for the renewal of the promises of baptism are provided in recently revised service books of the Lutheran, Episcopalian, Presbyterian, and Methodist churches (perhaps in others as well), and some thinking in the Roman Catholic church takes a similar direction.

One conviction that informs these new rites is that nothing should qualify the completeness of baptism. Baptism is not partial admission into Christ and his people. One is not *merely baptized.* A single-stage rite represents the christological wholeness of baptism. Such renewing of the promises of baptism as one may do subsequent to baptism itself is not initiatory, but is a voluntary action by a competent Christian person. (Following from this principle, several churches, in their recent baptismal rites, have, for the first time, associated with the baptismal action explicatory prayers and gestures signifying the Holy Spirit. Fullness of meaning is carried forth by fullness of sign.)

It might be noted that churches of the believer's baptism tradition, although they do not, of course, have a rite of confirmation to complement infant baptism, may, without compromising their distinctive understanding of baptism, find congenial a formal, repeatable act of renewing baptismal promises. The experience of Christians within the baptized life is much the same in all communions, and it may well be supported by similar pastoral measures.

Some occasions of renewing one's baptismal vows belonge to the ordered life of communal worship:

IHS Symbol—Simple Form. Another form of the ancient IHS abbreviation that represents Jesus' name.

Baptism is closely linked with the Holy Communion; what is begun in baptism (birth) is sustained in the Eucharist (feeding). Thus, every partaking in the eucharistic bread and wine may be thought of as a renewing of baptism.

As one is present at the baptism of someone else and takes part in the corporate statement of the baptismal promises, one's own promises are renewed.

The baptismal promises may be restated by a congregation at times, such as the Easter Vigil, even if there are no actual baptisms.

Every time one says the Apostles' Creed, one is put in touch with the baptismal covenant.

In addition to such occasions which belong to the structured, more or less schedulable life of the community, the renewing of the promises of baptism may be called forth by events in the unique biography in faith of any Christian.

Several churches list three occasions for renewing the baptismal promises: confirmation, reception, and reaffirmation.

(1) *Confirmation* is understood as the first occasion on which someone who was baptized at a young age makes a public avowal of Christian faith. Important things happen deep in the religious awareness of young people. Persons differ, and social situations vary. Yet the prolonged crisis of growing up and coming into adulthood in today's society has, for members of the faith community, a spiritual aspect, often intense and life-shaping. The church should help persons understand what is happening in the light of the will of God—help them find a vocabulary. It should welcome moments of new religious awareness and self-dedication and provide ways in which such moments can be interpreted and celebrated. Confirmation can serve such a pastoral function. A new stirring in a Christian believer's conscious in relation with God is referred to the fundamental starting point of that relation: baptism. One's present stands in creative bonding with one's past—a defining past even in which God has pledged to be forever faithful.

(2) *Reception* refers to the occasions (frequent in a mobile, individualistic society) on which persons who have been affiliated with one Christian communion seek, as baptized adults, to identify with another—carrying out the commitments of baptism in a new community of faith. Such per-

sons are welcomed through joining, not in something specific to the new denomination, but through reaffirming, in a new and chosen society of believers, the common Christian promises. These promises provide a mark of recognition and continuity in an occasion of some personal discontinuity.

It is important to note that even though the service books use three terms, the persons in all three categories are doing the same thing—renewing the covenant of baptism.

(3) Thus the third category, *reaffirmation*, may bring to expression occasions which do not fit the relatively defined terms *confirmation* and *reception*. Much experience of Christian life in the modern age is troubled and discontinuous. Alternative periods of commitment and disengagement, ecstasy and dullness may alternate with one another; periods of active life in the church may be followed by disillusion and dropping out, and then return. The renewing of the fundamental promises of baptism may be used to mark a person's restoration after a period of lapse. Such an occasion should not be carried out in such a way as to seem penitential. Whatever regret and struggle may have preceded it, the public event should be joyful and welcoming.

Christian experience is marked not only by times of return, but by times of discovery, rededication, and fresh beginnings, in one's spiritual life. These can be recognized in the life of a church by assisting persons to touch, at moments of newness, their basic starting place, baptism. Most churches which have entered this pastoral/liturgical opportunity in their recent service books have not been very prescriptive about how it is to be used, leaving the matter up to congregational experience and pastoral imagination. The Presbyterian church, however, has listed persons for which such a rite would be suitable: persons making public profession of faith, persons who have been estranged from the church, a congregation making a corporate act of renewal, the sick and the dying, those engaged in pastoral counseling, and those being received as members by transfer. Such a list should not seem complete and limiting, but rather suggestive of the possibilities that one communion sees in the public renewal of the promises of baptism.

Daniel B. Stevick

189 ✦ A Liturgy for the Renewal of the Baptismal Covenant

The following service invites worshipers to recall their own baptism, to renew their promises of faith to God, and to hear again God's promises and provisions for them as his people. The text is based on a service in Holy Baptism and Services for the Renewal of Baptism *formulated by the Office of Worship for the Presbyterian Church (U.S.A.) and the Cumberland Presbyterian Church. It is similar to texts used in several Protestant denominations.*

Renewal of Baptism for _____ a Congregation

SENTENCES FROM SCRIPTURE

It is appropriate that this service be led by the minister from the baptismal font or pool, which should be filled with water.

After the sermon has been preached, the Minister, using one or more of the following Scriptures, says:
Hear these words from Holy Scripture:
Know therefore that the Lord your God is God,
the faithful God who keeps covenant and steadfast love
with those who love God
and keep God's commandments. (Deuteronomy 7:9)

God has showed you what is good;
and what does the Lord require of you
but to do justice, and to love kindness,
and to walk humbly with your God? (Micah 6:8)

Once you were darkness,
but now you are light in the Lord;
walk as children of light . . .
and try to learn what is pleasing to the Lord.
   (Ephesians 5:8, 10)

The congregation stands, as the minister continues:
Sisters and brothers in Christ,
our baptism is the sign and seal
of our cleansing from sin,
and of our being grafted into Christ.
Through the birth, life, death, and resurrection of Christ,
the power of sin was broken
and God's kingdom entered our world.

Through our baptism we were made citizens of
  that kingdom,
and freed from the bondage of sin.
Let us celebrate that freedom and redemption
through the renewal of our baptism.

RENUNCIATION AND AFFIRMATION

I ask you, therefore,
once again to reject sin,
to profess your faith in Christ Jesus,
and to confess the faith of the church,
the faith in which we were baptized.

Do you renounce evil,
and its power in the world,
which defies God's righteousness and love?
I renounce them.

Do you renounce the ways of sin
that separate you from the love of God?
I renounce them.

Do you turn to Jesus Christ
and accept him as your Lord and Savior?
I do.

Do you intend to be Christ's faithful disciple,
obeying his word, and showing his love,
to your life's end?
I do.

With the whole church,
let us confess our faith.

The congregation affirms the faith in the words
  of the Apostles' Creed:

I believe in God, the Father almighty,
    creator of heaven and earth.
I believe in Jesus Christ, his only Son, our Lord.
    He was conceived by the power of the Holy
      Spirit
      and born of the Virgin Mary.
    He suffered under Pontius Pilate,
      was crucified, died, and was buried.
    He descended to the dead.
    On the third day he rose again.
    He ascended into heaven,
      and is seated at the right hand of the
        Father.
    He will come again to judge the living and
      the dead.
I believe in the Holy Spirit,
    the holy catholic church,

    the communion of saints,
    the forgiveness of sins,
    the resurrection of the body,
    and the life everlasting. Amen.

The minister leads the people in prayer, saying:

Let us pray.
God of life and goodness.
we praise you for claiming us through our baptism
and for upholding us by your grace.
We remember your promises given to us in our
    baptism.
Strengthen us by your Spirit,
that we may obey your will
and serve you with joy;
through Jesus Christ our Lord.
Amen.

The minister may place his or her hand into the
water of the font, lift up some water, let it fall back
into the font, and then make the sign of the cross
over the people, while saying:

Remember your baptism and be thankful.
In the name of the Father and of the Son and of
the Holy Spirit.
Amen.

The minister may invite persons who wish to receive the laying on of hands to come and kneel at
the font. The sign of the cross may be traced upon
the forehead of each person and may include the
anointing with oil. Laying both hands upon the
head of each person in turn, the minster says:

O Lord, uphold [Name] by your Holy Spirit.
Daily increase [him, her] your gifts of grace:
the spirit of wisdom and understanding,
the spirit of counsel and might,
the spirit of knowledge and the fear of the Lord,
the spirit of joy in your presence,
both now and forever.

The candidate answers:
Amen.

or

Defend, O Lord, your servant [Name]
with your heavenly grace,
that [he, she] may continue yours forever,
and daily increase in your Holy Spirit more and
    more,
until [he, she] comes to your everlasting kingdom.

The Candidate answers:
Amen.

The service concludes with the exchange of peace:

Minister: The peace of Christ be with you.
And also with you.

A celebration of the Lord's Supper may follow.

Commentary

Recent liturgical reforms and theological writings have emphasized the importance of a Christian piety shaped by our baptism. Christians need always to bear in mind their basic commitment of allegiance to Christ and God's fundamental saving act in Christ. There is no more powerful symbol of these truths than Christian baptism. Thus, many churches have used liturgical texts similar to the one printed here as a powerful means of recalling the images of baptism.

This practice is often used in conjunction with important pastoral moments: when a new member is welcomed into the church or when an estranged member is welcomed back; when a member of the congregation makes a renewed commitment of faith or pledge of Christian service; or when a member is facing illness, death, or another personal crisis.

This practice is also an important part of services of the Christian year, especially Easter Vigil and Pentecost. These services highlight themes integral to the nature and meaning of baptism, including our dying and rising with Christ in our baptism and our baptism into the Holy Spirit. This liturgy of renewal of baptism allows the congregation to claim their participation in the benefits of Christ's resurrection and the coming of the Holy Spirit.

This service in no way intends to repeat what happened at baptism. Baptism is not something that can be undone or lost. Nor does the service intend to minimize the importance of baptism, by repeating its images at even more occasions within the congregation's life. Worship leaders should exercise care in the planning of such renewal services so that they are always perceived as an act which recalls one's own baptism and appropriates its reality for the present. Thus, the service tends to magnify the importance of the first baptism, not to lessen it.

Suggestions for Appropriation

Worship leaders should inform the congregation well in advance of occasions for the renewal of baptism vows. Appropriate scriptural texts may be recommended for personal devotional use prior to the service. Romans 6:1-5 may be recommended as one such passage for an Easter baptismal renewal.

This service may be accompanied by any of the many baptismal hymns included in recently published hymnals. Easter hymns may also be used whenever the renewal is observed.

The congregation may speak the three sections of the Apostle's Creed as a response to a question from the worship leader, "What do you believe concerning the Father (and the Son, and the Holy Spirit, respectively)?" This recalls ancient practice at baptismal services (see the liturgy by Hippolytus in this series).

Commentary by John D. Witvliet

190 • GUIDELINES FOR PLANNING A SERVICE OF THE RENEWAL OF THE BAPTISMAL COVENANT

Planning for the renewal of baptism must be undertaken with the need of the local worshiping community in mind. This article reflects on this service of renewal and proposes guidelines for the worship planning process.

Participants and Setting

In most churches, the guiding of the act of the renewal and the voicing of the surrounding prayers will be in the hands of local clergy—the same person who has been pastor and counselor will be celebrant. (The Episcopal church reserves this presiding role at occasions of individual renewing of baptismal promises for the bishop.)

The churches which are introducing this action commend the use of sponsors, who personalize the support of the congregation.

Clearly, this act should be observed at a service where the congregation can give its welcome and pledge its continuing care. Whatever depths of unshared individual experience it may touch, the serious public reaffirmation of the common promises touches also the uniting, originating bonds in the shared life of a community of faith.

It would seem advisable to correlate the occasions for such acts of public reaffirmation with high moments of the church year. By locating them so they would take some of their meaning from the christological structure of the church's ritual shaping of time—a factor which might keep them from being seen in merely biographical or psychological contexts. In most instances, correlation with the festivals and seasons of the Year of Grace would locate these actions on a Sunday morning service of Word and sacrament.

The Actual Promises

The reaffirmation is meant to tie one's present to one's deep past. The promises should be those of the baptism rite, probably without any addition or deletion. These promises must be basic, economically worded, and long-wearing. As the common, church-making promises, they should be said by the entire congregation, even though the reason for saying them may grow out of one person's specific experience. The persons who are making particular reaffirmation say the promises with their fellow Christians; the congregation says them with ones for whom the act has special and to some extent unshared significance. All are put in touch with their baptism and its pledges.

There will usually be serious, soul-searching events behind the public reaffirmation. Sometimes such circumstances and struggles will be widely known in the congregation; at other times, they will be quite private. It would seem best to observe a public reticence concerning what brings each person to this moment in Christian experience. If the liturgical leader becomes chatty, or if the person making reaffirmation makes a speech in those cases in which personal revelation may be justified, it may call attention to those other cases in which too much said may be unwise at best or damaging at worst. Objectivity suits the occasion.

The promises should include the Apostles' Creed, the form consented to by each Christian at baptism from the earliest generations of the church. The Apostles' Creed is an account of God and of divine redemption and promise, based on the apostolic preaching. In many churches in recent years, the creed has been joined, at baptism, with a few elemental pledges on the part of each Christian. If such promises to faithfulness in Christian duties are capable of being said by a diversified congregation, in a variety of situations, over a period of years, they must be basic in content and carefully worded. An idiosyncratic, preachy, overstated body of words will not wear well. Persons differ as to how articulate they are. Some sincere Christians who seek to restate the commitments of their baptism may be quite halting, especially in public. Rather than put them in an awkward position, it would seem best to keep the promises in dialogical form: the presiding person asking "Do you believe. . . ?"; Will you. . . ?"; and the person reaffirming replying "I do" or "I will." Lest the exchange seem bathed in unreality, the promiser's words should probably include a simple recognition of human weakness and of the difficulty of Christian obedience in our time. Words to the effect of "I will . . . God helping me" would be suitable.

Daniel B. Stevick

191 ✦ BIBLIOGRAPHY ON THE RENEWAL OF THE BAPTISMAL COVENANT

The Book of Common Worship. Louisville: Westminster/John Knox, 1993. Refer to pages 431–490 for the Presbyterian baptismal rite.

Book of Occasional Services. New York: Church Hymnal Corp, 1988. Refer to pages 132–134 for the Episcopal baptismal liturgical rite.

Buchanan, Colin O. "The Renewal of Baptismal Vows." _Studia Liturgica_ 17 (1987): 47–51; and _The Renewal of Baptismal Vows._ Nottingham, U.K.: Grove Books, 1993. Refer to these work for a general description of baptismal renewal vows.

Holy Baptism and Services for the Renewal of Baptism: Supplemental Resources. Philadelphia: Westminster, 1985. Refer to Presbyterian baptismal renewal rite.

Occasional Services. Minneapolis, Augsburg, and Philadelphia: Board of Publication Lutheran Church in America, 1978. Refer to pages 23–26 for the Lutheran baptismal renewal rite.

The United Methodist Book of Worship. Nashville: United Methodist Publishing House, 1992. Refer to pages 111–114 for the Methodist baptismal renewal rite.

PART FOUR

The Lord's Supper

One of the most profound events in the life of Jesus was the supper he shared with his disciples on the eve of his death. At that supper, Jesus commanded his disciples to share this meal until he comes again. For centuries the church has followed this command, sharing the Supper of the Lord, eating the bread and drinking the cup as a witness to the death and resurrection of Jesus. No sacred action has been as significant for the life of the church as the Lord's Supper. Every worship tradition has developed theologies and liturgies for the Lord's Supper—attesting to the rich diversity in the church. Our own century has witnessed a convergence of the theology and practice of the Lord's Supper—attesting to the essential unity of the church. The following chapters outline the history, theology, and practice of the Lord's Supper.

✍ NINE ✍

History of the Lord's Supper

Developed from Jewish models, the liturgical form of the Christian Eucharist was well established in the earliest centuries. Although embellishments took place in the fourth century, a remarkable continuity with earlier practices is visible. The liturgies of the major Eastern cities replaced local liturgies in the East beginning in the fourth century, while in the West the liturgy of Rome dominated much later (in the ninth century and following).

In the early church, eucharistic theology developed against the background of controversies over the Trinity, Christ's human and divine natures, and the goodness of creation. In the Middle Ages, controversies over the exact nature of Christ's presence in the elements of bread and wine emerged, leading to the scholastic doctrine of transubstantiation in the thirteenth century. Eucharistic devotion flourished during the late Middle Ages.

Decrying what they perceived as abuses, Protestant Reformers themselves split over the nature of Christ's presence in the elements of bread and wine: Luther insisted on the real, corporeal presence of Christ; Zwingli and others insisted on the mere recalling of Christ's sacrifice in the human mind and heart (memorialism). Calvin occupied the middle ground with his doctrine of Christ's spiritual presence. In response, the Roman Catholic Council of Trent (1545–1563) reaffirmed transubstantiation and the sacrificial nature of the Eucharist. These doctrines continue to flourish in Western churches today.

A variety of eucharistic liturgies are employed by Christians in the Eastern churches. These groups tend to follow regional traditions (Syrian, Byzantine, Armenian, Alexandrian) rather than doctrinal lines.

---

192 ◆ THE LORD'S SUPPER IN THE EARLY CHURCH

The early church established the patterns for the theology and practice of the Lord's Supper that have largely been recovered in our century. Many of the recent developments in the renewal of worship can be understood by examining the early history of the Lord's Supper.

Although Christian eucharistic practice was clearly well established during the first three centuries, written documentation is sparse since liturgical patterns were taught orally and were written down only when circumstances required. The Christian Eucharist developed from the Jewish prayer of blessing (*berakah*). As the love feast (*agape* fellowship meal) became separated from the Eucharist of bread and wine, elements of the

Last Supper tradition were absorbed into the eucharistic prayer.

A wider variety of written sources survive from the period after the persecution which ended early in the fourth century. In West Syria (Antioch), Egypt, and East Syria (Edessa), the eucharistic liturgy was embellished as standardized forms emerged in the great central cities replacing a wide variety of local liturgies. In the Latin West, several regional liturgies survived until the Roman practice was made standard in the Carolingian empire (ninth century).

The central concern of eucharistic theology during this era was not the question of when and how the bread and wine became the body and blood of Christ (a ninth-century controversy) or whether the Eucharist repeated Christ's sacrifice on Calvary (a controversy of the eleventh century onward). Instead, the theology of the eucharistic action was employed to argue for the goodness of physical creation; the role of that creation in redemption through Christ's incarnation, death, and resurrection; and the possibility for Christians to participate in the new life initiated by God in the covenant sacrifice of Christ.

As Christianity penetrated the elite circles of the late Roman empire, the setting for the Eucharist also changed. Yet, although grand basilicas replaced the house churches of the period of persecution, the most striking characteristic of the first five centuries is precisely the degree of continuity preserved amid accommodation to changing circumstances.

The Ancient Church

No study of the Lord's Supper in the ancient church can fail to note how central the Eucharist is in the surviving evidence of the earliest stages of the Christian movement. Even where not explicitly stated, Christian communities understood that their life as a new people of God was confirmed and effected in the meals held on the Lord's Day. At these meals, the "taking, blessing, breaking, and giving" of bread and wine was a memorial action by which those baptized into the death and resurrection of Christ were sustained by their weekly eucharistic participation in his body and blood through the action of the Spirit (1 Cor. 11:17ff.; 12:12ff.). Here one clearly sees the inheritance from Israel, whose Passover and Sabbath meals, with the synagogue meetings, sustained the life of the people and told the story of Israel's origin and purpose. In the case of the Christians, however, membership in the *ekklesia,* the community of those "called forth," was not by blood, but by faith in the God whose new covenant in the death of the Messiah, Jesus, was memorialized in the eucharistic action.

The present article focuses on the fourth century. By the early fourth century, the essential shape of the Christian Eucharist had already been established with remarkable consistency. The actual meal, the original setting for the "taking, blessing, breaking, and giving" described in Paul's first letter to the Corinthians and in the Didache (*c.* 100–150), survived in the noneucharistic *love feast* (the agape meal). The evening love feast was no longer associated with the Eucharist in places where the Lord's Day was assumed to begin at sunrise (Gentile practice), rather than at sunset of the day before (Jewish practice). Moreover, in circumstances of active persecution, elaborate meal preparations may have carried some risk.

With the separation of the evening love feast from the Eucharist, the prayers of blessing over the bread and wine were conflated into a single eucharistic prayer—now actually including the Last Supper tradition, the *words of institution* ("the Lord Jesus on the night he was betrayed . . ."), as found in the Apostolic Tradition of Hippolytus (*c.* 215). Moreover, after some disagreement about the relationship between the Jewish Passover and the Christian paschal feast (Easter), it became customary to celebrate a Lord's Day as the Christian Passover after the date of the Jewish Passover and to make this the principal occasion on which catechumens were baptized and admitted to the eucharistic fellowship (as in Justin Martyr, *First Apology* [*c.* 160]; see chapter 62 and following). This gave a striking definition to the Lord's Day observance throughout the year. The normal Lord's Day Eucharist was prefaced with a simple order of Scripture readings, preaching, and prayer adapted from the synagogue service. All of this was intended to reiterate and instill the history of salvation, for the church was called to be a part of that history.

The rite shaped in this way was still commonly called *eucharistia,* the Greek equivalent of the Hebrew *berakah* (the blessing prayer). Latin Christians used this word in transliterated form, as they did in the case of other words with special Christian significance. However, they also referred to it in theological writings as the *coena dominicalis* (the Lord's Supper), and later, more popularly, as *missa* (Mass), perhaps because it followed the formal *dismissal* of the catechumens. In the course of our period, Greek Christians came to call it *leitourgia* (work of the people) because it was the public work of the people of God.

It is tempting to think that the cessation of the persecutions at the beginning of the fourth century and the eventual recognition of Christianity as the official religion of the imperial Roman government by the successors of Constantine worked a wholesale change in the liturgical life of the churches. Certainly accommodation to the new circumstances of freedom, even popularity, is found in liturgical developments. Yet the effort to maintain continuity with what had gone before is even more striking. This article will address the complex phenomenon of accommodation to the new context and continuity with old patterns.

Fourth-Century Sources

To understand early Christian liturgy, one must remember that, like its Jewish and pagan counterparts, it was a formal oral phenomenon. The liturgy was not written down in prayer books, sacramentaries, or missals. But neither was it extemporaneous in the modern sense. Worshipers had to follow the established order, contents, and even the specific language of the liturgy (doubtless with local, even personal modifications) precisely because it was not written down. Like a play without a written script, the words and actions of the principal actors had to be learned well by the entire cast so that all could take their appropriate parts. The sources for our knowledge of these first three centuries (e.g., Justin Martyr, Hippolytus) were the occasional written descriptions of what was said and done.

The vastly enlarged body of sources from the fourth and following centuries are of this same sort. In the new circumstances of the time, it was increasingly important to set down what had been or ought to be said and done. These burgeoning sources record materials not hitherto committed to writing. They also suggest how that material could be adapted to the new situation.

Antioch and Egypt. Two such sources reflect the situation in the church of Antioch, the Syrian capital, and in the Egyptian churches as they struggled to find unity in relation to the church of Alexandria, the capital of Egypt. At Antioch, in the latter decades of the fourth century, the Apostolic Constitutions set down practices common to that area (including a revision of earlier written sources such as the Didache, and Hippolytus' Apostolic Tradition). They also describe the Eucharist of the Antiochene church itself. Here we find an enlarged service of Scripture reading, preaching, and prayer, as well as an elaborated eucharistic "taking, blessing, breaking, and giving" of the bread and wine. The latter includes a rich and lengthy eucharistic prayer (_anaphora_) drawn on the model of Hippolytus' prayer with its unified order—the blessing for the work of redemption in Christ; the Last Supper tradition; and the invocation of the Spirit upon the bread and wine. From

the enlarged role of deacons, who function as assistants to the bishop, one can conclude that an extensive congregation now gathered in space much more extensive than in the house churches of earlier centuries. Yet the simple structure of the rite shows great restraint in preserving the basic practices of the past.

While the Alexandrian Liturgy of St. Mark is known to us only in much later form, the early fourth-century Euchologion (prayer collection) of Bishop Serapion of Thmuis provides an invaluable link between that later rite and earlier Egyptian liturgical fragments. Serapion's eucharistic prayer itself is of a different structure from that of Hippolytus, with various prayers of blessing from early Jewish models roughly united around separate invocations of the Spirit on the congregation and on the bread and wine before and after the recital of the Last Supper tradition. Other prayers in Serapion's collection are designed for use in what seems to be an extensive prefatory service of Scripture reading, preaching, and prayer. This illustrates once again the dual concern for continuity and accommodation to new circumstances.

East Syria. Recent studies have given us access to the history of the eucharistic prayer of Mari and Addai, attributed as the traditional founders of the East Syrian Christian center of Edessa. In its reconstructed fourth-century form, the eucharistic prayer of Mari and Addai seems to have been used in a eucharistic rite not unlike that common at Antioch and elsewhere at this time. But its internal structure and language suggest very early Jewish Christian origins so that it stands with the Didache and the precursors of Serapion's Euchologion as witnesses to the primitive character of eucharistic blessing prayers. In a process associated with the name of the Antiochene John Chrysostom, bishop of Constantinople (398–407), the Antiochene rite was adopted by the church of the imperial capital, Constantinople. Thus the eucharistic prayer of Mari and Addai remained in use only in the churches east of Syria, many of which later became Nestorian.

The West. In contrast to the Eastern tendency to reorganize earlier eucharistic practices under the auspices of major Christian centers, in the West (Gaul and Spain, northwest Africa, Rome and other parts of Italy) one glimpses continued local diversity. From northwest Africa, indeed, there are no descriptive liturgical sources. One is dependent on allusions such as those found in the homilies of Augustine of Hippo to reconstruct these liturgies. They indicate that the Latin language rites of the area preserved the shape of those in use in the third century, with few embellishments. Our knowledge of the quite different Gallican and Mozarabic rites of Gaul and Spain comes from liturgical books of a much later date (e.g., the Missale Gothicum and the Bobbio Missal). They are marked by ceremonial embellishments, which may show contact with Eastern developments of the period, and by considerable seasonal variation in their rich, even florid, Latin prayer forms. These eucharistic rites are interesting because they reflect the practices of Western Europe before the promotion of the Roman rite by the emperor Charlemagne at the end of the eighth century.

The Eucharist of the church of Rome in this period presents a variety of puzzles. While the third-century Roman liturgical practices that are reflected in Hippolytus generally remain in evidence, the fourth-century replacement of Greek by Latin as the liturgical language of the Roman church apparently coincided with innovation in liturgical practice. The Roman books associated with the name of Gregory the Great (d. 604) that Charlemagne acquired still showed restraint and simplicity in comparison to the rites of Gaul and Spain. However, certain embellishments from Eastern sources are apparent: the singing of *Kyrie eleison* and *Gloria in excelsis* as an entrance rite; and the brief but elegant *collecta* (gathering prayers), attributed to Leo the Great (d. 461), to introduce the Scripture reading and preaching. But the novel feature of the Eucharist itself is the invariable eucharistic prayer (canon). Our earliest evidence for it may consist in allusions to it found in the De Sacramentis of Ambrose of Milan (d. 397). This prayer, or unified collection of prayers, has been thought to bear resemblance to that of Serapion, but has no explicit invocation of the Spirit on the bread and wine either before or after the recital of the Last Supper tradition. This unusual prayer, which came to be called the *Gregorian Canon of the Mass* (also known as the Roman Canon), supplanted the comparable Gallican prayers from the Carolingian era onward. This Gregorian Canon became the standard by which later medieval and Reformation theologians sought to interpret the meaning of the eucharistic action.

Catechetical and Homiletic Sources. Given the paucity of our evidence from actual liturgical descriptions, the wealth of homiletic and catechetical material from the fourth and later centuries is of particular importance for the study of eucharistic thought and practice. Especially worth notice are the mystagogical catecheses, in which those who had been baptized and had received Communion for the first time at the Paschal feast (Easter Vigil) were subsequently instructed in the Eucharist. Of these, those attributed to Cyril of Jerusalem (d. 386), Ambrose of Milan, and John Chrysostom are the most rewarding. But the whole body of this material is invaluable. It reflects the new circumstances in which public instruction was both possible and necessary.

Theology

Dispute regarding the Eucharist was a hallmark of the Reformation era, with all sides appealing to the ancient church on behalf of views for or against the sacrificial character of the rite, the status of the bread and wine as the body and blood of Christ, and so on. It is thus important to notice that quite different considerations occupied the attention of the early Christians—even where their writings seem to address topics that later became controversial. Chief among the considerations at the time was a desire to explain the eucharistic action simply as the means of participation in the new life initiated by God in the covenant sacrifice of Christ. For instance, Justin Martyr and others, developing themes already suggested in the New Testament letter to the Hebrews, argued, against Jewish exegetes, that the offering of the bread and wine was the true sacrifice prophesied in Malachi 1:10-12 and that this offering was sufficient because of the one sacrifice of Christ memorialized in the eucharistic action. Similarly, Irenaeus (fl. c. 180), arguing against Gnostic denials of the goodness of the physical creation, insisted that the prescribed use of bread and wine in the Eucharist (like that of water in baptism) proves the goodness and utility of the physical creation in the redemptive plan of God for the salvation of both body and soul. Even Origen (d. 253), for all his commitment to a Platonic concern for the spiritual character of the relation of the soul to Christ, develops his analysis of a spiritual eating and drinking as the inner meaning of the physical action which he assumes to be part of the Christian life.

The same way of eliciting the implications of the eucharistic action is evident in the theologians of the fourth and following centuries. In the East, where the Arian, or Trinitarian, controversy broke out, such theologians as Athanasius (d. 373) and Basil the Great (d. 379) emphasized the single operation of Father, Son, and Spirit in both the eucharistic and baptismal actions. This emphasis influenced the adjustment of the eucharistic anaphora to refer equally to the work of all three persons of the Godhead and led in particular to the stress laid on the invocation (epiklesis) of the Spirit as affecting the making of the bread and wine into vehicles of communion with Christ. In the West, Ambrose of Milan's remarks to the newly baptized about the bread and wine becoming the body and blood of Christ by the "word of prayer" (presumably referring to the repetition of the Last Supper tradition), were later contrasted with Augustine's dramatic description, also for recently baptized, of the bread and wine now seen by them upon the holy Table for the first time as becoming spiritually, or symbolically, the body and blood of Christ. But even if—and it is highly improbable—Augustine thought he was saying something different from Ambrose, their fundamental interest is in the reality of participation in the body and blood of Christ in the Eucharist, rather than the transformation of the bread and wine.

Only later, beginning with the revival of theological interest in the Carolingian era (ninth century), did Western attention shift to questions about the transformation of the bread and wine. Later still, under the influence of the expiatory view of the sacrifice of Christ associated with the name of Anselm of Canterbury (d. 1109), controversy centered on whether the sacrifice of Calvary was repeated in the eucharistic action.

Physical Setting

Much can be learned about the eucharistic celebrations of the fourth and later centuries from the physical evidence of the surviving buildings and from pictorial representations of what went on in them. While domestic houses remodeled for liturgical use (the *house churches*) continued in use, Christians began to construct eucharistic *aulae* (*halls*)—later called *basilicas* by Renaissance scholars, who noted their similarity to law courts.

Often of considerable size and elegance themselves, these halls were commonly part of larger complexes, which included baptisteries and related structures. Approached through an atrium, or courtyard, and thus separated from surrounding streets, the entire complex retained something of the domestic character of the house churches and embodied the ekklesia's sense of separation from the general society. Similarly, while the furnishings of these buildings could be grand, with raised podiums for the reading of the Scriptures and with columns with a canopy (*ciborium*) setting off the small tables (*mensae*) or altars, the officiants wore no distinctive vestments. Furthermore, the congregations continued to stand with them, holding up their hands in prayer (*orantes*) at the time of the eucharistic prayer. Pews and kneeling benches were unknown.

Once again, both accommodation and continuity are visible. While a new grandeur often attended the setting of the eucharistic action, the "taking, blessing, breaking, and giving" were done with deliberate simplicity, recalling the earlier centuries and distinguishing Christian rites from those of classical paganism.

Much is omitted here, including not only the variety of eucharistic rites and their settings, but also the problems arising from Christianity becoming popular. Among these problems is the failure of the baptized to receive Communion with the regularity expected by their bishops. Yet, the striking feature of the period is the conscious and unconscious concern to continue setting forth the eucharistic memorial with integrity amid changed circumstances.

Lloyd G. Patterson

193 • The Lord's Supper in the Medieval West and the Modern Roman Catholic Church

Both the texts of the various prayers and directions for eucharistic practice survive from about the seventh century onward. The early Middle Ages was characterized by growing awe surrounding the sacrificial presence of Christ at the eucharistic altar. Controversies over the exact nature of Christ's presence in the elements of bread and wine broke out during the ninth century, with the spiritualized interpretation of Ratramnus of Corbie, being rejected in favor of the insistence on Christ's physical presence by Pascasius Radbertus. As scholastic theology developed in the medieval universities, the theology of transubstantiation emerged. Transubstantiation states that the substance of the bread and wine is changed into Christ's body and blood, but the perceptible accidents of bread and wine remain unchanged.

Transubstantiation is often misunderstood. It does not teach a crude physical presence of Christ in the eucharistic elements. Aristotelian philosophy—used by the scholastic theologians—often is at the root of this confusion. Aristotle classified things into three different categories: substance, accidents, and matter. Scholastic theologians used Aristotelian categories to explain the doctrine of transubstantiation. Thus, the physical material of the bread and wine is not changed into Christ's body and blood. Instead, the substance (i.e., the reality, the essence) of bread ceases to be the reality of bread and becomes the reality of Christ. In the context of the doctrine of transubstantiation, one might best refer to a sacramental presence *of Christ, rather than a physical or carnal presence of Christ in the Eucharist. In response to Lutheran and Zwinglian understandings of Christ's presence in the Eucharist, the Council of Trent reaffirmed the sacrificial character of the Mass and the theology of transubstantiation.*

Historical studies and renewed efforts to explain the nature of sacramental grace have led to changes in Roman Catholic eucharistic theology and liturgy since the Second Vatican Council. The Roman Catholic liturgical renewal of the nineteenth and twentieth centuries is one element contributing to sacramental and liturgical renewal in some Protestant denominations.

While the origins of a specifically Western or Latin liturgical tradition are difficult to trace, at least from the third century those trends which are later clearly identified with Western practice can be detected. Both Tertullian (*c.* 160–220) and Cyprian of Carthage (d. 258) seem to be speaking of a Latin liturgy when writing about the Eucharist. But these early rites and practices display a great deal of diversity even though the Apostolic Tradition of Hippolytus (*c.* 215), for example, argues for the primacy of Roman eucharistic traditions. For a long time it was supposed that all Western rites had a common source in Rome and

spread from there to outlying areas in a systematic way as pagan peoples were converted to Christianity. More recently, however, scholars have come to see that the lines of liturgical influence are more complex. Important ritual developments clearly took place in other Christian centers and were subsequently returned to Rome to influence eucharistic practice there. In any case, neat distinctions between West and East, Roman and non-Roman, are difficult to make in this early period of liturgical development.

Eucharistic Documents

We can be slightly more certain about Western eucharistic practice in the sixth to seventh centuries, since some documentary sources for this period exist. Early evidence for the beginnings of Western eucharistic practice is found in liturgical books containing the various prayers used by presiders. Several of these collections, known as sacramentaries, have survived. Generally their contents follow the course of the church year, providing texts for each celebration in the calendar. Although the earliest such manuscript (the so-called Leonine Sacramentary) dates from the seventh century, at least some of its liturgical material may be of a much earlier date. Analysis of these collections reveals the existence of a number of different euchological traditions, with Roman, Milanese, Spanish, Celtic, and Gallican books each expressing their own eucharistic personality.

Still later, but sometime before the eighth century, a group of liturgical documents called Ordines begins to appear, providing fuller information about how the Eucharist was actually celebrated in Rome in the early Middle Ages. The Ordines provide the practical, ceremonial details for all participants in the liturgy. When added to the prayers of the sacramentaries, the directions in the Ordines give a picture of both eucharistic words and actions for various occasions. Often these books also contain important historical and political addenda.

Eucharistic Theology and Practice in the Early Middle Ages

Throughout this early period, despite the vigor of local varieties in celebration, there was a growing tendency toward the standardization of the liturgy as authority came to be centered at Rome.

At the same time, eucharistic theology emphasized the sacrificial aspects of the Mass, the localized presence of Christ in the bread and wine, and allegorical interpretations of the action at the altar. Because of these trends, a sense of awe and reverence surrounding the Eucharist grew to dominate popular piety. The idea that ordinary communicants were unworthy to handle the body and blood of Christ in the form of bread and wine was fueled by an emphasis on penitence, resulting in the gradual decline of frequent Communion of the laity. Gazing upon the Eucharist at the moment of consecration was understood to be sufficient to produce a salvific effect. At the same time, the belief was strong that the Eucharist was a representation of the propitiatory sacrifice of Christ. This belief, in turn, led to the expectation that it might be practically employed to bring about desired objectives.

The theological poles of medieval eucharistic debate can be clearly seen in the controversy between the ninth-century monks. In the first systematic treatise devoted solely to the Eucharist, Pascasius Radbertus (*c.* 785–860) describes the ways in which Christ is present in the elements of bread and wine in extremely realistic and physical terms. Ratramnus of Corbie (d. *c.* 868) responded and attacked the carnal view of the Real Presence in favor of a more symbolic and spiritualized interpretation. In the end, Ratramnus' view was condemned as failing adequately to safeguard the doctrine of the Real Presence. The next three centuries saw an increasing identification of the bread and wine with the physical body and blood of Christ. Abuses of eucharistic practice were not uncommon.

By the eleventh century, the structure of the eucharistic rite had reached a certain stability in the West. Roman control had asserted itself over provincial control of ecclesiastical matters. Because of this control, the Eucharist, as it was celebrated in Rome (and particularly as it was celebrated by the bishop of Rome), came to be normative for the rest of the Christian West. But while in Rome large numbers of liturgical personnel were available, in outlying areas a single priest might be called upon to conduct the eucharistic rites alone. The variety of service books for each participant caused certain difficulties. The dissemination of Roman missals, which brought together the prayers, ceremonial directions, the sung parts of the Mass, and readings collected from a variety of liturgical books, not only made the celebration by a single person easier, but also further encouraged the uniformity of eucharistic rites and ceremonies according to Roman patterns.

Eucharistic Theology in the Late Middle Ages

Popular distortions of eucharistic theology and particularly the grossly carnal interpretation of the elements of bread and wine caused the thirteenth-century scholastics to give it special consideration. In 1215, the Fourth Lateran Council used the term *transubstantiation* to describe the change of bread and wine into the body and blood of Christ. However, Thomas Aquinas (1225–1274) was the first person to systematically describe transubstantiation by applying Aristotelian philosophical categories to the Eucharist. Aquinas proposed that while what is perceptible (the *accidents* of bread and wine) remains unchanged, the essential reality (the *substance*) is transformed into the body and blood of Jesus Christ. But even though transubstantiation was originally put forward to combat an overly realistic view of eucharistic presence, its philosophical nuances were difficult to translate into common terms. In the centuries which followed, transubstantiation came to be itself increasingly associated with the carnal presence of Christ in the elements of bread and wine.

By the time of the sixteenth-century Reformation, several trends in eucharistic theology and practice had crystallized. Because of the fear of defiling the body and blood of Christ, lay persons received Communion infrequently. Since the thirteenth century, the chalice had been withheld from them. However, eucharistic piety was high. Such popular devotions as benedictional exposition of the Blessed Sacrament, perpetual adoration, and the feast of Corpus Christi can trace their roots to the late Middle Ages. Because the Mass was thought to make present the propitiatory sacrifice of Christ, the number of Masses were multiplied to ensure an abundance of saving grace. Many religious houses, as well as parish clergy, made their living from the Mass stipends paid by groups and individuals who wished the Eucharist to be offered to bring about desired consequences for them—especially the early release of their souls from purgatory. Although Roman eucharistic practice tended to dominate, some local variety in rites, texts, and lectionaries remained.

The Catholic Reformation and the Eucharist

At the same time, the Catholic Reformation (often called the Counter-Reformation) left its own mark on eucharistic practice and piety. An ecumenical council convened at Trent (1545–1563) sought to curb abuses and to settle matters which the success of Protestantism in Europe had thrown into question. Several of the council's sessions dealt directly with the Eucharist. At the second meeting of the council (1551), the theology of the Eucharist was more precisely defined. Both Lutheran and Zwinglian positions were specifically rejected. Later sessions reaffirmed the sacrificial character of the Mass. The issue of Christ's presence in the elements was addressed at the third meeting of the council (1562). The council determined that the cup was properly denied to the laity because the whole Christ was present in both bread and wine.

One important result of the council deliberations was the establishment of the Congregation of Sacred Rites. Aiming at the standardization of public worship according to the council's decrees and aiming, as an ultimate goal, at a uniform liturgy for all of Roman Catholicism, the council immediately undertook the reform of liturgical books, including the missal. In the end, the rites of the Tridentine Missal (1570) embodied what was current eucharistic practice in the city of Rome and essentially ignored the diverse, local liturgical heritage of the church. Although some of these local rites (and especially those in France) continued to be used after Trent, the rites of the Tridentine Missal formed the official eucharistic liturgy of the Roman Catholic church until the Second Vatican Council undertook revision nearly four centuries later.

Contemporary Roman Catholic Eucharistic Thought and Influence

In the twentieth century, a renewal of attention to the Eucharist has taken place among many Western Christians. In Roman Catholicism, historical studies uncovered the earlier variety in eucharistic practice and documented the accumulation of devotional adjuncts. The Second Vatican Council sought to restore the Eucharist to the center of the Christian life by attempting to strip away the extraneous liturgical material in the eucharistic rites, to simplify rubrics, to recover ancient signs and symbols, to adapt eucharistic practice to indigenous cultures, and to elicit the "full, conscious, active participation" of the faithful. At the same time, eucharistic theology underwent a similar renewal, with such classic works as Edward Schillebeeckx's *Christ the Sacrament of the Encounter with God* (1960) providing a systematic reflection on the Christocentric nature of sacramental grace. It is this more relational understanding of the Eucharist which underlies the Second Vatican Council's Constitution on the Sacred Liturgy (December 4, 1963), as well as the new eucharistic prayers which began to appear in 1967.

In some of the Protestant churches, too, the Eucharist has been the subject of renewed interest in the late twentieth century. Beginning in the 1960s, the Roman Catholic liturgical agenda began to affect the revisions of Protestant services of the Lord's Supper. Historical studies and ecumenical contacts have facilitated some interdenominational convergence in eucharistic theology and practice. Most American Lutherans and Episcopalians have sought to reintroduce the Eucharist as the main Sunday service, and some Methodists and Presbyterians also view this as a desirable goal. But many American Protestants, especially those with strong ties to revivalist worship patterns and Enlightenment sacramental theology, have remained relatively untouched by these trends. Noneucharistic worship remains the norm. Most of the ecclesiastical descendants of the Reformers, however, have begun to search for their eucharistic roots in the early church and in the Continental and English Reformations, and have found a balance between ecumenical convergence and authentic Protestant diversity.

Susan J. White[7]

194 ♦ THE LORD'S SUPPER IN THE EASTERN CHURCHES

Although the Eastern churches divided in the fifth century between those that accepted the Christological formula of Chalcedon (Eastern Orthodox churches) and those that rejected it (non-Chalcedonian Eastern churches, particularly the Nestorians and Monophysites), the regional liturgies that had developed before

Chalcedon continued to be used by Christians on both sides of this ecclesial divide. The following paragraphs classify and interrelate the Syrian, Byzantine, Armenian, and Alexandrian traditions.

Eastern Liturgies after Constantine

In the post-Constantinian period, the eucharistic liturgy in the East underwent a process of standardization, the result of a complex dynamic of cultural, theological, and political factors. With the consolidation of ecclesiastical power under the major urban centers of Antioch, Alexandria, Jerusalem, and Constantinople came the consolidation and further assimilation of local liturgical uses to those of the urban centers. As the various local uses either survived or died out, the major liturgical traditions were formed. These traditions, in their turn, influenced the liturgical practices of other areas.

As regards the eucharistic liturgy, the developments of this period consisted of the filling-in of what have been termed the _soft points_ of the eucharistic _ordo_—the places where in the early liturgies there was only unaccompanied action, e.g., the entrance of the clergy into the church; the kiss of peace and the transfer of the eucharistic gifts; and the fraction, Communion, and Dismissal rites. These points of unaccompanied action in the pre-Constantinian eucharistic rites were in this period covered over with liturgical chant and prayer. These liturgical units of action covered with chant and prayer eventually disintegrated, leaving behind the liturgical flotsam and jetsam found in today's Eastern eucharistic liturgies. In this process of growth of liturgical units, those elements of greatest antiquity often were eliminated in favor of more recent elements: For example, while the act of Communion in the Byzantine rite seems at one time to have been covered by an antiphonal psalm, today only the antiphon of that psalm remains (the _koinonikon_).

Unfortunately, much of the history of the eucharistic liturgies of each Eastern liturgical tradition remains unknown. Paucity of texts and, where texts are available, lack of reliable critical editions make any satisfactory reconstruction of a general history of the Eucharist in the East impossible. This article has more modest aims: (1) to outline the liturgical traditions of the East and some of the circumstances of their evolution; (2) to outline briefly some of the major factors in the development of the Eucharist in the East; and (3) to give a thumbnail sketch of the major sources for and points in the history of the eucharistic liturgies of each Eastern liturgical tradition, as far as these factors are known.

The Liturgical Traditions

In 395 the Roman Empire was divided into Eastern and Western halves, the consolidation of a process begun in 293 with the partition of the Empire into four prefectures. The Eastern half of the Empire contained four cities which were to become the centers of the Eastern patriarchates: Antioch, center of the civil diocese of the Orient; Alexandria, center of the civil diocese of Egypt; Constantinople and Jerusalem, raised to the level of patriarchal seat in 381 and 451, respectively. During the fourth and fifth centuries, the liturgical usages of the cities, towns and villages surrounding these ecclesiastical centers unified more and more around the usages of the patriarchates.

Some liturgical traditions, however, developed partially or entirely outside the jurisdiction of the Roman Empire. The Chaldean, or East Syrian eucharistic rite developed primarily within the Persian Empire, and the Armenian rite grew up against the backdrop of constant power struggles between the two superpowers of late antiquity, the Roman and Persian Empires.

The result of this process of liturgical unification is the group of four basic Eastern liturgical traditions known today: (1) Syrian (East Syrian, West Syrian, and Maronite); (2) Byzantine; (3) Armenian; and (4) Alexandrian (Coptic and Ethiopian).

The eucharistic liturgies of the East are today celebrated by both Orthodox and Catholic churches (with the sole exception of the Maronite rite, which is celebrated only by Eastern rite Catholics). These liturgies are celebrated in a wide variety of languages, both classical and modern: from Greek, Syriac, Coptic, Slavonic, and Armenian to Arabic, various modern European languages, Chinese, Japanese, Malayalam, various Siberian and North American Indian languages, and English. While originally these rites were restricted to specific geographical locales, they are now found worldwide, the result both of missionary activity and of the Eastern Christian diaspora.

Influences Upon Development of the Traditions

One could list many influences upon the development of the liturgical traditions of the East and, hence, their eucharistic liturgies. We list six here: (1) the great dogmatic controversies of the early church, particularly the councils of Ephesus (431) and Chalcedon (451)—the acceptance or rejection of those decisions eventually determined the ecclesiastical divisions and practices of the various Eastern churches; (2) monasticism in its many forms existing in late antiquity—liturgical practices often traveled via monks, who were always on the go, traveling the length and breadth of the inhabited world; (3) pilgrimage to the holy city of Jerusalem—pilgrims often brought back to their native lands hagiopolite practices; (4) geography—either facilitated or hindered the spread of missionary activity and lines of commerce and communication; (5) the Roman and Persian Empires—either against or for which many different churches acted and reacted. (In addition, the influence of the Byzantine Empire eventually caused the abandonment of native eucharistic rites in favor of the Byzantine rite); (6) individuals—whose work often helped along the evolution or establishment of liturgical practices, e.g., Basil the Great, Iso'yabh III, or Gregory the Illuminator, to name three.

The Eucharistic Liturgies

We shall now turn to the individual rites themselves, in the following order: Syrian (East Syrian, West Syrian, and Maronite); Byzantine; Armenian; and Alexandrian (Coptic and Ethiopian). The treatment of the Syrian and Alexandrian traditions is preceded by a brief introduction.

The Syrian Tradition. On the basis of investigations into the East Syrian (or Chaldean), West Syrian, and Maronite eucharistic and baptismal liturgies, the Jesuit liturgist William Macomber has posited the existence of three, possibly four, liturgical traditions in Greater Syria and Persia at the beginning of the fifth century, centered upon Antioch, Jerusalem, and Edessa, with a possible fourth tradition existing in the Persian church. Reaction to the councils of Ephesus in 431 and Chalcedon in 451 set in motion the process of liturgical isolation and fusion which led to the eucharistic liturgies of the East Syrian, West Syrian, and Maronite rites, as we shall see below.

East Syrian. The Chaldean rite of today, used by members of the church of the East (often erroneously called *Nestorians*) and by Eastern rite Catholics in India, Iraq, and the United States, is one development of the ancient rite of Edessa, a city located on the eastern frontier between the Roman and Persian Empires. Edessa was the center of Syriac-speaking Christian culture and had been evangelized by the end of the second century at the latest. The form of Christianity which developed in Edessa was of a truly Semitic idiom, and the eucharistic liturgy which emerged from Edessa likewise bore the marks of its Judeo-Christian ancestry.

The Chaldean eucharistic rite was the first to be standardized, a process which began in the fifth century and ended in the seventh or eighth century. The Council of Ephesus in 431 condemned the teaching of Patriarch Nestorius of Constantinople, and began the process of the Persian church's ecclesiastical separation, formalized at the Synod of Beth Lapat in 484. Thus, the eucharistic liturgy of the church of the East developed without substantial influence from outside liturgical practices.

The Chaldean tradition is rich in liturgical commentaries. The model for all Chaldean commentators is the liturgical commentary of Theodor of Mopsuestia. Although he did not comment upon the Chaldean eucharistic service, per se, his method of interpreting each liturgical action in terms of the events of Christ's life was to be paradigmatic for later Chaldean liturgical commentary. Some important figures are Narsai, Gabriel bar Liphah Quatrayer (615–616), and an anonymous commentator of the mid-to-late ninth century. Later commentaries on the eucharistic service do not add anything new to these earlier works.

The first reference to the rite occurs in the canons of the first general synod of the church in Persia, held at Seleucia-Ctesiphon in 410. There, the bishops call for a standardization of the eucharistic rite of the Western rite used by bishops Marutha (of Martyropolis in the Roman Empire) and Isaac (of Seleucia). It is a strong possibility that this Western rite is that of Edessa.

In the sixth century, Catholicos Mar Aba I (540–552) added the anaphoras of Theodor of Mopsuestia and Nestorius to the eucharistic liturgy, translating them from the Greek. Catholicos Iso'yabh III

(650–659) was largely responsible for the final standardization of the Chaldean rite through his editions of the Taksa (the euchology for priests), the Hudra (the antiphonary for Sundays), and his commentary on the ceremonies of the office, eucharistic liturgy, and other liturgical rites. Iso'yabh may have eliminated the institution narrative from the anaphora of Addai and Mari, which he is said to have shortened. He may also have eliminated other eucharistic prayers from the Taksa.

Missionaries of the church of the East spread through Central Asia to India and China by the seventh century. When the Portuguese arrived in South India in the sixteenth century, they found Christians there using the Chaldean rite. The remainder of the sixteenth and seventeenth centuries saw the unification of these Malabar Christians with the see of Rome and their splintering into a variety of churches, some using the liturgical forms provided by the Portuguese, others placing themselves under the jurisdiction of the Jacobite Patriarch of Antioch (and, hence, using the Liturgy of St. James, now known as the Malankara rite), and yet others returning to the Catholicos of the church of the East. Today, the majority of Malabar Christians are Eastern-rite Catholics, and their eucharistic liturgy has been restored following the Second Vatican Council. Chaldean-rite Catholics in Iraq and the United States have also had their rite revised, but more conservatively than the Malabar rite. Finally, the Liturgy of Addai and Mari continues to be used by a very small remnant of the church of the East in Iraq, Iran, and the United States.

West Syrian. Reaction to the Council of Chalcedon cut across all three liturgical traditions of fifth-century Syria. For at least a century after the council, both Chalcedonians and non-Chalcedonians continued to celebrate the Eucharist according to the rite of their region. Chalcedonians were found in the cities of southern Syria and maritime Syria as well as Palestine. Eventually, these primarily Greek-speaking groups gave up the Liturgy of St. James for the Byzantine rite. These groups are termed *Melkites,* from the Syriac *malka* or Arabic *malek* meaning "king," for of course the Byzantine emperor adhered to the Christological definition of Chalcedon and attempted to require adherence to Chalcedon in all areas under Byzantine control or influence.

The non-Chalcedonians, or Monophysites, were found in the Aramaic-speaking population from northern Syria to Mesopotamia. The liturgy celebrated by these non-Chalcedonian groups became what is today known as the *West Syrian* or Jacobite liturgy (from the name of the organizer of the Monophysite church, the Syrian monk Jacob Baradai, who died in 578). The West Syrian tradition has a very large number of anaphoras (scholars count anywhere from seventy to one hundred), not all of which are in use today. The eucharistic liturgy is not entirely of West Syrian origin; it is a mixture of Greek elements from the eucharistic rites of Jerusalem (its anaphoral structure) and Antioch (the basic framework of the liturgy), which was soon translated into Syriac, and Edessa (metrical hymns). The Jacobites continued to borrow from Maronite and Byzantine sources in subsequent centuries.

The principal commentators upon the Jacobite eucharistic rite are: Jacob of Edessa (640–708), in his letter to Thomas the Presbyter; Moses bar Kepha (813–903); George of the Arabs (724); and Dionysius bar Salibi (d. 1171).

Maronite. It was once thought that the Maronite eucharistic rite was simply a branch of the West Syrian rite, because it shares much in common with the Liturgy of St. James. However, it is now believed that Aramaic-speaking Chalcedonians in Syria, especially in Lebanon and the Orontes Valley, were able to preserve a form of the ancient eucharistic rite of Edessa, as the features of the Maronite eucharistic liturgy which are most characteristically Maronite are not held in common with St. James, but rather with the Chaldean eucharistic rite. This ancient Edessene rite, however, has been overlaid through the centuries with borrowings from the Jacobite and Latin eucharistic rites. For example, the Maronite rite today includes anaphoras ascribed to some of the champions of the Monophysite cause, such as Philoxenus of Mabboug and Dionysius bar Salibi, to name two. Other Jacobite borrowings seem to be the sedro-form of prayer, and a preparatory part of the rite which seems to have been borrowed in the late fifteenth century or early sixteenth century, when a Maronite was elected Monophysite Patriarch of Antioch. Contact with the crusaders produced union with the see of Rome in 1182, although the firm union was not established until the sixteenth century. From the twelfth century, Latinisms began to be introduced into the Maronite Mass,

St. Athanasius. Athanasius, Bishop of Alexandria, is known as the "Father of Orthodoxy" because of his clear defense of the doctrine of the Trinity against the Arians. His symbol, a Bible resting between two pillars, is derived from the idea that his work was drawn from the Bible and was a pillar of orthodox teaching.

culminating in the Latinization under Patriarch Rizzi in the seventeenth century. Subsequent centuries have seen the restoration of the old form of the Maronite rite.

The Byzantine Tradition. The eucharistic liturgy of the Great Church of Constantinople is the most widespread Eastern rite in existence today. It is impossible to give any more than a cursory glance over the rich history of the eucharistic liturgies of this tradition: St. Basil, St. John Chrysostom and the Liturgy of the Presanctified. Thanks to the work of the Jesuit liturgists Juan Mateos and Robert Taft, the history of this rite is one of the most well known.

The first mention of a rite of Constantinople is during the period of Chrysostom's episcopate (397–404). It seems that the eucharistic liturgy at that time basically followed the liturgy of Antioch. It seems that the earliest liturgical influences upon the eucharistic rite of Constantinople were Antiochene and Cappadocian, since many of the city's early bishops came from those two areas.

The first commentary on the Byzantine eucharistic service is the Mystagogia of St. Maximus the Confessor, written between about 628–630. The next two witnesses to the eucharistic liturgy are the Historia Ecclesiastica of Patriarch St. Germanus of Constantinople (d. *c.* 730), and the Barberini Codex gr 336, which dates from about 800. What these three sources show is that during the seventh to the ninth centuries the Byzantine eucharistic liturgy underwent considerable growth and evolution, precisely at the so-called soft points of the rite: the preparation of the gifts was removed from a point just before the great entrance to completely before the entire liturgy, and a service of three antiphons, derived from the stational liturgy of the city, grew up immediately before the liturgy of the Word. During that time, more ancient elements in the service were either eliminated or moved in favor of the newer elements: The Old Testament reading vanished, as did the prayers over the penitents and the psalmodic elements of the service.

The Byzantine eucharistic rite reached its definitive synthesis in the tenth century, as witnessed by the tenth-century Typicon of the Great Church. The service underwent subsequent monastic influence, most notably in the form of the beginning and end to the service, taken from the Palestinian monastic office in force in Constantinople from the fall of the city in 1204. By the fourteenth century, the eucharistic rite had received the form it has today.

The Armenian Tradition. Armenia was evangelized simultaneously from Caesarea in Cappadocia in the West, and Edessa in the South. While the East Syrian influence perdured primarily in the calendar, the Cappadocian eucharistic liturgy formed the basis for the nascent Armenian eucharistic liturgy.

At the beginning of the fifth century, the anaphora of St. Basil the Great was translated into Armenian; this anaphora was later erroneously ascribed to Gregory the Illuminator, the apostle to Armenia, who had received his training in Cappadocia. Toward the end of the fifth century, four other Caesarean anaphoras were translated from Greek into Armenian: Catholicos Sahak, Gregory of Nazianzus, Cyril, and Athanasius.

Further Byzantine influence on the Armenian eucharistic rite took place from the seventh century, in spite of Armenian attempts to prevent it. The reason for this continuing Byzantinization can perhaps be attributed to the presence of strong groups within the Armenian hierarchy and monastic ranks whose theological views approximated those of the Byzantines.

Sometime after the tenth century, the Liturgy of St. Basil was translated again into Armenian. But with the tenth-century ascendancy of the Liturgy of St. John Chrysostom over the Liturgy of St. Basil in Constantinople, the Liturgy of St. John Chrysostom was adopted by the Armenians, as well as the Liturgy of the Presanctified. The time of the Crusades saw contact between Armenians and Latins, whom the Armenians welcomed. From the twelfth to the fourteenth centuries, some Latin features entered the Armenian service.

Both Chosroes the Great (c. 950) and St. Nerses of Lambron (d. 1198) wrote commentaries on the Armenian eucharistic liturgy. The eucharistic service in use today is that of St. Athanasius.

The Alexandrian Tradition. Two Egypts existed side by side in late antiquity: Lower Egypt, whose center was the great city of Alexandria, the center of Hellenic, philosophical Christianity; and Upper Egypt, the cradle of monasticism and the Coptic-speaking populace of the countryside, the center of a popular Christianity based upon wisdom sayings, asceticism, and ritual. After the Council of Chalcedon (451), the city of Alexandria remained in Chalcedonian hands, while the center of non-Chalcedonian power shifted to the monasteries. One monastery in particular became a powerful center of Monophysite Coptic Christianity: the Monastery of St. Macarius in Wadi al-Natrun, in Scetis near the Nile Delta in Lower Egypt. The patriarchal seat in Alexandria was occupied by both Chaldeconian and non-Chalcedonian patriarchs after Chalcedon.

Coptic. The Greek Liturgy of St. Mark appears to have been used by Melkites in Egypt until the twelfth century when, under Byzantine influence, they adopted the Byzantine eucharistic service (as did Melkites in Syria and Palestine).

However, among Monophysites the Liturgy of St. Mark was translated into Coptic and underwent further influence from Coptic monastic practice and Syrian liturgical practice, which came via the Syrian Jacobite monks who made their homes in Egypt, as well as the general ecclesiastical intercourse between Syrian and Egyptian Jacobites.

The first Coptic dialect used by the Egyptian Christians was Sahidic, which attained its classical form at the White Monastery in Upper Egypt, during the reign of Abbot Shenoute (c. 383–451). However, as the Monastery of St. Macarius gained more prominence as a fortress of non-Chalcedonian Christianity following Chalcedon, the Bohairic Coptic dialect used there began slowly to supplant the earlier Sahidic texts. Eventually, Bohairic became the only Coptic dialect used in worship.

Today's eucharistic rite is essentially that of Scetis. In the twelfth century, Patriarch Gabriel II Ibn Turayk (1131–1145) decreed that all local versions of the eucharistic prayer be suppressed, and that only three anaphoras be used throughout the entire Coptic church: St. Mark (also known as St. Cyril), St. Basil, and St. Gregory. In the fifteenth century, Patriarch Gabriel V composed his Liturgical Order (1411), still in use today. This work, along with *The Lamp of Darkness* of Abu al-Barakat (fourteenth century), are two of the most important commentaries on the Coptic eucharistic liturgy.

Ethiopian. The historic date of the Christianization of Ethiopia is 340. It appears that Coptic and Syrian missionaries penetrated into the country, and that by the fifth century monasticism had been established in Ethiopia. At the time of Chalcedon, the Ethiopians sided with the Monophysites. About the same time, the famous Nine Saints are said to have arrived in Ethiopia, beginning the work of translating Coptic, Greek and Syriac literature into Ge'ez, the classical form of the Ethiopian tongue. The head of the Ethiopian church, the abuna, was a Coptic monk chosen and sent from Egypt. In 1948, this relationship with the Coptic church was changed when the Ethiopian church was allowed a native abuna, consecrated in 1959.

The history of the Ethiopian eucharistic service is almost completely unknown, as it is perhaps the least-studied eucharistic liturgy of any in the East. Scholars have identified at least twenty different Ethiopian anaphoras of Syrian, Alexandrian, and Ethiopian origin—one of the most intriguing being the Anaphora of Our Lady.

Given the strong ties between the Coptic church and the Ethiopian church, one can posit a strong Coptic influence upon the structure and content of the Ethiopian eucharistic service. Observers have also noted in the practices of this church the presence of elements seeming to originate in Judaism. However, given the great gaps in our knowledge of Ethiopian history (especially from 650 to 1270), reconstruction of the history of any of the Ethiopian eucharistic liturgy will be difficult at best. Clearly, the Ethiopian eucharistic liturgy presents a fascinating field of study for future scholars of liturgy.

Grant Sperry-White[8]

195 • THE LORD'S SUPPER IN THE REFORMATION ERA

Martin Luther insisted that Christ's body and blood are really present in the Eucharist. On the other hand, the Swiss and South German Reformers, who initiated what became the Reformed tradition, believed Christ was present only symbolically in the minds and hearts of those participating in the Eucharist. Between these two positions, John Calvin later insisted on a real but wholly spiritual presence of Christ. All Protestant Reformers accented the role of preaching and insisted that lay people receive both bread and wine.

The medieval combination of eucharistic piety and abuse set the stage for the radical reevaluation for the Eucharist by those in the sixteenth century who sought a reformation of the church. The Reformers' concern with the centrality of the Word of God and their insistence on justification through faith alone and the priesthood of all the baptized put the Eucharist at the center of Reformation debate. In "An Open Letter to the Christian Nobility of the German Nation" (1520), Martin Luther (1483–1546) argued that "the status of a priest among Christians is merely that of an office-holder." This redefinition of priesthood undercut the current theology of the sacraments, particularly the sacrifice of the Mass, and laid the foundations for the eucharistic theology and practice of all the Reformation churches.

In *The Babylonian Captivity of the Church* (1520), Luther continued his attack on current eucharistic piety and practice by criticizing transubstantiation and the denial of the cup to the laity. The presence of Christ in the Eucharist, according to Luther, was like the presence of fire in a heated bar of iron, in which "every part is both iron and fire"; in the same way, Christ's body and blood are wholly present in the eucharistic bread and wine. With regard to Communion,

Luther argued that since Christ gave both bread and cup to his original disciples at the Last Supper, his present-day disciples deserve nothing less. Luther's *Formula Missae* (1523) and *Deutsche Messe* (1525–1526), although both quite conservative rites, shaped the Eucharist according to his Reformation principles.

But others of the period desired a more thoroughgoing reformation of the church, and thus of the Lord's Supper. Swiss Reformers Ulrich Zwingli (1484–1531), Martin Bucer (1491–1551), and John Oecolampadius (1482–1531) found that Luther's retention of the carnal presence of Christ in the elements of bread and wine left too much opportunity for theological and practical abuse and moved in the direction of a more symbolic and memorialistic view of the Eucharist. At the Marburg Colloquy (1529), Luther, arguing the conservative side, and the more radical Swiss Reformers were unable to come to agree on the matter of eucharistic presence, marking the fracture of the Reformation into distinct theological camps. John Calvin (1509–1564), the Reformer of the church at Geneva, attempted to moderate the Swiss and Lutheran views of the eucharistic presence, arguing that Christ is truly, albeit spiritually, received by those who faithfully partake of the bread and wine.

The various Reformers could agree, however, on a number of practical matters regarding the Lord's Supper, and especially on the necessity making the cup *and* bread available to the laity, the reading and preaching of Scripture at each celebration of the Lord's Supper, and the commitment that no Eucharist be held without communicants present. Reformation eucharistic rites simplified greatly their medieval predecessors. Increased participation of the laity was facilitated by a vernacular liturgy and the addition of responses. Although the intention was to return to the practices of the primitive church, certain elements of pre-Reformation piety remained, such as the heavily penitential emphasis. The Reformers had hoped that a weekly service of the Lord's Supper might be instituted. But since most people were used to receiving Communion infrequently (once a year was common), the celebration of the Eucharist quarterly was all that generally could be achieved.

Susan J. White[9]

196 ◆ THE LORD'S SUPPER AMONG RADICAL PROTESTANTS (1525–1900)

A cluster of believers' church movements offered an alternative view of Protestant approaches to the Lord's Supper. Although most of them espoused a non-sacramental, memorialist understanding of Christ's presence (more precisely, absence) in the bread and wine, they nonetheless developed intense forms of Communion piety. Much of their practice was inspired by an attempt to return to primitive Christian practice, which they were convinced had been memorialistic rather than sacramental.

Different approaches to the Lord's Table often reflect different understandings as to where and how Christ is present in its celebration. For medieval Catholicism, Christ's body and blood were directly present in the bread and wine. This took place through an act, transubstantiation, which priests alone could perform. The Reformation rejected so direct an identity, along with the priority it granted priests over the laity. Still, the largest Reformation traditions preserved Christ's presence in the elements in modified form. For Lutherans, Christ's body was "in, with, and under" the bread and wine. For Calvinists, the Holy Spirit imbued them with the risen Christ's spiritual reality. Only for Zwinglians, who emphasized the Supper's memorial character, was Christ perhaps absent from the elements themselves.

The seventeenth and eighteenth centuries, however, brought increasing emphasis on the rational, over against the aesthetic and ceremonial, aspects of faith. Under the Enlightenment's influence, talk of supernatural presence in physical elements sounded increasingly superstitious. In nineteenth-century North America, faith was spread largely through popular evangelical movements whose informality often clashed with sacramentalism. In practice, if not in theory, many Protestants were experiencing something like Christ's real absence from the Table by early in this century.

Yet there are numerous indications that Christ was experienced quite intensely during the Supper in movements outside the main streams. Since these movements, which came to clearest expression as free churches, formally affirmed Zwinglian memorialism and developed little explicit eucharistic theology, they often appear to affirm absence, too. Reexamined in light of today's revived liturgical interests, however, they offer unexpected insights into Christ's presence at the Table. Space permits examination of only a few and several surprising comparisons with current Catholic emphases.

Sixteenth-Century Anabaptists

For the Anabaptists of the Reformation period, the Communion bread and wine were simply bread and wine. The Lord's Table was a simple fellowship meal which memorialized Jesus' death. Yet Anabaptists denied Christ's physical presence in the elements in order to stress his deeper mystical presence throughout the whole celebration. The bread, said Melchior Hoffman, functions like the ring a bridegroom gives his bride; it conveys and enacts his desire to become one flesh, one spirit, one passion with her. As Christ gives himself for spiritual feeding, our nature is transformed by his, much as physical food is assimilated by ours.

For Anabaptists, Christ's presence was also communal. As Jesus shares himself through bread and wine, we are sharing them with each other. This means pledging to live and die for each other, as Jesus did for us. The Table thus binds us together as one body (1 Cor. 10:17). Sometimes it was accompanied, as at the Last Supper, by footwashing, a symbol of mutual servanthood (John 13:1-20) and the kiss of peace. For true unity to reign, conflicts had to be settled before or during the celebration (Matt. 5:23-24; 18:15-17).

Severe persecution soon drove Anabaptists into remote areas. On the other hand, Europe's non-Catholic population gathered into Lutheran and Reformed state churches. However these Protestant state churches' increasing formalism and rationalism left many spiritually dry. Within these churches the Pietist movement developed, stressing experiential and practical Christianity over formal ceremony and theology. The Pietist movement spawned two free churches that revitalized the Lord's Table.

The Church of the Brethren (Dunkers)

The German Baptist Brethren movement, originating among Radical Pietists in the German Palatinate in 1708, consciously placed itself in the Anabaptist stream of thought. Biblical study convinced them that the original Supper had been a three-part ceremony held in the evening and that it, therefore, must always be celebrated that way. Due to its complexity, this ceremony, collectively called the love feast, took place infrequently—often just once a year. Yet this rendered it more, rather than less, significant. Participants often traveled great distances for a weekend of fellowship and nurture. A prior deacon's visit or preparatory service sought to make everyone right with God and their fellows. (North American Mennonites also adopted some of these patterns.)

Since about 1770, the order of the love feast, held as a Saturday event, has been as follows: First comes footwashing, symbolizing cleansing and commitment to mutual servanthood. It concludes with the kiss of peace or the right hand of fellowship. Second comes what Brethren call the Lord's Supper, a simple but adequate communal meal (others usually call it an agape meal), preceded by a simple grace. Third is Communion, the sharing of bread and wine. Brethren call it a memorial and a proclamation, and state that Christ is not literally in the elements. These affirmations, however, are rarely discussed. Emphasis falls on breaking pieces from flat loaves of unleavened bread and serving each other from a common cup (individual cups are now commonly used). The brethren then pledge to live in peace and unity, following the Cross until the end.

Several decades later, Pietist impulses helped form the Moravian Church, so named because it incorporated remnants of the fifteenth-century Czech Brethren (Unitas Fratrum), whose eucharistic understandings resembled the Reformed. Later contacts with Reformed churches and American evangelicalism strengthened a memorialist emphasis. Initially, however, Moravians sought to be a Pietist fellowship within the Lutheran church, celebrating the Lord's Table in those congregations. Moravians continue, like Luther, to encourage taking "this is my body" at face value—yet adding that memorialism, consubstantiation, and even transubstantiation can be valid interpretations. At bottom, as among Anabaptists and the Brethren, the Lord's Table, for the Moravians, is to be experienced and lived out, not extensively thought about.

Early Moravians prepared carefully for Communion, especially through speaking about their spiritual state to spiritual leaders—not dissimilar to the Brethren's visit of a deacon. Since they usually communicated in Lutheran churches, their own Communions were often simple, including singing, spontaneous prayers, the kiss of peace, and hymns of unity. Their distinctive communal lifestyle, however, gave rise to other services which eventually influenced the Lord's Table. Moravians developed love feasts, which recall the New Testament·agape meals, as occasions for sharing food, songs, sometimes foot washing, and usually experiences. Often these were held in *choirs*, groups of one's peers which were especially close knit. Moravian hymnody and worship stressed the Lamb's blood and the body's unity, so that love feasts, though they could center on many themes, often emphasized these.

When the Moravians became an independent church, Communion occurred every fourth Sunday. Love feasts came on preceding Saturdays, becoming preparatory services for Communion which included concerns such as the preparatory speaking. Though love feasts remained separate and nonsacramental occasions, the Moravians' frequent spiritual absorption in Jesus' sufferings and the body's unity at these occasions markedly shaped the overall experience of the Lord's Table.

The Disciples of Christ

The North American Restoration, or Disciples movement, arising in the early nineteenth century from Presbyterianism, stressed the Lord's Table as a memorial and a proclamation. Yet, Alexander Campbell's careful biblical investigations highlighted additional elements (including the mandate that the Table be celebrated every Sunday, the day of the Resurrection—a custom quite dissimilar to that of the Brethren).

Campbell insisted that one whole loaf be used—that it actually be broken and that it be passed among the participants as one cup later would be. Without this decisive emphasis, the ceremony would be lost: the actual breaking and outpouring of Jesus' body and blood, and hence his radical self-giving; the direct, joint participation of each member in the benefits of Jesus' sacrifice; and the essential oneness of Jesus' body, and therefore of the church. These Communion acts led into prayers for fellow Christians, the poor, and evangelization; a collection for the needy; and sharing for mutual edification. In calling the Table a remembrance, Campbell meant the biblical anamnesis, which brings the realities concerned into the present. In calling for its weekly celebration, he stressed our need for regular nourishment from the Table.

Commonalities

Though the four above traditions differ, each regards the Lord's Table as a series of acts in which the whole community participates. If Christ does not reside directly in the elements, this hardly means that he is not really present. Those who concentrate on the elements (or the words of institution or the individual's faith alone) are looking in the wrong places. For Christ is surely present among the participants—present in the breaking, sharing, eating, drinking, and mutual pledging. Christ is personally and actively present: self-bestowing, cleansing, energizing, challenging, healing, and uniting.

Strikingly similar emphases are heard among some recent Catholic theologians. Transubstantiation, they argue, misconstrued Christ's Real Presence as a presence in particular objects. Medieval Catholicism, they continue, turned the Eucharist into a priestly act, distant from the worshiping congregation. However, Christ is present throughout worship, among all the participants, bestowing himself from the beginning, and not only present when the elements are raised.

Many of these Catholic theologians call Jesus' presence in the elements transignification. They point out that when an object (e.g., a ring) takes on a unique function in a relationship (e.g., a marriage), this object can validly be called something else (e.g., the bridegroom's *heart* or *self*) without physically changing. The object's signification alters radically, though its material substance remains the same. The sixteenth-century Anabaptist Melchior Hoffman, comparing Communion bread with a wedding ring, noted that it functioned like this.

Due to formalism, rationalism, and their own Zwinglian memorialism, the free churches discussed here, similar to many Protestants, often experience Christ's eucharistic absence. Liturgical renewal among more sacramental churches, however, has aroused the free churches to be concerned about this absence. These theologically articulate groups sometimes suggest that Christ might be present amid the actions and the participants around the Table—the very sort of pres-

ence often richly experienced in these free-church traditions.

Thomas Finger

197 ✦ CONVERGENCE AT THE TABLE

Creative thinking about the presence of Christ in the Eucharist in the twentieth century has been largely devoted to overcoming the ecumenical impasse on eucharistic presence inherited from previous times, especially the Reformation era in the sixteenth century. One of the consequences of ecumenical dialogue has been a reconsideration of the positions of medieval scholastic theologians and Protestant Reformers. One of the best surveys of the issues discussed remains Hermann Sasse's This is My Body *(Minneapolis: Augsburg, 1959).*

A Protestant Impasse

All the Protestant Reformers rejected the scholastic dogma of transubstantiation in the sixteenth century, while the Council of Trent reaffirmed it for the Roman Catholic church. This way of understanding the Real Presence of Christ grew slowly but logically out of the controversies over Christ's eucharistic presence during the ninth through eleventh centuries, and was promulgated as dogma by the Fourth Lateran Council in 1215. The teaching that the *substance* of the bread and wine changed into the body and blood of Christ while the *species* remain unchanged was given philosophical underpinning through use of Aristotelian categories by the great scholastic theologians of the thirteenth century. This scholastic teaching was affirmed by the Council of Trent, which condemned those who deny that a transubstantiation takes place in which "the species of bread and wine only remain."

The Protestant movement itself became divided over the issue of the Real Presence. Luther and Zwingli reached an impasse on this issue at the Marburg Colloquy in 1529. Luther doggedly clung to the words of Christ, "This is my body. This is my blood," while Zwingli held that the body of Christ could only be localized in heaven. Calvin later tried to find a middle way between Luther and Zwingli, although this entailed a rejection of both Luther's literal interpretation of the words of institution and Zwingli's figurative interpretation. According to Calvin, there is no corporeal presence of the body of Christ in the sacrament, as Luther held, for the body of Christ is locally circumscribed in heaven. Yet "we are spiritually fed," i.e., our souls are fed with the body and blood of the Lord. We can participate in the body and blood of Christ by raising our hearts to heaven (Calvin here appealed to the *sursum corda* of the classic eucharistic prayers.) The Reformed churches in Switzerland were never able to replace Zwingli's eucharistic theory and practice with Calvin's. Lutherans insisted on the *sacramental union* of Christ's body and blood "in, with, and under" the bread and wine in order to affirm that God in Christ meets us where we are, "deep in the flesh"; we do not ascend to where Christ is at the right hand of the Father.

Protestant Revisions

There had been some compromise on issues related to the sacrament of the altar in the Wittenberg Concordat of 1536, drafted largely by Philipp Melanchton (d. 1560) and Martin Bucer (d. 1551). But it was not until the twentieth century that something of an inter-Protestant breakthrough occurred in the Leuenberg Concordat of 1967. In this document the key idea that seemed to end the impasse was that the Real Presence was no longer to be "grasped in a static or physical manner"; *body* and *blood* designate the person of Jesus Christ. The accord is not established by agreement in any certain mode of Christ's presence in the bread and wine, but in an understanding of what happens during the celebration of the Supper. The Real Presence is grasped in a dynamic and actualist fashion. This understanding overcomes *the myth of locality,* whether this is the Lutheran "localization of the sacramental gifts in the elements" or the Calvinist localization of Christ's body in heaven.

It has been suggested that the German Lutheran-Reformed consensus achieved at Leuenberg was possible because of the perceived need of a common front against the Roman Catholic church. The results of the Leuenberg agreement have not been received by all Lutherans, including those in Germany. Nevertheless, the shift of attention from objects to events had its corollary in the teachings of the Second Vatican Council. *The Constitution on the Sacred Liturgy* (1963) broadened the focus on the Real Presence from an almost exclu-

sive concentration on the elements to the whole eucharistic action. Within that it specified four distinct modes of Christ's presence: in the Word, in the presiding minister, in the bread and wine, and in the assembly. This teaching advanced the question of Christ's eucharistic presence in a significant way by considering the purpose of Christ's presence among us: It is to be present *pro nobis,* on our behalf. "Christ indeed always associates the Church with Himself in the truly great work of giving perfect praise to God and making men holy" (I:7).

Catholic Revisions and Ecumenical Convergence

This teaching was possible because in the years before the Second Vatican Council attempts were made by Catholic theologians to translate the term *transubstantiation* into categories of contemporary phenomenology. Terms such as *transignification* (changed meaning) and *transfinalization* (changed purpose) were explored by Eduard Schillebeeckx in *The Eucharist* (New York: Sheed and Ward, 1968; see chapter 2) and Joseph Powers in *Eucharistic Theology* (New York: Herder and Herder, 1967; chapter 4); however, such ideas had been practically precluded by Pope Paul VI's encyclical *Mysterium fidei* (1965). Lutheran theologians had responded to the Leuenberg agreement by asking how Christ's presence as a person relates to the not-very-dynamic and decidedly physical presence of the objects of bread and wine about which the promises of the presence were actually made. So too, papal reflection noted that both meaning and purpose would be vitiated if the reality itself were not radically transformed.

These nagging concerns had to be incorporated into the final draft of the statement of the Faith and Order Commission of the World Council of Churches, *Baptism, Eucharist, Ministry,* finalized in Lima, Peru, in 1982. In this document, the council agreed that "the Eucharistic meal is the sacrament of the body and blood of Christ, the sacrament of his Real Presence. Christ fulfills in a variety of ways his promise to be always with his own. . . . But Christ's mode of presence in the Eucharist is unique. Christ said over the bread and wine of the Eucharist: 'This is my body. . . . This is by blood.' What Christ declared is true, and this truth is fulfilled every time the Eucharist is celebrated. The church confesses Christ's real, living, acting presence in the Eucharist" (Eucharist, par. 13).

Persisting Questions— Possible Answers

In the World Council of Churches' statement on the Eucharist, the ideas of the eucharistic meal as "sacrament of the body and blood of Christ" and "sacrament of his real presence" are linked together. But how the person of Christ, his body and blood, and the meal elements coincide is left unspecified. Indeed, the official commentary to this passage states: "Many churches believe that . . . the bread and the wine . . . become, in a real though mysterious manner, the body and blood . . . of the living Christ. . . . Some other churches . . . do not link that presence so definitely with the signs of bread and wine." In fact, some churches, especially in the Reformed communion, do not make this link at all.

There probably can be no profitable dialogue between those who affirm Real Presence (in some way) and those who affirm _real absence_. Among those who affirm Real Presence, there is some division between those who affirm the presence of _someone_ and those who affirm the presence of _something_. A breakthrough might occur if the question is asked: In what way is a person also an object? Whatever I am as a person, I am also a body; and my body is my availability, indeed my vulnerability, to others. I can give myself to others only bodily, and my body, thus given, may be misused by those to whom I give it. Jesus may mean by saying, "This is my body," "this is me, and I give myself to you." However, it is only as a body that Christ can give himself, and that body can be—and was—abused. There is also an element of sacrifice involved in this offer. The institution of the Lord's Supper is linked with the atoning sacrifice of Christ in all four New Testament institution accounts. Because of the possibility of superstitious abuse of the sacrament and because such a close identification brings with it a confrontation with the presence of Christ's sacrifice, some Protestants are thus hesitant to accept too strong an identification of Christ's Real Presence with the elements of bread and wine. But, if one can accept the idea that a person must also be a body, a proposition to which Catholicism has faithfully clung, it may be that agreement can be

reached on how to avoid abuses of the sacrament, which is the true Protestant concern. If so, it is possible that a true ecumenical breakthrough on the understanding of Christ's eucharistic presence may be achieved.

Frank C. Senn

198 • BIBLIOGRAPHY ON THE HISTORY OF THE LORD'S SUPPER

Bouley, Allan. _From Freedom to Formula: Evolution of the Eucharistic Prayer from Oral Improvisation to Written Texts._ Studies in Christian Antiquity #21. Washington D.C: Catholic University of America Press, 1981.

Bowmer, John. C. _The Sacrament of the Lord's Supper in Early Methodism._ Westminster: Dacre Press, 1964.

———. _The Lord's Supper in Methodism, 1791–1960._ London: Epworth, 1961.

Burr, David. _Eucharistic Presence and Conversion in Late Thirteenth-Century Franciscan Thought._ Transactions of the American Philosophical Society #74, pt. 3. Philadelphia: American Philosophical Society, 1984. Includes Franciscans who denied that transubstantiation was needed to explain eucharistic presence.

Clark, Francis. _Eucharistic Sacrifice and the Reformation._ London: Darton, Longman, and Todd, 1960; 2d ed. Oxford: Blackwell, 1967. Argues that the rejection of eucharistic _sacrifice_ by Protestants was based on a distorted view of Catholic teaching of the time. Roman Catholic.

Costen, Melva Wilson. _African American Christian Worship._ Nashville: Abingdon, 1993. See chapter 5 on the sacraments and ordinances of worship.

Dix, Gregory. _The Shape of the Liturgy._ 1945; Revised edition with expanded notes by Paul V. Marshall. New York: Seabury, 1982. Dix, an Anglican Benedictine monk, traces the development of the Christian Eucharist from the Jewish table fellowship and Passover ritual. Dix argues that the basic form of the Christian eucharistic sacrament can be authentically traced to the Last Supper, i.e., that Jesus established the form of the Eucharist as it has been practiced ever since. Dix's argument is not accepted by all scholars in all its details, but it remains a fundamental starting point for studying the development of the Christian Eucharist.

Dugmore, Clifford W. *The Mass and the English Reformers*. London: Macmillan, 1958. An important historical study that includes a sketch of sacramental theology before the Reformation, making it a much broader resource than its title suggests.

Elert, Werner. *Eucharist and Christian Fellowship in the First Four Centuries*. St. Louis: Concordia, 1966.

Empie, Paul C., and James I. McCord, eds. *Marburg Revisited: A Reexamination of Lutheran and Reformed Traditions*. Minneapolis: Augsburg, 1966.

Foley, Edward. *From Age to Age: How Christians Celebrated the Eucharist*. Chicago: Liturgy Training Publications, 1991. Study of the history of how worship affected ordinary people. Uses architecture, music, books, vessels, theology and so on. Illustrated.

Holifield, E. Brooks. *The Covenant Sealed: The Development of Puritan Sacramental Theology in Old and New England, 1570–1720*. New Haven, Conn.: Yale University Press, 1974.

Jasper, R(onald) C(laude) D(udley), and Geoffrey Cuming. *Prayers of the Eucharist*. 3d ed. New York: Pueblo Publishing, 1987. A translation of the most significant eucharistic liturgies in the history of the church.

Jungmann, Josef A. *The Mass of the Roman Rite: Its Origins and Development*. New York: Benziger, 1949. The most complete single survey of the history of Roman Catholic liturgy and sacraments in the form of a detailed commentary on the Mass, preceded by a survey of its history.

Lindberg, Carter, trans. and ed. "Karlstadt's Dialogue on the Lord's Supper." *Mennonite Quarterly Review* 53 (Jan. 1979): 35–78.

Mersch, Emile. *The Whole Christ: The Historical Development of the Doctrine of the Mystical Body in Scripture and Tradition*. Trans. John R. Kelly. London: Dennis Dobson, 1938; originally published as *Le corps mystique du Christ*. Louvain: Museum Lessianum, 1936. Roman Catholic.

McDonnell, Kilian. *John Calvin, the Church, and the Eucharist*. Princeton, N.J.: Princeton University Press, 1967.

McLaughlin, R. Emmet. *Caspar Schwenckfeld, Reluctant Radical: His Life to 1540*. New Haven, Conn.: Yale University Press, 1986.

McCue, James F. "The Doctrine of Transubstantiation from Berengar through Trent: The Point at Issue." *Harvard Theological Review* 61 (1968): 385–430.

Macy, Gary. *The Banquet's Wisdom: A Short History of the Theologies of the Lord's Supper*. New York and Mahwah, N.J.: Paulist Press, 1992.

———. *The Theologies of the Eucharist in the Early Scholastic Period: A Study of the Salvific Function of the Sacrament according to the Theologians, c. 1080–1220*. Oxford: Clarendon, 1984.

Rattenbury, John Ernest. *The Eucharistic Hymns of John and Charles Wesley*. London: Epworth Press, 1948.

Rempel, John D. *The Lord's Supper in Anabaptism*. Scottdale, Pa.: Herald Press, 1993. The only full study of eucharistic theology among the sixteenth-century Anabaptists, pointing out that not all Anabaptists had a purely memorialist (Zwinglian) understanding of the Eucharist but that a spiritualist interpretation dominated on all sides.

Rordorf, Willy, et al. *The Eucharist of the Early Christians*. Trans. by Matthew J. O'Connell. New York: Pueblo Publishing, 1978; originally published in Paris: Beauchesne, 1976.

Rubin, Miri. *Corpus Christi: The Eucharist in Late Medieval Culture*. Cambridge: Cambridge University Press, 1991. A careful study of how the Eucharist was perceived and practiced in the later Middle Ages on the eve of the Protestant Reformation.

Sheerin, Daniel J., ed. *Message of the Fathers of the Church*. Vol. 7, *The Eucharist*. Wilmington, Del.: Michael Glazier, 1986. A fine collection of documents regarding the Eucharist from the major early church writers. Essential for serious study.

Spinks, Bryan. *Freedom or Order? The Eucharistic Liturgy in English Congregationalism, 1645–1980*. Allison Park, Pa.: Pickwick Publications, 1984.

Stevenson, Kenneth W. *Eucharist and Offering*. New York: Pueblo Publishing, 1986. A survey of the history of eucharistic liturgies.

Walker, Michael J. *Baptists at the Table: The*

Theology of the Lord's Supper Amongst English Baptists in the Nineteenth Century. Didcot, U.K.: Baptist Historical Society, 1992.

See also the bibliographies on the theology and practice of the Lord's Supper. Many of those volumes include sections on the history of the Lord's Supper.

TEN

Theologies of the Lord's Supper

From the early church's firm belief in the Real Presence of the risen Christ in the Eucharist have developed a variety of Eastern Orthodox, Catholic, and Protestant explanations of how this mystery takes place (or, as Radical Reformation Protestants asserted, if any change at all occurs). Eastern Orthodox churches generally avoid complex theological and philosophical explanations. In the West, modern Roman Catholic theologians have searched for biblical language to explain this mystery, notably, the Pauline language about being inserted into Christ. They continue to uphold the doctrine of transubstantiation, which teaches the sacramental and substantial (real)—but not carnal or physical—presence of Christ.

Reformed (Calvinist) theology recognizes Christ's real and spiritual presence, but resists the idea that the sacrament is efficacious in and of itself. Anglicans assert Real Presence in a variety of ways, ranging from a position very close to the Roman Catholic doctrine of transubstantiation to an explanation that emphasizes the occasion when the bread and wine are received by the believer. With his roots in the Anglican tradition, John Wesley considered the Lord's Supper a powerful sacrament even while emphasizing inner renewal and sanctification.

The radical Protestant memorialist viewpoint of the Anabaptists and Ulrich Zwingli continues to be held by the groups descended from the Anabaptists (Mennonites and others), as well as by some mainline Protestants, many evangelicals, and all Pentecostal churches. However, each of these groups recognizes something worthy of reverence and devotion in the Communion service.

199 ◆ AN EARLY CHURCH THEOLOGY OF THE LORD'S SUPPER

Christian writers of the first two centuries affirmed, without attempting a theological explanation for the fact, that the risen Christ is present in the eucharistic action that transforms those who receive it.

——————— Christ's Presence ———————

What can be said confidently about the theology of the Lord's Supper in the earliest centuries is that the writings available to modern researchers attest to the conviction that the risen Christ is present in the eucharistic action and assembly. What cannot be said with confidence is how in the earliest eras this presence was explained philosophically, if indeed it was. What must be avoided (though frequently it happens) is the attempt to read back into those times later explanations and controversies, particularly the medieval and Reformation debates about Christ's presence in the Eucharist.

Certainly the understanding of the early centuries was related to the Lukan affirmation that the risen Lord "was known to them in the breaking of bread" (Luke 24:35, KJV), and to the concept of *anamnesis* behind the eucharistic formulations of Luke and Paul.

The Didache (*c.* 100–150) affirms, "To us you have granted spiritual food and drink for eternal life through your child Jesus" (10:3); speaks of "the life and knowledge which you have made known to us" (9:3); and speaks of "the knowledge and faith and immortality which you have made known to us." However, these statements, together with the cry *maranatha* "our Lord, come;" (10:6) can be interpreted broadly, rather than as specific references to eucharistic presence.

Hence, the first clear post–New Testament source on the Eucharist is Justin Martyr's *Dialogue with Trypho* (c. 150) (see chapters 65–67). In the *Dialogue,* Justin asserts the Eucharist to be the one true sacrifice acceptable to God; but Christ's presence in the Eucharist is not clearly implied. In the *First Apology* 66:2, however, Justin affirms:

> For we do not receive these things as common bread or common drink; but just as our Savior Jesus Christ, being incarnate through the Word of God, took flesh and blood for our salvation, so too we have been taught that the food over which thanks have been given by the prayer of the Word who is from him, from which our flesh and blood are fed by transformation, is both the flesh and blood of that incarnate Jesus.

Thus the work of Christ in the historical Incarnation and in the Eucharist are inextricably linked without elaboration as to how this can occur. It is clear, however, that Justin sees this as a teaching handed down—not as his own invention.

The Transformation of the Recipient

Further, the linkage between Christ in the Incarnation and Christ in the Eucharist is to be understood. Whatever happens or does not happen in the transformation of the bread and wine, Christ's presence in the Eucharist is a source of transformation (*metabolen*) of the worshipers. Whether this is ethical transformation (as may be inferred from Justin's later reference to sharing with all in need) or ontological transformation—or both—is also not specified.

It is likely that for Justin, the work of the *logos,* the Word, is crucial in any eucharistic transformation; certainly this is true in Irenaeus (c. 180). For Irenaeus states that "the mingled cup and the manufactured bread receives the Word of God, and the Eucharist of the blood and body of Christ is made, from which things the substance of our flesh is increased and supported. . . ." (*Against Heresies*, 5.2.3). Irenaeus also asserts that earthly bread "when it receives the invocation (*epiklesis*) of God is no longer common bread, but the Eucharist, consisting of two realities, earthly and heavenly"; and from this our bodies receive incorruption, "having the hope of resurrection to eternity" (4.18). Similarly for Ignatius of Antioch (c. 115), the Eucharist is the "medicine of immortality" (*To the Ephesians,* 20). However in none of these instances is there a hint of an explanation as to how the physical bread becomes more than bodily food.

A plethora of references throughout the writers of the period confirms the early church's affirmation that, through the bread and cup of the Eucharist, the faithful have a particular means of apprehending the presence of their Lord. Justin's reference to an accompanying transformation of people is less evident in other literature of the early church, and may represent his distinctive and enduring contribution to eucharistic teaching.

Laurence Hull Stookey

200 • An Eastern Orthodox Theology of the Lord's Supper

Although Eastern Orthodox theology insists as firmly as Roman Catholics in the West that the bread and wine become the body and blood of Christ, Orthodox theologians have not attempted the theological and philosophical explanations of how this happens that are characteristic of Catholic and Protestant controversies in the West. According to Orthodox theology, the eucharistic assembly is the essence of what it means to be the church. Worthy participants enter on the path of transformation by grace into becoming a new creature and partaking of the divine nature.

The Eucharistic Action

Since ancient times, Orthodox Christians have made no effort to explain the Holy Communion beyond the words of the Holy Scriptures. Paul wrote, "Is not the cup of thanksgiving for which we give thanks a participation in the blood of Christ? And is not the bread that we break a participation in the body of Christ?" (1 Cor. 10:16). Christ said, "Take and eat; this is my body," and "This is my blood of the covenant, which is poured out for many for the forgiveness of sins" (Matt. 26:26-27) when he instituted the Eucharist. For this reason, the Orthodox church teaches that the bread and wine are not ordinary bread and wine, but that they become the body and blood of Christ. However, the Orthodox church has always considered the sacrament a mystery beyond the comprehension of the human mind. Thus, Orthodox theologians make no effort to use rational or scientific terms to explain the change of bread and wine into the body and blood of Christ. Accordingly, Orthodox Christians reject Roman Catholic and Protestant efforts to understand the Eucharist as attempts to explain a mystery that cannot be explained. Thus the doctrines of transubstantiation, consubstantiation, the Real Presence, or symbolic interpretations of the sacrament find no place in Orthodoxy, because they fail to properly appreciate the mystical nature of Holy Communion.

Orthodox and Roman Catholic eucharistic piety and theology differ in several ways. The Orthodox church has always treated the consecrated bread and wine with great reverence, but has never developed the cult of the sacrament found in Roman Catholicism. The Orthodox church reserves the sacrament for the Communion of the sick, but has no equivalent to the Roman Catholic benediction of the blessed sacrament or the exposition. Orthodox theologians also reject the Roman Catholic teaching that the repetition of the words of Christ at the Last Supper transform the bread and wine into his body and blood. Instead, they consider the invocation of the Holy Spirit, the *epiklesis,* the climax of the change that begins when the priest prepares the bread and wine at the beginning of the service. Orthodox Christians view the Eucharist as a sacrifice of praise and thanksgiving. Paul wrote, "For whenever you eat this bread and drink this cup, you proclaim the Lord's death until he comes" (1 Cor. 11:26). Thus the Orthodox church also considers the Eucharist a commemoration of the life-giving death and resurrection of Christ. However, it has never developed the medieval Roman Catholic doctrine of the sacrifice of the Mass.

Corporate and Personal Transformation

Holy Communion is so central to Orthodoxy that Orthodox theologians define the church as a eucharistic assembly. For the Orthodox, the Lord's Supper or the divine liturgy is not simply another service, but the essence of what is to be the church. Echoing the words of Paul, "Because there is one loaf, we, who are many, are one body, for we all partake of the one loaf" (1 Cor. 10:17), Or-

thodox Christians believe that the Eucharist unites separate individuals into one body, the body of Christ, the church. The priest prays not only for the Holy Spirit to descend on the bread and wine, but also to descend on the assembly of believers, which becomes the body of Christ through participation in the divine liturgy. The Eucharist is not merely an earthly event for Orthodox Christians, but an ascent to join the company of heaven as they worship before the throne of God. Many aspects of salvation are found in the divine liturgy. The faithful hear the proclamation of the gospel through the readings from the Scriptures and the sermon. They profess their faith in the risen Lord. They also enter into an intimate relationship with the saving Christ, who feeds them with his own body and blood.

In his eucharistic discourse in the Gospel of John, Christ said, "Whoever eats my flesh and drinks my blood remains in me, and I in him" (John 6:56). Consequently, the Orthodox believe that those who partake worthily enter into an intimate personal relationship with Christ, an essential part of salvation. Orthodox Christians believe that salvation is more than the forgiveness of sins or eternal life; instead salvation is deification, the transformation of the believer through grace into a new creature and partaker of the divine nature (2 Pet. 1:4). Thus, Orthodox Christians believe that forgiveness of sins, and the gift of eternal life, are fruits of the sacrament. They also believe that Holy Communion is not only the transformation of bread and wine, but also the transformation of the believer through communion with Christ.

Orthodox Christians take very seriously Paul's warning: "Whoever eats the bread or drinks the cup of the Lord in an unworthy manner will be guilty of sinning against the body and blood of the Lord" (1 Cor. 11:27). At times, they have so exaggerated the sacred nature of the Eucharist that many Orthodox Christians received Holy Communion only a few times a year. Today, most Orthodox authorities encourage frequent Communion. However, those who participate in the sacrament carefully prepare themselves with prayer, fasting, and regular sacramental confession.

Thus, Holy Communion is central to Eastern Orthodoxy. The Eastern Orthodox church teaches that the Holy Spirit transforms the bread and wine into the real body and blood of Christ. However, they consider the change a mystery that must be approached through faith, not through human reason. They so emphasize the sacrament that they define the church as a eucharistic assembly. The worship of the divine liturgy defines the church, which receives its very being through communion with the risen Lord. Orthodox Christians consider Holy Communion an important part of the mystery of salvation—the union with Christ, which transforms the believer into the image and likeness of God and into a partaker of the divine nature. Finally, Orthodox consider Holy Communion sacred. Thus, they only approach the sacrament through repentance, prayer, and fasting.

John W. Morris

201 ✦ A ROMAN CATHOLIC THEOLOGY OF THE LORD'S SUPPER

The application of modern methods of biblical scholarship by Roman Catholic scholars since 1943 has been credited with renewing Catholic theology of the Eucharist. Although some early twentieth-century explanations of the meaning of the Eucharist were rejected by papal encyclicals as spiritualizing abandonments of historic belief in Christ's Real Presence, no consensus has emerged regarding language that would offer an alternative to the scholastic terminology of transubstantiation (material, substance, accidents), yet remain entirely faithful to the Roman Catholic tradition of Christ's Real Presence. Some have applied Pauline language about insertion into Christ's saving activity to both baptism and the Eucharist.

The Impact of the Biblical Movement

Twentieth-century Catholic theologians have continued to address traditional topics pertaining to the celebration of the Eucharist, especially: the sacramental presence of Christ; the representation of the sacrifice of Christ; and the role of the ordained minister (presbyter) in relation to the universal priesthood of all believers. Their work has been influenced by developments in philosophy and the human sciences, but especially by the biblical movement.

For centuries prior to the biblical movement, Catholic theologians followed the method of first establishing the official teaching of the church on the Eucharist and then searching the Scriptures for support of the teaching. The purpose of this method was to show how a respective teaching related to all other teachings of faith in a harmonious whole. Even though pastoral application was a genuine concern, it was not in the forefront of the theological account. While this approach clearly provided insight into the development of doctrine (teaching), it tended to give the impression that dogmatic formulations, and even lesser statements by the Pope, were somehow immune to the passing of time and to different historical situations.

The biblical movement, which had begun many years earlier among the Reformation churches, enhanced Catholic theology and led to the publication of the encyclical *Divino afflante spiritu* by Pope Pius XII in 1943. This circular letter to the church affirmed the importance and use of the historical-critical method in the study of the Scriptures, and of their centrality in making an account of the convictions of faith and the practices of the church.

This new method recognizes the Scriptures as expression of the faith of the church and, in turn, as the norm for evaluation of all subsequent theological discourse. The following questions guide this new method. In responding to the pastoral needs in a given cultural-historical setting, as well as to the needs of sound reason, how well does a given teaching serve the Word of God in Scripture? In view of both the lived tradition of the past, as well as the data of Scripture, does a teaching need reassessment in order to respond to valid current needs? This more recent method in making an account of the faith and practice of the church has the advantage of making the original revelation more intelligible, as well as of paying due attention to Christian life itself as a source of insight.

Theological Reevaluations

By the 1930s, theologians had begun a critical study of the dogma of Christ's presence under the forms of bread and wine, in such a way as to be faithful to the witness of Scripture, as well as to respond to recent philosophical questions. Eucharistic doctrine up until that time had been shaped by the questions and philosophy of the ninth-through-eleventh-century eucharistic controversies. In those centuries, some theologians had seemed to reduce the consecrated bread and wine to mere signs or symbols which, for the eyes of faith, only pointed to the presence of Christ in heaven. By the thirteenth century, theologians conceptually secured the Real Presence of Christ on the basis of the analogy with substantial changes in material beings, but with the following difference. Whereas material beings undergo changes in substantial form, the bread and wine become the body and blood of Christ by a complete change of being. Only the outward appearances remain. It must be noted that the desire was to defend the biblically grounded faith-conviction of the church: Christ is really present, and this implies real change. Any explanation is by way of analogy.

Some early twentieth-century theologians wanted to respond to the pastoral questions regarding the meaning of eucharistic food—the sacramental presence of Christ inviting the believer to faith. They reasoned that, if God changes the meaning of bread and wine, this entails a change of being. Therefore, the eucharistic bread and wine only have the meaning-for-us of Christ's saving presence.

Papal Responses

In the encyclical *Humani generis* (1951), Pope Pius XII rejected this approach because it seemed to spiritualize Christ's eucharistic presence (i.e., reduce it to only subjective meaning for the believer) and to set aside the scholastic theology of substantial change—thus, the Real Presence. In response, literature appeared which continued to depart from scholastic philosophical language, but instead considered a theology of conversion of elements. In the encyclical *Mysterium Fidei* (1965), Pope Paul VI asserted that any change of meaning for the believer is grounded on a change in the being of the elements of bread and wine. In so doing, the Pope implicitly acknowledged the inadequacies of the explanation grounded in scholastic philosophical language and opened the door to further theological development in making an account of the faith of the church.

Since 1965, no common approach to the dogma of transubstantiation, i.e., the real transformation of the bread and wine into the body and blood of Christ has emerged. However, theologians have compared the eucharistic conversion to the In-

carnation; just as the *logos* took flesh by the power of the Spirit, so the risen Lord takes up the bread and wine in the power of the Spirit as a corporeal means of saving presence. At the same time, Catholic theologians stress that the presence of Christ in the believer by faith is the necessary condition for a fruitful reception of the sacrament of faith.

Insertion into Christ's Saving Activity

To the extent that Catholic theology has retrieved the Pauline understanding of baptism (see especially Rom. 6) as insertion by the Spirit into the death of the Lord to the glory of the Father with all others who are baptized, it has been able to more profoundly make an account for the Eucharist as the offering of the one-for-all sacrifice of Christ by the church, i.e., Christ and his members. This retrieval of the New Testament theology of the church not only enables a richer appreciation of the presence in the Christian of the gift of the participation in the Spirit of Christ's faith, but also of the Spirit as the condition for the possibility of the active, trusting faith of Christians. Hence, it is recognized that the presence in the believer of faith comes about by the gift of insertion into Christ's saving activity on the cross by the power of the Spirit to the glory of God with all other baptized members. In the celebration of the Eucharist, the baptized offer to the Father not another sacrifice, but the one eternal sacrifice of Christ, into which they have been baptized by the power of the Spirit.

Priest and Presider: Liturgical Reform

This understanding of the origin of the church situates the role of the ordained minister at the Eucharist in radical baptismal relationship to all others who share in the universal priesthood of all believers. The ordained minister fulfills the valid need for leadership in the most important act of worship of the church. By convening the church, proclaiming the Scriptures and the eucharistic prayer (prayer of praise and thanksgiving), the presider serves the crucial role of calling the church to its origin, the cross of Christ; to its present situation, being in Christ for the peace and salvation of all the world; and to its hope, the recapitulation of all things in Christ. The presider acts in the name of the church in that the church deputes the ordained minister to act in the person of Christ, the one head of the church. As such, the presider can be said to be a sacrament of the church—Christ and his members. From this perspective, the ordained minister has the responsibility to reconcile the members of the body to themselves, i.e., to be the body of Christ in history.

The *Constitution on the Sacred Liturgy* (1963) issued by the Second Vatican Council mandated the reform of the liturgy, the public worship of the church. The fruits of the biblical movement and the liturgical movement have yielded benefit for all the churches of the Western Christian tradition in the reforms of orders of worship. The tremendous consensus on the topics of sacramental presence, the representation of the sacrifice of Christ, and the meaning of ordained ministry in relation to the celebration of the Eucharist are obvious in the Lima Document of the World Council of Churches in 1982. Such a consensus is the work of the Spirit enabling the churches to recognize and overcome those issues which have divided them since the sixteenth century.

Theresa Koernke

202 ✦ A Lutheran Theology of the Lord's Supper

A distinctive Lutheran theology of the Lord's Supper arises out of Luther's evangelical understanding of sacrament as well as two specific matters of controversy in the sixteenth century—the sacrifice of the Mass and the presence of Christ at the Supper. Luther's own writings and the Lutheran confessional documents of the sixteenth century are the principal sources for this theology.

A Sacrament of Promise and Command

In Lutheran theology, the Lord's Supper is one of two chief sacraments (together with baptism). In opposition to the medieval scholastic theology of sacrament, which understood the supper as an efficacious sign of grace (*efficax signum gratiate*) working by means of the ritual action of the Mass (*ex opere operato*), Luther and his followers for-mulated a theology of the Lord's Supper within a concept of the sacrament determined by an emphasis on the activity of God's Word and the role of faith. The Word of God in the sacrament is both a word of command and a word of promise. The words of Christ, recorded in Scripture, provide the mandate for what Christians do at the Lord's Supper; they also proclaim the promise of God which lies at the heart of the supper. Moreover, the word of the sacrament is, as Augustine said, a visible word. At the Lord's Supper, it is the earthly elements of bread and wine in the context of the entire sacramental action that give visibility to God's Word. Corresponding to the activity of God's Word in the sacrament is the sacrament's reception by faith. Faith receives what God promises in the Supper, and in this conjunction of the Word of God and faith the sacrament has its effect. Thus, the sacrament of the Lord's Supper is a means of grace. In its deepest sense, the Lutheran interpretation of the Supper as a sacrament under the categories of the Word of God and faith understands the Lord's Supper as a means by which the living Christ, who is God's Word, encounters faithful people of God.

Sacrifice Rejected, Yet Real Presence Affirmed

Other characteristic features of Lutheran theology of the Lord's Supper emerged from the controversy with Rome over the sacrifice of the Mass. Luther condemned the idea of the sacrifice of the Mass for two specific reasons. In the first place, it had allowed the Mass to become a particular kind of work by which people sought God's favor and assistance through the performance of religious ceremony. In keeping with the doctrine of justification by faith, Luther taught that the Lord's Supper is an exercise of faith, not a ceremonial work to obtain some benefit from God. In the second place, the Mass as a sacrifice misconstrued the very nature of the Supper as sacrament. It is a benefit (*beneficium*), not a sacrifice (*sacrificium*). The Supper is a gift to be received by faith, rather than an offering made to God by the priest for the spiritual well-being of the living and the dead. It is the gift of forgiveness. The Supper contains and visibly enacts God's promise of forgiveness in order that it might be faithfully received. It is also the gift of communion in Christ through the reception of his body and blood. The sacramental elements are received in faith, not presented to God as an offering. In accordance with the Lord's own command, the bread is for eating and the cup is for drinking, not for sacrifice.

Lutheran theology of the Lord's Supper is also characterized by the doctrine of the Real Presence of Christ. Luther rejected the doctrine of transubstantiation for a number of reasons. First of all, he argued that the Scriptures are clear that bread and wine remain genuine bread and wine; their substance is not changed. Luther also questioned the notion of a change in the elements of bread and wine because this belief was linked with a claim about the power of the priest to bring it about. Furthermore, Luther insisted that Christ's presence at the Supper was a mystery and that transubstantiation as the official teaching of the church violated that mystery because it made a specific explanation—one that relied on Aristotelian categories of thought—binding for theology and faith. Despite these concerns about the doctrine of transubstantiation, Luther did not give up the belief that at the Supper the bread and wine are the true body and blood of Christ. This insistence on the Real Presence of Christ at the Supper emerged fully in debates with the Zurich Reformer Zwingli, which divided the adherents of the Reformation.

The classic Lutheran position states that the true body and blood of Christ are present "in, with, and under" the elements of bread and wine. This presence exists through the power of God's Word, which proclaims and promises Christ's presence to those who receive the sacrament. Lutheran adherence to the Real Presence seeks to protect the mystery of Christ's presence at the Supper without prescribing a specific explanation (and, for this reason, the Lutheran position should not be labeled *consubstantiation*). The scriptural foundation for this teaching lies in Christ's own words from the institution narrative ("This *is* my body"), which Luther felt constrained to take quite literally. Although the Real Presence cannot be explained, it can be understood with the help of Christological categories. The personal union of the human and divine natures of Christ itself provides a fitting analogy for the sacramental union of Christ's body and blood with the elements of bread and wine.

Three Latin tags further delineate the Lutheran doctrine of the Real Presence, particularly in relation to Reformed theologies of Christ's presence at the Supper. The *manducatio oralis* (oral eating) affirms that Christ's body and blood are received orally in the eating and drinking of the sacramental bread and wine and not in some spiritual or incorporeal way. The *manducatio indignorum* (eating of the unworthy) assures the objectivity of Christ's presence in its claim that Christ's presence is not dependent upon faith; even those without faith receive the body and blood of Christ. Finally, there is the Lutheran interpretation of the early church's theology of *communicatio idiomatum* (the *communication of attributes* between the divine and human natures of Christ). In response to the attempt of Reformed theologians to dismiss the Real Presence with the claim that the humanity of Christ is located in heaven and consequently cannot be present in the sacramental elements, Luther and his followers argued by referring to the communicatio idiomatum that Christ's humanity now shares the omnipresence (or ubiquity) characteristic of his divinity. Thus, it is possible for Christ's body and blood to be present at earthly altars. Through the Word of God, this presence becomes a saving presence to be received by faith.

Thomas H. Schattauer

203 ◆ A REFORMED THEOLOGY OF THE LORD'S SUPPER

For the Reformed tradition, the bread and wine are signs that point to Christ's spiritual presence, but have no power apart from the accompanying Word of God. Christ is divinely present. However since his ascension, his humanity has been localized in heaven. In order to protect the sovereign freedom of God, Reformed theology resists both Lutheran and Catholic views of the objective efficacy of the sacrament. The Lord's Supper is neither a converting sacrament, nor mere ceremony. It renews and seals Christ's promise to us, exercises Christian's faith, and incites growth in the Christian life.

Sign and Substance

For the Reformed, Jesus Christ, the sole mediator between God and man, is personally present today, governing and sustaining the church through the Word of God and two sacraments. The sacraments are accessories to the preaching of the Word of God, which establishes the church. Recognizing the believer's anxiety and weakness, God employs these physical signs of grace throughout the church's history to confirm his promised grace and to claim for himself all of us, soul and body.

Christ instituted the Lord's Supper as a sign that, through his death and resurrection, he fulfills the new covenant, establishing reconciliation between wayward humans and a holy God (Matt. 26:28). All the components of this service—the basic foods, the breaking of the bread, the distribution, and the eating as a community—powerfully signify Christ as the believers' spiritual life and present nourishment.

The Reformed insist that the bread and wine are physical signs which have no power in themselves, but point to Christ's spiritual presence. In this symbolic view, the Word must accompany the elements. The Word constitutes the elements as a sacrament by identifying the promised reality this service mirrors.

With this definition, the Reformed reject transubstantiation and adoration of the consecrated elements, considering a failure to distinguish sign and substance as idolatrous. Characteristically, the Reformed identify idolatry as any tendency to trust in something created, instead of worshiping God, who is spirit.

Christ's Presence

The substance of the Lord's Supper is "Christ communicating himself with all his benefits to us" (Belgic Confession [1561]: art. 35). This sacrament does not just intellectually remind the believer of Christ; "here the faithful . . . have such union with Christ Jesus as the natural man cannot apprehend" (Scots Confession [1560]: chap. 21). Even though his human body is in heaven, the Spirit "transfuses life into us from the flesh of Christ" (*Calvin's Tracts* 2:249).

With this thesis, the Reformed reject the Arminian conception of the Lord's Supper as an ordinance. Frequently, Zwingli is also labeled a memorialist on the ground that he views the elements as bare signs representing what is absent. Recent scholarship questions this assessment of the later Zwingli. Certainly, he affirms that this ceremony brings to mind historical events. However, believers are not confined to that sphere. Those "taught inwardly by the Spirit . . . know and

believe that Christ suffered for us: it is they alone who receive Christ" (*Exposition of the Faith*, Library of Christian Classics 24:261). Since "the true body of Christ is present by the contemplation of faith" (*The Latin Works of Huldreich Zwingli* 2:49), the believer comes "to the Lord's Supper to feed spiritually upon Christ" (*Exposition of Faith* 24:259). As Locher documents, Zwingli's idea of recollection is not that of the Enlightenment, but instead the Augustinian concept of *memoria*, in which the Spirit illuminates the mind and makes Christ present (Gottfried W. Lochner, *Zwingli's Thought: New Perspectives* [Leiden: E. J. Brill, 1981], 222–24).

This understanding of Jesus' personal presence contests the Lutheran view. Since the benefits of salvation are mediated solely by Christ, the Lutherans argue that the divine and even the human nature must be locally present with the elements. First, the Reformed point out that the hypostatic union grounds the unity of the two natures of Christ and Christ's presence in the Eucharist. Just as Jesus' human nature has salvific efficacy for humans only through his deity, in the same way, Jesus' human nature can spiritually nourish humans through the Spirit's work in the Eucharist. Second, Scripture carefully demonstrates that Jesus' humanity is like ours, not ubiquitous, but delimited by place (Luke 24:6; Mark 16:6). Furthermore, Scripture demonstrates that Jesus' human nature is now in heaven (Acts 1:9-11). In addition, through the Supper believers "proclaim the Lord's death until he comes" (1 Cor. 11:26). Thus Jesus' words of institution must be interpreted figuratively . Third, if Christ's humanity is not like ours, the salvation of humanity is endangered.

God's Grace

The Reformed also underscore God's sovereign freedom and the reality of grace. Since the Lord's Supper depends entirely on Christ's initiative, the signs carry no power in themselves. Rather, the Spirit freely creates faith in us and links us to the person of Jesus Christ through the sign. The elements, then, are the instruments Christ uses to make believers partakers of himself.

According to medieval theology, the priest's sacrificial work and the church's oblation to God in the Mass were instrumental for imparting and perfecting Christ's benefits. The Reformed repudiate this view as promoting justification by works. The church has nothing meritorious to offer God. Christ is the sole mediator; his sacrifice is unique and its efficacy eternal. This sacrament is a supper, not a sacrifice; served at a table, not an altar. Nor are others needed to transmit Christ's benefits (*Calvin's Tracts* 2:184), for Christ is present in his Word and sacraments. Moreover, the church's oblation is not meritorious, but a response of gratitude for Christ's prior and present work (Calvin, *Institutes* 5.18.16). Simply put, we live by grace solely through Christ's work.

This Reformed distinctive also opposes the Lutheran view. Seeking to preserve the objectivity and truthfulness of God's promise in the Lord's Supper, Luther maintains that wherever this visible Word is presented, Christ is automatically present. Consequently, he concludes that even the wicked feed on Christ (*monducatio impiorum*), but receive judgment. Reformed theologians reject this reciprocal linking of sign and substance, because it precludes God's sovereign freedom and the Supper as a means of *grace*. They also reject the other extreme that separates the sign and substance dualistically because it suggests that God's Word is deceptive. Generally, the Reformed follow Calvin's proposal: "If the Lord truly represents the participation in this body through the breaking of the bread, there ought not to be the least doubt that he truly presents and shows his body." But faith alone apprehends this objective reality. Thus, only if the Spirit has already created faith can one feed on Christ (*Institutes* 4.17.10).

Purpose

The Reformed do not elevate the Lord's Supper to a converting sacrament, nor reduce it to a bare ceremony mandated by our Lord. Christ instituted the Lord's Supper for nourishing the believer in the following three ways.

First, speaking through the words of institution, Christ declares that his sacrifice at Calvary, which ratified the covenant long ago, was given for believers. Through communion with believers, Christ renews and seals that original promise. Now, "I see with my eyes that the bread of the Lord is broken for me and that the cup is shared with me" (Heidelberg Catechism [1563]: 75).

Second, the Lord's Supper exercises our faith and incites growth in the Christian life. Traditionally, the Reformed emphasize Paul's exhortation to "examine" oneself (1 Cor. 11:28). The Scots Confession even "fences in" the table (chapter 23). The point is that communion with Christ presupposes believers who are conscious of their sinfulness, repentant, aware that Christ is the sole source of eternal life, and endeavoring to make their "whole life conformable to . . . Christ" (Calvin, *Calvin's Tracts* 2:174). Because Christ is present here, faith is "kindled and grows more and more, and is refreshed by spiritual food" (Second Helvetic Confession [1566]: chap. 21).

Having been assured of reconciliation and empowered by Christ—despite being sinners—the Lord's Supper now issues in acts of gratitude, *eucharistia,* for Christ's work: "a spiritual oblation of all possible praise unto God" (Westminster Confession of Faith [1646]: chap. 29.2) and "a fervent love towards God and our neighbor" (Belgic Confession: art. 35). The church gratefully demonstrates Christ's love to others by "coalescing into one body" and "regarding a brother as a member—eye, hand or foot . . ." (Zwingli, *The Latin Works of Huldreich Zwingli* 3:394). While originating in God's action, this sacrament concludes with believers attesting to the reality of their faith.

Timothy R. Phillips

204 ✦ An Anglican Theology of the Lord's Supper

Anglicans believe in the Real Presence of Christ in the Eucharist. They reject any doctrine of a crudely material presence. The Thirty-nine Articles, the sixteenth-century Anglican statement of doctrine and polity, also rejected the less crudely materialist Catholic doctrine of transubstantiation. The following paragraphs outline four ways that Anglicans explain Christ's real, sacramental presence.

Real But Not Carnal or Local Presence

The Anglican Communion (sixty million worldwide) is catholic and evangelical. It is catholic in that its creeds, sacramental theology, and polity (episcopacy) conform to the undivided church prior to the East/West division of the eleventh century. At the same time, the English church has concluded that the main doctrinal developments of the Protestant Reformation, such as the authority of Scripture and the necessity of personal faith, are also part of the ancient faith. These catholic and evangelical threads are reflected in the Anglican view of the presence of the bread and wine.

The Anglican Communion advocates the Real Presence of Christ regarding the Eucharist. When Christ says, "This is my body. . . . This is blood" (Matt. 26:26, 28), referring to the bread and the wine of the Lord's Supper, he declares his presence. No attempt is made to explain away Real Presence, for this would be, as someone has said, "The real absence of Christ." The Word of God clearly calls the church to believe that it really and truly feeds on Christ in the Holy Communion. This is a mystery, not able to be fully comprehended by the human mind (a mystery no less than other doctrines such as the Trinity and the relationship between the deity and the humanity of Christ). Nevertheless, this presence is to be acknowledged and affirmed.

Anglicans hasten to add the qualification that Real Presence is not physical or local, as the doctrine called transubstantiation is often thought to teach. (See "The Lord's Supper in the Medieval West," chapter 9; transubstantiation was in fact aimed at countering a crude doctrine of Christ's physical, local presence in the Eucharist.) The Thirty-nine Articles confessional statement of the Anglican Church state in article 28, "Transubstantiation (or the change of the substance of bread and wine) in the Supper of the Lord, cannot be proved by holy writ; but is repugnant to the plain words of Scripture, overthroweth the nature of a sacrament, and hath given occasion to many superstitions."

Any notion that the elements of Communion change into the physical body and blood of Christ—not simply into the substance of Christ—goes beyond the statements of Scripture, for the Bible only tells Christians that the bread and wine are his body and blood, and not how that occurs. If the elements become the physical reality, then they cease to be a sacrament, a sign. Granted, the Eucharist is more than a sign in that grace is applied through it (hence a sacrament), but if the bread and wine become the physical body and blood, then the elements become less than a sign. Despite the effort by medieval theologians to counter such crudely corporal interpretations, such interpretations reappeared from time to time and led to abuses of the elements themselves.

Although the Anglican Communion has upheld the real-yet-mystery view of presence, this view has been understood in a variety of ways. Apart from those who would simply leave Real Presence as a mystery and go no further, there are four main views.

First, the Anglo-Catholic understanding of presence (the more Roman Catholic and Eastern Orthodox view) advances a view of real sacramental change that rejects any crude theory of physical or material changes. At the Conference on Anglo-Catholic Theology in London in 1927, the following position was stated:

> After consecration it [bread] is changed, . . . not by any change in anything which can be correlated in terms of electrons, but by the addition of opportunities of spiritual experience in that, by devout communion, we are made partakers in Christ. We are guilty of gross materialism if we think of the Host, or Chalice, in terms only of their physical properties, as purely physical objects, rather than in terms also of the opportunities of spiritual experience they afford, opportunities which are no less fundamental, and which are infinitely more significant (A. E. Taylor and Will Spens, *The Real Presence* [London: Anglo-Catholic Congress, 1927]).

This statement is careful to avoid a materialist change but pushes for some sort of change in a real sense. The distinction between spiritual and physical is not pressed, nor is the material considered to be more real than spiritual.

A second view of the sacramental presence of Christ is known as virtualism. "As used in the Sacrament they [the elements] have the 'virtue' of Christ's body and blood, inasmuch as they are vehicles of Christ's gifts to the soul, though they cannot be ontologically identified with what they convey" (Oliver C. Quick, *The Christian Sacraments* [London: Nisbet & Co., 1927, 1995], 206). The virtue of Christ is applied when the Holy Spirit descends to the sacraments at the *epiklesis*, the invocation of the third person of the Trinity, the Spirit. This application of Christ's virtue has been considered as taking place at the service as a whole, at the consecration itself through an additional prayer before or after the canon, or upon the reception of the elements into the faithful recipient. Virtualism is sometimes called a memorialist view. However, virtualism should not be

St. Basil the Great. One of the three great Cappadocian Fathers of the fourth century, Basil lived an ardent ascetic life and is often regarded as the father of the monastic tradition. His symbol is a scroll on which is written (in Greek): "The ascetic life is both difficult and perilous."

confused with Zwinglianism, a position that believes in no special presence relative to the Eucharist in the service proper or in the person. The *epiklesis*, historically an Eastern Orthodox distinctive, has also come into Anglicanism at different times, particularly as one of the emphases of the Anglo-Catholic movement of the last century. This prayer was incorporated into the 1928 version of the Prayer Book. Modern versions often make the *epiklesis* optional.

A third view of the Real Presence of Christ is another variation of an Eastern Orthodox emphasis that was taught by John Calvin, who was quite influenced by the Eastern church Fathers. Calvin built on the verse, "Let us draw near with a true heart . . . not neglecting to meet together . . . all the more as you see the Day drawing near" (Heb. 10:22-25). This mystical drawing near was Calvin's understanding of the *sursum corda*, a historical statement in virtually all eucharistic services that is based on the previous Scripture and is translated, "Lift up your hearts." According to the Reformer at Geneva, the *sursum corda* teaches that Christ is really present at the Eucharist because the church draws near to him in the heavenlies in a mysterious sense. The ascended Lord is at the head of the table. This ascension position can also be combined with any or all of the other approaches to Christ's presence in the Eucharist.

A fourth view of presence in Anglicanism is receptionism, the most popular conviction among many evangelicals since the Reformation. This opinion maintains that the elements become the body and blood of Christ when actually received by faith and not until then. They remain simple elements of bread and wine when taken in unbelief.

All of these views of presence are represented in the Anglican Communion, a large and comprehensive church. The Anglican church believes in a true Real Presence, even though there are various ways of understanding the reality of this presence. It rejects a physical transformation of the elements. It thus affirms in the Articles of Religion: "The Body of Christ is given, taken, and eaten, in the Supper, only after an heavenly and spiritual manner. And the means whereby the Body of Christ is received and eaten in the Supper, is Faith." As such, the Anglican Communion embraces the Catholic as well as the evangelical position in its belief in Christ's presence in the bread and wine.

Ray R. Sutton

205 ◆ An Anabaptist Theology of the Lord's Supper

The sixteenth-century Anabaptists followed Ulrich Zwingli, the Reformer of the city of Zurich, where the first wing of Anabaptism originated, in viewing the Lord's Supper as a memorial, or sign, of Christ's death. However, they believed that Christ was profoundly present in their hearts, even if the bread and wine were not the vehicles to accomplish that presence. Their emphasis on the Lord's Supper as a simple fellowship underscores the fundamentally communal nature of their theology of the Eucharist.

A Sign of Inward, Spiritual Union with Christ

Like the Protestant Reformers, the sixteenth-century Anabaptists denied that Communion bread and wine are Jesus' literal body and blood. The bread, they insisted, is simply bread; the wine is simply wine; and the Lord's Supper is a simple fellowship meal—not a ritual. Anabaptist leaders, some of whom had been associated with Ulrich Zwingli, employed his language, calling the Lord's Supper a memorial, or sign, of Jesus' death. As such the Lord's Supper expressed, above all, the divine love.

It may seem as if the Lord's Supper, for the Anabaptists, was simply a reminder of a past event. However, in denying what seemed to them a crude, mechanical identification of Christ's presence with the eucharistic elements, they were seeking to stress a profound notion of his presence. This presence was both spiritual and communal.

Anabaptists frequently claimed, as did some late medieval sacramentarians, that eating and drinking are often used figuratively in Scripture to mean believing and trusting. Consequently, all who truly receive Christ by faith partake of his flesh and blood in the most important sense (esp. John 6:25-71). Many Anabaptist writers expressed this in deep mystical language. Jesus, said Melchoir Hoffman, gives himself as a bridegroom to a bride, lovingly uniting his innermost heart with ours. Just as the food humans absorb becomes one with our nature, Hans Denck and Dirk Philips affirmed that so too we absorb, and are transformed by, his divine nature (though we do not, of course, literally become God). Such a union, clearly, can arise only through active spiritual communion, never through mechanical reception of physical elements. When they stressed that the Lord's Supper was a sign, Anabaptists often meant a sign of this kind of spiritual reality, and not only of a historical event. But if Christ could be eaten and drunk in a wholly spiritual, inward way, why should one celebrate the outer ceremony at all? Some contemporaries of the Anabaptists, called Spiritualists, actually dispensed with it. But Anabaptists refused to dispense with it. Why?

The Communal Dimension

When believers gather around the Lord's Supper, not only does Christ share himself with them through the bread and wine. Believers also share bread and wine with each other. And through this sharing, believers are drawn more closely together as a community. "Because there is one bread, we who are many are one body, for we all partake of the one bread" (1 Cor. 10:17, RSV). Anabaptists often recalled an image found as early as the Didache (*c.* 100–150): As individual grains must be broken and ground to make a loaf, and individual grapes pressed to make wine, so must Christians die to themselves and be transformed to make up Christ's body.

The Lord's Supper, then, was also an occasion on which fellow Christians openly pledged themselves to each other. While Christ was offering himself to each one fully, even unto death, so did each Anabaptist, strengthened by Christ's presence, offer to share burdens and possessions with, and even to die for, the others. Since such gatherings were extremely illegal, participants knew that they might soon be dying for each other quite literally—as after the original Last Supper.

The Lord's Supper, then, could be celebrated rightly only among those willing to serve, love, and walk with each other. Footwashing, which expressed this willingness and which had accompanied the original Supper (John 13:1-20), was sometimes included. Failing to discern the body (1 Cor. 11:29) meant participating without this attitude. Conflicts, accordingly, had to be dealt with before or in the context of the Supper (following the order of Matt. 18:15-17; cf. Matt. 5:23-24).

When the Anabaptists denied Christ's physical presence in the bread and wine, they meant to point towards a more profound presence which was, on one hand, mystical. They experienced Jesus' life and love, poured out decisively on the cross, transforming them in the present at the deepest levels. And since they experienced this as they shared bread and wine, Jesus' presence was also communal. (Their insistence that the Supper be a fellowship meal, not a ritual, was designed to enhance this communal sense.) Further, since this sharing involved commitment to live and die for each other, Christ's presence was, or at least pointed towards, what we today call ethics.

The Lord's Supper, to be sure, memorialized a specific, bloody, historical event. But in its celebration, Christ was also really present. Where? Christ was not literally in the elements, was not simply in the words of institution, and was not merely in the individual's faith considered by itself. Christ's Real Presence was first and foremost communal.

Thomas Finger

206 ✦ A Wesleyan Theology of the Lord's Supper

To John Wesley, the Lord's Supper was a powerful sacrament. He believed that even repentant unbelievers could take of the bread and cup and find salvation. Above all, Communion was a means of santification by which believers are transformed into the image of Christ.

Wesley's Understanding of the Eucharist

In his eucharistic thought, John Wesley (1703–1791), the founder of Methodism, was consciously and faithfully Anglican. As such, in his Articles of Religion for the Methodists, he took over verbatim the twenty-eighth article of the Anglican Thirty-nine Articles of Religion (1563), which rejected transubstantiation to be a senseless opinion hurtful to piety (_Works of John Wesley_ 7:64; 9:278). He was just as strongly opposed to Luther's view of consubstantiation. He insisted that Christ is bodily present in heaven and not on the Table in either the Catholic or Lutheran sense.

However, Wesley did believe in the Real Presence of Christ in the Eucharist, putting him in opposition to Zwingli's memorialist view as well. Much of the eucharistic teaching of John and Charles Wesley is found in the volume of _Hymns on the Lord's Supper_, which they first published in 1745. As a preface to the hymnbook, Wesley printed an abridgment of Daniel Brevint's _Christian Sacrament and Sacrifice_, the structure of which forms the outline for the grouping of the hymns under three categories: a memorial of Christ's past sufferings, a means of present graces, and a pledge of future glory. If the first sounds Zwinglian, the other two counter that impression. In spite of some memorialist language in Wesley, he does not conform to the Zwinglian model. The Lord's Supper is a real means of grace. At the Table, there is a real communion with the living Christ and a real reception of his body and blood,

albeit in a spiritual—not physical—manner. In the sacrament, believers receive not only the sign of Christ's body, but along with the sign the thing signified—namely, all the benefits of his incarnation and passion.

Wesley's view is one of "Spiritual Presence" closer to that of Calvin than to that of either Luther or Zwingli. This reflects his Anglican heritage, because Cranmer's eucharistic thought was arguably closer to Calvin's than to that of the other Continental Reformers. But Wesley's conception of _spiritual presence_ differs somewhat from Calvin's. Whereas Calvin spoke of the presence of Christ's body in terms of _power_, mediated to us by the Holy Spirit (_Institutes_ 4.17.24–33), Wesley stresses the presence of Christ in terms of his _divinity_—the whole Trinity being present in the Supper bestowing the benefits of Christ's redemptive act (see _Hymns on the Lord's Supper_, nos. 53 and 155).

The Lord's Supper as a Converting Ordinance

Wesley looked upon the Lord's Supper as a _converting_ sacrament. An unconverted person could come to the Table with a repentant heart and find forgiveness. "Inasmuch as we come to his table, not to give him any thing, but to receive whatsoever he sees best for us, there is no previous preparation indispensably necessary, but a desire to receive whatsoever he pleases to give. . . . No fitness is required . . . but a sense of our state, of our utter sinfulness and helplessness" (_Works_ 1:280). In such cases, the act of receiving the bread and the cup could be the very means of conversion, not merely something added to it.

Although Wesley's followers have never practiced closed Communion in the sense of barring from Communion those from other denominations or theological persuasions, not all have been comfortable with their progenitor's belief that an unbeliever may be converted to Christ by coming to the Lord's Supper. But Wesley insists that "the Lord's Supper was ordained by God, to be a means of conveying to men either preventing, justifying, or sanctifying grace, according to their several necessities" (_Works_ 1:280). Thus, the Lord's Supper is a means of preventing grace to restrain them from sin, of justifying grace to show their sins forgiven, and of sanctifying grace to renew their souls in the image of God.

Sanctification

The idea of sanctifying grace lies at the heart of Wesley's eucharistic thought. It was in his emphasis on sanctification that Wesley made one of his most significant contributions to both Christian theology and Christian spirituality. In his sermon on "The Duty of Constant Communion," he says: "As our bodies are strengthened by bread and wine, so are our souls by these tokens of the body and the blood of Christ. This is the food of our souls: This gives strength to perform our duty, and leads us on to perfection" (*Works* 7:148). Sanctification, in its broadest sense, is the gracious life-long process by which Christians are transformed into the image of Christ (2 Cor. 3:18) and conformed to his likeness (Rom. 8:29). Wesleyanism understands the Eucharist to be that means of grace, instituted by Jesus Christ, to which we are invited for repentance, for self-examination, for renewal, for spiritual sustenance, for thanksgiving, for fellowship, for anticipation of the heavenly kingdom, and for celebration in our pilgrimage toward perfection in the image of Christ. All these are involved in our sanctification, and all these are benefits available to us at the Table of the Lord.

Rob L. Staples

207 ◆ A RESTORATION VIEW OF THE LORD'S SUPPER

Churches that make up the Restoration movement share a desire to be called Christians only, *with no further label and no exclusive doctrines. Therefore, a church of the Restoration movement will call itself* Christian *or a* church of Christ *in the generic sense, not the sectarian sense. The Restoration plea is to restore the unity and practice of New Testament Christianity. Restoration churches have pursued differing options in how to carry out that plea, but all of the churches share a common heritage in the Restoration movement. Furthermore, they also share a common view of the Lord's Supper.*

Restoration churches look to uphold the ordinances of Christ, but have little regard for the ordinances of the later church. They seek direct command or apostolic precedent for church polity and practice. Hence, their practice of the Lord's Supper is generally an attempt to emulate the first-generation church's practice. The following is a summary of the theological position of the Restoration movement's approach to the Lord's Supper: It is instituted by Christ as an open, weekly memorial meal, which symbolizes the body and blood of Christ. Christ is present in the meal, but only spiritually. The meal provides opportunity for believers to commune with the Lord as they celebrate an enactment of the very center of the gospel, the death, burial and resurrection of the Lord (1 Cor. 15:3-4). What follows is a further explanation of this summary.

The Supper Was Instituted by God. The Supper was not a later addition of the church. Jesus himself said, "Do this." Therefore, it is a binding practice. However, in the eyes of Restorationists, later church practice made the meal an elaborate religious rite. Restorationists' practice is as simple and straightforward a service as possible within the corporate assembly.

The Supper Is Open. Churches of the Restoration movement practice open Communion. That is, a communicant need not be a member of the group to participate. Many of the churches print a notice in the bulletin to that effect. They make it known that if one is an immersed believer, they are neither specifically invited nor barred from the Table. Each person partakes according to his or her own conscience.

The Supper Is Celebrated Weekly. Jesus did not specify how often to eat; only to remember him by it. However, there seems to be apostolic precedent for at least a weekly Lord's Supper in the book of Acts (Acts 2:42; 20:7). Furthermore, Restorationists will be quick to point out that the breaking of the bread was perhaps the primary reason for the assembly of the church at Troas. "On Sunday, we all met together to eat the Supper of the Lord" (Acts 20:7, *Simple English Bible* [SEB]). Some Restoration movement churches even call their Sunday services "Lord's Supper Assemblies" or some such title to clearly represent this sentiment. Some of the churches resist allowing the Lord's Supper to be served at any time other than the Lord's Day; but at the very least, virtually none of the churches celebrate less often than once a week.

The Supper Is a Memorial. Jesus said, "Eat this to remember me," and "Drink this to remember me. Every time you drink this, you will be remembering me" (1 Cor. 11:24-25, SEB). The aspect of Jesus that is remembered is multifold, but mostly it has to do with his being an atoning sacrifice for sin (1 John 2:2).

The Supper Is a Meal. The meal involves breaking unleavened bread (Acts 2:42; 20:7; 1 Cor. 10:16). Some churches use small individual pieces of bread for convenience and public health, while others use larger loaves from which members actually break a piece. The meal also involves "the fruit of the vine." Restorationists see little consequence in whether it is wine or grape juice. However, members are able to serve themselves at the Feast, and this they see as significant. Each Christian is invited to approach the throne boldly, with no mediator other than Jesus himself.

Many of the churches also give attention to the symbolic detail of using the loaf for the Communion service. "Though there are many of us, we are one body. There is one loaf, but all of us share this one loaf" (1 Cor. 10:17, SEB). A few even use one cup, since one cup is mentioned in the Gospel accounts. Almost invariably churches will use bread without leaven, based on Paul's statement in 1 Corinthians 5:6-8.

The Supper Symbolizes the Body and Blood of Christ. The Lord said, "This bread is my body" (Matt. 26:26, SEB). Restorationists do not see the bread as literally Christ's body, but as the footnote in the *Simple English Bible* says, it *represents* his body. He did not say, "This *becomes* my body," but that it is. The bread, then, is a memorial of Calvary. Likewise, the fruit of the vine symbolizes the blood of Christ. Jesus said, "This is my blood" (Matt. 26:28). Again this is understood metaphorically. Since he was still physically present with them at the institution, he must have meant this in a spiritual sense.

Christ Is Spiritually Present. Jesus had promised that "Wherever two or three people have gathered in my name, I am there" (Matt. 18:20, SEB). In the same sense, Christ is also *there* at the meal. There is no need for invoking his presence; Restorationists acknowledge him as there, in the assembly, in the bread, in the cup, and in the heart. In a real sense, Christ is present at the table, but only in a spiritual sense.

The meal then involves discerning the body and blood of the Lord. "If someone is eating and drinking without recognizing the meaning of the body of Christ, he is condemning himself by eating and drinking!" (1 Cor. 11:29, SEB). The Communion service involves a clear recognition of not just the presence of Christ, but also the meaning of his sacrifice. The service also might involve recognizing that the church is the physical body of Christ and the person's relationship to that earthly body (see 1 Cor. 10:17, SEB).

The Supper Is a Time of Communion. "The cup of blessing which we bless is the sharing of Christ's blood, isn't it? When we all break off a piece of bread, it is the sharing of Christ's body isn't it?" (1 Cor. 10:16, SEB). Christ actually became sin for us, so we can become right with God in Christ (2 Cor. 5:21, SEB). Thus Restorationists understand Christ's presence in a physical meal to mean that they have more intimate contact with the forgiveness offered through the body of Christ.

The Supper then involves a time of self-examination. "Each person must look deeply into his own heart. Then he should eat the bread and drink from the cup in the right way" (1 Cor. 11:28, SEB). Participants are to make certain that they approach the meal in holiness, that they are recognizing the substitutionary atonement of Christ for their sins, that they are determined to honor Christ in their lives, and that they are confessing and renouncing sin in their lives. Forgiveness does not come from the Table itself, but forgiveness is celebrated in the feast.

The cup is also a new covenant between God and humankind. Jesus said, "This cup is God's new agreement in my blood which is being poured out for you" (Luke 22:20, SEB). An agreement is made between two parties. One party agrees to give the other party forgiveness and eternal life, and the second party agrees to die to self and serve the Master/Giver. In the Lord's Supper, the covenant is renewed weekly.

The Supper Is a Celebration. "The cup of blessing which we bless is the sharing of Christ's blood, isn't it?" (1 Cor. 10:16, SEB). The Communion service is more than a memorial service for an honorable death; it is a personal celebration of rejoicing, thanksgiving, and blessing. While Restoration churches would cringe at the use of the word *Eucharist* for the Lord's Supper, they would readily embrace the positive concept of this celebration.

The Supper Enacts the Center of the Gospel. "Every time you eat this bread and drink from this cup, you are telling about the Lord Jesus' death, until he returns" (1 Cor. 11:26, SEB). The proclamation is not so much one of evangelistic preaching as it is confession in the assembly. Through participation in the meal, Christians glory or boast in the cross (Gal. 6:14). The Cross is the center of the proclamation, as it is of the gospel (1 Cor. 1:23). The proclamation looks forward as well as backward. Paul writes, "You are telling about the Lord Jesus' death, until he returns" (1 Cor. 11:26, SEB). The Supper is a memorial of his death; and it is to be a perpetual memorial interrupted only by his return.

Restoration movement churches celebrate the Lord's Supper weekly, for that seems to be apostolic practice. They take openly, in keeping with the Restoration plea for unity in essential matters. They take simply, reflecting their bias away from later developments (*corruptions*) of the church. And they take commemoratively, recognizing Christ's spiritual presence, but otherwise seeing the meal as a symbolic memorial of his death.

Ken Read

208 • AN EVANGELICAL THEOLOGY OF THE LORD'S SUPPER

Some evangelical Protestants have reappropriated central elements of the pre-Reformation church's understanding of the Lord's Supper: a memorial of Christ's death that is also a genuine means of grace and Christ's ontological Real Presence. They insist also that God's sovereignty be affirmed and that the Lord's Supper be understood as pointing toward the ultimate banquet in heaven. Laden with such profound meaning and power, this sacrament requires careful preparation to keep it from being trivialized or routinized.

Evangelical Reappropriation of the Catholic tradition

With the triumph of Enlightenment rationalism in Western society, evangelical churches in general have tended to discard the sacramental and mystical dimensions of the Lord's Supper, thereby reducing it to a bare memorial rite or an *agape* meal. But another strand in the evangelical movement is concerned to retrieve the higher view of the sacraments espoused in the magisterial Reformation as well as in early Pietism and Puritanism. There is here a willingness to draw upon the insights of Catholic tradition, though with discrimination. These evangelicals propose a restatement of the Lord's Supper that is firmly anchored in Holy Scripture but respectful of church tradition.

From the perspective of evangelical catholicity, the Lord's Supper is first of all an abiding memorial of the atoning death of Jesus Christ. It is a commemoration of his vicarious sacrifice on the cross, not an extension or continuation of this sacrifice, much less a repetition. Instead, the Holy Supper is a sign and witness of Christ's once-for-all sacrifice for sin, made efficacious by the Holy Spirit in faith and obedience. It is also an occasion in which we present our sacrifices of praise and thanksgiving to the living God in gratefulness for God's act of redeeming love in Jesus Christ.

Again, the Lord's Supper signifies a participation in the body and blood of Christ and personal communion with the living Christ by the power of his Spirit. Although believers do not contribute or add to Christ's atoning sacrifice, they receive its benefits through hearing and believing, eating and drinking, confessing and celebrating. The Lord's Supper is not simply a testimony of grace but a means of grace by which we enter into Christ's passion and victory mystically and vicariously.

In the history of the churches of the Reformation, a conflict arose as to whether the finite can receive and bear the infinite (*finitum capax infiniti*). Those on the Reformed side argued that the finite in and of itself cannot bear the infinite, but it can be penetrated and used by the infinite to reach sinful humanity with the message of grace. The elements of bread and wine, just as the words of the sermon, or of Scripture, have no power in and of themselves. But they can communicate the grace of God by virtue of being laid hold of by the Spirit in the act of confession and celebration.

Real Presence in Light of God's Freedom

Those who stand in the tradition of the Protestant Reformation can indeed affirm the Real Presence of Christ in the eucharistic meal. It is not a physical presence, but still a bodily presence, for in the eating and drinking believers make contact with the whole person of Jesus Christ, his body and Spirit. Christ is present not simply in our memories, but ontologically, as the personal Spirit who encounters believers not only in the elements, but in the whole action of the Eucharist.

Catholic evangelicals contend that the Lord's Supper should be celebrated in the context of public worship. The sacrament is under the Word, not vice versa. Without interpretation, ritual is reduced to a magical rite believed to work automatically. Preaching is the more fundamental means of grace. Through the power of the gospel proclamation, the visible Word becomes effectual for our salvation. In an authentic evangelical theology, the visible Word is subordinated to the proclaimed Word; at the same time, the proclaimed Word is fulfilled in the visible Word.

It is also important to affirm the freedom of God in all his dealings with sinful humanity. God is free to speak God's Word in both sermon and sacrament, but is also free to withhold the Word of God. If believers truly hear the real Word of God, if we meet the living Christ in this holy meal, a miracle has taken place. Since grace does not find its goal except in faith and obedience, the participants' response is necessary if the Holy Supper is to be a means for their sanctification and redemption.

—— Looking toward the Supper ——

Finally, the Holy Supper should be seen as an eschatological banquet. In this celebration, participants look forward to the time when they will eat and drink anew with their Savior—when he comes again in power and glory (Matt. 26:29; 1 Cor. 11:26). They have been buried with Christ in his death; they will be raised with him in his resurrection (Rom. 6:5, 8).

With the Reformers, I advocate an open, but not indiscriminate Communion—open to all who confess their sins and believe, closed to those who have not made a public profession of faith or who openly lead immoral lives and show no sign of contrition (see Heidelberg Catechism, Q. 82). Holy Communion presupposes self-examination and repentance. While the ideal is weekly observance, in the present secular milieu I recommend monthly observance to allow for serious preparation for this holy meal.

Evangelicals need to steer clear of both ceremo-

nialism, which reduces the Supper to a ritual performance, and rationalism, which confers on the symbols a merely social value. Evangelicals should be alert to the dangers of both sacramental objectivism and mystical subjectivism. The mere performance of the rite does not make it significant for faith, but the personal encounter with the living Christ makes the rite come alive for faith.

Donald G. Bloesch

209 • A Pentecostal Theology of the Lord's Supper

Although Pentecostal churches view the Communion service as a symbolic remembrance, rather than a sacramental action, they recognize it as a powerful part of their worship life. Time, place, and manner vary widely. In recent years Communion is being celebrated more frequently and with greater liturgical intentionality in some Pentecostal churches.

—— A Vital Worship Practice —— Understood Memorialistically

Celebration of the Lord's Supper is one of the two ordinances practiced by most Pentecostals. An exception is the Church of God (Cleveland, Tennessee) which also holds to the ordinance of footwashing, which may be joined to the celebration of Communion. For many years, some pastors and congregations would never hold Communion without footwashing.

Within Pentecostalism, the celebration of the Lord's Supper has been most frequently referred to as Communion. In previous decades, the term _Lord's Supper_ also was used regularly. Neither carried any special connotations or theological implications.

Even from the beginning years of the various Pentecostal denominations, Communion has been regarded as a vital worship practice in the local church. Participation in this rite is seen as an obedient remembrance of Christ's death and atonement for humanity's sins. It is also considered to be a reflection of the believer's relationship with the Lord Jesus Christ. It symbolizes the appropriation of the benefits of Christ's death to the repentant sinner's life.

Pentecostals have not attributed any particular

spiritual significance to Communion other than its being a symbolic remembrance. However, within the ministry, it has become very evident that no other sign act carries such tremendous spiritual impact. Individuals who regularly appear to be untouched by the ministry of the Word and song become exceptionally honest when faced with the need for introspection before the Communion elements. But this observation has not caused any real turning to the dynamic presence view.

Variety in Manner, Time, and Setting

The atmosphere for the celebration of Communion has generally leaned toward the somber, serious introspection of self and remembrance of Christ's suffering. In more recent decades, some pastors have begun to emphasize the joyous aspect which can also accompany this ceremony. Through the sorrow of Christ's suffering and our repentance, great joy follows. This pattern has been incorporated into many services through the use of themes which emphasize victory or rejoicing and through the emphasis on praise after participation.

The bread used to represent the body in this celebration varies greatly from one congregation to another. Its range includes leavened bread, unleavened bread, and various commercially produced wafers. Each congregation uses either what the pastor prefers or what has been used traditionally. However when it comes to representing Christ's blood, Pentecostals have almost exclusively used grape juice. This practice is due to the insistence on total abstinence from all alcoholic beverages.

Individual Pentecostal denominations have encouraged the celebration of the Lord's Supper, without dictating the time and frequency of observance. In the early decades of the movement, congregations tended to observe Communion once or twice a year at the most. New Year's Eve watch night services are favorite occasions.

Renewed Attention to the Lord's Supper

A renewed sense of the importance of Communion has seen a marked increase in the frequency of observance. More and more Pentecostal churches participate on a quarterly basis, while a few celebrate monthly. This new practice is especially true where congregations have incorporated some liturgical aspects into their worship services. Sunday morning Communion has also become more of the norm.

Along with the increase in frequency, some variation in the method of observance is developing. These changes in method are a definite result of the worship renewal movement, with its emphasis on both creativity and relevancy. Communion while kneeling at the altar, seated at tables in the fellowship hall, or even in small groups are occasionally seen; however, the standard method still is that of serving the congregation while they are seated in their pews.

Pentecostals practice open Communion. Any born-again believer, regardless of denominational membership or preference, is welcome to participate, even if they are just visiting. They are encouraged to participate as a reminder that Christ's church is not a divided body.

Pentecostal pastors have been encouraged to administer Communion under the patronage of the local church rather than allowing any individual to hold a Communion celebration. Communion services are held in college chapels as part of the overall spiritual experience; however, individual lay celebrations without the presence of an ordained minister are not encouraged.

Jerald Daffe

210 ✦ A CHARISMATIC THEOLOGY OF THE LORD'S SUPPER

Charismatic churches affirm the importance of the Lord's Supper, although it is not always a central feature of their worship services. Many discussions about the Lord's Supper among charismatic Christians have centered around the actual practice of the Lord's Supper.

The celebration of the Lord's Supper is one of the earliest expressions of Christian worship, predating the writing of the first New Testament documents by twenty years. Like water baptism, Holy Communion is viewed by some groups within the charismatic movement as a sacrament, a holy mystery of God that imparts grace. Others see Communion as an ordinance or memorial instituted by Christ and carried out in obedience. These two perspectives are, in many ways, determined by the theology of the denomination to which the group belongs or from which the group has emerged. While there is a great variety in the frequency and style of celebration, the majority view of both charismatic and Pentecostal churches falls on the side of the ordinance. Holy Communion, then, has not been given a significantly high priority in practice.

Except for individuals and groups that still maintain their connection and activity within formal liturgical churches, the Eucharist (which means _thanksgiving_) has been stripped of most written liturgy and is celebrated in a more spontaneous manner. A few Pentecostal groups have developed a standard approach to Communion, but most of them, along with non-aligned ministries, charismatic fellowships, and independent churches, have endorsed a bias against any structure in worship. This has produced an approach to the Eucharist which inhibits the use, effectiveness, and appreciation of written prayers and other liturgical structures. The emphasis on the "now work" of the Spirit encourages a more informal method of celebration that meets the need of the moment. The consecration and distribution of the Communion elements usually takes place by offering a spontaneous prayer over the bread and the cup, utilizing a theme developed during the service or other topics. No standard design of the liturgy or concern for the physical posture of the communicant is required.

The use of the wafer or host (found in many mainline churches) has not been continued by most charismatic or Pentecostal churches, who prefer the use of bread loaves, crackers, or other forms of leavened and unleavened bread. One reason given is that the loaf of bread is more symbolic of the unity of the body, than the individual wafer.

Perhaps the most sensitive area, with respect to the Last Supper, is the use of grape juice instead of fermented wine. While the balance of biblical and historical scholarship confirms the use of fermented wine in the early celebrations of the Eucharist, Pentecostal and most charismatic groups have adamantly adopted the use of an unfermented substitute. The Pentecostal conviction stands consistent with their declaration of total abstinence from all alcoholic beverages. From this position, the issue of wine versus juice is seen as irrelevant or that Jesus' use of wine was merely an accident of history. A few still believe that the wine in Scripture was not actually fermented. Whatever reasons are given, most would argue that the elements are not as important as what they symbolize.

Charismatic groups generally use an unfermented juice as well. Many who have come into the charismatic movement from evangelical or holiness expressions of faith were used to grape juice as the normative symbol and have simply continued encouraging this practice. Some charismatic leaders have even contended that fermented wine is an inconsistent representative of the incorruptible blood of Christ.

As a rule, both Pentecostal and charismatic churches celebrate Holy Communion once a quarter or once a month. In rare instances, weekly Communion is celebrated.

Randolph W. Sly

211 ♦ Bibliography on the Theology of the Lord's Supper

A Biblical Theology of the Lord's Supper

Benoit, P., Jacques Dupont, and others. _The Eucharist in the New Testament: A Symposium._ Trans. E. M. Stewart. Baltimore: Helicon, 1964.

Delorme, Jean, et al. _The Eucharist in the New Testament._ Baltimore: Helicon, 1964.

Jeremias, Joachim. _The Eucharistic Words of Jesus._ Philadelphia: Trinity Press International, 1991. A classic study by a widely respected biblical scholar.

Kilpatrick, G. D. _The Eucharist in Bible and Liturgy._ The Moorhouse Lectures 1975. New York: Cambridge University Press, 1983. Prefers sacrifice over against sacrament and covenant models for contemporary eucharistic interpretation.

Kodell, Jerome. _The Eucharist in the New Testament._ Wilmington, Del.: Michael Glazier, 1988.

Smith, Dennis E., and Hal E. Taussig. _Many Tables: The Eucharist in the New Testament and Liturgy Today._ Philadelphia: Trinity Press, 1990.

Schweitzer, Eduard. _The Lord's Supper According to the New Testament._ Trans. Joseph M. Davis. Philadelphia: Fortress Press, 1971.

Systematic and Pastoral Theologies of the Lord's Supper

Arndt, Elmer J. F. *The Font and the Table*. London: Lutterworth, 1967. A Reformed scholar looks at the sacraments, with special attention to the architectural setting for baptism and the Lord's Supper.

Balasuria, Tissa. *The Eucharist and Human Liberation*. Maryknoll, N.Y.: Orbis Books 1979. An Asian liberationist perspective on the Eucharist. Roman Catholic.

Bouyer, Louis. *Eucharist: Theology and Spirituality of the Eucharistic Prayer*. Notre Dame, Ind.: Notre Dame University Press, 1968. Roman Catholic.

Brilioth, Yngve. *Eucharistic Faith and Practice: Catholic and Evangelical*. London: SPCK, 1930. A Lutheran scholar with an ecumenical focus.

Buxton, Richard F. *Eucharist and Institution*. London: Alcuin Club, 1976.

Cabie, Robert, ed. *The Church at Prayer*. Vol. 2, *The Eucharist*. Collegeville, Minn.: Liturgical Press, 1986. Roman Catholic.

Crockett, William R. *Eucharist: Symbol of Transformation*. New York: Pueblo Publishing, 1989. Concerned with the relationship of the Eucharist and issues of justice.

Cullman, Oscar, and F. J. Leenhardt. *Essays on the Lord's Supper*. Richmond: John Knox, 1958.

Davies, Horton. *Bread of Life and Cup of Joy: Newer Ecumenical Perspectives on the Eucharist*. Grand Rapids: Eerdmans, 1993. A fine survey of theological motifs in current theological discussions of the Eucharist; helpful as an introduction to the current debate.

Deiss, Lucien. *It's the Lord's Supper: Eucharist of Christians*. New York: Paulist Press, 1976.

Dunnet, Dolores E. "The Eucharist: Representative Views." *Journal of the Evangelical Theological Society* 32:1 (1989): 63–72. Basically an evangelical case for worship renewal and eucharistic renewal.

Empie, Paul C., and T. Austin Murphy, eds. *Lutherans and Catholics in Dialogue*. Vol. 3, *The Eucharist as Sacrifice*. Minneapolis: Augsburg, 1974.

Hay, Leo, O.F.M. *Message of the Sacraments*. Vol. 3a, *Eucharist: A Thanksgiving Celebration*. Collegeville, Minn.: Liturgical Press/Michael Glazier Books, 1989.

Hellwig, Monika A. *The Eucharist and the Hunger of the World*. New York: Paulist Press, 1976. A valuable discussion of liturgy and justice, with special attention to the Eucharist.

Heron, Alasdair I. C. *Table and Tradition: Toward an Ecumenical Understanding of the Eucharist*. Philadelphia: Westminster, 1983. A concise historical study of the development of eucharistic theology by a Reformed (Calvinist) theologian, covering both patristic, medieval, and Reformation positions.

Lee, Bernard J. *Alternative Futures for Worship*. Vol. 3, *Eucharist*. Collegeville, Minn.: Liturgical Press, 1988.

Keiffer, Ralph A. *The Message of the Sacraments*. Vol. 3, *Blessed and Broken: The Contemporary Experience of God in the Eucharist*. Wilmington, Del.: Michael Glazier, 1982.

Martimort, Aime-Georges. *The Church at Prayer: The Eucharist*. Shannon, Ireland: Irish University Press, 1973. Roman Catholic.

Marshall, I. Howard. *Last Supper and Lord's Supper*. Grand Rapids: Eerdmans, 1980. A summary of recent New Testament scholarship on the Lord's Supper.

Mascall, Eric Lionel. *Corpus Christi*. 2d ed. London: Longmans, 1965. Anglican.

Nichols, Aidan, O.P. *The Holy Eucharist*. San Francisco: Ignatius Press, 1991.

O'Carroll, Michael, ed. *Corpus Christi: A Theological Encyclopedia of the Eucharist*. Wilmington, Del.: Michael Glazier, 1988.

Orthodox Perspectives on Baptism, Eucharist, and Ministry. Brookline, Mass.: Holy Cross Orthodox Press, 1985.

Power, David N. *The Eucharistic Mystery: Revitalizing the Tradition*. New York: Crossroad, 1992. A significant theological treatise by a widely respected Roman Catholic liturgical theologian.

Powers, Joseph M. *Eucharistic Theology*. London: Burns and Oates, 1968.

Ratzinger, Joseph Cardinal. *Feast of Faith*. San Francisco: Ignatius Press, 1986.

Reumann, John. *The Supper of the Lord: The New Testament, Ecumenical Dialogues, and Faith and Order on Eucharist*. Philadelphia: Fortress, 1985.

Schmemann, Alexander. *The Eucharist: Sacrament of the Kingdom*. Crestwood, N.Y.: St. Vladimir's Seminary Press, 1988.

Smolarski, Dennis C. *Eucharistia: A Study of Eucharistic Prayer*. New York: Paulist Press, 1983.

Stookey, Laurence Hull. *Eucharist: Christ's Feast with the Church.* Nashville: Abingdon, 1993.

Thurian, Max. *The Eucharistic Memorial.* 2 vols. London: Lutterworth, 1960–1961. Reformed-ecumenical perspective from the Taizé community.

———. *The Mystery of the Eucharist: An Ecumenical Approach.* Trans. Emily Chisholm. Grand Rapids: Eerdmans, 1981. A brief general survey of the various historic and theological understandings of the Eucharist, sensitive to both Eastern and Western practice.

von Allmen, Jean Jacques. *The Lord's Supper.* London: Lutterworth, 1969. A respected Reformed scholar's examination of the theology of the Lord's Supper.

Wainwright, Geoffrey. *Eucharist and Eschatology.* London: Epworth, 1971. Methodist/Ecumenical.

Willimon, William. *Sunday Dinner: The Lord's Supper and the Christian Life.* Nashville: The Upper Room, 1981. An easily accessible volume written by a Methodist minister.

Theological Studies of the Practice of the Lord's Supper

Deiss, Lucien. *The Mass.* Collegeville, Minn.: Liturgical Press, 1992. Roman Catholic.

Eucharistic Liturgy. Geneva: World Council of Churches, 1988. The eucharistic liturgy for the plenary session of the Faith and Order Commission in Lima, 1982, is published as a small booklet for use in ecumenical settings. Contains the full service.

Fink, Peter E. *Eucharistic Liturgies: Studies in American Pastoral Liturgy.* Paramus, N.J.: New Press, 1969.

Galley, Howard E. *The Ceremonies of the Eucharist: A Guide to Celebration.* Boston: Cowley Publications, 1989. A handbook for liturgical celebration based on the 1979 *Book of Common Prayer,* dealing with the furnishings of the sanctuary, role and vesture of clergy, singers, servers, and so forth; celebration of the Eucharist step-by-step; Eucharist and baptism; deacon's liturgy; liturgy when a bishop visits a parish; and rites of ordination. Author played leading role in revision of *The Book of Common Prayer* and other volumes.

Hatchett, Marion. *Commentary on the American Prayer Book.* New York: Seabury Press, 1981. A theological and liturgical commentary on the 1979 *Book of Common Prayer,* including a discussion of each sacramental liturgy.

McKenna, John H. *Eucharist and Holy Spirit: The Eucharistic Epiklesis in Twentieth Century Theology (1900–1960).* Great Wakering, England: Mayhew-McCrimmon, 1975.

Mitchell, Leonel L. *Praying Shapes Believing.* Minneapolis: Winston, 1985. A theological commentary on the 1979 *Book of Common Prayer,* including a discussion of each of the sacramental rites.

O'Connell, John Berthram. *The Celebration of Mass: A Study of the Rubrics of the Roman Missal.* Rev. ed. Milwaukee: Bruce Publishing, 1956. Although this book is largely concerned with the precise instructions for carrying out the Roman Catholic Mass in its pre-Vatican II form, it sheds much light on Roman Catholic understandings of the sacraments along the way.

Pfatteicher, Philip. H. *Commentary on the Lutheran Book of Worship: Lutheran Liturgy in its Ecumenical Context.* Minneapolis: Augsburg Fortress, 1990. Includes a commentary on the eucharistic liturgy.

Senn, Frank C., ed. *New Eucharistic Prayers: An Ecumenical Study of Their Development and Structure.* New York: Paulist Press, 1987.

Smolarske, Dennis C. *Eucharistia: a Study of the Eucharistic Prayer.* New York: Paulist Press, 1982.

Watkins, Keith. *Celebrate with Thanksgiving: Patterns of Prayer at the Communion Table.* St. Louis: Chalice Press, 1991. A Disciples of Christ scholar examines liturgies for the Lord's Supper.

See also the bibliographies on the history and practice of the Lord's Supper and the bibliography on the sacraments, ordinances, and sacred actions of the church.

The Practice of the Lord's Supper

Although the liturgies of the Orthodox, Roman Catholic, Anglican, and certain Protestant communions may seem forbiddingly complex to members of nonliturgical Protestant traditions, the heart of the Communion service in all the liturgical groups is the great prayer of thanksgiving and blessing over the bread and wine. The prayer's roots extend all the way to the Jewish liturgy Jesus himself used. A combination of scholarly research and interconfessional discussion has brought a large degree of consensus about the main outlines of the Great Prayer of Thanksgiving in the early church, which in turn has enabled the Faith and Order Commission of the World Council of Churches to reach a remarkable consensus about the shape of a common eucharistic prayer. The fruits of this research and discussion, together with guidelines for constructing one's own form of this basic prayer, are offered in the following pages.

212 • THE HEART OF COMMUNION

The Great Prayer of Thanksgiving follows a pattern given to us by Jesus himself, who built upon Jewish models. Although the various churches have different versions of this prayer, a basic, fourfold structure found already in the Gospel accounts of the Last Supper is common to all: taking bread, giving thanks, breaking and pouring, and distributing.

The Eucharistic Prayer

What is the Great Prayer of Thanksgiving, and what does it have to do with worship?

Although that title, and another term, the *eucharistic prayer,* may sound unfamiliar to some of us, the prayer itself is not. It is a prayer all of us have joined in many times—the central prayer in the celebration of Holy Communion. *Eucharist* is the New Testament Greek word for *thanksgiving.* So the eucharistic prayer is often called the Great Prayer of Thanksgiving. It is a unique prayer with a distinctive pattern, provided by the Lord Jesus Christ himself on the very first Easter.

As Jesus walked to Emmaus with two of his disciples that day, he recounted the story of salvation: "And beginning with Moses and all the prophets, he interpreted to them in all the scriptures the things concerning himself" (Luke 24:27, RSV). Then, when he was eating with them, he did four more specific things: he *took* the bread, he *blessed* it, he *broke* it, and he *gave* it to them. As soon as he did those things, they recognized him.

It is no wonder their eyes were opened; only three days earlier, in the Upper Room, they had seen that same fourfold pattern, *taking, blessing, breaking,* and *giving* (Matt. 26:26; Mark 14:22; Luke 22:19). And later, we discover in the passage we call the Institution (1 Cor. 11:23-26), the Lord delivered the identical pattern to the apostle Paul.

Two Kinds of Blessing

The blessing that was a part of those early Suppers was not some magical formula. It was a specific kind of prayer that first blessed God, and then asked God to bless the food.

We know the first kind of blessing from Psalm 103: "Bless the Lord, O my soul, . . . and forget not all his benefits." This attitude of blessing God was an important part of the traditional Passover liturgy that Jesus and his disciples would have followed in the Upper Room. It was especially connected with the third cup of wine, the Cup of Blessing. As Jesus and the disciples celebrated the Passover together, Jesus would have recited a prayer (well-known to his disciples), thanking God for creation and then for redemption, recounting the history of salvation, and using phrases from the Psalms. We don't know what Jesus prayed at Emmaus, and we are not certain what Paul prayed at Corinth, but we do know, from patristic documents, that the early Christian church developed its eucharistic prayers out of these Jewish roots.

We know the second kind of blessing from hearing children at the dinner table: "Lord, bless this food and drink for Jesus' sake. Amen." Jesus pronounced this kind of blessing at the feeding of the five thousand. He would also have pronounced it in the Upper Room as another part of the Passover liturgy, praying for God's blessing on the unleavened bread and on the cups of wine. This type of blessing, therefore, also became part of the early eucharistic prayers.

But before long, members of the early church began insisting that the blessing of the Lord's Supper should be more special than the general meal-time blessing used in the Jewish Passover. Since this was a special kind of bread and wine—since it was the communion of his body and blood in which Christ could be recognized—these early Christians wanted the blessing of Jesus' actual presence. They asked that Jesus Christ would be as fully present as he had been at Emmaus—not only in the elements, but even more as the host of the meal, offering himself up to his disciples, just as he did in the Upper Room. They asked the Holy Spirit to come down and accomplish this miracle, a request we call the *epiklesis*.

Thus, although the earliest Christians continued to use the Jewish forms for worship, gradually these Jewish roots began to bear new fruit. The Passover prayers were rearranged into the more unified eucharistic prayer, which included the request for Jesus' presence at the supper.

Although there are many different versions of this prayer, all of them have one basic structure, framed in Jesus' fourfold pattern:

(1) Take the bread and wine.
(2) Give thanks.
   Sursum corda: "Lift up your hearts"
   Bless God for creation
   Bless God for redemption
   Sanctus and Benedictus: "Holy, Holy" and
     "Blessed Is . . ."
   Institution from 1 Corinthians 11:23
   Epiclesis of the Holy Spirit
   The "Sacrifice of Thanksgiving" (Ps. 116:17; Rom. 12:1)
   The Lord's Prayer
(3) Break the bread (fraction), pour out the wine.
(4) Give them to Christ's disciples (distribution).

Some versions of the prayer put the *sanctus* earlier; some inserted intercessions, some skipped the *epiklesis;* and some added a reference to the Second Coming. The medieval Roman version lost the *epiklesis* and most of the thanksgiving. Protestant liturgies scattered the prayer's parts throughout the whole Communion form.

The Pattern of the Creed

Is the Great Prayer of Thanksgiving essential to a proper celebration of the Supper? Put it this way: No other pattern available to us gets us closer to Jesus' model. Nor is any other pattern closer to the message of the gospel. The same Trinitarian pattern that summarizes the gospel promises in the Apostles' Creed (creation, redemption, *epiklesis*) provides the structure for the Great Prayer. So when you pray the Great Prayer of Thanksgiving, you are praying the gospel promises, and you are walking with Jesus on the Emmaus road as he recounts the history of salvation.

A good eucharistic prayer gives thanks for creation and then for redemption, moving through Christ's conception and virgin birth to his suffering and death and then to his resurrection and ascension. Then, because of the Ascension, the prayer claims fellowship with Christ and entrance into heaven itself, and the local congregation dares to join the worship around the throne when it sings the Sanctus and Benedictus (taken from Ps. 118; Isa. 6; and Rev. 4). The congregation begins to experience the Holy Spirit, who miraculously unites *the holy catholic church* in heaven and on earth and works *the communion of the saints* around the Table.

The prayer then asks that, in our remembering and by the Spirit, the Lord Jesus himself might be present, that the bread and wine might be what Jesus said they'd be, and that through the working of faith the congregation might fully share in Christ. Usually, the prayer ends in a note of praise.

Holy Communion is many things, and it has many benefits, but all are lost unless prayer is at the heart of it—not just any prayer of the preacher's own invention, but a biblically patterned prayer. If you need to shorten your Communion service, or make it less didactic and more direct and powerful, don't cut out that biblical fourfold pattern and its prayer. Without that prayer, the Lord's Supper is nothing but a ceremony or an empty chancel drama.

Prayer is how we open wide the mouths of our souls for God to feed us. It is in prayer that we "lift up our hearts to God," and it is that Great Prayer of Thanksgiving that takes the roof off the church and even lets the angels in.

Daniel Meeter[10]

213 • THE PRAYER OF THANKSGIVING

Scholars played an important role in rediscovering how central the eucharistic prayer was in the very earliest history of the church. Although the earliest texts of the eucharistic prayers often survive only in fragments embedded in later works, diligent comparison has permitted the piecing together of the model prayer of thanksgiving given by Hippolytus of Rome (c. 215).

When Christians assemble to celebrate the Lord's Supper, they take the bread and cup in memory of Jesus. Just as Jesus at the Last Supper said a prayer of thanksgiving or blessing, Christians, too, have a prayer of thanksgiving, whose diverse elements are listed as follows in the Ecumenical Consensus Statement _Baptism, Eucharist and Ministry_ (Faith and Order Paper 111. [Geneva: World Council of Churches, 1982]; para. 27 of the Eucharist): (1) thanksgiving to the Father for the marvels of creation, redemption, and sanctification; (2) the words of Christ's institution of the sacrament according to the New Testament tradition; (3) the memorial of the great acts of redemption, passion, death, resurrection, ascension, and Pentecost, which brought the church into being; (4) the invocation of the Holy Spirit on the community and the elements of bread and wine; (5) the consecration of the faithful to God, a reference to the communion of the saints; (6) the prayer for the return of the Lord and the definitive manifestation of the kingdom; and (7) the amen of the whole community.

A concrete realization of these elements of the prayer of thanksgiving is found in the Lima Liturgy, the prayer of thanksgiving, used for the first time at the 1982 plenary session of the Faith and Order Commission in Lima, Peru, and subsequently at the Sixth General Assembly of the World Council of Churches in Vancouver in 1983.

The recovery of the prayer of thanksgiving has been one of the principal outcomes of the contemporary liturgical movement in the Western churches throughout the world. As a result of the sixteenth-century Reformers' great dissatisfaction with the Roman canon, many liturgical orders whose origins lie in the Reformation separated the narrative of the institution of the Eucharist from its place in the prayer of thanksgiving in favor of reciting one of its four scriptural accounts before the distribution and reception of Holy Communion. This had the effect also of distributing elsewhere in the service as separate prayers what could have formed part of a unified prayer of thanksgiving and, in some cases, adding didactic exhortations.

Modern liturgical historians played a great role in the recovery of a prayer of thanksgiving in the West. Scholars studied the implications of the brief description of the presider's _prayers and thanksgiving_ in Justin Martyr's _First Apology,_ (see chapters 65–67; [c. 150]), commented on the model episcopal prayer of thanksgiving proposed in the _Apostolic Tradition_ (c. 215) of Hippolytus of Rome, drew attention to the variety of prayers of thanksgiving in the Eastern rites, and began to present theories on the origins and development of the prayer of thanksgiving.

In 1968 the Roman Catholic church, whose Eucharist had a single prayer of thanksgiving (Roman Canon) for nearly fifteen hundred years, introduced three new optional eucharistic prayers. This introduction was a major step in contemporary liturgical reform. The Roman Canon, which had been a major obstacle to ecumenical dialogue because of its heavy use of the language of offering, was now only one of several eucharistic prayers approved for the Roman rite. This accomplishment of the Commission, which was appointed to implement the liturgical reforms of the Second Vatican Council's _Constitution on the Liturgy,_ influenced favorably the work of several liturgical committees engaged in recovering a prayer of thanksgiving for their own churches.

John Barry Ryan

214 ♦ A COMMON TEXT FOR THE PRAYER OF THANKSGIVING

The prayer of thanksgiving that follows was prepared for the plenary session of the Faith and Order Commission of the World Council of Churches in Lima, Peru, in 1982. The liturgy of which this eucharistic prayer is a part was first celebrated on January 15, 1982. The aim of the liturgy was to illustrate the theological achievement of the Faith and Order document Baptism, Eucharist and Ministry (BEM). *(Although the Roman Catholic Church, unlike the Orthodox churches, does not participate generally in the World Council of Churches, Roman Catholic theologians did participate in this project of the Faith and Order Commission.) This prayer is important because it offers a modern way of giving thanks that is tied to historical precedent. It is not presented here to be slavishly reproduced, but to serve as a guideline for the preparation of the prayer of thanksgiving in the local church. Each congregation should adapt it to its own worship practices.*

_____ The Basic Pattern: The Liturgy _____ of the Eucharist

17. PREPARATION

OFFICIANT: Blessed are you, Lord God of the universe, you are the giver of this bread, fruit of the earth and of human labor, let it become the bread of Life.

CONGREGATION: **Blessed be God, now and for ever!**

OFFICIANT: Blessed are you, Lord God of the universe, you are the giver of this wine, fruit of the vine and of human labor, let it become the wine of the eternal Kingdom.

CONGREGATION: **Blessed be God, now and for ever!**

OFFICIANT: As the grain once scattered in the fields and the grapes once dispersed on the hillside are now reunited on this table in bread and wine, so, Lord, may your whole Church soon be gathered together from the corners of the earth into your Kingdom.

CONGREGATION: **Maranatha! Come Lord Jesus!**

18. DIALOGUE

PRESIDER: The Lord be with you.

CONGREGATION: **And also with you.**

PRESIDER: Lift up your hearts.

CONGREGATION: **We lift them up to the Lord.**

PRESIDER: Let us give thanks to the Lord our God.

CONGREGATION: **It is right to give him thanks and praise.**

19. PREFACE

PRESIDER: Truly it is right and good to glorify you, at all times and in all places, to offer you our thanksgiving O Lord, Holy Father, Almighty and Everlasting God. Through your living Word you created all things, and pronounced them good. You made human beings in your own image, to share your life and reflect your glory. When the time had fully come, you gave Christ to us as the Way, the Truth, and the Life. He accepted baptism and consecration as your Servant to announce the good news to the poor. At the last supper Christ bequeathed to us the Eucharist, that we should celebrate the memorial of the cross and resurrection, and receive his presence as food. To all the redeemed Christ gave the royal priesthood and, in

The Lord's Supper. In nonliturgical traditions, the symbols of the Lord's Supper are usually a loaf of bread and a single cup or chalice.

loving his brothers and sisters, chooses those who share in the ministry, that they may feed the church with your Word and enable it to live by your sacraments. Wherefore, Lord, with the angels and all the saints, we proclaim and sing your glory:

20. SANCTUS

CONGREGATION: **Holy, Holy, Holy. . . .**

21. EPIKLESIS I

Presider: O God, Lord of the universe, you are holy and your glory is beyond measure. Upon your Eucharist send the life-giving Spirit, who spoke by Moses and the prophets, who overshadowed the Virgin Mary with grace, who descended upon Jesus in the river Jordan and upon the apostles on the day of Pentecost. May the outpouring of this Spirit of Fire transfigure this thanksgiving meal that this bread and wine may become for us the body and blood of Christ.

CONGREGATION: **Veni Creator Spiritus!**

22. INSTITUTION

PRESIDER: May this Creator Spirit accomplish the words of your beloved Son, who, in the night in which he was betrayed, took bread, and when he had given thanks to you, broke it and gave it to his disciples, saying: "Take, eat: this is my body, which is given for you. Do this for remembrance of me." After supper he took the cup and when he had given thanks, he gave it to them and said: "Drink this, all of you: this is my blood of the new covenant, which is shed for you and for many for the forgiveness of sins. Do this for the remembrance of me." Great is the mystery of faith.

CONGREGATION: **Your death, Lord Jesus, we proclaim! Your resurrection we celebrate! Your coming in glory we await!**

23. ANAMNESIS

PRESIDER: Wherefore, Lord, we celebrate today the memorial of our redemption: we recall the birth and life of your Son among us, his baptism by John, his last meal with the apostles, his death and descent to the abode of the dead: we proclaim Christ's resurrection and ascension in glory, where as our Great High Priest he ever intercedes for all people; and we look for his coming at the last. United in Christ's priesthood, we present to you this memorial: Remember the sacrifice of your Son and grant to people everywhere the benefits of Christ's redemptive work.

CONGREGATION: **Maranatha, the Lord comes!**

24. EPICLESIS II

PRESIDER: Behold, Lord, this Eucharist which you yourself gave to the church and graciously receive it, as you accept the offering of your Son whereby we are reinstated in your covenant. As we partake of Christ's body and blood, fill us with the Holy Spirit that we may be one single body and one single spirit in Christ, a living sacrifice to the praise of your glory.

CONGREGATION: **Veni Creator Spiritus!**

25. COMMEMORATION

OFFICIANT: Remember, Lord, your one, holy, catholic, and apostolic church, redeemed by the blood of Christ, reveal its unity, guard its faith, and preserve it in peace. Remember, Lord, all the servants of your church: bishops, presbyters, deacons, and all to whom you have given special gifts of ministry. (Remember especially . . .)

Remember also all our sisters and brothers who have died in the peace of Christ, and those whose faith is known to you alone: guide them to the joyful feast prepared for all peoples in your presence, with the blessed Virgin Mary, with the patriarchs and prophets, the apostles and martyrs . . . and all the saints for whom your friendship was life. With all these we sing your praise and await the happiness of your kingdom where with the whole creation, finally delivered from sin and death, we shall be enabled to glorify you through Christ our Lord;

CONGREGATION: **Maranatha, the Lord comes!**

26. CONCLUSION

PRESIDER: Through Christ, with Christ, and in Christ, all honor and glory is yours, Almighty God and Father, in the unity of the Holy Spirit, now and for ever.

CONGREGATION: **Amen.**

27. THE LORD'S PRAYER

OFFICIANT: United by one baptism in the same Holy Spirit and the same body of Christ, we pray as God's sons and daughters:

CONGREGATION: **Our Father . . .**

28. THE PEACE

OFFICIANT: Lord Jesus Christ, you told your apostles: Peace I leave with you, my peace I give to you. Look not on our sins but on the faith of your church. In order that your will be done, grant us always this peace and guide us towards the perfect unity of your kingdom for ever.

CONGREGATION: **Amen.**

PRESIDER: The peace of the Lord be with you always.

CONGREGATION: **And also with you.**

OFFICIANT: Let us give one another a sign of reconciliation and peace.

29. THE BREAKING OF THE BREAD

PRESIDER: The bread which we break is the communion of the body of Christ, the cup of blessing for which we give thanks is the communion in the blood of Christ.

30. LAMB OF GOD

CONGREGATION: **Lamb of God, you take away the sins of the world, have mercy on us. Lamb of God, you take away the sins of the world, have mercy on us. Lamb of God, you take away the sins of the world, grant us peace.**

31. COMMUNION

32. THANKSGIVING PRAYER

In peace let us pray to the Lord: O Lord our God, we give you thanks for uniting us by baptism in the body of Christ and for filling us with joy in the Eucharist. Lead us towards the full visible unity of your church and help us to treasure all the signs of reconciliation you have granted us. Now that we have tasted of the banquet you have prepared for us in the world to come, may we all one day share together the inheritance of the saints in the life of your heavenly city, through Jesus Christ, your Son, our Lord, who lives and reigns with you in the unity of the Holy Spirit, ever one God, world without end.

CONGREGATION: **Amen.**

33. FINAL HYMN

34. WORD OF MISSION

35. BLESSING

PRESIDER: The Lord bless you and keep you. The Lord make his face to shine on you and be gracious to you. The Lord look upon you with favor and give you peace. Almighty God, Father, Son and Holy Spirit, bless you now and forever.

CONGREGATION: **Amen.**

--- **Commentary** ---

A first step in understanding the prayer of thanksgiving is a knowledge of its constitutive elements and their arrangement. Although there is much diversity in contemporary eucharistic prayers, it is possible to give a general overview of their elements and at the same time take into account variations.

After the Table has been prepared with bread and wine, the presider and the congregation engage in a traditional brief dialogue, which in many recent prayers goes:

The Lord be with you
And also with you;
Lift up your hearts
We have lifted them up;
Let us give thanks to the Lord our God
It is right to give our thanks and praise.

The form and probably many of the words of this very old dialogue go back to Jewish table prayer. Its function at the Lord's Supper is to alert the congregation to a new phase in its worship and unite it as the priestly people, who offer praise and thanksgiving to God.

The presider begins the prayer by taking the congregation's response and expanding it into a prayer of thanksgiving to God. It is customary to see this part of the prayer, called a preface, in conjunction with the congregational response that follows it, the "Holy, holy, holy . . ." Many prayers of thanksgiving have variable prefaces and other variable parts within a fixed framework. It is not uncommon to find in the contemporary reform a prayer into which one of dozens of variable prefaces may be inserted to accommodate it to a feast day, a liturgical season, or a church service such as a wedding or a funeral.

The specific content of the preface varies from prayer to prayer. Some prayers begin with a sort of contemplation of the greatness and mercies of God; others start with thanking God for creating the universe and those who inhabit it; and still others praise God through recalling what God has accomplished through the prophets and through Jesus Christ.

The congregational response to this acknowledgment of God's greatness is the "Holy, holy, holy . . ." inspired by Isaiah 6:3, the basis for Revelation 4:8. Added to this is a verse from Matthew 21:9, whose source is Psalm 118:26, "Blessed is He who comes in the name of the Lord! Hosannah in the highest!" These responses bring together both the worship of the most Holy God and God's messenger, Jesus the Savior, while at the same time joining the time-bound earthly celebration to the eternal heavenly celebration of the angels

and saints. This Sanctus/Benedictus unit is preceded by a customary introductory formula and is often followed by a brief prayer that takes up one of its words such as *holy* or *full* and gives it a theological development, however brief. In some prayers of thanksgiving, this development serves as a transition to a recollection of the deeds of Jesus Christ, which culminates in the account of the institution of the Eucharist the night before he died. Often this institution narrative is a conflated version, rather than a direct importation of any of the four scriptural accounts.

In many prayers of thanksgiving, the institution narrative is followed immediately by a congregational acclamation of remembrance of the death and resurrection of Jesus Christ, prompted by the phrase, "Do this in memory of me." The presider also briefly continues in this mode of remembrance, called in Greek the *anamnesis*, which in many prayers is accompanied by some expression of offering the bread and the cup, as in the third-century eucharistic prayer of the Apostolic Tradition of Hippolytus. The Roman Rite's Eucharistic Prayer II adapts the eucharistic prayer of Hippolytus as "this life-giving bread, this saving cup." Other contemporary prayers pointedly omit such offering, although the Lima Liturgy has, "We present to you this memorial."

The invocation of the Holy Spirit, often known by its Greek name of *epiklesis*, follows. In general, the Holy Spirit may be invoked upon the presider, the congregation, and the gifts of bread and wine. In some prayers of thanksgiving, notably in the Roman and Alexandrian traditions but also in the Lima Liturgy, the Holy Spirit is invoked upon the gifts of bread and wine before the institution narrative and upon those who will partake of them only after the institution narrative. However, the Byzantine prayers of thanksgiving, called *anaphoras* (prayers of offering), and most prayers of thanksgiving of contemporary Reformation churches, have a single unified *epiklesis* after the *anamnesis*. The fundamental purpose of the *epiklesis* is to ensure that the action of the congregation is the action of the Holy Spirit, who is the agent of spiritual transformation of the congregation and its gifts. The Faith and Order Commission speaks of this when it refers above to the consecration of the faithful to God.

In most contemporary prayers of thanksgiving, intercessions for the living and the dead, the church and the world, together with some reference to the communion of saints follow the *epiklesis*. Older prayers of thanksgiving, notably the Roman canon, situate some of these intercessory prayers following the Sanctus. In some *anaphoras*, these prayers receive an extended development. The modern tendency is toward brevity, not duplicating intercessions that take place at other parts of the service.

The prayer closes with a doxology, a short hymn of praise, and an expression of glory to God, usually expressed in a Trinitarian fashion. The congregational response to all this is called the great amen. In this way the prayer is rounded out, since it begins in praise and ends in praise.

In many orders, the prayer of thanksgiving may be preceded by some Table setting prayers or prayers of approach. After the prayer of thanksgiving, some or all of the following elements are customary: the Lord's Prayer, the exchange of peace (in some orders done after the liturgy of the Word), the fraction rite, and the invitation to Holy Communion.

In the ongoing liturgical reform, efforts are being made in several areas. Having recovered the prayer of thanksgiving, some churches are attempting to recover it as a sung prayer. Musicians have composed music for the entire prayer. Other churches, notably in Africa and Asia, see a need for inculturating the prayer of thanksgiving so that it may not seem to be imported from an alien tradition. Finally, under the impetus of feminist studies, others are experimenting with divesting the prayer of its patriarchal language so that it may be radically inclusive. This is perhaps the most difficult task to be achieved.

John Barry Ryan

215 ✦ GUIDELINES FOR PREPARING COMMUNION PRAYERS

We find two main patterns for the prayer of thanksgiving at Communion services. One focuses primarily on Jesus' words of institution at the Last Supper, as reported by Paul; the second employs the words of institution, but embeds them in the story of God's saving action. With these main outlines in mind, worship committees in churches that lack prescribed liturgies can construct prayers of consecration that are faithful both to the broad tradition of the church dating back to the apostolic times, while also remaining faithful to their own tradition.

Instructions

There are two ways of constructing services of the Eucharist (the thanksgiving) or the Holy Communion or the Lord's Supper. One way might be called the warrant form. Warrant means authorization. What is essential in this form is to cite the authorization for the conduct of the Supper, which very frequently comes from 1 Corinthians 11:23-27. A statement about the memorial character of the event and the spiritual preparedness of the communicants might follow. Fundamentally, this service roots its sanction in the dominical (referring to Lord) words of the institution, either from Paul or from one of the Gospel narratives of Jesus' meal in the Upper Room. Generalizations are hazardous, but that aside, this form is used frequently in generic Protestantism and/or in churches most often referring to the Supper as an ordinance.

A second way of constructing services of the Eucharist might be called narrative form. More elaborate in form and sequential in structure, this form roots the authorization not just in the dominical words of institution, but in the story of Jesus' life and work, of which the authorizing words are only a part. To be included as well in this form is God's providential work in creation, in the election and exodus of Israel, in sending prophets, in the concrete acts of human service rendered by Jesus, in his meals, in the people whom he encountered, and culminating in the Passion-Easter events. This form is inclusive of the entire Scriptures, of various kinds of texts and stories, and of tradition's use of these materials, facilitating the ongoing praise of God. Again, generalizations are hazardous, but that aside, this form is usually used in the liturgical churches, who most often designate the Supper as a sacrament. Being story in form, this order of service is doxological, not didactic, in character.

Clearly, the use of the narrative form enjoys widespread acceptance, as is evidenced in the study of the new hymnals and pastor's handbooks/books of worship published by various denominations. Some reasons need to be noted for this convergence. First, biblically, the story-form dominates, since the Bible contains a story consisting of stories. Second, it is noted that in the Bible, God is praised by having the deeds of God recited back to God; by doing so, the community keeps the memory of God's mighty deeds alive and perpetuates that memory. Third, the work of God began with creation, not with redemption; with Israel, and not with the church. The implication is that the same God who created the world redeemed it. Fourth, and as a direct result of the preceding point, the work of Jesus Christ cannot be reduced to what happened during Holy Week. There is a story of Jesus' life and work that contextualizes Holy Week, so that by the time Easter occurs, one can discern that the risen Lord is the crucified Jesus, and the crucified Jesus is the risen Lord. Furthermore, one discerns that this Jesus is the one whose prophetic ministry did not win him approval, but accusation. Fifth, eschatology, the doctrine of the Last Things, the blessed hope, the vision of a new heaven and a new earth, is a major biblical theme. The Eucharist "shows forth the Lord's death until he comes," according to Paul. This is so because the resurrection of Jesus Christ is the end of death and the "beginning of a new world," according to the Epistle of Barnabas (*c.* A.D. 130). Hence the Eucharist previews the marriage supper of the Lamb, when all of the people of God will be gathered with Abraham and Sarah; all other patriarchs, matriarchs, prophets, prophetesses, priests, and rulers; and all others like the youthful—but believing—blessed Virgin Mary and the aged and persistent Simeon who waited for the "consolation of Israel." To this list of biblical names and the stories in which they are embedded, we can add our names and our stories. Sixth, as awareness of the roots of the church's praying and believing become more widely known, people come to see that this mode of praying enables people to live where Saint Augustine said that most of life takes place—between memory and hope.

A eucharistic prayer of my own is printed below with commentary. It is for use in a parish. This prayer takes two things for granted. First, as noted by Gregory Dix, the shape of the eucharistic act has four parts: Jesus took bread (and cup), gave thanks, broke (by implication, poured the cup), and distributed them to the disciples. Second, the giving of thanks also acquired a *shape*. This shape can be learned easily; this shape frees people to put the tradition in conversation with the contemporary—to be rooted, yet reaching out.

When the writing of the eucharistic prayer is carried out in worship committees, in consonance with the constitutional and confessional integrity of each tradition, that committee stands a good chance to become a vigorous Bible study group and a group soon to learn that liturgical theology connects immediately with those who live between memory and hope. I think such committees are the place where theological and spiritual depth meet; where head, heart, and hand meet; and where work and prayer meet. Here ancient dualism between nature and grace, body and spirit, secular and sacred, creation and redemption, Roman Catholic and Protestant, and liturgy and evangelism have a chance of being seen, not as antitheses and alternatives, but as complementary companions.

Now, the prayer will be considered. Please note that various parts of the Service below are interspersed with commentary. You might want to discuss the occasions other than a Sunday morning service when the Eucharist would be appropriate in your settings, e.g., weddings, funerals, wedding anniversaries, church anniversaries, diocesan or conference gatherings of churches in annual conferences, etc. How would a eucharistic celebration affect those gatherings differently than having the conventional services of worship or ceremonies? This gets at the issue of what is unique about a Eucharist celebration.

Ignatius of Loyola (d. 1556) spoke of praying with the church—not just for it, but with it. What I have tried to offer is a way of praying with the church by using Scripture, scriptural patterns, and a traditional shape that does not sacrifice freedom to form. Rather, this prayer releases people to make connection between the foundational and the lived experience and in this way to praise the God who makes all things new—not least of all by enabling people to have thankful hearts.

Sample Prayer with Commentary

Greeting

LEADER: The Lord be with you.
CONGREGATION: **And also with you.**

Commentary: This greeting recalls Jesus' Easter greeting (John 20:21, 26), except that in John "peace" is substituted, and the closing greetings of Paul (1 Cor. 16:23; 2 Cor. 13:13). Mary is greeted similarly by the angel (Luke 1:28).

Sursum Corda

LEADER: Lift up your hearts.

CONGREGATION: **We lift them to the Lord.**

LEADER: Let us give thanks to the Lord our God.

CONGREGATION: **It is always right to give God thanks and praise.**

Commentary: This sets the shape of the event as it establishes the task of praising God. Praise belongs here in addition to thanks because, as Claus Westermann points out, biblical Hebrew lacked a word for thanks. Hence, Israelites expressed thanks by telling a story to the person receiving the appreciation, detailing the events, words, and experiences, which evoked the joy and gratitude (*Praise and Lament in the Psalms*, trans. Keith Crim and Richard Soulen [Atlanta: John Knox, 1981], 25–26). Narrative is thus intrinsic to a biblical mode of giving thanks (and by extension read 1 Kings 8:15, 21; 1 Sam. 25:39; Pss. 89; 41; 106; Eph. 1:3ff; 1 Pet. 1:3ff, and 2 Cor. 1:3ff). The Latin subheading means, "Lift up your hearts."

Preface, Sanctus, and Benedictus

It is always right, good, and proper that we should give you thanks and praise, O gracious Father. But now, in this season of Pentecost, we thank you for the Holy Spirit whom you sent through your Son to bring to our remembrance all he said and did, and who enables us to love and serve with this same Spirit. Therefore, with angels and archangels and all the host of heaven we praise your name saying:

CONGREGATION: **Holy, Holy, Holy, Lord of hosts, Heaven and earth are full of your glory; Hosanna to the Lord most high, Blessed is the one who comes in the name of the Lord. Hosanna in the Highest!**

Commentary: This is the introduction to the eucharistic prayer. It (1) locates the season of the church year (in this case it is Pentecost), and (2) designates the gift of God's grace and providence celebrated during that season of the year. This, then, is a major theological statement set forth as a doxology.

The word *sanctus* means "holy." Its threefold form is derived from several scriptural texts and settings: Isaiah 6:3, Mark 11:9-10; and Revelation 4:8. This hymn is envisioned by the writer of Revelation 4:8 as the heavenly hymn in which the church joins to sing as part of its unbroken fellowship with the communion of saints. Note that this establishes the eschatological dimension of the Eucharist early in the rite. The word *benedictus* means "blessed," and is not part of all of the patristic liturgies. It is found in the Palm Sunday acclamation of Jesus (Matt. 21:9; Mark 11:9; and Luke 19:38).

Dialogue (Thanksgiving)

LEADER: Gracious God, we thank you for your desire to create us and have friendship with others other than yourself. How glad it makes us to be in your image and after your likeness. How freeing it is to see others in the same way: made of the same clay by one and the same potter.

Commentary: The praise of God continues as the story forming the nucleus of this Eucharist is told, reciting God's graciousness back to him and recalling it for the people so that their hearts can overflow with gratitude and generosity.

CONGREGATION: **How majestic is your work in all the earth.**

LEADER: When you created us you provided for our necessities.

CONGREGATION: **For place, a garden; for food, plants and animals; for companions, Adam for Eve, Eve for Adam. Every need supplied—praised be your name in all the earth.**

LEADER: Humans sinned, violated trust, presumed on good will, exploited the abundance of creation, and took advantage of others. We lost our place, displaced our companions, and misplaced commitments. Needs unknown at creation were generated.

CONGREGATION: **How stressful it is when life is out of place. Have mercy on us.**

LEADER: But when we had lost our place, misplaced our trust, and displaced others, you sent your Son to take his place beside us. He crossed cultures—from heaven to earth, eternity to time—and lived on our turf, learning to be a son. Speaking our language, he was apprenticed to a carpenter, and befriended any who needed him; eventually, he was crucified in our place.

CONGREGATION: **All made from the same clay, we are redeemed by the same cross. How majestic is your grace in all the earth.**

LEADER: And so, dear God, you have called us to take our places beside others, to cross cultures to their turf, to learn to live there, for that place and those people, to leave home and make a new home as your Son did for us.

CONGREGATION: **Spirit of God, give us grace to do so.**

The Anamnesis and Words of Institution

LEADER: And now with great thanksgiving we recall the first apostle, the Sent-One, Jesus Christ, who on the night when he was betrayed took bread, and when he had given thanks he broke it and said, "This is my body which is for you. Do this in remembrance of me." In the same way also he took the cup after supper, saying: "This cup is the new covenant in my blood. Do this as often as you drink it, in remembrance of me. For as often as you eat this bread and drink this cup, you proclaim the Lord's death until he comes.

Commentary: Anamnesis means "memorial." Specifically, Jesus Christ is the content of this memory and of this representation of God's work in Jesus Christ for us. The words of the institution contain the specific warrant for what the church is doing at this meal. The offerings of bread and wine, the bread often baked by various members of the congregation, can be brought forward during the offertory of gifts. Families who provide the eucharistic gifts can bring them forward to the table along with those carrying the other gifts.

Acclamation

CONGREGATION: **Christ had died! Christ is risen! Christ will come again!**

Epiklesis or Invocation of the Holy Spirit

LEADER: Come Holy Spirit upon us and upon these gifts that they may be what Jesus said they were: his body and blood, broken, shed for us, and gifts of God for the people of God. Maintain us in this bond of unity until the entire church is gathered into the heavenly country from which there is neither exile nor need for immigration and where the feast has room for all.

Commentary: Epiklesis means "to call upon," and in this case, the Holy Spirit is called upon to do the special work of the Spirit's office in relation to this event in the same way that the Holy Spirit is asked to take the words of Christ and use them effectively in the lives of believers. The Eucharist is a word-event attached to specific gifts of Creation (bread and wine) which Jesus asked his followers to use as a means of access to his promises. It is the Holy Spirit's work to take Jesus' words and deeds and apply them to others. Jesus was conceived by the Holy Spirit (Luke 1:35), received the Spirit at baptism (Luke 3:21-22), was led by the Spirit into the wilderness (Luke 4:1ff), preached by the Spirit (Luke 4:16ff), and offered up his life in the Spirit (Heb. 9:14).

The same Spirit which came upon Jesus is called upon to enable this work which Jesus commands us to do, so that it might truly accomplish that which he purposed in commanding that it be done.

According to the church traditions, there might be variation as to whether the Spirit is invoked more on the people than on the gifts or vice versa. In some traditions, intercessions are offered at this point.

Note again how eschatology is prominent here with the anticipation of gathering the whole people of God in the consummation of all things. The gift of the Holy Spirit is in itself a sign of the last days (Acts 2:17; Rom. 8:18-26; 2 Cor. 1:21-22; Eph. 1:8-14).

Doxology

LEADER: By Jesus Christ, and with Him and

in Him, in the unity of the Holy Spirit all honor and glory is yours, Almighty Father, now and forever.

CONGREGATION: **Amen.**

Commentary: This is the Trinitarian conclusion of the prayer, in praise of the one God whose work in creation and redemption, Israel and the church, nature and grace will come to fruition in God's own time, for which we wait even as we carry on the work Jesus has commissioned us to do.

Lord's Prayer

LEADER: And now as our savior Christ has taught, we are bold to pray:

CONGREGATION: **Our Father . . .**

Agnus Dei

Commentary: Agnus Dei means "lamb of God." This portion of the liturgy is to be sung. Again the best resources are hymnals and books of contemporary liturgical forms. Pertinent Scripture texts are Isaiah 53:7, John 1:29, and Revelation 5:6ff. One version is the following:

> Praise to the Lamb!
> Jesus, Lamb of God, have mercy on us;
>   Jesus, Lamb of God,
> give us your peace.

John Weborg

216 ✦ AN INCLUSIVE LANGUAGE PRAYER OF THANKSGIVING

This eucharistic prayer uses traditional structure and elements to frame abundant biblical imagery, located especially in the verbs. The liturgical and biblical traditions are enlivened by ancient metaphors and poetic euphony and rhythm. In addition, this text seeks to be inclusive of the experience of a wide variety of Christians in its imagery. The prayer is not one of penitence or catechizing, but of genuine praise and intercession. It is hoped that while each line sounds familiar, the effect of the prayer will be to call us back to yet another image of grace.

It is indeed right,
from east to west, from north to south,
in all the seasons of our life,
to give thanks to you, O God, O Living One.

[use this sentence or replace with proper preface:]
Dwelling beyond time and space, you abide among us, embracing the world with your justice and love.
And so, with all the baptized of every race and land,
with the multitudes in heaven
and the countless choirs of angels,
we praise your glorious name
and join their unending hymn:
HOLY, HOLY, HOLY, LORD, GOD OF POWER AND MIGHT,
HEAVEN AND EARTH ARE FULL OF YOUR GLORY.
  HOSANNA IN THE HIGHEST.
  BLESSED IS HE WHO COMES IN THE NAME OF THE LORD.
  HOSANNA IN THE HIGHEST.

Holy God,
holy and mighty one,
holy and immortal:
you we praise and glorify
you we worship and adore.

You formed the earth from chaos;
you encircled the globe with air;
you created fire for warmth and light;
you nourish the lands with water.

You molded us in your image,
and with mercy higher than the mountains,
with grace deeper than the seas,
you blessed the people of Israel
and cherished them as your own.

That also we, estranged and dying,
might be adopted to live in your Spirit,
you called to us through the life and death of Jesus,
who in the night he was betrayed,
took bread, and gave thanks;
broke it, and gave it to his disciples, saying:
Take and eat, this is my body, given for you.
Do this for the remembrance of me.
Again, after supper, he took the cup, gave thanks,
and gave it for all to drink, saying:
This cup is the new covenant in my blood,
shed for you and for all people
for the forgiveness of sin.
Do this for the remembrance of me.

Together as the body of Christ,
we proclaim the mystery of his death:

CHRIST HAS DIED. CHRIST IS RISEN. CHRIST WILL COME AGAIN.

Holy God,
holy and merciful one,
holy and compassionate,
with this bread and cup we remember your Son,
the first-born of your new creation.
We remember his life lived for others,
and his death and resurrection,
which renewed the face of the earth.
We await his coming
when, with the world perfected through your wisdom,
all our sins and sorrows will be no more.
AMEN. COME, LORD JESUS.

Send upon us and this meal your Holy Spirit,
whose breath revives us for life,
whose fire rouses us to love.
Enfold in your arms all who share this meal.
Nurture in us the fruits of the Spirit,
that we may be a living tree,
sharing your bounty with all the world.
AMEN. COME, HOLY SPIRIT.

Holy and benevolent God,
receive our praise and petitions,
as Jesus received the cry of the needy,
and fill us with your blessing,
until, needy no longer and married to your love,
we feast forever in the triumph of the Lamb:
through whom all glory and honor are yours,
O God, O Living One, with the Holy Spirit,
in your holy church, now and forever.
AMEN.

Gail Ramshaw

217 ✦ BIBLIOGRAPHY ON THE PRACTICE OF THE LORD'S SUPPER

For a collection of liturgies from various worship traditions, see *Baptism and Eucharist: Ecumenical Convergence in Celebration,* edited by Max Thurian and Geoffrey Wainwright (Grand Rapids: Eerdmans, 1983).

For examples of Baptist eucharistic liturgies, see Jesse Jai McNeil, *Minister's Service Book for Pulpit and Parish* (Grand Rapids: Eerdmans, 1993), 34–42; and Alec Gilmore, Edward Smalley, and Michael Walker, *Praise God: A Collection of Material for Christian Worship* (London: Baptist Union, 1980).

For Disciples' (Christian Church—Disciples of Christ) Lord's Supper liturgies, see Keith Watkins, ed., *Celebrate with Thanksgiving: Patterns of Prayer at the Communion Table* (St. Louis: Chalice Press, 1991), and *Thankful Praise: A Resource for Christian Worship* (St. Louis: CBP Press, 1987).

For the Christian Reformed Church, see *The Psalter Hymnal* (Grand Rapids: CRC Publications, 1987), 972–87.

For the Episcopal eucharistic liturgy, see *The Book of Common Prayer* (New York: Church Hymnal Corporation, 1979), 316–412.

For Evangelical Lutheran Church in America's Lord's Supper liturgies, see *Lutheran Book of Worship* (Minneapolis: Augsburg; and Philadelphia: Board of Publication, Lutheran Church in America, 1978), 57–120.

For Lutheran Church–Missouri Synod's Lord's Supper liturgies, see *Lutheran Worship* (St. Louis: Concordia, 1984), 149–71.

For Methodist eucharistic rites, see *The United Methodist Book of Worship* (Nashville: United Methodist Publishing House, 1992), 33–80.

For an Orthodox eucharistic liturgy, see *An Orthodox Prayer Book,* edited by Fr. N. M. Vaporis (Brookline, Mass.: Holy Cross, 1977); and *The Divine Liturgy according to St. John Chrysostom* (Minneapolis: Light and Life Publishing, 1989).

For Presbyterian Church–USA and Cumberland Presbyterian Church's Lord's Supper liturgies, see *The Book of Common Worship* (Louisville: Westminster/John Knox, 1993), 33–85; 126–156; also see *The Service for the Lord's Day: Supplemental Resources* (Philadelphia: Westminster, 1984).

For Reformed Church in America's perspective, see *Worship the Lord* (Grand Rapids: Eerdmans, 1987), 2–13.

For the Roman Catholic eucharistic liturgy, see *The Roman Missal: The Sacramentary* (New York: Catholic Book Publishing, 1974).

For United Church of Christ Lord's Supper liturgies, see *Book of Worship: United Church of Christ* (New York: Office of Church Life, 1986), 29–95.

PART FIVE.

Sacred Actions for the Seasons of Life

The Christian faith has implications for every aspect of life. From birth to death, Christians bear witness to Jesus Christ, whose death and resurrection give new meaning to each. This section presents liturgies for three important passages in the life of the believer: dedication, marriage, and death. In each case, they are accompanied by descriptions of their history and theology and suggestions for worship planning. These are important actions for the life of the church. They are important for the pastoral ministry of the church to new parents, to engaged couples, and to grieving friends and family. They are also significant for the church's witness to the world: Many non-Christians will come to worship only at services of dedication (or baptism), marriage, and funerals of friends and family. The church has an important responsibility to plan a service that is sensitive both to the theological vision to which the Scripture and history of the church bear witness and to the pastoral needs of the families, friends, and the congregation.

❧ TWELVE ❧

Child Dedication

Believers' churches baptize only those who make a conscious profession of personal faith in Christ. Yet they recognize the importance of nurturing spiritually children reared by believing parents within the Christian community. The ceremony of child dedication offers one way to symbolize the fact that children of Christian parents in some sense belong to the Christian community even though they are not baptized.

218 • HISTORICAL ORIGINS AND DEVELOPMENT OF CHILD DEDICATION

Although its origins are obscure, the modern practice of dedicating children to God appears to have originated among Anglo-American revivalist Congregationalists and Baptists in the eighteenth century.

Dedication of children or infants is a practice commonly found in churches which practice only adult or believers' baptism. The rite of child dedication is known by various titles in different Christian communities; it may be called family dedication, child presentation, blessing of children, or a service of thanksgiving and covenant.

Origins

The historical origins of the practice of child dedication are difficult to determine. In the mid-nineteenth century, David Benedict reported a 1790 reference to a rite of "devoting of children," and suggested that it was a widespread practice among Baptists in Virginia and North Carolina. He describes a ceremony in which the mother, as soon as possible after birth, took the child to church, where the minister either held the infant or laid hands on it, thanked God for his mercy, and prayed the Lord's blessing upon the child (David Benedict, *Fifty Years Among the Baptists* [1859], 122–23).

Benedict theorized the rite had originated among the "New Light" Congregationalists of New England who emerged from the Great Awakening earlier in the century. These revivalists, while not rejecting infant baptism outright, tended to restrict it to cases where at least one parent was a committed Christian and church member. In the setting of frontier evangelism, remote from established congregations and regular Christian instruction, few candidates for infant baptism would have met this qualification. There is also evidence that child dedication was practiced in England from about the middle of the nineteenth century.

As with much in the history of Christian worship, the practice of infant dedication evidently preceded its theological justification. Scriptural precedent, however, is often found in the presentation of Jesus in the temple at the age of eight days, when he was blessed by the aged prophetic figures Anna and Simeon (Luke 2:22-38). Samuel's dedication to the Lord by his mother Hannah also comes to mind (1 Sam. 1:24-28), although this was in fulfillment of her pledge specifically committing him to the Nazirite vow (1 Sam. 1:11). Jesus' own action in blessing children brought to him, laying his hands on them, and praying for them (Matt. 19:13-14), is paradigmatic for the ceremony of child dedication.

Among baptistic or revivalist groups, the practice of other churches in the greater community may have influenced the development of a ceremony for dedication of children. The churches of the Reformation—Presbyterians and Lutherans—along with those of Anglican heritage—Episcopalians and Methodists—all continued the rite of infant baptism. Worshipers in churches practicing only believers' baptism may have desired a comparable rite of passage for their children, an act symbolic of the beginning of their spiritual pilgrimage as members of the church family. The result was a ceremony which carefully avoided the terminology of baptism, but accomplished the same end as a rite of initiation. Christians who practiced infant baptism sometimes referred to the earlier Baptist practice of "devoting of children" as "dry Christening."

Changing views of the relation of children to the church family were reflected in the publication, in 1847, of Horace Bushnell's *Christian Nurture*. Bushnell, a New England Congregationalist, taught that children of Christian parents should grow up with the sense of always having been a Christian and not be required to testify to a singular conversion experience in order to be received by the church. While those who practiced believers' baptism could not have accepted all the implications of Bushnell's views, perhaps they saw child dedication as a way of recognizing the general principle of Christian nurture.

---------------- **Meaning** ----------------

Christian nurture is, in fact, the foundational concept for the practice of child dedication today in most churches. The language of child dedication services reflects the expectation that the child will mature within the nurturing context of church and family, in preparation for the time when he or she will confess personal faith in Christ and commit to himself or herself in baptism. This hope is articulated differently in various communities and congregations. Sometimes the focus is on the continuity of Christian training and the gradual unfolding of faith through the ongoing work of God in the life of the child. In other cases, human depravity receives greater recognition, with the need for repentance and conversion before the child will be ready for believers' baptism.

Form and Occasion. Whatever the view of the significance of child dedication, services in most churches follow a similar format. The family is introduced to the church with some statement about their role in the church or their relationship to its members. Various theological statements are made concerning the church's, or pastor's, understanding of what is or is not taking place in the dedication of a child. There may be prepared readings and responses for the minister, parents, and congregation, with the congregation often pledging to support the parents in the task of Christian nurture and witness. The minister will hold the child or otherwise touch it, and invoke the Lord's blessing upon parents and child in prayer.

In smaller churches, infant or child dedication may take place whenever a family has a new child to be presented. In larger churches, families are usually grouped for dedication on scheduled Sundays. Some churches may incorporate child dedication into a special worship service devoted to the theme of Christian nurture and maturing in the faith, perhaps in conjunction with an annual popular observance such as Mother's Day or Father's Day. Where dedication services are held rather infrequently, special announcements or bulletin notices may call attention to recent births in member families as they occur.

Pulpit-centered churches, especially those with broadcast ministries, have the greatest difficulty incorporating child dedication as an act of worship; there is the tendency to abbreviate the rite in the interest of moving quickly to some other phase of the service. In other churches, the pastoral leadership gives greater attention to child dedication as a part of corporate worship. A minister may, for example, carry the child into the congregation, introducing the child especially to people with particular involvement in those ministries which will be the first to touch the child's life as a member of the church family. Parents, grandparents, and other family members appreciate this more personalized approach.

Richard C. Leonard

219 ◆ A THEOLOGY OF CHILD DEDICATION

Child dedication is a nonsacramental rite observed by churches which practice only believers' baptism. Theologically and in other ways, it parallels infant baptism as a ceremony marking the child's entrance into the Christian community and the beginning of his or her journey along the path of Christian nurture and training.

As a practice, child dedication is a corollary to believers' or adult baptism, since it is observed in most cases only in churches which do not baptize infants or children. Child dedication usually looks forward to the time when the child, having been trained and guided by the nurture of church and home, will make his or her own responsible decision to be baptized in confession of faith in Christ.

Dedication and Baptism

Theologically, however, the language and thrust of child dedication is similar to that found in the infant baptism services of many churches, especially those not in the liturgical-sacramental tradition. The language of infant or children's baptism in these churches is usually the language of Christian nurture. Since the child is unable to confess faith in Christ, the parents do so in his or her behalf, and pledge themselves, along with the congregation, to provide a Christian environment to influence the maturing child. This environment will eventually lead to an adult commitment to Christ and his or her church through an act such as confirmation or covenanting. Exactly the same purpose is served by the rite of child dedication, except that the commitment of Christian parents to the nurture of the child is to be ratified in the child's later life, not in confirmation or church membership, but in believer's baptism. Thus, child dedication and infant baptism are equal, although they are sacramental or nonsacramental, depending on one's point of view.

The exception to this parallel occurs when infant or child baptism is understood, not as a pledge by the parents or sponsors, but as an act _ex opere operato_. That is, the very act of baptism, by a recognized ecclesiastical authority using water and the Trinitarian formula, is believed to accomplish a work in the spiritual realm—in particular the regeneration of the child's life in cleansing the child from the taint of original human sin. In this more highly sacramental understanding, the parents' commitment to raise the child in the faith of Christ is not the operative factor in baptism. Infant or child dedication is not a parallel to this type of regenerative baptism. However, even some churches which accept the theology of baptismal regeneration also incorporate the language of Christian nurture into the rite.

Since there is no single theology of infant baptism within the Christian community, the dedication of children cannot be viewed simply as an antithesis to baptism. Churches which practice child dedication in place of baptism often include

a disclaimer, stressing that the ceremony of dedication does not accomplish regeneration nor establish the child's spiritual position. Thus George Hill, a Baptist, wrote, "The idea that the spiritual life of the child is secured, or directly aided, by such a service is scarcely less objectionable than the doctrine of baptism regeneration" (quoted in Gideon G. Yoder, _The Nurture and Evangelism of Children_ [1959], 136–37). However, such a disclaimer could be equally applicable to infant baptism as practiced within the Christian nurture framework.

Theologies of Dedication

Thus, there is a certain tension within the effort to provide a theological justification for child dedication or presentation. At one end of this tension is the understanding that a person becomes part of Christ and his church through repentance and a faith commitment; at the other pole is the recognition that the spiritual environment in which children mature is a major factor in their appropriation of the life of Christian discipleship.

The issue for a theology of child dedication is the question of who children are before God, and what their status is within the body of Christ. The issue is reflected within Scripture itself. On one hand, "folly is bound up in the heart of a child" (Prov. 22:15) and "childish ways" must be left behind as we mature (1 Cor. 13:11); on the other hand, "children [are] a reward" from the Lord (Ps. 127:3), and believers must become like little children to enter the kingdom of heaven (Matt. 18:3). The New Testament touches only briefly upon the status of children within the church, in the suggestion that the decision of both Cornelius (Acts 10:47-48) and the Philippian jailer (Acts 16:33) to be baptized also incorporated their households into the family of the faithful. Furthermore, the New Testament also touches on this status when Paul remarks that Timothy's faith was a heritage from his mother and grandmother (2 Tim. 1:5) and that "from infancy you have known the holy Scriptures, which are able to make you wise for salvation through faith in Christ Jesus" (2 Tim. 3:15).

Several writers representing churches which practice believers' baptism and child dedication have attempted to address the question of the status of children within the church. Keith Watkins, a Disciples of Christ scholar, considers children to be "catechumens or learners, people who are in the process of developing that maturation of life and spirit which will enable them to make their own appropriate commitment to Christ" ("Children in Worship," *Encounter* [Summer 1983]: 272). He compares the church to a family, in which children are full members, but are not expected to have the same responsibility as parents. The child's role in the life of the church is appropriate to his or her stage of development, an anticipation of the time when a full participation in the church's life becomes possible.

William E. Hull, a Baptist minister, approaches the issue from the perspective of personal salvation history, understood in terms of both covenant and conversion. In Hull's view, whereas the child born into an Israelite family was part of the covenant through solidarity with his family, tribe, and nation, the New Testament community "shifted the focus from birth to new birth, from covenant to conversion, from group solidarity to individual decision." Child dedication is the affirmation that the child is holy in virtue of his or her solidarity with a Christian home (cf. 1 Cor. 7:14). As the child's salvation history unfolds, however, he or she may be expected to affirm a commitment to this spiritual heritage in baptism in middle or later childhood. But this salvation history should continue beyond baptism to mature to an adult stage of full ownership of the Christian faith ("The Child in the Church," in *Celebrating Christ's Presence Through the Spirit*, ed. Cyril E. Brandt and Ruby J. Burke [1981]). Thus, both child dedication and believers' baptism are signposts along a pilgrimage which, ideally, continues throughout the life of the Christian.

The British Baptist scholar G. R. Beasley-Murray sees the child as included in two solidarities: solidarity with Adam in human sin and solidarity with the Second Adam in justification. Both solidarities are chosen: Corporate sin engulfs humanity but expresses itself through individual acts of transgression; salvation in Christ is also corporate, but becomes a reality when the individual chooses to trust in Christ ("The Theology of the Child," *American Baptist Quarterly* [December 1982]: 200). This view has less in common with the Christian nurture paradigm than others previously described because it places greater emphasis on the interruption of the child's experience in a moment or period of conversion. Nevertheless,

Beasley-Murray accepts the concept of dedication of children, not on biblical grounds, but as a way of recognizing the place of children in the church family as those being instructed in the faith.

In summary, the rite of dedication or presentation of children has a theological foundation similar to that of infant baptism as practiced within the orbit of a philosophy of Christian nurture. It is not, however, a counterpart to infant baptism understood as an act of cleansing from sin and regeneration.

Although the focus of this discussion has been upon the question of the understanding of the role and place of the child in the life of the church, the act of child dedication has to be understood also as a statement about the place and role of parents or other adult sponsors in the body of Christ. The ceremony of dedication is, functionally, an opportunity for parents, younger couples in particular, to signify their solidarity with the whole church and their commitment to its mission and purpose—a commitment which they hope and intend to instill in their children. The theology of child dedication, therefore, belongs within the larger context of the theology of the laity, or the whole people of God.

Richard C. Leonard

220 • A LITURGY FOR CHILD DEDICATION

The ceremony of infant or child dedication is observed by churches which practice believers' baptism; these churches typically are free churches which do not follow a detailed or historic liturgy. As a result, considerable variation may be found in the format of child dedication services. The following is a suggested pattern based on practice in several congregations.

Since the rite of the dedication of children is a public testimony by the parents of their intent to raise their child in the Christian faith, with the hope that he or she will one day make a personal commitment to Christ in baptism, the ceremony is almost always included as part of the regular Sunday worship of the gathered church. The act of dedication or presentation may come at any convenient point in the service. Because dedication usually signifies the beginning of the child's pilgrimage of Christian instruction, however, an

IHS Symbol with Cross. The IHS symbol is often combined or intertwined with the cross, as shown above.

appropriate point for the ceremony would be just preceding the Scripture lesson and sermon.

Order for Child Dedication

Introduction of the child (children) and parents

Statement of the purpose and meaning of dedication

Charge to parents and their response

Blessing or prayer for the child (children), involving holding or touching the child by the officiant

Response of the congregation

Benediction or concluding prayer

Commentary

The officiant, in most churches an ordained minister, calls forward those families presenting children for dedication. In a larger congregation especially, the minister may briefly introduce the parents, mentioning the history of their association with the congregation, their current roles and responsibilities, and their relationships to other members or visitors who may be present (such as grandparents or brothers and sisters of the child being dedicated).

The minister may offer Scripture quotations, such as Psalm 127, 1 Samuel 1:24-28, Matthew 19:13-14, or selected verses from Luke 2:21-40, which speak of the biblical precedent for child dedication and the historic regard for children, in biblical faith, as a blessing from the Lord. The minister may then explain the meaning of dedication as an act which anticipates the child's later baptism in conscious confession of faith in Jesus Christ, through Christian nurture by parents, the congregation, and the larger family of God. The minister may stress the special importance of training in the Holy Scriptures.

The officiant may then address the parents, charging them with their responsibility as examples of godly living and custodians of the child's spiritual development. The parents may be given an opportunity to respond with a testimony to their own faith in Christ and an acceptance of the charge laid upon them. This is most effective where the parents, the father in particular, are able to address the congregation in spontaneous and personal witness.

The minister then lays hands upon the child, or each child in turn, or preferably holds the child, and invokes the Lord's blessing upon the child and Lord's favor and wisdom upon the parents. The minister may also make a statement receiving the child into the congregation of Christ's flock; this can be effectively symbolized by carrying the child into the midst of the congregation during this portion of the service.

When all children have been dedicated in this manner, the officiant may invite the congregation to respond in a brief act (in the church bulletin) affirming support for the parents in their task and welcoming the child into the concern of the family of God. Where time and custom permit, spontaneous expressions from members of the congregation (blessing, prophecy, words of encouragement) may occur. The officiant may then close the service of dedication with a brief prayer or benediction, inviting the congregation to greet the parents and their children following the worship service.

Richard C. Leonard

221 • Bibliography on Child Dedication

See the bibliographies on the history and theology of baptism for the several entries regarding the issue of the baptism of children.

THIRTEEN

Marriage

The sacred action of Christian marriage is often likened to the relationship that Christ has with his church, for it is a covenant between a man and a woman that joins them as one. The following chapter explores the history and theology of Christian marriage and provides sample services for this joyful occasion.

222 ♦ HISTORICAL ORIGINS AND DEVELOPMENT OF CHRISTIAN MARRIAGE

Despite challenges from some quarters, Judaism and the early Christians considered marriage a good gift from God, part of God's good creation. Marriage is considered a sacrament by both Eastern Orthodox and Roman Catholic Christians. The Orthodox permit divorce under certain conditions; most Protestant denominations, for whom marriage is a covenant rather than a sacrament, permit divorce under a broader range of circumstances.

—————— Marriage in the Bible ——————

The Old Testament portrays the God Yahweh as the creator of 'adam, man and woman (Gen. 1:27; 5:2). The fact that Yahweh names male and female together 'adam, humankind, founds their equality as human beings. They are equally "bone of bone, flesh of flesh" (Gen. 2:23). It is only because they are equal that they can marry and become one person, in Hebrew "one body" (Gen. 2:24). As a gift of the Creator, marriage is good (Gen. 1.31) and has a religious significance in Israel. Since it is from God, it relates man and woman to God. God not only created 'adam sexual and for marriage, but also blessed him and her and marriage, and made them good. It is because God made them male and female to become one body (Gen. 2:24) that Yahweh later declares, "I hate divorce . . . so do not be faithless" (Mal. 2:16, RSV).

Central to the Hebrew people's notion of its special relationship with God was the idea of the covenant. Yahweh is the God of Israel; Israel is the people of God. Together Yahweh and Israel

form a communion of grace and salvation. Four of Israel's great prophets, Hosea, Jeremiah, Deutero-Isaiah, and Ezekiel, speak of this relationship in terms drawn from marriage. They preach about the covenant relationship of Yahweh and Israel in terms of a marriage to an unfaithful wife. They find in the marriage between a man and a woman an image in which to represent the relationship of Yahweh's covenant with Israel. On a superficial level, the marriage of Hosea and Gomer is like many other marriages. On a more profound level, it serves as prophetic symbol, revealing and celebrating in representation the covenant relationship between Yahweh and Israel.

This conception of marriage as a prophetic symbol of a mutually faithful covenant is continued in the New Testament, with a minor change. Rather than presenting marriage as a symbol of the covenant between Yahweh and Israel, the letter to the Ephesians presents it as an image of the covenant between Christ and the church. The writer takes over a household code from tradition, but he critiques it in Ephesians 5:21 challenging the absolute authority of any one Christian group over any other—of husbands, for instance, over wives. He establishes a basic attitude for all Christians, an attitude of mutual giving way, so that their fundamental attitude may be to give reverence to Christ.

As Christians are all admonished to give way to one another, it comes as no surprise that a wife is to give way to her husband (Eph. 5:22). What does come as a surprise, both then and now, is that a husband is to give way to his wife. That follows from the general instruction that Christians are to give way to one another. It follows also from the specific instruction given to husbands. That instruction is not that "the husband is the head of the wife," but rather that *in the same way* that the Messiah is the head of the church is the husband the head of the wife."

A Christian husband's headship over his wife is an image of Christ's headship over the Church. Since *diakonia*, or *service*, is Christ's way of exercising authority (Mark 10:45) and since it was as a servant that "Christ loved the church and gave himself up for her" (Eph. 5:25), a Christian husband is instructed to be head over his wife by serving and giving himself up for her. She is instructed, by implication, to do the same for him. Authority modeled on that of Christ does not mean domination; it means service. Christian spouses become servants one to the other. It is thus that their marriage becomes a prophetic symbol of the covenantal servant relationship between Christ and his church (Eph. 5:32). Divorce and remarriage are prohibited in the New Testament because God, in the beginning, made them male and female to become one body (Mark 10:8-9; Matt. 19:5-6).

Teaching about Marriage in the Early Church

The Christian church soon moved out of its parent Jewish culture into a Graeco-Roman one which reshaped the biblical doctrine about marriage. To understand Christian marriage today, we must first understand the early church's teaching. The early and anonymous Epistle to Diognetus (second century) portrays the general Christian situation. "Neither in region nor in tongue nor in the social institutions of life do Christians differ from other men. . . . They take wives as all do." Clement of Alexandria (d. c. 215) employs a simple argument to show that marriage is good. Since there is only one God, who is good, and since marriage was created by that good God, it is also good. Irenaeus (fl. c. 180) employs the same argument in his refutation of the Gnostics. He accuses those who oppose the essential goodness of marriage of finding fault with the God "who made male and female for the begetting of men."

Already in the second century, in his apology for Christians, Justin (d. c. 165) had replied to Roman accusations about the sexual immorality of Christians by insisting that "either we marry only to have children or, if we do not marry, we are continent always." But Clement goes much further, arguing that the only purpose for sexual intercourse is to beget a child and that any other purpose must be excluded. Origen (d. c. 254) agrees, arguing that the man who has sexual intercourse only with his wife, "and only for the sake of children," is truly circumcised.

Two Fathers left the Western church with a theology of marriage that controlled Christian thinking for centuries. The lesser one is Tertullian who, in a first book, *To A Wife*, exhibits the same ambivalence to sexuality and marriage that is evident in the early church. He grants that, in the beginning, marriage was necessary to populate the earth, but argues that when the end of the world is near there is no need for such activity. One might think that Tertullian has no time for marriage. In a second book under the same title, however, he writes the most beautiful lines on Christian marriage one could hope to find. "What a bond is that of two faithful who are of one hope, one discipline, one service. . . . They are truly two in one body, and where there is one body there is also one spirit." One would think that between the first and second books, Tertullian had found a wonderful wife.

One reaches in the writings of Augustine, the great bishop of Hippo (d. 430), insight into the nature of marriage that was to mold the doctrine of the Latin church down to our day. Augustine's basic statement about sexuality and marriage is ubiquitous, firm, and clear. Contrary to those heretics who hold that sexuality and marriage are evil, he insists that sexuality and marriage were created good by a good God, and cannot lose their intrinsic goodness. He specifies the good of marriage as threefold and teaches that even after the Fall the marriages of devout Christians still contain this threefold good: spousal fidelity, offspring, and sacrament, by which he means the indissolubility of marriage.

Medieval Developments

Two actions by Pope Stephen II in 751 symbolized changes underway for centuries in the Catholic church. He approved of the palace revolt of Pepin against the king of the Franks, and he invited Pepin to Italy to liberate it from the Lombards. In these actions, Roman ecclesial practices crossed into northern Europe as part of an emerging Holy Roman Catholic empire. A church that was originally Palestinian, then Graeco-Roman, became decisively European. There was, however, no corresponding change in the theology of marriage, for the theological method of the time was to collect the opinions of the Fathers and then comment upon them. In the year 850, therefore, the theology of marriage had not advanced beyond where Augustine left it in 430. Marriage is good because it was created by the good God. Divorce is not permitted, to say nothing of remarriage.

Though marriage remained a secular institution and church participation in weddings was not required until the eleventh century, an old question continued to be raised: When is a marriage valid and, therefore, indissoluble? The ancient Roman answer was well-established: when it is initiated by free consent. The answer in the new Holy Roman empire, influenced by northern European customs, conflicted with that answer: The first act of sexual intercourse after the wedding makes marriage. Because these customs raised serious

Marriage. The sacred rite of baptism is symbolized by the clasping of two hands. Sometimes a third hand is seen above them with the thumb and first two fingers extended in benediction. This represents the blessing of the triune God upon the marriage.

questions for a church committed to the proposition that a valid marriage was indissoluble, a definitive answer had to be found. It was found in a compromise suggested by the canonist Gratian in the middle of the twelfth century: Marriage is initiated by free consent, and it is consummated and made indissoluble by sexual intercourse following consent.

Early scholastic theologians did not doubt that marriage was a sign of grace, only that it was a cause of grace. They hesitated, therefore, to include it among the sacraments of the church. The Dominicans Albert the Great (d. 1280) and Thomas Aquinas (d. 1274) had no such doubts. In his commentary on Peter Lombard's theological textbook, Albert characterizes as "very probable" the opinion which holds that marriage "confers grace for doing good . . . specifically that good a married person should do." In his commentary on the same textbook, Thomas asserts as "most probable" the opinion that "marriage, in so far as it is contracted in faith in Christ, confers grace to do those things which are required in marriage." In the _Summa Theologiae_, he lists marriage among the seven sacraments with no doubt whatever and, by the time of the Protestant Reformation, theologians universally held that marriage was a sacrament.

Marriage in the Reformation

The theology of marriage offered by the Reformers was in contrast to the scholastic theology they despised. Marriage, Martin Luther (d. 1546) taught in the _Babylonian Captivity_ (1520), was created by God as an institution of this world, not as a sacrament. It belongs under the jurisdiction of civil authority, not under that of the church which has taken it captive. Philipp Melanchthon (d. 1560), acknowledged as _the_ theologian of the first Lutheran generation, confirms this antisacramental approach to marriage. In his commentary on article 13 of the Augsburg Confession (1530), he defines sacrament as a rite which has "the command of God and to which the promise of grace has been added." Applying the Reformation principle of _sola scriptura_, "Scripture alone," he then argues that there are only three such sacraments, "baptism, the Lord's Supper, and absolution." John Calvin (d. 1564) follows the same line of argument in his dismissal of marriage as a sacrament.

Marriage in the Twentieth Century

Though they differ in the theological language they use about marriage, the contemporary churches agree that it is not only a social, but also a religious reality. They believe it places spouses in a context of grace. The Catholic traditions express this grace-context in their teaching on marriage as sacrament, that is, as a prophetic symbol in and through which the church proclaims and celebrates that presence of God in Christ known as grace. The Roman Catholic church distinguishes two dimensions of that sacrament. There is first the wedding ceremony, which ritualizes the free giving of consent by which two Christians establish a marriage. There is secondly the married life of the couple, which establishes their consent in a lifelong partnership of love. In ordinary language, both these actions are named *marriage;* in Catholic theological language, both are also named *sacrament.*

The Orthodox tradition insists that, since marriage is a sacrament of the church, not a legal contract, the minister of the sacrament is the presiding priest. The Roman Catholic tradition, since it insists that marriage is a contract as well as a sacrament, insists that the minister of the sacrament is the contracting couple. The Roman tradition, based on its reading of Jesus' statements on divorce and remarriage, continues to discourage divorce and to prohibit remarriage in the church. The Orthodox tradition, based on its readings of the sayings of Jesus in the entire gospel story, accepts divorce and remarriage under certain circumstances. The liturgical ritual for a second marriage, however, is not the joyful ritual it is for a first marriage, but a ritual of sadness for the failure of the first marriage and of sorrow for any sin connected with that failure.

Though John Calvin did not accept marriage as a sacrament, he did accept it as a sign of the covenant between Christ and the church. The Reformation traditions have followed him in this teaching, accepting marriage as a covenant. In this covenant, spouses commit themselves mutually to a life of intimate partnership in abiding love. They commit themselves to explore together the religious depths of their shared life and to respond to those depths in the light of their common Christian faith. They commit themselves to abide in covenant and in love and to withdraw from them only when their partnership has ceased to exist and when all available means to restore it have been exhausted. Though most Protestant traditions, on the basis of their understanding of the Gospels, now permit divorce and remarriage, no one should doubt that their theology of marriage as covenant and as a sign of the covenant between Christ and the church does situate marriage in the context of grace every bit as much as the Catholic theology of sacrament. Marriage, indeed, along with the family or the little church that proceeds from it, represent the high point of the Christian vocation.

223 ✦ A THEOLOGY OF MARRIAGE

Marriage in Western culture is viewed as a loving partnership for the whole of life, intended both for the welfare of the partners and the procreation and nurture of children. Christian marriage adds to this a perspective on marriage as an image of God's covenant relationship with the church.

Western European Marriage

This first section is about the theology of marriage and asks three questions: What is marriage, what is marriage for, and how does marriage come to be? The answer to the first question has been dominated by a Roman definition found in the *Digesta* of the Emperor Justinian (sixth century). "Marriage is a union of a man and a woman and a communion of the whole of life" (23, 2, 1). The definition would be clear if the phrase, "whole of life," were not ambiguous. This phrase can mean everything that the spouses have, and then it implies that nothing is left unshared between them. It can mean as long as life lasts, and then it can imply that marriage is a lifelong commitment. Over the years, these two meanings have been so interwoven that marriage has come to be regarded as the union of a man and a woman which commits them to the sharing of all their goods throughout the whole of their life. I will return to this matter of the whole of life in a moment.

Marriage, then, is a union, a partnership of a man and a woman for the whole of their life. But what is the partnership for? Again, in the Western world, there has been no doubt. Marriage has two ends, the marital well-being of the spouses and the procreation and upbringing of children. In the thirteenth-century, there arose a question about the relationship of these two ends. It was answered by arranging them hierarchically, establishing the procreation of children as the primary end and the well-being of the spouses as the secondary end. When a conflict between the ends arose, the secondary well-being of the spouses had to give way to the primary end of procreation. That hierarchy and subordination of ends was continued most constantly in the Catholic Church until the Second Vatican Council introduced a change.

In its document on *The Church in the Modern World*, the Second Vatican Council (1963–1965) refused to employ the long-traditional terminology about primary and secondary ends. It taught explicitly that procreation "does not make the other ends of marriage of less account" and that marriage "is not instituted solely for procreation" (n. 50). The same discussion about the laws of marriage was repeated in the 1983 revision of the Roman Catholic *Code of Canon Law*, with the same result. It is clear that, in the latter half of the twentieth century, by deliberated choice, the Catholic tradition has come into line with the other Christian traditions on this point. Marriage is for both the mutual well-being of the spouses and for the procreation and nurture of children, without either of these ends taking precedence over the other.

The third questions arises, namely, how does marriage come to be? The obvious answer is in a wedding; but that answer is not precise enough. For a marriage to be validated, only one moment of the wedding counts, the solemn moment of giving consent. "I, John, take you, Amanda, for my lawful wife, to have and to hold, from this day forward, for better, for worse, for richer, for poorer, in sickness and in health, until death do us part." When Amanda has given the same consent, she and John are pronounced "husband and wife." If this moment of free consent is missing, or is seriously flawed in any way, there is no valid marriage, there is no legal union, for free consent makes marriage. A marriage appearing to result from a wedding is null, that is, not valid, from the moment of seriously flawed free consent. A later declaration of nullity, called an annulment, does not make a marriage invalid. It merely declares that it was always legally invalid, appearances to the contrary notwithstanding. Since the free consent of

the spouses makes their marriage, all the Western churches teach that the spouses, not the witnessing church minister, are the ministers of marriage to one another.

The consensual phrase, "until death do us part," returns us to our consideration of "the whole of life." It has become almost fashionable to scorn that phrase because, it is said, unconditional promises covering the whole of life are not possible. To promise something for next week is one thing, runs the argument, but to promise it for fifty years from now is quite another. Only conditional promises made on the condition that nothing substantially changes in either spouse, continues the argument, can be made with any binding weight. The Christian churches, including those that countenance divorce and remarriage, refuse to accept that argument. They hold that marriage is for the whole of life; that it is intended to be dissolved only by death. We must briefly consider this question.

The claim that the marriage vow "until death do us part" is impossible is, quite simply, false. A man and a woman can commit themselves unconditionally, for commitment is a statement of present, not future, intention. Principles, freely chosen and lovingly embraced now, can continue to be freely chosen and lovingly embraced fifty years hence even in substantially changed circumstances.

Consider soldiers going off to war. Soldiers value life, liberty, and comfortable living as much as any other man and woman, but they do not value just any life. They value the life of honor and fidelity at any cost. Those who marry make that same commitment to love, honor, and fidelity, "until death do us part." For Christians of all denominations, that commitment acquires distinctive firmness from their equal commitment to the Christ they confess as Savior and to his teaching on marriage and divorce (Mark 10:11-12; Matt. 5:32; 19:9; Luke 16:18).

In summary, then, in the Western world, marriage is looked upon as a loving partnership for the whole of life created by free consent and ordered equally to the mutual well-being of the spouses and to the procreation and nurture of children. Christians accept that description of marriage as a foundation, and on that foundation build something more. I will now consider what more they add to it.

Christian Marriage

Religions are always on the lookout for ways to image God and God's relationship to humankind. Since the idea of their special relationship to God, arising out of the covenant, was central to the self-understanding of the Israelites, it is not difficult to understand that they would choose a human reality to image and symbolize the covenant relationship. It is not difficult, either, to understand that the reality they chose was that human reality of permanent and exclusive relationship called marriage. The prophet Hosea was the first to speak of marriage as image of the covenant.

Hosea interprets his marriage to his wife Gomer as a prophetic symbol, making visible in representation the covenant between God and Israel. Besides being a human and secular institution, Hosea's parable declares, marriage is also a religious symbol, symbolizing the abiding love and covenant between God and Israel. Lived from this perspective of faith, Christians today state that marriage is a two-storied reality. On a first story, it signifies the covenant partnership of the whole of life between this man and this woman. On a second story, it signifies in representation the abiding covenant partnership of God and Israel.

The word *covenant* is today both a Protestant and a Catholic word to characterize a marriage between Christians. It is not a randomly chosen word. It is, rather, an ancient theological word, conjuring up for Christian spouses echoes of the biblical covenants between God and God's people and between Christ and Christ's people. Covenant, however, is more than just a biblical echo; it is also an intensely personal commitment. Covenants engage persons to mutual services; covenants are for the whole of life; covenants are religious realities, witnessed by God; and covenants can be made only by adults who are emotionally and spiritually mature. To designate a marriage between Christians as a covenant marriage is to imply that it is not only an echo of the two biblical covenants but also an extension and a participation in both. It is precisely this idea that leads the Catholic churches to speak of Christian marriage also as a sacrament.

The classical Catholic definition of sacrament, an outward sign instituted by Christ to give grace, can be explicated with respect to marriage. To say that a marriage between Christians is a sacrament is to say that it is a two-storied reality. On a first story, the human and secular story, it proclaims and makes visible the steadfast love and partnership for the whole of life between a Christian man and a Christian woman. On a second story, the religious and symbolic story, it images and makes visible the steadfast love and communion between Christ and his church.

Any man and woman committing in marriage to one another announce before witnesses: "I love you and I give myself to you." A couple committing to one another in a Christian marriage say that, but they also say more. They say: "I love you as Christ loves the church and I give myself to and for you as Christ gives himself to and for the church" (cf. Eph. 5:25). A Christian marriage is, therefore, more than just a secular marriage; it is more than just a human covenant. It is also a religious marriage and a religious covenant. God and God's Son are present in it—third partners in it, from its beginning.

This presence of grace in its most ancient catholic sense, namely the presence of the saving God, is not something extrinsic to the marriage. It is something essential to it, something without which it would not be a Christian marriage at all. Of course, a Christian marriage makes visible the mutual love of a Christian man and woman. It also makes visible in representation their love of Christ and their covenant to make their marriage an image of Christ's covenant with the church. In this sense, Christian marriage may be defined as a sacrament, an outward sign of the presence of the God of grace.

224 ♦ An Ecumenical Liturgy for a Christian Marriage

The following marriage rite is brief and may be used in a variety of settings, although a Christian marriage service should be held in the place where the community of faith gathers for worship.

ENTRANCE

As the people gather, music appropriate to the praise of God may be offered. At the appointed time the bride, groom, and other members of the wedding party enter and come and stand before the minister. The families of the bride and groom may stand with the couple.

During the entrance of the wedding party, the

people may stand and sing a psalm, hymn, or spiritual song. Or an anthem may be sung, or instrumental music played.

Sentences of Scripture

(The minister calls the people to worship, either before or after the Entrance, using one of the following, or another appropriate verse from Scripture.)

1 (1 John 4:16)
God is love,
and those who abide in love,
abide in God,
and God abides in them.

2 (Ps. 118:24)
This is the day that the Lord has made;
let us rejoice and be glad in it.

3 (Ps. 106:1)
O give thanks, for the Lord is good.
God's love endures forever.

Statement on the Gift of Marriage

(The minister says:)
We gather in the presence of God
to give thanks for the gift of marriage,
to witness the joining together of N. and N.,
to surround them with our prayers,
and to ask God's blessing upon them,
so that they may be strengthened for their life
    together
and nurtured in their love for God.

God created us male and female,
and gave us marriage
so that husband and wife may help and comfort
    each other,
living faithfully together in plenty and in want,
in joy and in sorrow,
in sickness and in health,
throughout all their days.

God gave us marriage
for the full expression of the love between a man
    and a woman.
In marriage a woman and a man belong to each
    other,
and with affection and tenderness
freely give themselves to each other.

God gave us marriage
for the well-being of human society,
for the ordering of family life,
and for the birth and nurture of children.

God gave us marriage as a holy mystery
in which a man and a woman are joined together,
and become one,
just as Christ is one with the church.

In marriage, husband and wife are called to a new
    way of life,
created, ordered, and blessed by God.
This way of life must not be entered into carelessly,
or from selfish motives,
but responsibly, and prayerfully.

We rejoice that marriage is given by God,
blessed by our Lord Jesus Christ,
and sustained by the Holy Spirit.
Therefore, let marriage be held in honor by all.

Prayer

(The minister says:)
Let us pray:
Gracious God,
you are always faithful in your love for us.
Look mercifully upon N. and N.,
who have come seeking your blessing.
Let your Holy Spirit rest upon them
so that with steadfast love
they may honor the promises they make this day,
through Jesus Christ our Savior.
Amen.

(The congregation may be seated.)

Declarations of Intent

(The minister addresses the bride and groom individually, using either A or B:)

A
N., understanding that God has created, ordered, and blessed the covenant of marriage,
do you affirm your desire and intention to enter this covenant?

Answer: _I do._

B
(If both are baptized, the following may be used:)
N., in your baptism
you have been called to union with Christ and the church.
Do you intend to honor this calling
through the covenant of marriage?

Answer: _I do._

Affirmations of the Families
(The minister may address the families of the bride and groom:)

N., N. [Names of family members],
do you give your blessing to N. and N.,
and promise to do everything in your power to uphold them in their marriage?

(The families of the bride and groom answer:)

1
We (I) give our (my) blessing
and promise our (my) support.

or

2
We (I) do.

(The families of the bride and groom may be seated.)

Affirmation of the Congregation
(The minister may address the congregation, saying:)
Will all of you witnessing these vows
do everything in your power
to uphold N. and N. in their marriage?

Answer: *We will.*

(A psalm, hymn, spiritual song, or anthem maybe sung.)

Reading from Scripture
(The following, or a similar prayer for illumination, may be said:)

God of mercy,
your faithfulness to your covenant frees us to live together
in the security of your powerful love.

Amid all the changing words of our generation,
speak your eternal Word that does not change.
Then may we respond to your gracious promises
by living in faith and obedience;
through our Lord Jesus Christ.
Amen.

(One or more Scripture passages are read.)

Sermon
(After the Scriptures are read, a brief sermon may be given.)

(A psalm, hymn, spiritual song, or other music may follow.)

Vows
(The people may stand.)

(The minister addresses the couple:)
N. and N.,
since it is your intention to marry,
join your right hands,
and with your promises
bind yourselves to each other as husband and wife.

(The bride and groom face each other and join right hands. They in turn then make their vows to each other, using A or B.)

A
(The man says:)
I, N., take you, N., to be my wife;
and I promise,
before God and these witnesses,
to be your loving and faithful husband;
in plenty and in want;
in joy and in sorrow;
in sickness and in health;
as long as we both shall live.

(The woman says:)
I, N., take you, N., to be my husband;
and I promise,
before God and these witnesses,
to be your loving and faithful wife;
in plenty and in want;
in joy and in sorrow;
in sickness and in health;
as long as we both shall live.

B
(The man says:)
Before God and these witnesses,
I, N., take you, N., to be my wife,
and I promise to love you,
and to be faithful to you,
as long as we both shall live.

(The woman says:)
Before God and these witnesses
I, N., take you, N., to be my husband,
and I promise to love you,
and to be faithful to you,
as long as we both shall live.

Exchange of Rings (or Other Symbols)
(If rings are to be exchanged, the minster may say to the couple:)

What do you bring as the sign of your promise?

(When the rings are presented, the minister may
say the following prayer:)
By your blessing, O God,
may these rings be to N. and N.
symbols of unending love and faithfulness,
reminding them of the covenant they have made
this day,
through Jesus Christ our Lord.
Amen.

(The bride and groom exchange rings using A or
B or other appropriate words. The traditional
Trinitarian formula should be omitted for both the
bride and groom if one of the marriage partners
is not a professing Christian.)

A

(The one giving the ring says:)
N., I give you this ring as a sign of our covenant,
in the name of the Father,
and of the Son,
and of the Holy Spirit.

The one receiving the ring says:
I receive this ring as a sign of our covenant,
in the name of the Father,
and of the Son,
and of the Holy Spirit.

B

(As each ring is given, the one giving the ring
says:)
This ring I give you,
as a sign of our constant faith
and abiding love,
in the name of the Father,
and of the Son,
and of the Holy Spirit.

Prayer

(The couple may kneel.)

(One of the following prayers, or a similar prayer,
is said:)
Let us pray:

1

Eternal God,
Creator and preserver of all life,
author of salvation, and giver of all grace:
look with favor upon the world you have made
  and redeemed,
and especially upon N. and N.

Give them wisdom and devotion
in their common life,
that each may be to the other
a strength in need,
a counselor in perplexity,
a comfort in sorrow,
and a companion in joy.

Grant that their wills
may be so knit together in your will,
and their spirits in your Spirit,
that they may grow in love and peace
with you and each other
all the days of their life.

Give them the grace,
when they hurt each other,
to recognize and confess their fault,
and to seek each other's forgiveness
and yours.

Make their life together
a sign of Christ's love
to this sinful and broken world,
that unity may overcome estrangement,
forgiveness heal guilt,
and joy conquer despair.

Give them such fulfillment of their mutual love
that they may reach out in concern for others.

[Give to them, if it is your will,
the gift of children,
and the wisdom to bring them up
to know you,
to love you,
and to serve you.]

Grant that all who have witnessed these vows today
may find their lives strengthened,
and that all who are married
may depart with their own promises renewed.

Enrich with your grace
all husbands and wives, parents and children,
that, loving and supporting one another,
they may serve those in need
and be a sign of your kingdom.

Grant that the bonds by which all your children
are united to one another
may be so transformed by your Spirit
that your peace and justice may fill the earth,
through Jesus Christ our Lord.
Amen.

2
Eternal God,
without your grace no promise is sure.
Strengthen N. and N.
with patience, kindness, gentleness,
and all other gifts of your Spirit,
so that they may fulfill the vows they have made.
Keep them faithful to each other and to you.
Fill them with such love and joy
that they may build a home of peace and welcome.
Guide them by your Word
to serve you all their days.

Help us all, O God,
to do your will in each of our homes and lives.
Enrich us with your grace
so that, supporting one another,
we may serve those in need
and hasten the coming of peace, love, and justice
    on earth,
through Jesus Christ our Lord.
Amen.

Lord's Prayer
(The minister invites all present to sing or say the
    Lord's Prayer:)
As our Savior Christ has taught us, we are bold to
    say:
(All pray together.)

or

Our Father in heaven,
hallowed be your name,
your kingdom come,
your will be done,
on earth as in heaven.
Give us today our daily bread.
Forgive us our sins
as we forgive those who sin against us.
Save us from the time of trial
and deliver us from evil.
For the kingdom, the power, and the glory are
    yours
now and forever. Amen.

or

Our Father, who art in heaven,
hallowed be thy name,
thy kingdom come,
thy will be done,
on earth as it is in heaven.
Give us this day our daily bread;

and forgive us our debts,
as we forgive our debtors;
and lead us not into temptation,
but deliver us from evil.
For thine is the kingdom,
and the power, and the glory, forever.
Amen.

Announcement of Marriage
(The minister addresses the congregation:)
Before God
and in the presence of this congregation,
N. and N. have made their solemn vows to each
    other.
They have confirmed their promises by the join-
    ing of hands
[and by the giving and receiving of rings].
Therefore, I proclaim that they are now husband
    and wife.

Blessed be the Father and the Son and the Holy
    Spirit now and forever.

(The minister joins the couple's right hands.)

(The congregation may join the minister in saying:)
Those whom God has joined together
let no one separate.

CHARGE AND BLESSING

Charge to the Couple
(The minister addresses the couple, using one of
the following:)

1 (See Col. 3:12-14)
As God's own,
clothe yourselves with compassion,
kindness, and patience,
forgiving each other
as the Lord has forgiven you,
and crown all these things with love,
which binds everything together in perfect harmony.

2 (Col. 3:17)
Whatever you do, in word or deed,
do everything in the name of the Lord Jesus,
giving thanks to God through him.

Blessing
(The minister gives God's blessing to the couple
and the congregation, using one of the following:)

1 (See Num. 6:24-26)
The Lord bless you and keep you.
The Lord be kind and gracious to you.
The Lord look upon you with favor
and give you peace.
Amen.

2

The grace of Christ attend you,
the love of God surround you,
the Holy Spirit keep you,
that you may live in faith,
abound in hope,
and grow in love,
both now and forevermore.
Amen.

(A psalm, hymn, spiritual song, or anthem may be sung, or instrumental music may be played, as the wedding party leaves.)

Book of Common Worship[11]

225 ◆ A Liturgy for a Marriage Service

This section presents a very simple marriage service accompanied by a commentary to highlight its theological meanings.

"Let us worship God."

Commentary: It is made clear from the outset that this wedding is not merely a civil ceremony but, more importantly, also a religious one, in which the role of the God who is grace is as central as the roles of the spouses. God is confessed throughout the ceremony as the one who guarantees the fidelity of the spouses.

"Friends, marriage is established by God. In marriage, a man and a woman willingly bind themselves in love, and become one even as Christ is one with the church, his body."

Commentary: This declaration embodies three theological ideas: (1) Marriage is part of God's creation and is therefore *good* (cf. Gen. 1:27-28); (2) Valid marriage requires that there be free consent, that the spouses "freely bind themselves"; (3) Christian marriage is modeled on the covenantal union of Christ and church—the spouses are to be one "as Christ and church are one."

"We have not loved one another as you commanded. We have been quick to claim our own rights and careless of the rights of others. We have taken much and given little. . . . O God, strengthen us in love, so that we may serve you as a faithful people."

Commentary: The great commandment for Christian spouses, as for all Christians, is the commandment of love (cf. Matt. 22:39). This prayer confesses our shortcomings and asks strength [grace] for love and fidelity. Love, as one would expect for the followers of Jesus (cf. Mark 10:45), is specified as service and giving way (cf. Eph. 5:21-23).

Now lessons, relating to marriage and its meanings, are read from Old and New Testaments. A sermon explains them. Having been reminded to "Be subject to one another out of reverence for Christ" (Eph. 5:21), each spouse then speaks the words of free consent. "[Name], I promise with God's help to be your faithful husband/wife, to love and serve you as Christ commands, as long as we both shall live."

Commentary: These words represent the core of the ceremony, the giving of the free consent required for the validity of the marriage presented by the readings and the sermon. That they are given for the whole of life, "as long as we both shall live," is clear. The ring, the traditional symbol of unbroken fidelity, is given in pledge of this promise. The mutual exchange of rings better symbolizes the call of both spouses to be faithful.

"Love is slow to lose patience, it looks for a way of being constructive. It is not possessive. . . . it does not pursue selfish advantage. It is not touchy. . . . Love knows no limit to its endurance, no end to its trust, no fading of its hope; it can outlast anything. It still stands when all else has fallen."

Commentary: This prayer confesses, in echoes of Paul's words in 1 Corinthians 13, both the difficulty of love for the children of Adam and the nature of love for the followers of the new Adam, Christ. It underscores the life-long character of Christian love, which "still stands when all else has fallen."

The Lord's Prayer is recited.

Commentary: The spouses join hands to symbolize their union. The entire congregation should also join hands to symbolize their union in God in Christ, whose prayer they recite.

"[Name] and [Name], you are now husband and wife according to the witness of the holy catholic church and the law of the state. Become one. Fulfill your promises. Love and serve the Lord."

Commentary: The minister here acknowledges what all the Western churches confess; namely, that the spouses minister marriage to one another. The Eastern Orthodox, of course, teach that the presiding priest alone is the minister. Note again the injunction to Christian love as mutual service.

"What God has united man must not divide" (cf. Matt. 19:6).

"The grace of the Lord Jesus, the love of God, and the fellowship of the Holy Spirit, be with you all. Amen."

Commentary: The solemn biblical injunction and the closing doxology emphasize two theological facts, the life-long nature of Christian marriage and the Trinitarian grace which is its strength. Note that the presence of God frames the ceremony from beginning to end. It is this presence of grace, in the ceremony and throughout marriage, that moves the Catholic church to speak of both as sacraments.

226 ✦ GUIDELINES FOR PLANNING A MARRIAGE SERVICE

The preceding discussion underscores the main elements to be symbolized and therefore included in a Christian wedding service. When woven together after careful planning, they create a service that follows the general outline described below.

The Entrance Procession. The Entrance procession at a wedding is a form of the Entrance procession of the ministers at Sunday worship. Since the marrying couple are the ministers of marriage, they should walk together in this procession, preceded by the best man and the maid of honor, their parents, and the presiding church minister. The long-traditional wedding procession in which the bride enters with her father, preceded by her bridesmaids, to be handed over to her husband, derives from a time when a marriage was the transfer of a woman from the legal authority of her fa-

ther to that of her husband. Since few brides, hopefully few couples, see marriage in this light today, this traditional procession is best replaced by the ministerial procession that has been described.

An Opening Prayer. Most marriage services offer options from which the couple, in consultation with the presiding minister, can choose prayers which highlight that their marriage is not only a civil but more especially a religious and Christian ceremony.

Scripture Readings and Explanatory Sermon. Again, most marriage services offer a selection of marriage-related Old and New Testament readings, from which a couple may select those that best speak the Word of God to their marriage. There is need today, I feel, to make a special plea for the reading of Ephesians 5:21-32 properly understood and explained. This is a text which underscores the covenantal and sacramental dimensions of Christian marriage; it is also a text which is regularly scorned by contemporary women because of the offensive phrase "the husband is the head of the wife as Christ is the head of the church" (v. 23). The text is offensive when one focuses on the words "the husband is the head of the wife." The true Christian focus, however, falls on "as (that is, in the same way as,) Christ is head of the church." How Christ is head of the church needs to be carefully explained in a sermon. He is head, not in the manner of a divine-right monarch or master, but as a servant (cf. Mark 10:45; Matt. 23:11; Luke 22:26). A Christian husband is called to be head of his wife by being her radical servant, and she is summoned to be his radical servant. Mutual service, in imitation of the Christ they confess as Lord, is not an idea Christian spouses should ever scorn.

The Exchange of Consent. The exchange of consent, as already explained, is the central and essential part of the ceremony and should, therefore, be planned in order to achieve careful clarity. Since the wedding ring symbolizes unbroken fidelity to the marital promises and since the marriage ceremony emphasizes the equal call and obligation of both spouses to remain faithful, the exchange of rings has become a common practice and is a better symbol than the former tradition of giving a single ring to the bride.

Concluding Rites. The ceremony concludes with a blessing of the new spouses and of the children that may be born from their union. There should also be some praise of and thanksgiving to the Trinitarian God who is at the center of their marriage. Again, there are options here from which the spouses may choose to give the ceremony their own Christian stamp.

Michael Fowler

227 ✦ BIBLIOGRAPHY ON THE MARRIAGE SERVICE

Biddle, Perry H. _Abingdon Marriage Manual._ Rev ed. Nashville: Abingdon, 1987. Includes five denominational marriage service liturgies with commentary.

Bromiley, Geoffrey W. _God and Marriage._ Grand Rapids: Eerdmans, 1980. A theological discussion of marriage.

Christianse, James L. _The Minister's Marriage Handbook._ Old Tappan, N.J.: Revell, 1985. Includes ten liturgies for the marriage service.

Cooke, Bernard, ed. _Alternative Futures for Worship._ Vol. 5, _Marriage._ Collegeville, Minn.: Liturgical Press, 1988. A discussion of the future of marriage in the Roman Catholic tradition.

Glusker, David, and Peter Misner. _Words for Your Wedding._ San Fransico: Harper, 1986. Includes five denominational marriage service liturgies with a variety of additional textual options.

Hatchett, Marion. _Commentary on the American Prayer Book._ New York: Seabury Press, 1981. A theological and liturgical commentary on the 1979 _Book of Common Prayer,_ including a discussion of the marriage liturgy.

Hogan, Richard M., and John M. LeVoir. _Covenant of Love: Pope John Paul II on Sexuality, Marriage, and Family in the Modern World with a Commentary on Familiaris Consortio._ 2d ed. San Francisco: Ignatius Press, 1992. Originally published by Doubleday, 1985.

Haughton, Rosemary. _The Theology of Marriage._ Butler, Wis.: Clergy Book Service, 1971.

John Paul II. _Theology of Marriage and Celibacy: Catechesis on Marriage and Celibacy in the Light of the Resurrection of the Body._ Preface by Donald W. Wuerl. St. Paul Editions, 1986.

Journal of the Liturgical Conference 4:2 (Spring 1984). Issue is devoted to the topic of marriage.

Meyendorf, John. _Marriage: An Orthodox Perspective._ 2d ed. Crestwood, N.Y.: St. Vladimir's Seminary Press, 1975.

Mitchell, Leonel L. _Praying Shapes Believing._ Minneapolis: Winston, 1985. A theological commentary on the 1979 _Book of Common Prayer,_ including a discussion of the marriage rite.

Orsy, Ladislas. _Marriage in Canon Law: Texts and Comments, Reflections and Questions._ Wilmington, Del.: Michael Glazier, 1986.

Pfatteicher, Philip. H. _Commentary on the Lutheran Book of Worship: Lutheran Liturgy in Its Ecumenical Context._ Minneapolis: Augsburg Fortress, 1990. Includes a commentary on the marriage liturgy.

Reformed Worship 16 (June 1990). Theme of issue is on Christian marriage.

Reformed Liturgy and Music 20: 3 (Summer 1986). A theme of issue is on marriage.

Robinson, Geoffrey. _Marriage, Divorce and Nullity: A Guide to the Annulment Process in the Catholic Church._ Collegeville, Minn.: Liturgical Press, 1988.

Schillebeeckx, Edward. _Marriage._ 2 vols. Kansas City: Sheed and Ward, 1985. An extended theological study by a prominent Roman Catholic theologian of this century.

Stevenson, Kenneth. _Nuptial Blessing: A Study of Christian Marriage Rites._ New York: Oxford University Press, 1983.

Thomas, David M. _The Message of the Sacraments._ Vol. 5, _Christian Marriage: A Journey Together._ Wilmington, Del.: Michael Glazier, 1983.

Willimon, William H. _Worship as Pastoral Care._ Nashville: Abingdon, 1979. See chapter on Christian marriage service.

For marriage service liturgies representative of distinct traditions, see:

- For a Baptist or free church service, see Jesse Jai McNeil, _Minister's Service Book for Pulpit and Parish_ (Grand Rapids: Eerdmans, 1993), 44–49. See also many of the books listed below.

- For the Christian Reformed Church's service, see _The Psalter Hymnal_ (Grand Rapids: CRC Publications, 1987), 1007–1012.

- For an ecumenical service, see _A Christian Celebration of Marriage: An Ecumenical Lit-_

urgy, prepared by the Consultation on Common Texts (Philadelphia: Fortress, 1987).

- For the Episcopalian service, see *The Book of Common Prayer* (New York: Church Hymnal Corporation, 1979), 423–38.

- For the Evangelical Lutheran Church in America's service, see *Lutheran Book of Worship* (Minneapolis: Augsburg; Philadelphia: Board of Publication, Lutheran Church in America, 1978), 202–6.

- For the Lutheran Church–Missouri Synod's service, see *Lutheran Worship—Agenda* (St. Louis: Concordia, 1984), 120–33.

- For the Mennonite service, see Gary and Lydia Harder, *Celebrating Christian Marriage* (Newton, Kans.: Faith and Life Press; Scottdale, Pa: Mennonite Publishing House, 1980).

- For the Methodist service, see *The United Methodist Book of Worship* (Nashville: United Methodist Publishing House, 1992), 115–38.

- For the Presbyterian service, see *The Book of Common Worship* (Louisville: Westminster/John Knox, 1993), 841–93; and *Christian Marriage: Supplemental Liturgical Resource 3* (Philadelphia: Westminster, 1986).

- For the Reformed Church in America's service, see *Worship the Lord* (Grand Rapids: Eerdmans, 1987), 30–36.

- For the Roman Catholic rite, see *The Rites,* vol. 1 (New York: Pueblo Publishing, 1983).

- For the United Church of Christ's service, see *Book of Worship: United Church of Christ* (New York: Office of Church Life, 1986), 321–56.

❧ FOURTEEN ❧

The Funeral

The Christian attitude toward death, based on hope and confidence in Christ's victory over death, was one of the most important ways Christianity differed from the ancient culture into which it was born. As Christianity became inculturated in the Middle Ages, Christian rites surrounding death and burial were among the most important ways that an entire culture, however imperfectly, took on the impress of the Christian faith. Despite the ambivalent and even bleak regard of death in modern society, Orthodox, Catholic, and Protestant funeral services continue to proclaim the Christian hope of resurrection.

228 ◆ HISTORICAL ORIGINS AND DEVELOPMENT OF THE FUNERAL

Christian rituals related to death did not begin at the funeral service. Dying itself was surrounded by many Christian rites. During the Reformation, Protestants' sharp attacks on the medieval beliefs in purgatory and intercession for the deceased eventually shifted attention in the modern world away from a preoccupation with death to a widespread ignoring of the reality of death.

——— Death in Human Cultures ———

Rituals are formative experiences—the means by which a community expresses for itself and hands on to others its significant beliefs. The funeral, encompassing all of the rites related to death and burial, embodies a community's understanding of death and the afterlife.

An historical survey of the funeral properly begins with the anthropological data on the burial customs of indigenous peoples of *undeveloped* areas of the world. Like those peoples whose artifacts date back to antiquity, these peoples often view death with fear, not hope, and look upon the corpse with aversion, not affection. Since the human unconscious cannot fathom the possibility of its own death, it generally attributes the ending of life to some malicious intervention.

Even though death is feared in all cultures, in less complex societies people have developed a distinct pattern which helps them cope with the inevitability of death—not tribal customs, but personal rituals which have taken shape over the course of time.

Sensing death's approach, the person calls for family and friends to assemble. Gathering around the dying person, they listen attentively to his or her last words, recognizing them to be words filled with wisdom, either accumulated over the years or inspired in the moment. At the gathering, the business of distributing property is first attended to, and then the person assumes the posture for quietly awaiting death.

When the person dies, the family usually buries the corpse out of superstition, not respect. Some believe that an unburied corpse cannot rest in peace, and is consequently doomed to wander the earth, presumably haunting friends and relatives. Others fear that evil spirits inhabit the corpse, and therefore want those evil ones put underground as soon as possible and kept there. It has even been suggested that the tombstone originated as an added precaution to prevent roaming corpses.

——— Death in Judaism ———

Although there are no written records of a Jewish liturgy of burial dating before the ninth century A.D., what scattered references there are to burial rites in Judaism always reflect realism and simplicity. Jesus, for example, was buried according to Jewish custom. Although the nearness of the Sabbath, coupled with fear of the authorities, prevented his friends from anointing the body in the usual way, both the synoptic and the Johannine gospels, while differing in specific details, record that his body was wrapped in linen, with myrrh and aloes between the bands (Matt. 27:59; Mark 15:46; Luke 23:53, 56; 24:1; John 19:39-40), and laid to rest in the tomb.

The Jews viewed dead bodies as unclean and therefore disposed of them before going back to prayers or going on with business as usual. Mourners were forbidden to work, bathe, or have sexual intercourse for up to as long as thirty days. Male mourners were served a "meal of comfort" (*labra'ah*) after the funeral, consisting of eggs and lentils, prepared by friends and neighbors and served with wine.

The *Kaddish*—the sanctification—gives a synthesis of Jewish theology with regard to death. Originally the concluding prayer of the synagogue liturgy, the Kaddish is an eschatological prayer similar to the Lord's Prayer. In addition to being prayed during the funeral, traditionally the Kaddish must be recited every day for eleven months following the death of a parent, blood relative, or spouse.

Early Christian Funeral Customs

In the early days of the Christian community, when Roman influence was strongest, funeral customs show an attraction to the mystery cults of the East as well as the practices of Egypt. Initially, Christians and pagans were buried side by side in cemeteries, with only decorations or inscriptions to distinguish one from the other. Early symbolism depicted Jesus as tending sheep, fishing, or presiding over the heavenly banquet. In time, however, as the theology of death became more paschal in character, symbols of deliverance began to predominate. Jesus' miracles, particularly the raising of Lazarus and the curing of the blind man, were popular representations.

There are records of funeral meals as customary in early Christianity, which probably had their origin in the Roman custom of graveside feasts, rather than in the Jewish meals of comfort held in the homes of the mourners. Roman funeral meals were connected with either the belief that the dead needed nourishment or the idea that the tedium of the death would be relieved by such feasts. Often they became occasions of such raucous behavior that most of our knowledge of them is derived from various bishops' condemnations of them. Their condemnations addressed the scandal that such excesses caused. In contrast, bishops encouraged prayer vigils, fasting, and gifts to the needy as more appropriate customs to develop.

The weeping and wailing associated with mourning, as well as black mourning garments, were also considered to be un-Christian because despair, rather than hope, was seen as their primary motivation. Consequently, devout Christians developed more appropriate means of expressing their grief, replacing weeping and wailing with singing psalms and hymns.

From the writings of the Fathers, one learns of other un-Christian behavior that was gradually adapted to reflect more accurately the theology of the Christian community. One example of this was the Christian custom of placing eucharistic bread in the corpse's mouth. This custom probably traced its origin to the mystery cults, where a coin was placed in the mouth of the deceased, so that he or she would be able to pay the fare to Charon on the ferry across the river Styx.

The oldest Roman ritual for death and burial (*Ordo* 49) dates from the seventh century. Rather than a highly structured ritual, the *Ordo* actually presents an outline for the service. The ritual consisted of two parts: the first part, which ritualized death, took place in the home of the deceased; the other, a burial ritual, took place in the church and cemetery.

For Christian burial, when death appeared to be imminent, the Christian was given the Eucharist, as a token of the resurrection he or she was about to experience. From that time until the moment of death, family and friends would read the Passion narrative to the one dying. When they thought the soul was about to leave the body, those gathered in prayer would respond, "Come, saints of God, advance angels of the Lord. . . ." Then, after reciting Psalm 113, they would pray, "May the choir of angels receive you."

After death, the body was placed on a litter and carried in procession to the church. There the community recited an office, consisting of Psalms, using the poignant antiphon: "May the angels lead you into paradise, may the martyrs welcome you and guide you into the holy city Jerusalem." While reciting Psalm 117, the procession continued on its way, escorting the body to the cemetery, and responding, "Open the gates for me, and once I am within I shall praise the Lord."

Medieval, Reformation, and Modern Practices

Parallel to the peaceful, paschal vision of the Christian's final journey were harsh scenes of final judgment for those who died unrepentant. God and the company of angels stood guard before the heavenly court. In medieval culture, the art of Christian death became the subject of a body of devotional literature. This _ars moriendi_ (art of dying) tradition was intended to help people face death with confident hope in Christ's salvation but, at the same time, warn against complacency, overconfidence, hypocrisy, and impiety.

Protestant Reformers believed that medieval Christian belief in purgatory, intercession of saints, and prayers for the dead were theologically wrong. As a result, in Protestant circles and, by extension in modern Northern European culture generally, what happens to people after death ceased to be a central topic of theological and religious conversation. Protestant funerals proclaimed the victory of Christ over death, but preoccupation with preparing for death during life and with dying a holy death was not characteristic of Protestants as it had been and continued to be for Catholics.

In modern times, the funeral has undergone another transition. Standing within a culture which would rather deny death's reality and power, the Christian churches understand the funeral more as a means of ministry to the grieving, rooted in the community's theology of death, than an opportunity only to honor the deceased.

Julia Ann Upton

229 • A THEOLOGY OF THE FUNERAL

The Christian funeral must find ways to affirm Christian belief in Christ's victory over death, commend the deceased to God's mercy, and comfort the survivors.

The key question to ask in focusing on the theology of the funeral is, "What belief does this ritual express regarding the community's understanding of God?" Egyptian pyramids and neolithic passage tombs stocked with food and material treasures tell us that those communities believed in a life beyond physical death which they imagined to be similar to earthly life. Christian funerals, by contrast, ought to express the community's belief in eternal life—that the dead have passed beyond the suffering, trials, and needs of bodily life into the realm of God where every tear will be wiped away (Rev. 21:4). If the assembly is clad in black, weeping, wailing, and not participating in the ritual at all, it is difficult to imagine that they believe their dead have triumphed and are living in heavenly bliss. There will, of course, be cultural differences regarding mourning customs, but they shouldn't negate the community's foundational beliefs.

During the Second Vatican Council (1962–1965), when the Roman Catholic bishops of the world examined the Catholic funeral liturgy, they saw just such a conflict between the church's theology of death and the ritual that was supposed to be expressing that theology. They saw that the paschal character so essential to Christian faith was not clearly seen in the rituals of death and burial. As a result, all of the rituals related to death and burial were revised in the _Order of Christian Funerals_ (1989).

Christians believe that God rewards the good, but punishes the wicked, so another important theological element of the funeral is commending the deceased to God's mercy, confident that God reads the heart, and is therefore more just than humans can even imagine.

A third important theological element of the funeral is acknowledging the deep grief of the assembly, their desire to comfort one another, and their desire to be comforted by God through the church's ministry. Regardless of the circumstances of death, someone they love has died, and the mourners stand in need of consolation. The funeral ritual, therefore, should not deny that reality, but address it. The American way of death, about which so many sociologists have written, is often a denial of death's ultimacy, where corpses are turned into mannequins, reposed in a tableau of pretense. The Christian way of death needs to witness the belief that death is not endless sweet repose, but the doorway through which the Christian passes into new life.

Julia Ann Upton

230 ◆ A Liturgical Order for the Christian Funeral

The following funeral liturgy is designed as a service of witness to the resurrection of Jesus Christ. Like every service of Christian worship, it is rooted in the paschal mystery, the death and resurrection, of Christ.

ENTRANCE

Gathering

(The pastor may greet the family. Music for worship may be offered while the people gather.)

(The coffin or urn may be carried into the place of worship in procession, in which case the pall may be placed on it outside the place of worship with these words:)

Dying, Christ destroyed our death.
Rising, Christ restored our life.
Christ will come again in glory.
As in baptism *Name* put on Christ, so in Christ may *Name* be clothed with glory.

Chi Rho. Shown above are two versions of the chi rho symbol (the Greek letters X and P). The chi rho is an abbreviation for the name of the Lord Jesus Christ. The chi rho symbols above appear on early burial inscriptions, lamps, and coins.

Here and now, dear friends, we are God's children.
What we shall be has not yet been revealed;
but we know that when he appears, we shall be like him, for we shall see him as he is.
Those who have this hope purify themselves as Christ is pure.

THE WORD OF GRACE

(If the coffin or urn is carried into the place of worship in procession, the pastor may go before it speaking these words, the congregation standing. Or if the coffin or urn is already in place, the pastor speaks these or other words from in front of the congregation.)

Jesus said, I am the resurrection and I am the life.
Those who believe in me, even though they die, yet shall they live, and whoever lives and believes in me shall never die.
I am Alpha and Omega, the beginning and the end, the first and the last.
I died, and behold I am alive for evermore, and I hold the keys of hell and death.
Because I live, you shall live also.

Greeting

Friends, we have gathered here to praise God and to witness to our faith as we celebrate the life of *Name*.
We come together in grief, acknowledging our human loss.
May God grant us grace, that in pain we may find comfort, in sorrow hope, in death resurrection.

(If there has been no procession, the pall may be placed at this time.)

(Whether or not the pall is placed at this time, the sentences printed above under **Gathering** may be used here if they were not used earlier.)

Hymn or Song

Prayer

(One or more of the following or other prayers may be offered, in unison if desired. Petition for God's help, thanksgiving for the communion of saints, confession of sin, and assurance of pardon are appropriate here.)

The Lord be with you
And also with you.
Let us pray.

O God, who gave us birth,
you are ever more ready to hear than we are to
    pray.
You know our needs before we ask, and our igno-
    rance in asking.
Give to us now your grace, that as we shrink be-
    fore the mystery of death, we may see the light
    of eternity.
Speak to us once more your solemn message of
    life and of death.
Help us to live as those who are prepared to die.
And when our days here are accomplished, en-
    able us to die as those who go forth to live, so
    that living or dying, our life may be in you, and
    that nothing in life or in death will be able to
    separate us from your great love in Christ Jesus
    our Lord. Amen.

Eternal God,
we praise you for the great company of all those
    who have finished their course in faith and now
    rest from their labor.
We praise you for those dear to us whom we name
    in our hearts before you.
Especially we praise you for _Name,_ whom you
    have graciously received into your presence.
To all of these, grant your peace.
Let perpetual light shine upon them;
and help us so to believe where we have not seen,
    that your presence may lead us through our
    years, and bring us at last with them into the
    joy of your home not made with hands but eter-
    nal in the heavens; through Jesus Christ our
    Lord. Amen.

(The following prayer of confession and pardon
may also be used:)

Holy God, before you our hearts are open, and
    from you no secrets are hidden.
We bring to you now our shame and sorrow for
    our sins.
We have forgotten that our life is from you and
    unto you.
We have neither sought nor done your will.
We have not been truthful in our hearts, in our
    speech, in our lives.
We have not loved as we ought to love.
Help us and heal us, raising us from our sins into
    a better life, that we may end our days in peace,
    trusting in your kindness unto the end;
through Jesus Christ our Lord, who lives and

reigns with you in the unity of the Holy Spirit,
one God, now and for ever. Amen.

Who is in a position to condemn?
Only Christ, Christ who died for us, who rose for
    us, who reigns at God's right hand and prays
    for us.
Thanks be to God who gives us the victory
    through our Lord Jesus Christ.

Psalm 130
(Psalm 130 may be sung or spoken.)

Proclamation and Response

Old Testament Lesson
(One or both of the following or another lesson
may be read: Isaiah 40:1-8; Isaiah 40:28-31)

Other Suggested Scripture Readings
Exodus 14:5-14, 19-31: Israel's deliverance
Isaiah 43:1-3a, 5-7, 13, 15, 18-19, 25; 44:6, 8a: God
will deliver
Isaiah 55:1-3, 6-13: Hymn of joy

Psalm 23
(Psalm 23 may be sung or spoken.)

New Testament Lesson
(One of the following or another lesson may be
read: 1 Corinthians 15:1-2a, 12, 16-18, 20, 35-38a,
42b-44, 54-55; Revelation 21:1-7; Romans 8:1-2, 11,
14, 17-18, 28, 31-32, 35-39.)

Other Suggested Scripture Readings
2 Corinthians 4:5-18: Glory in God
Ephesians 1:15-23, 2:1-10: Alive in Christ
1 Peter 1:3-9, 13, 21-25: Blessed by God
Revelation 7:2-3, 9-17: The multitude of the redeemed

Psalm, Canticle, or Hymn

Gospel Lesson
(The following or another lesson may be read:
John 14:1-4, 18-19, 25-27)

Other Suggested Scripture Readings
Luke 24:13-35: Jesus at Emmaus
John 11:1-4, 20-27, 32-35, 38-44: The raising of
Lazarus

Sermon
(A sermon may be preached, proclaiming the
gospel in the face of death. It may lead into,
or include, the following acts of naming and witness.)

Naming
(The life and death of the deceased may be gathered up in the reading of a memorial or appropriate statement, or in other ways, by the pastor or others.)

Witness
(Pastor, family, friends, and members of the congregation may briefly voice their thankfulness to God for the grace they have received in the life of the deceased and their Christian faith and joy.)

(Signs of faith, hope, and love may be exchanged.)

Hymn or Song

Creed or Affirmation of Faith

Commendation
(If the Committal is to conclude this service, it may be shortened and substituted for the Commendation.)

Prayers
(One or more of the following prayers may be offered, or other prayers may be used. They may take the form of a pastoral prayer, a series of shorter prayers, or a litany. Intercession, commendation of life, and thanksgiving are appropriate here.)

God of us all, your love never ends.
When all else fails, you still are God.
We pray to you for one another in our need, and
    for all, anywhere, who mourn with us this day.
To those who doubt, give light; to those who are
    weak, strength; to all who have sinned, mercy;
    to all who sorrow, your peace.
Keep true in us the love with which we hold one
    another.
In all our ways we trust you.
And to you, with your Church on earth and in
    heaven, we offer honor and glory, now and for
    ever. Amen.

O God, all that you have given us is yours.
As first you gave *Name* to us, now we give *Name*
    back to you.

(Here the pastor, with others, standing near the coffin or urn, may lay hands on it, continuing:)

Receive *Name* into the arms of your mercy.
Raise *Name* up with all your people.
Receive us also, and raise us into a new life.
Help us so to love and serve you in this world that
we may enter into your joy in the world to come.
Amen.

Into your hands, O merciful Savior, we commend
    your servant *Name*.
Acknowledge, we humbly beseech you, a sheep
    of your own fold, a lamb of your own flock, a
    sinner of your own redeeming.
Receive *Name* into the arms of your mercy, into the
    blessed rest of everlasting peace, and into the
    glorious company of the saints of light. Amen.

(The pastor may administer Holy Communion to all present who wish to share at the Lord's table, the people using A Service of Word and Table III or one of the musical settings, and the pastor using An Order for Holy Communion. Otherwise, the service continues as follows:)

Prayer of Thanksgiving
God of love, we thank you for all with which you
have blessed us even to this day:
for the gift of joy in days of health and strength
and for the gifts of your abiding presence and
promise in days of pain and grief.
We praise you for home and friends, and for our
baptism and place in your Church with all who
have faithfully lived and died.
Above all else we thank you for Jesus, who knew
our griefs, who died our death and rose for our
sake, and who lives and prays for us.
And as he taught us, so now we pray.

The Lord's Prayer
(All pray the Lord's Prayer.)

Hymn

Dismissal with Blessing
(The pastor, facing the people, may give one or more of the following, or other, Dismissal with Blessing: Hebrews 13:20-21; Ephesians 3:18-19)

A Service of Committal follows at the final resting place.

AN ORDER FOR HOLY COMMUNION
This order may be included in the Service of Death and Resurrection. It is our tradition to invite all Christians to the Lord's table, and the invitation should be extended to everyone present; but there should be no pressure that would embarrass those who for whatever reason do not choose to receive Holy Communion.

Taking the Bread and Cup

(The pastor, standing if possible behind the Lord's table, facing the people from this time through Breaking the Bread, takes the bread and cup; and the bread and wine are prepared for the meal.)

The Great Thanksgiving

The Lord be with you.
And also with you.
Lift up your hearts. (The pastor may lift hands and keep them raised.)
We lift them up to the Lord.
Let us give thanks to the Lord our God.
It is right to give our thanks and praise.

It is right, that we should always and everywhere give thanks to you, Father Almighty *(almighty God)*, Creator of heaven and earth;
through Jesus Christ our Lord, who rose victorious from the dead and comforts us with the blessed hope of everlasting life.

And so, with your people on earth and all the company of heaven we praise your name and join their unending hymn:

(The pastor may lower hands.)

Holy, holy, holy Lord, God of power and might, heaven and earth are full of your glory. Hosanna in the highest! Blessed is he who comes in the name of the Lord. Hosanna in the highest!

(The pastor may raise hands.)

Holy are you, and blessed is your Son Jesus Christ.
By the baptism of his suffering, death, and resurrection you gave birth to your Church, delivered us from slavery to sin and death, and made with us a new covenant by water and the Spirit.
When the Lord Jesus ascended, he promised to be with us always in the power of your Word and Holy Spirit.

(The pastor may hold hands, palms down, over the bread, or touch the bread, or lift the bread.)

On the night in which he gave himself up for us, he took bread, gave thanks to you, broke the bread, gave it to his disciples, and said:
"Take, eat; this is my body which is given for you. Do this in remembrance of me."

(The pastor may hold hands, palms down, over the cup, or touch the cup, or lift the cup.)

When the supper was over he took the cup, gave thanks to you, gave it to his disciples, and said:
"Drink from this, all of you; this is my blood of the new covenant, poured out for you and for many for the forgiveness of sins.
Do this, as often as you drink it, in remembrance of me."

(The pastor may raise hands.)

And so, in remembrance of these mighty acts in Jesus Christ, we offer ourselves in praise and thanksgiving as a holy and living sacrifice, in union with Christ's offering for us, as we proclaim the mystery of faith:

Christ has died; Christ is risen; Christ will come again.

(The pastor may hold hands, palms down, over the bread and cup.)

Pour out your Holy Spirit on us, gathered here, and on these gifts of bread and wine.
Make them be for us the body and blood of Christ, that we may be for the world the body of Christ, redeemed by his blood.

(The pastor may raise hands.)

By your Spirit make us one with Christ, one with each other, and one in communion with all your saints, especially *Name* and all those dear to us, whom we now remember in the silence of our hearts.

(A time of silence for remembrance.)

Finally, by your grace, bring them and all of us to that table where your saints feast for ever in your heavenly home.

Through your Son Jesus Christ, with the Holy Spirit in your holy Church, all honor and glory is yours, almighty Father *(God)*, now and for ever. Amen.

The Lord's Prayer

The pastor's hands may be extended in open invitation.
And now, with the confidence of children of God, let us pray:
(The pastor may raise hands.)
(All pray the Lord's Prayer.)

Breaking the Bread

The pastor, still standing behind the Lord's table

facing the people, breaks the bread and then lifts the cup, in silence or with appropriate words.

Giving the Bread and Cup

Dismissal with Blessing
(One of the following or other scriptures may be read: 1 Peter 1:3-9; John 12:24-26)

Committal
(Standing at the head of the coffin and facing it [preferably casting earth on it as it is lowered into the grave] the pastor says:)

Almighty God, into your hands we commend your *son/daughter Name,* in sure and certain hope of Resurrection to eternal life through Jesus Christ our Lord. Amen.

This body we commit to the ground *(to the elements, to its resting place),* earth to earth, ashes to ashes, dust to dust.

Blessed are the dead who die in the Lord.
Yes, says the Spirit, they will rest from their labors for their deeds follow them.

(One or more of the following or other prayers is offered:)

Gracious God, we thank you for those we love but see no more.
Receive into your arms your servant *Name,* and grant that increasing in knowledge and love of you, *he/she* may go from strength to strength in service to your heavenly kingdom; through Jesus Christ our Lord. **Amen.**

Almighty God, look with pity upon the sorrow of your servants, for whom we pray.
Amidst things they cannot understand, help them to trust in your care.
Bless them and keep them.
Make your face to shine upon them, and give them peace. **Amen.**

O Lord, support us all the day long of our troubled life, until the shadows lengthen and the evening comes, and the busy world is hushed, and the fever of life is over and our work is done.
Then in your mercy grant us a safe lodging, and a holy rest, and peace at the last; through Jesus Christ our Lord. **Amen.**

Eternal God, you have shared with us the life of *Name.*

Before *he/she* was ours, *he/she* is yours.
For all that *Name* has given us to make us what we are, for that of *him/her* which lives and grows in each of us, and for *his/her* life that in your love will never end, we give you thanks.
As now we offer *Name* back into your arms, comfort us in our loneliness, strengthen us in our weakness, and give us courage to face the future unafraid.
Draw those of us who remain in this life closer to one another, make us faithful to serve one another, and give us to know that peace and joy which is eternal life; through Jesus Christ our Lord. **Amen.**

(The Lord's Prayer may follow.)

(A hymn or song may be sung.)

(The pastor dismisses the people with the following or another blessing:)
Now to the One who is able to keep you from falling, and to make you stand without blemish in the presence of God's glory with rejoicing, to the only God our Savior, through Jesus Christ our Lord, be glory, majesty, power, and authority, before all time and now and forever. **Amen.** (Jude 24-25)

United Methodist Book of Worship[12]

231 ✦ A BASIC LITURGY FOR A FUNERAL

The following is an outline for an informal funeral service that reflects the themes described in the articles above.

Song. Beginning with a song that expresses in a simple and meaningful way the feelings of those gathered together for the funeral immediately draws the community together more powerfully than when words alone are used. Some suggested songs are:
"Sometimes I Feel like a Motherless Child"
"O God Our Help in Ages Past"
"Amazing Grace"
"Lord of All Hopefulness"
"Wondrous Love"

Prayer. The prayer, offered by the person leading the funeral liturgy, should address God as those gathered understand God, commend the deceased to God's embrace, and ask comfort for those grieving. The leader should also be particularly conscious of the circumstances of death. In other words, one does not pray for a deceased infant in the same way one prays for a person who has rounded out eighty years; nor does one pray for a person released after a long suffering in the same way one prays for person taken suddenly from the family and friends' midst by accident or suicide.

Readings. Some suggested biblical readings are: Wisdom 3:1-9; Isaiah 25:6a, 7-9; Lamentations 3:17-26; Romans 5:5-11; 8:31b-35, 37-39; 14:7-9; 2 Corinthians 4:14–5:1; Philippians 3:20-21; 1 John 3:1-2; Luke 24:13-35; John 5:24-29; 11:32-45.

Response. Each reading should be followed by some type of response by the assembly, but first there should be a silent pause for reflection. Psalms 23, 25, 27, 42, and 148 are particularly appropriate. The community could recite the entire Psalm together, alternate sides, or repeat a short refrain between each strophe. A simple chant like "Jesus Remember Me" (Taizé/GIA Publications) could also be sung as a response.

Witness. Storytelling, or faith-sharing, about the deceased can be an important means of supporting the spirits of those who grieve. Christian hope is based on the confident belief that life is not ended, but changed. By being given an opportunity to share precious memories, family and friends hold on to the conviction that their dead are still with them, in their new life.

Intercessory Prayer. When the time for sharing seems to be drawing to a close, the leader can invite those gathered to pray for their needs and the needs of all who grieve in petitions such as these:

> We pray that our brother/sister [Name] may be joined to the company of saints at the heavenly banquet.

> We pray that all those whose hearts are heavy with sorrow may know comfort.

> We pray that the burden of sickness and suffering may be lightened by compassion and love.

To each petition the assembly can respond, "O God, hear us in word or song."

Lord's Prayer. The intercessory prayer should conclude by inviting the assembly to join together and pray as Jesus taught us. If it seems appropri-ate, the leader can invite those gathered to join hands as they pray.

Conclusion. The leader can conclude the service by inviting those gathered to embrace each other in the peace of Christ. If there is to be another service, or a continuation of those services, at the gravesite, the leader should invite the assembly to continue the journey there.

The graveside service should consist of at least a song of farewell and prayer committing the body of the deceased to the earth. The ancient Christian hymn _In paradisum_ is most appropriate:

> May the angels lead you in paradise;
> may the martyrs come to welcome you;
> and take you to the holy city,
> the new and eternal Jerusalem.

The leader then prays in these or similar words:

> With faith and confidence that life is changed, not ended, we commend the body of [Name] to the ground [or the deep, or the element, or its resting place—depending on the circumstances of interment].

> Lord, you wept at the tomb of your friend Lazarus. Comfort us now as we take our leave in sorrow.

If interment takes place immediately, the mourners can throw a handful of dirt or flowers into the grave reverently.

The final words should be addressed to the assembly:

> May the God of love and mercy
> wipe every tear from our eyes,
> and lead us to walk in ways of peace.

Julia Ann Upton

232 ✦ GUIDELINES FOR PLANNING THE FUNERAL

Since the liturgical celebrations of the funeral bring together family and friends who are experiencing deep grief, the ritual itself should minister to these people. Therefore, the ritual should be attentive to all the senses; be marked by beauty, dignity, and reverence; and with simplicity invite the participation of the assembly.

The Word of God ministers to the grieving as it proclaims the paschal mystery and comforts the sorrowful. Although nonbiblical readings should not replace Scripture, they can be used in addition to biblical readings. John Donne's sonnet "Death Be Not Proud" and Anne Sexton's "Awful Rowing Toward God" are two examples of religious poetry suitable for a funeral. The Psalms are particularly responsive to the needs and moods of the community, expressing the depths of grief as well as the heights of praise. These ancient songs cut through time and culture to touch the core of human longing. Psalm 23 ("The Lord is my shepherd") is often prayed or sung at funerals because of its comforting pastoral motif.

The *Order of Christian Funerals*, the *Lutheran Book of Worship*, and *The Book of Common Prayer* provide a variety of prayers that capture the unspoken prayers and hopes of the assembly and respond to their need for consolation. The prayers of intercession even more directly address the needs of the deceased, those who mourn, and the entire assembly. Models are provided in the ritual books which can be adapted to particular circumstances as needed.

Because of its power to evoke strong feelings, music has an important place in all funerals. Songs can console and uplift the mourners by their references to the paschal character of Christian death and the community's share in Christ's victory.

There is also a place for reverent silence in the funeral rites which can evoke awe as the community stands in the face of the mystery of death.

Other Christian symbols can be used effectively, although local custom will dictate the degree to which each speaks in the funeral rites:

Candles serve as a continuous reminder of Christ's victory, along with our share in that victory, recalling both the Easter celebration and baptism when the newly baptized receive the light of faith.

Water sprinkled on the coffin at the beginning of the funeral liturgy likewise recalls the Christian's incorporation into Christ's death and resurrection through the waters of baptism.

Incense can be used in the funeral rites to lend greater dignity to the celebration. It gives visual expression to our prayers as they rise to God, while being attentive to the sense of smell as well.

A *Bible or book of the Gospels* placed on or near the coffin can symbolize the deceased's fidelity to God's Word.

The *cross* with which the Christian is first marked in baptism, may also be placed on or near the coffin.

Flowers, subtle reminders that life and beauty transcend present suffering, also enhance the celebration.

The colors used should reflect Christian hope, without negating human grief. White in American culture, therefore, is more appropriate than black.

Processions, with pallbearers carrying the coffin, have a significance as the family and friends of the deceased go from one ritual to the next, from funeral home to the place of burial. They recall not only early Christian funerals, but also the journey that is human life and the Christian pilgrimage to the heavenly Jerusalem.

Julia Ann Upton

233 ♦ BIBLIOGRAPHY ON THE FUNERAL SERVICE

Atchley, E. G. Cuthbert. *Ordo Romanus Primus*. Trans. Latin and English. London: 1905. Contains the medieval funeral rite. For a critical edition of the Latin text, see M. Andrieu, *Les Ordines Romani du haut Moyen Age* (Louvain: 1931–1961).

Cieslak, William. *Console One Another: Commentary on the Order for Christian Funerals*. Washington, D.C.: Pastoral Press, 1990.

Curley, Terence P. *Console One Another: A Guide for Christian Funerals*. Kansas City, Mo.: Sheed and Ward, 1993.

Dallen, James. *The Funeral Liturgy*. Glendale, Ariz.: Pastoral Arts Associates of North America, 1980.

Fitzgerald, William. *Speaking About Death: Poetic Resources for Ministers of Consolation*. Chicago: ACTA Publications, 1990.

Hatchett, Marion. *Commentary on the American Prayer Book*. New York: Seabury Press, 1981. A theological and liturgical commentary on the 1979 *Book of Common Prayer,* including a discussion of the funeral liturgy.

Irion, Paul E. *The Funeral: Vestige or Value?* Nashville/New York: Abingdon, 1966.

Kreeft, Peter. *Love Is Stronger than Death*. Ann Arbor, Mich.: 1979; San Francisco: Ignatius, 1992. Excellent discussion of a theological perspective on death.

Langford, Andy. *Your Ministry of Planning a Christian Funeral*. Nashville: Discipleship Resources, 1989. A pamphlet with advice for both worship planners and family members of the deceased.

Marchel, Michael. _Parish Funerals_. Chicago: Liturgy Training Publications, 1987.

Mitchell, Leonel L. _Praying Shapes Believing_. Minneapolis: Winston, 1985. A theological commentary on the 1979 _Book of Common Prayer_, including a discussion of the funeral rite.

Owusu, Vincent Kwame. _The Roman Funeral Liturgy: History, Celebration, and Theology_. Nettetal: Steyler, 1993.

Pfatteicher, Philip. H. _Commentary on the Lutheran Book of Worship: Lutheran Liturgy in its Ecumenical Context_. Minneapolis: Augsburg, 1990. Includes a commentary on the liturgy for the burial of the dead.

Powell, Geoffrey. _Liturgy of Christian Burial: An Introductory Survey of the Historical Development of Christian Burial_. London: SPCK, 1977.

Reformed Worship 24 (June 1992). Theme of issue is on funerals.

Reformed Liturgy and Music (Fall 1986). Theme issue.

Rowell, Geoffrey. _The Liturgy of Christian Burial_. London: Alcuin, SPCK, 1977. An introductory survey of the history of Christian funerals.

Rutherford, Richard. _The Death of a Christian: The Rite of Funerals_. Rev. ed. New York: Pueblo Publishing, 1990.

———. _The Order of Christian Funerals: An Invitation to Pastoral Care_. Collegeville, Minn.: Liturgical Press, 1990.

Sloyan, Virginia. _A Sourcebook About Christian Death_. Chicago: Liturgy Training Publications, 1990.

Sparkes, R., and Richard Rutherford. "The Order of Christian Funerals: A Study in Bereavement and Lament." _Worship_ 60:6 (1986): 499–510.

Temple of the Holy Spirit: Sickness and Death of the Christian in the Liturgy. New York: Pueblo Publishing, 1983.

Vander Zee, Leonard. _In Life and In Death: A Pastoral Guide for Funerals_. Grand Rapids: CRC Publications, 1992.

For representative funeral liturgies, see:

- For a Baptist and free church liturgy, see Jesse Jai McNeil, _Minister's Service Book for Pulpit and Parish_ (Grand Rapids: Eerdmans, 1993), 61–85.

- For the Christian Reformed Church's liturgy, see Leonard Vander Zee, _In Life and In Death: A Pastoral Guide for Funerals_ (Grand Rapids: CRC Publications, 1992).

- For the Episcopalian liturgy, see _The Book of Common Prayer_ (New York: Church Hymnal Corporation, 1979), 469–510.

- For the Evangelical Lutheran Church in America's liturgy, see _Lutheran Book of Worship_ (Minneapolis: Augsburg; Philadelphia: Board of Publication, Lutheran Church in America, 1978), 206–14.

- For the Lutheran Church–Missouri Synod, see _Lutheran Worship—Agenda_ (St. Louis: Concordia, 1984), 169–96.

- For the Mennonite liturgy, see Melvin D. Schmidt, _Funerals and Funeral Planning_ (Newton, Kans.: Faith and Life Press; and Scottdale, Pa.: Mennonite Publishing House, 1980).

- For the Methodist Church's liturgy, see _The United Methodist Book of Worship_ (Nashville: United Methodist Publishing House, 1992), 139–72; _A Service of Death and Resurrection: The Ministry of the Church at Death_ (Nashville: Abingdon, 1979).

- For a Presbyterian liturgy, see _The Book of Common Worship_ (Louisville: Westminster/John Knox, 1993), 905–47; and _The Funeral: A Service of Witness to the Resurrection: Supplemental Liturgical Resource 4_ (Philadelphia: Westminster, 1986).

- For the Reformed Church in America's liturgy, see _Worship the Lord_ (Grand Rapids: Eerdmans, 1987), 42–49.

- For the Roman Catholic liturgy, see _Order of Christian Funerals_ (Collegeville, Minn.: Liturgical Press, 1989); and _The Rites_, vol. 1 (New York: Pueblo, 1983).

- For the United Church of Christ's liturgy, see _Book of Worship: United Church of Christ_ (New York: Office of Church Life, 1986), 357–90.

PART SIX

Sacred Actions in the Life of the Worshiping Community

Throughout the history of the church, worshipers have marked significant occasions in the life of their community by actions which bear witness to their dependence on God and testify to the significance of Jesus' death and resurrection for the life of their community. The following chapters describe many of the most significant of such actions. As you read and study these chapters, note how each is a manifestation of an important theological insight; how the history of each action reveals its meaning and significance for the Christian community; and how these insights and meanings continue to shape the practice of these actions today. For when they are performed properly, these actions are not an end in themselves, but rather point to the larger reality of God's work in Jesus Christ and in the worshiping community.

✒ FIFTEEN ✒

Ordination and Commissioning

From the beginning, Christians have set apart (consecrated) leaders by invoking the Holy Spirit through prayer and the laying on of hands. Initially this was done by the apostles whom Jesus himself had chosen. Although not all Christian groups view a chain of successive imposition of hands reaching back to the apostles as crucial, nearly all Christian groups employ already ordained ministers in the ordination ceremony. All Christian groups, in their practices, do recognize some special status for their leaders, even if they reject a clergy-laity distinction theologically.

234 ✦ HISTORICAL ORIGINS AND DEVELOPMENT OF ORDINATION IN THE WEST

In the New Testament, leaders were set apart for ministry by the laying on of hands accompanied by prayer. Although elaborate ceremonies emerged that were later eliminated by the Protestant Reformers, laying on of hands with a prayer for consecration remained a constant characteristic of ordination.

Ordination in the New Testament

Comparatively little is said in the New Testament about the rites by which the leaders of the church were commissioned for their ministry. This is not surprising, since ministry in the New Testament period was still undergoing development and change. We find references to the Twelve and to the apostles in the Gospels (Matt. 10:1-5; Mark 3:14-19; Luke 6:13), and to apostles, prophets, and teachers in 1 Corinthians 12:28. Acts and the Epistles speak of leaders (Heb. 13:7), presbyters, or elders (*presbuteroi*, 1 Pet. 5:1; James 5:14; Acts 11:30), teachers (Gal. 6:6), overseers, i.e., bishops (*episcopoi*, Acts 20:17, 28; Phil. 1:1; Titus 1:5ff), and ministers (*diakonoi*, Phil. 1:1; 1 Tim. 3:1ff). These various titles represent charismatic ministries and offices common in the Pauline communities, as well as more institutionalized forms of office which seem to have existed in the Jerusalem community. A common characteristic of these offices or ministries is that the apostles and their successors appointed individuals to fill them (see Titus 1:5) and that they originated from the apostles or were associated with them (see Acts 6:1ff; 11:30; 14:23). In Acts, appointment to an office or ministry is by the imposition of hands (*epithesis ton cheiron*) and through an associated confirmation by the Holy Spirit (Acts 13:2; 20:28). In the Pastoral Epistles, imposition of hands is also mentioned as a means of recognizing a ministry exercised prophetically (1 Tim. 4:14) or of appointing a person to a ministry or office (2 Tim. 1:6).

The actual rites of ordination mentioned in Acts and the epistles of Paul contain no liturgical texts and the barest of descriptions. In Acts 6:1-6, we are told of the selection of seven men to serve the needs of the widows of the Hellenists in Jerusalem. They are selected by the community and presented to the apostles, who pray over them and lay hands on them. Acts 13:2-3 describes how Paul and Barnabas were set apart for their ministry: "Then, completing their fasting and prayer, they laid hands on them and sent them off." Paul and Barnabas, during their first missionary journey, appointed presbyters in each church and "with prayer and fasting, commended them to the Lord in whom they had put their faith" (Acts. 14:23). This practice of praying over and laying hands on those to be appointed as ministers is also alluded to in the two letters to Timothy (1 Tim. 4:14; 5:22; 2 Tim. 1:6; 4:1-8). This pattern formed the core of the ordination rites of the church as they were developed and elaborated over the centuries.

——— Ordination in the Early Church ———

The most ancient ordination rite of the church is that of Hippolytus of Rome (c. 225), and is contained in his Apostolic Tradition. Hippolytus provides us not only with a description of the ordination of a bishop, but also with ordination prayers for bishops, presbyters, and deacons. The rubrics contained in the Apostolic Tradition and the prayers, especially that for the ordination of a bishop, have had a great influence on ordination rites in both the Eastern and the Western churches. The ordination prayer of Hippolytus for a bishop is presently being used by the Episcopal and Roman Catholic churches in their revised ordination rites. The ordination rite of Hippolytus takes place on a Sunday, in the context of the celebration of the Eucharist. The bishop is chosen by the people, and those bishops who are present give their consent. The bishops silently lay hands on the bishop-elect, while the members of the presbyterate stand by in silence. One of the bishops, in the name of all, says the prayer of ordination while continuing to lay hands on the bishop-elect for the episcopacy. The prayer is addressed to the "God and Father of our Lord Jesus Christ" and recalls that God has established ministers for the church. A brief *epiklesis* (invocation of the Holy Spirit) follows which asks God to:

> Pour forth now that power which is from you, of the princely Spirit which you granted through your beloved Son Jesus Christ to your holy apostles, who established the church in every place as your sanctuary, to the unceasing glory and praise of your name.

The prayer continues with intercessions for the new bishop. The bishop is to feed the flock and exercise a blameless high priesthood by unceasingly praying and offering the holy gifts of the church. The bishop is to forgive sins. All this is done through the servant/child Jesus Christ. After the ordination prayer, all exchange the kiss of peace with the new bishop, and the bishop proceeds to receive the offerings of the people from the deacons and then proclaims the eucharistic prayer.

Similar prayers are provided for the ordination of presbyters or deacons. The prayer for presbyters indicates that the role of the presbyter is to assist the bishop in the governance of the church. Hippolytus notes that "When, moreover, a presbyter is ordained, let the bishop lay his hand on his head, while the presbyters also touch him . . ." Hipplytus continues by stating that when a deacon is ordained, only the bishop lays hands on the candidate for the deacon's office:

> For he is not ordained for the priesthood, but for serving the bishop, . . . For he is not a member of the council of the clergy, but attends to responsibilities and makes known what is necessary to the bishop; not receiving the common spirit of the presbyter. . . . Wherefore, let the bishop alone make him a deacon; on a presbyter, however, the presbyters as well should also lay on their hands, because of the common and like spirit of the clergy. For the presbyter has only this power to receive; he does not on the other hand have power to give. Because of this, he does not ordain clergy; he rather is to put his seal on the ordination of a presbyter while the bishop ordains.

The fifth-century *Statuta ecclesiae antiqua*, which were probably written in Gaul, substantially reproduces the directions of Hippolytus in canons 2, 3, and 4. All three texts speak of the imposition of hands as the central act. All bishops present impose hands on a new bishop; the bishop and presbyters present lay hands on the new presbyter; and the bishop alone lays hands on the deacon. Eventually these texts became rubrics that were prefixed to the ordination rites of the medieval pontificals (books of rites used by bishops).

The actual terminology used for ordination in the early church changes over a period of time. The pagan term for election by a show of hands, *cheirotonein*, is in the New Testament and in early Christian writings. This term is eventually replaced by the term *cheirepithesia* which refers to the imposition of hands. By the fourth-century, a distinction is made between the imposition of hands performed by a priest, *cheirothetei*, and ordination which was performed by the bishop, *cheirotonei*. Thus the emphasis changes from raising the hand to elect the candidate for an office to that of imposing or laying hands on the one elected to the office of ministry. This distinction between election and ordination is manifested in the later ordination rites, which either presume a previous election of the candidate or have a brief rite of election by the bishop with the consent of the people at the beginning of the rite.

Ordination Rites of the Roman Sacramentaries and Ordines

In the sixth, seventh, and eighth centuries, the ordination rites are found in the ancient sacramentaries (books containing the prayers of the ministers) of the Roman church and the church in Gaul as well as in the collections of rubrics known as the *Ordines Romani*. The *Sacramentary of Verona* (*Sacramentarium Veronense*), also known as the *Leonine Sacramentary* (fifth to sixth centuries), contains the texts of the ordination prayers for bishops, priests, and deacons. As is common in the early liturgical books, no rubrics are provided, and it is necessary to go to the Ordines Romani, 34–40, for the rubrics. The ordination of the bishop of Rome took place before the *Gloria,* at the opening of the Mass, while the ordination of presbyters and deacons occurred between the Epistle and Gospel in the first part of the Mass. The ordination of the bishop begins with two collects, whereas the rites for presbyters and deacons have an invitatory and collect, which originally probably introduced and concluded the litany of the saints. By the seventh to eighth centuries, the collect and invitatory followed the litany. The ordination prayer followed the collect.

The ordination prayers, which are totally unrelated to those of Hippolytus, are filled with allusions to the ministry of the high priests, the priests and Levites of the Old Testament. In a characteristic Roman fashion, they are preoccupied with the *cursus honorum* or progression of honor from a lesser dignity to a greater one. There is no reference to the laying on of hands in the Verona Sacramentary itself, and, in fact, the Ordines Romani are not always clear about the matter. They do mention that the book of the Gospels was held over the head of the one being ordained bishop of Rome, but nothing is said about the bishops present imposing hands on the bishop-elect's head. When the pope ordained bishops, the pope alone laid hands on them. Nevertheless, it is probably safe to assume that the imposition of hands took place at Rome during the ordination prayer for deacons and presbyters.

In this early period of the Roman ordination rites, the candidates were clothed in the vestments of their order before they were presented for ordination. After their ordination, deacons and presbyters took their places with their fellow deacons and presbyters for the remainder of the liturgy.

As the Roman liturgy spread north into Gaul, it began to be intermixed with rites and prayers taken from this region. The resulting hybrid rite eventually returned to Rome and affected the subsequent Roman liturgical books. The *Gelasian Sacramentary* and the *Missale Francorum* reflect this mixed form of the Roman ordination rites. In addition to the Roman prayers, these books contain prayers of Gallican origin. The Gallican ordination rites of the fifth or sixth century probably consisted of an admonition to the faithful and the clergy, a bidding or invitatory, and the prayer of consecration. These consecration prayers are more centered on Christ and on the notions of ministry in the New Testament rather than those of the Roman tradition. In the case of the presbyter, an anointing of the hands followed the ordination prayer. In the Missale Francorum and the Gelasian Sacramentary, the Roman prayers are followed by the Gallican texts so that there is a doubling of ordination rites. A choice was probably made at first between the Roman texts and the Gallican texts, but eventually both were recited, one set after the other. The anointing of the hands of the priest seems to have come from the Celtic church, and then, to have been passed on to the church in Gaul. It was not until after the ninth century that this practice was accepted by the Roman church. The eighth to tenth century English ordination rites have an anointing of the deacon's hands and an anointing of both the hands and head of the presbyter.

Medieval Ordination Rites

By the end of the ninth century, the imposition of hands occurred in silence before the prayer of ordination, rather than during it. In some manuscripts the rubrics infer that the imposition of hands also continued throughout the ordination prayers.

A basic structure had evolved by the tenth century, in which the Roman and Gallican prayers were separated from each other by the vesting of the newly ordained minister and the presentation of symbols or instruments of office. Accordingly, the pastoral staff and ring were given to the bishop; the chalice and paten were given to the presbyter; and the book of the Gospels were given to the deacon. The incorporation of the presentations into the ordination rites for bishops, presbyters, and deacons began a change that would eventually lead theologians and bishops to regard them as the essential act of ordination, rather than the imposition of hands before or during the ordination prayer.

The thirteenth-century ordination rites were elaborated in a more theatrical manner than hitherto. The ordination rites for a bishop began with a formal presentation of the candidate, an examination, and the profession of faith. After the gradual (the Psalm after the Epistle), there was an invitation to prayer followed by the litany of the saints, the imposition of the Gospels on the head of the bishop-elect, and the imposition of hands by the consecrating and co-consecrating bishops with the words "accipe spiritum sanctum" (receive the Holy Spirit). The ordination prayer was interrupted by the singing of the hymn "Veni Creator" while the head of the bishop-elect was anointed. The ordination prayer then continued. After the prayer, the hands of the new bishop were anointed, and the new bishop was presented with the pastoral staff, ring, and book of the Gospels. The ordination rite proper concluded with the kiss of peace.

In the rite for the ordination of a presbyter, a whole new series of rites was added. As in the rite for the ordination of a bishop, there was a presentation which was followed by the election of the new priest at the beginning of the rite. The ordination prayer was preceded by the imposition of hands and followed by the vesting of the new priest. The new priest's hands were anointed, and the new priest was then presented with the chalice and paten. A second imposition of hands took place after Communion and the recitation of the creed. This imposition of hands was accompanied by an imperative formula, *accipe spiritum sanctum* (receive the Holy Spirit), which had previously been used in various places in connection with the first imposition of hands. The use of such a formula is a reflection of the medieval concept that the forms for the sacraments should be declarations rather than prayers. Following the imposition of hands, the back of the chasuble was lowered (which hitherto had been pinned up). The new presbyter then made a promise of obedience, received the kiss of peace, and was admonished concerning the manner of celebrating Mass. The bishop concluded the rite by giving the newly ordained priest a *penance* (usually the recitation of a series of Psalms) and the final bless-

ing. In a sense, these post-Communion rites form a second ordination rite at the end of Mass.

The most significant change in the rite for the ordination of a deacon was the division of the ordination prayer into two parts by the imposition of hands and a formula beginning, "accipe . . ." ("receive . . ."). After the new deacon was vested in a stole and a dalmatic, the new deacon was presented with the book of the Gospels. The Gallican ordination prayer was used to conclude the rite.

In the thirteenth century, the practice of the newly ordained bishop concelebrating with the consecrating bishop became common. A form of concelebration is also found in the rite for the ordination for presbyters. The newly ordained priests were invited to come near the altar, and from the offertory on, they read all the prayers of the Mass in a low voice, as if they were celebrating individually. Both newly ordained bishops and priests received Communion from the presiding bishop.

Reformation Ordination Rites

At the time of the Reformation, the continental Reformers stripped away all that they considered to be unbiblical in the ordination rites. As a result, the rites consisted, with local variations, of a reading from Scripture, a long admonition, the laying on of hands with an imperative formula, and a prayer for the ministry of the church. Unfortunately, the epicletic and eucharistic nature of the ordination prayers of consecration were lost and replaced by a questionable medieval concept of ordination using a formula rather than a prayer. Vesting, anointing, and the presentation of symbols of office generally disappeared, with the exception of the giving of a Bible to the one being ordained.

In England, the ordination rites were also revised. Much of the traditional structure of the rite was retained, but duplications were omitted, as were anointings and the presentation of vestments. The giving of the Bible or New Testament was retained, but after the first revision, the presentation of the chalice and paten was omitted. The Anglican rites also reflected the medieval preoccupation with the use of a formula for the imposition of hands, and the ordination prayer became a general prayer for the ministry of the church.

A few "New-Testament-only" groups, e.g., the

Plymouth Brethren, reject the idea of set-apart ministry as a post–New Testament innovation and hence an illegitimate practice. Other groups, e.g., the medieval Waldenses, the sixteenth-century Anabaptists (with their Mennonite, Amish, and Hutterite descendants), and some evangelical, independent Bible churches and Pentecostal groups claim to reject any distinction between clergy and laity, but in practice do view their ministers and leaders as somehow distinct from non-ministerial laity. They have gradually developed the equivalent of ordination ceremonies, even if they lack a theology to undergird them.

Contemporary Ordination Rites

The rites for the ordination of bishops, presbyters, and deacons of the Roman Catholic church were revised in 1968. In the revised rites, the imposition of hands by the bishop and the ordination prayer of consecration are clearly the central features. All three ordination rites begin with the celebration of the liturgy of the Word of the Eucharist. The ordination rites take place after the Gospel. The candidates for the diaconate and presbyterate are presented to the bishop, and elected by the bishop. The people give their consent. The rite for the ordination of a bishop begins with the hymn "Veni Creator," which is followed by the presentation of the bishop-elect and the reading of the apostolic mandate. All three rites then follow with the homily and the examination of the candidate. The examination is followed in the rites for deacons and presbyters by a promise of obedience to the bishop and the bishop's successors. All three rites continue with an invitation to prayer, the litany, and a concluding prayer. The laying on of hands then takes place in silence. The presbyters join the bishop in imposing hands on candidates for the presbyterate, and all bishops present lay hands on the bishop-elect. In each rite, the ordination prayer of consecration is then sung or recited. After the prayer, the new bishop's head is anointed with chrism. Deacons and presbyters are vested by members of their new order with the dalmatic and stole (for deacons) or the chasuble and stole (for presbyters). A new bishop is then presented with the book of the Gospels, ring, miter, and pastoral staff. New presbyters have their hands anointed with chrism and are presented with the offerings (bread on the paten and wine and water in the chalice), which have been brought to the bishop by the faithful. A deacon is given the book of the Gospels by the bishop. The new bishop is seated in the episcopal chair, if the bishop is ordained in the cathedral in which the bishop will serve. The ordination rites proper end with the kiss of peace given to the new minister by the bishop and other members of the diaconate, presbyterate, or episcopate. At the ordination of a bishop, the new bishop is led through the congregation, after the post-Communion prayer while the "Te Deum" or another similar hymn is sung, in order to bless the people. A new bishop who is ordained in the new bishop's own cathedral takes over the presidency of the Eucharist; otherwise the bishop takes the first place among the concelebrants. New presbyters concelebrate with the bishop, and new deacons carry out their diaconal functions during the liturgy of the Eucharist.

An example of the revised rite of the Episcopal church, for the ordination of priests, contained in _The Book of Common Prayer_ (1979), is given below in "A Liturgy for Episcopal Ordination." This liturgy shares many features in common with the revised Roman rites.

The United Methodist Church published its revised ordination rites in _The United Methodist Book of Worship_ (1992). The new rites are very similar to those of the Episcopal church. In the rite for the ordination of elders, the presentation of the candidates takes place at the beginning of the liturgy. After the liturgy of the Word, there is an address on the office and functions of the order being conferred, which leads into an examination of the candidate. This is followed by an invitation to prayer and the singing of a hymn to the Holy Spirit. The laying on of hands takes place during the ordination prayer which follows the hymn. The prayer itself is a reworking of the Episcopal ordination prayer. Immediately after the prayer, a Bible is presented to the new elder, and, if desired, a stole and/or chalice and paten may be given to each new elder. The orders of ministers entering the ministry of the United Methodist Church from another denomination may be recognized. Unlike the Roman and Episcopal rites, provision is made for the ordination to conclude without the celebration of the Lord's Supper. However, the rite as presented presumes that the Eucharist will normally be a part of the service. The new elders remain with the bishop and assist him or her during the celebration of the Lord's Supper.

The Roman, Episcopal, and United Methodist rites reflect a return to the more ancient traditions of the undivided church. A good example of this is the use in all three churches of Hippolytus' prayer of consecration for a bishop. This prayer has replaced the traditional texts formerly used in these churches.

All these new ordination rites reflect the common pattern that has emerged as a result of the contemporary liturgical renewal. In these new ordination rites, the central portion of the liturgy for ordination follows the proclamation of the Word of God and leads into the liturgy of the Eucharist. The laying on of hands and the prayer of consecration take their rightful place as the principal rites. The rites of vesting and presentation of symbols of office clearly take a second place.

235 ◆ A Theology of Ordination in the West

The main distinction among Christians in the question of ordination remains the matter of apostolic succession of bishops, who in turn are responsible for ordination of other ministers. Roman Catholics, Anglicans, and the Eastern Orthodox believe in a direct succession of ordination from the time of the apostles. Other churches, even though they have leaders they call bishops, do not view them in direct apostolic succession. The ecumenical consensus statement on Baptism, Eucharist, and Ministry *(1982) attempts to rejoin the two positions by referring to a general continuity in apostolic ministry.*

——— Catholic and Anglican Positions ———

Throughout history, the church's understanding of the meaning of ordination has changed according to the particular theological presuppositions current at the time. The Reformation was a period in which a wide variety of interpretations of ordination and ecclesiastical ministry flourished within the church. After the Reformation, the Roman Catholic church continued to speak of ordination as a sacrament which conferred a permanent and ontological change (sacramental character) in the minister. The various churches that sprung from the Reformation generally rejected

ordination as a sacrament and the notion of sacramental character.

The Roman Catholic and Anglican churches stressed that it was essential that a bishop in apostolic succession alone confer ordination. Apostolic succession, as it was then understood, meant that an unbroken line of bishops ordaining their successor through the imposition of hands could be traced back to the apostles. Many of the Reformed churches rejected this requirement of tactile succession as well as the necessity of having bishops as the ministers of ordination. The ordination of presbyters by other presbyters/ministers became normative, and in some communities, the local community ordained its own ministers.

The Catholic and Anglican churches continued a threefold ministry of bishops, presbyters (priests), and deacons, whereas many of the Reformed communities established one order of ministers (pastors) or a twofold ministry of ministers and deacons.

——— Ecumenical Statements on Ordination ———

In 1982, the Commission on Faith and Order of the World Council of Churches published *Baptism, Eucharist, and Ministry* (hereafter *BEM*), a statement that attempts to provide an ecumenical agreement on the two dominical sacraments of baptism and the Eucharist and also on ministry in the church. Numbers 39–55 of the *BEM* address the meaning of ordination, the act of ordination, the conditions for ordination, and a way towards the mutual recognition of the ordained ministries. What follows is a summary of the main points of *BEM* regarding ordination. They reflect a growing ecumenical convergence on the nature and meaning of ordination.

BEM first explores the meaning of ordination and begins by stating that:

The Church ordains certain of its members for the ministry in the name of Christ by the invocation of the Spirit and the laying on of hands (1 Tim. 4:14; 2 Tim. 1:6); in doing so it seeks to continue the mission of the apostles and to remain faithful to their teaching. The act of ordination by those who are appointed for this ministry attests the bond of the church with Jesus Christ and the apostolic witness, recalling that it is the risen Lord who is the true ordained and bestows the gift. (*BEM* 39)

Ordination is thus seen as the action of God and the church, "by which the ordained are strengthened by the Spirit for their task" and are supported by recognition and prayers of the congregation (_BEM_ 40).

In speaking of the act of ordination, _BEM_ underlines the ancient practice of ordaining ministers in the "context of worship and especially of the Eucharist." Ordination is an act of the whole community and not merely that of a particular ecclesiastical order of ministry. "The act of ordination by the laying on of hands of those appointed to do so is at one and the same time invocation of the Holy Spirit (_epiklesis_); sacramental sign; acknowledgment of gifts and commitment" (_BEM_ 41). Traditionally, ordination is done by bishops or those who exercise oversight (_episkope_) in the community.

The act of ordination expresses the action of the community in praying for the gift of the Spirit for the one chosen to be a minister of the church. "It is an invocation to God that the new minister be given the power of the Holy Spirit in the new relation which is established between this minister and the local Christian community and, by intention, the church universal" (_BEM_ 42). At the same time, it "is a sign of the granting of this prayer by the Lord who gives the gift of ordained ministry" (_BEM_ 43). It is God who acts in ordination through the church. "Although the outcome of the church's _epiklesis_ depends on the freedom of God, the church ordains in confidence that God, being faithful to his promise in Christ, enters sacramentally into contingent, historical forms of human relationship and uses them for his purpose" (_BEM_ 43). "Ordination is a sign performed in faith that the spiritual relationship signified is present in, with, and through the words spoken, the gestures made, and the forms employed" (_BEM_ 43). This is what Catholic tradition means when it refers to ordination as a sacrament. Ordination is an acknowledgment on the part of the church. It is an acknowledgment "of the gifts of the Spirit in the one ordained, and a commitment by both the church and the ordained to the new relationship" (_BEM_ 44). The church "acknowledges the minister's gifts and commits itself to be open towards these gifts" (_BEM_ 44). Those ordained likewise "offer their gifts to the church and commit themselves to the burden and opportunity of new authority and responsibility" (_BEM_ 44).

And lastly, through ordination the new ministers "enter into a collegial relationship with other ordained ministers" (_BEM_ 44). Hence, the new minister is spoken of as being a part of the order of bishops, the order of presbyters (priests, ministers), or the order of deacons.

236 • A LITURGY FOR EPISCOPAL ORDINATION

The following liturgy for the ordination of a priest is taken from the 1979 revision of The Book of Common Prayer _of the Episcopal Church (USA)._

Concerning the Service

When a bishop is to confer Holy Orders, at least two presbyters must be present.

From the beginning of the service until the offertory, the bishop presides from a chair placed close to the people, and facing them, so that all may see and hear what is done.

The ordinand is to be vested in surplice or alb, without stole, tippet, or other vesture distinctive of ecclesiastical or academic rank or order.

When the ordinand is presented _his_ full name (designated by the symbol N.N.) is used. Thereafter, it is appropriate to refer to _him_ only by the Christian name by which _he_ wishes to be known.

At the offertory, it is appropriate that the bread and wine be brought to altar by the family or friends of the newly ordained.

At the Great Thanksgiving, the new priest and other priests stand at the altar with the bishop, as associates and fellow ministers of the sacrament, and communicate with the bishop.

The family of the newly ordained may receive Communion before other members of the congregation. Opportunity is always given to the people to communicate.

The Service

A hymn, psalm, or anthem may be sung.

The people standing, the bishop says:
Blessed be God: Father, Son and Holy Spirit.
PEOPLE: **And blessed be his kingdom, now and for ever. Amen.**

In place of the above, from Easter day through the day of Pentecost:

BISHOP: Alleluia, Christ is risen.
PEOPLE: **The Lord is risen indeed. Alleluia.**

In Lent and on other penitential occasions

BISHOP: Bless the Lord who forgives all our sins.
PEOPLE: **His mercy endures for ever.**
BISHOP: Almighty God, to you all hearts are open, all desires known, and from you no secrets are hid: Cleanse the thoughts of our hearts by the inspiration of your Holy Spirit, that we may perfectly love you, and worthily magnify your holy name; through Christ our Lord. Amen.

The Presentation

The bishop and people sit. A priest and a lay person, and additional presenters if desired, standing before the bishop, present the ordinand, saying:

[N.], Bishop in the Church of God, on behalf of the clergy and people of the Diocese of [N.], we present to you [N.N.] to be ordained a priest in Christ's holy catholic church.

BISHOP: Has *he* been selected in accordance with the canons of this church? And do you believe *his* manner of life to be suitable to the exercise of this ministry?
PRESENTERS: We certify to you that *he* has satisfied the requirements of the canons, and we believe *him* to be qualified for this order.

The bishop says to the ordinand:

Will you be loyal to the doctrine, discipline, and worship of Christ as this church has received them? And will you, in accordance with the canons of this church, obey your bishop and other ministers who may have authority over you and your work?

ANSWER: I am willing and ready to do so; and I solemnly declare that I do believe the Holy Scriptures of the Old and New Testaments to be the Word of God, and to contain all things necessary to salvation; and I do solemnly engage to conform to the doctrine, discipline, and worship of the Episcopal Church.

The Ordinand then signs the above Declaration in the sight of all present.

All stand. The bishop says to the people:

Dear friends in Christ, you know the importance of this ministry, and the weight of your responsibility in presenting [N.N.] for ordination to the sacred priesthood. Therefore, if any of you know any impediment or crime because of which we should not proceed, come forward now, and make it known.

If no objection is made, the bishop continues:

Is it your will that [N.] be ordained a priest?

The people respond in these or other words:
It is.

BISHOP: Will you uphold *him* in this ministry?
The people respond in these or other words:
We will.

The bishop then calls the people to prayer with these or similar words:

In peace let us pray to the Lord.

All kneel, and the person appointed leads the Litany for Ordinations, or some other approved litany. At the end of the litany, after the Kyries, the bishop stands and reads the Collect for the Day, or the following Collect or both, first saying:

The Lord be with you.
PEOPLE: **And also with you.**
BISHOP: Let us pray.

O God of unchangeable power and eternal light: Look favorably on your whole church, that wonderful and sacred mystery; by the effectual working of your providence, carry out in tranquility the plan of salvation; let the whole world see and know that things which had grown old are being made new, and that all things are being brought to their perfection by him through whom all things were made, your Son Jesus Christ our Lord; who lives and reigns with you, in the

Ordination. *An ancient symbol of ordination is the stole. Modern symbols of ordination include a head upon which hands are laid or a chalice set upon the Bible.*

unity of the Holy Spirit, one God, for ever and ever. **Amen.**

THE MINISTRY OF THE WORD

Three lessons are read. Lay persons read the Old Testament lesson and the Epistle.

The readings are ordinarily selected from the following list and may be lengthened if desired. On a major feast, or on a Sunday, the bishop may select readings from the Proper of the Day.

Old Testament: Isaiah 6:1-8; or Numbers 11:16-17, 24-25 (omitting the final clause)
Psalm 43 or 132:8-19
Epistle: 1 Peter 5:1-4;* or Ephesians 4:7, 11-16; or Philippians 4:4-9
*It is to be noted that where the words *elder, elders,* and *fellow elder* appear in the translations of 1 Peter 5:1, the original Greek terms *presbyter, presbyters,* and *fellow presbyter* are to be substituted.

The Reader first says:
>A Reading (Lesson) from _____ .
>A citation giving chapter and verse may be added.

After each reading, the Reader may say:
>The Word of the Lord.
>PEOPLE: **Thanks be to God.**

or the Reader may say:
>Here ends the reading (Epistle).

Silence may follow.

A Psalm, canticle, or hymn follows each reading.

Then, all standing, the deacon, or if no deacon is present, a priest reads the Gospel, first saying:
>The Holy Gospel of our Lord Jesus Christ according to _____ .
>PEOPLE: **Glory to you, Lord Christ.**

Gospel: Matthew 9:35-38; or John 10:11-18; or John 6:35-38

After the Gospel, the Reader says:
>The Gospel of the Lord.
>PEOPLE: **Praise to you, Lord Christ.**

The Sermon

The congregation then says or sings the Nicene Creed:

>We believe in one God, the Father, the Almighty
>>maker of heaven and earth,
>>of all that is, seen and unseen.

>We believe in one Lord, Jesus Christ,
>>the only Son of God,
>>eternally begotten of the Father,
>>God from God, Light from Light,
>>true God from true God,
>>begotten, not made,
>>of one Being with the Father.
>>Through him all things were made.
>>For us and for our salvation
>>he came down from heaven:
>>by the power of the Holy Spirit
>>he became incarnate from the Virgin Mary,
>>and was made man.
>>For our sake he was crucified under Pontius Pilate;
>>he suffered death and was buried.
>>On the third day he rose again
>>>in accordance with the Scriptures;
>>he ascended into heaven
>>>and is seated at the right hand of the Father.

He will come again in glory to judge the
living and the dead,
and his kingdom will have no end.
We believe in the Holy Spirit, the Lord, the
giver of life,
who proceeds from the Father and the Son.
With the Father and the Son he is worshipped and glorified.
He has spoken through the Prophets.
We believe in one holy catholic and apostolic Church.
We acknowledge one baptism for the forgiveness of sins.
We look for the resurrection of the dead,
and the life of the world to come.
Amen.

The Examination

All are seated except the ordinand, who stands
before the bishop. The bishop addresses the
ordinand as follows:

My *brother*, the church is the family
of God, the body of Christ, and the
temple of the Holy Spirit. All baptized
people are called to make Christ
known as Savior and Lord, and to
share in the renewing of his world.
Now you are called to work as a pastor, priest, and teacher, together with
your bishop and fellow presbyters,
and to take your share in the councils of the church.

As a priest, it will be your task to
proclaim by word and deed the Gospel of Jesus Christ, and to fashion
your life in accordance with its pre-
cepts. You are to love and serve the
people among whom you work, caring alike for young and old, strong
and weak, rich and poor. You are to
preach, to declare God's forgiveness
to penitent sinners, to pronounce
God's blessing, to share in the administration of Holy Baptism and in the
celebration of the mysteries of Christ's
body and blood, and to perform
the other ministrations entrusted to
you.

In all that you do, you are to nourish Christ's people from the riches of
his grace, and strengthen them to

glorify God in this life and in the life
to come.

My *brother*, do you believe that you
are truly called by God and his church
to this priesthood?

ANSWER: I believe I am so called.
BISHOP: Do you now in the presence of the
church commit yourself to this trust
and responsibility?
ANSWER: I do.
BISHOP: Will you respect and be guided by the
pastoral direction and leadership of
your bishop?
ANSWER: I will.
BISHOP: Will you be diligent in the reading
and study of the Holy Scriptures, and
in seeking the knowledge of such
things as may make you a stronger
and more able minister of Christ?
ANSWER: I will.
BISHOP: Will you endeavor so to minister the
Word of God and the sacraments of
the New Covenant, that the reconciling love of Christ may be known and
received?
ANSWER: I will.
BISHOP: Will you undertake to be a faithful
pastor to all whom you are called to
serve, laboring together with them
and with your fellow ministers to
build up the family of God?
ANSWER: I will.
BISHOP: Will you do your best to pattern your
life [and that of your family, *or* household, *or* community] in accordance
with the teachings of Christ, so that
you may be a wholesome example to
your people?
ANSWER: I will.
BISHOP: Will you persevere in prayer, both in
public and in private, asking God's
grace, both for yourself and for
others, offering all your labors to
God, through the mediation of Jesus
Christ, and in the sanctification of the
Holy Spirit?
ANSWER: I will.
BISHOP: May the Lord who has given you the
will to do these things give you the
grace and power to perform them.
ANSWER: Amen.

The Consecration of the Priest

All now stand except the ordinand, who kneels facing the bishop and the presbyters who stand to the right and left of the bishop.

The hymn, "Veni Creator Spiritus" or the hymn "Veni Sancte Spiritus" is sung.

A period of silent prayer follows, the people still standing.

The bishop then says this Prayer of Consecration:

> God and Father of all, we praise you for your infinite love in calling us to be a holy people in the kingdom of your Son Jesus our Lord, who is the image of your eternal and invisible glory, the firstborn among many brethren, and the head of the church. We thank you that by his death he has overcome death, and, having ascended into heaven, has poured his gifts abundantly upon your people, making some apostles, some prophets, some evangelists, some pastors and teachers, to equip the saints for the work of the ministry and the building up of his body.

Here the bishop lays hands upon the head of the ordinand, the priests who are present also laying on their hands. At the same time the bishop prays:

> Therefore, Father, through Jesus Christ your Son, give your Holy Spirit to [N.]; fill *him* with grace and power, and make *him* a priest in your church.

The bishop then continues:

> May *he* exalt you, O Lord, in the midst of your people; offer spiritual sacrifices acceptable to you; boldly proclaim the gospel of salvation; and rightly administer the sacraments of the New Covenant. Make *him* a faithful pastor, a patient teacher, and a wise councilor. Grant that in all things *he* may serve without reproach, so that your people may be strengthened and your name glorified in all the world. All this we ask through Jesus Christ our Lord, who with you and the Holy Spirit lives and reigns, one God, for ever and ever.

The people in a loud voice respond:

> **Amen.**

The new priest is now vested according to the order of priests.

The bishop then gives a Bible to the newly ordained, saying:

> Receive this Bible as a sign of the authority given you to preach the Word of God and to administer his holy Sacraments. Do not forget the trust committed to you as a priest of the church of God.

The bishop greets the newly ordained.

The Peace

The new priest then says to the congregation:

> The peace of the Lord be always with you.

PEOPLE: **And also with you.**

The presbyters present greet the newly ordained; who then greets family members and others, as may be convenient. The clergy and people greet one another.

THE CELEBRATION OF THE EUCHARIST

The liturgy continues with the offertory. Deacons prepare the Table.

Standing at the Lord's Table, with the bishop and other presbyters, the newly ordained priest joins in the celebration of the Holy Eucharist and in the Breaking of the Bread.

After Communion

In place of the usual post-Communion prayer, the following is said:

> Almighty Father, we thank you for feeding us with the holy food of the Body and Blood of your Son, and for uniting us through him in the fellowship of your Holy Spirit. We thank you for raising up among us faithful servants for the ministry of your Word and Sacraments. We pray that [N.] may be to us an effective example in word and action, in love and patience, and in holiness of life. Grant that we, with *him*, may serve you now, and always rejoice in your glory; through Jesus Christ your Son our

Lord, who lives and reigns with you and the Holy Spirit, one God, now and for ever. Amen.

The bishop then asks the new priest to bless the people.

The new priest says:

The blessing of God Almighty, the Father, the Son, and the Holy Spirit, be among you, and remain with you always. *Amen.*

A deacon, or a priest if no deacon is present, dismisses the people.

Let us go forth into the world, rejoicing in the power of the Spirit.

PEOPLE: **Thanks be to God.**

From Easter Day through the Day of Pentecost "Alleluia, Alleluia" may be added to the dismissal and to the response.

THE LITANY FOR ORDINATIONS

For use at Ordinations as directed. On Ember Days or other occasions, if desired, this litany may be used for the prayers of the people at the Eucharist or the Daily Office, or it may be used separately.

God the Father,
Have mercy on us.
God the Son,
Have mercy on us.
God the Holy Spirit,
Have mercy on us.
Holy Trinity, one God,
Have mercy on us.
We pray to you, Lord Christ.
Lord, hear our prayer.
For the holy church of God, that it may be filled with truth and love, and be found without fault at the Day of your Coming, we pray to you, O Lord.
Lord, hear our prayer.
For all members of your church in their vocation and ministry, that they may serve you in a true and godly life, we pray to you, O Lord.
Lord, hear our prayer.
For [N.], our Presiding Bishop, and for all bishops, priests, and deacons, that they may be filled with your love, may hunger for truth, and may thirst after righteousness, we pray to you, O Lord.
Lord, hear our prayer.
For [N.], chosen bishop [priest, deacon] in your church, we pray to you, O Lord.
Lord, hear our prayer.
That *he* may faithfully fulfill the duties of this ministry, build up your church, and glorify your name, we pray to you, O Lord.
Lord, hear our prayer.
That by the indwelling of the Holy Spirit *he* may be sustained and encouraged to persevere to the end, we pray to you, O Lord.
Lord, hear our prayer.
For *his* family [the members of *his* household *or* community], that they may be adorned with all Christian virtues, we pray to you, O Lord.
Lord, hear our prayer.
For all who fear God and believe in you, Lord Christ, that our divisions may cease and that all may be one as you and the Father are one. We pray to you, O Lord.
Lord, hear our prayer.
For the mission of the church, that in faithful witness it may preach the Gospel to the ends of the earth, we pray to you, O Lord.
Lord, hear our prayer.
For those who do not yet believe, and for those who have lost their faith, that they may receive the light of the Gospel, we pray to you, O Lord.
Lord, hear our prayer.
For the peace of the world, that a spirit of respect and forbearance may grow among nations and peoples, we pray to you, O Lord.
Lord, hear our prayer.
For those in positions of public trust [especially _____], that they may serve justice and promote the dignity and freedom of every person, we pray to you, O Lord.
Lord, hear our prayer.
For a blessing upon all human labor, and for the right use of the riches of

creation, that the world may be freed from poverty, famine, and disaster, we pray to you, O Lord.
Lord, hear our prayer.

For the poor, the persecuted, the sick, and all who suffer; for refugees, prisoners, and all who are in danger; that they may be relieved and protected, we pray to you, O Lord.
Lord, hear our prayer.

For ourselves; for the forgiveness of our sins, and for the grace of the Holy Spirit to amend our lives, we pray to you, O Lord.
Lord, hear our prayer.

For all who have died in the communion of your church, and those whose faith is known to you alone, that, with all the saints, they may have rest in that place where there is no pain or grief, but life eternal, we pray to you, O Lord.
Lord, hear our prayer.

Rejoicing in the fellowship of [the ever-blessed Virgin Mary, (blessed N.) and] all the saints, let us commend ourselves, and one another, and all our life to Christ our God.
To you, O Lord our God.

Lord, have mercy.
Christ, have mercy.

Lord, have mercy.

At ordinations, the bishop who is presiding stands and says:

The Lord be with you.
PEOPLE: **And also with you.**
BISHOP: Let us pray.

The bishop says the appointed Collect.
When this Litany is used on other occasions, the Officiant concludes with a suitable Collect.

——— Additional Directions ———

At All Ordinations. The celebration of the Holy Eucharist may be according to Rite One or Rite Two. In either case, the rubrics of the service of ordination are followed. The summary of the law, the Gloria in excelsis, the prayers of the people after the creed, the general confession, and the usual post-Communion prayer are not used.

At the presentation of the ordinand, the declaration "I do believe the Holy Scriptures . . ." is to be provided as a separate document to be signed, as directed by Article VIII of the Constitution of this church and by the rubrics in each of the ordination rites. (When there are more ordinands than one, each is to be presented with a separate copy for signature.)

The hymn to the Holy Spirit before the prayer of consecration may be sung responsively between a bishop and the congregation, or in some other convenient manner.

If vestments or other symbols of office are to be dedicated, such blessing is to take place at some convenient time prior to the service. The following form may be used:

V.   Our help is in the name of the Lord;
R.   **The maker of heaven and earth.**
V.   The Lord be with you.
R.   **And also with you.**
        Let us pray.
        Everliving God, whose power is limitless, we place before you, with our praise and thanks, *these tokens* of your servant's ministry and dignity. Grant that [N.], who has been called to leadership in your church, and bears *these signs*, may faithfully serve you and share in the fullness of your life-giving Spirit; through the high priest and good shepherd of us all, Jesus Christ our Lord. Amen.

At the Ordination of a Bishop. Following the consecration prayer, and while the new bishop is being clothed with the vesture of the episcopate, instrumental music may be played.

Following the presentation of the Bible and the formula "Receive the Holy Scriptures . . ." a ring, staff, and mitre, or other suitable insignia of office may be presented.

During the eucharistic prayer, it is appropriate that some of the consecrating bishops and representative presbyters of the diocese stand with the new bishop at the altar as fellow ministers of the sacrament.

The newly ordained bishop, assisted by other ministers, distributes Holy Communion to the people. When necessary, the administration may take place at several conveniently separated places in the church.

After the pontifical blessing and the dismissal, a hymn of praise may be sung.

The bishops who are present are not to depart without signing the Letters of Consecration.

At the Ordination of a Priest. Reasonable opportunity is to be given for the priests present to join in the laying on of hands.

The stole worn about the neck, or other insignia of the office of priest, is placed upon the new priest after the entire prayer of consecration is completed and immediately before the Bible is presented. Afterwards, other instruments or symbols of office may be given.

If two or more are ordained together, each is to have *his* own presenters. The ordinands may be presented together, or in succession, as the bishop may direct. Thereafter, references to the ordinand in the singular are changed to the plural where necessary. The ordinands are examined together.

During the prayer of consecration, the bishop and priests lay their hands upon the head of each ordinand. During the laying on of hands, the bishop alone says over each ordinand: "Father, through Jesus Christ your Son, give your Holy Spirit to [N.]; fill *him* with grace and power, and make *him* a priest in your church." When they have laid their hands upon all the ordinands, the bishop continues: "May they exalt you, O Lord, in the midst . . ."

A Bible is to be given to each new priest, and the words "Receive this Bible . . ." are to be said to each one.

All the newly ordained take part in the exchange of the peace, and join the bishop and other priests at the altar for the Great Thanksgiving. Similarly, all the new priests break the consecrated bread and receive Holy Communion.

At the Ordination of a Deacon. The stole worn over the left shoulder, or other insignia of the office of deacon, is placed upon the new deacon after the entire prayer of consecration is completed and immediately before the Bible is given.

If two or more are ordained together, each is to have *his* own presenters. The ordinands may be presented together, or in succession, as the bishop may direct. Thereafter, references to the ordinand in the singular are changed to the plural where necessary. The ordinands are examined together.

During the prayer of consecration, the bishop is to lay hands upon the head of each ordinand, and say over each one: "Father, through Jesus Christ your Son, give your Holy Spirit to [N.]; fill *him* with grace and power, and make *him* a deacon in your church." After laying hands upon all the ordinands, the bishop continues "Make them, O Lord, modest and humble. . . ."

A Bible is to be given to each new deacon, and the words "Receive this Bible . . ." are also to be said to each one.

After participating in the peace, the deacons go to the altar for the offertory. If there are many deacons, some assist in the offertory and others administer Holy Communion. One, appointed by the bishop, is to say the dismissal.

When desired, deacons may be appointed to carry the sacrament and minister Holy Communion to those communicants who, because of sickness or other grave cause, could not be present at the ordination.

If the remaining elements are not required for the Communion of the absent, it is appropriate for the deacons to remove the vessels from the Altar, consume the remaining elements, and cleanse the vessels in some convenient place.

Commentary

Concerning the Service. These notes give additional information to those involved in the planning and the actual celebration of an ordination. Further directions common to all the ordination rites are given at the end of the ordination services.

(1) In keeping with ancient Western tradition (from at least the late third century) other presbyters (priests) participate in the ordination of a presbyter by joining the bishop in laying hands on the candidate in the context of the prayer of ordination.

(2) The bishop should be clearly seen by the congregation during the rites of ordination. The placement of the bishop's chair will be determined by the arrangement of the chancel. If necessary, provision should also be made for a microphone at the chair so that the bishop may be heard throughout the rite.

(3) The candidate wears the basic vestments common to both lay and ordained ministers, namely, the cassock and surplice or the alb. The

alb has become the common ecumenical vestment and is more appropriate than the (cassock and) surplice. After the imposition of hands, the distinctive vestment(s) appropriate to the order of presbyters is given to the new priest, e.g., stole (and chasuble).

(4) The candidate is addressed by his or her full name only at the initial presentation, thereafter only by the first name or the name by which the candidate wishes to be called.

(5) Since the celebration of an ordination is primarily a celebration of the church and its ministry, undue attention should not be given to the family of the candidate. Nevertheless, it is appropriate for the family or friends of the new priest to participate in the service by presenting the bread and wine for the Eucharist. The new priest may also exchange the peace with his or her family.

(6) According to the ancient rites for ordination, the new priest joins the ranks of the other presbyters immediately at the end of the ordination rite. The new priest stands with the other presbyters at the altar for the eucharistic prayer. This is traditionally referred to a concelebration. In the early form of concelebration, the presbyters did not verbally participate in the recitation of the prayer of thanksgiving, but signified their participation as presbyters by their presence near the bishop, by wearing the vestments of their order, and by gesture (extending their hands over the gifts or in the gesture of prayer).

(7) The reception of the sacrament by the people should not be limited in any way. A sufficient amount of bread and wine should be consecrated, and provision should be made to ensure that there are enough ministers to distribute the Eucharist to the people. The family of the new presbyter may receive Holy Communion before the remainder of the congregation.

The Ordination of a Priest. The ordination rite begins in the usual way with the singing of a hymn, psalm, or anthem. The bishop then says or sings the introductory acclamation and the collect for purity. The Gloria, the Kyrie, and Trisagion are omitted from the ordination service, and their place is taken by the presentation of the candidate.

The Presentation. The first part of the ordination rite begins with the presentation of the candidate(s).

Normally each candidate is presented by a presbyter and a lay person, but there may be additional presenters, lay or clerical. Care should be taken that the presentation not be overdone. The purpose of this portion of the rite is to ensure that the candidate has been called to ordination by the church, that he or she has been properly prepared to undertake the ministerial office, and leads a life appropriate to the ministry. The candidate, in turn, is asked to make the declaration required by church law that he or she will be faithful to the doctrine, law, and worship of the Episcopal church and will be obedient to the bishop and other lawful supporters.

The declaration is given to the candidate in a written form, and the candidate signs it in the presence of the bishop and the congregation.

The bishop then addresses the people and asks for their assurance that there are no reasons why the candidate should not be ordained. They are then asked if they wish the candidate to be ordained and if they will support him or her in the exercise of the ministry. The congregation may respond to the questions using the words provided, or in other appropriate words. It is only with this final approval by the people that the bishop proceeds with the ordination.

The bishop invites the people to pray, using the words provided or in his own words, and the Litany for Ordinations is then sung or recited. Another suitable litany may be used. The candidate kneels during the litany; alternatively, the candidate might lie prostrate in humble prayer. It was the ancient tradition of the church for the people to stand for prayer during the season of Easter and on Sundays. If this practice is followed, the candidate kneels and the people stand. The litany constitutes the prayer of the people for the candidate and is one of the basic elements of the ordination rite. It expresses the church's prayer for the one who will exercise its ministry. The bishop concludes the litany with a collect.

The collect of the day or the one in the ordination rite may be used. Although both prayers may be said, one after the other, it is probably best to use only one.

The Ministry of the Word. The usual pattern of a reading from the Old Testament, New Testament (Epistle), and Gospel is followed. The readings may be chosen from those given in the ordination rite or, on Sundays or feasts, the readings of the day may be chosen. When the readings of the day are used, it may be appropriate for one of the ordination readings to also be used. In such cases, it is usually better to replace the second reading with one of the ordination readings, since the first reading and Gospel are usually related.

The sermon is normally based on the Scripture readings and should relate them to the ministry of the church and the order presbyter (priest) which is being conferred. The Nicene Creed is sung or recited immediately after the sermon.

The Examination. The ordination rite continues with the examination of the candidate, who stands before the bishop. The bishop first addresses the candidate and explains the duties and responsibilities of a priest. In light of the explanation of the office of priest, the bishop then asks the candidate a series of eight questions:

> Are you called by God and the church to the priesthood?
>
> Do you commit yourself to responsibilities of the priesthood?
>
> Will you respect and follow the directions of the bishop?
>
> Will you read and study the Scriptures?
>
> Will you properly proclaim the Word of God and administer the sacraments?
>
> Will you be a faithful pastor for the building up of the church?
>
> Will you pattern your life on the teaching of Christ?
>
> Will you pray in public and private for yourself and others?

The bishop concludes with the wish that the candidate be assisted by the Lord's grace to keep all that has been promised.

The Consecration of the Priest. The central act of the ordination now takes place. The candidate kneels before the bishop. The presbyters present stand to either side of the bishop in such a way that the people can clearly see what is taking place.

The consecration of the priest begins with a hymn invoking the Holy Spirit—"Veni Creator Spiritus" or "Veni Sancte Spiritus." Both these hymns are found in *The Hymnal 1982*, nos. 502, 504, and 226.

Before the prayer of consecration is begun, there is a period of silence which continues the prayer for the Holy Spirit begun in the hymn.

The prayer of consecration is a return to the ancient practice of the church. In the 1928 Prayer Book, the ordination prayer is very general, and the imposition of hands is accompanied by a separate imperative formula which emphasizes the role of the bishop. The new prayer of consecration incorporates a large part of the prayer of the previous Prayer Book, but adds to it a specific invocation of the Holy Spirit, during which hands are laid on the candidate by the bishop and participating presbyters. Since the bishop and presbyters lay hands on the candidate at the same time, care should be taken that the candidate not be obscured from the view of the people by all the priests surrounding him or her.

The prayer concludes with a series of intercessions, which pray that the one being ordained may faithfully exercise the various aspects of the priestly ministry.

The remaining rites help to explain the significance of what has just taken place. The new priest is first vested in a stole worn around the neck and hanging before the chest. If desired, a chasuble may also be given. The chasuble is not used if the cassock and surplice is worn. A Bible is given to the priest, and, if desired, other signs of office may be presented, e.g., a chalice and paten. These presentations are reminders that the priest is to proclaim the Word of God and to administer the sacraments.

In keeping with the ancient ordination rites, the bishop greets the new priest, welcoming him or her into the ministry of the church.

The Peace. The new priest performs his or her first ministerial act by greeting the people. The presbyters present greet the priest, who is now associated with them in the order of the priesthood. Others present may also greet the priest. It should be noted that this greeting is, in fact, the exchange of the peace which concludes the ordination rite and prepares for the Eucharist which now follows. The members of the congregation greet one another in the customary manner.

The Celebration of the Eucharist. The altar is prepared, and the gifts of the people are received in the usual way. The new priest joins the bishop and presbyters at the altar for the Great Thanksgiving and the Breaking of the Bread. The new presbyter may also assist in the distribution of the Eucharist.

After Communion. This proper post-Communion prayer replaces those contained in the Holy Eucharist: Rite One or Rite Two. In addition to thanking God for the Eucharist which has just been received, the prayer also gives thanks for the gift of the new priest to the church and prays for the faithful exercise of his or her ministry.

The liturgy concludes with the new priest blessing the people at the invitation of the bishop. Although the blessing is normally not required when Rite Two is used, it is mandatory on this occasion. The people are then dismissed in the usual way.

The Litany for Ordinations. The litany serves several purposes during the ordination rite. It is the intercessory prayer of the congregation for the one(s) being ordained. It also takes the place of the usual prayers of the people which normally conclude The Word of God and are omitted in the ordination service.

Additional Directions. These additional rubrics follow the ordination rites and deal with several matters in greater detail than the brief rubrics of the rites.

At All Ordinations. (1) The ordination rites take place during the celebration of the Eucharist, which may follow either Rite One or Rite Two. Since the ordination rites take place in the context of the Eucharist, several changes need to be made in the eucharistic liturgy. The ordination rites have their own introductory rites, which replace those of the Eucharist. Because the litany is used, the prayers of the people are omitted. The general confession is omitted, and the proper ordination post-Communion prayer replaces those of the eucharistic liturgy.

(2) Each candidate is to have a printed copy of the Declaration, which is signed by the candidate during the service.

(3) The hymn to the Holy Spirit may be sung in a variety of ways: responsorially between the bishop and people, by all together, alternately by the choir and congregation, etc.

(4) Vestments and other symbols of office are not blessed during the ordination rites, and such a blessing is not really necessary. However, if a blessing is desired, it is done using the prayer provided here at a convenient time before the service.

At the Ordination of a Priest. (1) The presbyters present may participate in the laying on of hands. However, the particular circumstances, e.g., the number of priests, the size of the chancel, etc., may require that the number of priests participating in the laying on of hands be limited.

(2) The new priest is vested with a stole alone or with a stole and a chasuble after the prayer of consecration. Other symbols of office are presented after the Bible is given to the new priest. Eucharistic vessels (chalice or paten), oil stocks, or pyx are appropriate symbols for presentation at this time. Nevertheless, only the presentation of the Bible is required by the rite.

(3) When several candidates are ordained together, they may be presented individually and may have individual presenters, or the candidates may be presented as a group.

(4) The presbyters join the bishop in the laying on of hands, but the bishop alone says the prayer. This is done for each candidate, and the bishop continues the prayer of consecration only after all have received the imposition of hands with its corresponding portion of the prayer.

(5) The formula for the presentation of the Bible is said individually for each priest when several are ordained at the same time.

(6) The newly ordained priests all participate in the peace, stand at the altar for the Great Thanksgiving and assist in the Breaking of the Bread, and receive Communion. Whether they participate in the celebration at any other way will depend on the bishop and local custom.

The Book of Common Prayer

237 • GUIDELINES FOR PLANNING AN ORDINATION

The following guidelines are intended especially for those whose churches do not have a required ordination service. They may also be of assistance to those who must use a particular liturgy.

(1) The ordination should be carefully planned in consultation with the candidate and, if possible, with the presiding minister.

(2) Care should be taken to insure that the ordination will manifest the full variety of the ministries and orders of the church. The liturgical roles normally exercised by lay persons should not be taken over by clergy.

(3) Since music is a basic part of the liturgical celebration, the music for the ordination liturgy should be carefully integrated into the whole celebration.

(4) The celebration of an ordination is a celebration of the whole church and not merely of an individual and his or her family. The service should be planned so that the congregation can actively participate throughout the celebration.

(5) The liturgy for an ordination normally includes the following elements, although not necessary in this order: presentation of the candidate, proclamation of the Word of God, sermon/homily, examination of the candidate, prayer for the candidate by the congregation, ordination prayer with the laying on of hands, presentation of symbols of office, exchange of the peace, and celebration of the Eucharist.

(6) In churches where vestments are used, the candidate usually wears the basic ministerial vestment, without a stole, from the beginning of the service. The white alb is rapidly becoming the basic vestment common to all ministers. Other vestments, e.g., a stole, may be given to the new minister after the ordination prayer and the imposition of hands. A minister (elder, presbyter, priest) wears the stole so that it passes around the neck and the ends hang pendant in front. A deacon wears the stole over the left shoulder so that it passes across the chest and back and is fastened on the right side.

(7) The presentation of the candidate generally takes place at the beginning of the service or after the sermon. It may include a request to ordain the candidate, the assent of the people, and prayer for the candidate (litany or some other prayer). This portion of the service should be kept relatively simple and not appear to be a canonization of the candidate.

(8) The proclamation of the Word of God should follow the usual pattern of the church. It is appropriate that readings be proclaimed from the Old Testament, the New Testament (other than the Gospels), and from one of the Gospels. Many churches have specific readings that are assigned for ordinations. The readings other than the Gospel are read by lay persons in many churches.

(9) The readings are followed by a sermon on the readings; it ought to relate also to the ordination which is about to take place. In some churches it will incorporate a charge to the candidate, or this will follow as a separate element.

(10) An examination of the candidate takes place. Various questions are asked of the candidate on his or her willingness to live a life in keeping with the order of ministry being conferred, and whether he or she will faithfully carry out the responsibilities of his or her new office.

(11) Prayer for the candidate may take the form of a hymn to the Holy Spirit or a litany (if this has not preceded this point in the service).

(12) The ordination prayer and the laying on of hands form a single unit. The first portion of the prayer recalls the ministry of Christ and his gift of the ministry to the church. The laying on of hands may take place in silence before the prayer or during the prayer itself. It is preferable that when the laying on of hands takes place during the ordination prayer, it be accompanied by an invocation of the Holy Spirit to confer the particular order of ministry. If there is more than one candidate, the laying on of hands and invocation should be repeated for each candidate. If a bishop is being ordained, other bishops participate in the laying on of hands on the candidate. If a minister (elder, presbyter, priest) is being ordained, other members of that order of ministry participate in the laying on of hands. The presiding minister alone lays hands on a candidate for the diaconate. The other ministers who participate in the laying on of hands should stand in such a way as to not block the view of the people. The portion of the prayer after the imposition of hands should include intercessions that the new minister be given by God the gifts necessary for carrying out his or her new ministry.

(13) The new minister may be vested as indicated above. Other symbols of office, such as a Bible and/or chalice and paten, may be given to the new minister. Care should be taken that these presentations not seem more important than the laying on of hands and the ordination prayer.

(14) The ordination portion of the service concludes with the presiding minister giving the new minister the peace (right hand of fellowship). The other ministers present may also greet the new minister.

(15) It is appropriate that the service continue with the celebration of the Eucharist (Lord's Supper, Holy Communion). The newly ordained minister may assist the presiding minister, or, when

appropriate, preside at the celebration of the Eucharist.

Alan Detscher

238 • BIBLIOGRAPHY ON ORDINATION AND COMMISSIONING

Bradshaw, Paul. _Ordination Rites of the Ancient Churches of East and West._ New York: Pueblo Publishing, 1990.

————. _The Anglican Ordinal._ Alcuin Club Collections. London: SPCK, 1971.

Buchanan, Colin Oglivie. _Modern Anglican Ordination Rites._ Alcuin Club Collections. Nottingham, England: Grove Books, 1987.

Campbell, Dennis. _The Yoke of Obedience: The Meaning of Ordination in United Methodism._ Nashville: Abingdon, 1988.

Cooke, Bernard. _Ministry to Word and Sacraments: History and Theology._ Philadelphia: Fortress Press, 1980.

Cowan, Michael A., ed. _Alternative Futures for Worship._ Vol. 6, _Leadership Ministry in Community._ Collegeville, Minn.: Liturgical Press, 1988.

Hatchett, Marion. _Commentary on the American Prayer Book._ New York: Seabury Press, 1981. A theological and liturgical commentary on the 1979 _Book of Common Prayer,_ including a discussion of the ordination rite.

Haendler, Geit. _Luther on Ministerial Office and Congregational Function._ Philadelphia: Fortress Press, 1981.

Lawson, Albert Brown. _John Wesley and Christian Ministry._ London: SPCK, 1963.

Lienhard, Joseph T. _Ministry:The Message of the Sacraments._ Vol. 8, _Message of the Fathers of the Church._ Wilmington, Del.: Glazier, 1984.

Mitchell, Nathan, O.S.B. _The Message of the Sacraments._ Vol. 6, _Mission and Ministry: History and Theology in the Sacrament of Order._ Wilmington, Del.: Michael Glazier, 1982.

Mitchell, Leonel L._Praying Shapes Believing._ Minneapolis: Winston, 1985. A theological commentary on the 1979 _Book of Common Prayer,_ including a discussion of the ordination rites.

Moede, Gerald F. _The Office of Bishop in Methodism._ New York: Abingdon, 1964.

Mosemann, John H. _Ordination, Licensing, and Installation._ Newton, Kan.: Faith and Life Press; Scottdale, Pa.: Mennonite Publishing House, 1983.

Power, David N. _Gifts That Differ: Lay Ministries Established and Unestablished._ New York: Pueblo Publishing, 1980.

Vos, Wiebe, and Geoffrey Wainwright, eds. _Ordination Rites._ Rotterdam, Netherlands: Liturgical Ecumenical Trust, 1980.

Warkentin, Marjorie. _Ordination: A Biblical-Historical View._ Grand Rapids: Eerdmans, 1982. A biblical, historical, and theological study by a Baptist lay person.

For representative ordination liturgies see:

• For Baptist and free church traditions, see Jesse Jai McNeil, _Minister's Service Book for Pulpit and Parish_ (Grand Rapids: Eerdmans, 1993), 106–40.

• For the Christian Reformed Church, see _The Psalter Hymnal_ (Grand Rapids: CRC Publications, 1987), 992–1006.

• For Episcopal, see _The Book of Common Prayer._ (New York: Church Hymnal Corporation, 1979), 551–556.

• For Evangelical Lutheran Church in America, see _Occasional Services_ (Minneapolis: Augsburg; Philadelphia: Board of Publication, Lutheran Church in America, 1982), 192–203.

• For the Lutheran Church–Missouri Synod, see _Lutheran Worship—Agenda_ (St. Louis: Concordia, 1984), 205–37.

• For the Mennonites, see John H. Mosemann, _Ordination, Licensing, and Installation_ (Newton, Kans.: Faith and Life Press; Scottdale, Pa.: Mennonite Publishing House, 1983).

• For the Methodists, see _The United Methodist Book of Worship_ (Nashville: United Methodist Publishing House, 1992), 652–713.

• For the Reformed Church in America, see _Worship the Lord_ (Grand Rapids: Eerdmans, 1987), 50–55.

• For Roman Catholic, see _The Rites,_ vol. 2. (New York: Pueblo Publishing, 1980).

• For the United Church of Christ, see _Book of Worship: United Church of Christ_ (New York: Office of Church Life, 1986), 391–446.

SIXTEEN

Reconciliation

The following pages deal primarily with the history of the sacrament of reconciliation in the West and, after the Protestant Reformation, in the Roman Catholic church. From the New Testament onward, Christians were convinced that sin disrupted relationships with God and within the church. Hence the church was responsible to deal with sin. From the broader topic of how the church maintains discipline, the following pages focus more narrowly on post-baptismal confession of sin and reconciliation with the church.

239 ◆ HISTORICAL ORIGINS AND DEVELOPMENT OF RECONCILIATION IN THE WEST

Baptism is the primary means of reconciling sinners to God. But what happens when Christians fall into sin after baptism? In the sacramental traditions of Eastern Orthodoxy and Roman Catholicism, the Eucharist itself has been a means of restoring relationship with God and other Christians. But highly visible or habitual sinning required special attention if the integrity of the Christian community was to be maintained. In the Western tradition this led to the sacrament of penance: confession, absolution, and satisfaction for wrongs done. Although Protestants rejected many aspects of this sacramental practice, they retained a deep concern about church discipline and used both individual and corporate means to maintain discipline. In recent decades, Roman Catholic practices have changed markedly. Recently, Protestant groups have largely replaced formal church discipline with pastoral counseling. (For a renewed emphasis on corporate repentance in one wing of Protestantism, see chapter 19, "The Solemn Assembly.")

Biblical Practices

Saint Paul is the apostle of reconciliation, and the ministry of Christians, as he describes it, is particularly characterized by the word *reconciliation*. The context of Paul's reference to the centrality of reconciliation for Christians comes from a marriage situation in which spouses separate for a time—at least with an abstinence from sexual intercourse—and then come back together (1 Cor. 7:11). A secular, legal usage of reconciliation between husband and wife provides a symbol of a relationship action which takes place between God and human persons—both individually and communally; between God and the world God created; and between humans themselves.

Reconciliation is not used as a specialized vocabulary word in the Hebrew Scriptures. But the action described by the phrase "to reconcile" permeates the story of God's creative act and God's interactive history with the human race. In its beginnings, God's creation is pictured as becoming separated from God by the disobedience of the first man and woman (generating a hostile environment in which they earn their bread in sweat and toil; Gen. 3), but with God's promise that they would come back together again. In a second creation account depicting the story of Noah and the Flood (Gen. 6–9), once again there is the recognition of God's separation from all creation, but with a rainbow promise of a faithful, reconciling presence that would never destroy the world and its inhabitants again. From the stories of Abraham and Sarah to that of Moses and Zipporah, the covenant relationship of God and the people of God permeates the Hebrew Scriptures. Yet, the history of the Israelite people is one of broken relationships always being repaired and restored at the initiative of God. Another strong image is that of the spousal or marriage relationship between God and humankind, which takes in all the struggles of separation and coming back together, all too familiar even in the most special of love relationships (Hos. 2:16-22). The penitential rites developed in the Mosaic tradition all look to the reconciliation of human beings with God.

Within this biblical setting, Paul can readily adopt the language of reconciliation. God is reconciling each one of us in Christ Jesus (2 Cor. 5:18). In Christ, God is reconciling the whole world to God's self (Col. 1:20). Because of our faith in Jesus, believers are to be reconciled to one another and to God (Eph. 2:16). Because of the faith of believers, they find themselves called to a ministry of reconciliation (2 Cor. 5:18). Reconciliation, then, emphasizes the return, the coming back together after some kind of alienation, separation, or rejection—identified as human sin. The Bible stresses God's initiative in the process of reconciliation and the invitation to humans, not only to respond but also in Jesus to become cooperators in his mission of reconciling.

Early Church Rigorism and Public Repentance

As reflected in the Acts of the Apostles, the first Christians realized this sense of reconciliation in the profession of Jesus as Savior and in being baptized in his name through the water and the Spirit. The early Christians as they gathered in their first assemblies (*ecclesia*, the term later translated "church") rejoiced in their sense of being a new creature and this world being a new creation—all related to God in Christ Jesus (2 Cor. 5:17). The definitiveness of the reconciliation even through Jesus' life, death, and resurrection was made clear when the candidates stepped forward to be immersed in the unrepeatable rite of baptism for the forgiveness of sins. The Christian community realized another moment in this reconciliation with God and one another each time they entered into the celebration of the breaking of the bread (Eucharist); at the same time they also experienced themselves caught up with Jesus in the reconciliation ministry.

But a problem arose when the various civil persecutions of the early Christians became the occasion for a number of people either to reject their newfound faith or to perform some pagan ritual act which compromised it. In the early second century of the Christian era, the church developed a more elaborate form of reconciliation in order to deal with sinful members of the community. Baptized members who had sinned seriously and thereby publicly affected the community—for example, apostates, those unfaithful in marriage (adulterers), and those who had cut short the life of another person (murderers)—came forward for another ritual act of reconciliation, a coming back after baptism to God and to the community, the church.

This ritual action established an order of penitents, similar to the already established order of catechumens in the early church. This action brought the repentant sinner, by stages of a penitential process, back to full communion with the church. It truly was a ministry of the local church, with an emphasis on the prayer, fasting, and almsgiving support of the community members, in addition to the penance of the repentant sinner. On a schedule similar to that for catechumens, the individual penitents entered into the process usually on Ash Wednesday by the confession of their sins, ordinarily to the bishop (*episcopus*). The confession was followed by the laying on of hands by the minister as a gesture of both exorcism and solidarity, then by the taking on of a lengthy penance by the penitent person, sometimes for life (often including the repudiation of a military career and a total abstinence from sexual relations). Finally came the celebration of receiving absolution from the bishop and a welcome back into the community Eucharist on Holy Thursday. This so-called second baptism, now not of water but of tears, was very rigorous because it was lengthy and could only be entered upon once by a penitent person. Because of difficulty of the penitential process, many people waited until their deathbed to use their only chance to enter this rite.

This specialized practice of reconciliation, eventually referred to as a canonical penance, flourished in the church from the late second through the fifth centuries. Those who had sinned seriously were required to take advantage of this rite for their participation in the church; otherwise they suffered excommunication. Most Christians continued to experience reconciliation less formally and publicly for the sin in their lives through a variety of ways—prayer, fasting, almsgiving, spiritual guidance from another, and participation in the Eucharist.

The Origins of Private Confession

Beginning sometime in the fifth century, because of a tradition present in the Irish monasteries—a tradition of a reflective monastic practice prevalent even earlier in the Christian churches of the Middle East—another ritual action of reconciliation developed as a response to human sinfulness. It seems to have grown out of the practice of monks who sought direction for their spiritual development by telling their faults as well as virtues to a spiritual father. Eventually, this monastic practice became common among all church members. The process involved the individual's confessing of their sins, ordinarily to a priest, whenever they had committed a serious sin; speaking to the confessor in private; accepting a penance proper to the offense; and then receiving the sign of forgiveness. Each confessor, even the inexperienced or ill-educated, was helped in making the penance appropriate to the sins confessed by referring to books called penitentials, which listed various kinds of sins commonly confessed with appropriate penances. This became known as the tariff practice of penance, since it built upon the notion of paying a specific tax or tariff for specific violations of civil law (the punishment fitting the crime). Not only did the rite lose its communal setting, but even the concept of sin became more private, as a code violation with the consequences of incurring an individual debt. This debt had to be paid in order for it to be absolved.

As a nod to some kind of community context, the development of substitutes or commutations for the penances imposed slowly became common. In order to reduce the length of time for penance or to relieve its severity, the church extended the possibility of substitutes to the penitent, generally called indulgences. The prayers and good works of other church members, the unused merits of saints' lives, or even the superabundant fruits of Christ's own sacrifice were promised to increase the worth of the lesser penitential act performed by the repentant sinner, and thereby satisfy so many days, months, or even years of penance performed according to the norms of the penitential books. Eventually, such substitutions or indulgences for penitential acts led to the abuses of the fifteenth- and sixteenth-century church.

From Ireland, this form of reconciliation spread throughout Christian Europe. This private penance only briefly struggled for legitimacy with the older form represented in the order of penitents, since this canonical penance had fallen into disuse among the Christian faithful. The new rite, called Celtic penance, offered the advantage of frequency and ready availability. However, at the same time, the rite in its stress on the private nature of penance appeared to mitigate the community context and involvement. The prominence of the confession of sins, which enabled the confessor to assign appropriate penance, led to the popular name confession, especially from the eighth century onwards.

Medieval and Reformation Reforms

The decrees of the Fourth Lateran Council in 1215 recognized this rite of confession and absolution, identified officially as the sacrament of penance, as the ordinary means of ecclesiastical forgiveness. But the sacrament still tended popularly to be called confession, from the emphasis given in the Irish church development. The Fourth Lateran Council, in its decrees on penance, imposed a requirement for all Christians guilty of serious sin to confess to a priest annually before Easter Communion.

In the late medieval church, confession and absolution were the normal means for supporting the repentant and reconciling the sinner. The Protestant Reformers, beginning with Luther in the early sixteenth century, generally rejected this sacrament of penance, often claiming that the Fourth Lateran Council had invented it. Martin Luther's call for reform in the church returned to the emphasis on baptism and Eucharist as the normal means of our reconciliation with God and the community. Although he remained ambiguous about its place in the Christian life, he tended to devalue the ritual action of penance, but still retain it. Calvin and other Reformers focused reconciliation in baptism, the Eucharist, and in some private, non-sacramental actions, thereby eliminating penance. The concern of the Reformers was to let no human action, even a church ritual action, obscure the total efficacy of Jesus' salvific act and the absolute gratuity of God's grace, especially in the act of reconciliation.

The Council of Trent in the sixteenth century made some attempt to clarify church belief and practice and so marked another stage in the development of the sacrament of penance, especially in its stance towards the Reformation movements represented by Luther and Calvin. The Council of Trent reaffirmed the decrees of the Fourth Lateran Council, thereby highlighting the importance of confession and absolution in the reconciliation of the individual Christian sinner with God. The elements of the ritual action remained the same, but penance was no longer needed to be completed before the priest absolved the sinner. This remained the common practice in the Roman Catholic church until the Second Vatican Council (1962–1965).

Although, as noted above, some of the Protestant Reformers desired to see aural confession of sin retained, they taught that sins could be legitimately confessed to another lay person. Anglicans included public, corporate confession of sins with absolution in their eucharistic liturgies. John Calvin and the Reformed tradition laid great emphasis on a disciplined church even while rejecting sacramental confession. The Anabaptists and their descendants (Mennonites, Amish, Hutterites) adamantly rejected the very idea of aural confession and priestly absolution as a post–New Testament corruption of the Christian gospel. They advocated private admonition of wayward members by other members based on Matthew 18. If this private admonition went unheeded, the congregation would take action to excommunicate the wayward member.

In practice, however, aural confession of sins to another person gradually disappeared in all Protestant groups. Its place was taken by various forms of corporate church discipline. As part of the catholicizing trend in Anglicanism after the sixteenth century, especially during the nineteenth century, aural confession of sins to a priest with absolution and penance became more common, although it still remains the exception among Anglicans.

Modern Reforms

In 1963, in the *Constitution on the Sacred Liturgy,* the council called for a reform of the sacra-
ment of penance that would clearly show the social and ecclesial nature and effects of the sacrament. On December 2, 1973, the Rite of Penance was promulgated; the Roman Catholic community in the United States began to use the new rite in 1977. Although the decree tended to use the terminology of penance and reconciliation interchangeably, reconciliation appears to be the favored term in better expressing the Christian reality. The ritual action of reconciliation takes on three approved forms. The first form is that of the individual persons confessing to the priest minister. However, the ritual setting is focused more on a dialogue, with appropriate Scripture being read aloud and providing the context for the confession of their sins. The second form is a group or community entering into a Bible service reflection, with possibly a communal examination of conscience, but with individual confession and absolution followed often by a common penance for all the participants. The third form is aimed at the group or community entering into the ritual action, with Scripture reflections and common examination of conscience. This form requires no individual confession of personal sins, but rather a general acknowledgment of sinfulness from all the participants followed by a general absolution by the priest minister. In addition, a number of models of communal celebrations of reconciliation without absolution are given in an appendix of this decree.

The introduction of these new ritual actions of reconciliation has left this particular sacrament still not well understood or utilized. At a special synod of bishops called by Pope John Paul II in 1983, the subject was penance and its place in the contemporary world. In the apostolic exhortation called "Reconciliation and Penance" subsequently published on December 2, 1984, Pope John Paul II stated clearly that penance in Christian life is to be related to reconciliation with God, with oneself, and with others. He stressed the profoundly personal character of the sacrament, adding emphasis to the first two ritual forms of individual confession of sins. At the same time, the Pope restricted the use of the third ritual form for highlighting a social and an ecclesial context of general reconciliation.

An understanding of the development of reconciliation in its many forms, but focused in a specialized ritual action, has led Christians today to a greater appreciation of its theology, ministry, and celebration. The Christian mystery of reconciliation is key to understanding God's relation to us all, redemption in Christ, conversion, the church, and its life of worship and ministry to sinners.

David L. Fleming

240 ♦ A Western Theology of Reconciliation

Sin estranges and alienates people from God and each other, but God reconciles the world to himself through Christ. Christians celebrate their reconciliation to God in Christ by means of baptism and the Eucharist. Yet, admission of guilt and genuine sorrow for sin, as made evident in fasting, almsgiving, and other acts, are part of the way the church deals with sin after baptism.

Paul and the Theology of Reconciliation in Christ

The message of Jesus is a message of reconciliation. His words, his actions, in fact his whole life, death, and resurrection are concerned with re-establishing a loving relationship between God and the individual; between individuals as brothers and sisters to one another; and between humankind and the world God created. Reconciliation forms an integral part of gospel living.

Reconciliation can be understood simply from its secular usage as a coming back together, a restoration of harmony after some separation or alienation (e.g., Acts 7:26; Moses trys to reconcile his countrymen who are fighting among themselves). To be reconciled also means to be at peace within oneself in relation to a situation or circumstance (e.g., 2 Sam. 13:39; David's becoming reconciled to the death of his son Amnon).

Paul becomes the theologian of reconciliation. His use of the term puts it into a complex relationship with redemption, salvation, and justification. The very use of reconciliation to describe the relationship between God and human beings acknowledges the human awareness of some kind of alienation or separation. In Colossians 1:21, Paul describes Christians before their redemption as "estranged and hostile in mind, doing evil deeds" (NRSV). In Romans 5:10, these people are

described as "enemies" of God. Reconciliation is the result of God's initiative in Christ: if by Jesus' death we as Christians have been reconciled, Paul reflects then how "much more surely, having been reconciled, will we be saved by his life" (Rom. 5:10, NRSV). In 2 Corinthians 5:17-21, Paul repeats that "in Christ God was reconciling the world to himself." The effect on us, Christians, is that we are reconciled by God's action; for our part, we must receive the gift. So Paul begs us to "be reconciled to God" (2 Cor. 5:20, NRSV). Not only is reconciliation a gift we freely receive from God, but in so doing we are also entrusted by God with this message of reconciliation. As Paul boasts, we have been given by God the ministry of reconciliation. Paul in Colossians reminds us again that although God has now reconciled us, this gift of reconciliation demands that we remain steadfast in the faith, "without shifting from the hope promised by the gospel" (Col. 1:23, NRSV). God is the initiator of reconciliation. In the life, death, and resurrection of Jesus, God has completed this divine action of reconciliation. The responsibility of humans is to receive the gift offered. In addition, as Christians, we must be faithful in order not to reject the gift. Furthermore, we are entrusted with preaching the gospel message of reconciliation. We are to be ministers of reconciliation, ambassadors of Christ. The action of God in Jesus not only affects the relationship of human beings with God, but also affects the relationships between persons and groups, particularly joining together Jews and Gentiles into the one body of Christ (Eph. 2:16). Reconciliation focuses first on the initiative and the definitive action of God, and then on our human response and the ongoing conversion within the community of faith. Finally, Paul envisions the created world in solidarity with sinful humankind, rejoicing in the reconciliatory gift. Paul proclaims that through Jesus "God was pleased to reconcile to himself all things, whether on earth or in heaven, by making peace through the blood of his cross" (Col. 1:20, NRSV).

Paul's theological vision builds on God's dealing with humankind from the very beginning, as the Hebrew Scriptures testify to it. From the creation story in which everything, including man and woman, is created and declared good by God, the Scriptures testify about the movement of these first humans, by their disobedient choice, away from and to alienation from the God, who had intimately walked with them in the garden. The rest of the Hebrew Scriptures consist of a single long narrative of God's continual reaching out to human beings, who consistently choose to do evil and to reject the life and love which God offers. If the Hebrew Scriptures tell us a story of humanity's or our sins, they also relate our human attempt to acknowledge our sins, to make amends, and to expiate the wrongs which we have done. And so, for example, the Mosaic ritual outlines expiatory sacrifices and other rites, such as the wearing of sackcloth and ashes, which give direction to human admission of guilt and to our readiness to receive God's forgiving love.

Jesus' life, death, and resurrection are God's definitive action to offer forgiveness and to establish reconciliation with God forever. No sin is so great as to stand outside the scope of God's forgiveness. No person, regardless of age, sex, ethnic origin, or whatever else divides humanity, is excluded from the reconciliation God offers in Jesus. There is recognition, then, that sin is the breakdown of relationship between God and humanity, a breakdown between us as human persons, a breakdown also between us and our world. Christian faith believes that God in Jesus heals these division and establishes a love union so wonderful that Paul identifies it as making us a new creation (2 Cor. 5:17).

Baptism and Eucharist; Confession and Penance

Granted the need for reconciliation and God's provision of this reconciliation through Jesus, how have we as Christians understood our own entrance into reconciliation with God? Being baptized has always meant the personal receiving of God's reconciling gift. And so we are baptized into Jesus. This primary step establishes the *new creation* relationship between God and baptized individuals. Another major step in reconciliation is the baptized Christian's participation in the Eucharist. Not only do we as Christians remember and enter into the central reconciling act of Jesus' own life, but we also identify with Jesus in Communion and so find ourselves in communion with all the members of the community.

These two major moments in reconciliation, baptism and the Eucharist, are celebratory in that they focus on the restoration of union, of new creation, and of life. But there is another aspect

Chi Rho with Alpha and Omega. The above symbol from the ancient catacombs combines two familiar symbols for Christ—the chi rho and the alpha and omega.

to reconciliation in which the focus is more on the confession of faults or sins that cause the breakdown of the reconciliatory relationship and on the performance of penance to mark the sincerity of our human response to these sins. Fasting, almsgiving, and various acts of penance such as self-inflicted pain have traditionally been a part of a penitent's reconciliation. Admission of guilt, of being a sinner, is an even more central piece. As the early Christian church discovered, certain sins by its members were not only public offenses against God, but they also were disruptive or harmful to the life of the community. The only recourse seemed to be excommunication—a declaration that these persons had cut themselves off from the community of faith by their sinful action. The three most common sins eliciting this response of excommunication were apostasy, adultery, and murder.

The church in its reflection on the words of Jesus about forgiving seventy times seven times slowly came to identify a certain ritual action specifically aimed at the confession of serious sin and at forgiving repentant sinners and receiving them back into the community and its Eucharist. At first, it was a ritual action to be experienced only once in life after baptism. Later development in the church identified the ritual action as one that could be used as often as necessary. The elements of this ritual action remain the same, even if there was some slight change in the ordering of elements in its earliest days. The sacramental elements are the confession of sins; the absolution or forgiveness of sins by the priest minister; and some sort of penance performed to demonstrate a firm purpose of amendment.

Today, the important areas which need to be developed in the theology of reconciliation are threefold. First, we as Christians need to better understand the ecclesial and social nature of reconciliation in its various forms. Second, we need to develop a greater appreciation for creating reconciliation rites as an integral part of ecclesial worship. Finally, we must forge a true union of celebration between an individual's reconciliation and the church's mission of reconciliation.

David L. Fleming

241 ✦ A LITURGY FOR RECONCILIATION

Lent and Advent are the two penitential seasons of the church year. They are times of preparation and waiting. The most important way we as Christians prepare for the coming of the Christ, the one who reconciles us, is to examine ourselves and repent of sin. The following liturgy is set within the context of Advent. By changing the prayers and Scripture readings, it can be suitably modified for other seasons of the year.

─────────── **The Service** ───────────

Opening Hymn

Greeting and Introduction
May the Lord's grace, mercy, and peace be with you.

We need to need Jesus. Reconciliation is the church's attempt to have us all enter into the many centuries of longing in the human heart until the coming of Christ. Too easily we presume Jesus in our Christian lives. We, too, need to know our deep need of his coming in our lives. . . . again and again and again.

Opening Prayer
God of mercy and love, you sent your only Son to redeem us and your Spirit to fill us with life. Touch our minds and hearts with the saving power of your word. Stir up in us our need for Jesus our Savior. Strengthen our desire to seek out and live the way of life to which he calls you. We ask this in Jesus' name. Amen.

First Scripture Reading
Isaiah 6:1-8

Response
Either an appropriate Psalm or a hymn

Second Scripture Reading
Luke 1:39-45

Homily

A Litany of Confession
Let us turn to God and beg his forgiveness.
> For having thought too little about who you are and our need for you:
> **Forgive us, Lord.**
> For not having sought the kind of freedom you offer us:
> **Forgive us, Lord.**
> For reaching out for a salvation only in terms of our own preferences and interests:
> **Forgive us, Lord.**
> For not having noticed people who are sad:
> **Forgive us, Lord.**
> For having so often lacked understanding for others:
> **Forgive us, Lord.**
> For having evaded our calling as Christians:
> **Forgive us, Lord.**
> For having been so full of ourselves and our own wants:
> **Forgive us, Lord.**
> For the absence of peace among us:
> **Forgive us, Lord.**
> For failing to share our life with those who need it:
> **Forgive us, Lord.**
> For retreating from our responsibilities and going our own way:
> **Forgive us, Lord.**
> For having lived with so little confidence in the future which you will give us:
> **Forgive us, Lord.**

Let us pray:
For the fearfulness of our love, for all our sins of selfishness and self-sufficiency, we ask your forgiveness, Lord. May we know this forgiveness which you offer us. May this new heart which you

promise to create in us be felt in our lives and in our community. We ask this in Jesus' name. Amen.

A Confession and Absolution Sign

Proclamation of Praise for God's Mercy (a sung penance)

Final Prayer
O God, you gladden us year after year with the promise of our redemption. Grant, we pray, through the intercession of Mary the mother of Jesus, John the Baptist his herald, and all the holy ones—the women and men who have waited for and proclaimed his coming—that we who now prepare for the Christmas coming of our redeemer may also welcome him without fear when he comes as our judge. We ask this in Jesus' name. Amen.

Final Blessing and Dismissal
May the Lord bless you and keep you. **Amen.**
May he let his face shine upon you and be gracious to you. **Amen.**
May he lift up his countenance to you and give you peace. **Amen.**
May almighty God bless you, the Father and the Son and the Holy Spirit. **Amen.**
Let us go forth in the love and peace of Christ. **Thanks be to God.**

Closing Hymn

Commentary

Opening Hymn. The hymn should be appropriate to the Advent season and should help gather the community in a unified spirit ready for the call to be reconciled. One example might be "O Come, O Come, Emmanuel."

Greeting and Introduction. The greeting and the introduction could be done by the presiding minister. There is also the possibility of another minister introducing the reconciliation theme. The greeting reminds us that it is God who calls and gathers worshipers. The introduction focuses on the particular need of reconciliation at this time. The introduction should attractively invite all present to ready their hearts.

Opening Prayer. Since the introduction has invited the participants to ready their hearts, the presiding minister sums up the prayer in words

that once again help focus their need for forgiveness and their desire for reconciliation.

First Scripture Reading. A lector or another minister proclaims the Word of God. The first reading is taken from any part of the Bible other than the Gospels. Once again, the biblical selection should be appropriate to the focus of the service.

Response. The community is to be actively involved in some form of response to God's Word. The recitation or chanting of a Psalm or the singing of a hymn provides a way of establishing a dialogue between God and the community of faith.

Second Scripture Reading. The second reading is a passage from one of the Gospels; it can be proclaimed by the presiding minister or by another.

Homily. The presiding minister is ordinarily the homilist, allowing the Word of God to be a light in the midst of darkness and a sword which pierces through the human situation. Pastoral advice, exhortation, and guidance make up the homilist's contribution to the participant's lives.

A Litany of Confession. The confessional litany is usually led by a lector or minister other than the presiding one. The litany stimulates a kind of examination of conscience for the individual. At the same time, the litany is an attempt to capture the sense of mutual support of all in the community in the church's task of reconciliation and forgiveness.

A Confession and Absolution Sign. The active participation of the community members is elicited by some sort of movement or gesture. For example, each person could come forward to be sprinkled with cleansing water by the presiding minister, or each could come forward to kiss a cross. There is also the possibility of each penitent's coming forward to the presiding minister and declaring, "I am a sinner. I confess [mentioning one repented sin]." It is important that the presiding minister sum up the effect of the repentant gesture by declaring God's forgiving and welcoming love after all come forward. There is also the possibility that individual absolution can be declared as each comes forward.

Proclamation of Praise for God's Mercy. After the presiding minister has spoken God's mercy on the repentant sinner, the dialogue is once more engaged by means of a hymn or a common prayer of the community. This hymn or prayer should speak of a purpose of amendment and a thanksgiving to God for mercy.

Final Prayer. The presiding minister sums up once again the prayer of the community in its thanks and in its resolution for living the Christian faith with greater fidelity.

Final Blessing and Dismissal. The presiding minister speaks God's blessings on the community members as they individually and as an ecclesial identity enter into their ordinary flow of life.

Closing Hymn. The closing hymn is again appropriate to the season and to the service, e.g., "Wake, Awake, the Night is Dying." The ecclesial identity and the social support of each person of the community for the other are symbolized by the blending of voices in a song of praise to God.

Daniel L. Fleming

242 ♦ GUIDELINES FOR PLANNING A SERVICE OF RECONCILIATION

The service of reconciliation should be planned with the needs of the local worshiping community in mind. The following checklist highlights concerns which should be addressed by worship planners.

(1) A service of reconciliation celebrates redemption, justification, and salvation in which God forgives us seventy times seven through the life, death, and resurrection of Jesus. It is a Christian celebration because, through our faith in Jesus, we as Christians are being reconciled to God and to one another. A service of reconciliation can never be only an individual event, but must somehow encompass both the personal and also the wider ecclesial and social dimensions. As the word reconciliation indicates, the service of reconciliation celebrates a return to harmony after that harmony has in some way been disrupted ("How can we who died to sin go on living in it?" [Rom. 6:2, NRSV]).

(2) A service of reconciliation can focus on:
   (a) the individual, where the disharmony is within oneself;
   (b) the interpersonal, where the disharmony is between and within persons, families, churches, ethnic groups, or nations;
   (c) the cosmic, where the disharmony is between humankind and the world of creation.

(3) The basic elements of a reconciliation service include:
   (a) an introduction, which focuses on the disharmony;
   (b) the proclamation of the Word of God, which confronts the evil and declares God's judgment and mercy;
   (c) the call to forgiveness and healing and the response of the penitent by some sort of confession and sign of amendment;
   (d) the forgiveness being declared;
   (e) the response of praise and thanksgiving.

(4) Partners within the service of reconciliation are:
   (a) the community, which as the whole church and as a priestly people acts in different ways in the work of reconciliation, especially by praying, interceding, supporting, and so on;
   (b) the repentant sinner, who may be any hurting member of the community or even the total ecclesial community seen as a group;
   (c) the presider, the minister, or the confessor, who in the name of the community, though also a sinner, conducts the service for an individual or for a group, by presenting God's Word, calling to repentance, receiving the confession, speaking God's Word of forgiving love, and rejoicing in God's mercy.

David L. Fleming

243 ♦ BIBLIOGRAPHY ON RECONCILIATION

Braswell, Mary. *The Medieval Sinner: Characterization and Confession in the Literature of the Middle Ages.* Cranbury, N. J.: Fairleigh-Dickinson University Press, 1983.

Collins, Mary, and David Power. *The Fate of Confession.* Concilium 198. Edinburgh: T. & T. Clark, 1987.

Cooke, Bernard. *Reconciled Sinners: Healing*

Human Brokenness. Mystic, Conn.: Twenty-Third Publications, 1986.

Crichton, J(ames) D(unlop). *The Ministry of Reconciliation: a Commentary on the Order of Penance 1974.* London: Geoffrey Chapman, 1974.

Dallen, James. *The Reconciling Community: The Rite of Penance.* New York: Pueblo Publishing, 1986.

————. *Removing the Barriers: The Practice of Reconciliation.* Chicago: Liturgy Training Publications, 1991.

Favazza, Joseph A. *The Order of Penitents: Historical Roots and Pastoral Future.* Collegeville, Minn.: Liturgical Press, 1988.

Fink, Peter E. *Alternative Futures for Worship.* Vol. 4, *Reconciliation.* Collegeville, Minn.: Liturgical Press, 1988.

Gula, Richard M. *They Walk Together Again: The Sacrament of Reconciliation.* New York: Paulist Press, 1984.

Hamelin, Leonce. *Reconciliation in the Church: A Theological Pastoral Essay on the Sacrament of Penance.* Collegeville, Minn.: Liturgical Press, 1980.

Halligan, Francis Nicholas. *Sacraments of Reconciliation: Penance, Anointing of the Sick.* Staten Island, N.Y.: Alba House, 1973.

Hellwig, Monika K., ed. *The Message of the Sacraments.* Vol. 4, *Sign of Reconciliation and Conversion: The Sacrament of Penance for Our Times.* Wilmington, Del.: Michael Glazier, 1982.

Jennings, Theodore. *The Liturgy of Liberation: The Confession and Forgiveness of Sins.* Nashville: Abingdon, 1988.

Kennedy, Robert J., ed. *Reconciliation: The Continuing Agenda.* Collegeville, Minn.: Liturgical Press, 1987.

Mick, Lawrence E. *Penance: The Once and Future Sacrament.* Collegeville, Minn.: Liturgical Press, 1988.

Perales, Jorge. "The Service of the Indulgentia: Light on the Rite of General Confession and Absolution." *Worship* 62:2 (March 1988): 138–53.

von Speyr, Adrienne. *Confession.* San Francisco: Ignatius Press, 1982.

Tentler, Thomas N. *Sin and Confession on the Eve of the Reformation.* Princeton, N.J.: Princeton University Press, 1977.

Theisen, Jerome P. *Community and Disunity: Symbols of Grace and Sin.* Collegeville, Minn.: St. John's University Press, 1975.

Consult also these representative reconciliation liturgies:

• For the Episcopal church, see *The Book of Common Prayer* (New York: Church Hymnal Corporation, 1979), 447–52.

• For the Evangelical Lutheran Church in America, see *Lutheran Book of Worship* (Minneapolis: Augsburg; Philadelphia: Board of Publication, Lutheran Church in America, 1982), 193–97.

• For the Lutheran Church–Missouri Synod, see *Lutheran Worship—Agenda* (St. Louis: Concordia, 1984), 137–44.

• For a Presbyterian order, see *The Book of Common Worship* (Louisville: Westminster/John Knox, 1993), 905–47, 1005–1022.

• For the Roman Catholic church, see *The Rites,* vol. 2 (New York: Pueblo Publishing, 1980).

• For the United Church of Christ, see *Book of Worship: United Church of Christ* (New York: Office of Church Life, 1986), 268–322.

SEVENTEEN

Anointing of the Sick

Anointing with oil is an act of trust and dependence on God. Throughout the history of the church, anointing has been used at a variety of occasions including confirmation and ordination. But the most frequent use of anointing with oil has been reserved for the anointing of the sick. When the sick person is anointed in the presence of the worshiping community, the whole community declares that it places its trust on God alone for healing. The following articles describe the history and theology of this action, as well as provide a liturgy to accompany it. In these articles, note the significance of the scriptural references to anointing.

244 • HISTORICAL ORIGINS AND DEVELOPMENT OF ANOINTING THE SICK WITH OIL

Anointing with oil is one of the oldest human rituals. It is frequently mentioned in Scripture and played an important role in the life of the early church. This article traces the history of this sacred action, concentrating on the ancient and medieval periods.

Ancient peoples used olive oil in several ways. Shepherds poured it on the scratched and wounded heads of sheep entering the fold at eventide (Ps. 23:5). Kings, prophets, and priests were anointed as a consecration to their sacred tasks. In the Scriptures, Aaron and his sons are anointed at the initiation of the Levitical priesthood (Lev. 8:30); both Saul and David are anointed to their kingships (1 Sam. 10:1; for Saul; and 1 Sam.16:13; 2 Sam. 2:4; 5:3; for David); and Elijah was instructed to anoint Elisha as a prophet (1 Kings 19:16). Both men (2 Sam. 12:20) and women (Ruth 3:3) employed oil as a cosmetic. It appears that a good host was expected to pour oil on the heads of his guests as a courtesy. Jesus administers a rebuke to the Pharisee who fails to anoint his head when he goes to dine in that man's home (Luke 7:44-46).

Anointing for Healing

By New Testament times the medicinal use of oil was common. Jesus tells the story of a Samari-tan who finds a robbery victim left for dead along the roadside and pours wine and oil on his wounds (Luke 10:33-34). The wine was probably used for disinfecting, and the oil as a healing agent.

It is not clear when anointing with oil began to be practiced for affecting supernatural healing. The Gospel writers do not record any instance in which Jesus used oil for this purpose; although in one case, he applied a mud plaster (John 9:6). Mark's gospel states, however, that Jesus' disciples were to anoint sick persons with oil for healing when they went out to proclaim the appearance of the kingdom of God (Mark 6:13).

In the first century, anointing with oil was clearly associated with prayer for healing. Referring to a practice with which his readers were obviously familiar, James directs that persons afflicted with illness call for the church elders to pray for them and anoint them with oil (James 5:14), adding that the sick person will be raised up and his sins forgiven through these actions (v. 15).

Early Christian writings contain accounts of both exorcisms and healings of persons, who were deformed, paralyzed, and afflicted with illnesses which were not imminently fatal, as a result of anointing with oil and prayer. Although the James passage is not specifically cited in these accounts, it is reasonable to assume that this passage provides the background for them.

Rituals of Anointing

Historically, the church has differentiated between anointing as a liturgical act and the gift of healing mentioned by Paul in his first letter to the Corinthians (1 Cor. 12:9, 28, 30). In his *Liber de praescriptionibus*, Tertullian condemns the heretical practice of allowing women to teach, cast out evil spirits, and promise healing (chap. 41 [PL 2:69]). Since Tertullian would have understood that the gift of healing as given by God and, thus, not regulated by the church, his polemic must have been directed specifically against the institutional practice of healing by the laity.

By the beginning of the third century, the blessing of oil for use in healing rituals had become an established Christian custom. A reference in the *Apostolic Tradition* of Hippolytus contains a prayer to be used in the Mass in which God is requested to imbue the oil with healing power. Hippolytus does not specify whether people applied the oil to themselves, ingested it, or were anointed by a religious official. In the *Sacramentary of Serapion,* there are prayers to be said over both oil for anointing and water to be consumed for the healing of illness and casting out of demons (*De visitatione infirmorum* 2:4). A similar prayer for consecrating both oil and water is found in the *Testamentum Domini nostri Jesu Christi*. No liturgy can be found for applying the oil or drinking the water. This absence may indicate that the efficacy was thought to be in the elements themselves. Thus, they could be administered by the common people as well as by clerics.

Although directions are given for praying over the sick, there is no direct reference in the third- and fourth-century *Canons of Hippolytus* to anointing with oil. An allusion to anointing can be inferred, however, from a mention in canon 222 of preparing vases for the sick (see L. Duchesne, *Origins of Christian Worship* [1904], 537–39); it is possible that these were vases of anointing oil.

The Council of Laodicea (A.D. 367) provided for the anointing of repentant heretics in order that they might be received back into the fellowship of the church. This practice is not linked with James' instruction and is apparently not derived from his epistle.

From the fifth to the eighth century, anointing with oil was commonly used for both healing and exorcism. Some documents from this period specifically relate anointing to the forgiveness of sin.

It appears that the oil had to be blessed by the bishop in order to be considered effective, but the act of anointing was often carried out by the lay people. Although no instructions are given for the method of anointing, it was usually accompanied by prayer or invoking the name of the Lord. Sometimes the oil was applied to the afflicted person; sometimes he or she merely touched it; and on some occasions it was consumed as a drink.

In both the Eastern and Western church, anointing for healing was widely practiced from the eighth century to the Middle Ages. However, during this period it began to be viewed as preparation for death, rather than being primarily a means of healing. Subsequently, anointing was usually accompanied by the sacraments of penance and/or Communion. The many liturgies that developed for such anointings frequently required the reading of a psalm or litany or the recitation of the Lord's Prayer; some required the laying on of hands. In addition to the shift in emphasis, a change took place in laws regulating its administration. All of this period's documents that are available indicate that only the priests were allowed to perform what was now considered to be a sacrament of the church.

Sacramental Practice

The theology of anointing for extreme unction, which began with liturgical reform under Charlemagne, became formalized during the Middle Ages. The emphasis of this sacrament was on forgiveness of sin. Many instructions were written on the way this sacrament was to be administered. These instructions allow for the possibility that physical healing may take place as a result of this sacrament, since the removal of sin would necessarily have a beneficial effect on the body. However, spiritual healing was of primary concern, since the sacrament was performed only in extreme cases when death was probable.

The emphasis on anointing for extreme unction rather than for physical healing is still apparent in the Roman Catholic church. Indeed, its official interpretation of James' instructions for anointing and prayer for healing is that they refer to preparation for death. Since this anointing is considered to be a sacrament, the church allows only ordained priests to administer it.

Many Protestant churches which do not anoint *in extremis* practice anointing for healing in accordance with James 5:14-15. Anointing is a regular occurrence in churches of the Pentecostal and charismatic traditions, which believe in supernatural healings as a gift of the Holy Spirit.

Janice E. Leonard

245 • THE DEVELOPMENT OF ANOINTING IN THE MODERN CHURCH

This article traces the history of anointing since the Protestant Reformation in the sixteenth century. Note how each development in the history of anointing was based on larger theological discussions.

The Protestant Reformers of the sixteenth century envisioned the purification and renewal of medieval European Christianity according to the doctrinal and experiential norms, which they saw contained in the Scriptures and the first five centuries of early Christian tradition. Remarkably, however, for all the profound theological, ecclesiastical, and societal change brought about by the Reformation, the ancient Christian rite of anointing for healing received little positive attention from leading Protestant thinkers. They rejected the Catholic sacrament of the extreme unction as unbiblical and ,for the most part, consigned supernatural _gifts of healing_ to the apostolic age. While Rome was accused of misinterpreting James 5:14-15, no correct Protestant exposition of the text was set forth. Trying to remedy the problem of misuse with non-use, the Reformers replaced the service of extreme unction with a service for the visitation of the sick. The Anglican _Book of Common Prayer,_ which shaped all the Reformed churches, denied the sick person both anointing and the laying on of hands. Luther did, however, appear to recognize James 5 as a prescription to be followed in praying for the physically ill and mentally disturbed, though he did not sanction the practice as a sacrament.

The emergence of post-Reformation, nonconformist, sectarian religious movements in England, on the European continent, and in North America during the seventeenth and eighteenth centuries was accompanied by a revival of anointing with oil in association with healing prayer. Early English and American Baptists practiced the rite, recounting their success, especially in cases of mental illness. The German Baptist Brethren (also called Dunkers), who originated in the early eighteenth century and later emigrated to Pennsylvania, reinstituted anointing with oil and prayer for healing as one of several New Testament practices they claimed a divine, scriptural call to recover. Modeling themselves after their Anabaptist Swiss Brethren forbearers, nineteenth-century Old Order Mennonites, who settled mostly in Pennsylvania, also observed the rite of anointing the sick. Later Mennonite groups, such as the Mennonite Brethren in Christ, followed the same tradition of anointing with oil.

Though eighteenth-century evangelical awakenings in England and America were characterized by miraculous healings, the practice of anointing per se received minimal attention. John Wesley acknowledged that the practice had been lost to the church due to unbelief, but at the same time, showed little effort to recover and integrate it with his ministry of healing prayer. Ironically, few of the groups which grew out of the First Great Awakening, most notably the Methodists, showed much sustained interest in either healing prayer or anointing with oil.

The Second Awakening of the early nineteenth century bore more lasting results regarding the restoration of anointing for healing. Many of the denominations of Wesleyan persuasion, which were derived from the camp meeting movement on the American frontiers, continue to teach and practice to some degree the anointing of the sick: the Wesleyan Church, the Free Methodist Church, the Church of the Nazarene, and the Church of God (Anderson, Indiana).

The practice of unction for healing assumed new importance toward the close of the nineteenth century as a trans-Atlantic, interdenominational holiness and healing movement gained momentum in England and America. Captain R. Kelso Carter, who authored an early manifesto for the holiness/healing movement entitled _The Atonement for Sin and Sickness_ (1884) continued to practice anointing the sick with oil, even after subsequently publishing some retractions of his earlier radical views on healing. The Bethshan International Conference on Divine Healing and True Holiness, which convened in London in 1885, featured a special public anointing service as part of its week-long series of meetings. Prominent clergymen of varying denominational backgrounds who espoused a holiness/healing spirituality also endorsed healing prayer with the anointing of oil. Dr. A. J. Gordon, the prominent Baptist pastor in Boston, Dr. A. B. Simpson, founder of the Christian and Missionary Alliance, and Andrew Murray, the well-known South African theologian, all wrote widely disseminated books on healing which highlighted the practice of anointing. R. A. Torrey, the famed American lawyer turned revivalist, wrote in the same vein at the turn of the twentieth century. The present Statement of Faith of the Alliance Church, which was founded by A. B. Simpson, represents one of the earliest formal evangelical recommendations of "prayer for the sick and anointing with oil as . . . privileges for the church in this present age" (art. 8).

The advent of Pentecostalism with its Holiness roots at the outset of the twentieth century spawned a new worldwide family of Pentecostal denominations that affirmed the doctrine of healing through prayer, symbolized in anointing with oil. Some of these churches, such as the Elim Pentecostal Churches of Britain, even enshrined the rite of anointing for healing as an ordinance alongside baptism and the Lord's Supper. The James 5 liturgy of healing prayer and anointing with oil became standard fare in various Pentecostal denominations around the world, thus raising the profile of the rite in modern Christendom.

Though not as influential as in Pentecostalism, twentieth-century developments within historic denominations regarding the rite of anointing are also noteworthy. In 1905, Emmanuel Church, an established congregation in Boston, witnessed an attempted synthesis of counseling, anointing, and prayer by several physicians and psychiatrists. Other organizations followed suit. Simultaneously, the Guild of Health was founded in Britain, inspiring healing practices primarily among Anglican and Episcopalian churches.

In the United States, the Order of the Nazarene (1910) was established in Boston by Reverend Henry Wilson with a similar agenda in mind. Other organizations followed. The Order of Saint Luke, the Physician (established in 1947), which had its beginnings in 1929 with the ministry of Dr. John Gayner Banks; Camps Farthest Out (c. 1930), established by Glenn Clarke; and the Sanford Schools of Pastoral Care (1955), associated with the healing ministry of Agnes Sanford, all sought to promote anointing with oil and prayer for the sick within traditional denominations.

At the ecclesiastical level, the twentieth century has seen the reintroduction of unction and laying on of hands into the mainstream of the church's life. Both the 1928 revised edition of *The Book of Common Prayer* of the American Episcopal Church and the Scottish Episcopal Prayer Book (1929) included a service of unction. Also, the 1962 revised Prayer Book of the Anglican Churches of Canada contains an anointing service with prayers for the healing of the whole person. During the 1950s and 1960s official studies of sacramental healing were undertaken in the denominations of the American Episcopals, the Presbyterians, and the Lutherans, including also the United Church of Canada and the Church of England. Paralleling these developments in Protestantism, the Second Vatican Council in 1962 prepared the ground in Roman Catholicism for the creation of a "continuous rite" of anointing for the sick, complementing the sacrament of the extreme unction administered immediately prior to death.

The widespread circulation of healing spirituality during the past twenty years, generated by a proliferation of renewal movements and healing ministries of differing orientations, has served to raise transdenominational consciousness as to the necessary and legitimate place of unction for healing within the life and ministry of the church. As a result, even churches with no liturgical tradition of a healing rite have seen fit to develop healing services which include healing prayer in conjunction with the anointing with oil and the laying on of hands.

Charles Nienkirchen

246 • A Theology of Anointing with Oil

Anointing with oil is action frequently mentioned in Scripture. This article traces these references and explains the theological significance of the image of ritual anointing that these passages establish.

The Source of Sickness

Biblical writers have always presupposed a connection between sickness and sin. At the initiation of the covenant, Yahweh promises Israel that if they will obey the terms of the covenant Yahweh will not bring upon them the illnesses brought upon Egypt (Exod. 15:26; Deut. 7:15). This statement reflects ancient covenant structure in which curses of various kinds, including physical ailments, are the result of violation of the covenant stipulations, whereas blessings of good health and prosperity will accompany compliance.

The Old Testament is filled with references to God's punishment upon disobedient people in the form of plague and illness. As the great King of the covenant, source of all blessings and cursings, Yahweh maintained sovereignty over every facet of life including sickness, healing, and death. Both Abraham and Isaac petitioned the Lord to open the wombs of their barren wives (Gen. 15:2-3; 25:21). Hezekiah prayed that his life would be spared and he would be healed (2 Kings 20:1-3). David fasted and prayed for the life of his newborn son (2 Sam. 12:15-17). In addition, the prophets both healed the sick and raised the dead through the power of the Lord.

Anointing as Consecration

Anointing with oil is not mentioned in connection with healing in the Old Testament but it is used extensively in acts of consecration. Aaron and his sons were set apart for the priesthood (Exod. 29:21), and the entire tabernacle consecrated for the service of the Lord with a sprinkling of special holy oil (30:26). The kings of Israel had oil poured over their heads to signify their having been chosen by the Lord for the monarchy (1 Sam. 10:1; 16:13). Even prophets were sometimes anointed for their special function as spokesmen for Yahweh and the covenant (1 Kings 19:16).

Although the physical act of anointing is performed by a designated person, it derives its significance from the idea that the Lord is the one who ultimately anoints. Religious leaders are often referred to as "the anointed of the Lord" (1 Sam. 12:3; 24:6). A psalm addressed to the king contains the phrase, "God, your God, has set you above your companions by anointing you with the oil of joy" (Ps. 45:7), and another quotes Yahweh as saying of David, "With my sacred oil I have anointed him" (Ps. 89:20). An unnamed psalmist exults at the great acts of God, singing, "Thou hast exalted my horn like that of the wild ox; I have been anointed with fresh oil" (Ps. 92:10, NASB).

Parallelism in this verse suggests that the singer equates victory over enemies with God's favor as typified in God's anointing.

Jesus as God's Anointed

The writer of Hebrews interprets Psalm 45 as a reference to Jesus (Heb. 1:8-9), thereby identifying him as the Lord's anointed, *par excellence*. John records this anointing in his record of Jesus' baptism, during which the Holy Spirit descended in the form of a dove and remained on Jesus (John 1:32). In Matthew's gospel Jesus is the servant prophesied by Isaiah who is anointed with the Holy Spirit (Matt. 12:18; Isa. 42:1-4); Luke records Jesus' own testimony that he fulfills a similar prophecy from Isaiah 61:1 (Luke 4:18-19). Peter says that God has made Jesus "both Lord and Christ" (Acts 2:36). *Christ* is the Greek equivalent of the Hebrew *Messiah,* meaning "anointed one," and that Jesus is now the source of anointing with the Holy Spirit for all who believe in him (v. 38). In the New Testament, then, the anointing with the Holy Spirit seems to have taken the place of a literal anointing with oil for those commissioned by the Lord.

Healing in the New Testament

Jesus' appearance as the embodiment of the new covenant is accompanied by miracles or healing, a sign of God's blessing and presence among God's people. These miracles are a fulfillment of the ministry for which he is anointed (Matt. 11:3-5). Although the record does not show that Jesus himself used oil in this connection, his disciples, in carrying out his commission to announce the kingdom of God, anointed with oil when they healed the sick (Mark 6:13).

During the first century, the practice of anointing for healing apparently became established in the Christian church. James recommends it in his epistle (James 5:14) without going into detail about the way in which it was to be performed. This reference suggests that James' readers were familiar with the practice of anointing for healing—it was not new or different.

Oil as a Type of the Holy Spirit

From the references cited above, it seems clear that the oil of anointing is a type of the Holy Spirit. This is indisputably true in the case of anointings for consecration, and can be assumed when anointing is done for physical or spiritual healing.

The use of a symbol for the Holy Spirit emphasizes the healer's awareness that he or she is not the possessor of healing power; rather, it is only when the Holy Spirit is mediated to the afflicted individual that healing can take place. Applying oil for healing appears to have a meaning similar to that of invoking the name of Jesus when praying for the sick. The healer is acting as an agent for the Lord, affecting healing by Christ's authority or in Christ's name. Thus James instructs the elders to anoint with oil in the name of the Lord.

Within the confines of Trinitarian theology, a person might wonder whether it is the Holy Spirit or Jesus Christ who is the healer. A distinction between the two is not made in Scripture. In Hebrew, the word for spirit is *ruah* and its Greek equivalent is *pneuma*; both words can also be translated "wind" or "breath." The Holy Spirit is the holy wind or breath; it is equivalent to the Word of God. David sings:

> By the word of the LORD were the heavens made,
> their starry host by the breath of his mouth.
> (Ps. 33:6)

If Jesus is the Word of God (John 1:1), he is one with the breath or Spirit of God. Indeed, the Spirit is known as "the Spirit of the Lord" (Luke 4:18) and the "Spirit of Christ" (Rom. 8:9; 1 Pet. 1:11), as well as "the Spirit of God" (Eph. 4:30). Paul says that the Lord *is* the Spirit (2 Cor. 3:17). Supernatural healing is one of the gifts of the Holy Spirit listed by Paul (1 Cor. 12:9, 28, 30).

Conclusion

There is no clear indication of the origin of anointing with oil for healing, although anointing for consecration and commissioning is known from Old Testament times. Both Old and New Testaments make a connection between anointing with oil and the power and presence of the Holy Spirit of God. Thus, one can say that oil becomes a type of the Holy Spirit and the breath of Christ. When oil is applied to an individual and combined with prayer, it releases the power of the healing Christ on behalf of the sufferer. Hence healing is carried out in the name of Jesus through the power of the Holy Spirit which become one and the same.

Janice E. Leonard

247 • A Liturgy for Anointing of the Sick

This service allows for a local congregation to focus on the needs of its members who may be suffering physically, emotionally, or spiritually. The outline of the service follows a traditional order of service, with entrance, proclamation, confession and assurance, and prayers. Following the prayers, members of the congregation are given the opportunity to receive anointing with oil or the laying on of hands. These acts are powerful symbols of God's presence with the people of God. In the face of adversity, the service of anointing gives opportunity for a bold declaration of faith and trust in God, for a recalling of God's promises, and for communal prayers for the suffering.

The Service

ENTRANCE

Greeting
LEADER: The grace of our Lord Jesus Christ and the love of God and the communion of the Holy Spirit be with you all.

PEOPLE: **Amen.**

Opening Sentence
LEADER: The apostle Paul said, "Do not conform yourselves to the standards of this world, but let God transform you inwardly by a complete change of your mind."

Hymn

SERVICE OF PROCLAMATION

Scripture Readings
Old Testament Reading: Genesis 1:26-31 or 2 Kings 5:1, 8-15; Psalms 20; 23; 91; 103; 145:13-21

New Testament Epistle: Acts 3:1-10; Hebrews 12:1, 2; James 5:13-16; 1 John 1:5–2:2; 5:13-15

New Testament Gospels: Matthew 8:1-17; 9:2-8; Mark 6:7-13; 10:46-52; Luke 17:11-19; John 9:1-22

Sermon

SERVICE OF RECONCILIATION

Call to Confession
LEADER: Jesus said, "Ask, and it will be given; seek, and you will find; knock, and it will be opened to you."

PEOPLE: **For everyone who asks receives, and those who seek find, and to each who knocks it will be opened.**

LEADER: Friends in Christ, God knows our needs before we ask and in our asking prepares us to receive the gift of grace. Let us open our lives to God's healing presence and forsake all that separates us from God and neighbor. Let us be mindful both of our personal sin and of our communal sins of family, class, race, and nation.

Confession

Silent Personal Prayers, followed by:

LEADER: Let us confess our sins together.

PEOPLE: **(Ps. 51:1-12)**

Assurance of Pardon

LEADER: If we confess our sins, God is faithful and just and will forgive our sins and cleanse us from all unrighteousness. Brothers and sisters, in Jesus Christ, we are forgiven.

PEOPLE: **Thanks be to God!**

SERVICE OF PRAYER

Intercessory Prayers

The Lord's Prayer

SERVICE OF ANOINTING (or laying on of hands)

Thanksgiving over the Oil (not used in a service of laying on of hands)

LEADER: O God, our Redeemer, giver of health and salvation, we give you thanks for the gift of oil, used by prophets and apostles as a sign of your grace and favor. Send your Spirit now, we pray, that those who receive this anointing in repentance and faith may be made well in accordance with your will; through Jesus Christ, our Lord. Amen.

Invitation

LEADER: Those who desire to be anointed (or to receive the laying on of hands) now come forward. During this time, may we all be united in prayer for those seeking God's healing.

Act of Anointing

Unction. Unction is symbolized by the vessel which holds the oil for anointing.

LEADER: (spoken to each who is anointed) [Name], as I anoint you, so may God grant you the powerful presence of the Holy Spirit. With infinite mercy, may God forgive your sins, release you from suffering, and restore you to health and strength. May God deliver you from all evil, preserve you in all goodness, and bring you to everlasting life; through Jesus Christ our Savior. Amen.

[or] Laying on of Hands

LEADER: (spoken to each upon whom hands are laid) [Name], we lay our hands on you in the name of our Lord and Savior Jesus Christ. May God grant you the powerful presence of the Holy Spirit, forgiving your sin, releasing you from suffering, and restoring you to health. May God deliver you from all evil, preserve you in all goodness, and bring you to everlasting life; through Jesus Christ our Savior. Amen.

Prayer of Thanksgiving

LEADER: Let us pray.

PEOPLE: **We give praise and thanks to you, O God! In Jesus Christ, you have given us life; brought ministry, forgiveness, healing, and peace; commanded the disciples to heal the sick; and continued the healing ministry among us to this day. Keep us mindful of your love and mercy that we may be faithful throughout all our days. We pray in the name of Jesus Christ, our Lord. Amen.**

SERVICE OF HOLY COMMUNION

SERVICE OF DISMISSAL

Charge

LEADER: Go in peace to love and serve God.

Hymn

Benediction

LEADER: May God bless you and keep you. May God's face shine upon you and be gracious to you. May God look upon you with kindness and give you peace.

PEOPLE: **Amen.**

Adapted from The Book of Worship[13]

——————— Commentary ———————

The act of anointing has a rich history in the Christian faith. In the Old Testament, anointings frequently accompanied blessings and ceremonies which indicated a passing of royal power. The New Testament also refers to anointing. The title *Christ* itself means "the anointed one"; Christians are those who share in Christ's anointing. In addition, a specific occasion for anointing is described explicitly in James 5:14-16:

> Is any one of you sick? He should call on the elders of the church to pray over him and anoint him with oil in the name of the Lord. And the prayer offered in faith will make the sick person well; the Lord will raise him up. If he has sinned; he will be forgiven. Therefore confess your sins to each other and pray for each other so that you may be healed. The prayer of a righteous man is powerful and effective.

This passage mentions several important acts which should be present in a service of healing: prayers of petition, anointing with oil, and confession of sin. Each of these are acts of humility, that place reliance not on self, but on God. They are also acts of faith, which do not doubt the power of God to affect healing. Finally, they are able to be communal acts, offered within the context of a community of faith.

Worship planners and church leaders should introduce such services of anointing with care, especially to congregations not accustomed to this practice. First, this clear scriptural directive in James should be noted and explained. In addition, the relationship of this act to the sacraments should be explained. In most church traditions, anointing is not a sacrament, even though it uses a physical element to demonstrate or symbolize a spiritual reality. The exact nature of this relationship will depend upon the sacramental theology of a given church. Finally, the nature of the service should be explained to the congregation, including a description of basic outline of the liturgy, an indication of those for whom the anointing is intended, and a description of the way in which the anointing will take place.

——————— Suggestions for Planning ———————

The needs of those who will be anointed may be communicated to the congregation prior to the service so that all may be in prayer for them.

All of the elders or similar office-bearers of the congregation may be involved in the act of anointing or laying on of hands.

Olive oil is traditionally used in anointing. It may be placed in a small bowl prior to the service or poured from a small flask or pitcher into a bowl just prior to the prayer of thanksgiving for the oil.

The service of anointing should proceed at a careful pace, allowing for periods of silent prayer and reflection.

The reading from James 5 should be included in all services of anointing.

During the anointing, the congregation may offer silent prayer or join in singing a hymn or petition for God's healing presence. Alternatively, psalms may be read or sung, by a solo reader or by a cantor or by a choir. The psalms listed in the service of proclamation are all appropriate for use at this point.

Following the anointing, the worship leader

may offer a prayer of petition on behalf of those sick and suffering who were not able to be present for the service.

A hymn of trust may follow the anointing, such as "There is a Balm in Gilead," "How Firm a Foundation," or "Come, Ye Disconsolate."

Commentary by John D. Witvliet

248 • GUIDELINES FOR PLANNING AN ANOINTING SERVICE

The following guidelines provide liturgical and pastoral rationale for planning an anointing service.

Anointing with oil for healing is usually done in the context of worship, although it can take place in any appropriate setting. At a given point in the service the minister may invite all those in need of healing to come to the altar or another designated area. The congregation may continue to sing songs of worship led by the chief musician or minister of music during the anointing service.

Usually a minister or an elder of the church will approach the person for whom the minister is to pray and ask the nature of the complaint. He or she may then apply olive oil to an index finger from a small bottle or flask and touch it to the sufferer's forehead, sometimes marking it in the shape of the cross. The minister or elder then places one or both hands on the person's head, or on the afflicted areas of the body where proper or appropriate to do so, and prays for healing from the specific ailment in the name of Jesus. The prayer might be as follows:

In the name of Jesus, I speak (or command) healing for this (brother/sister) from (the sickness). I ask that all symptoms of this ailment be removed, never to return. Be healed in the name of Jesus!

If the officiant has reason to believe the problem to be of demonic origin, the officiant will ask the candidate for healing to renounce all association with the occult in Jesus' name. The person may say:

By the power of the name of Jesus, I (complete name), renounce all occult activity in which I may have engaged. I turn my back on Satan and accept deliverance in Jesus' name.

The officiant might then pray in the following manner:

Spirit of infirmity (or name of illness), I command you in the name of Jesus Christ to come out of (him/her) and never to return. Satan, you have no authority over this child of God; you were defeated at the cross. Come out in the name of Jesus.

It is common in churches which practice the gifts of the Holy Spirit for those being prayed for to fall backward to the floor following the prayer, where they might lie for several minutes. This phenomenon is known variously as falling under the power or being slain in the Spirit. Such churches usually have people ready to catch those being anointed and lower them to the floor to break their fall and prevent injury.

When the anointing for healing takes place in a home or other private setting, the same procedure can be followed. If olive oil is not available, vegetable or mineral oil can be substituted.

Janice E. Leonard

249 • BIBLIOGRAPHY ON THE ANOINTING OF THE SICK

Buchanan, Colin Oglivie. _Liturgy for the Sick: The New Church of England Services._ Nottingham, England: Grove Books, 1983.

Empereur, James L., S.J. _The Message of the Sacraments._ Vol. 7, _Prophetic Anointing: God's Call to the Sick, the Elderly, and the Dying._ Wilmington, Del.: Michael Glazier, 1982.

Fink, Peter E. _Alternative Futures for Worship._ Vol. 7, _Anointing of the Sick._ Collegeville, Minn.: Liturgical Press, 1988.

Frost, Evelyn. _Christian Healing: A Consideration of the Place of Spiritual Healing in the Church of Today in Light of the Doctrine and Practice of the Ante-Nicene Church._ London: Mowbray, 1954.

Gusmer, Charles W. _And You Visited Me: Sacramental Ministry to the Sick and Dying._ New York: Pueblo Publishing, 1984.

———. _The Ministry of Healing in the Church of England: An Ecumenical and Liturgical Study._ Great Wakering, England: Mayhew-McCrimmon, 1974.

Halligan, Francis Nicholas. *Sacraments of Reconciliation: Penance, Anointing of the Sick.* Staten Island, N.Y.: Alba House, 1973.

Israel, Martin. *Healing as Sacrament.* London: Darton, Longman, and Todd, 1985.

Kelsey, Morton T. *Healing and Christianity in Ancient Thought and Modern Times.* New York: Harper and Row, 1973.

Knauber, Adolf. *Pastoral Theology of the Anointing of the Sick.* Collegeville, Minn.: Liturgical Press, 1975.

Poloma, Margaret M. *The Assemblies of God at the Crossroads: Charisma and Institutional Dilemmas.* Knoxville: University of Tennessee Press, 1989. See especially chapter 4: "Divine Healing in the Pentecostal Experience."

Puller, Frederick William. *The Anointing of the Sick in Scripture and Tradition.* London: SPCK, 1904.

Rahner, Karl. *The Anointing of the Sick.* Denville, N.J.: Dimension Books, 1970.

Richards, John. *The Question of Healing Services.* London: Daybreak, 1989.

Representative liturgies for services of healing include:

- For the Episcopal church, see *The Book of Common Prayer* (New York: Church Hymnal Corporation, 1979), 453–461.

- For the Evangelical Lutheran Church in America, see *Occasional Services* (Minneapolis: Augsburg; Philadelphia: Board of Publication, Lutheran Church in America, 1982), 89–102.

- For the Lutheran Church–Missouri Synod, see *Lutheran Worship—Agenda* (St. Louis: Concordia, 1984), 145–53.

- For the Methodist church, see *The United Methodist Book of Worship* (Nashville: United Methodist Publishing House, 1992), 613–30.

- For the Roman Catholic church, see *The Rites,* vol. 2 (New York: Pueblo Publishing, 1980).

- For the United Church of Christ, see *Book of Worship: United Church of Christ* (New York: Office of Church Life, 1986), 296–320.

✦ EIGHTEEN ✦

Footwashing

A connection between footwashing and the Lord's Supper has survived both in the liturgical church's Maundy Thursday rites and in the regular Communion practices of many smaller denominations that understand its practice as a form of literal obedience to the New Testament. It has always been understood as a statement of humility and loving service to one's neighbor.

250 ✦ HISTORICAL ORIGINS AND DEVELOPMENT OF FOOTWASHING

At the Last Supper Jesus gave special meaning to an ordinary custom of the Mediterranean world. Associated with the Lord's Supper and with baptismal rites in the early church, footwashing survived as part of the bishop's Maundy Thursday ritual, as a regular practice in monasteries, and as part of court ceremonial. At the same time, based on John 13, medieval and Reformation sects retained footwashing as a regular part of the Communion liturgy.

From Mediterranean Custom to Monastic and Royal Ceremony

Although practiced by more than one hundred denominations in North America, liturgical footwashing—"the sacrament that almost made it"—remains an enigma to many modern religious persons. Even among practitioners, who are chronologically and usually geographically removed from first-century Palestinian culture, the ritual's meaning is polyvalent.

The bodily practice of washing another person's feet has its origins in an Eastern custom of hospitality and was practiced throughout much of the ancient world. On dusty roads in warm, oriental climates, travelers' sandal-clad feet quickly became dirty, so many hosts provided bathing basins for their arriving guests. Hospitality was emphasized when the hosts personally washed their guests' feet, or had their servants perform the act. Mediterranean physicians also sometimes washed and massaged the feet of ill persons before applying restorative oils. Cleanliness was thought necessary to avoid such diseases as leprosy, and—as is often the case—what personal health demands, religion readily sanctions. Hebrew Scriptures speak of this original practice of sanitary self-cleansing (e.g., Gen. 18:4; 19:2; 24:32; Judg. 19:21) and of the washing by a host (1 Sam. 25:41), as well as of the religious requirement of ritual footwashing for priests (Exod. 30:18-21; 40:30-32; 2 Chron. 4:6).

Three references to footwashing can be found in canonized Christian writings of the first century. One reference is in Luke 7:36-50, the story of the delinquent host and the gracious woman. A second is in 1 Timothy 5:9-10, where footwashing is a qualification for a widow's enrollment into the care of the church—she must have "washed the feet of the saints, relieved the afflicted and devoted herself to doing good in every way."

The third and most important reference in canonical Christian Scriptures is John 13:1-20, where after the Supper, Jesus washes the feet of his disciples, instructing them to follow his example and wash each other's feet. In the Hellenistic world, the unpleasant task of washing feet often was performed by slaves, so Jesus' reported act would be have considered extraordinary. Footwashing practitioners sometimes refer to this fourth gospel pericope as the institution of footwashing as a church sacrament or ordinance. In any event, most scholars agree that, based on the 1 Timothy and the John passages, footwashing was practiced at least in Ephesus and in the

The Washing of Feet. The washing of feet is often portrayed by a clay water vessel and a towel draped at its side.

Johnannine community of the first century.

Several second- and third-century church Fathers, including Irenaeus (fl. 180), Clement of Rome, Cyprian (d. 258), Clement of Alexandria (d. *c.* 215), and Tertullian (d. *c.* 220), imply that the liturgical practice of footwashing was practiced in their time. Athanasius (d. 373) charges bishops to wash the feet of weak priests three times a year—at Easter, Pentecost, and Epiphany.

Ambrose (d. 397) makes it evident that the practice was used as a postbaptismal ceremony in some areas. While not practiced in the church at Rome, some bishops and clergy washed neophytes' feet in Ambrose's time, especially in Turin, Gaul, North Africa, and possibly Syria. "I am simply recommending our own rite," says Ambrose about footwashing. "I wish to follow the Roman Church in everything: but we too are not devoid of common sense." Other church Fathers indicating some ritual footwashing include Augustine (d. 430) and John Chrysostom (d. 407).

The forty-eighth canon of the Synod of Elvira (306) in Spain forbids the practice of footwashing following baptism, so apparently the rite had been practiced in some places there. Ironically, bishops at the seventeenth Synod of Toledo (694) in Spain said "washing the feet at the feast of *Coena Domini* which has fallen into disuse in some places must be observed everywhere."

By the ninth century, postbaptismal footwashing was virtually extinct, but the ritual took on new life in medieval monasteries. Benedict's Rule (sixth century) made provision for regular liturgical footwashing as a mark of humility, as well as for hospitable footwashing for visitors. That Bernard of Clairvaux (1090–1153) recommended the practice is evident in one of his sermons to monastics.

Apart from its regular liturgical role in monastic life, footwashing became a part of ecclesiastical and secular court ritual during the Middle Ages. It was employed at coronations of kings and emperors and installations of popes and other leaders. In these ceremonies, the one about to be crowned or installed publicly washed the feet of twelve old, usually poor, lay persons or priests as a sign of humility. In the church and in the courts, it also became associated with Maundy Thursday observances celebrated by leaders washing the feet of those of lower status.

Survival as a Sectarian Communion Ritual

Medieval sectarian groups preserved the link between footwashing and the Lord's Supper, undoubtedly in part because of their focus on following the New Testament practice literally (John 13). The Albigenses and Waldenses, eleventh- and twelfth-century sects in southern France, Italy, and elsewhere, conducted footwashing ceremonies. The former group practiced footwashing following the Lord's Supper as a response to Jesus' example. Itinerant preachers among the Waldenses washed each other's feet upon arrival at congregations as a gesture of humility and hospitality.

Sixteenth-century Anabaptists picked up the practice of footwashing at the Communion service, perhaps from predecessor sects, but more likely directly from John's gospel account. From the time of their inception to today, some Anabaptist groups have practiced footwashing either as a Communion ritual or as a hospitable practice for visiting church leaders. Pilgram Marpeck (c. 1495–1556), a mining engineer who was influential in the Swiss and South German Anabaptist churches, made repeated references to footwashing in his writings, ranking the practice with baptism, forgiveness of sins, teaching, the Lord's Supper, and the laying on of hands. The Dutch Anabaptist leader Dirk Philips (1504–1568) suggested that footwashing is among the ordinances which distinguish the "true church" from "all false and anti-Christian congregations."

Martin Luther and other Reformers, in their few scattered references to liturgical footwashing, suggested that it simply distinguishes a kind of fanaticism and peculiarity. After stating clearly that "we have nothing to do with feetwashing with water," Luther went on to admonish those with other convictions: "If you wish to wash your neighbor's feet, see that your heart is really humble, and help every one in becoming better."

Modern Revivals

In the late twentieth-century, footwashing remains a local practice in both Catholic and mainline Protestant religious communities. Where it is practiced, the ritual usually is part of Maundy Thursday celebrations. Smaller Protestant denominations including some Mennonite and Baptist bodies, the Church of God (Anderson, Ind.), and the Church of the Brethren practice footwashing infrequently as part of a love feast Communion or Lord's Supper. Even among these latter groups, the practice is waning in many congregations, partly as the result of acculturation, embarrassment about peculiar customs, and lack of educational materials that explore footwashing's meanings. A full-scale retrieval of the never-universal practice is unlikely, although one may expect continued, meaningful observance of footwashing in the worship services of some historic practitioners as well as in liturgically innovative religious groups.

Keith A. Graber Miller

251 • A THEOLOGY OF FOOTWASHING

Because of the ambiguity stemming from differences between the Johannine and synoptic accounts in the New Testament, the relationship between footwashing, the Lord's Supper, and baptism has been variously interpreted. The rite has been understood to symbolize purification, humility, and service to one's neighbor.

Ambiguous New Testament Evidence

Theological interpretations of footwashing's rich meaning vary considerably, both in historical and contemporary liturgical settings. Theological and ethical emphases embodied in the practice include humility, cleansing, forgiveness, renewal, discipleship and service. In some fellowships, the Lord's Supper and footwashing are preceded the previous week by a time of "making things right" with God and sisters and brothers in the church (Matt. 5:23-24), so that the basin and towel have come to signify reconciliation.

Footwashing's polyvalence is the result of ambiguity in the primary founding document (John 13); multiple local understandings emerging through the nonuniversality of the practice; cultural transformations which make footwashing's practical purpose less apparent; and the burden on the bodily practice itself to carry the weight of interpretation.

It is noteworthy, first of all, that no account of footwashing is included with the Corinthian or synoptic Gospels' narratives of the Lord's Supper. Nor, inexplicably, is the institution of the Lord's Supper included in the Johannine passage. Secondly, most scholars believe the John 13 passage itself represents a combination of two different Johannine traditions. Verses fourteen through seventeen suggest that by washing the disciples' feet Jesus was setting an example of self-sacrificing humility. However, verses six through ten indicate that what Jesus did in the footwashing is essential if the disciples are to gain a heritage with him (v. 8), and apparently this action cleanses them of sin (v. 10). It is also unclear whether understanding is to come only after the Resurrection (v. 7) or if understanding is possible now (vv. 12, 17). Thus, from the founding text at least two different interpretations are possible: the need for regular spiritual cleansing and the admonition to be humble.

In a provocative reconstruction of the passage, Oscar Cullmann suggests that the footwashing refers both to baptism and to the Eucharist. In religious history, water is often symbolically associated with spiritual cleaning or, in Christian contexts, baptism. For Ambrose, footwashing was linked with the baptism of neophytes as a "special help of sanctification," even though "in baptism all guilt is washed away." Led by Augustine, many Latin writers since the fourth century, including a few modern Roman Catholic scholars, see a reference to penance in verse ten: "The one who has bathed does not need to wash, except for his feet." The latter clause is a disputed one, and its inclusion or exclusion greatly colors possible interpretations.

Humility and Service

Washing of feet as a mark of servility appears in Jewish rabbinical literature. In the footwashing practice among members of the medieval Christian ecclesiastical and political hierarchy, and among members of medieval monastic groups, humility is the most obvious strand of emphasis. Most modern commentators see no sacramental significance in footwashing, but consider it a lesson in humility. These scholars usually believe the footwashing story and Jesus' injunction to "wash one another's feet" is to be taken figuratively rather than literally.

Other contemporary interpretations include viewing footwashing as a "symbolic act of eschatological hospitality," receiving the disciples into the place where Jesus was going (Hultgren); as a preparation for the martyrdom, which Jesus' disciples were willing to face, analogous to the anointing of Jesus' feet by Mary (Matt. 26; Weiss); or as a prophetic action distinguishing "the community which Jesus calls into existence from the power structures so universal in human society" through "the love of friendship expressing itself in joyful mutual service for which rank is irrelevant" (Schneiders).

With most modern footwashings being enacted by all congregants rather than only the political or church hierarchy, the theme of mutual service may make more intuitive sense than humility or spiritual cleansing. For egalitarian practitioners, humility is slightly less evident because the ritual's symbolic meaning is less discontinuous with existing relationships among those who wash and those who are washed—in contrast to historic relationships between kings, princes, popes, and bishops and those whose feet they washed. Likewise, members of Christian fellowships have no calling to perform spiritual cleansing on one another, even though water does signify such cleansing.

For some Protestant denominations, the practice's meaning has shifted, even though performance of the ritual has remained relatively unchanged. For example, among twentieth-century Mennonites, the ordinance has generally shifted its meaning from passive cleansing (purification) or equally passive humility toward active service. This is a nuanced shift away from the ritual's agent-centeredness toward other- or act-centeredness and reflects Mennonite's modern movement toward engagement with their world, rather than withdrawal into pure communities.

Because of footwashing's multiple, interrelated symbolic possibilities, contemporary liturgical footwashings may emphasize cleansing, forgiveness, renewal, humility, discipleship, reconciliation or service, or may combine the various theological and ethical themes into a coherent whole.

Keith A. Graber Miller

252 • A Liturgy for Footwashing

While some denominations and congregations include footwashing in their regular Communion or Lord's Supper celebrations, other practitioners include the rite only in their Maundy Thursday services. The following liturgy could be adapted for Passion Week or other occasions. In most footwashings, the sign-act itself embodies its own meaning, so the liturgical rhetoric may be minimal, assuming that leaders have provided some prior teaching about footwashing's history, development, and theological and ethical emphases. The liturgy given here also assumes footwashing's association with a larger celebration of the Lord's Table (for example, see "A Common Text for the Great Thanksgiving" in chapter 9), but details on the rest of the Communion service are not included here. The footwashing liturgy begins after the gathering, greeting, opening prayers, reading of Scripture, and celebration of the Lord's Table, all of which ought to be sensitive to footwashing themes. The introductory remarks, litany, and prayer are only examples of how one might provide interpretation.

The Service

Introductory Comments

LEADER: The washing of one another's feet, following the example of Jesus when he washed the feet of his disciples, is a symbol of our need for renewed cleansing and forgiveness, made possible by the love of God and the grace of the Lord Jesus Christ. In it we see the majesty of God, who always stoops to lift our burdens and cleanse our sins, empowering us to live freely. Through washing another's feet, we also commit ourselves to lives of service, in the spirit of Christ, who took on human form, humbling himself in cross-bearing service to others. By kneeling and washing, we express the love which serves human needs, both within our fellowship and beyond these walls. Hear, then, the Word of the Lord.

Gospel Lesson
John 13:1-17

Silent Meditation

Footwashing Litany

LEADER: O Eternal Wisdom, O Vulnerable God,
we praise you and give you thanks,
because you laid aside your power as
   a garment
and took upon yourself the form of a
   slave.

PEOPLE: **You became obedient unto death,**
even death on a cross,
receiving authority and comfort
from the hands of a woman;
for God chose what is weak in the
   world
to shame the strong;
and God chose what is low and de-
   spised in the world
to bring to nothing things that are.

ALL: **Therefore, with the woman who**
   gave you birth,
the women who befriended you and
   fed you,
the woman who anointed you for
   death,
the women who met you, risen from
   the dead,
we praise you.

LEADER: Blessed is our brother Jesus,
who on this night, before Passover,
rose from the Supper, laid aside his
   garments,
took a towel and poured water,
and washed his disciples' feet, saying
   to them:
"If I, your Lord and Teacher,

have washed your feet,
you also ought to wash one another's
   feet.
If you know these things,
blessed are you if you do them.
If I do not wash you,
you have no part in me."

PEOPLE: **Lord, not my feet only**
but also my hands and my head.

ALL: **Come now, tender Spirit of God,**
wash us and make us one body in
   Christ;
that, as we are bound together
in this gesture of love,
we may no longer be in bondage to
   the
principalities and powers
that enslave creation,
but may know your liberating peace
such as the world cannot give. Amen.

(From _Hymnal: A Worship Book_)

The Footwashing

Commentary: The footwashing may begin with a brief announcement of procedure—where basins and towels are located, how persons should pair up, or a request that participants return to their seats following the washing. These announcements should be limited—teaching about specifics related to the rite should take place in an earlier setting or should be listed somewhere in the bulletin.

Often the rite takes place in relative silence, with participants speaking only in hushed tones—and, most likely for new practitioners, nervous titters. Footwear may be removed at the benches, or more likely, near the basins.

Footwashing may be done either in pairs or in rows. In row washing, an appointed person may kneel before each basin and wait for a person to be seated in the chair in front of the basin. The appointed one places that person's feet in the basin one at a time, lifts and dries each foot, and rises. The person whose feet have been washed kneels and washes the feet of the next person waiting in line. Persons who have had their feet washed and have washed the feet of another may be seated and replace their footwear. The feet of the one who began the footwashing will be washed last.

In pair-washing, persons select someone with

whom they want to wash feet by tapping them on the shoulder, asking them quietly, or nodding to the other. This may be a friend, a person with whom they've recently reconciled, a visitor, or anyone else in the fellowship. Usually persons wash only same-sex partners, although this is not always the case. Depending on the level of modesty desired, basins may be placed in the open auditorium or in more private educational classrooms. Participants take turns at the basins. The washer stoops in front of the other person, takes her foot in her hand, and rinses it with water, drying it with a towel. After both feet are washed, the two switch positions, and the washer becomes the washed. After both have washed, they stand and hug, exchange a handshake or the "holy kiss" (Rom. 16:16), and speak affirmingly to the other— e.g., "God bless you." Participants then replace their footwear and return to their seats.

Hymns of Commitment

Commentary: After people begin reassembling in the sanctuary or auditorium, hymn-singing may lead the group back into corporate worship and allow others to return to their seats unobtrusively.

Unison Closing Prayer
Blessed are you, O God
You set aside
> this bread as a sign of your Son's broken
> body,
> this cup as a sign of his shed blood,
> this basin as a sign of his servanthood.
Through them you have made us partakers of
> Christ
> and of one another.
As we go forth, give us grace
> to count others better than ourselves,
> to love our enemies,
> to seek peace.
Send the Spirit of truth to keep alive in us
> what Jesus taught and did,
> who lives and reigns with you and the Holy
> Spirit,
One God, forever and ever. Amen.

Benediction

253 ♦ GUIDELINES FOR PLANNING A FOOTWASHING SERVICE

Congregational leaders planning their first liturgical foot- *washing may take comfort in recognizing that the rite's traditions allow for tremendous flexibility and creativity. As with other symbolic religious acts, there is no one right way to celebrate footwashing.*

Because of footwashing's cultural strangeness, pastors and other church leaders may encounter some resistance to including footwashing with the Maundy Thursday or Lord's Supper services. Some may suggest that washing the feet of others is foreign to their daily experience so it cannot carry meaning in Christian worship. However, the bodily practice itself—stooping, touching the feet of another, and kneeling before another—continues to indicate a kind of humbling of oneself. With persons washing each other's feet, the practice primarily suggests mutual service with another. And while practitioners' feet are usually clean when they come to the basin, water continues to signify—as it does in baptism—spiritual cleansing, forgiveness, and renewal.

Those planning a footwashing service need to decide beforehand whether persons will wash in pairs or in rows; what level of modesty is appropriate for the parish or congregation; and whether men and women may be mixed in the washing or segregated. Planners are discouraged from making the service more palatable by substituting handwashing for footwashing, partly because handwashing has its own religious history.

Church leaders should be sensitive to the special needs of persons with disabilities, as well as those who choose not to participate in the footwashing. If pair-washing is chosen, service planners at first may want to observe the pairing process, then search out persons who do not have partners so that no interested person is excluded.

To celebrate footwashing, a fellowship will need a sufficient number of basins or tubs, perhaps one for every fifteen persons. Sometime just before or during the service, the basins may be placed in various open spaces throughout the auditorium or sanctuary, or in educational classrooms. A small stack of towels should be placed near each basin.

Because footwashing is new to many people, some explanation of not only the theological and ethical symbolism, but procedural arrangements is needed. It is best if, during the service itself, announcement of procedures is limited. Service planners may include in the bulletin a succinct explanation of how footwashing is celebrated, and of where basins are located. In addition, it would be helpful if church leaders could use the educational hour during preceding weeks to discuss the history, development, and theology of footwashing. Some fellowships may choose to include footwashing in a small-group worship service before introducing the practice into formal, corporate worship. Then those already experienced could serve as mentors or examples in the designated basin areas.

In some religious traditions, footwashing services are accompanied by an offering for the alms or outreach fund. In combination with the ritual, church leaders may also consider asking participants to sign a covenant committing themselves to a specified amount of concrete voluntary service during the coming months or year.

No one would expect to conduct flawlessly a first-time footwashing service, with the unusual demands and clumsy gestures the symbolic act necessitates. Service planners will need to be flexible and good-humored in their efforts and integrate learning from initial celebrations into later footwashings.

Keith A. Graber Miller

254 ✦ BIBLIOGRAPHY ON FOOTWASHING

Bender, Harold S. "Footwashing." *Mennonite Encyclopedia II*. Scottdale, Pa.: Herald, 1955.

Hultgren, Arland J. "The Johannine Footwashing (13:1-11) as Symbol of Eschatological Hospitality." *New Testament Studies* 28:4 (October 1982): 539–46.

Miller, Keith A. Graber. "Mennonite Footwashing: Identity Reflections and Altered Meanings." *Worship* 66:2 (March 1992): 148–70.

Jeffrey, Peter. "*Mandatum Novum Do Vobis*: Toward a Renewal of the Maundy Thursday Footwashing Rite." *Worship* 64:2 (1990): 107–41. Deals with controversy over washing women's feet on Maundy Thursday in recent years in Roman Catholic dioceses.

Schnieders, Sandra M. "The Footwashing (John 13:1-20): An Experiment in Hermeneutics." *The Catholic Biblical Quarterly* 43:1 (January 1981): 76–81.

Thomas, John Cristopher. *Footwashing in John 13 and the Johannine Community*. Sheffield, U.K.: Journal for the Study of Old Testament Press, 1991.

Weiss, Harold. "Footwashing in the Johannine Community." *Novum Testamentum* 21 (October 1979): 298–325.

For representative footwashing liturgies see:

• *The Book of Occasional Services* (New York: Church Hymnal Corporation, 1988), 91.

• *Book of Worship: United Church of Christ* (New York: Office of Church Life, 1986), 197–206.

❧ NINETEEN ❧

The Solemn Assembly

Fasting and prayer have been marks of repentance for Jews and Christians for millennia. Wednesdays and Fridays were fast days for Christians since the earliest centuries of Christian history. Four times a year, the Ember days (the Wednesday, Friday, and Saturday after December 13; the day after the first Sunday of Lent; the day after Pentecost Sunday; and the day after September 14) were special days for repentance and fasting. The most rigorous monastic orders followed a more restricted diet between September 14 and Easter than during the rest of the year, and mandated strict fasts on bread and water certain days of the week throughout much of the year. Protestants in Germany observe a day of prayer and fasting each autumn; the day is also an official national holiday in many countries with Protestant state churches.

The following pages describe a recent movement among Southern Baptists to encourage congregations to hold a weekend day of prayer, fasting, and repentance. Although to some degree these efforts build on the American tradition of camp meetings and revivals, the solemn assembly movement places greater emphasis on fasting than has been customary in American revivalism in recent times. In this sense, this movement reaches back to the colonial Puritan approach to revival, which, in turn, has roots in European Protestantism.

255 ◆ HISTORICAL ORIGINS AND DEVELOPMENT OF THE SOLEMN ASSEMBLY

Solemn national assemblies for prayer, fasting, and repentance are described in the Old Testament Scriptures. In America, local and national leaders have called for days of prayer and fasting at times of crisis and when they perceive a need for repentance by the entire society. In 1989 Southern Baptist leaders issued a call to prayer and solemn assembly.

Biblical Basis for the Solemn Assembly

Holy convocations and/or solemn assemblies may be described as a day or days in which God's followers come together under concerned leadership to confess sins and to be brought into a renewed relationship with God. Worshipers confess both personal and corporate sins which have separated them from God. The spirit of the solemn assembly may be found in 2 Chronicles 7:14, "if my people who are called by my name, will humble themselves and pray and seek my face and turn from their wicked ways then I will hear from heaven and will forgive their sin and will heal their land." This is the biblical intention of the solemn assembly: confession, forgiveness of sin, personal restoration, national blessing, and the healing process.

The concept of solemn assembly emanates mainly from Old Testament literature. The terminology does not appear in the New Testament largely for two reasons. The first reason is that New Testament Christian leaders and writers were Jews (some exceptions being noted) who practiced Jewish custom while being Christians. They knew about holy days and solemn assemblies. Therefore, there was no real need to deal with solemn assemblies. The second reason has to do with the constant and ongoing confession of sin believed to be necessary for an appropriate relationship with God the Father as taught in New Testament literature. Practicing this teaching made even mentioning solemn assemblies unnecessary, since they were called only in the case of gross personal and corporate sin. In addition to these two reasons, the national and religious life of Israel had been interrupted by the defeat and pagan rule of the country. Israel was not a free nation. In the face of Roman rule, calling a solemn assembly would have been extremely difficult.

The Old Testament records at least twelve solemn assemblies, if the Old Testament revivals are equated with solemn assemblies. The term *solemn assembly* is sometimes but not always used. The following is a listing of these solemn assemblies:

Exodus 33:7-11
1 Samuel 7:5-6
2 Samuel 6:14-19 (1 Chronicles 13:1–16:43 [same event])
2 Chronicles 15:9-15
2 Chronicles 29:5-29
2 Chronicles 34:31-33
Ezra 6:16-22
Ezra 8:21-23; 9:5-15; 10:7-12
Nehemiah 8:1-12
Joel 1:14; 2:12-17, 19, 28-29

The solemn assemblies of the Old Testament all have several things in common. First, Israelites turn away from God and involve themselves in sins. Second, God then sends some form of corrective or remedial judgment upon the people. Third, the leader or leaders of the people become burdened, recognize the judgment, and see the cause as sin. The fourth common element is the action taken by the leaders. This is usually a call to repentance in the form of a solemn assembly. There is no more vivid expression of the burden felt by the leader than can be found in Exodus 32:32: "But now, please forgive their sin—but if not, then blot me out of the book you have written." It should be noted that God directs the leader to call a solemn assembly. This is no mere human plan to deal with a personal and collective crisis.

In considering the biblical material relative to the solemn assembly, the term holy convocation must be considered. The two terms are often used in connection with the same event. Leviticus 23:8 designates the seventh day of the Passover as a holy convocation, and in Deuteronomy 16:8 the same event on the same day is called a solemn assembly. The same is true in several Old Testament passages. Both terms are necessary to convey fully the concept of a special day or a season when confession of sin and a turning to God are the emphases. There are eight days prescribed in the Old Testament, which are recognizable as holy convocations or solemn assemblies. They are:

The first day of the Feast of the Passover
The seventh day of the Feast of the Passover
The Feast of First Fruits
The Feast of Trumpets
The Day of Atonement
The first day of the Feast of Tabernacles
The eighth day of the Feast of Tabernacles
The Sabbath Day

These eight days were observed annually at specified times. The solemn assemblies were also called when made necessary by radical departures from God. These observances served to help the people maintain their essential relationship with God. As has been stated, Christians in the New Testament period continued to observe many, if not all, of these days. An example of this is the New Testament Christian Jew who worshiped on the Sabbath (Saturday) in the synagogue and also on the first day of the week (Sunday) in celebration of the Resurrection. In the upper room experience, Jesus celebrated the Passover with his disciples. He then celebrated with them that meal which is observed by Christian groups under differing names such as, the Lord's Supper, Communion, and others. This meal is seen by many as a New Testament example of a holy convocation or a solemn assembly. Jesus said in that instance, "let a man so examine himself . . ." In this statement, he was suggesting that the confession of sin should be done before one partake of the meal, whether as a memorial or in some other context. Therefore, in the minds of many, the New Testament Christian does what the Old Testament saint did in solemn assembly as he or she observes this practice or ordinance, the Lord's Supper. This understanding in no way precludes the possibility of calling holy convocations or solemn assemblies at other times.

Southern Baptist Solemn Assemblies

Religious and secular history document the fact that solemn assemblies have been a part of

America's national religious past. National leaders from the time of the New England Puritans to the nineteenth-century Civil War called solemn assemblies for the purpose of confessing personal and corporate sin, as well as for the purpose of seeking God during times when God was perceived to be judging the people. Many sermons for such assemblies have been recorded and preserved, thus informing and guiding successive generations. The solemn assembly was abandoned sometime during the latter part of the nineteenth century and the first quarter of the twentieth century, because it was perceived as an Old Testament activity which held no value for New Testament Christianity. Southern Baptist use of solemn assemblies has been of relatively recent origin, beginning in 1989 with a "Call to Prayer and Solemn Assembly: A Timely Proclamation for our Nation's Churches . . . from Southern Baptist Leaders" (September 17, 1989).

This document was prepared by prayer leaders representing every board, auxiliary, and commission in Southern Baptist Convention headquarters. The one-page document was mailed to Baptist state leaders and distributed through the state conventions to local churches. The National Prayer Corps issued a Call to Prayer and Solemn Assembly on national television. This, according to some, was the beginning of the Southern Baptist Convention involvement in the solemn assembly movement.

Perhaps Southern Baptist involvement did begin formally and officially in the manner described. However, a number of Southern Baptists other than the National Prayer Leaders were working on similar material and ideas prior to the televised national call. One writer developed a paper entitled "A Journey into Prayer and Solemn Assembly" as a model for the implementation of solemn assemblies in Baptist churches (see "Guidelines," below, for details). Other individuals were working and developing materials in the area of prayer. Often these ideas were taken up by existing movements, such as the lay renewal process which was firmly established in such state conventions as Texas. In that state, the Baptist men's organization had taken the lead in the lay renewal process. This group was ready to begin working with the concept of the solemn assembly and providing leadership in a few churches. These early efforts in the state of Texas cannot be seen as

solemn assemblies. Many weekend meetings were held and called solemn assemblies, but they were not solemn assemblies because they did not meet the biblical criteria for planning, introducing, and conducting solemn assemblies. They also did not meet biblical criteria in terms of the final results. The same story can be told with regards to other state conventions and the churches in them. However, all of the individuals who were working in the area of renewal, prayer for revival, solemn assembly, and other areas were motivated basically by the same convictions. These were:

(1) God is holy and hates sin.
(2) America has turned away from God.
(3) America has become a very sinful nation.
(4) God has begun America's judgment.
  (a) The judgment is currently remedial in nature.
  (b) If repentance does not occur, the judgment will become final.
(5) The only hope America has is prayer and revival.
(6) National revival is needed.
(7) Extraordinary commitment to prayer is needed.

As different individuals and groups prayed, sought God, planned, and developed materials, events were taking place within the life of the Southern Baptist Convention which indicated that God's Spirit was moving and that God intended to do something through the Southern Baptists. Throughout the year of 1989, a new fervor developed to seek God at the national level, at the state level, in conferences, in retreats, and in local churches. Since that time, the movement which began and held so much hope for revival has slowed. There seem to be several reasons for the slowing, among them the following:

(1) Churches have been reluctant to become involved in planning and conducting solemn assemblies.
(2) Southern Baptist churches are at the saturation point in trying to accommodate programs fostered by national and state conventions.
(3) There is considerable difference of opinion as to who should conduct a solemn assembly and where.
(4) Most local church leaders do not have the sophistication to develop an awareness of personal

and corporate sin to the level necessary for a solemn assembly to be successful.

(5) The authority to call a solemn assembly and to require all church members to attend is lacking in Southern Baptist churches.

(6) When God begins a work by the Spirit, God will surely close the work down if humans begin to take credit for what is happening, rather than giving credit to God's Holy Spirit.

Even though progress toward solemn assemblies and national revival has slowed, there continues to be some effort in this direction. Because God has promised to honor repentance and recommitment, the solemn assembly continues to be a biblically sound process which holds much hope for the present as well as for the future.

P. Preston Graham

256 ◆ A THEOLOGY FOR THE SOLEMN ASSEMBLY

The solemn assembly movement is based on 2 Chronicles 7:14. In this passage the people of Israel were challenged to fast and pray and in doing so repent of their wicked ways. This national approach is applied in the solemn assembly movement to an individual congregation based on New Testament Christian practices.

While progress toward actually holding solemn assemblies seems to have slowed down, individuals who have given themselves to a study of spiritual awakenings seem to feel that there still is hope for a major awakening in the near future. If it is indeed as J. Edwin Orr, author and student of awakenings, has stated, America and the world may be on the threshold of widespread spiritual awakening. His premise is that awakenings do not come suddenly, but come after a considerable period of preparation. Preparation and petition for awakening has been occurring for over ten years now in fairly heavy concentration within evangelical groups, both in America and abroad. The solemn assembly is a part of this activity.

But what of the theology of solemn assembly? Is this a theologically sound concept? Where does the concept of solemn assembly begin?

The Bible says, "In the beginning God . . ." (Gen. 1:1), and again the Bible says, "In the beginning was the Word . . . and the Word was God" (John 1:1). These passages, then, are the beginning of the concept of solemn assembly. It begins with the fact of an eternal God, a preexistent God, whose crowning achievement in the creative acts was the creation of humanity. A quick review of the Genesis account of Creation reveals that God made humanity in "his own image." Humans were made like God, especially in the sense that they were sinless and that they were given a free will. Humanity at some point after Creation rebelled and disobeyed God. Now with sin in their life, brought about by exercising their free will in the wrong direction, humans need to free themselves from that sin and guilt. At this point, several characteristics of God must be considered which impact the concept of the solemn assembly. First, God is above sin. That is, God is high, holy, and almighty. Second, God does not consider sin a light matter, and denounces sin. Third, God is just. When there is sin, God punishes that sin. Fourth, God is loving and merciful. Perhaps the first solemn assembly of the Old Testament occurred in Genesis 3:9, "But the Lord God called to the man." God called for confession of sin, rebuked the sinners, judged them, and made a covering for them. The Lord God called a solemn assembly in order to deal with these first two humans in their sins, and God continues to issue the call to solemn assembly.

There are two or three other strands which must be grasped and followed in developing the theology of the solemn assembly. Genesis shows how God dealt with God's first creation, with the original man and woman. Afterwards, God chose a people. Out of all the thousands upon the face of the earth, God began to call a people to be the people of God. God did this through Abram and Sarai. The story begins in Genesis 12 and fills the entire book of Genesis. The rest of the Old Testament is largely an account of God's efforts to get the people of Israel to love and serve him out of their own free wills. This story is interspersed with accounts of a rebellious people who often moved away from God to gross sin, to rebellion and apostasy. Solemn assemblies for the purpose of confession of sins and a return to God were called by leaders of the people who were inspired by God.

Thus, the entire theology of the solemn assembly may be summarized by the verse in 2 Chronicles 7:14, "If my people, who are called by my name, will humble themselves and pray and seek my face and turn from their wicked ways then I will hear from heaven and will forgive their sins and will heal their land."

God continued to call the people of God (the nation Israel) to repentance until the sin of rebellion and related sins became such that God finally let Israel go its own way. However, God did not let the Israelites go or turn them over to their own lust without making one final attempt to rescue them. In Christ, God provided the perfect atonement for sins and the washing of regeneration by the blood of this "Lamb without spot or blemish." Even though Israel of antiquity rejected God's provision for their atonement, God continues to call the people of God to solemn assembly, that is, to a meeting of accountability with God. Now, however, the people of God have become a spiritual Israel, purchased by the blood of Christ. This spiritual Israel consists of all races from many nations.

As for verses in the New Testament which embody the theology of solemn assembly, there are many. A selected example is 1 John 1:9, "If we confess our sins, he is faithful and just and will forgive us our sins . . . purify us from all unrighteousness." This verse and its theology applies not only to the individual, but also to congregations as well. That is why in the exercise of the solemn assembly, individual confession of sin is emphasized as well as the confession of corporate sins

committed by the assembly. The plan or liturgy for the solemn assembly as seen in the Old Testament patterns cited earlier can be adapted for use by New Testament Christians. The following articles demonstrate Christian adaptations of these Old Testament patterns.

P. Preston Graham

257 ♦ GUIDELINES FOR PLANNING A WEEKEND SOLEMN ASSEMBLY

This example of planning and holding of a weekend solemn assembly comes from Southern Baptists in Texas. The movement in Texas grew out of several retreats for leaders of Texas Baptist men's groups at which the Holy Spirit caused a spirit of revival to break out, leading to brokenness, repentance, confession, and prayer.

Motivation

It is unnecessary that one point to conditions in this great nation, America, to begin to lay out the motivation behind the hunger and thirst in God's people to see a revival and renewal in the churches and among God's people. God's judgment is pending because of rampant evil, and because the people of God are far from God. Whether this will be a final judgment or a remedial kind of judgment upon those who call themselves Baptists hangs in the balance. However, it need not be either, if the letter and the spirit of 2 Chronicles 7:14 can be carried to the churches, and if the people will act upon that verse along with other Scriptures. The motivation is the absolute necessity for God's people to turn from their sins to become truly God's people. The hands of the clock of God's judgment stand at five minutes until midnight, and the clock keeps ticking away. Will we as Christians make a serious effort to do God's bidding and return to God, or will we go on as if God's eyes could not see and God's ears could not hear—as if the stench of our filthiness did not reach God's sensitive holy nostrils?

This is the burden and the purpose for "A Journey into Prayer and Solemn Assembly." We, as the people of God, need to seek God's face and to ask permission to become involved in what God

Chi Rho with Greek Cross. The figure above, seen in the catacombs, combines the chi rho with a Greek cross.

is trying to do, not in the sense of "God, let me do something for you," but in the sense of "God, let me be involved in what you are doing."

––––––– **Description of the Weekend** –––––––

This "Journey into Prayer and Solemn Assembly" is designed as a weekend effort. It could be repeated annually or about every eighteen months, as deemed necessary. The weekend is to be characterized by solemnity. The effect desired is the "beauty of holiness." This statement should not to be misconstrued to mean that a self-righteousness is sought. Instead, this weekend is an effort to follow the instructions of 2 Chronicles 7:14, in order to let God come to humble, confession-seeking people with all the beauty of God's presence. It is an effort to experience the *shekannah glory.* It is not an effort to seek some kind of spiritual high for the sake of the high. It is not an effort to twist God's arm to get God to turn from what God purposes. It simply is an effort to do what the Word tells God's people to do in order that God will visit the people of God once again, empowering and sending out representatives to a lost, waiting world.

There is no outside leadership team for the church on this weekend. The only visitors to the church would be a prayer leader and the prayer leader's spouse and, in most cases, a music leader and the music leader's spouse. They are a praying team, working and praying with the pastor and the pastor's spouse. Provision for these visitors should be made to minimize the care church members need to extend toward them.

The pastor of the church will assume a major role in this weekend as the pastor follows and works beside the prayer leader. Deacons will be involved in their true function as servants, and church members themselves will carry along the activities of the weekend through clearly prepared instructions and group activities.

Preparation for the weekend should begin at least one month before the actual weekend. Three months of preparation would be better.

A detailed description of the events and activities of this weekend follows.

Twelve weeks before the anticipated weekend, institute the following:

Start a ten-week study about prayer.

Through preaching and/or teaching, begin to emphasize the need for humility, confession of sin, and prayer.

Teach about the solemn assembly through sermons, etc.

Begin to publicize the weekend journey and, as led by the Holy Spirit, indicate that the weekend will include a solemn assembly on Saturday afternoon and a twenty-four hour liquid fast.

Two weeks before the weekend journey, begin prayer groups:

Have each groups talk among themselves.

Have the groups study material about the solemn assembly.

Have the groups study material on fasting.

Have the groups study other related topics.

Pray for the weekend set for the church to come together in solemn assembly.

One week before the weekend journey, leaders should:

Announce again the weekend and emphasize that a solemn assembly on Saturday afternoon will be a vital part of the weekend experience.

Urge the entire church to attend the entire weekend.

Emphasize the conviction and purpose behind the weekend.

Stress that there will be no team to care for and only one meal to prepare.

Remind the people that the fast begins on Friday at 6:00 P.M. and continues through Saturday until 6:00 P.M. The fast is to be a liquid fast. Since milk is considered a solid, it should not be used as a liquid during the weekend fast.

Remind church members that all food preparation should be done on Thursday or during the day on Friday and put in the refrigerator or freezer. No food preparation should take place on Friday after 6:00 P.M.

No work is to be done during the time between Friday at 6:00 P.M. and Saturday at 6:00 P.M. If labor is necessary to care for small children and people who are ill, it should be kept to a minimum and, if possible, arranged to be carried out by someone not involved in the meetings.

This weekend is to be set aside as a sacrifice unto God and should be given over to meditation, Bible reading, and prayer.

Explain that the weekend begins on Friday at 6:00 P.M. with the fast and that the people will assemble at the church at 7:00 P.M. for the first meeting.

Walk the people through Saturday: the continuing of the fast and the Saturday morning teaching session at 9:00 A.M., followed by a reflection session in homes at 10:30 A.M. (No food should be served, only liquids.)

Stress that the time between 11:30 A.M. and 2:00 P.M. on Saturday should be a continuation of the fast, Bible reading, prayer, and meditation.

All the people should plan to be present for the solemn assembly, which begins sharply at 2:00 P.M. Explain to the people that the fast will be broken by the communal meal, which will be the agape feast, followed by the Lord's Supper. The meal will consist of simple foods which have been prepared before 6:00 P.M. on Friday and have been refrigerated or frozen.

The teaching time will occur near the end of the communal meal, while the people are still around the tables, and will include teaching through interpreting and through congregational sharing.

The communal meal should be a time of rejoicing with one another, and the teaching time should be a time of joy and praise.

Adults and youth should be informed that they are to assemble in the auditorium on Sunday at the normal Sunday school hour for a recapitulation and teaching time.

Provision must be made for children too young to be in the teaching time at the Sunday school hour. I suggest that workers be borrowed from sister churches, so that all church members may participate in the teaching time.

There will be a break between the Sunday school hour teaching time and the preaching hour.

Sunday morning preaching hour will be given to a brief teaching period, followed by a time of public commitment.

The Sunday evening service will begin at the time that discipleship training usually is scheduled. The pastor will lead the people in worship with sermon, testimonies, and commitment.

The Journey into Prayer and Solemn Assembly

Friday: Prayer leader and music leader arrive at the church prior to 7:00 P.M. (There is no team for this weekend.)

People assemble in church auditorium for teaching at 7:00 P.M. Teaching session will include:

Introduction to the weekend
Definition of prayer (both talking and listening)
Conditions for effective prayer
Hindrances to effective prayer

8:00 P.M.: People will move to small groups for a related activity.

Small groups will be asked to select a leader after prayer, if the leader has not been appointed previously.

Leader will take the group through the activity/ activities (see "Activity Sheet for Friday Night" below).

People will return to auditorium for reports and prayer.

Saturday: People assemble in church auditorium for teaching at 9:00 A.M. Teaching session will be on "Following Jesus in prayer."

10:00 A.M.: People will move to homes for reflection session.

10:30 A.M.: At the reflection session in homes (no food, only liquid refreshment will be served), leader will take the group through the activity/ activities (see "Activity Sheet for Saturday Morning" below).

11:30 A.M.: People will be encouraged to go home for rest/meditation/prayer.

2:00 P.M.: People will return to the church to participate in the solemn assembly (see "Solemn Assembly Activity Sheet for Saturday Afternoon" below).

6:00 P.M.: People will move to the dining area. People break fast and rejoice in their liberation from sin as they participate in a structured communal meal, or agape feast, followed by the Lord's Supper. (See instructions for the communal meal under "Solemn Assembly Activity Sheet for Saturday Afternoon" under the subheading below.)

Activity Sheet for Friday Night

The person who was selected by the church to be a Friday night group leader should take the activity sheets to the group meeting place. When the small group has assembled, the leader should hand the sheets to each person present.

LEADER: Before our Lord chose the twelve who were to be closer to him on earth than anyone else, he prayed all night and then selected the twelve. We shall engage in prayer to ask God to teach us tonight.

The leader prays or calls upon someone else to pray.

Group activity

LEADER: (Read or call upon someone else to read the following account.) An engineer had retired from a rather large company. Later, the company called him to come back to serve as a consultant to help them find out why a key piece of equipment would not work properly. He returned to the company and spent about fifteen minutes looking at the equipment; then, after drawing a sketch of the equipment, he drew an "X" at one spot and wrote at the bottom of the sketch, "Fix this." He sent the company a bill for $10,000.00 for the service rendered. The company official who received the bill was a bit put out and returned the bill with a note, "Please itemize." The engineer returned the bill itemized in this way: "For inspecting the equipment and drawing an 'X,' $1.00. For knowing where to place the 'X,' $9,999.00." (Note: This story by Don Gibson, Director of Renewal Ministry, Texas Baptist Men.)

LEADER: Like the engineer, God knows where to place th "X" when equipment needs to be fixed. Has God, or is God, drawing some "X's" in your life? Read one item at a time. Allow time for each person to complete each item as it is read before going on to the next item.

(1) Turn your sheet over and draw a circle to represent your life.
(2) Place a cross at the center if you are born again and know it.
(3) Think about your life. Place "X's" in the circle to show where God has indicated that some fixing was or is needed.
(4) Think about what each of those "X's" mean. (Allow time.)
(5) Draw a circle around the "X" representing the last time that God touched a spot in your life. (Allow time.)
(6) Invite group sharing about their circles and the "X's" in their lives. (Allow time.)
(7) Close with prayer.

Activity Sheet for Saturday Morning

HOST:

(1) Assemble the group, then ask someone to read 2 Chronicles 7:14.
(2) Read the following: "When God's people become cold, often hard, and distance themselves from God, they are courting disaster. Isaiah 59:2; Psalm 66:18; and 1 Peter 3:12 all say that sin separates us from God."
(3) Call upon someone to read each of the above-stated verses.
(4) Say, "When we are separated from God by our sins, the enemy Satan can inflict all manner of destructive things upon us. But, thank God, he has made a way of escape for us."
(5) Call upon someone to read (a) 1 John 1:7-9, and (b) Hebrews 10:17.
(6) Say, "God no longer requires the blood of bulls and goats in order to forgive us our sins. In 2 Chronicles 7:14, we read what God tells us we are to do."
(7) Say, "We will spend a few moments in prayer before we begin the selected activity. Will you pray for this time together?" (Pause.) "Will you pray for the effects of and the results of this weekend?" (Pause.) "Will you invite the Holy Spirit to be present and to lead us in our activity?" (Pause.) "Father, we pray these things in the name of Jesus. Amen."

Activity

HOST:

Read, then pause after each question. Count slowly to yourself, saying "one and two, and three, and four . . . until you have reached sixty." Or, pause for one minute if you choose to use a watch. Move on to the next question.

(1) If you only had one prayer that you could pray, what would it be?
(2) If you only had two prayers you could pray, what is the second one?
(3) If you only had three prayers you could pray, what is the third one?

Consider the things you would pray about. Was any of the three for things? For others? Of praise or thanksgiving? For our church? For our pastor?

(4) As you have listened to the Holy Spirit, what has the Spirit said to you about your prayers and your prayer life? Pause for responses.
(5) What do you consider to be the greatest need of our church that should be lifted to the Father in prayer?
(6) We are going to dismiss with prayer; but, before we do, is there anyone who needs to share something with this group?

Host: Remind everyone to continue in fasting/ meditation/study/ prayer. Remind everyone to be in the auditorium by 2:00 P.M. sharp. Call on someone to voice a dismissal prayer.

Alternate Activity for Saturday Morning
Host:
Lead the group or enlist another member of the group to lead.

LEADER: (Read the following:)
There was an old man, a very wise old man, who lived in a village. A group of the local young people who assembled were led by a somewhat rebellious youth. He said, "Let's prove that the old man is not so wise by giving him a question which he cannot answer." He caught a small bird, and the group went to the old man. The leader held the bird cupped in his hand so that no part could be seen. He said, "Old man, what do I have in my hand?" The old man answered, "My son, you have a small bird." Somewhat startled by the old man's answer, he then asked another question, "Is it alive or dead?" If the old man should answer, "It is dead," he intended to open his hand to let the bird fly away. If the old man should say, "It is alive," he intended to crush the life out of the bird to show a dead bird. The old man paused for a moment; then, looking straight into the eyes of the lad, he answered, "My son, you have to decide. The bird is in your hands."

Lead in prayer or call upon someone else to pray. The prayer should be a prayer that God, through the Holy Spirit, will teach through the reading of this simple story and this time of sharing together.

Ask the following questions. Suggest that anyone may give a verbal response as the Holy Spirit leads. Assure the group that no one will be called upon for a response. Pause after reading each question. (Count slowly, silently saying "one and two and three and four" etc. until sixty is reached. Then move on to the next question. If a watch is used, allow one minute for response before moving on to the next question.) After a person comments, always ask, "Is there another response?" or something similar.

Questions (Pause at least one minute between questions.)
(1) Did the Holy Spirit say anything to you during the reading of this simple story?
(2) Who might the old man represent?
(3) What has God placed in your hands?
(4) Are you allowing that thing to live and produce?
(5) Is there anything in your hands that you are about to crush?
(6) How do you feel about having to decide what you will do with what God has placed in your hands?

LEADER: Remind the group to continue in fasting/Bible study/prayer and to return at 2:00 P.M. to the church auditorium. Close with prayer.

Solemn Assembly for Saturday Afternoon

PASTOR: I now declare this to be a God-ordained solemn assembly. Let there be no frivolity. Instead, let there be a solemnity, not that God desires to see long faces; but rather, the Lord does delight in the humility of his people. Too long have we taken for granted the sovereignty of God. Too long have we come together with a lack of reverence and a respect for the God of the universe, the Creator of all things, the Sustainer of life, and the Redemptor of mankind. Oh, God of our salvation, look down upon us, honor and bless

that which we do in your presence
this day.
LET THE SOLEMN ASSEMBLY BEGIN!

Music leader sings or leads appropriate hymn.

PASTOR: Please stand in honor of God's Word.
Listen as the Word of God is read in
your hearing and respond after each
reading. Our prayer leader will lead
you in each response.

At this point the pastor will begin reading select
verses of Scripture. Then the prayer leader will
lead the people in response after the reading of
each Scripture.

PASTOR: Hear, O heaven, and give ear, O earth:
for the Lord has spoken, I have nour-
ished and brought up children, and
they have rebelled against me.

RESPONSE: **We have indeed been a rebellious
people.**

PASTOR: The ox knoweth his owner, and the
ass his master's crib: but Israel doth
not know, my people doth not consider.

PEOPLE: **We are the sheep of his pastures.**

PASTOR: Ah, sinful nation, a people laden with
iniquity, a seed of evil doers, children
that are corrupt: they have forsaken
the Lord, they have provoked the
Holy One of Israel unto anger, they
are gone backwards.

PEOPLE: **Oh, Lord, we are filled with iniquity
and we are backslidden from thee.**

PASTOR: Why should ye be stricken any more?
Ye will revolt more and more: the
whole head is sick, and the whole
heart faint.

PEOPLE: **We have despised thy correction,
our Father and our God.**

PASTOR: From the sole of the foot even unto
the head there is no soundness in it;
but wounds and bruises, and putre-
fying sores: they have not been
closed, neither bound up, neither
mollified with ointment.

PEOPLE: **Father in heaven, we suffer the
wounds of our sins.**

PASTOR: Your country is desolate, your cities
are burned with fire: your land,
strangers devour it in your presence,

and it is desolate, as overthrown by
strangers.

PEOPLE: **Strangers are in possession of our
inheritance.**

Music leader motions or asks the people to be
seated. He or she then reads:

And the daughter of Zion is left as a
cottage in a vineyard, as a lodge in a
garden of cucumbers, as a besieged
city. Except the Lord of hosts had left
unto us a very small remnant, we
should have been as Sodom, and we
should have been like unto Gomorrah.
Hear the word of the Lord, ye rulers
of Sodom; give ear unto the law of
our God, ye people of Gomorrah.

Music leader then sings or leads appropriate
hymn.

The pastor motions or asks the people to rise,
then reads:

To what purpose is the multitude of
your sacrifices unto me? saith the
Lord: I am full of the burnt offerings
of rams, and the fat of fed beasts; and
I delight not in the blood of bullocks,
or of lambs, or of he goats.

PEOPLE: **He hath shewed thee, O man, what
is good; and what doth the Lord require of thee, but to do justly, and
love mercy, and walk humbly with
thy God?**

PASTOR: When ye come to appear before me,
who hath required this at your hand,
to tread my court?

PEOPLE: **We have offered polluted bread
upon the altar of God, even our
lives.**

PASTOR: Bring no more vain oblations; incense
is an abomination unto me; the new
moons and Sabbaths, the calling of
assemblies, I cannot abide, away with
it; it is iniquity, even the solemn
meeting.

PEOPLE: **Who can stand in the hill of the
Lord? He that hath clean hands and
a pure heart.**

PASTOR: And when ye spread forth your hands,
I will hide mine eyes from you: yea,
when ye make many prayers, I will not

PEOPLE: hear: Your hands are full of blood.

PEOPLE: **For the eyes of the Lord are over the righteous, and His ears are open unto their prayers; but the face of the Lord is against them that do evil.**

PASTOR: If we confess our sins, He is faithful and just to forgive us our sins, and to cleanse us from all unrighteousness. The blood of Jesus Christ his Son cleanseth us from all sin.

PEOPLE: **Oh, Lord, we would be cleansed.**

PASTOR: Wash you, make you clean; put away the evil of your doings from before mine eyes; cease to do evil; learn to do well; seek judgment; relieve the oppressed, judge the fatherless, plead for the widow. Come now, let us reason together, saith the Lord: though your sins be as scarlet, they shall be as white as snow; though they be red like crimson, they shall be as wool.

PEOPLE: **We are coming Lord, coming now to thee.**

The pastor motions for the people to be seated.

Music leader sings "Though Your Sins Be As Scarlet."

PASTOR: We have come to a time in this solemn assembly for the humbling of ourselves, the confession of our individual sins, and the seeking of God's face. Let us read again that familiar passage found in 2 Chronicles 7:14. Let us read together:

        If my people, who are called by my name, will humble themselves and pray and seek my face and turn from their wicked ways, then I will hear from heaven and will forgive their sin and will heal their land.

PASTOR: Let us pray. (Pastor then leads in prayer.)

        This is a very solemn time of seeking God. Please remain still and quiet. Let there be no talking. If there should be a need for physical relief, move very quietly and see that no more than two are three are moving at the same time. Take care of the physical need and then return quietly to your place. Everyone, now with bowed heads, begin to seek the Lord. Sheets of paper have been prepared and are here at the front, along with pencils. When you are ready, slip quietly from your seat, come to the altar to pray. List by name those sins that you wish to confess, pray for forgiveness, and deposit the slip in the basket at the altar. Later in the service, these will form a part of our solemn assembly as we burn them together, signifying God's forgiveness and liberation. Remember this is a list of your individual sins and is between you and God. No one else will read your list of personal sins. Now, as you bow before God, we will let the Holy Spirit tell us when to move on to the next part of the service.

Music leader sings softly "Grace That Was Greater Than All Our Sins."

After a sufficient length of time, the pastor should move the service to the next phase, which will be a confession of corporate sin.

PASTOR: In the days of Joel, when a solemn assembly was called, every class of people was called to be present to participate: the congregation, the elders, children, nursing infants, the bridegroom, the bride, priest, and ministers. The result of this participation in the confession of the corporate sins of God's people was that God extended his healing hand of mercy and blessing so that the people were made to rejoice. Listen carefully as I read from select passages (Joel 1:13-14; Joel 2:12-18; and Joel 2:25). Our deacons will now rehearse in our ears and before God those corporate sins which our church has committed. God convicted us of these corporate sins in our prayer groups which we had prior to this solemn assembly. Several deacons now will come and take part in the reading of the list.

The pastor should review the lists from which the deacons read to make sure there is no duplication of corporate sins. Each deacon should read a list then drop it into the basket for burning before God. When all the corporate sins have been read, the pastor will begin again.

PASTOR: Now therefore if you will obey my voice indeed, and keep my covenant, then ye shall be a peculiar treasure unto me above all people: for all the earth is mine: and ye shall be unto me a kingdom of priests, a holy nation.

PEOPLE: **All that the Lord hath spoken we will do.**

The pastor should lead in an appropriate prayer and afterward instruct the people concerning the burning of the basket of confessed sins as well as the communal meal and the observance of the Lord's Supper. If the burning takes place in the sanctuary, make provision for the safety of people and building. Consider the amount of smoke which will be generated, and take precautions not to trigger smoke detectors which might summon the fire department. City codes should be considered and any special permissions secured. The assembly could adjourn to a nearby parking area for the burning. After the burning of the sins, the people are to go directly to the dining area in a reverent manner for the communal meal and the Lord's Supper.

Burning the Sin Offering

Whether burning the sin offering is conducted in the sanctuary, on the parking lot, or in some other designated area, it should be a very serious meaningful activity.

LEADER: We have assembled ourselves in this place to continue the solemn assembly. Those individual sins which each of us confessed as we wrote them on slips of paper and placed them on the altar are in this container. Also, those corporate sins which you as a church identified and confessed are in this container. We remember that the holy Word of God teaches us that at the moment we confess our sins and claim the cleansing blood of Jesus, those sins are forgiven, gone, remembered no more by our heavenly Father. According to God's Word, we need do no more. But we are at this time, in this place, going to burn these lists of our individual and corporate sins in a symbolic reminder that God destroyed them through the blood of Jesus. As the flames from these pages lead upward and as the smoke curls toward the heavens, let us remember the confessed sins that they represent.

PRAYER LEADER: Their sins and iniquities will I remember no more.

PASTOR: Let us remember that the blood of bulls and goats, rams and heifers, pigeons and turtle doves is not required to cleanse us from our sins.

PRAYER LEADER: As far as the east is from the west, so far hath he removed our transgressions from us.

PASTOR: There is therefore now no condemnation to them which are in Christ Jesus, who walk not after the flesh, but after the Spirit.

PRAYER LEADER: Would all of you respond after me: **Forgetting those things which are behind, and reaching forth unto those things which are before, I press toward the mark for the prize of the high calling of God in Christ Jesus.**

PASTOR: (While lighting the papers) If the Son has made you free, you are free indeed.

(People should very reverently watch as the paper burns.)

The pastor should lead in a prayer of thanksgiving and praise for the forgiveness of the sins of the people. The pastor then asks the people to go reverently to the dining area for the communal meal and Lord's Supper, after asking God to bless the food.

The Communal Meal and the Lord's Supper

Before the people enter the dining area, food has been grouped according to meats, vegetables, salads, desserts, breads, and drinks. Deacons already have been appointed to serve the people. As much as possible, disposable materials should be used. As soon as the people have had sufficient time to eat, deacons clear the tables of the disposable goods and cover the remaining food with clean tablecloths. As soon as the tables are cleared, the Lord's Supper begins.

Music leader sings "We Will Break Bread Together."

At this point, the pastor takes charge, and the deacons assist. As the deacons bring in whole loaves of bread, the pastor comments that tonight members shall partake of the Lord's Supper as closely as possible to the way it was done in the Upper Room, except that Jesus broke the break himself and served it. However, he might have torn free a piece of bread before passing it on, just as will be done tonight. The pastor reads 1 Corinthians 11:23-24 and blesses the bread. Deacons pass the loaves of bread down the tables, letting each loaf go as far as it will before starting another loaf. The congregation at the tables will tear off a piece of bread, large enough for several bits, and will eat it, remembering the sacrifice of our Lord.

Music leader sings a Communion hymn or song.

The pastor reads 1 Corinthians 11:25-26 and blesses the cup. The deacons pass the grape juice.

After the elements have been distributed, the music leader sings again.

Finally the prayer leader concludes with a teaching session.

P. Preston Graham

Works Cited

1. Bob Creslak, "A Ritualizer Looks at Ritual," *Modern Liturgy* 8:6 (1981): 6.
2. Robert Webber, *God Still Speaks* (Nashville: Thomas Nelson, 1980), 143–152.
3. Bernard Cooke, "Sacraments," *New Dictionary of Sacramental Worship* (Collegeville, Minn.: Liturgical Press, 1990), 1116–1117.
4. Ibid., 1117–1119.
5. Michael J. Farley, "Sacraments in the Eastern Church," *New Dictionary of Sacramental Worship,* 1125–1126.
6. Ibid.
7. Susan J. White, "Eucharist, History of, in the West," *New Dictionary of Sacramental Worship,* 416–422.
8. Grant Sperry-White, "Eucharist, History of, in the East," *New Dictionary of Sacramental Worship,* 410–416.
9. White, "Eucharist," 418–419.
10. Daniel Meeter, "The Heart of Holy Communion," *Reformed Worship* 22 (Winter 1992): 34–36.
11. Presbyterian Church USA, et al., *Book of Common Worship* (Louisville: Westminster/John Knox, 1993), 841–851.
12. Adapted from the *United Methodist Book of Worship* (Nashville: United Methodist Publishing House, 1992), 141–157.
13. Adapted from *The Book of Worship* (Cleveland: United Church of Christ Office for Church Life and Leadership, 1986), 309–320. Used by permission.

Index

IN MEMORIAM

Larry J. Nyberg

1949–1993

Distinguished Project Editor
who suddenly entered into the kingdom
as his editorial work on
The Complete Library of Christian Worship
was nearing completion